Anglo-Saxon England 20

Her mon mæg giet gesion hiora swæð

ANGLO-SAXON ENGLAND
20

Edited by
MICHAEL LAPIDGE
University of Cambridge

MALCOLM GODDEN
University of Oxford

SIMON KEYNES
University of Cambridge

PETER BAKER
Emory University

MARTIN BIDDLE
University of Oxford

DANIEL CALDER
University of California, Los Angeles

ROBERT DESHMAN
University of Toronto

KLAUS DIETZ
Freie Universität Berlin

ROBERTA FRANK
University of Toronto

HELMUT GNEUSS
Universität München

FRED ROBINSON
Yale University

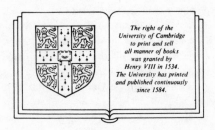

*The right of the
University of Cambridge
to print and sell
all manner of books
was granted by
Henry VIII in 1534.
The University has printed
and published continuously
since 1584.*

CAMBRIDGE UNIVERSITY PRESS

Cambridge

New York   Port Chester   Melbourne   Sydney

Published by the Press Syndicate of the University of Cambridge
The Pitt Building, Trumpington Street, Cambridge CB2 1RP
40 West 20th Street, New York NY 10011-4211, USA
10 Stamford Road, Oakleigh, Victoria 3166, Australia

© Cambridge University Press 1991

First published 1991

Typeset by
Servis Filmsetting Ltd
Manchester

Printed in Great Britain by
Dotesios Ltd Trowbridge

ISBN 0 521 41380 X
ISSN 0263-6751

SUBSCRIPTIONS: Anglo-Saxon England (ISSN 0263-6751) is an annual journal. The subscription price (including postage) of volume 20 is £52 for UK institutions (US$89 in USA and Canada), £38 (US$56 in USA and Canada) for individuals ordering direct from the Press and certifying that the annual is for their personal use. Copies may be sent airmail where applicable for £7 extra (orders to Cambridge only – dollar subscription price *includes* air delivery to North America). Orders, which must be accompanied by payment, may be sent to a bookseller, subscription agent, or direct to the publishers: Cambridge University Press, The Edinburgh Building, Shaftesbury Road, Cambridge CB2 2RU. Orders from the USA or Canada should be sent to Cambridge University Press, 40 West 20th Street, New York, NY 10011-4211, USA.

Back volumes: £47.00 (US$91.00 US and Canada) each available from Cambridge or the American Branch of Cambridge University Press.

A catalogue record of this book is available from the British Library.

Contents

List of illustrations   *page* vii

Settlement mobility and the 'Middle Saxon Shift': rural
   settlements and settlement patterns in Anglo-Saxon England   1
   H.F. HAMEROW *The University of Durham*

Adultery in early Anglo-Saxon society   19
   THEODORE JOHN RIVERS *Rego Park, New York*

The Liudhard medalet   27
   MARTIN WERNER *Temple University, Philadelphia*

The Werden 'Heptateuch'   43
   B.C. BARKER-BENFIELD *The Bodleian Library, Oxford*

The uncarpentered world of Old English poetry   65
   EARL R. ANDERSON *Cleveland State University*

The use of modal verbs in complex sentences: some developments
   in the Old English period   81
   HIROSHI OGAWA *The University of Tokyo*

Anonymous polyphony and *The Wanderer*'s textuality   99
   CAROL BRAUN PASTERNACK *The University of California at
   Santa Barbara*

The geographic list of *Solomon and Saturn II*   123
   KATHERINE O'BRIEN O'KEEFFE *Texas A&M University*

Latin learning at Winchester in the early eleventh century: the
   evidence of the Lambeth Psalter   143
   PATRICK P. O'NEILL *University of North Carolina at Chapel
   Hill*

Poetic language and the Paris Psalter: the decay of the Old
   English tradition   167
   M.S. GRIFFITH *New College, Oxford*

v

A new Latin source for the Old English 'Three Utterances'
exemplum   187
    MARY F. WACK *Stanford University* and CHARLES D.
    WRIGHT *The University of Illinois at Urbana-Champaign*

Wulfstan's *De Antichristo* in a twelfth-century Worcester
manuscript   203
    J.E. CROSS *The University of Liverpool*

A pair of inscribed Anglo-Saxon hooked tags from the Rome
(Forum) 1883 hoard   221
    JAMES GRAHAM CAMPBELL *University College London* and
    ELISABETH OKASHA *University College, Cork*, with an
    introductory note by MICHAEL METCALF *Ashmolean*
    Museum, Oxford

Bibliography for 1990   231
    CARL T. BERKHOUT, *The University of Arizona*
    MARTIN BIDDLE, *Hertford College, Oxford*
    MARK BLACKBURN, *Gonville and Caius College, Cambridge*
    SARAH FOOT, *Gonville and Caius College, Cambridge*
    ALEXANDER RUMBLE, *The University of Manchester*
    and SIMON KEYNES, *Trinity College, Cambridge*

Index to volumes 16–20   281

*Abbreviations listed before the bibliography (pages 231–3) are used throughout the
volume without other explanation*

Illustrations

PLATES

between pages 54 and 55

I*a*   Bishop Liudhard medalet from church of St Martin, Canterbury, obverse. Liverpool, Mayer Collection

I*b*   Bishop Liudhard medalet from church of St Martin, Canterbury, reverse. Liverpool, Mayer Collection

II   Reliquary of Sainte-Croix, Poitiers

III   Byzantine ivory of the Last Judgment. London, Victoria and Albert Museum

IV   Coptic textile with jewelled Cross. Minneapolis Institute of Arts

V   Sancta Sanctorum reliquary, outer cover. Patriarchal cross on Paradise-Golgotha. Vatican, Museo Sacro

VI   Syro-Palestinian ivory pyxis. Cleveland Museum of Art

VII   J. Gritsch, *Quadragesimale* ([Strassburg, 1495]) (private collection)
a Contemporary stamped binding; front cover
b 'Hook' of lower paste-down: (original recto) Num. XXXIII.43–55
c 'Hook' of lower paste-down: (original verso) Num. XXXV.3–13

VIII   Rome (Forum) hoard, pair of silver hooked tags, inscribed (a) +DOM-NOMA, and (b) RINOPAPA+

IX   London, Upper Thames Street, bone 'motif-piece'

FIGURES

1	Mucking: plan of the settlement	*page* 4
2	Words for 'lord' in *The Paris Psalter*, *Beowulf* and *Genesis A*	169
3	Use of weak nouns in *The Paris Psalter*, *Beowulf* and *Genesis A*	171
4*a*	Distribution of Class I weak verbs in *The Paris Psalter*, *Beowulf* and *Genesis A*	173
4*b*	Distribution of Class II weak verbs in *The Paris Psalter*, *Beowulf* and *Genesis A*	173

ACKNOWLEDGEMENTS

By permission of the Trustees of the British Museum the design on the cover is taken from the obverse of a silver penny issued to celebrate King Alfred's occupation and fortification of London in 886

Permission to publish photographs has been granted by the National Museums and Galleries on Merseyside (pls. Ia, Ib), the Trustees of the Victoria and Albert Museum, London (pl. III), the Minneapolis Institute of Arts (pl. IV), the Biblioteca Apostolica Vaticana (pl. V), the Cleveland Museum of Art (pl. VI), the Trustees of the Bodleian Library, Oxford (pl. VII), the Museo Nazionale, Rome (pls. VIIIa, VIIIb), and the Museum of London (pl. IX).

Material should be submitted to the editor most convenient regionally, with these exceptions: an article should be sent to Martin Biddle if concerned with archaeology, to Robert Deshman if concerned with art history, to Simon Keynes if concerned with history, numismatics or onomastics, and to Michael Lapidge if concerned with Anglo-Latin or palaeography. Whenever a contribution is sent from abroad it should be accompanied by international coupons to cover the cost of return postage. A potential contributor is asked to get in touch with the editor concerned as early as possible to obtain a copy of the style sheet and to have any necessary discussion. Articles must be in English.

The editors' addresses are:

Professor P. S. Baker, Department of English, Emory University, Atlanta, Georgia 30322 (USA)

Mr M. Biddle, Hertford College, Oxford OX1 3BW (England)

Professor D. G. Calder, Department of English, University of California Los Angeles, Los Angeles, California 90024 (USA)

Professor R. Deshman, Graduate Department of History of Art, University of Toronto, Toronto, Ontario M5S 1A1 (Canada)

Professor K. Dietz, Institut für Englische Philologie, Freie Universität Berlin, Gosslerstrasse 2–4, 1000 Berlin 33 (Germany)

Professor R. Frank, Centre for Medieval Studies, University of Toronto, Toronto, Ontario M5S 1A1 (Canada)

Professor H. Gneuss, Institut für Englische Philologie, Universität München, 8000 München 40, Schellingstrasse 3 (Germany)

Professor M. R. Godden, Pembroke College, Oxford OX1 1DW (England)

Dr S. D. Keynes, Trinity College, Cambridge CB2 1TQ (England)

Professor M. Lapidge, Department of Anglo-Saxon, Norse and Celtic, University of Cambridge, 9 West Rd, Cambridge CB3 9DP (England)

Professor F. C. Robinson, Department of English, Yale University, New Haven, Connecticut 06520 (USA)

Settlement mobility and the 'Middle Saxon Shift': rural settlements and settlement patterns in Anglo-Saxon England

H. F. HAMEROW

The traditional image of the stable Anglo-Saxon village as the direct ancestor of the medieval village is no longer tenable in view of growing evidence for settlement mobility in the early and middle Saxon periods. Indeed, it now appears that most 'nucleated' medieval villages are not the direct successors of early, or even middle Saxon settlements, and that nucleation itself appears to be a remarkably late phenomenon.[1]

In response to a recent burst of interdisciplinary attention to the settlements and settlement patterns of Anglo-Saxon England,[2] this paper reviews the evidence for settlement mobility in the Anglo-Saxon landscape, most strikingly in evidence at the settlement complex excavated at Mucking, Essex. The implications of this mobility for the development of the later Saxon landscape are then considered, with particular regard to the 'Middle Saxon Shift' model which supposes the widespread displacement of rural settlements in the seventh and early eighth centuries, often to agriculturally superior settings, and a concomitant reorganization of territorial units.

The first Anglo-Saxon settlement to be adequately recorded was that of Sutton Courtenay, Berkshire, excavated by E. T. Leeds in the 1920s.[3] Leeds managed to salvage a number of so-called 'sunken huts' from a gravel quarry. The dug-out floors of these huts provided the only evidence of non-ecclesiastical Anglo-Saxon building known at the time, and it was concluded, understandably, that they were dwellings. Since then numerous Anglo-Saxon settlements have been excavated, albeit incompletely and generally under

---

[1] C. Taylor, *Village and Farmstead* (London, 1983).

[2] The high profile of archaeology within the wider spectrum of settlement studies is apparent in *Anglo-Saxon Settlements*, ed. D. Hooke (Oxford, 1988), the contributors to which evaluate the results of archaeological excavation and survey within the same topographical context as place-name and charter evidence. The present study owes a considerable debt to this book, as will be apparent.

[3] E. T. Leeds, 'A Saxon Village at Sutton Courtenay, Berkshire', *Archaeologia* 73 (1923), 147–92; 'A Saxon Village at Sutton Courtenay, Berkshire: Second Report', *Archaeologia* 76 (1926–7), 59–80, and 'A Saxon Village at Sutton Courtenay, Berkshire: Third Report', *Archaeologia* 112 (1947), 79–94.

unsatisfactory conditions. These have revealed that sunken huts were generally ancillary to a wide range of ground-level timber buildings or halls, including some of considerable sophistication.[4]

For example, the plan of the sixth- and seventh-century settlement excavated at Cowdery's Down, Hampshire, reveals an orderly and prosperous settlement, presumably of high status.[5] The excavator divides the settlement into three phases, the largest and final phase apparently housing a population of at least sixty. Many of the buildings lay within fenced enclosures, but the largest halls, presumably the 'chiefly' residences, lay just outside the enclosures with smaller buildings arranged inside. While the position of individual buildings shifted within these enclosed yards and the final phase saw considerable expansion and the construction of new buildings, the farmsteads essentially occupied the same parcels of land throughout the *c.* 150 year lifespan of the settlement.

A very different kind of settlement was excavated at West Stow, in the flood plain of the river Lark in Suffolk.[6] Excavations there uncovered a much higher proportion of huts to halls (67:7), which ranged in date from the fifth century to the seventh. The halls have been interpreted as the focal points for family units, each with one or two huts around it at any one time. The excavator has suggested that these buildings represent the progressive shifting of the same three farmsteads in the course of some two and a half centuries.[7]

The settlement of Catholme, on the river Trent near Burton, consisted of at least eight enclosed farmsteads, with two trackways running through the village. The excavation yielded few datable artefacts, but radiocarbon dates suggest that it may have been occupied from the late fifth century to the tenth.[8] At Catholme, the same holdings remained where they were first established, despite repeated rebuilding of individual structures. This planning and stability is in sharp contrast to West Stow with its shifting farmsteads, and, as I shall argue, appears to be atypical of Anglo-Saxon rural settlements generally.

This tiny sample of excavated settlements is hardly representative, but it does reflect the tremendous diversity of Anglo-Saxon rural communities. This

[4] For a general overview of the archaeology of Anglo-Saxon rural settlements, the standard reference remains: P. Rahtz, 'Buildings and Rural Settlements', *The Archaeology of Anglo-Saxon England*, ed. D. Wilson, 2nd ed. (Cambridge, 1981), pp. 49–98. A valuable update has been provided by M. Welch, 'Rural Settlement Patterns in the Early and Middle Anglo-Saxon Periods', *Landscape Hist.* 7 (1985), 13–24.
[5] M. Millett, 'Excavations at Cowdery's Down, Basingstoke, 1978–1981', *Arch J* 140 (1983), 151–279, fig. 27.
[6] S. West, *West Stow: the Anglo-Saxon Village*, 2 vols., East Anglian Archaeol. 24 (Ipswich, 1985).   [7] *Ibid.* II, fig. 301.
[8] S. Losco-Bradley and H. Wheeler, 'Anglo-Saxon Settlement in the Trent Valley: Some Aspects', *Studies in Late Anglo-Saxon Settlement*, ed. M. Faull (Oxford, 1984), pp. 101–14.

diversity is suggestive of a socio-economic hierarchy, but the archaeological evidence is as yet insufficient to define this hierarchy more closely, or to establish whether there is regional variation. Only excavation of more settlements on a large scale can ultimately resolve these questions. Increasingly severe restrictions imposed on the funding of archaeological excavation make the achievement of this goal in the near future unlikely. One Anglo-Saxon settlement has, however, been excavated on a truly large scale, that of Mucking, in south-east Essex.

Crop-marks first revealed the archaeological potential of the Mucking settlement complex, situated on the 100′ gravel terrace overlooking the Thames estuary.[9] Excavations took place between 1965 and 1978 under the direction of M. U. Jones and W. T. Jones, in advance of quarrying. In the course of those thirteen years, a highly complex multi-period archaeological landscape was revealed, spread across some fifty acres. Area excavation on this scale remains unparalleled in England. With its two pagan cemeteries, at least fifty-three post-hole buildings and over two hundred sunken huts, Mucking remains by far the most extensive Anglo-Saxon settlement excavated to date in England.[10] It is, furthermore, virtually the only Anglo-Saxon settlement known from excavation which we can be confident was settled during Myres's 'phase of transition, AD 410–450', and was continuously occupied at least to the beginning of the eighth century.[11]

The distributions across the site of datable metalwork, and of local and imported pottery, clearly indicate that the plan of the settlement can be divided into sectors of various date, as indicated in fig. 1. The boundaries shown on

---

[9] M. U. Jones, V. Evison, and J. N. L. Myres, 'Crop-mark Sites at Mucking, Essex', *AntJ* 48 (1968), 210–30. The following section is based on H. Hamerow, 'Anglo-Saxon Pottery and Spatial Development at Mucking, Essex', *Berichten van de Rijksdienst voor het Oudheidkundig Bodemonderzoek* 37 (1987), 245–73.

[10] M. U. Jones and W. T. Jones, 'The Crop-mark Sites at Mucking, Essex, England', *Recent Archaeological Excavations in Europe*, ed. R. Bruce-Mitford (London, 1975), pp. 133–87; H. Hamerow, 'Mucking: the Anglo-Saxon Settlement', *CA* 111 (Sept. 1988), 128–31.

[11] During the early years of the excavations, it was suggested that a substantial settlement of barbarian mercenaries – *foederati* – had been stationed at Mucking in the late fourth or early fifth century, to protect London and reinforce the strained defences of the *civitates*. While the hypothesis is historically plausible, it rests upon rather tenuous assumptions regarding the early date and supposed military affiliations of certain types of late Roman metalwork, so-called 'Romano-Saxon pottery' and other pottery types. Many of these assumptions have since come under serious criticism. In short, while the hypothesis that Anglo-Saxon Mucking originated as a federate settlement cannot be dismissed, the archaeological evidence is insufficient to prove it. See J. Morris, review of J. N. L. Myres and B. Green, *The Anglo-Saxon Cemeteries of Caistor-by-Norwich and Markshall, Norfolk*, in *MA* 18 (1974), 225–32; S. Hawkes, 'Some Recent Finds of Late Roman Buckles', *Britannia* 5 (1974), 386–93; and W. Roberts, *Romano-Saxon Pottery*, BAR, Brit. Ser. 106 (Oxford, 1982).

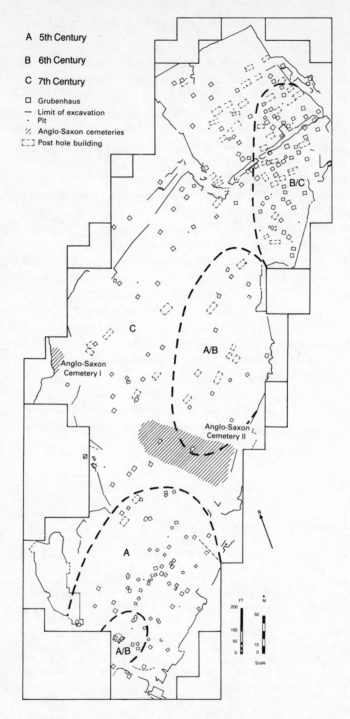

A 5th Century

B 6th Century

C 7th Century

□ Grubenhaus
— Limit of excavation
· Pit
╱ Anglo-Saxon cemeteries
⌐ ⌐ Post hole building

B/C

C

A/B

Anglo-Saxon
Cemetery I

Anglo-Saxon
Cemetery II

A

N

A/B

FT   M

200   50

100   10

50   0

Scale

Fig. 1   Mucking: plan of the settlement

fig. 1 should not be viewed as absolute (it cannot, for example, be assumed that every building in phase 'A' is fifth-century in date), but rather as demarcating broad phases of settlement as suggested by the distribution of artefacts.[12]

An unambiguous picture of shifting settlement is provided by this plan, and for the first time in England we can identify what archaeologists and geographers on the continent have termed a *Wandersiedlung* – literally, a wandering settlement.[13] There is no evidence for discontinuous or abrupt shifts; instead, a gradual change in the focus of the settlement is indicated, occurring perhaps one farm at a time.

Such mobility is discernible at other English settlements, most strikingly at West Stow, as already noted; but also at New Wintles Farm, Oxon., and Purwell Farm, Oxon. Excavations at Walton and Pennylands in Buckinghamshire revealed settlements dating primarily from the fifth century to the seventh, but more recently, both sites have yielded a number of eighth-century finds. The middle Saxon settlements at Wicken Bonhunt, Essex, and Maxey, Northamptonshire, both yielded small quantities of early Saxon pottery from outlying features, suggesting continuous but shifting development.[14] Such shifting, however, is most clearly defined at Mucking. Professor Waterbolk has defined two types of settlement shift:[15] the first occurs when the main building within a farm complex shifts within its yard or property; the second, when the entire settlement relocates. Because properties as such cannot be identified with any certainty at Mucking, it is unlikely that the first type of shift can ever be recognized there. It is quite clear, however, that the extent, location and layout of the settlement as a whole changed substantially in the course of the fifth to seventh centuries.

In the initial phase of settlement (fig. 1, 'A'), the southwestern sector of the terrace was the focus for relatively dense occupation; some huts were rebuilt

---

[12] The archaeological basis of this phasing is described in detail in H. Hamerow, *Mucking: the Anglo-Saxon Settlement*, English Heritage Monograph (London, 1991).

[13] H. Jankuhn, 'Die eisenzeitlichen Würzeln unserer mittelalterlichen Dörfer', *Die Kunde* 37 (1986), 93–103.

[14] West, *West Stow* II, fig. 30; F. Berisford, 'The Early Anglo-Saxon Settlement Sites in the Upper Thames Basin with Special Reference to the Area around Cassington and Eynsham' (unpubl. B. Litt. dissertation, Oxford Univ., 1973), pp. 40 and 42–3; M. Farley, 'Saxon and Medieval Walton, Aylesbury: Excavations 1973–74', *Records of Buckinghamshire* 20 (1976), 153–290, at 167, and 'The View from the Hill: Middle Saxon Settlement in Buckinghamshire', paper presented to conference on Middle Saxon England (1990); K. Wade, 'A Settlement Site at Bonhunt Farm, Wicken Bonhunt, Essex', in *Archaeology in Essex to A.D. 1500*, ed. D. Buckley, CBA Research Report 34 (London, 1980), 96–103; P. Addyman, 'A Dark-Age Settlement at Maxey, Northamptonshire', *MA* 8 (1964), 20–73, at 40.

[15] H. T. Waterbolk, 'Mobilität von Dorf, Ackerflur und Gräberfeld in Drenthe seit der Latènezeit: archäologische Siedlungsforschungen auf der nordniederländischen Geest', *Offa* 39 (1982), 97–137, at 103.

on roughly the same spot up to three times, an indication that occupation of this area was of considerable duration. Remnant prehistoric, and especially Roman, ditches (and perhaps surviving hedges) seem to have conditioned the layout of this early phase, as many of the huts were dug alongside these ditches.

In the succeeding phase, probably sometime in the sixth century (fig. 1, 'A/ B'), the main focus of settlement shifted to the north, just beyond Anglo-Saxon cemetery II. This phase of settlement appears to have been smaller, presumably briefer in duration, and certainly more dispersed than that of the initial occupation.

The third phase of settlement (fig. 1, 'B/C'), corresponding roughly to the sixth and seventh centuries, may have overlapped chronologically with this central scatter of buildings; the settlement still lay along the terrace edge, but had moved further to the northeast. Occupation was again comparatively dense, and some of the buildings appear to have been crudely aligned.[16] In the course of the seventh century the settlement shifted away from the edge of the terrace westward. The largest huts were found in this phase, and seem to represent widely dispersed, single farmsteads. The parish church of Mucking lies two kilometres northeast of the excavation, off the terrace, near a creek; it is possible that part of the Anglo-Saxon settlement moved down the slope in that direction as well. Crop-marks, however, gave no indication of this, and excavation there has not been possible.

We must therefore imagine Mucking not as a single, sprawling village, but rather as a shifting hamlet, at times perhaps more than one. It consisted of a conglomeration of single farmsteads without clearly defined properties, common boundaries or trackways. The spatial relationships of these farm-steads, ranging from clustered to dispersed, presumably reflect varying degrees of social interaction; at certain phases, the settlement appears to have been a relatively integrated community, while in the final phase of settlement there can have been few communal arrangements.

A number of *Wandersiedlungen* have been excavated on the Continent, and it is to these settlements that we must turn for the best comparative data for Mucking. Continental methods of excavation, whereby large areas are stripped of plough soil, are particularly well suited for revealing the layouts of shifting settlements. A number of these large-scale settlement excavations have been published, notably those of Wijster and Odoorn in Drenthe;

---

[16] The fact that so few post-hole buildings are recorded from phase 'A' is almost certainly due to necessarily incomplete excavation in advance of quarrying which took place in this part of the site.

Flögeln and Gristede in Lower Saxony; and Nørre Snede and Vorbasse in central Jutland.[17]

Around the medieval village of Vorbasse, for example, a series of settlements spanning the first century B.C. to the eleventh century A.D. have been excavated, lying up to 500 metres apart. In Denmark, as in Germany and the Netherlands, archaeologists have defined territories which were continuously occupied from the pre-Roman Iron Age to the early medieval period; yet rarely did the settlements, field systems, and cemeteries within these territories remain on the same spot for much more than a century. Indeed, in Denmark, stable settlements are known only since the eleventh and twelfth centuries.[18] We may now be reasonably certain that a similar pattern of shifting settlement was often the case in early and middle Saxon England, at least in lowland regions. The causes of this mobility, and of the apparent stability (*Platzkonstanz*) of a few settlements,[19] remain obscure. The gradual shifting of these settlements presumably relates to agricultural practice; the use, for example, of former house sites and farmyards as arable has been demonstrated at Vorbasse.[20]

To return to Mucking, population size has obvious relevance for any consideration of the development of the Mucking settlement, and here the evidence from the cemeteries is crucial. Up to sixty-three burials, all inhumations, were recovered from Cemetery I. Cemetery II, lying 150 metres to the east, contained over 750 burials, roughly one-third inhumations and two-thirds cremations. As the phasing of the settlement demonstrates, there is not a

---

[17] W.A. van Es, *Wijster: a Native Village Beyond the Imperial Frontier*, Palaeohistoria 11 (1967); H.T. Waterbolk, 'Odoorn im frühen Mittelalter', *Neue Ausgrabungen und Forschungen in Niedersachsen* 8 (1973), 25–89; P. Schmid, 'Ländliche Siedlungen der vorrömischen Eisenzeit bis Völkerwanderungszeit im niedersächsischen Küstengebiet', *Offa* 39 (1982), 73–96; D. Zoller, 'Die Ergebnisse der Grabung Gristede, Kr. Ammerland, 1971–73', *Neue Ausgrabungen und Forschungen in Niedersachsen* 9 (1975), 35–57; T. Hansen, 'Nørre Snede', *Jnl of Danish Archaeol.* 1 (1982), 181; S. Hvass, 'Vorbasse: The Development of a Settlement through the First Millennium A.D.', *Jnl of Danish Archaeol.* 2 (1983), 127–36.

[18] Jankuhn, 'Die eisenzeitlichen Würzeln', pp. 93–103; M. Müller-Wille, 'Siedlungs- und Flurformen als Zeugnisse frühgeschichtlicher Betriebsformen der Landwirtschaft', *Geschichtswissenschaft und Archäologie: Untersuchungen zur Siedlungs-, Wirtschafts- und Kirchengeschichte*, ed. H. Jankuhn and R. Wenskus (Sigmaringen, 1979), pp. 355–72, at 365.

[19] The settlements of Cowdery's Down and Catholme, for example, appear to have been relatively stable. Cowdery's Down, however, was not founded until the sixth century, and appears to have been both short-lived and of high status. At Catholme, it may be that the planned layout of the settlement orginated at a later phase of occupation.

[20] S. Hvass, 'Die Völkerwanderungszeitliche Siedlung Vorbasse, Mitteljütland', *Acta Archaeologica* 49 (1979), 61–112, at 108; S. Hvass, 'Die Struktur einer Siedlung der Zeit von Christi Geburt bis ins 5. Jahrhundert nach Christus: Ausgrabungen in Vorbasse, Jütland, Dänemark', *Studien zur Sachsenforschung* 2 (1980), 161–80, at 179.

simple equation between two cemeteries and two settlements, as was originally imagined. Only a thorough analysis of the cemeteries may eventually explain why there were two essentially contemporary burial grounds apparently serving the same community. Assuming that both cemeteries relate to the excavated settlement, a crude comparison of the number of buildings with the number of burials suggests an undifferentiated average population of between eighty-five and one hundred, with at least nine to ten post-hole buildings and fourteen sunken huts in use at any one time.[21]

What few demographic data we have for this period indicate that a community of this size was exceptional. Yet the lack of any clear internal organization, and the absence of large, 'high status', or obviously central buildings, generated the hypothesis in the early years of the excavation that Mucking was a 'pioneer' settlement, a first landfall for storm-tossed immigrants from Lower Saxony. The grave-goods of the founders of Anglo-Saxon Mucking and their descendants, however, reflect considerable wealth and a distinct social hierarchy, belying the rather impoverished appearance of the settlement.[22]

The affluence and social hierarchy apparent in the cemeteries at Mucking are thus not reflected in the arrangement and size of the buildings. So few associated settlements and cemeteries have been excavated, however, that it would be premature to attempt a detailed model to explain this contrast in social terms. It is nevertheless of interest to note that at Hjemsted in southwest Jutland, a prosperous-looking fourth- to fifth-century settlement consisting of large, sophisticated timber buildings was associated with burials which contained remarkably few precious items. Another apparently prosperous and carefully planned settlement is that of Wijster, in Drenthe. Here, too, the excavator remarks of the associated fourth- and fifth-century burials that 'the poverty of the grave goods is striking'.[23] The evidence is far from conclusive, however, and a number of possible solutions may be offered for this contrast

[21] This sort of demographic analysis is fraught with ambiguity, however. For example, it seems certain that there may originally have been many more post-hole buildings at Mucking than were recorded, and some of those recorded may not have functioned as living quarters; estimates of the life spans of people and houses in early Anglo-Saxon England remain, furthermore, little more than educated guesses. A more detailed demographic analysis is attempted in Hamerow, *Mucking*.

[22] An elaborate silver-inlaid bronze belt-set or *cingulum*, several sword burials and imported glass vessels excavated from the cemeteries are among the grave-goods illustrated in Jones and Jones, 'The Crop-Mark Sites at Mucking, Essex', pls. xxvii–xxviii and figs. 58–62.

[23] P. Ethelberg, *Hjemsted: en gravplads fra 4. & 5. årh. e. kr.* (Haderslev, 1986); W. Haarnagel and P. Schmid, 'Siedlungen', in *Siedlungen im deutschen Küstengebiet vom 5. Jh. v. Chr. bis zum 11. Jh. n. Chr.*, ed. G. Kossack, K.-E. Behre and P. Schmid, 2 vols. (Bonn, 1984) I, fig. 78; and van Es, *Wijster*.

between settlements and their associated cemeteries. At Wijster, for example, the small numbers of excavated burials dating to the fourth and fifth centuries are insufficient to have peopled the buildings in the settlement. They thus appear to represent only a fraction of the total population, and richer burials may be located elsewhere.[24]

At Mucking, we see the reverse situation, namely cemeteries containing a considerable number of well-furnished burials, associated with an unremarkable settlement.[25] Bishopstone, Sussex, and West Stow are virtually the only other English sites of this period where both settlement and cemetery have been excavated extensively, and (at least in part) published. Here too, the settlements appear to have consisted of small, essentially undifferentiated buildings, but were associated with a number of well-furnished burials.[26]

Could the apparently haphazard layout and humble buildings of the Mucking settlement be a reflection of socio-economic stress and instability? Such stress may have led to the investment of wealth in the burial of the dead in order to establish an ancestral presence on the land, and thus, as Bullough has suggested, assert the community's claim to local resources.[27] Alternatively, the lack of any obvious structure or planning within the settlement may simply reflect the absence of an overall, regulating authority.

A causal link between socio-economic stress and the phenomenon of 'poor' settlements associated with 'rich' burials must of course remain a hypothetical formulation. Ancestral ties could, however, also offer an explanation for the otherwise puzzling reluctance of the Mucking settlers to abandon the poor soils and windswept conditions of the terrace, initially settled perhaps through compulsion or for strategic reasons.[28] The importance of ancestor worship in the relationship between early Germanic communities and the land has recently been discussed by several scholars. Bullough, for example, has called attention to the link between the burial of ancestors and the property rights of kin expressed in certain early law codes.[29] Chapelot and Fossier have noted the importance of the spatial relationship between cemeteries and settlements, and suggest that the latter frequently moved about a 'sacred zone', while the cemeteries remained essentially static. They see the ultimate abandonment of

---

[24] van Es, *Wijster*, p. 503; see also M.D. Schön, 'Gräberfelder der römischen Kaiserzeit und frühen Völkerwanderungszeit aus dem Zentralteil der Siedlungskammer von Flögeln, Ldkr. Cuxhaven', *Neue Ausgrabungen und Forschungen in Niedersachen* 18 (1988), 181–297, at 233.

[25] Statistical evaluation of the Mucking cemeteries is in progress (S. Hirst and D. Clarke, forthcoming).

[26] West, *West Stow*. It seems unlikely, however, that the whole of the settlement was excavated.

[27] D. Bullough, 'Burial, Community and Belief in the Early Medieval West', *Ideal and Reality in Frankish and Anglo-Saxon Society*, ed. P. Wormald (Oxford, 1983), pp. 177–201, at 194–5.

[28] Hamerow, *Mucking*.   [29] Bullough, 'Burial, Community and Belief', p. 195.

pagan cemeteries and their replacement by burials around a church as the 'breaking of the religious link between the land belonging to the dead and that of the living', although as R. K. Morris has noted, this process was a gradual one.[30]

The findings at Mucking can be summarised as follows: first, that the settlement belonged to the category of *Wandersiedlungen*, long familiar from continental excavations; second, that the Mucking settlement, though mobile, continued to utilize the same burial grounds for some three centuries; and third, that the density of Anglo-Saxon settlements and burials in the immediate vicinity of Mucking, and place-name evidence,[31] suggest that this shifting occurred not at random, but within a territorial unit, and possibly within the framework of a regional administration.

The abandonment of its ancestral territory by the Mucking community, and the breaking of the link between pagan cemeteries and their associated settlements, must ultimately be related to more generalized changes in the Anglo-Saxon landscape. Several interrelated factors lay behind these changes. In the first place, increases in the power of dynastic chiefdoms and religious foundations must have had a profound impact on the pattern of rural settlement in many areas. The monastery of Tilbury, for example, founded by St Cedd *c.* 653, must have lain a scant 3 km from the Mucking settlement. Population growth has also been suggested by a number of scholars, most recently by T. Unwin, as a catalyst for settlement nucleation, although we lack the demographic data from England needed to test this model.[32] Finally, the changing pattern of middle and late Saxon settlement has also been explained in terms of agricultural advances which made new, heavier soils available for

---

[30] J. Chapelot and R. Fossier, *The Village and House in the Middle Ages* (London, 1985), p. 41; R.K. Morris, *The Church in British Archaeology* (London, 1983). The recognition that the majority of pre-conversion cemeteries are adjacent to their associated settlement finds further confirmation in the recent publication of Anglo-Saxon settlement/cemetery complexes at Puddlehill, Bedfordshire; Spong Hill, Norfolk; and West Heslerton, N. Yorkshire. See C. L. Matthews and S.C. Hawkes, 'Early Saxon Settlements and Burials on Puddlehill, near Dunstable, Bedfordshire', *ASSAH* 4 (1985), 59–115, fig. 1; C. Hills, K. Penn and R. Rickett, *The Anglo-Saxon Cemetery at Spong Hill, North Elmham Part IV: Catalogue of Cremations*, East Anglian Archaeol. 34 (Gressenhall, 1987), fig. 133; and D. Powlesland, 'Excavations at Heslerton, North Yorkshire 1978–82', *ArchJ* 143 (1987), 53–173, at 143, fig. 70.

[31] Especially the proximity of place-names in *-gē*. See N. Brooks, 'The Creation and Early Structure of the Kingdom of Kent', *The Origins of Anglo-Saxon Kingdoms*, ed. S. Bassett (Leicester, 1989), pp. 55–74; Hamerow, *Mucking*.

[32] T. Unwin, 'Towards a Model of Anglo-Scandinavian Rural Settlement in England', *Anglo-Saxon Settlements*, ed. Hooke, pp. 77–98, at 80; Müller-Wille, 'Siedlungs- und Flurformen'; M. Hughes, 'Rural Settlement and Landscape in Late Saxon Hampshire', *Studies in Late Anglo-Saxon Settlement*, ed. Faull, pp. 65–80, at 74.

cultivation; the laying out of open fields, for example; or environmental changes, such as soil erosion or changing water tables.[33]

A model, often called the 'Middle Saxon shift', has gained wide acceptance as an explanation for the apparent differences between the settlement patterns of early and late Saxon England. The concept of a 'Middle Saxon shift' in settlement was developed most fully in 1981 by C. Arnold and P. Wardle as a theoretical framework for the development of early and middle Saxon rural settlement patterns. Their study builds on earlier work, especially that of D. Bonney, which suggested that the distribution of pagan Saxon burials in some cases reflected embryonic territories, and that these territories could be related to later administrative structures, namely parish boundaries.[34] The basis of their model may very briefly be summarised as follows:

1. That early Anglo-Saxon settlements and cemeteries are situated on light, relatively poor soils, often in elevated locations, such as hilltops or terraces.

2. That early place-name elements, in contrast, are located on richer soils, often in valleys, and often not associated with pagan cemeteries.

3. That these pagan cemeteries tend to be located on or near parish boundaries.

The authors infer a widespread shift in settlement from poor, elevated locations to prime sites, often on heavier soils in river valleys; this shift, they claim, finds archaeological confirmation in the desertion of settlements founded in the fifth and sixth centuries, and the emergence of new centres in the seventh and eighth centuries. This process did not merely involve the 'relocation of settlements within a defined land unit, but the reorganization of such territorial units, some of whose new boundaries later became fossilized as parish boundaries', leaving earlier settlements on the margins of these new territories. The authors suggest a change in 'land use requirements' as the cause of the proposed shift.[35]

---

[33] Berisford, 'The Early Anglo-Saxon Settlement Sites in the Upper Thames Basin', p. 22; D. Hall, 'The Late Saxon Countryside: Villages and their Fields', *Anglo-Saxon Settlements*, ed. Hooke, pp. 99–122, at 102–3; Welch, 'Rural Settlement Patterns in the Early and Middle Anglo-Saxon Periods', pp. 21–2.

[34] C. Arnold and P. Wardle, 'Early Medieval Settlement Patterns in England', *MA* 25 (1981), 145–9; D. Bonney, 'Pagan Saxon Burials and Boundaries in Wiltshire', *Wiltshire Archaeol. Magazine* 61 (1966), 25–30; D. Bonney, 'Early Boundaries and Estates in Southern England', *Medieval Settlement*, ed. P. Sawyer (London, 1976), pp. 72–82.

[35] Arnold and Wardle, 'Early Medieval Settlement Patterns in England', p. 148. New data from excavation and surveys are often fitted too readily into the framework offered by the 'Middle Saxon shift'. Thus, the results of the recent 'East Anglian Kingdom Survey' which has identified numerous potential settlements primarily from surface scatters of finds and pottery have provisionally been interpreted as reflecting 'a clear fall in the number of sites between the fourth and fifth centuries, a steady growth throughout the later fifth and sixth followed

This attempt to view Anglo-Saxon settlement patterns within a dynamic topographical context represented an important advance. Yet the evidence adduced for the widespread abandonment of settlements by the early eighth century is, as will be argued, inconclusive, and the introduction of open fields at such an early date has been shown to be essentially untenable. These problems have been addressed in a detailed and lucid critique by Martin Welch.[36] It may nevertheless be useful to re-examine the Middle Saxon shift model here, in view of the new evidence from Mucking.

Andrew Russel has recently tested the model set forth by Arnold and Wardle statistically against 34 East Anglian settlements.[37] His results reveal that while early Saxon settlements may in general lie closer to parish boundaries than do parish churches, both tend to be located closer to the edges than to the centre of the parish. This is certainly true at Mucking. While 23% of early Saxon settlements lie within 400 metres of the parish church, only 17% are more than 2 km distant. Russel concludes that the predominant factor in determining the location of early settlements was their proximity to running water, and that it was along these water courses that the medieval parish boundaries were often drawn. In view of the chronological gaps between pagan burials, church sites of the Late Saxon period and parish boundaries which often did not crystallize before the twelfth century, it is hardly surprising that attempts to relate them topographically are frequently inconclusive.[38]

Regarding the foundation of 'new centres' in the seventh and eighth centuries as proposed by Arnold and Wardle, this phenomenon may in many cases be more apparent than real, and a consequence of the limited size of field surveys and excavations. Russel makes an important, if obvious, point: 'If the settlements were continuously shifting across the landscape, or coalescing from a dispersed settlement pattern, searching a small area will produce finds mostly of one period of occupation.'[39] Mucking is a perfect example: had only its northernmost sector been excavated, Mucking would no doubt have been

---

by a shift in the seventh century, and then a dramatic increase in the ninth and tenth centuries'. See J. Newman, 'East Anglian Kingdom Survey: Final Interim Report on the South East Suffolk Pilot Field Survey', *Bull. of the Sutton Hoo Research Committee* 6 (April, 1989), 17–19.

[36] Welch, 'Rural Settlement Patterns in the Early and Middle Anglo-Saxon Periods', pp. 19–21.

[37] A. Russel, 'Early Anglo-Saxon Ceramics from East Anglia: A Microprovenience Study' (unpubl. Ph.D. thesis, Univ. of Southampton, 1984), pp. 96–114. I am grateful to Dr Russel for allowing me to refer to his work.

[38] This is not to say that such relationships did not exist. For example, 'early estate groupings' can be shown to have influenced the formation of parish boundaries in the south-west: see D. Hooke 'Introduction: Later Anglo-Saxon England', *Anglo-Saxon Settlements*, ed. Hooke, pp. 1–8, at 5.   [39] Russel, 'Early Anglo-Saxon Ceramics from East Anglia', p. 112.

hailed as one of the 'new centres' founded in the seventh century. In other words, as Arnold and Wardle themselves warned, we are in danger of confusing a continual process of shifting settlement with a single event.[40] It thus seems imprudent to posit a major displacement and reorganization of rural settlements on the basis of the apparent desertion of sites such as Bishopstone, Cassington and Eynsham in the seventh and eighth centuries, and to disregard the possibility of steady migration.

A shift from hilltops to valleys, or from light, marginal soils, to heavy, 'prime' soils is thus inadequate to explain the supposed abandonment 'before the end of the eighth century' of virtually all excavated settlements founded in the fifth and sixth centuries.[41] The difficulty archaeologists have in dating settlements of this period undoubtedly lies behind many of these apparent 'desertions'. The paucity of grave-goods and the virtual disappearance of pottery in large parts of southern England by the end of the seventh century greatly complicate the recognition of seventh- and eighth-century contexts.[42] It is therefore necessary to re-examine the 'negative evidence' which is often adduced when proposing the abandonment of a settlement, particularly in light of recent work in East Anglia.

The first Anglo-Saxon pottery to be wheel-turned and mass-produced was manufactured in the Ipswich area between the mid-seventh and mid-ninth centuries. It was distributed relatively widely within East Anglia, and the possibilities for identifying East Anglian settlements of the elusive late seventh and eighth centuries are, therefore, promising. Indeed, the 'East Anglian Kingdom Survey' which has taken place in conjunction with the recent excavations at Sutton Hoo, has already produced impressive results, although these must necessarily be regarded as preliminary. The survey has located numerous potential settlements, including several major surface scatters of Ipswich Ware in the vicinity of parish churches. The distribution of

---

[40] Arnold and Wardle, 'Early Medieval Settlement Patterns in England', p. 147.

[41] *Ibid.*

[42] The transition, for example, from grass-tempered pottery, usually associated with the 'pagan' Saxon period, to the earliest 'shelly' wares of the Upper Thames valley, cannot be dated with any precision. Excavations at St Aldates, Oxford, suggest that the shelly wares were already developed by the late eighth- or early ninth-century, but there is no securely dated, stratified sequence linking these wares with the grass-tempered pottery of the fifth to seventh centuries. See B. Durham, 'Archaeological Investigations in St Aldates, Oxford', *Oxoniensia* 42 (1977), 83–203. The difficulties of dating late-seventh- and eighth-century contexts are addressed by: Arnold and Wardle, 'Early Medieval Settlement Patterns in England', p. 147; A. Meaney and S. Hawkes, *Two Anglo-Saxon Cemeteries at Winnall*, Soc. of Med. Archaeol. Monograph Ser. 4 (London, 1970); R. Hodges, *The Hamwih Pottery: the Local and Imported Wares*, CBA Research Report 37 (London, 1981), 53; H. Hamerow, 'The Pottery and Spatial Development of the Anglo-Saxon Settlement at Mucking, Essex' (unpubl. D. Phil. dissertation, Oxford Univ., 1987), p. 99.

these sites is apparently distinct from that of early Anglo-Saxon pottery scatters. Very few of these scatters of early pottery produced significant quantities of Ipswich Ware, leading to the conclusion that 'a shift in location probably came in the seventh century'.[43] The dating of Ipswich Ware, however, is imprecise, and there seems no reason to assume that these scatters should date to the seventh century, rather than to the eighth century, or even later. Further, the presence of Ipswich Ware as a surface scatter need not preclude the existence of an earlier, more friable, pottery component which has not survived. In the absence of excavation, the date and nature of these sites remain untested.

Outside East Anglia, Ipswich Ware is much less common, and may be restricted to 'special' settlements. Mucking, for example, produced coins dating to c. 685, but only two cross-joining sherds of Ipswich Ware. Ipswich Ware was recorded in some quantity, however, from the presumably monastic settlement at Barking and the apparently 'high status' settlement at Wicken Bonhunt.[44] Alan Vince has observed that the absence of Ipswich Ware from rural settlements along the Thames seems due, not to their abandonment by the late seventh century, but rather to patterns of trade. Thus, 'once again, we have no means of identifying the majority of middle Saxon settlements in the Thames valley since if the settlement was not involved in long-distance trade its pottery assemblage might be indistinguishable from that of an early Saxon settlement'.[45]

A number of pioneering regional surveys make it clear, furthermore, that early Anglo-Saxon settlements were usually not located on poor soils in marginal, high locations, but on the contrary, followed the Romano-British settlement of 'prime' land in river valleys.[46] In this regard, recent research in Hampshire, comparing early and middle Saxon settlement patterns to late Roman topography, as well as to the administrative and agrarian organization suggested by pre- and post-Conquest charters, has proven particularly fruitful. One of the first micro-topographical studies of rural Anglo-Saxon settlement was undertaken by Professor B. Cunliffe for the area around the village of

[43] Newman, 'East Anglian Kingdom Survey'.

[44] K. Wade, 'A Settlement Site at Bonhunt Farm', *Archaeology in Essex to A.D. 1500*, ed. D. Buckley, CBA Research Report 34 (London 1980), 96–103; D. Priddy, 'Excavations in Essex 1986', *Essex Archaeol. and Hist.* 18 (1987), 104.

[45] A. Vince, 'New Light on Saxon Pottery from the London Area', *The London Archaeologist* 4.16 (Autumn, 1984), 431–9.

[46] The distribution of early Kentish settlements, for example, appears to have been strongly influenced by the position of Roman roads and trackways, water courses and fertile soils. See A. Everitt, *Continuity and Colonization: the Evolution of Kentish Settlement* (Leicester, 1986), *passim*; and S. Hawkes, 'Anglo-Saxon Kent c. 425–725', *Archaeology in Kent to A.D. 1500*, ed. P. Leach, CBA Research Report 48 (London, 1982), fig. 28.

Chalton.[47] Since elaborated upon by M. Hughes,[48] the model proposed involves the foundation of early Saxon hill-top communities (in this instance, Church Down and Catherington) and their abandonment by the ninth century, to be replaced by valley settlements (in this instance, Chalton, Idsworth and Blendworth) by the time of the Domesday survey. Cunliffe prefers a model of migrating settlement, involving the gradual eclipsing of at least some early communities by a series of 'satellite' settlements, to one of abrupt abandonment.

The pattern of early Saxon settlement in Hampshire has since been shown to be more complex, and to have been conditioned in part by the Roman landscape. Place-names in *-hām*, denoting 'a village community', are considered to represent in many cases the earliest phase of Anglo-Saxon settlement. The topographical distribution of the *-hām* element reveals a variety of correlations between these names, Roman settlements of various kinds and Roman roads in the Midlands, East Anglia, Kent, Surrey and Sussex.[49] In Hampshire, although pagan Saxon cemeteries show no clear correspondence to Roman settlement, the relationship of place-names in *-hām* to the latter is unmistakable. How this relationship should be interpreted is less clear, and, as Martin Biddle has noted, the cause of such correlations between early Anglo-Saxon place-names and Romano-British settlement undoubtedly varied from region to region.[50]

More recently, archaeological survey and excavation in the Meon valley in Hampshire have revealed a fourth-century building, sixth-century burials, and a middle to late Saxon settlement all within 400 metres of one another, reflecting considerable mobility within a restricted area. The potential for territorial analyses in this region is further enhanced by the quality of the charter evidence.[51]

While the correlation between Romano-British and early Saxon settlement patterns is thus becoming more clearly defined, the contrast between the dispersed pattern of early Saxon settlement and the increasingly nucleated

---

[47] B. Cunliffe, 'Saxon and Medieval Settlement-Pattern in the Region of Chalton, Hampshire', *MA* 16 (1972), 1–12.

[48] Hughes, 'Rural Settlement and Landscape in Late Saxon Hampshire', p. 112.

[49] M. Gelling, *Signposts to the Past* (London, 1978), p. 112; B. Cox, 'The Significance of the Distribution of English Place-Names in *-hām* in the Midlands and East Anglia', *JEPNS* 5 (1973), 15–73; Hawkes, 'Anglo-Saxon Kent *c.* 425–725'; J. McN. Dodgson, 'Place-Names from *hām*, Distinguished from *hamm* Names, in Relation to the Settlement of Kent, Surrey and Sussex', *ASE* 2 (1973), 1–50.

[50] M. Biddle, 'Hampshire and the Origins of Wessex', *Problems in Economic and Social Archaeology*, ed. G. Sieveking, I. Longworth and K. Wilson (London, 1976), pp. 323–42, at 332 and fig. 2.

[51] M. Hughes, 'The Meon Valley Landscape Project', *Soc. for Landscape Stud. Newsletter, 1988*, pp. 7–10.

pattern apparent in much of England, if not by the time of Domesday Book, then certainly by 1200, still requires interpretation. Steady settlement 'drift' is insufficient to explain it. A growing number of excavations and surface surveys confirm Hurst's observation, made already in the early 1970s, that while late Saxon settlements often lie beneath medieval villages, they do not in turn overlie early or middle Saxon settlements. For example, David Hall's work in Northamptonshire reveals that early Anglo-Saxon settlements closely followed the pattern of Romano-British settlement; this pattern, however, is 'quite unlike that of later villages'.[52] In his survey of 152 parishes, 82 early to middle Saxon sites lay well away from 'present vills', while only 14 medieval villages yielded evidence of early or middle Saxon occupation. Only one deserted late Saxon settlement was identified.

The Fenlands of Norfolk have yielded further evidence for a significant nucleation of settlement occurring in the late Saxon period. Apart from two middle Saxon sites, Walton and Walpole, which occupied topographically desirable positions and developed into late Saxon villages, the remaining six middle Saxon settlements produced little or no late Saxon material.[53] The evidence for early Anglo-Saxon settlement in this region, however, remains intractably sparse.

The 'second' settlement shift identified by M. Hughes in Hampshire between the eighth and eleventh centuries thus finds parallels in the regional models discussed above, despite a certain degree of variability in different landscapes, and under different political and economic constraints.[54] Any substantial reorganization of territorial units in the seventh and eighth centuries (as distinct from an *expansion* of settlement at this time), however, remains in question. If a widespread shift or nucleation of settlement is inferred, then there is no reason to suppose that this process began any earlier than the late eighth or ninth century, later than archaeologists, at any rate, have tended to believe.[55]

It seems increasingly likely that this 'shift' was not simply from marginal to

---

52 J. G. Hurst, 'The Changing Medieval Village in England', in *Man, Settlement and Urbanism*, ed. P. J. Ucko, R. Tringham and G. W. Dimbleby (London, 1972), pp. 531–40; D. Hall, 'The Late Saxon Countryside: Villages and their Fields', *Anglo-Saxon Settlements*, ed. Hooke, pp. 99–122, at 100–1.

53 R. Silvester, *The Fenland Project 3*, East Anglian Archaeol. 45 (Ipswich, 1988), 158.

54 Hughes, 'Rural Settlement and Landscape in Late Saxon Hampshire', p. 76.

55 C. Taylor, *Village and Farmstead*, p. 120. Also, R. Dodgshon, *The Origins of British Field Systems: an Interpretation* (London, 1980), p. 110. W. J. Blair has observed that this transition from scattered settlement (i.e. multi-vill estates scattered across *parochiae*) to nucleated settlement (i.e. villages based on 'cellular' manors) seems in many cases to have been associated with the breaking up of multiple estates from the ninth to eleventh centuries. See W. J. Blair, 'Minster Churches in the Landscape', *Anglo-Saxon Settlements*, ed. Hooke, pp. 35–58, at 56.

prime locations, or from dispersed to nucleated settlements, but involved a fundamental change from essentially mobile to essentially stable communities. This process was undoubtedly closely related to changes in agrarian organization, in particular the desirability of nucleated settlement for the efficient maintenance of open-field farming.[56]

With the recognition of settlement mobility as an essential factor in determining rural settlement patterns in early and middle Saxon England, the still widely held view that 'the only sites available for total excavation are precisely the minor sites, or the "failed" sites, which were abandoned', seems less persuasive.[57] It is important that these settlements not be regarded as atypical or 'failed' communities, but instead as the by-products of a natural, indeed 'typical' pattern of migrating settlement. The fact that so few Anglo-Saxon settlements have been excavated on a large scale has led to a distorted perception of settlement patterns; hypotheses of desertion and 'gaps' in settlement are frequently offered as explanations when incomplete excavation is more likely to blame. Surface survey, no matter how thorough, can rarely exclude the disconcerting possibility that the missing phase of settlement lies in the next field. The implications for excavation and survey strategies, and for presumed correlations between early place-names and settlements, should be obvious.

As our understanding of the processes of estate formation and settlement nucleation in the late Saxon period increases, the nature of earlier settlement types and patterns remains elusive. More large-scale excavation of individual settlements and their associated cemeteries, combined with regional field surveys, are desperately needed if we are to understand how the shifting settlements which predominated in the early Anglo-Saxon landscape resolved themselves into the estate pattern which 'was to survive to the present day and establish the administrative pattern of the rural landscape for the next 1000 years'.[58]

---

[56] D. Hooke, *The Anglo-Saxon Landscape: the Kingdom of the Hwicce* (Oxford, 1985), p. 144. Medieval villages could also shift, of course, although this generally involved the expansion, contraction, or complete relocation of villages, rather than the gradual drifting characteristic of the *Wandersiedlungen* of this earlier period. See C. Taylor, 'Aspects of Village Mobility in Medieval and Later Times', *The Effect of Man on the Landscape: the Lowland Zone*, ed. S. Limbrey and J.G. Evans, CBA Research Report 21 (London, 1978), 126–34.

[57] S. Hawkes, 'The Early Saxon Period', *The Archaeology of the Oxford Region*, ed. G. Briggs, J. Cook and T. Rowley (Oxford, 1986), pp. 64–108, at 85.

[58] D. Hooke, 'Regional Variation in Southern and Central England in the Anglo-Saxon Period and its Relationship to Land Units and Settlement', *Anglo-Saxon Settlements*, ed. Hooke, pp. 123–52, at 151. I am grateful to John Blair, Martin Welch and Alan Vince for their comments on an earlier version of this article. I also wish to thank the Department of Medieval and Later Antiquities of the British Museum, and English Heritage, for granting free access to the Mucking archive. I gratefully acknowledge the support of the Mary Somerville Research Fellowship, Somerville College, Oxford.

Adultery in early Anglo-Saxon society: Æthelberht 31 in comparison with continental Germanic law

THEODORE JOHN RIVERS

As in other societies, adultery was a punishable offence among the Germanic peoples. Although it is a topic which has commanded considerable attention, it has been given attention not so much because it deals with family law and its significance to social history, as because it concerns the treatment of women. But closely related to the question of women, of course, is that of how men view each other. Even as early as Tacitus,[1] evidence exists that Germanic women were treated with respect, and were subject to the protection or *mundium* of male relatives. Although exaggerated, the account in the *Germania* gives us some understanding of the role of Germanic women in respect of betrothal, marriage and family life. But it also leaves us with questions to which we most likely will never find answers.

Adultery in early Germanic society was an offence which only married women could commit, and therefore only married women could be held liable for punishment.[2] Because a wife was under the *mundium* of her husband, the crime of adultery entitled the husband to retribution for his wife's liaisons, but punishment for this crime took various forms. Among the Visigoths, Burgundians and Lombards, the outraged husband could kill his wife and her lover with impunity when he caught them *in flagrante delicto*,[3] but the laws also permitted the adulteress and her lover to be delivered into the custody of the outraged husband to be dealt with as the latter saw fit.[4] The need for

---

[1] *Germania*, trans. M. Hutton, rev. E.H. Warmington, Loeb Classical Library, rev. ed. (Cambridge, MA, 1970), chs. 18–20.

[2] H. Brunner, *Deutsche Rechtsgeschichte*, ed. C.F. von Schwerin, 2nd ed., 2 vols. (Berlin, 1906–28) II, 854.

[3] *Lex Visigothorum* (hereafter *L. Visig.*) III. 4. 1 and III. 4. 3, in *Leges Visigothorum*, ed. K. Zeumer, MGH, Legum sectio I: Leges nationum Germanicarum 1 (Hannover, 1902), 147–8. *L. Visig.* III. 4. 9 (*Leges Visigothorum*, ed. Zeumer, pp. 150–1) required the adulteress to be delivered to a husband's wife for punishment if the wife's husband was convicted of adultery, and seems to contradict the view expressed by Brunner (above, n. 2).

[4] *L. Visig.* III. 4. 4 (*Leges Visigothorum*, ed. Zeumer, p. 149). *Leges Burgundionum (Liber Constitutionum)* LXVIII. 1, in *Leges Burgundionum*, ed. L.R. de Salis, MGH, Legum sectio I: Leges nationum Germanicarum 2. 1 (Hannover, 1892), 95; K.F. Drew, *The Burgundian Code*

retribution was evident because the husband's honour was slighted when his wife had committed adultery. If the adulterous wife was not killed, the adulterer was compelled to make restitution to the husband with payment of the wife's wergeld.[5]

The laws which allow the outraged husband to have the power of life and death over his wife and lover, it may be assumed, imply the absence of the church's influence. When the church did acquire an influence in Germanic society, not only did the husband lose the power of life and death over the adulterous couple, but he was also included for the first time within the group of possible offenders.[6] The laws which first signalled this change, although we can be sure that they are somewhat belated, were Lombardic, notably Grimwald 6 (of the year 668) and Liutprand 130 (733).[7] In other words, adultery acquired a new meaning when the church began to exert its authority among the Germanic peoples. But the king also became a beneficiary of the growing influence of the church, because as the secular arm of authority, he was entitled to receive part of the required payment.

Anglo-Saxon law on adultery appears to be significantly different. For whereas retribution for adultery in Germanic society was graduated according to the wergeld of the woman with whom one had committed adultery (as evident, for example, in Bavarian law),[8] payment for adultery among the Anglo-Saxons was directly proportionate to the class of the offended husband. This distinction is first evident in the laws of Æthelberht of Kent, and was still applicable three centuries later in the West Saxon laws of Alfred.

We must bear in mind, of course, that the relatively 'late' arrival of

(Philadelphia, 1949), p. 68. *Edictus Rothari* 212, in [*Leges Langobardorum*, ed. F. Bluhme and A. Boretius], MGH, Leges (in Folio) 4 (Hannover, 1868), 51–2; K. F. Drew, *The Lombard Laws* (Philadelphia, 1973), p. 93. See also *Alfred* 42. 7, in *Die Gesetze der Angelsachsen*, ed. F. Liebermann, 3 vols. (Halle, 1903–16) I, 77. There are parallels to Roman law, notably *Lex Romana Visigothorum* XXVII. 1 (*Pauli Sent*. II. 27. 1), in *Lex Romana Visigothorum*, ed. G. Haenel (Leipzig, 1849), p. 372, and *Leges Burgundionum* (*Lex Romana*) XXV, in *Leges Burgundionum*, ed. de Salis, p. 146.

5 *Lex Baiwariorum* VIII. 1, in *Lex Baiwariorum*, ed. E. von Schwind, MGH, Legum sectio I: Leges nationum Germanicarum 5.2 (Hannover, 1926), 353; T. J. Rivers, *Laws of the Alamans and Bavarians* (Philadelphia, 1977), p. 138.

6 Likewise, V. L. Bullough and J. Brundage, *Sexual Practices and the Medieval Church* (Buffalo, NY, 1982), p. 132, add that the church tried to replace justified homicide, when a spouse was caught red-handed, with monetary payment.

7 *Leges Langobardorum*, ed. Bluhme and Boretius, pp. 94 and 162–3; Drew, *The Lombard Laws*, pp. 134 and 201–2. However, Liutprand 130 adds that if a husband encouraged his wife to commit adultery so that he could kill her *in flagrante delicto* as a scheme to possess her property, the husband, if convicted, was compelled to pay her wergeld.

8 Assuming, of course, that the adulteress or the adulterous couple was not killed *in flagrante delicto*. For the Bavarian law, see above, n. 5.

Christianity in England may have contributed in some way to the different development of Anglo-Saxon society, in comparison with that of the continental Germanic peoples. For the church only gradually acquired the authority to influence native law. Its slow, yet persistent, influence was evident in England as well as on the Continent. There were no sweeping changes that the church brought to bear on family law, property law, or the law of obligations. It was equally slow in its definition of kingship.[9] Therefore, it is not wholly accurate to say that Germanic custom was put into writing because of the influence of Roman culture, although the codifying of Germanic law is commonly attributed to Roman example. Rather, we would be more accurate in saying that these customs were written down because of the influence and presence of the church; that is, Christianity used the written word, however slow it might have been, as a means for the codification of customary law. And the influence of the church itself, of course, was built upon Roman example. The church was the intermediary between the literacy of Roman law and the orality of Germanic law.

Despite its rendition into writing, the laws of the first English lawgiver, Æthelberht of Kent, show only minor influence by Christianity, since the majority of these laws are pagan. Admittedly, those laws which are easily identifiable as Christian appear at the beginning of the body of Æthelberht's laws, which was not uncommon practice.[10] The laws which immediately follow show no Christian influence, although it is impossible to demonstrate such influence beyond a doubt when the church's presence is not immediately detectable.[11]

Nevertheless, we are principally concerned with *Æthelberht*, ch. 31, which deals with adultery. The law says:

Gif friman wið fries mannes wif geligeþ, his wergelde abicge 7 oðer wif his agenum scætte begete 7 ðæm oðrum æt þam gebrenge.[12]

If a freeman lies with the wife of a freeman, he is to atone with his [or her][13] wergeld, and to obtain another wife with his own money, and bring her to the other's home.[14]

---

[9] Similar views are expressed in J. M. Wallace-Hadrill, *Early Germanic Kingship in England and on the Continent* (Oxford, 1971), p. 39.

[10] It is common to many of the Anglo-Saxon laws, in addition to the Alamannic and Bavarian.

[11] We must question the overly optimistic view regarding the influence of Christianity upon Æthelberht's laws taken by J. Imbert, 'L'influence du christianisme sur la législation des peuples francs et germains', *Conversione al cristianesimo nell' Europa dell' alto medioevo*, SettSpol 14 (1967), 365–96, at 367.   [12] Liebermann, *Gesetze der Angelsachsen* I, 5.

[13] 'Her' is not explicit in Whitelock's translation, but is included in the earlier translation in *The Laws of the Earliest English Kings*, ed. F. L. Attenborough (Cambridge, 1922), p. 9.

[14] *English Historical Documents, c. 500–1042*, ed. D. Whitelock, 2nd ed., Eng. Hist. Documents 1 (London, 1979), 393.

Despite Æthelberht's conversion to Christianity (*c.* 601)[15] as well as the
presence of the church in Kent, the punishment for adultery described in ch.
31 had not yet advanced to that stage when the new meaning of adultery, in
which a married man could also be held liable, had been defined by the church.
Æthelberht 31 itself is a famous law and has become the focal point of
considerable historical scholarship. It is also problematical, not only because
of the ambiguity of its language, but also because of its dissimilarity from
other laws regarding adultery. In fact, the ambiguity of the wergeld payment is
the main reason why this law is unlike all other Germanic laws that punish the
same offence. Although the text seems to be quite straightforward, interpretations vary widely: it is arguable that the adulterous freeman paid the wergeld
of the outraged husband;[16] that he paid his own wergeld;[17] or that he paid the
wergeld of the adulterous woman.[18]

As divergent as the readings are that would variously identify the wergeld
as the husband's or the adulterer's, there is nonetheless no reason to suppose
that the wergeld of the wife is required. Because other laws that punish
adultery are different from *Æthelberht* 31, the language of the retributive clause
('he is to atone with his wergeld . . .') appears to be in need of correction. Such
a correction would bring *Æthelberht* 31 into line with all other Germanic laws
concerning adultery. But there is no justification why this should be done, for
not only is the language of the law clearly against it, but *Alfred* 10,[19]

15 The reference in Bede, *HE* I.26, is ambiguous regarding the year of Æthelberht's
conversion: *Bede's Ecclesiastical History of the English People*, ed. B. Colgrave and R.A.B.
Mynors (Oxford, 1969), p. 76.
16 See my 'A Reevaluation of Æthelberht 31', *Zeitschrift der Savigny-Stiftung für Rechtsgeschichte*,
Germanistische Abteilung 93 (1976), 315–18. R. Hill, 'Marriage in Seventh-Century
England', in *Saints, Scholars and Heroes: Studies in Medieval Culture in Honour of Charles W. Jones*,
ed. M.H. King and W.M. Stevens, 2 vols. (Collegeville, MN, 1979) I, 67–75, at 70, also
considers this interpretation.
17 This interpretation is an old one. See, for example, *Ancient Laws and Institutes of England*, ed.
B. Thorpe, 2 vols. (London, 1840) I, 11, and W.E. Wilda, *Geschichte des deutschen Strafrechts*
(Halle, 1842), p. 827. Much scholarship has followed, including such well-known historians
as R. Sohm, *Das Recht der Eheschliessung aus dem deutschen und canonischen Recht* (Weimar, 1875),
p. 76, and F. Roeder, *Die Familie bei den Angelsachsen*, Studien zur englischen Philologie 4
(Halle, 1899), 136–7.
18 That the wife's wergeld is paid is also an old interpretation. See J. Grimm's review of *Ancient
Laws and Institutes of England*, ed. Thorpe, in *Göttingische gelehrte Anzeigen* (1841), 345–60, at
353–4, to which we should add *Die Gesetze der Angelsachsen*, ed. R. Schmid, 2nd ed. (Leipzig,
1858), p. 5, as well as his footnote to ch. 31, and E. Rosenthal, *Die Rechtsfolgen des Ehebruchs
nach kanonischem und deutschem Recht. Eine rechtsgeschichtliche Abhandlung* (Würzburg, 1880), p.
55. This interpretation is also upheld in *Laws of the Earliest English Kings*, ed. Attenborough,
p. 177, n. 31.1. More recently, C. Fell, *Women in Anglo-Saxon England and the Impact of 1066*
(London, 1984), p. 64, also subscribes to this interpretation, but her discussion presents no
analysis of *Æthelberht* 31 and makes no reference to the law's complexity and ambiguity.
19 'If anyone lies with the wife of a man of a twelve-hundred wergeld, he is to pay to the husband
120 shillings; to a man of a six-hundred wergeld 100 shillings is to be paid; to a man of the *ceorl*

promulgated three centuries after *Æthelberht* 31, still attests to the custom in the earlier law.

Continental laws from the sixth, seventh and eighth centuries indicate that the wife's wergeld was required from the adulterer when she was convicted of adultery. But these laws must be differentiated from those discussed above which allowed the husband to kill his wife outright when she was caught *in flagrante delicto*.[20] The adulterer was required to pay for his liaison with another's wife, whether she was caught in the act,[21] or was falsely accused.[22] In either case, payment of the woman's wergeld was required. Even when convicted of incest with a close relative or a sister-in-law, the adulterer was compelled to pay the woman's wergeld.[23] Although ontologically responsible for her own crime, a wife did not directly pay for it because her husband held her *mundium*. The adulterer compensated the husband for his loss when the wife's *mundium* was jeopardized, although a wife may have suffered her own form of punishment, since it is possible that her husband may have taken his hand to her and that to this act the law lent a deaf ear.[24]

All the continental laws referred to above required the adulterer to compensate with the woman's wergeld. But these laws conflict with *Æthelberht* 31; that is, they indicate that the situation in England was totally different from that on the continent. *Æthelberht* 31 manifests a different temperament and a different people. It shows a people who were influenced by Christianity very gradually, whose marital institutions appear to have been less stable than those on the continent, and who were noted for their unusual marital customs, such as the marriage of a son with his stepmother.[25]

Nevertheless, *Æthelberht* 31 specifies that the adulterer was required to

[common freeman] class 40 shillings is to be paid.' *Gesetze der Angelsachsen*, ed. Liebermann I, 56. English translation in *English Historical Documents*, ed. Whitelock, p. 411. The same compensatory ratio in *Alfred* 10 is also evident in *Alfred* 18.2 and 18.3. The direct relationship linking the atonement for adultery with the value of an individual's wergeld in *Alfred* 10 is considered meaningless by Rosenthal, *Die Rechtsfolgen des Ehebruchs*, p. 56, n. 1.

20 See above, n. 3.

21 *Lex Baiwariorum* VIII. 1 (*Lex Baiwariorum*, ed. von Schwind, p. 353).

22 Grimwald 7, in *Leges Langobardorum*, ed. Bluhme and Boretius, p. 402.

23 *Leges Burgundionum* (*Liber Constitutionum*) XXXVI (*Leges Burgundionum* ed. de Salis, p. 69). See also *Lex Frisionum* IX. 10, in *Lex Frisionum* ed. K. A. Eckardt and A. Eckhardt, MGH, Fontes iuris Germanici antiqui 12 (Hannover, 1982), 48.

24 The church also remained silent when the husband, desiring to stay with his wife, reprimanded her. *Penitentiale Theodori*, II.xii.11, in *Councils and Ecclesiastical Documents Relating to Great Britain and Ireland*, ed. A. W. Haddan and W. Stubbs, 3 vols. (Oxford, 1869–78) III, 200 (II.xii.12 in J. T. McNeill and H. M. Gamer, *Medieval Handbooks of Penance*, Columbia Univ. Records of Civilization 29 (New York, 1938), 209).

25 Bede, *HE* I.27 and II.5, in *Bede's Ecclesiastical History*, ed. Colgrave and Mynors, pp. 84 and 150 respectively. Also see Asser, *De rebus gestis Ælfredi*, ch. 17, in S. Keynes and M. Lapidge, *Alfred the Great: Asser's 'Life of King Alfred' and Other Contemporary Sources* (Harmondsworth, 1983), p. 73.

furnish another wife for the outraged husband and was to bring her to the husband's home,[26] or at least to be responsible for the cost of the second marriage.[27] Since the adulterer was required by law to find a replacement for the wife found guilty of adultery (assuming that the husband found the new woman to his liking and that he wanted to part with his wife), it may be inferred that this replacement would most likely have a wergeld equal to that of the adulterous wife. But it seems illogical for the adulterer to furnish both a new wife for the husband and also pay the wife's wergeld, since payment of the latter probably was equal to the procurement of the new wife.[28] The outraged husband either received the payment of the wife's wergeld, as evidently happened on the Continent, or received a new woman in place of the adulterous wife. Even on the Continent, where Christianity had a greater influence, divorce from an adulterous wife was discouraged so that the husband remained with his wife while still entitled to receive monetary payment from the adulterer. In England, on the other hand, payment of the husband's wergeld would have compensated him for the loss of honour and would recompense him for the brideprice[29] which he had paid to his wife's guardian in order to bind and legalize the marriage. And payment of the husband's wergeld would of course be required in addition to the procurement of the new wife. Clearly, it was the husband who suffered a loss when his wife was convicted of adultery, and it was the husband who was compensated accordingly. The adulterous wife, however, when rejected by her husband, returned to her father. In some cases, perhaps, the husband mourned little if his wife was guilty of adultery,[30] for example in the event that the adulterous wife married the adulterer.

Eventually, the bishops became the custodians of marital fidelity. Since the church regarded as legitimate only those marriages contracted between two partners within the recognized degree of consanguinity, any violation of this

---

[26] See A. Schultze, 'Das Eherecht in den älteren angelsächsischen Königsgesetzen', *Berichte über die Verhandlungen der Sächsischen Akademie der Wissenschaften zu Leipzig, phil.-hist. Klasse* 93.5 (1941), 1–79, at 73–4; cf. *Æthelberht* 77. See also *Gesetze der Angelsachsen*, ed. Liebermann I, 7.

[27] H.D. Hazeltine, 'Zur Geschichte der Eheschliessung nach angelsächsischem Recht', in *Festgabe für Dr. Bernhard Hübler ... zum 70. Geburtstage am 25. Mai 1905* (Berlin, 1905), pp. 249–84, at 271.

[28] Among the continental Saxons, the brideprice was equal to the woman's wergeld. See *Lex Saxonum* 40, in [*Leges Saxonum*, ed. K. von Richtofen and K.F. von Richtofen], MGH, Leges (in Folio) 5 (Hannover, 1875–89), 69–70. Cf. *Lex Saxonum* 43 and 49 (*ibid.* pp. 71–2 and 74).

[29] Comparative anthropology indicates that the woman's brideprice, not her person, was purchased. L. Lancaster, 'Kinship in Anglo-Saxon Society', *Brit. Jnl of Sociology* 9 (1958), 230–50 and 359–77, at 243. This view is in sharp contrast with D.M. Stenton, *The English Woman in History* (London, 1957), pp. 8 and 11.

[30] Even Attenborough, *Laws of the Earliest English Kings*, p. 177, says that it was not difficult to please an injured husband.

stability, such as adultery, became a matter of church concern. This condition is most evident in the penitentials,[31] which also found their way into the eleventh-century laws of Cnut.[32] In particular, Cnut's laws required that a wife or husband guilty of adultery were to be placed under the custody of the bishops for retribution and penance.[33]

It should be apparent that before their adoption of Christianity, the Germanic peoples had no standardized law of adultery. Although the laws extant from many Germanic peoples are similar, there was no law of adultery that was common to all.[34] *Æthelberht* 31 seems to present extenuating conditions when a wife was found guilty of adultery, because it required a restitution different from the continental laws concerning the same offence. But while some of the marital customs of the Anglo-Saxons were unusual, at least by continental standards, the requirement in Æthelberht's code that the adulterer had to pay the husband's wergeld was perhaps no more than a custom which had its roots in the pagan past.

---

[31] In addition to the penitential of Theodore, see also the penitential of Egbert, notably IV. 8–9, in *Councils and Ecclesiastical Documents*, ed. Haddan and Stubbs III, 420.

[32] It seems quite probable that Cnut's laws were promulgated under the direction of Wulfstan, archbishop of York and bishop of Worcester, as argued by Dorothy Whitelock, 'Wulfstan and the Laws of Cnut', *EHR* 63 (1948), 433–52, and 'Wulfstan's Authorship of Cnut's Laws', *EHR* 70 (1955), 72–85.

[33] II Cnut 53.1, and 54.1: *Gesetze der Angelsachsen*, ed. Liebermann I, 349.

[34] And similarly, the view expressed in F. Pollock and F. W. Maitland, *The History of English Law Before the Time of Edward I*, 2nd ed., 2 vols. (Cambridge, 1895) II, 437.

The Liudhard medalet

MARTIN WERNER

Although it is a precious and rare material testament to the introduction of Christianity to Anglo-Saxon England, the Liudhard medalet (pl. I) has received surprisingly little scholarly attention.[1] It is scarcely known to art historians.[2] The aim of this paper is to draw attention to the emblem on the reverse of the issue, and to offer an hypothesis on its meaning. Discovered 'some years' before 1844 with other gold coins – looped for suspension as if for a necklace of medalets – and jewellery in or near the churchyard of St Martin's, Canterbury,[3] and published in 1845,[4] the medalet recently has been convincingly assigned to a group of grave goods deposited c. 580–90.[5] Besides the coin in question, the group included an Italian *tremissis* of Justin II, a Germanic *tremissis* of unsure origin, a Merovingian *solidus* struck by Leudulf at *Ivegio vico* and two *tremisses* from southern France, the first from Saint-Bertrand-de-Comminges, the second from Agen.[6] Today these objects are in Liverpool,

---

[1] Cat. no. 7018, Rolfe-Mayer Coll., Merseyside Co. Museums, Liverpool. Mounted for suspension, the coin alone has the weight of a *tremissis*.

[2] So little known that M. Schapiro and Seminar, 'The Miniatures of the Florence Diatessaron (Laurentian MS Or. 81): their Place in Late Medieval Art and Supposed Connection with Early Christian and Insular Art', *Art Bull.* 55 (1973), 494–531, at 524, n. 158, mistakenly placed the medalet in the Crondall hoard (c. 650).

[3] For discussion of site, see S.E. Rigold, 'The Sutton Hoo Coins in the Light of the Contemporary Background of Coinage in England', in *The Sutton Hoo Ship Burial* I, ed. R.L.S. Bruce-Mitford (London, 1975), 653–77, at 655.

[4] The circumstances of discovery are vague, but three of the coins (the Italian *tremissis* of Justin II, the Liudhard medalet and the Germanic *tremissis*) were first exhibited by W.H. Rolfe at a meeting of the Numismatic Society in 1844 (*NChron* 6 (1844), Proceedings, 27–8) and were published the same year by C. Roach Smith in the *Collectanea Antiqua* 1 (London, 1848), 63–4, pl. XXII (although the bound volume of the *Collectanea* is dated 1848, its fascicules were being published from 1843 on). Shortly after this, Rolfe procured an additional five pieces, and the hoard was published as a whole in 1845; C. Roach Smith, 'Merovingian Coins, etc. Discovered at St Martin's near Canterbury', *NChron* 7 (1845), 187–91, pl. VIII.

[5] Because one of the coins is more greatly worn than the others and has a loop of a type found elsewhere only in a seventh-century setting, S.C. Hawkes, in S.C. Hawkes, J.M. Merrick and D. Metcalf, 'X-Ray Fluorescent Analysis of Some Dark Age Coins and Jewellery', *Archeometry* 9 (1966), 98–138, esp. 104–6, 120 and 134, argues for two groups comprising the assemblage, the first deposited c. 580, the second c. 630. However, as P. Grierson, 'Addenda et Corrigenda', in his *Dark Age Numismatics* (London, 1979), p. 5, points out, it is not likely that two supposedly conterminous graves, one proposed as approximately fifty years later than the first, should each have contained unique coins of the same age (c. 570-580).

[6] Cf. P. Grierson, 'The Canterbury (St Martin's) Hoard of Frankish and Anglo-Saxon Coin-Ornaments', *BNJ* 27 (1953), 39–51, at 49 (repr. in his *Dark Age Numismatics*); M. Warhurst,

and Philip Grierson has persuasively argued for the inclusion of a Merovingian *tremissis* in the Bibliothèque Nationale, Paris, as once forming part of the deposit.[7] Most likely all the coins of the Canterbury group were issued during the second half of the sixth century.

A bust figure wearing a pearled diadem and draped in a garment of delicate material faces right on the obverse of our medalet. Above is a backwards running inscription which when turned around reads LEVARDVS EPS. The reverse is dominated by a double-barred cross on a rounded base. Its upper arm, barely shorter than the crossbeam, supports two pendants. In turn, the crossbeam carries little vertical bars on its ends. Placed upside down above the cross are the letters AA, chevron-barred, and to each side NINΛ; below we read VΛV. A dotted line circles obverse and reverse.

Modern scholarship perceives the obverse inscription as 'Leudardus Episcopus', and identifies the bishop so named as Liudhard, the chaplain, according to Bede, who accompanied the Frankish princess Bertha to England upon her marriage to Æthelberht, king of Kent.[8] Notwithstanding Liudhard's Frankish background, his coin has but tenuous connection to sixth-century Merovingian issues. As is true for other of the Canterbury coins, its fabric, obverse bust type and inscription share some few similarities with Visigothic and southern Gaulish coinage,[9] but its reverse design is essentially without numismatic precedent.[10]

Ancient British Issues and Later Coins from English, Irish and Scottish Mints to 1279, with Associated Foreign Coins, SCBI 24 (London, 1982), xvi–xvii; P. Grierson and M. Blackburn, *Medieval European Coinage* I: *The Early Middle Ages (5th–10th Centuries)* (Cambridge, 1986), pp. 122–4.

[7] *Tremissis* from Oloron (Pyrenées-Atlantique); Grierson, 'Canterbury Hoard', p. 49; Grierson and Blackburn, *Coinage*, p. 122; Warhurst, *Ancient British Issues*, p. xvii.

[8] Understanding the obverse inscription as LYVDARDVS EPS, D.B. Haigh, 'Notes on the Old English Coinage', *NChron* ns 9 (1869), 177–8, and *idem*, 'Notes in Illustration of the Runic Monuments of Kent', *AC* 7 (1872), 233, became the first to link it to the Bishop Liudhard mentioned by Bede. G.C. Brooke, *English Coins*, 3rd ed. (London, 1950), p. 3, emended the reading to LEVDARDVS. As Grierson, 'Canterbury Hoard', p. 41, points out, 'the reading is not open to doubt and the dates of the other coin ornaments fit in with the period to which Liudhard's residence in England may be assigned'. Local Canterbury tradition, as recorded by the fourteenth-century monk William Thorne (*Chronicle of Saint Augustine's Abbey, Canterbury*, trans. A.D. Davis (Oxford, 1934), p. 18), gives Liudhard's bishopric as Senlis.

[9] For these connections, see Grierson, 'Canterbury Hoard', pp. 42–59, who notes that the dominions of Charibert, Bertha's father, included Agen, Oloron and St Bertrand-de-Comminges – towns represented by coins in the hoard. A flourishing trade between Kent and the Garonne region may be partial explanation for the migration of coins to Canterbury. See also below, n. 38.

[10] However, Blackburn informs me that he believes the idea of a reverse design featuring a large cross may have been inspired by the coinage of Tiberius II (578–82), perhaps indirectly by way of Visigothic issues. *Solidi* issued early in the reign of Tiberius II display a large cross-on-steps; his *tremisses* sometimes have a cross potent with bars at the ends of the arms. Similarly,

Despite the lack of any well defined continental affiliation, C.H.V. Sutherland postulates the creation of the coin by a competent, if barely literate, Frankish member of Liudhard's household.[11] More plausible are the arguments for Jutish manufacture at Canterbury, which Margaret Deanesly[12] and Philip Grierson have presented.[13] They have drawn attention to such things as the absence of retrograde inscriptions from contemporary Merovingian coinage, and the runic characteristics of the lettering on our issue. There can be little doubt that at Canterbury Liudhard employed a local craftsman to manufacture his gold coin – the earliest known Anglo-Saxon coin. But to what purpose?

Although several unusual sixth-century Merovingian coins feature the name of a king, and although the Visigoths began to put the king's name on their coins *c.* 580–3, there seem to be no Merovingian or Visigothic gold coins of this date with the name of a bishop.[14] Very likely it was Liudhard himself who thought of using such an inscription with a bust type obviously borrowed from imperial coinage,[15] so that it is not surprising to discover the reverse design to be equally anomalous. The cross is especially large and elaborate. Its size, unbroken continuity, pendants and small bars, and especially the clear attachment of its base to the exergual line, give the emblem the character of an altar cross.

Before taking up this issue we must first examine several relevant passages in Bede's *Historia ecclesiastica gentis Anglorum*. At one point (*HE* I.25), the author writes of Æthelberht's welcome of the mission sent by Pope Gregory:

cross-on-steps designs with arms ending as pronounced wedges appear on the second coinage of the Visigothic king Leovigild introduced *c.* 584; cf. Grierson and Blackburn, *Coinage*, p. 442, no. 210.

[11] C.H.V. Sutherland, *Anglo-Saxon Gold Coinage in the Light of the Crondall Hoard* (London, 1948), p. 32.

[12] M. Deanesly, 'Canterbury and Paris in the Reign of Æthelberht', *History* 26 (1941), 97–104, at 100, points out: 'The method used at the date was to prepare a plain, circular 'flan' of the precious metal: to lay it, heated, on an anvil or carved die, to lay the other above and 'strike' the top die until the design appeared on both sides of the flan. If the carver of the die, however, taking some coin as his model, carved the head looking in the same direction, and the legend round the head running from left to right, as his model, he would find that his new coin would come out with the head turned in the other direction (which would not matter) and with the legend 'retrograde' running from right to left. This is what happened to Liudhard's coin; it happened occasionally in all early coinages: but it certainly would not have happened if a Frankish moneyer had made it for Liudhard, for they were experienced and turned out no retrograde legends at this date.'

[13] Grierson, 'Canterbury Hoard', p. 42.

[14] Cf. Grierson and Blackburn, *Coinage*, pp. 128–31.

[15] The diadem is clearly copied from imperial coins, and, as Blackburn has pointed out to me, the drapery may be similarly inspired, for the band with pellets running down it is often found on contemporary imperial issues.

Some knowledge of the Christian religion had already reached him because he had a Christian wife of the Frankish royal family whose name was Bertha. He had received her from her parents on condition that she should be allowed to practise her faith and religion unhindered, with a bishop named Liudhard whom they had provided for her to support her faith.[16]

Subsequently (I.26) we are told that:

There was near by, on the east of the city, a church built in ancient times in honour of St Martin, while the Romans were still in Britain, in which the queen who, as has been said, was a Christian, used to pray.[17]

Bede goes on to inform us that Æthelberht became king in 560,[18] and Gregory of Tours, who was acquainted with Bertha's mother Ingoberga, in his *Liber historiae Francorum* says of the year 589:

In the fourteenth year of king Childebert, queen Ingoberga, the widow of Charibert [†567] departed this life . . . and having consulted me she bequeathed certain things to the church of Tours and the basilica of S. Martin there . . . being as I judge in her seventieth year of her age, and leaving behind an only daughter, whom the son of a certain king of Kent had taken in marriage.[19]

Because Gregory implies that Æthelberht was not yet king at the time of his marriage, it has been assumed that he married Bertha not long before 560.[20] Recently, however, Nicolas Brooks, noting the improbably long reign of fifty-six years which Kentish chronological tradition assigns to Æthelberht, and the marriage in *c*. 561 of Charibert and Ingoberga, has argued that Bede's 560 accession date is an error and that Æthelberht must have married Bertha in the late 570s or the 580s – certainly before Ingoberga's death in 589.[21] Presenting a slightly different chronology, Ian N. Wood has come to a similar conclusion.[22] Given our hypothesis of Canterbury creation for the Liudhard medalet, this must mean the coin was struck between *c*. 578 and 589. We shall find that this late sixth-century dating bears directly on an interpretation of the double-barred cross on the reverse.

Notwithstanding a paucity of early examples, before the close of the sixth

---

16 *Bede's Ecclesiastical History of the English People*, ed. B. Colgrave and R. A. B. Mynors (Oxford, 1969), pp. 72–5.
17 *Ibid.* p. 77.   18 *Ibid.* p. 148; also *Anglo-Saxon Chronicle*, s. a. 565, 618.
19 *Liber historiae Francorum* (hereafter *HF*) IX. 26, ed. W. Arndt and B. Krusch, MGH, SS rer. Merov. I, 116. See also *ibid.* p. 382.
20 Cf. Deanesly, 'Canterbury', pp. 98–9, and Sutherland, *Crondall Hoard*, p. 29, n. 1, for *c.* 560 dating.
21 N. Brooks, *The Early History of the Church of Canterbury* (Leicester, 1984), p. 6.
22 I. N. Wood, *The Merovingian North Sea* (Alingsås, 1983), pp. 15–16.

century the double-barred or patriarchal cross had established itself as the acknowledged symbol of the True Cross, the Cross upon which Christ was crucified.[23] Its upper bar exemplifying the title board above the Saviour's head, the emblem appears in several reliefs at the Justinianic monastery of St Catherine, Mt Sinai;[24] and it decorates the cover or outlines the container for the wooden fragments of three reliquaries of contested but probable Early Christian date: the Metropolitan Museum's Fieschi-Morgan staurothec,[25] the Vatican Sancta Sanctorum reliquary box,[26] and the reliquary of the convent of the Holy Cross, Poitiers (pl. II). Of these, the last named is of the highest interest, for it is directly associated with St Radegund, founder of the Poitiers convent and stepmother of Bertha's father Charibert.

Born a Thuringian princess in 519, Radegund was orphaned early and compelled to marry the brutal Frankish king Clothar. Well educated and deeply pious, upon Clothar's murder of her brother, she fled the palace at Soissons to become a consecrated nun. After numerous vicissitudes, with her repentant husband's reluctant support she established her convent in Poi-

---

[23] For literature on the cult of the True Cross and the patriarchal cross emblem, see M. Werner, 'The Cross-Carpet Page in the Book of Durrow: the Cult of the True Cross, Adomnan and Iona', *Art Bull.* 72 (1990), 174–223.

[24] Crosses in relief appear above loopholes in the central bay of the southeast wall of the monastery. Those at left and centre have large tituli slightly separated from the uprights. The tituli ends are shaped like the *tabulae ansatae* employed as title boards in contemporaneous Syro-Palestinian Crucifixion scenes. On either side of the central cross at Mt Sinai are kneeling lambs representing the apostles, martyrs and the faithful as the paradisical flock who drink from the rivers of paradise–Golgotha; see G. H. Forsyth and K. Weitzmann, *The Monastery of St Catherine at Mt Sinai: the Church and Fortress of Justinian* (Ann Arbor, MI, 1965), pls. Vb and VIIIa.

[25] The Fieschi-Morgan staurothec has on its face a cloisonné image of Christ on the Cross. The interior has a patriarchal cross-shaped compartment for the cross fragments. Some specialists have assigned the work a date as late as *c.* 1000, but recent opinion has centred on a date considerably earlier. Thus M. E. Frazer, in *The Age of Spirituality: Late Antique and Early Christian Art, Third to Seventh Century*, ed. K. Weitzmann (New York, 1979), pp. 635–6, placed the staurothec in early eighth-century Palestine, and A.D. Kartsonis, *Anastasis* (Princeton, 1986), pp. 94–123, advocated a date in the first part of the ninth century.

[26] A wooden pilgrim's box containing minor relics from the Holy Land labelled 'from the place of the life-giving resurrection', its inner cover is painted with scenes from the life of Christ. A patriarchal cross within a mandorla and raised on Golgotha hill appears on the outer cover. Two staves (probably representing the lance and staff respectively held by Longinus and Stephaton) are crossed in front of the Cross. In the upper half of the panel is the inscription IC XC; below we read AΩ. The work has been variously dated, but most cogent are the iconographical arguments in favour of sixth-century Palestinian creation offered by K. Weitzmann, 'Loca Sancta and the Representational Arts of Palestine', *Dumbarton Oaks Papers* 28 (1974), 31–55, at 49 See also G. Vikan, *Byzantine Pilgrimage Art* (Washington, 1982), pp. 18–20.

tiers.[27] In view of the raging and bloody royal and ecclesiastical feuds of the day, and the precipitous decline of the Latin tradition in western and southern Gaul (a tradition she much admired), Radegund must have regarded herself as the bearer of Christian enlightenment to half-civilized barbarians.[28] Certainly she modelled her life on that of Helena, the mother of Constantine the Great, who at an advanced age founded churches on the Mount of Olives and in Bethlehem and was believed to have discovered the True Cross in Jerusalem. Like the Augusta Helena, Radegund was dedicated to the acquisition of sacred relics and most particularly wanted a relic of the wood of the True Cross.[29] Unable to locate a Cross fragment in Gaul, she sent a delegation with this charge to Constantinople. Successful in their entreaties to Justin II and the Empress Sophia, the pilgrims returned with a magnificent reliquary of the True Cross and other treasures.[30] First displayed in the chapel of a monastery Radegund had founded at Tours, the imperial gifts were brought to Poitiers in 569. An elaborate reception was organized, and to commemorate the occasion Radegund's Italian chaplain, the poet Venantius Fortunatus, wrote one or more hymns to the Cross later to become part of the Latin liturgy.[31] Miracles and cures were soon attributed to the relics including,[32] as a remedy for fever,

---

[27] For her life, see two prose biographies: *Vita S. Radegundis libri duo* (1) by Venantius Fortunatus, (2) by the nun Baudonivia, MGH, SS rer. Merov. II; Gregory of Tours, HF IX. 39 and 42 (*ibid.* I, 393–6 and 401–4). See also 'Radegonde', *Dictionnaire d'archéologie chrétienne et de liturgie*, XIV, cols. 2044–55; 'Poitiers', *ibid.* 1319–24; F. Brittain, *Saint Radegund* (Cambridge, 1928); L. Coudanne, 'Baudonivie, moniale de Sainte-Croix et biographe de sainte Radegonde', *Etudes Merovingiennes*, Actes des Journées de Poitiers, 1–3 May 1952 (Paris, 1953), pp. 45–9.

[28] Cf. P. R. L. Brown, *Relics and Social Status in the Age of Gregory of Tours* (Reading, 1977), p. 20; P. Riché, *Education and Culture in the Barbarian West, Sixth through Eighth Centuries*, trans. J. Contreni (Columbia, SC, 1962).

[29] B. M. Peebles, 'Fortunatus, Poet of the Holy Cross', *American Church Monthly* 38 (1933), 153–66, draws attention to the important collection of relics Radegund had assembled even before she established the Convent of the Holy Cross.

[30] For an examination of Radegund's motives in requesting relics of the True Cross, see E. Delaruelle, 'Sainte Radegonde, son type de sainteté et la chrétienté de son temps', *Études Merov.*, pp. 65–74. Also useful is A. Cameron, 'The Early Religious Policies of Justin II', *Stud. in Church Hist.* 13 (1976), 51–68. Underlining Radegund's interest in Helena is Gregory of Tours' reference to the latter's journey to Jerusalem, her discovery of the True Cross, etc., in HF I. 36 (MGH, SS rer. Merov. I, 51).

[31] Gregory of Tours, HF IX. 40 (MGH, SS rer. Merov. I, 396–7); HF X. 15 (MGH, SS rer. Merov. I, 425–6); *idem, In gloria martyrum*, HF I. 5 (MGH, SS rer. Merov. I, 489–90); Baudonivia, *Vita S. Radegundis*, HF II. 14, 16 (MGH, SS rer. Merov. II, 386–9); Venantius Fortunatus, *Ad Iustinum et Sophiam Augustos*, 55–9, ed. F. Leo, MGH, Auct. antiq. IV.1, 277. Venantius Fortunatus wrote three hymns on the Cross, *ibid.* 27–35. *Vexilla regis* was composed for the procession that welcomed the Cross relics to Poitiers, but the other two,

the use of water in which a silk textile employed as wrapping for the Cross fragments had been washed.[33]

These remarkable events occurred perhaps a decade before Bertha's departure for Kent. Their undoubted renown and phyletic association, as well as the possibility of contact between Bertha and her mother's friend Gregory (who became bishop of Tours in 593), would seem to assure word of them reaching the princess with relative dispatch. Moreover Liudhard himself may have been in communication with Tours during his Canterbury tenure. St Martin was patron saint of the Franks and of the kings of Paris; Gregory of Tours wrote of his life and compiled an uncritical list of his miracles.[34] Therefore, it is more than likely that Liudhard rededicated the Roman church of St Martin soon after arriving in Canterbury[35] – and would have sent to Tours for relics of the saint. On this point, let us note that a side chapel was named for St Martin in SS Peter and Paul, Canterbury (where Bertha was buried),[36] and the near certainty of Tours being on Augustine's route to Kent in the 590s.[37] A flourishing trade between Kent and Gaul underlines these connections.[38]

Only the central part of the sixth-century Byzantine reliquary brought to

though inspired by the reception, may have been composed later; *Vexilla regis prodeunt, ibid.* 34–5; *Crux benedicta nitet, ibid.* 27; *Pange lingua gloriosi, ibid.* 27–8.

[32] Particularly interesting is Gregory's report of a supernatural boiling up of oil in a lamp in the same oratory as housed the Cross relics at Tours: *In gloria martyrum,* HF I. 14 (MGH, SS rer. Merov. I, 498). A similar event occurred later in connection with the Cross relics at Poitiers: *In gloria martyrum, ibid.* I. 5 (MGH, SS rer. Merov. I, 489–90); HF IX. 40 (MGH, SS rer. Merov. I, 396–7).

[33] *In gloria martyrum,* I. 6 (MGH, SS rer. Merov. I, 492). See further M. Vieillard-Troiekouroff, 'Les monuments religieux de Poitiers d'après Grégoire de Tours', *Etudes Merov.,* pp. 285–92.

[34] *De virtutibus sancti Martini episcopi,* III–VI, MGH, SS rer. Merov. I, 584–660. See also Venantius Fortunatus, *Vita S. Martini,* MGH, Auct. antiq. IV.1, 292–370.

[35] Cf. *Bede's Ecclesiastical History,* ed. Colgrave and Mynors, p. 76, n. 2.

[36] HE II. 5, ed. Colgrave and Mynors, p. 150. For references to possible connections between Canterbury and Tours, see M. Deanesly, 'Early English and Gallic Minsters', *TRHS* 4th ser. 13 (1941), 25–69, at 42; J. M. Wallace-Hadrill, 'Rome and the Early English Church: Some Questions of Transmission', *SettSpol* 7 (Spoleto, 1960), 519–48, at 532–6.

[37] Entered into the Pontifical Register for July 596, the letters written by Pope Gregory to the members of Augustine's mission and to bishops and others in a position to protect them along the route indicate a journey following the Rhône and Loire to Tours; *S. Gregorii Magni Registrum Epistularum,* ed. D. Norberg, 2 vols., CCSL 140–140A (Turnhout, 1982) II, 961–2.

[38] The many Frankish objects buried in Kent add credence to the idea that Æthelberht's marriage was political confirmation of the significant commercial intercourse between Kent and Gaul; cf. Hawkes, 'X-Ray', p. 120. See further A. R. Lewis, *The Northern Seas* (Princeton, 1958), pp. 65, 71–3 and 104–5; Brooks, *Early History,* p. 7, n. 17; Wood, *North Sea,* pp. 17–18. See P. Grierson, 'Commerce in the Dark Ages: a Critique of the Evidence', *TRHS* 5th ser. 9 (1959), 123–40, for mention of contacts at the St Denis fair.

Poitiers survives – a square face displaying the wooden Cross fragments in a double-barred cross-shaped cavity in a setting of foliate scrolls in cloisonné.[39] Recalling the scarcity of contemporaneous East Christian examples of the patriarchal cross, and noting the absence of the emblem from continental Latin productions before 600, it seems reasonable that we acknowledge the strong likelihood of the Poitiers reliquary being the instrument of introduction of the patriarchal cross symbol to the West. Equally important is the Liudhard medalet, for it displays the earliest extant double-barred cross of northern creation. This extraordinary iconographic circumstance, together with the family and ecclesiastic associations examined above, emphatically suggests a connection between reliquary and coin: the Canterbury medalet – at least in part – must owe its existence to Liudhard's wish to commemorate Radegund's acquisition of a magnificent reliquary of the True Cross. Thus the explanation for the employment of a previously unknown cross type in the remote Germanic kingdom of Kent is to be found in the historical events of the sixth century and clearly implies that the Liudhard coin was issued after 569.

Yet specific parallel between the reliquary and coin crosses does not extend beyond reference to the patriarchal cross: in our Canterbury issue the outlines of a simple double-barred cross act as a scaffold for a more complex arrangement wherein the cross rises from an elliptical base and is decorated with pendants, bars and circle. This last mentioned motif – framing the junction of upright and major crossbeam – was undoubtedly meant to represent a wreath. Significantly, the combination of patriarchal cross and wreath-circled crossing is without precedent in Early Christian art. Only in middle Byzantine and later productions do such crosses again appear – in

---

[39] The reliquary was recorded as a triptych in 1740: Poitiers, Coll. Munic., dom Fonteneau 547, fol. 196. During the Middle Ages the reliquary was kept in a small châsse of Carolingian creation, but if we follow Gregory of Tours (*In gloria martyrum*, I. 5 (MGH, SS rer. Merov. I, 489–92)) it was originally protected by a silver chest; cf. M. Conway, 'St Radegunde's Reliquary at Poitiers', *Art Jnl* 3 (1923), 1–12. Doubts have been cast on the long-standing sixth-century dating of the surviving reliquary face, with A. Frolow, *La Relique de la vraie croix* (Paris, 1961), p. 179, proposing a post-Iconoclastic substitution for the original staurothec. However, most modern scholarship supports the traditional attribution; cf. references in K. Wessel, *Byzantine Enamels* (Shannon, 1967), p. 8; and Werner, 'Cross-Carpet Page', p. 183, n.29. It should be noted that as regards East Christian coinage, the patriarchal cross type is first to be found on issues of Justinian II; J.D. Breckenridge, *The Numismatic Iconography of Justinian II (685–695, 705–711 A.D.)*, Num. Notes and Monographs 144 (New York, 1959), pl. 1 (12); A. Frolow, *Les Reliquaires de la vraie Croix* (Paris, 1965), p. 131, n. 4. Blackburn has kindly informed me that a gold *solidus* of Theodosius II (C.C. Vermeule, 'Roman Numismatic Art, A.D. 300–400', *NCirc* 65 (1957), 5, fig. 7), long thought to picture the Emperor holding a patriarchal cross, was not so intended but results from a fault in the die-cutting, 'the line forming the shaft of the cross having slipped a little too far, going past the wedge at the top of the cross and so looking a bit like a double barred cross'.

association with the *Hetoimasia* throne in Last Judgement and other scenes (pl. III). Symbolic representation of the Godhead, the *Hetoimasia* admits of several levels of meaning dependent on attributes and context, but often gives emphasis to the importance of the three persons of the Trinity and the eschatology of the Apocalypse.[40] In this setting the double-barred cross with wreath (or diadem)[41] at major crossing refers to Christ's crucifixion, his resurrection and the Second Coming.[42]

Because many of the mid-Byzantine *Hetoimasia* crosses and that on the Canterbury medalet have exact congruity, the latter cannot have been a fortuitous or accidental invention. By the fifth century, the 'empty throne' (together with gold diadem, *sudarium*, gospelbook, apocalyptic roll, Lamb, Chi-Rho, jewelled (single-barred) cross etc.) figures in numerous mosaics and reliefs.[43] In several instances the jewelled cross rises through the diadem. This, together with the existence of the Liudhard emblem, prompts thoughts of a lost sixth-century *Hetoimasia* with a wreathed patriarchal cross such as became popular five centuries later.[44]

[40] See T. von Bogyay, 'Zur Geschichte der Hetoimasie', *Akten des XI. Internationalen Byzantinestenkongresses München, 1958*, ed. F. Dölger and H. G. Beck (Munich, 1962), pp. 58–61; G. Schiller, *Ikonographie der christlichen Kunst* III, *Die Auferstehung und Erhöhung christi* (Gütersloh, 1971), 193–202.

[41] For wreath and cross symbolism, cf. T. Klauser, 'Aureum Coronarium', *Reallexikon für Antike und Christentum* I (1950), cols. 1010–20; G. Schiller, *Iconography of Christian Art* I (New York, 1971), 100–1, 131 and 133–4; R. Turcan, 'Girlande', *Reallexikon für Antike und Christentum* XI (1981), cols. 1–23.

[42] Early Christian belief held that those parts of the Crucifixion Cross that touched Christ miraculously ascended to heaven to become the cross of the Second Coming, the *signum filii hominis* (Matt. XXIV.30). Leo the Great's eighth homily on the Passion (*Sermo* liv. 6, PL 54, 340–1) preserved in the Roman Breviary as the homily for matins of the *Exaltatio*, says that in gazing upon the Crucified Christ we should see the dazzling splendour of the Cross – Christ's Judgement throne. And the early Latin *Adoratio* hymns often refer to the eschatological cross of the Second Coming and Last Judgement.

[43] For examples and iconographic analysis, see B. Brenk, *Tradition und Neuerung in der christlichen Kunst des ersten Jahrtausends: Studien zur Geschichte des Weltgerichtsbildes* (Vienna, 1966), pp. 38–40 and 218–20; J. Engemann, 'Images parousiaques dans l'art paléochretien', in *L'Apocalypse de Jean: Traditions exégétiques et iconographiques IIIe–XIIIe siècles*, ed. P. Petraglio *et al.* (Geneva, 1979), pp. 73–107.

[44] That *Hetoimasia* representations with wreathed patriarchal crosses existed before the eleventh century is uncertain. Examples are incomplete or cannot be precisely dated. Thus there is the marble relief on the north façade of San Marco, Venice. Restored in the thirteenth century, it features the *Hetoimasia* supporting a medallion with the Lamb. Six lambs and a palm tree appear on either side and a Greek inscription identifies the lambs as the apostles. At the centre of the throne on a half-circular base is a wreathed patriarchal cross. Archaic in appearance and iconography, the relief has been variously dated from the sixth to the eleventh century, with Schiller, *Iconographie* III, 197, placing it in the ninth century, and O. Demus, *Die Skulpturen von S. Marco in Venedig*, Centro Tedesco di Studi Veneziani/Deutsches Studienzentrum in Venedig 3 (1979), no. 62, and Belting, 'Ein Gruppe konstantinopler Reliefs aus dem XI. Jahrhundert', *Pantheon* 30 (1972), 271, n. 14, in the eleventh.

But while this possibility cannot be ruled out, a more likely premise posits dependence of the wreathed patriarchal cross on interposition and not *Hetoimasia* evolution. That is to say, the cross type was probably developed in an iconographic context separate from the *Hetoimasia*, and was at some point (ninth or tenth century?) substituted for the earlier single-barred wreathless cross. The absence of a throne as setting for the cross on our medalet is some indication of this, and even more compelling is evidence attesting to the formulation of the type within the framework of early Palestinian *loca sancta* iconography. Indeed, it appears to have originated in a conjunction of two demonstrations conceived at the Martyrium of the Holy Sepulchre.

The first of these, the *Crux Gemmata* on stepped rectangular or square base, symbolized the jewelled cross erected in the fourth or fifth century on Golgotha hill to commemorate Christ's death and resurrection.[45] Of the numerous Early Christian representations of the Golgotha Cross there seems to be only one example with a wreath circling the crossing: that decorating a fifth- to seventh-century Coptic textile in the Minneapolis, Institute of Arts (pl. IV).[46] Here the *Crux Gemmata* proclaims the idea of Christ's personal victory and the eschatological glory ascribed to his death and return, an iconography reflective of the Palestinian cult of the True Cross and its ceremonies of Adoration and Veneration.

At Golgotha, the jewelled Cross stood within or adjacent to the church of Golgotha where on special occasions until the time of the Arab conquest the wood of the Crucifixion Cross and its titulus were displayed on the altar.[47] The

---

[45] Constantine the Great may have commissioned a commemorative cross for Golgotha hill, but if so it was replaced in the early fifth century by a gem-studded cross at the behest of Theodosius II; E. Dinkler, *Signum crucis* (Tübingen, 1967), p. 68; E.D. Hunt, *Holy Land Pilgrimage in the Later Roman Empire, A.D. 314–460* (Oxford, 1982), pp. 228–9, n. 49. A silver cross replaced the *Crux Gemmata* in 620; A. Grabar, *Martyrium* (Paris, 1946) III, 273–4. For discussion of representations, see A. Lapinski, 'La "Croix Gemmata" e il culto della Santa Croce – nei monumenti superstiti e nelle raffigurazioni monumentali', *Felix Ravenna* 3rd ser. 30 (1960), 5–62.

[46] Minneapolis, Institute of Arts, *The Art of Collecting: Acquisitions 1980–1985* (Minneapolis 1986), cat. no. 83.126 (p. 101). A Latin cross whose shaft terminates in a narrow tenon inserted into a stepped base is pictured on the textile. A wreath of leaves and fruit is centred behind the crossing. Its dimensions are such as to allow the flared ends of transom and shaft to extend beyond its outer profile. Sixteen gems are shown as set within the cross; nine circles decorate the base. Placed in each of the cantons shaped by cross arms and wreath is a tiny Greek cross, and vertical rows of floral designs flank the central emblem. For an iconographic analysis, see M. Werner, 'On the Origin of the Form of the Irish High Cross', *Gesta* 29 (1990), 98–110.

[47] Before 635 the primary relic of the True Cross was kept in the church of Golgotha at the extreme south end of the eastern portico of the forecourt of the Rotunda of the Holy Sepulchre. This church or chapel incorporated or stood next to an open tower-like construction set up above a ciborium over the Cross of Golgotha. Below or to one side was a

patriarchal cross emblem is directly symbolic of this most sacred relic and also alludes to the *locus sanctus* where it was kept.[48]

If the pendants, short vertical bars combined with the wreath on the Liudhard emblem (and the similar arrangements employed in later Byzantine insignia), are accepted as exemplary of the Golgotha Cross,[49] then, used along with the titulus of the True Cross, they effect a locution conflating two cross types which separately evoke two of the principal (and contiguous) *loca sancta* of the Holy Sepulchre – the monumental jewelled cross of Golgotha hill and the church of Golgotha with its primary relic of the Saviour's incarnation and crucifixion.

The Golgotha Cross was understood as rising at the centre of the world. An interpretation of the base of the Canterbury cross as a globe – the globe of world dominion such as support crosses in a number of sixth-century imperial images – would obviously underline this reference.[50] Yet such a reading is problematic. In the imperial compositions just cited, the crosses are of the usual single-barred variety and the supporting globes are almost inevitably large and perfectly ovoid. Contrarily, the base of the Kentish cross is elliptical and moundlike. In his cross hymns, Venantius Fortunatus often refers to the True Cross as the Tree of Life,[51] an identification regularly found in patristic literature and in the liturgy.[52] And there is good reason to interpret the scroll-work on the Poitiers reliquary face as meant as reference to the Tree of Life. More significantly, sometimes, as on one of the late sixth-century tin-lead

chapel alternately called the Niketerium or Tomb of Adam; C. Coüasnon, *The Church of the Holy Sepulchre in Jerusalem* (London, 1974), pp. 50–3; J. Wilkinson, *Pilgrims before the Crusades* (Warminster, 1977), pp. 175–9; W. E. Kleinbauer, in *Age of Spirituality*, pp. 650–1. For early pilgrims' descriptions of the service of veneration of the 'sacred wood' during the Good Friday rite at the Holy Sepulchre, cf. E. Franceschini and R. Weber, 'Itinerarium Egeriae', in *Itineraria et alia Geographica*, CCSL 175–6 (Turnhout, 1965), 27–90; P. Geyer, '*Itinerarium Antonini Placentini*', *ibid.* p. 139.   [48] Cf. Frolow, *La Relique*, pp. 124–36.

[49] See related *Crux Gemmata* types in Frolow, *Les Reliquaires*, pp. 39, 42, 46 and 48; Lipinski, 'Croix Gemmata', pp. 26, 30, 34, 36, 42–44, 47 and 49.

[50] For example, see J. Deer, 'Der Globus des spätrömischen und des byzantinischen Kaisers. Symbol oder Insigne?', *Byzantinische Zeitschrift* 54 (1961), 53–84; R. Grigg, '"Symphōnian Aeidō tēs Basileias": an Image of Imperial Harmony on the Base of the Column of Arcadius', *Art Bull.* 59 (1977), 469–82, at 472, n. 23.

[51] See above, n. 31. Further, J. Szövérffy, 'Crux Fidelis: Prolegomena to a History of the Holy Cross Hymns', *Traditio* 23 (1966), 6–12; Frolow, *La Relique*, pp. 179–80.

[52] We find in the New Testament an identification of the Tree of Life of Genesis, Ezekiel and Proverbs with the sacrificial and redemptive death of Christ (Rev. XXII.1–2); Golgotha is equated with Mt Zion as the heavenly abode where the Lamb is worshipped, the mount of the future paradise, from which flow the four rivers (Rev. XIV). Patristic literature and later tradition identify the Tree of Life as erected on the spot where Adam lived and died, and as the Tree which would carry the second Adam. It rose from Golgotha at the centre of the world. For literature, see Werner, 'Cross-Carpet Page', nos. 22–3.

ampules from the Holy Land, the cross, given a prominent titulus, is composed of palm trunks and appears to grow from a mound-shaped hill.[53] Particularly interesting is the cross painted on the outer lid of the Sancta Sanctorum reliquary box mentioned earlier, because, like the Liudhard emblem, it has a titulus and is straight-sided (pl. V). What is more, it is fixed into the curve of the hill of paradise – Golgotha.[54] Given the literary and visual evidence cited above – especially that of the Vatican box cover – it seems reasonable that we allow for the strong possibility of the elliptical base of the Liudhard cross being intended as symbolic of paradise – Golgotha hill. We would then be able to discover in the medalet reverse besides evocation of Golgotha, victory wreath, wood of the Crucifixion Cross and its titulus, reference to the metaphoric Tree of Life in the earthly paradise at the centre of the world.[55]

At this point it is important that we consider a related eventuality, namely that the medalet design depends on an exemplar which pictured the cross as if standing on an altar. The crucial detail permitting this hypothesis is the half circle above the base on our cross. Whereas the symmetrical lettering framing the emblem does not intrude into the central field and is simply meant to resemble a legend, the half circle sharply intersects the upright; together with the exergue, it may possibly have been intended to define a platform or table beneath the cross. For support for this interpretation we must turn to the carving on an early sixth-century pyxis in the Cleveland Museum.[56] Of Syro-Palestinian workmanship, the ivory displays the annunciation, entry into Jerusalem, raising of Lazarus and healing of the blind man as pairs of scenes centred on a baldachin raised on three steps. Beneath the central arch of the baldachin a hanging lamp is pictured above an altar on which rests a codex, and behind or more likely also on the altar is a cross; curtains over thymiateria are outlined beneath the side arches (pl. VI). The baldachin has been explained as symbolizing the Holy Sepulchre, its altar construed as replacing the Rotunda tomb so as to identify the latter with authentic church altars, an

---

[53] A. Grabar, *Ampoules de Terre Sainte* (Paris, 1958), pl. XXII. See also J. Fleming, 'Baum, Baüme', *Lexikon christlicher Ikonographie*, ed. H. Aurenhammer, 8 vols. (Rome, 1968–76) I, 89.   [54] See above, n. 26.

[55] Adding further complexity to the problem of the base of the Liudhard cross is the probability that sometimes the globe is equated with Golgotha hill. As example we cite a capital in the north side of the nave arcade in the sixth-century church of St Catherine, Mt Sinai; Forsyth and Weitzmann, *Mt Sinai*, pl. LXIIb. Carved in relief is a single-barred cross mounted on a celestial globe. The alpha and omega are suspended from the beam and below are two drinking lambs (at the rivers of Paradise). Vines grow from the top of the cross and connect to an adjacent Tree of Life. We are reminded of Venantius Fortunatus's reference to the eucharistic symbolism of the vine (John XV.5) and the identity of vine and Tree of Life in *Crux benedicta nitet*: 'Appenso et vitis inter tua brachia, de quo dulcia sanguineo vina valore fluent.' In this setting, there is an obvious correlation of globe with Golgotha hill.

[56] For analysis and bibliography, see A. St Clair, *Age of Spirituality*, pp. 579–80, no. 519.

association dependent upon the East Christian belief in the presence of the crucified Christ on the altar during the Eucharistic rite. In this view, the pyxis itself must have served as container for the host. All this is pertinent because close inspection reveals the baldachin altar as defined by a half circle above a horizontal line, a conception approximating that of half circle and exergue on our early Anglo-Saxon coin. Mindful of the symbolic Holy Sepulchre iconography of the ivory, it becomes difficult to credit this similarity as coincidental. Rather, we are led to speculate upon the existence of now lost sixth-century Syro-Palestinian monuments with presentations like those on the Cleveland pyxis save for the display of altar crosses of the Liudhard cross type with its emphatic references to the Passion, the Resurrection and the *loca sancta* of the Holy Sepulchre. Taking into account both the importance for the sixth-century Christian community we have assigned to the Poitiers reliquary and the specific points of comparison demonstrated between the Liudhard cross and East Christian examples, there seems no reason to reject the possibility that the medalet reverse depends upon the example of an altar cross representation introduced in association with the treasures brought to Poitiers. Besides ivories of the Cleveland pyxis type, textiles such as Gregory of Tours described as wrapping True Cross relics conceivably could have carried such designs.[57]

Moreover, although deprived of contemporary Latin example, we must not fail to consider the possibility that the Canterbury reverse was meant to represent a specific and identifiable double-barred altar cross. Such crosses do figure in post-Iconoclastic scenes of councils.[58] And if we translate the third canon of a church council held at Tours in 567 (*Vt corpus Domini in altari non imaginario ordine, sed sub crucis titulo componatur*)[59] as 'Let the Lord's body be placed on the altar [i.e. the eucharist be consecrated, the eucharistic action be carried out] not amid an arrangement of images, but under the sign of the cross', the last phrase seems to call for use of an altar cross.[60] Between 565 and

---

[57] See above, n. 33. Also worthy of note is Venantius Fortunatus's mention of textiles in the chapel where the fragments were kept at Tours as carrying the figure of a Cross; *Carmina* II.3 (MGH, Auct. antiq. IV.1, 32–3).

[58] Cf. a miniature in the tenth-century Menologium of Basil II (Vatican City, Biblioteca apostolica vaticana, gr. 1613, fol. 108); C. Walter, *L'Iconographie des conciles dans la tradition byzantine* (Paris, 1970), pp. 37–8, and frontispiece.

[59] *Concilia Galliae, A. 511–A. 695*, ed. C. de Clerq, CCSL 148A (Turnhout, 1963), 178.

[60] Here we follow the translation of R. A. Markus, 'The Cult of Icons in Sixth-Century Gaul', *JTS* ns 29 (1978), 151–7, at 154, who rejects the alternate translation favoured by de Clerq and others: 'Let the body of the Lord [understood as the consecrated eucharistic particles] be placed on the altar not in some arbitrary order [i.e. following the phantasy of the individual celebrant] but in the form of a cross.' Markus believes that *imaginario ordine* refers to sacred images and that the council was objecting to the use of *cancelli* with such images in Gaul. See also L. Nees, 'The Iconographic Program of Decorated Chancel Barriers in the Pre-Iconoclastic Period', *Zeitschrift für Kunstgeschichte* 46 (1983), 15–26, at 25–6.

568 Justin II sent a famous silver gilt (single-barred) cross containing a fragment of the True Cross to Rome.[61] The third canon of the 567 council (at which the strict rule of monastic enclosure introduced by Radegund at Poitiers was also approved)[62] suggests that interest in the acquisition of altar crosses was not confined to Rome. Is it possible that the Liudhard medalet recorded the acquisition of an altar cross sent by Justin II along with other treasures to Radegund in 569, or, perhaps, a locally crafted cross made to mark the occasion of the arrival of the relic?

We may never know the answer, and in any event must turn from consideration of developments in Gaul to inquire whether the medalet provides specific Canterbury witness beyond Liudhard's name and 'portrait'. We have already noted obvious biographical analogies between Radegund and the Augusta Helena. Of course, when dealing with distaff royalty, flattering comparison with Helena was something of a literary convention during these years. For example, on behalf of his patroness, Venantius Fortunatus wrote a panegyric to Justin II and Sophia, thanking them for their splendid gifts and comparing the two to Constantine and Helena (even referring to the discovery of the True Cross).[63] On her part, Bertha must have felt deep affinity with both Radegund and the Augusta. Though circumspect in her proselytizing, together with her chaplain she managed to keep Christianity alive in Kent for a decade or more before the arrival of the mission from Rome. Even when mildly chastising her for failing to convert Æthelberht before Augustine did, Pope Gregory pays homage to the queen in noteworthy fashion:

I have praised Almighty God, who has mercifully vouchsafed the conversion of the English as a reward for you. He once fired the hearts of the Romans for the Christian faith through Helena of holy memory, the mother of the most religious emperor Constantine; so now we believe that his mercy is at work in your majesty's zeal on behalf of the English. Indeed, you ought, already long ago, by your truly Christian wisdom to have inclined the mind of our glorious son, your husband, to follow the faith which you hold, for the sake both of his own and his people's salvation; in this way you would have reaped the reward of heavenly joy for his conversion and through him, for that of the whole people. Since your majesty, as we have said, is strong in the true faith and learned in letters, this should have been no prolonged or difficult task.[64]

---

[61] See C. Belting-Ihm, 'Das Justins Kreuz in der Schatzkammer der Petirskirche zur Rom', *Jahrbuch der römisch-germanischen Zentralmuseums, Mainz* 12 (1965), 142–66.

[62] This was the Rule of Caesarius of Aples, the first monastic rule for women and the first to insist that votaries be not permitted to leave the cloister from the time of their profession until the end of their life. Cf. Brittain, *Radegund*, p. 22.

[63] *Ad Iustinum et Sophiam Augustos*, 55–9 (MGH, Auct. antiq. IV.1, 275–8).

[64] *Ep.* XI. 35 (ed. Norberg, CCSL 140, 923–4). Translation by R. A. Markus, 'The Chronology

Thus we find support for the hypothesis that, borrowing cross symbiology of Palestinian origin closely identified with Bertha's illustrious kinswoman Radegund, and, paying tribute at the some time to the Frankish queen, Liudhard commissioned his gold coin in order to commemorate his accomplishments and that of his own queen who, 'strong in faith' like Helena, brought the True Cross to a profane and wicked world. Almost certainly only a few of the coins were issued – for use as Easter offerings – and one such, it would seem, became part of a necklace worn by a pious woman of the court.

It is difficult to avoid speculating on the likely effect a copy of the Canterbury coin may have had on the spread of the symbolism associated with the True Cross in Britain and Ireland.[65] Still relatively rare in the seventh and eighth centuries, the patriarchal cross is yet the dominant motif in one of the carpet pages in the Book of Durrow and another in the Book of Kells.[66] It is my belief that in both codices these cross-carpet pages belong to sequences intended to bring to mind *loca sancta* of the Holy Sepulchre and their liturgical associations.[67] Similarly, the Irish high cross, which has been interpreted as making reference to the Cross of Golgotha, has as its most characteristic feature the circled crossing – a motif anticipated in the Liudhard cross design. Nevertheless, as I have attempted to demonstrate elsewhere, the initiative for these Insular formulations does not seem to reside in the medalet arrangement.[68] In the end, apart from the insights it offers into Latin sixth-century history and iconography, perhaps all that can be said of the Liudhard medalet is that it is the first of many Insular monuments whose imagery reflects the influence of an iconography emanating from the Holy Sepulchre in Jerusalem and concerned with the Adoration and Veneration of the Cross of Crucifixion.

of the Gregorian Mission to England: Bede's Narrative and Gregory's Correspondence', *JEH* 14 (1963), 16–30, at 18–19.

[65] Some slight suggestion of Radegund's importance comes from 'Saint Regedun Street' in Canterbury. Known as 'Long Lane' up to 1794, it takes its name from an allegedly ancient bath called 'St Radegund's Bath'. Whether, in fact, the bath is as old as the sixth century is open to question. See Brittain, *Radegund*, pp. 67–70; R. Aigrain, 'Un ancien poème anglais sur la vie de Sainte Radegonde et le culte de Sainte Radegonde en Angleterre', *Etudes Merov.*, p. 5. More substantial is the evidence of the early influence of Venantius Fortunatus's poetry. The beginning and end of two of his poems were engraved in the seventh century on the wall of a basilica in Wessex; Aldhelm of Malmesbury knew of Venantius's writings. St. Columbanus's writings also reflect the Italian poet's influence, but whether the Irish saint read him at Bangor or later on the Continent is uncertain. See A. Cordoliani, 'Fortunat, l'Irlande et les irlandais', *Etudes Merov.*, pp. 34–43; and M. Lapidge, 'Appendix on the Poems in the Earlier Period', in R. W. Hunt, 'Manuscript Evidence of Knowledge of the Poems of Venantius Fortunatus in Late Anglo-Saxon England', *ASE* 8 (1979), 279–95, at 288–9.

[66] Cf. Werner, 'Cross-Carpet Page', pp. 190–222, for discussion of the importance of the cult in Dark Age Britain and Ireland. [67] *Ibid.* [68] Werner, 'Irish High Cross', pp. 101–7.

The Werden 'Heptateuch'

B. C. BARKER-BENFIELD

A Vulgate fragment from the Book of Judges was published by Michelle P. Brown in 1989 under the title 'A New Fragment of a Ninth-Century English Bible'.[1] The depleted bifolium – one trimmed leaf with its ragged, conjoint stub – had been sold at Christie's of London on 2 December 1987 (lot 137) for a hammer-price of £24,000 through Quaritch's to Prof. T. Takamiya of Tokyo. But the manuscript from which it derives is already recorded: the remains of thirty-two further leaves are preserved in Düsseldorf, Universitätsbibliothek, A. 19, and were published in the 1971 Supplement of *Codices Latini Antiquiores*.[2] Thirty-one of the leaves are more or less complete (some are conjoint), while the thirty-second consists of a top half only. Like the Tokyo fragment, they show all the signs of having been rescued from bindings; the trimming of many edges has created further minor losses of text throughout. They preserve text from each of the first seven books of the Old Testament.[3]

The Tokyo fragment had been consigned to the sale-room by the Roman Catholic Archdiocese of Los Angeles. The sale of *Medieval and Renaissance Manuscripts* on 2 December 1987 comprised the second part of the Estelle Doheny Collection from the Edward Laurence Doheny Memorial Library at St John's Seminary, Camarillo, California.[4] The library had been founded in 1940 by the Papal Countess Estelle Doheny (1875–1958) in memory of her late husband; she continued to enrich it with acquisitions such as the Judges fragment, which she bought from the New York dealer H. P. Kraus, perhaps

---

[1] *ASE* 18 (1989), 33–43, with pls. I–II.

[2] E. A. Lowe, *Codices Latini Antiquiores*, 11 vols. (with 2nd ed. of vol. II) and Supp. (Oxford, 1934–72; hereafter *CLA*), Supp., no. 1685, with plate of the upper part of the verso showing the start of Leviticus. *CLA* gives the Düsseldorf reference as 'Landes- und Stadtbibliothek A. 19'. The fragments are now the responsibility of the Heinrich-Heine-Universitätsbibliothek and I have been asked by the authorities there (to whom I am grateful for the loan of a microfilm) to state the following: 'Die Handschrift ist Dauerleihgabe der Stadt Düsseldorf an die Universitätsbibliothek Düsseldorf.' For an account of the Düsseldorf collections, see G. Karpp, 'Mittelalterliche Handschriften und Inkunabeln in der Universitätsbibliothek Düsseldorf', *Codices Manuscripti* 7 (1981), 4–13. The leaf containing the start of Leviticus, though reproduced by Lowe as part of A. 19, has a different shelfmark (Fragment K 16: Z 1/1) and was at one time in the Hauptstaatsarchiv (see below, pp. 45, n. 12, 46, n. 14 and 62, n. 87). [3] See Appendix (below, pp. 62–4), for details of the surviving contents.

[4] The catalogue of the first part (*Fifteenth-century Books including the Gutenberg Bible*), sold at Christie's of New York on 22 October 1987, includes a fuller account of Countess Doheny and her collections.

43

around 1953.[5] The Christie's sale-catalogue states its earlier provenance as 'From the collection of manuscript leaves of Dr E. A. Lowe'.

The 1971 'Supplement' to *CLA* was in effect a twelfth volume which gathered in both new finds and also some previously rejected candidates around the borderline at *CLA*'s cut-off date of A.D. 800. The last sentence of Lowe's Introduction, with its sentimental image of the good ship *CLA* sailing safely into port, is immediately followed by a Publisher's Note: 'E. A. Lowe died on 8 August 1969. He had seen proofs of all except the three indexes at the end of this volume.'[6] It may therefore be assumed that Lowe had passed the following direct reference which specifies the exact contents of the main Tokyo fragment in the entry for Düsseldorf A. 19 at Supp., no. 1685: 'The leaf containing Iudic. X.7–XI.26, formerly belonging to the library of Schloss Arenfels, is still to be located.' Evidently Lowe was unwilling to advertise his earlier ownership; perhaps he did not know of Countess Doheny's subsequent purchase. Schloss Arenfels, a thirteenth-century castle rebuilt in 1849 by the architect E. F. Zwirmer, lies at Bad Hönningen, not very far up the Rhine from Düsseldorf. During the first half of the twentieth century it was the home of Friedrich, Graf von Westerholt und Gysenberg (1877–1951), and his family. It is not clear from Lowe's statement whether he obtained the fragment directly from Schloss Arenfels himself.

Lowe's verdict that the fragment formerly in his own collection was from the same manuscript as the thirty-two Düsseldorf leaves can be confirmed from the physical evidence. The main Tokyo leaf now has twenty-four lines in each column, but Michelle Brown deduces from the text that three to four more lines have been trimmed away at the head.[7] Many of the Düsseldorf leaves show similar (less drastic) losses, but enough are sufficiently intact to prove that the regular number of lines per column was indeed twenty-eight.[8] The text indicates the loss of only one leaf between the last Düsseldorf leaf (ending at Judges III.21) and the Tokyo stub (starting at Judges V.5). A feature noted by Michelle Brown in the Tokyo fragment is the erasure of the

---

[5] The entry under the Doheny Library in W. H. Bond and C. U. Faye, *Supplement to the Census of Medieval and Renaissance Manuscripts in the United States and Canada* (New York, 1962), p. 14 (no. 59 [6558]), records that Countess Doheny obtained it from Kraus, but does not give a date. I assume that the Kraus catalogue cited at *CLA* Supp., p. 68, for no. 1685 ('*Fifty Select Books*, H. P. Kraus catalogue 60, p. 12, no. 7, New York, n.d. [ca. 1953]') in fact advertises the sale of the Doheny/Tokyo fragment, though I have not been able to see it.

[6] *CLA* Supp., p. xi.   [7] M. P. Brown, 'New Fragment', pp. 35 and 40.

[8] The severe trimming makes the evidence of measurements impossible to evaluate for the whole page and difficult even for the written space. *CLA* gives '270 × calculated ca. 225 mm.' as the average written space of both Düsseldorf and Tokyo leaves, while M. P. Brown ('New Fragment', p. 34) reconstructs the written space for the Tokyo fragment as 'approximately 274 × 209 mm.' Given that the line-lengths vary and most of the figures are estimates, the discrepancies seem insignificant.

last two letters of '-que' to produce an abbreviated form;[9] the same erasure occurs conspicuously throughout the Düsseldorf leaves.

The surviving decoration consists of plain but elegant calligraphic initials in ink, rarely more than two lines high, no doubt made in the course of writing; sometimes they are formed into simple, angular designs and occasionally ornamented further with minor decorative elements such as triangular patterns of three dots. Opening titles, closing titles and first lines are written in what Lowe calls 'black artificial uncial betraying familiarity with Anglo-Saxon script'. Those leaves of which the upper margins have not been trimmed often carry a running-title in the original Insular minuscule: 'liber.' on the verso, the name of the book in the genitive on the recto ('leuitici.', 'iosue' and 'iudicum.').

Besides Judges, Düsseldorf A. 19 contains fragments from Genesis, Exodus, Leviticus, Numbers, Deuteronomy and Joshua. It is therefore with some justice that Lowe sums up the contents as 'HEPTATEUCHUS (fragm.)', though this title still begs the question, considered by Michelle Brown with a list of biblical manuscripts from early Anglo-Saxon England, as to how much more of the bible the original manuscript may have contained.

The Kraus catalogue is the only reference supplied in *CLA*'s bibliography for Supp., no. 1685 and it is difficult to find much further published information about the Düsseldorf leaves. But *CLA* does at least indicate their medieval home: the Benedictine abbey of Werden (now Essen-Werden) on the Ruhr, in the diocese of Cologne. In 1989 Sigrid Krämer published a substantial list of surviving manuscripts from Werden's medieval library, including Düsseldorf A. 19 and thirty-one other Düsseldorf entries.[10] The list includes a number of entries dated to the eighth and ninth centuries, not to mention the sixth-century 'Codex Argenteus Upsaliensis' of the Gospels in Gothic.[11]

ARCHAEOLOGICAL CONTEXT: LATE MEDIEVAL BINDINGS FROM WERDEN

More detailed information about the archaeological context of A. 19 is given in the catalogue of a 1989 exhibition of Düsseldorf's treasures:[12] the fragments

---

[9] *Ibid.* p. 38 and n. 12.

[10] S. Krämer, *Handschriftenerbe des deutschen Mittelalters*, 2 vols., Mittelalterliche Bibliothekskatalogen Deutschlands und der Schweiz: Ergänzungsband 1 (Munich, 1989) II, 826–8 (arranged by modern location). Further detail is supplied by W. Stüwer, *Die Reichsabtei Werden an der Ruhr*, Germania Sacra NF 12, Die Bistümer der Kirchenprovinz Köln: das Erzbistum Köln 3 (Berlin and New York, 1980), 61–86 (arranged in roughly chronological order). For the route from Werden to Düsseldorf, see Karpp, 'Universitätsbibliothek Düsseldorf', pp. 7 and 9.   [11] See below, p. 53, n. 40.

[12] *Kostbarkeiten aus der Universitätsbibliothek Düsseldorf: Mittelalterliche Handschriften und Alte Drucke*, ed. G. Gattermann, Schriften der Universitätsbibliothek Düsseldorf 5 (Wiesbaden,

– perhaps from an Octateuch, Genesis to Ruth? – were released at the beginning of the twentieth century from bindings of the former monastic library at Werden, where their parchment had been cannibalized by the 'Klosterbuchbinder' of c. 1500. Archival evidence[13] confirms that the abbey maintained its own active bindery (*officina librorum*) from its acceptance of the Bursfeld reform in 1474 until around 1550: the accounts incorporate payments for leather, boards, chains, clasps and binders' tools.

It is not clear whether sufficient information was preserved at the time of their removal to identify all the individual source-bindings of the biblical fragments now.[14] On the leaf containing Deut. IV.45–VI.5, a reference in an italic hand of the sixteenth or seventeenth century to a passage of biblical commentary (on Matt. XXV.5) in which Nicholas de Lyra states his own date of writing may indicate the contents of its source-binding. Maybe Lowe's fragment from Schloss Arenfels derived from a binding in the castle library. But the source-binding of two of the Düsseldorf leaves is now identifiable in a private collection. The bound volume is a copy of the *Quadragesimale* of Johannes Gritsch ([Strassburg], 1495), an incunable which has the distinction of having been started by one anonymous printer and finished by another.[15] Its contemporary binding is of tanned leather decorated with blind stamps over wooden boards.[16] The former presence of two clasps of tanned leather and metal, which went from lower to upper board, is indicated by stations at the

1989), 18 (no. 2), with plate of the leaf containing the start of Leviticus under the shelfmark 'Fragment K 16: Z 1/1 (zu Ms. A 19, 1–26)'. The descriptions of the manuscripts are by G. Karpp.   13   Mentioned but not quoted by Stüwer, *Werden*, p. 56.

14   Stüwer, *Werden*, p. 64 (no. 15), says that the leaf containing the start of Leviticus derived from Werden records at the Hauptstaatsarchiv. The plate in *Kostbarkeiten* shows the oval stamp of the 'Hauptstaats-archiv Düsseldorf' at the centre of the lower margin, just to the left of the three characteristic holes of a chain-staple; at the lower edge of the plate, the stain of a leather turn-in is just visible. So if the leaf did come from the Werden archives, it had been used as the pastedown of a bound volume rather than as a limp wrapper. Oddly, Stüwer fails to mention the other 31 leaves in A. 19; one of them (see below, Appendix) was probably originally conjoint with the first Leviticus leaf and shows three matching chain-staple stains at its foot. It presumably derived from the same chained binding.

15   H *8078; Proctor 739; BMC I, 161 + 145; Goff G-508. Sig. a–z and A–E are in the type of the 'Printer of the 1493 *Casus Breves Decretalium*', F–M in that of the 'Printer of the 1483 Jordanus de Quedlinburg'.

16   See pl. VIIa. Unfortunately Werden is not one of the German monastic libraries covered by E. Kyriss, *Verzierte gotische Einbände im alten deutschen Sprachgebiet*, 4 vols. (Stuttgart, 1951–8). Two of the stamps appear to match those reproduced by W. H. J. Weale and L. Taylor, *Early Stamped Bookbindings in the British Museum* (London, 1922), pp. 68–9 (no. 155) and pl. XI, 14–15, from a British Library incunable bearing the Werden *ex libris* (Aquinas, *Secunda secundae* [Strassburg, c. 1474/77] = BMC I, 79, shelfmark IC 891); perhaps four other stamps also match and the overall lozenge patterns are similar, but each binding includes further stamps not found on the other. The pastedowns of the Aquinas are from a large, noted liturgical manuscript of fourteenth(?)-century German origin.

fore-edges. Legible offsets on the bare wood of the inside covers identify its former pastedowns as two trimmed leaves in Düsseldorf A. 19 containing text from the Book of Numbers.[17] One side of each pastedown had been folded by the binder into a 'hook' or broad stub which he then tucked around the adjacent gathering: these two parchment hooks still survive at their original stations in the incunable and contain the beginnings and ends of lines in the familiar Insular minuscule,[18] to augment the two Düsseldorf leaves (see pl. VII*b* and *c*).

The incunable retains no *ex libris* inscription assigning it definitely to Werden (leaf 'a1' and any preceding flyleaves are now missing):[19] but an early clue which may help to confirm its institutional home is the large 'lombardic' capital **H** (or possibly **N**), written in red on a lozenge of paper which is pasted onto the leather at the upper centre of the outside front cover.[20] Just above, a thin, horizontal band of lighter leather probably indicates the position of a lost title-label.[21] The spine also retains semi-legible fragments of several later paper labels.

In the Appendix (see below, pp. 62–4), I have made a tentative attempt from the microfilm of Düsseldorf A. 19 to establish a collation structure on the basis of textual and physical evidence. The microfilm shows some leaves still definitely joined as bifolia. Other visible clues – deposits of glue or paste, stains from leather turn-ins, marks of metal clasps and chain-staples, offsets of the Insular script itself – confirm that in the late medieval bindings a bifolium was often used as pastedown plus flyleaf. Some of the Düsseldorf leaves which are now singletons can also be paired into bifolia on the basis of such evidence. In all, perhaps twelve bifolia (including three where the joins are unconfirmed) were used as pastedown plus flyleaf in bindings of small folio size. At

---

[17] See below, Appendix.

[18] Num. XXIV.7–XXVI.7; and XXXIII.43–XXXV.13, see pl. VII*b* and *c*.

[19] Although the binding retains its original sewing and spine and is generally in good condition, it is clear that a certain amount of expert 'tidying' has been carried out (including trimming of the leather turn-ins), perhaps at the time when the pastedowns were removed. The split leather at the joints was further reinforced in 1989.

[20] See pl. VII*a*. A large red letter on the cover is mentioned as the 'old shelfmark' in Stüwer's descriptions of several Werden manuscripts: Berlin, Staatsbibliothek der Stiftung Preussischer Kulturbesitz, Lat. qu. 505 = Stüwer, *Werden*, no. 34, not listed by Krämer; Düsseldorf, Universitätsbibliothek, B. 81, B. 191 (including a printed book of 1484), E. 2 and E. 3 = Stüwer, nos. 25, 71, 22 and 38; Budapest, National Széchényi Library, Clmae 277 (including a printed item of [1506?]) = Stüwer, no. 76; Darmstadt, Hessische Landes- und Hochschulbibliothek, 93 = Stüwer, no. 58.

[21] Fifteenth-century parchment title-labels on the upper boards are mentioned in the catalogue descriptions of several stamped-leather bindings from Werden, e.g. Berlin, Staatsbibliothek der Stiftung Preussischer Kulturbesitz, Theol. lat. fol. 362 (Rose 308) and Wolfenbüttel, Herzog August-Bibliothek, Gud. lat. 125 (4429). See also below, n. 23.

least five of these pastedowns have the characteristic holes or stains at the centre of their lower edges for the nails or rivets of metal chain-staples: usually three round marks in a triangular pattern. Allowing four leaves per binding (one bifolium at each end), I estimate that these twenty-four Düsseldorf leaves might have been removed from a minimum of six bindings of small folio size, of which at least five were once chained.

Six further Düsseldorf singletons were used as pastedowns in bindings of similar small-folio size, but none (as far as can be seen from the microfilm) shows obvious chain-staple marks. The Gritsch incunable of 1495 accounts for two of them. That volume itself shows no sign of ever having been chained. The way its two pastedowns were cut and folded makes it clear that the binder used them as singletons: instead of providing pastedown plus flyleaf for each board, the Insular leaves were used only as pastedowns and were sewn firmly into the text-block structure through the folded 'hooks'. The sequence of biblical text suggests that the two pastedowns themselves once formed a bifolium; if so, the binder would simply have started work by taking a bifolium from the pile and cutting it in two. The six single pastedowns could thus have been taken from a minimum of three more bindings of small-folio size, including the Gritsch incunable.

The two remaining Düsseldorf fragments consist of one leaf folded in half to form the pastedown plus flyleaf for a binding of half the normal size, with the top half only of one further leaf used as a pastedown of similar half-size. These are the two earliest surviving fragments from Genesis and could have formed a bifolium; it seems reasonable to guess that they come from the same binding. This brings the total number of bindings from which the Düsseldorf leaves were rescued to a minimum of nine small folios and one small quarto.

It is clear that the Tokyo fragment was also redeployed for binding purposes. Michelle Brown minutely analyses the physical traces of its later history and suggests that its parchment was used in at least two successive bindings:[22] a larger binding with strap-and-pin fastening, perhaps of thirteenth- to fourteenth-century date, to account for three small copper-stained holes at what is now the upper centre of the main leaf; and a smaller limp cover to which the fragment was trimmed for use as a stiffener, to explain some prickings and a larger hole which goes through both the main leaf and its conjoint stub near the top of the gutter. To add to the difficulties of reconstruction, the edges appear to have been 'tidied' by (further?) trimming in modern times when the fragment retrieved its status as a valuable Insular/biblical specimen.

This sort of evidence is very hard to judge from photographs. But the theory of successive bindings gives the Tokyo fragment an unusually busy

[22] Brown, 'New Fragment', pp. 35–6.

after-life; I do not think it impossible that its scars derive instead from the same archaeological circumstances as those of the six single Düsseldorf pastedowns. In pl. II of Michelle Brown's article, the dark vertical lines visible on the verso of the main fragment are plainly glue-deposits showing the grain of a wooden board onto which it was once stuck as the pastedown. The stains and fragments of brown leather turn-ins (reduced by the modern trimming) probably belong to the same binding, more likely fifteenth-century than earlier since the colour of the leather suggests it was tanned rather than tawed. The strap-and-pin method of clasping belongs usually to a somewhat earlier period and ought to have left a parallel set of marks further down for the lower fitting. The photographs show no sign of chain-staple marks. Michelle Brown states that the glue-marks do not run over the stub, an observation consistent with the possibility that the Tokyo stub was hinged around an outside gathering like the 'hooks' in the Gritsch incunable: in relation to the turn-in stains, the stub is positioned correctly for this at what would have been the inner edge of the host binding. However, the Tokyo stub is much less neatly trimmed than the Gritsch hooks, the concurrent hole near the gutter in both leaf and stub may be too far in to have been caused by an endband and there is no ready explanation for the reported copper-stained holes.[23] It may be that the binding which carried the Tokyo fragment diverged early from the ten or more which contained the main group now at Düsseldorf. On the other hand, the biblical manuscript ought not to have reached its moment of dissolution much earlier than 1496;[24] it would be uneconomical to suppose that its carcase had already been supplying parchment for bindings of earlier centuries. Other surviving fragments from Werden suggest that the abbey was discarding a number of its early manuscripts at around the same period, especially those in Insular script. Their waste parchment was being re-used in bindings, as wrappers for the abbey's archives and even for rewriting as palimpsests.[25]

EARLIER LINKS WITH WERDEN

The founder of Werden was not English by birth, though he had long-term connections with the Anglo-Saxon missions to the Continent. The abbey was

[23] The Düsseldorf leaf containing Lev. II.2–IV.18 (re-used as a pastedown) has a small rectangular mark at approximately the position indicated by Michelle Brown for Tokyo's three copper-stained holes, about one third of the way down near the centre of the leaf. It looks like metal-damage, though it is difficult to envisage what metal fitting could have caused it. The British Library Aquinas (see above, n. 16) has the nail-holes for a horn label-cover at about this position on the outside front cover, but they form a more recognizable pattern.   [24] The colophon of the Gritsch incunable is dated 31 December 1495.
[25] See *CLA* VIII, no. 1070; A. Dold, 'Die zwei Palimpseste der Kgl. Universitätsbibliothek Bonn S 366 und S 367', *Zentralblatt für Bibliothekswesen* 35 (1918), 211–15; R. Drögereit, *Werden und der Heliand: Studien zur Kulturgeschichte der Abtei Werden und zur Herkunft des Heliand* (Essen, [1951]), p. 40 and n. 68.

established around 800 by the Frisian St Liudger (c. 742–809), first bishop of Münster. The first two Frisian priests to be ordained by Willibrord were Liudger's great-uncles[26] and he had been nurtured at Utrecht by Abbot Gregory in the traditions of Willibrord and Boniface. His education had been enriched by two visits to the school of York in Alcuin's time.

One of the earliest books from Werden to survive complete is Berlin, Staatsbibliothek der Stiftung Preussischer Kulturbesitz, Theol. lat. fol. 366 (Rose 276),[27] a manuscript of St Paul's Epistles in Insular script. Its survival will have been helped by the long-established tradition that its scribe was St Liudger himself. With some inconsistency, Lowe excluded it from *CLA* as being too late, but mentioned it in his analysis of the scripts of the 'Heptateuch' fragments at Supp., no. 1685: the script of the two fragments from the beginning of Genesis, which he distinguishes from the rest, 'is more akin to that of Berlin MS. Theol. lat. fol. 366, another Anglo-Saxon manuscript from Werden (not included in *C.L.A.*)'. The Berlin manuscript is in similar two-column format to the 'Heptateuch' fragments, but has smaller dimensions and fewer lines.[28] Distinctive (though not unique) features of its script are a prominent l which curls under the next letter and an x with a large, superfluous hook below on the left.[29] From the published photographs, the l and the x of the main 'Heptateuch' hand are quite different, though the two manuscripts do not seem very far apart in general style. An individual feature found in both manuscripts is the 'reversed, whiplash' form of capital Q noted by Michelle Brown in the Tokyo fragment.[30]

One striking parallel emerges from a single example in the most frequently reproduced page of the Berlin Epistles: the '-que' of 'atque' at Rom. I.12, originally written out in full, has been altered to the abbreviated form by the erasure of the last two letters.[31] The abbreviation is common enough, and

---

26 Altfrid, *Vita S. Liudgeri* I.5, ed. G. H. Pertz, MGH, SS 2 (Hannover, 1829), 406; see W. Levison, *England and the Continent in the Eighth Century* (Oxford, 1946), p. 62.

27 V. Rose and F. Schillmann, *Verzeichniss der lateinischen Handschriften der königlichen Bibliothek zu Berlin*, 3 vols., Die Handschriften-Verzeichnisse der königlichen Bibliothek zu Berlin 12–14 (Berlin, 1893–1919) II.i, 52–4; A. Chroust, *Monumenta Palaeographica: Denkmäler der Schreibkunst des Mittelalters*, 2nd ser. (Munich, 1907–17) III.xxii, pl. 7a (6r); H. Degering, *Die Schrift*, Wasmuths Werkkunst-Bücherei 6 (Berlin, [1929]), pl. 39 (69r); Drögereit, *Werden und der Heliand*, pp. 19–20 (no. 1), pl. 1 (6r); *Das erste Jahrtausend: Kultur und Kunst im werdenden Abendland an Rhein und Ruhr*, ed. V. H. Elbern, 3 vols. (Düsseldorf, 1962–4), Tafelband pl. 267 (76(77)r); Stüwer, *Werden*, p. 62 (no. 3). Lowe's own negatives now at the Bodleian include one of 3r.

28 Leaf-measurements 273 × 215 mm. (ex inf. Chroust); 2 cols., twenty-three lines.

29 B. Bischoff indicates in his review of Drögereit (*Anzeiger für deutsches Altertum und deutsche Literatur* 66 (1952), 7–12, at 8) that the hooked form of x appears also in the work of Fulda and Würzburg scribes. See also below, p. 57, n. 67.   30 Brown, 'New Fragment', p. 37.

31 Fol. 6rb18 (ink foliation), the page chosen by Chroust (see above, n. 27) and further reproduced by Drögereit, *Werden und der Heliand*, pl. 1, and by V. H. Elbern, *St. Liudger und die Abtei Werden. Gesammelte kunsthistorische Aufsätze* (Essen, 1962), pl. 6, facing p. 48.

some scribes and readers may have felt the need to distinguish '-que' from 'qu[a]e'; but '-que', fully written out, is not wrong as such, so the corrector must have been both fussy and persistent. An even closer parallel lies in the manner of erasure: in the Berlin example, the first minim of the u appears to have been left unerased, as though to form the abbreviation-sign;[32] the '-que' erasures throughout the 'Heptateuch' fragments are usually made in exactly the same way.[33]

While plain erasures are impossible to date, these are surely early rather than late, for they must belong to a period when manuscripts in Insular script were still being actively studied and when the Berlin manuscript was still being treated as a book rather than as a relic. The Werden *ex libris* in the Berlin Epistles is thought to be ninth-century and the earliest of its ascriptions to St Liudger not much later.[34] By contrast, the evidence connecting the 'Heptateuch' manuscript with Werden dates from the far end of the medieval period. But the duplication of the distinctive '-que' erasure may well be sufficient to lengthen the provenance back to a respectable antiquity: the two biblical manuscripts were being read and corrected in the same early environment, perhaps even by the same corrector.

The published attributions of the date and origin of the 'Heptateuch' fragments provide an object-lesson in palaeographic subjectivity. E. A. Lowe and G. Karpp, knowing the later provenance, suggest a date around 800 and tentatively assign the script to Werden.[35] Lowe's conclusion about the manuscript's origin is 'written probably in Werden, possibly in England' and in the small print he unfairly condemns the main hand as 'somehow lacking the typical Anglo-Saxon verve'. But Michelle Brown dates the Tokyo fragment somewhat later, to *c.* 825 to 850, and ascribes it on the basis of comparable English documents to greater Mercia.[36]

Similar discrepancies arise in the descriptions of the few early additions: Lowe notes 'small corrections in Caroline minuscule'; Michelle Brown refers to insertions in an Anglo-Saxon pointed minuscule script by a tenth-century

---

[32] This is clear in Chroust's fine plate, though in the later, poorer reproductions the half-erased form starts to look almost like a colon (which may indeed have been the effect intended).

[33] See the Gritsch fragment at pl. VII*b*, lines 1, 10 and 17.

[34] Drögereit, *Werden und der Heliand*, pp. 19–20, discusses the datings of the added inscriptions.

[35] Lowe at *CLA* Supp., no. 1685 ('saec. VIII–IX'); Karpp in *Kostbarkeiten*, no. 2 ('um 800'). J. Crick ('An Anglo-Saxon Fragment of Justinus's *Epitome*', *ASE* 16 (1987), 181–96, at 184 and n. 18) seems to attribute the 'Heptateuch' to Werden in the later eighth century; the early dating, not quite compatible with Werden's foundation *c.* 800, arises from her wish to cite its script as an example of Northumbrian influence on the Continent (*via* Echternach) alongside a genuinely Northumbrian product, London, British Library, Cotton Tiberius A. xiv (*CLA* Supp., no. 1703), which in turn receives a late dating. The London Bede is also cited by Drögereit, *Werden und der Heliand*, p. 75 and pl. 16c, for comparison with Werden manuscripts in script and decoration.   [36] Brown, 'New Fragment', p. 40.

hand.[37] The Tokyo fragment contains only slight additions, but the thirty-two Düsseldorf leaves display a wider sample: mainly corrections, but even the odd pen-trial. One early concern was to write out in words the numbers which were written in Roman numerals in the original text:[38] possibly an indication that the text was being prepared for public reading. The words 'Hec omitte', written at the start of one of the less rewarding genealogical passages of Numbers (XXVI.1), ought to be an instruction to a reader rather than to a scribe. One of the correcting hands is noticeably clumsy, but their letter-forms seem generally Caroline. My opinion, also contaminated by provenance, is that the additions are by German hands, sometimes perhaps as late as the tenth century.

THE EARLY MANUSCRIPTS OF WERDEN

For travelling Irish and English to giddy about Europe writing Insular script seems almost defiantly inconsiderate of the requirements of modern scholarship. Some earlier manuscripts preserved in continental foundations were certainly written in the British Isles and many later manuscripts in Insular script can be distinguished as second-generation continental products; but there are others where it is very hard to tell whether they were written in the British Isles or on the Continent, by English-born or by English-trained scribes. Textual relationships or the distinction between Insular and continental preparation of parchment offer no firm yardsticks: exemplars, skins and techniques can also travel. Saints and scribes are just as mobile and unclassifiable: St Liudger himself could be described as a third-generation continental product, but his own script will have been refreshed or recontaminated at York. Since the script of the 'Heptateuch' has been attributed both to England and to Germany, it would appear to be one of the Insular manuscripts on the cusp.

Pre-foundation books

In his 1977 Lyell Lectures at Oxford on 'The Insular System of Scripts *c.* 600– *c.* 850',[39] Professor Julian Brown stressed the relationships of continental to native Insular scripts not only in their origins but also in their ongoing development. Connections may be sought not only in the scribal training of the missionaries but also in the books they took with them or had sent later to their new foundations. Irish, Northumbrian and southern English origins are indicated in *CLA*'s attributions of the earliest books for which there is certain or probable evidence of later Werden ownership. Apart from the sixth-

---

[37] *Ibid.* p. 38.   [38] See the Gritsch fragment at pl. VII*c*, line 5, '[duo] milia'.
[39] Reviewed by B. C. Barker-Benfield in *TLS*, 27 January 1978, p. 100.

century Gothic Gospels,[40] there are fragments of perhaps eight books in Insular script which Lowe dates to the eighth century, before the foundation of the abbey. A collection of excerpts from Gregory's *Moralia* by Lathcen, an Irish monk of the seventh century, is ascribed to an eighth-century scriptorium 'presumably in Ireland'.[41] The other seven are assumed by Lowe to have been written in England. Four are ascribed to Northumbria: an abbreviated version of Cassiodorus's *Expositio psalmorum*[42] to the first half of the century, a miscellany including works of Chrysostom and the *Pastor Hermae* to the mid-century (arguments for Werden provenance weaker than most)[43] and copies of Orosius (*Historiae adversum paganos*)[44] and Isidore (*Etymologiae*)[45] to the second half. Another Isidore (*De ortu et obitu patrum, Allegoriae,* etc.)[46] and an unidentified theological work[47] were 'written presumably in England' with-

[40] Uppsala, Universitetsbiblioteket, DG 1 + Speyer, Dombibliotek *s.n.* (stray leaf, discovered 1970). The question of whether St Liudger might have obtained the 'Codex Argenteus' in its native Italy, in France or even in England has attracted speculation; but firm evidence for Werden provenance starts only with its discovery there by scholars of the later sixteenth century (see O. v. Friesen and A. Grape in the introduction to the facsimile, *Codex Argenteus Upsaliensis* (Uppsala, [1928]), pp. 83–8; Drögereit, *Werden und der Heliand*, pp. 18–19; Stüwer, *Werden*, pp. 61–2 (no. 1)).

[41] Fragments scattered between Düsseldorf and New York: *CLA* VIII, no. 1185 ('Landes- und Stadtbibl. B. 212 + Staatsarchiv S.N.') + XI, p. 22 (Columbia University Library, Plimpton 54); Stüwer, *Werden*, p. 63 (no. 7); further discussed and reproduced by Karpp in *Kostbarkeiten*, no. 1 (giving the shelfmark in the Universitätsbibliothek as 'Fragment K 1: B 212'). They had been re-used as wrappers on fifteenth-century Werden records.

[42] *CLA* Supp., no. 1786 ('Düsseldorf, Staatsarchiv Fragm. S.N.'): archival wrapper. Not listed by Stüwer or Krämer.

[43] *CLA* VIII, no. 1187 ('Düsseldorf, Landes- und Stadtbibl. B. 215 + C. 118 + Staatsarchiv Fragm. 20'). Omitted by Krämer, but listed by Stüwer, *Werden*, p. 62 (no. 2, 'Werdener Herkunft sehr wahrscheinlich'). Seven of the ten leaves were rescued from bindings of books belonging to the monastery of Beyenburg near Werden.

[44] *CLA* Supp., no. 1687 ('Düsseldorf, Staatsarchiv HS. Z. 4 nr. 2'). Krämer, *Handschriftenerbe* II, 827, gives the reference as Hauptstaatsarchiv, 'Fgm. K 19: Z 11–2 (Depos. in UB u. UB Fragm. K 14: 11)'. Not listed by Stüwer.

[45] *CLA* VIII, no. 1189 + Supp., p. 6 ('Düsseldorf, Staatsarchiv HS. Z. 4 nr. 3, 1 + Fragm. 28 + Gerleve (near Koesfeld), Stiftsbibliothek S.N.'); Stüwer, *Werden*, p. 63 (no. 8, 'Ein Fragment Werdener Provenienz wahrscheinlich'). In his Lyell Lectures, Julian Brown noted its similarity to one of the hands of *CLA* VIII, no. 1134 (Kassel, Landesbibliothek, Theol. fol. 21, later at Fulda) and compared both manuscripts to the Leningrad Bede (Public Library, Q. v. I. 18 = *CLA* XI, no. 1621).

[46] Düsseldorf, Universitätsbibliothek, B. 210. *CLA* VIII, no. 1184: second half of the eighth century, 'provenance not known'. Listed by Krämer, *Handschriftenerbe* II, 827, but not by Stüwer. For two further leaves, see B. Bischoff and V. Brown, 'Addenda to *Codices Latini Antiquiores*', *MS* 47 (1985), 317–66, at 358: from a Werden binding.

[47] *CLA* VIII, no. 1045 ('Berlin, Deutsche Staatsbibl. Fragm. 34 . . . saec. VIII', with corrections in ninth-century Caroline minuscule); Stüwer, *Werden*, p. 63 (no. 12). The two small fragments are from the fifteenth-century binding of Berlin, Staatsbibliothek der Stiftung Preussischer Kulturbesitz, Theol. lat. fol. 346 (Rose 298, *CLA* VIII, no. 1066); see below, p. 59 and n. 74.

out more specific localization, and a fragment of saints' lives was 'written presumably in South England, possibly in an Anglo-Saxon centre on the Continent' in the second half of the eighth century.[48] It seems all too easy to suggest a link between the four northern books and Liudger's education in Alcuin's York, but the *Vita S. Liudgeri* by Altfrid does state that when he finally returned from York to Utrecht around 772 he went 'bene instructus, habens secum copiam librorum'.[49]

Insular fragments, late-eighth or early-ninth century

By rights, the good ship *CLA* ought to have reached port without any stowaways from Werden's own scriptorium. If Lowe had scrupulously observed his cut-off date of 800, its coincidence with the abbey's approximate foundation-date should have made him exclude any manuscripts which he judged to have been written at Werden itself. But *CLA* does include fragments of Werden provenance in Insular minuscule from five further books for which the attributions teeter between the eighth and ninth centuries and between England and Germany: the 'Heptateuch' manuscript, itself; a canon law collection;[50] Jerome on Isaiah, and Bede's

---

[48] *CLA* VIII, no. 1068: fragment re-used in the fifteenth-century binding of a Werden manuscript, Berlin, Staatsbibliothek der Stiftung Preussischer Kulturbesitz, Theol. lat. fol. 355 (Rose 307). Drögereit, *Werden und der Heliand*, p. 25 (no. 6), pl. 5, suggests that this and other Berlin binding fragments of saints' lives (from Theol. lat. fol. 362 (308) and 367 (353)) came from the same 'Passionar' as a leaf re-used in the Bonn palimpsests (see above, p. 49, n. 25). Stüwer, *Werden*, p. 63 (no. 6) lists four unspecified Berlin fragments with a reference to *CLA* VIII, no. 1068. But the Insular script of the palimpsested leaf in Drögereit's pl. 5 (Bonn, Universitätsbibliothek, S. 367, 110v) looks later and more continental than that of the *CLA* plate. The various fragments of saints' lives ought to derive either from more than one Werden passional in Insular script or from one volume that was augmented later (see also below, p. 57 and n. 68).

[49] 'Well taught, having with him plenty of books', I.12 (MGH, SS 2, 408), quoted by Levison, *England and the Continent*, p. 141 and n. 4. On the date, see A. Schröer, 'Chronologische Untersuchungen zum Leben Liudgers', *Liudger und sein Erbe: dem siebzigsten Nachfolger des heiligen Liudger Clemens August Kardinal von Galen Bischof von Münster zum Gedächtnis*, 2 vols., Westfalia Sacra 1–2 (Münster, 1948–50) I, 85–138, at 105 and 138. Drögereit, *Werden und der Heliand*, p. 75, proposed that the manuscripts brought by Liudger from York are represented by the Berlin Epistles and its associated group; but Bischoff asserts in his review (p. 8) that these manuscripts cannot be earlier than around 800. See also Crick, 'Anglo-Saxon Fragment of Justinus', pp. 193–4.

[50] *Collectio Quesnelliana*, *CLA* VIII, no. 1188 ('Düsseldorf, Landes- und Stadtbibl. E. 32 . . . saec. VIII ex.'); Drögereit, *Werden und der Heliand*, pp. 25–6 (no. 7), pl. 6; Stüwer, *Werden*, p. 63 (no. 9, 'Werdener Herkunft wahrscheinlich'); not listed by Krämer. Lowe observes that 'the lower left limb of x turns to the right, a feature of many Northumbrian manuscripts' (*not* the hooked x of the Berlin Epistles), but also compares *CLA* IX, no. 1414 (Würzburg, Universitätsbibliothek, M. p. th. f. 47), a Würzburg manuscript with possible Kentish connections. Crick ('Anglo-Saxon Fragment of Justinus', pp. 186–7) cites the canon law

Ia Bishop Liudhard medalet from church
of St Martin, Canterbury, obverse.
Liverpool, Mayer Collection

Ib Bishop Liudhard medalet from church
of St Martin, Canterbury, reverse.
Liverpool, Mayer Collection

II Reliquary of Ste Croix, Poitiers

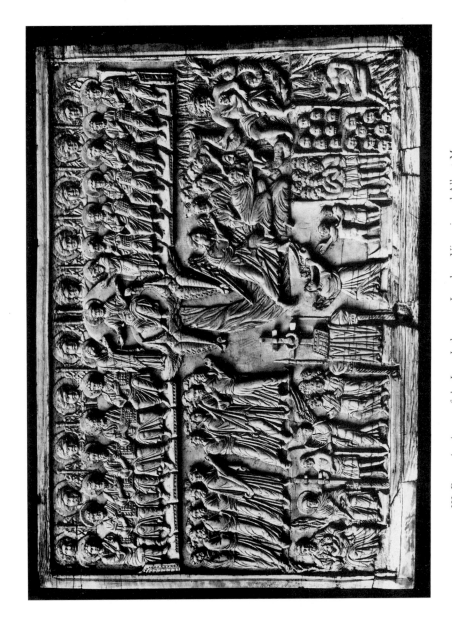

III Byzantine ivory of the Last Judgment. London, Victoria and Albert Museum

IV Coptic textile with jewelled Cross. Minneapolis Institute of Arts

V Sancta Sanctorum reliquary, outer cover. Patriarchal cross on Paradise-Golgotha.
Vatican, Museo Sacro

VI Syro-Palestinian ivory pyxis. Cleveland Museum of Art

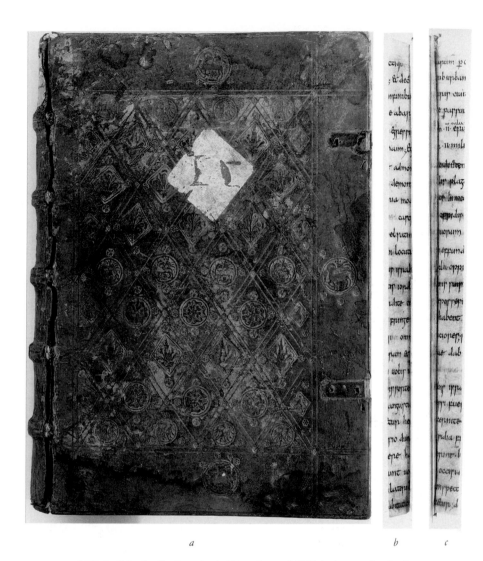

VII J. Gritsch, *Quadragesimale* ([Strassburg, 1495]) (private collection)
a Contemporary stamped binding; front cover
b 'Hook' of lower paste-down: (original recto) Numbers XXXIII.43–55
c 'Hook' of lower paste-down: (original verso) Numbers XXXV.3–13

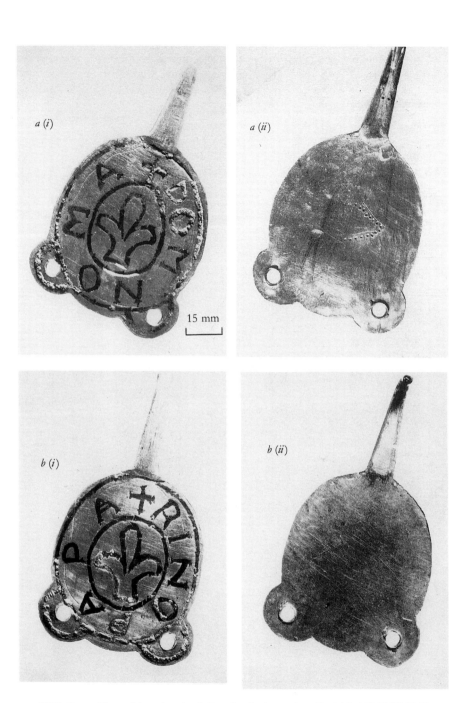

VIII Rome (Forum) hoard, pair of silver hooked tags, inscribed (*a*) +DOMNOMA, and (*b*) RINOPAPA+

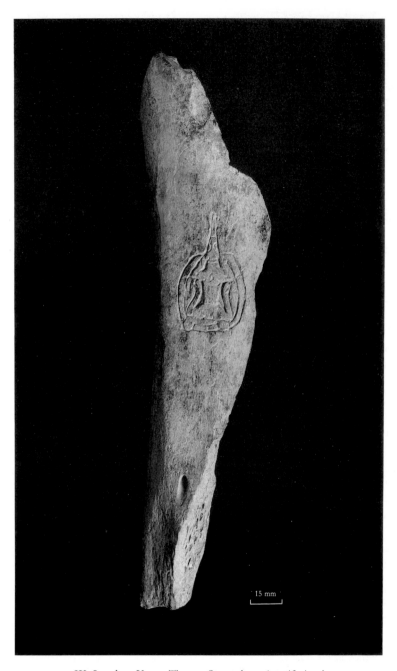

IX London, Upper Thames Street, bone 'motif-piece'

Homiliae;[51] and Gregory's *Dialogi*.[52] Lowe's individual assessments are rightly cautious; his verdict on the Canons, for example, is 'written in an Anglo-Saxon centre, probably on the Continent and possibly at Werden'. But it is an odd quirk of the play of evidence that these fragments scrape aboard *CLA* through the very weakness of their provenances, whilst complete and better-certified manuscripts are left out. In the preface to *CLA* VIII, Lowe throws caution to the winds and cites the fragments of the Canons and of Gregory's *Dialogi* as being 'in all probability' from Werden, in a list of Insular specimens 'certainly written on the Continent'.[53]

Insular manuscripts associated with the founders of Werden

Altfrid describes St Liudger as 'in scripturis sacris non mediocriter eruditus'[54] – just the sort of person to be particular about his 'qu[a]e's and '-que's – and the twelfth-century *Vita rhythmica S. Liudgeri* specifies a *Regula* (of St Benedict) and a psalter as having been written in his own hand.[55] Several books, especially biblical texts, were held to be autographs of Liudger and his brother Hildigrim in the later Werden tradition. Those that survive display an unfortunate multiplicity of hands, but all are in Insular script and some are better authenticated than others.

The inscriptions which assign the Berlin Epistles to Liudger are early.[56] To judge by its script, the manuscript could well have been written before the date of Liudger's death in 809. Its attribution to Liudger's own hand is far better

collection as a 'continental counterpart' of the Justinus fragments (see *CLA* IX, no. 1370), for which she tentatively accepts Lowe's attribution to Northumbria in the mid-eighth century; but since she uses the Werden connection to support that attribution, there is a danger of circularity.

51 *CLA* Supp., no. 1686 ('saec. VIII ex.') and no. 1688 respectively ('Düsseldorf, Staatsarchiv HS. Z. 4 nr. 1' and 'nr. 8'), both re-used as wrappers for sixteenth-century records concerning Werden dependencies. Both listed by Krämer, *Handschriftenerbe* II, 827–8 (Hauptstaatsarchiv, 'Fgm. K 19: Z 8–1' and 'Fgm. K 16: Z 4–2'). Stüwer, *Werden*, p. 64 (no. 16) lists a single leaf of anonymous homilies at Düsseldorf, perhaps a reference to the Bede. See also below, p. 61.

52 *CLA* VIII, no. 1070 (= Bonn, Universitätsbibliothek, S. 366, fols. 34, 41, palimpsested at Werden, *c.* 1500). A second fragment of the same text, *CLA* VIII, no. 1186 ('Düsseldorf, Landes- und Stadtbibl. B. 213'), is not listed by Krämer, but Stüwer (*Werden*, p. 64 (no. 14)) includes it as 'wahrscheinlich von Werdener Hss losgelöst' and Lowe slyly mentions Werden in his description without committing himself: 'Written either in England or in an Anglo-Saxon centre in Germany, like Werden. Provenance unknown.' It seems not unlikely that these two fragments are parts of the same book, though Lowe does not explicitly make the connection.

53 *CLA* VIII, p. vi. Here Lowe again treats the two Gregory fragments (nos. 1070 and 1186) as separate entries.

54 'Very learned in the holy scriptures', II.6 (MGH, SS 2, 413); see also A. Schröer, 'Das geistliche Bild Liudgers', *Das erste Jahrtausend*, ed. Elbern I, 194–215, esp. 210–11.

55 Line 985, quoted by Stüwer, *Werden*, p. 85 (nos. 3–4).   56 See above, p. 51 and n. 34.

warranted than that of a small gospelbook (Berlin, Staatsbibliothek der Stiftung Preussischer Kulturbesitz, Theol. lat. qu. 139 (Rose 259)),[57] perhaps somewhat later, which seems to stand apart from the other Insular manuscripts from Werden in script-style: its ligatures, sometimes very prominent, may betray a familiarity with continental cursive. The gospels has an early list of Werden relics and a 'treasure-binding' apparently portraying Liudger as bishop, but the late attribution to Liudger is refuted by a seventeenth-century inscription in the volume itself.[58] Another gospelbook attributed to Liudger, now lost, was last reported at Werden in 1718 by Martène and Durand.[59] Finally, to move from books supposedly written by Liudger to books owned by him, there are nineteenth-century reports of a gospelbook with an ivory cover showing scenes of the life of Christ, also now lost, which had been given to Liudger by a sister of Charlemagne.[60]

Hildigrim (I), Liudger's younger brother, was bishop of Châlons-sur-Marne from 802 until his death in 827. After his brother's death, he took over as head of the Werden community (809–27).[61] A copy of Gregory's *Homiliae in Ezechielem* (Berlin, Staatsbibliothek der Stiftung Preussischer Kulturbesitz, Theol. lat. fol. 356 (Rose 315))[62] ends with a long colophon in the first person, still in Insular script and apparently original: '. . . ego Hildigrimus indignus diaconus scribere coraui [= curaui?] ad utilitatem multorum, et auxiliante domino nostro Iesu Christo ad finem usque conpleui. Bonum opus nobis in uoluntate sit, a deo autem erit in perfectione.'[63] The general script-style clearly belongs to the same family as that of the Berlin Epistles and the colophon was traditionally accepted to mean that it was in Hildigrim's autograph. But

---

57 Chroust, *Monumenta*, 2nd ser. III.xxii, pls. 8a–b (64r, 61v: 215 × 145 mm., 27 long lines); Drögereit, *Werden und der Heliand*, pp. 28–9 (no. 11), pls. 9–10. Chroust's pl. 8b (= Drögereit's pl. 9) shows some original '-q.' for '-que' abbreviations by the scribe in the prefatory matter to Luke.

58 Stüwer, *Werden*, pp. 64–5 (no. 18).   59 *Ibid*. pp. 84–5 (no. 2).

60 *Ibid*. p. 84 (no. 1), last reported on its way to a private collection in England in 1852. Oxford, Bodleian Library, MS Douce 176 (*CLA* II, no. 238) is a gospel lectionary of *c*. 800 attributed to Chelles, where Charlemagne's sister Gisla was abbess, and its ivory cover shows scenes from the life of Christ. It is not certain when the ivory was married to the book and (unless there has been some deception) the later provenances do not tie up; but could Liudger's present have been a twin?

61 See Schröer, 'Chronologische Untersuchungen', p. 132, n. 29; Stüwer, *Werden*, pp. 298–9. Through his pioneering mission to the Halberstadt area, Hildigrim is mistakenly described as bishop of Halberstadt in some later traditions.

62 Chroust, *Monumenta*, 2nd ser. III.xxii, pls. 6a–b (2r, 1v: 312 × 215 mm., 25 long lines); Drögereit, *Werden und der Heliand*, p. 20 (no. 2), pls. 2 and 16a; Stüwer, *Werden*, pp. 62–3 (no. 5, 'geschrieben für Hildigrim').

63 Fol. 96v: 'I, Hildigrim, an unworthy deacon, took care of the writing for the use of many and brought the task to its end through the help of our Lord, Jesus Christ. Let our intention for the work be good, but it will be God who brings it to perfection.'

another scribe names himself as 'Ego Feluuald' in an acrostic poem in Insular script at the start of the manuscript: line 4, supplying the **F**, reads 'Folia conscripsi haec pauperum usibus apta . . .'[64] Neither the wording nor the published definitions of the hand(s) make the circumstances clear: the explanation that Hildigrim commissioned Felwald does not really seem to justify his colophon, unless the transition to the first person plural at the end is more literal than it seems. Nevertheless, Hildigrim's colophon is the most direct surviving statement from Werden's founding fathers about their activities in the making of books.

The other candidate for Hildigrim's own pen is a second copy of St Paul's Epistles (Hannover, Kestner-Museum Culem. I Nr. 1).[65] The tradition which makes Hildigrim its scribe is far later (sixteenth-century?) than that which assigns the Berlin copy to Liudger; but the scripts of the two copies seem fraternally close. The last leaf of the Hannover volume contains material from the psalms[66] and is claimed by Drögereit, perhaps correctly, as a fragment from a separate book; it is in Insular script, evidently from the same scriptorium.

Further Insular manuscripts of Werden provenance

The hooked **x** of the Berlin Epistles is found in both the Epistles and the psalter-fragment of Hannover, but not in the Gregory written by Felwald and/or Hildigrim.[67] It also appears in the remains of what may be another collection of saints' lives.[68] However, the extensive homiletic fragments in Insular script which supplied the bulk of the palimpsested parchment for Bonn, Universitätsbibliothek, S. 366 seem to be written in an altogether rougher and atypical style.[69] A fragment of the Easter cycle of Dionysius

---

[64] Fol. 1v: 'I, Felwald' and 'I wrote these leaves, fit for the uses of poor men . . .'

[65] Chroust, *Monumenta*, 2nd ser. III.xxii, pl. 7b (77v: 245 × 210 mm., 25 long lines), printed alongside the plate from the Berlin Epistles; Drögereit, *Werden und der Heliand*, pp. 20–3 (no. 3, two hands), pls. 3 and 16b; Stüwer, *Werden*, p. 63 (no. 11). The date is misprinted as 's. XV' by Krämer, *Handschriftenerbe* II, 828.

[66] Fol. 81: Ps. XVII.10–XVIII.33. Drögereit, *Werden und der Heliand*, pp. 23–4 (no. 5), pl. 4. Chroust (*Monumenta*, 2nd ser. III.xxii, text for pl. 7b) seems to take fol. 81 as part of the Epistles volume and it is ignored by Stüwer and Krämer.

[67] Bischoff, review of Drögereit, p. 8, takes its absence from the Gregory (as well as its appearance beyond Werden, see above, p. 50, n. 29) as evidence that Drögereit is wrong to pronounce it a Werden symptom. However, the Gregory is the only manuscript of the immediate group in which the hooked **x** is not reported; if Felwald was its scribe rather than Hildigrim, its absence seems less significant.

[68] The palimpsested fragment illustrated by Drögereit, *Werden und der Heliand*, pl. 5 = Bonn S. 367, 110v; see above, p. 54, n. 48.

[69] Drögereit, *Werden und der Heliand*, p. 27 (no. 9), pl. 7, cf. Stüwer, *Werden*, p. 77 (no. 74). The folio numbers are itemized by Dold, 'Palimpseste', p. 211. These are presumably the

Exiguus in continental Insular[70] is generally accepted as a product of Fulda, though annalistic entries relating to Werden were added not much later.

After Liudger's death in 809, the diffusion of his cult was not instantaneous; so his appearance as the last of the confessors in an apparently early litany in Cologne, Dombibliothek, 106 ought to be significant. Swithbert and Lebuin, his Anglo-Saxon predecessors in Frisia and Deventer, are also invoked, together with Cuthbert, Egbert, Bede and Willibrord.[71] The manuscript is a complex miscellany containing works of Alcuin and Bede, with hymns, litanies and other material, in a variety of script-styles and hands.[72] The contents approximate to materials sent by Alcuin to Arno of Salzburg in 802. In its time, Cologne 106 has been assigned to Alcuin's (or Rand's) Tours and to Hildebald's (or Jones's) Cologne. The liturgical hints towards Werden are supported by the palaeographical evidence of two Insular hands: the second in particular (Jones's hand 'Q', complete with hooked **x**) seems to match the style of the Liudger/Hildigrim group. But they are just two of the twenty or so hands which contributed to the miscellany; even the litany naming Liudger is by one of the subsidiary Caroline hands. The circumstances of its making must have been unusual: perhaps a conference of scholars whose scripts were too varied for them to have worked together for any length of time.[73]

---

fragments 'in Anglo-Saxon minuscule of a German type' which Lowe dismisses as seemingly ninth-century in his discussion of the palimpsested fragments of Gregory's *Dialogi* (*CLA* VIII, no. 1070). Dold suggests some textual connection with Hrabanus Maurus's commentary on St Matthew (completed by 821/2). To judge by his plate, Drögereit (p. 28 (no. 10), pl. 8) is probably right to identify fol. 193 of the palimpsest as deriving from another (homiletic?) book, in a more regular Insular script which still fails to match the style of the main Werden group.

70 *CLA* IX, no. 1234 ('Münster in Westph., Staatsarchiv Msc. I. 243 (foll. 3–10) . . . Saec. VIII ex.'). Drögereit, *Werden und der Heliand*, pp. 26–7 (no. 8, noting that the Werden entries are still in Insular style); listed by Krämer, *Handschriftenerbe* II, 828, but not by Stüwer. In his Lyell Lectures, Julian Brown observed that the script recalled *CLA* II, no. 146 + Supp., p. 19 (Fulda) and VIII, no. 1181 (unlocalized).

71 See M. Coens, *Recueil d'Études Bollandiennes*, Subsidia Hagiographica 37 (Brussels, 1963), 139–49.

72 See L. W. Jones, 'Cologne *MS. 106*: a Book of Hildebald', *Speculum* 4 (1929), 27–61, pls. I–VI; and Jones, *The Script of Cologne from Hildebald to Hermann*, The Mediaeval Academy of America, Publication 10 (Cambridge, MA, 1932), 40–3 (no. 7), pls. XXXI–XLV, esp. XL–XLII; Drögereit, *Werden und der Heliand*, pp. 31–5, pls. 11–12. After detailed analysis, Jones concluded that the manuscript had been 'parcelled out for simultaneous copying among seven scribes', of which two (hands 'N' and 'Q') were Insular, and supplemented by some thirteen or so further contemporary hands.

73 The idea of a temporary gathering of scribes, perhaps at Werden, is proposed by B. Bischoff, 'Panorama der Handschriftenüberlieferung aus der Zeit Karls des Grossen' (first published 1965), in his *Mittelalterliche Studien*, 3 vols. (Stuttgart, 1966–81) III, 5–38, at 7, n. 8. Earlier, Bischoff had been more dubious about Drögereit's suggestion that Cologne 106 had Werden connections (review, p. 9).

Early Caroline manuscripts of Werden provenance

The manuscripts in Caroline minuscule with later *ex libris* inscriptions of Werden include a few which are early enough to have been written at the same period as the Insular group. Berlin, Staatsbibliothek der Stiftung Preussischer Kulturbesitz, Theol. lat. fol. 346 (Rose 298)[74] is a copy of Augustine's *Tractatus in euangelium Iohannis* (pt 1) in Caroline and Maurdramnus minuscule of the turn of the century; Lowe describes it as 'written probably at Corbie, or possibly in a North-west German centre where scribes trained in the Corbie school were active, such as Werden . . .' This begs the question, but plainly Corbie is a major source, of books if not of scribes. Berlin, Staatsbibliothek der Stiftung Preussischer Kulturbesitz, Theol. lat. fol. 354 (Rose 312)[75] is a copy of Gregory's *Moralia in Job* (pt 6, bks 28–35), which Lowe says was 'written doubtless at Corbie' in the second half of the eighth century; restoration leaves were added at the turn of the eighth and ninth centuries in Maurdramnus half-uncial and Caroline minuscule, 'either at Corbie or by scribes trained there'. A Werden provenance is less secure for a third manuscript from the Corbie sphere of influence of the same period, a miscellany on Genesis including Alcuin's *Quaestiones* (Düsseldorf, Universitätsbibliothek, B. 3).[76] It has no *ex libris* of Werden and seems to have been at the neighbouring convent at Essen from the tenth century; but there was a tradition that it had been passed on to Essen from Werden and had originally been obtained by St Liudger himself. A somewhat later copy of Gregory's *Epistolae* (Berlin, Staatsbibliothek der Stiftung Preussischer Kulturbesitz, Theol. lat. fol. 322 (Rose 321))[77] is attributed by Bischoff to the Corbie scriptorium of the second third of the ninth century; it was at Werden by the twelfth century.

The manuscripts in Caroline minuscule which were certainly written at Werden later in the ninth century appear to show a blend of Insular and Corbie influence.[78] This no doubt indicates that the Corbie group of manuscripts was already in Werden's library at a very early period. But the evidence seems

---

[74] *CLA* VIII, no. 1066; Drögereit, *Werden und der Heliand*, p. 39; Stüwer, *Werden*, p. 64 (no. 13).

[75] Main manuscript = *CLA* VIII, no. 1067a; restoration leaves = no. 1067b. Drögereit, *Werden und der Heliand*, p. 30; Stüwer, *Werden*, p. 62 (no. 4: 'teils ags. Schrift' – but there is no mention of any Insular script in Lowe's descriptions).

[76] *CLA* VIII, no. 1183 ('saec. VIII–IX . . . pre-Caroline minuscule of the so-called Corbie ab-type . . . Written in the Corbie region'), cf. p. ix ('post ca. A.D. 798'); Drögereit, *Werden und der Heliand*, p. 23 (no. 4) (but see Bischoff's review, p. 8, noting that the binding is Essen's, not Werden's); Stüwer, *Werden*, p. 63 (no. 10); not in Krämer's list.

[77] Bischoff, review of Drögereit, p. 8; Stüwer, *Werden*, p. 67 (no. 30); listed by Krämer, *Handschriftenerbe* II, 826.

[78] Bischoff, review of Drögereit's *Werden und der Heliand*, p. 9, cf. pp. 11–12, diagnoses this mixture of influences in the scattered fragments of the 'Werden Glossaries' (Munich,

insufficient to prove that the Corbie-style manuscript of Augustine on John was actually written at Werden, or that the eighth-century Corbie copy of Gregory's *Moralia* was definitely repaired there. The same doubts apply to Werden's manuscript of Gregory's *Regula pastoralis* (Berlin, Staatsbibliothek der Stiftung Preussischer Kulturbesitz, Theol. lat. fol. 362 (Rose 308)), written in fine, early Caroline style and signed by one of its scribes, a Presbyter Harduinus whose work is known elsewhere.[79] As might be expected, Liudger's foundation was clearly drawing on continental as well as on Insular sources for its book supply; but how soon it started to import Caroline scribes as well as books is hard to tell. If Werden played host for the temporary 'write-in' of Cologne 106, its own community might have contributed both Insular and Caroline scribes; but the latter are more difficult to pick out amongst the throng of visitors.

CONCLUSIONS

Although the external evidence for the Werden provenance of the 'Heptateuch' and its contemporary Insular fragments is late, some similarities begin to emerge both amongst the fragments themselves and with the complete manuscripts which are more firmly linked to St Liudger and his circle. It seems likely that between them they preserve quite a fair amount of evidence for the Insular minuscule of Liudger's foundation in the early years of the ninth century. Nevertheless, it has to be admitted that the script of the 'Heptateuch' does not lie squarely in the centre of the group: *CLA*'s photograph scarcely does justice to its neat calligraphy, but the style does seem more compressed and less bold than the ideal model of Werden's early scriptorium. Its closest relative, to judge by the published photographs, is possibly the Hannover Epistles. Still, the script is not far off in 'grade' and intention: a cursive

Bayerische Staatsbibliothek, Cgm 187 III, etc.: Drögereit, pp. 35–7; Stüwer, *Werden*, p. 65 (no. 20)). The detection of similar influences in the scripts of the *Heliand* manuscripts provided the thrust of Drögereit's argument for their Werden provenance; but Bischoff has shown that it points more convincingly towards Corvey ('Die Schriftheimat der Münchener Heliand-Handschrift' (first published 1979), in his *Mittelalterliche Studien* III, 112–19, pls. I–II; see also pp. 103–4). See also now discussion in *The Epinal, Erfurt, Werden, and Corpus Glossaries*, ed. B. Bischoff, M. Budny, G. Harlow, M. B. Parkes and J. D. Pheifer, EEMF 22 (Copenhagen, 1988), 20–2 and 64.

79 Chroust, *Monumenta*, 2nd ser. III.xxii, pls. 9a–b; Drögereit, *Werden und der Heliand*, pp. 38–9; Stüwer, *Werden*, pp. 65–6 (no. 23). For Harduin's other manuscripts, see Bischoff, 'Panorama', p. 9, n. 18, cf. p. 11, n. 25. A fragment of an Insular passional was re-used in its fifteenth-century binding: see above, n. 48. Harduin of Saint-Wandrille, with whom Presbyter Harduinus is usually identified, died in 811.

minuscule written to a fair degree of formality and elegance. I concur with the verdict of Lowe and Karpp: the 'Heptateuch' was probably written at Werden in the early ninth century, maybe while the founder was still alive; but the possibility remains that it was an import from England.[80]

According to my notes, Julian Brown did not comment directly on the 'Heptateuch' fragments in his Lyell Lectures. But like Lowe, he did try to define the Insular script-style of Werden by picking out individual specimens from *CLA*. In the fourth Lyell Lecture on 12 May 1977, with all due hesitation, he named the Jerome and the Bede at *CLA* Supp., nos. 1686 and 1688,[81] as representatives of the Insular script-style of Werden. Like the 'Heptateuch' fragments, these fragments seem both less well documented and less central than the complete manuscripts in Insular script which failed to meet *CLA*'s criteria, the Gregory of Hildigrim/Felwald and the two manuscripts of the Pauline Epistles. But Julian Brown's general conclusion[82] holds good: a neat, stately minuscule inspired by good models of southern English cursive (his 'Type IIB') was developed around the turn of the century onwards in several Anglo-Saxon foundations in western Germany: Mainz, Fulda and Hersfeld as well as Werden.[83] His two Werden examples are not as large and bold as some of those from the other houses, but they share with them the elegance and formality which are also found in the 'Heptateuch' fragments.

In degree of intention, Julian Brown observed that this German style 'often *looks* and sometimes *is* "set" rather than "cursive"'. My notes indicate that almost in the next breath he turned to the Hatton mass-text and the Book of Cerne[84] as the closest English parallels for this rather formalized and calligraphic breed of cursive minuscule from the Insular scriptoria of western Germany. It is reassuring that a parallel with the Book of Cerne is precisely the conclusion reached by Michelle Brown in her study of the Tokyo fragment.[85] After the recent advances in the definition of ninth-century Insular script in

---

[80] If the origin and later date proposed by Michelle Brown are correct, the question arises of how the manuscript reached Werden from England: an opportunity to explore the continuing relationship of Werden to its Anglo-Saxon roots.

[81] See above, pp. 54–5 and n. 51.

[82] Following Bischoff's 1965 'Panorama' (see above, p. 58, n. 73). See also B. Bischoff, *Paläographie des römischen Altertums und des abendländischen Mittelalters*, Grundlagen der Germanistik 24, 2nd ed. (Berlin, 1986), 126–8, and Crick, 'Anglo-Saxon Fragment of Justinus', pp. 184–5.

[83] Julian Brown's examples included: Mainz, *CLA* I, no. 97; Fulda II, no. 146 + Supp., p. 19, recalling IX, no. 1234 and VIII, no. 1181; Hersfeld VIII, nos. 1144 and 1225.

[84] Respectively Oxford, Bodleian Library, Hatton 93 (*CLA* II, no. 241) and Cambridge, University Library, Ll. 1. 10 (not in *CLA*).

[85] Brown, 'New Fragment', pp. 38–40.

B. C. Barker-Benfield

England, it may now be time to take the continental survivals more into account, as Julian Brown had begun to do.[86]

APPENDIX

CONTENTS OF THE SURVIVING FRAGMENTS, WITH A TENTATIVE COLLATION[87]

Joins-code

| = still joined as a bifolium

⁝ = probably originally conjoint

⁝ = possibly originally conjoint

```
┌──────── (Düss. A. 19, fol. [15])  Gen. Prol. | quo pos[s]im[88] – end; chapter-headings I–LXIX
⁝  ┌ ─ ─ ─ ─  (One lost leaf?)
⁝  └ ─ ─ ─ ─  (One lost leaf?)
└──────── (Düss. A. 19, fol. [17])  Gen. III.13–16, III.22–IV.2; IV.8–13, 17–23 (top half only)
```

[86] *Postscript.* It was not until after completing this article that I read Rosamond McKitterick's important paper, 'Anglo-Saxon Missionaries in Germany: Reflections on the Manuscript Evidence', *Trans. of the Cambridge Bibliographical Soc.* 9 (1989), 291–329, which sets the process of reassessment of the relationship between English and continental Insular script well on its way. Dr McKitterick questions the underlying assumptions of Lowe's frequent references to 'Insular centres' and specifically cites (p. 297) the *CLA* entry for Düsseldorf A. 19 as an example of his subjectivity of judgement; her conclusion on the manuscript is nevertheless the same, that a Werden origin is likely but not completely certain. The Werden manuscripts, as I have outlined them, seem to fall into categories similar to those defined by Dr McKitterick at the earlier foundations of Würzburg and Fulda, including not only books in continental Insular script but also books which could have been written either in England or on the Continent, alongside others in contemporary continental scripts. As Cologne 106 may confirm at Werden, different scribal practices might have co-existed at such communities without immediate pressure towards assimilation and uniformity. Like Julian Brown, Dr McKitterick recognizes the possibility of continuing feed-back between England and the Continent in the development of Insular script in the early ninth century. The relative lateness of Werden's foundation may make the evidence of its Insular manuscripts particularly valuable.

[87] The microfilm (dated 28 September 1977) does not present the leaves in the order of the biblical text and the few folio numbers visible do not seem to follow consecutively. Nevertheless, the order of the microfilm sometimes seems relevant to the archaeological connections of the leaves as recovered from their intermediate bindings. In the chart, I have allocated to each Düsseldorf leaf my own folio-number in square brackets in the order of its appearance on the microfilm. The leaf at the start of Leviticus, of which the verso is illustrated by both Lowe and Karpp for its fine title-heading, is not present on the microfilm, perhaps because it arrived separately from the Hauptstaatsarchiv (see above, pp. 43, n. 2, 45, n. 12 and 46, n. 14). The information about the contents of its recto is taken from Stüwer, *Werden*, p. 64 (no. 15).

[88] Near the end of 'Desiderii mei . . .' = *Préfaces de la bible latine* [ed. D. De Bruyne] (Namur, 1920), p. 8, line 25.

(Düss. A. 19, fol. [18]) Gen. XXXIII.14–XXXV.6
(One lost leaf)
(Düss. A. 19, fol. [19]) Gen. XXXVI.29–XXXVII.32

(Düss. A. 19, fol. [20]) Exod. XXI.18–XXII.18
(One lost leaf?)
(One lost leaf?)
(One lost leaf?)
(One lost leaf?)
(One lost leaf?)
(One lost leaf?)
(Düss. A. 19, fol. [21]) Exod. XXIX.44–XXXI.6

(Düss. Fragm. K 16: Z 1/1) Lev. chapter-headings LXV–LXXXIX; I.1–II.2
(Düss. A. 19, fol. [1]) Lev. II.2–IV.18
(Düss. A. 19, fol. [5]) Lev. IV.18–VI.10
(Düss. A. 19, fol. [7]) Lev. VI.11–VII.33
(Düss. A. 19, fol. [3]) Lev. VII.33–IX.7
(Düss. A. 19, fol. [6]) Lev. IX.7–XI.10
(Düss. A. 19, fol. [2]) Lev. XI.10–XIII.4
(Düss. A. 19, fol. [4]) Lev. XIII.5–51

(Düss. A. 19, fol. [11] + Gritsch fragment) Num. XXIV.7–XXVI.7
(One lost leaf)
(Düss. A. 19, fol. [13]) Num. XXVI.61–XXVIII.17
(Düss. A. 19, fol. [8]) Num. XXVIII.17–XXIX.36
(Düss. A. 19, fol. [9]) Num. XXIX.36–XXX.24
(Düss. A. 19, fol. [14]) Num. XXXI.24–XXXII.22
(One lost leaf)
(Düss. A. 19, fol. [12] + Gritsch fragment) Num. XXXIII.43–XXXVI.13
(Düss. A. 19, fol. [22]) Num. XXXV.13–XXXVI.13; Deut., chapter-headings I–X
(Düss. A. 19, fol. [10]) Deut. chapter-headings X–end; I.1–8
(One lost leaf)
(One lost leaf)
(Düss. A. 19, fol. [16]) Deut. III.3–IV.9
(Düss. A. 19, fol. [23]) Deut. IV.9–45
(Düss. A. 19, fol. [24]) Deut. IV.45–VI.5
(Düss. A. 19, fol. [25]) Deut. VI.5–VII.20
(One lost leaf)
(Düss. A. 19, fol. [26]) Deut. IX.8–X.15
(Düss. A. 19, fol. [27]) Deut. X.15–XII.1
(One lost leaf)
(Düss. A. 19, fol. [28]) Deut. XIII.6–XV.6
(Düss. A. 19, fol. [29]) Deut. XV.5–XVI.22

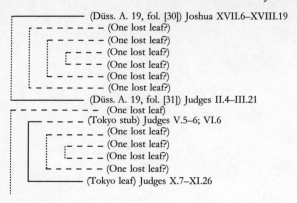

(Düss. A. 19, fol. [30]) Joshua XVII.6–XVIII.19
(One lost leaf?)
(One lost leaf?)
(One lost leaf?)
(One lost leaf?)
(One lost leaf?)
(One lost leaf?)
(Düss. A. 19, fol. [31]) Judges II.4–III.21
(One lost leaf)
(Tokyo stub) Judges V.5–6; VI.6
(One lost leaf?)
(One lost leaf?)
(One lost leaf?)
(One lost leaf?)
(Tokyo leaf) Judges X.7–XI.26

The uncarpentered world of Old English poetry

EARL R. ANDERSON

Cultural archaism is often thought of as a natural concomitant of oral tradition, and by extension, of a literature that is influenced by oral tradition.[1] In the case of Old English poetry, archaism might include residual pagan religious beliefs and practices, such as the funeral rites in *Beowulf* or the use of runes for sortilege,[2] and certain outmoded aspects of social organization such as the idea of a state dependent upon the *comitatus* for military security. An example often cited is the adaptation of heroic terminology and detail to Christian topics. The compositional method in Cædmon's 'Hymn', for instance, is regarded by many scholars as an adaptation of panegyric epithets to the praise of God,[3] although N. F. Blake has noted that heroic epithets in the poem could have derived their inspiration from the psalms.[4] In *The Dream of the Rood*, the image of Christ mounting the Cross as a warrior leaping to battle has been regarded variously as evidence of an artistic limitation imposed by oral tradition,[5] or as a learned metaphor pointing to the divine and human nature of Christ and to the crucifixion as a conflict between Christ and the devil.[6] The martyrdom of the apostles is represented as military conflict in

---

[1] This aspect of oral tradition is discussed by W. J. Ong, *Orality and Literacy: the Technologizing of the Word* (London, 1982), pp. 41–2.

[2] E. G. Stanley, *The Search for Anglo-Saxon Paganism* (London, 1975).

[3] Adaptation of secular panegyric in the 'Hymn' was proposed by C. L. Wrenn, 'The Poetry of Cædmon', *PBA* 32 (1946), 278–95, and K. Malone, 'Cædmon and English Poetry', *Mod. Lang. Notes* 76 (1961), 193–5. The formulaic character of the 'Hymn' was studied by F. P. Magoun, Jr, 'Bede's Story of Cædmon: the Case History of an Anglo-Saxon Oral Singer', *Speculum* 30 (1955), 49–63, and by D. K. Fry, 'Cædmon as a Formulaic Poet', *Forum for Mod. Lang. Stud.* 10 (1974), 227–47; and see also his 'The Memory of Cædmon', *Oral Traditional Literature: a Festschrift for Albert Bates Lord*, ed. J. M. Foley (Columbus, OH, 1981), pp. 282–93, and P. R. Orton, 'Cædmon and Christian History', *NM* 84 (1983), 163–70.

[4] N. F. Blake, 'Cædmon's Hymn', *N&Q* 207 (1962), 243–6.

[5] R. E. Diamond, 'Heroic Diction in *The Dream of the Rood*', *Studies in Honor of John Wilcox*, ed. A. D. Wallace and W. O. Ross (Detroit, MI, 1958), pp. 3–7.

[6] R. Woolf, 'Doctrinal Influences on *The Dream of the Rood*', *MÆ* 27 (1958), 137–53, repr. in her *Art and Doctrine: Essays on Medieval Literature*, ed. H. O'Donoghue (London, 1986), pp. 29–48; O. D. Macrae-Gibson, 'Christ the Victor-Vanquished in *The Dream of the Rood*', *NM* 70 (1969), 667–72; C. J. Wolf, 'Christ as Hero in *The Dream of the Rood*', *NM* 71 (1970), 202–10; A. L. Klinck, 'Christ as Soldier and Servant in *The Dream of the Rood*', *Florilegium* 4 (1982), 109–16; for the *miles Christi* theme, see M. A. Dalbey, 'The Good Shepherd and the Soldier of God: Old English Homilies on St Martin of Tours', *NM* 85 (1984), 422–34.

Cynewulf's *Fates of the Apostles*, Christ and his apostles as king and *comitatus* in Cynewulf's *Ascension*, and temptation by devils as a military attack in *Guthlac A*; these illustrate a point made by A.B. Lord concerning the nature of conservatism in oral tradition: 'tradition is not a thing of the past but a living and dynamic process which began in the past [and] flourishes in the present'.[7]

The dynamic nature of 'tradition' makes it difficult to isolate archaic substrata from contemporaneous culture. As a result we are left without a clear picture of the nature and extent of 'cultural archaism' in the poetry. We experience a parallel difficulty in assessing the nature and extent of 'archaic' language in cases where this is assumed to represent a special link with the past or with ancestors, as in Eskimo séance poetry[8] or in the heroic poems of Velema the Fijian, who presents his poetry as the words of ancestors speaking through him and who (according to his English translator) chose 'archaic words from his own background, words which he alone understands'.[9] As R. Finnegan has warned, in such cases the linguistic 'archaisms' may in fact be innovations, or else word-combinations and images 'that are long-established yet constantly developed and renewed'.[10] Without a detailed analysis of the contents of archaism, the general problem cannot be addressed here. In this essay I shall, however, present a detailed analysis of one instance of cultural archaism, which I shall call the 'uncarpentered' perspective in Old English poetry. My thesis is that although the real world of the Anglo-Saxons was 'carpentered' like our own, the world of Old English poetry is 'uncarpentered'.

In an initial attempt to explain what this means, we may adduce a poem by the American poet A.R. Amons, 'Corson's Inlet', in which a narrator represents himself in a meditative walk over sand dunes:

> I went for a walk over the dunes again this morning
> to the sea, . . .
> the walk liberating, I was released from forms,
> from the perpendiculars,
>   straight lines, blocks, boxes, binds
> of thought
> into the hues, shadings, rises, flowing bends and
>   blends of sight . . .

There are no straight lines in nature, not even in nature theoretically conceived. As Albert Einstein once put it, the universe is 'something like

---

[7] A.B. Lord, 'Characteristics of Orality', *Oral Tradition* 2 (1987), 62–4.

[8] *Peter Freuchen's Book of the Eskimos*, ed. D. Freuchen (London, 1962), p. 277.

[9] *The Flight of the Chiefs: Epic Poetry of Fiji*, ed. B.H. Quain (New York, 1942), p. 16.

[10] R. Finnegan, *Oral Poetry: its Nature, Significance and Social Context* (Cambridge, 1977), p. 111.

curved'. The round earth's corners can be imagined only as a paradox. A. Holder writes of 'Corson's Inlet' that the 'seaside setting works . . . against the idea of order. It is a place that resists straight lines, which the poem associates with forms and fixed, ordering thoughts. The waterline itself is inexact, shifting. Amons allows his mind to shift also – mental 'lines' cannot contain the complexity and constant changes of nature that he encounters in his walk over the dunes'.[11]

Nothing like 'Corson's Inlet' could have been composed by an Anglo-Saxon poet, first because Old English lacks the vocabulary of geometric forms upon which Amons depends, and second (more significantly) because the conceptual world of Old English poetry could never support a contrast between the experience of curves and circles and that of angles and straight lines. To borrow a term from cultural anthropology, the world of Old English poetry is 'uncarpentered', a world 'where manmade structures are a small portion of the visual environment and where such structures are constructed without benefit of carpenter's tools . . . Straight lines and precise right angles are a rarity.' In consequence, if geometrical figures are named they will tend to be curved rather than angular, such as are predominant in the environment. In a carpentered world, in contrast, manmade angular structures are prominent in the landscape and give rise to an expanded vocabulary of geometric forms that includes words for angular shapes.[12]

H.W. Burris, Jr recently developed support for this 'carpentered world hypothesis' through a comparative study of geometric figure terms in seventy-two languages. Among these, nine were found to have no geometric terms; thirteen had terms only for a circle or circularity; eleven had terms for a circle and a square or angularity; five had terms for a circle, a square or angularity, and a triangle; and thirty-nine had all these plus a rectangle.[13] These figures suggest that the evolution of geometric terms across languages can be predicted in terms of a five-stage development:

1	2	3	4	5
no terms	circle or curve	square or angularity	triangle	rectangle
(9)	(13)	(11)	(5)	(39)

---

[11] A. Holder, *A. R. Amons* (Boston, 1978), p. 46.
[12] M. H. Segall, D. T. Campbell and M. J. Herskovitz, *The Influence of Culture on Visual Perception* (New York, 1966), pp. 83–4.
[13] H. W. Burris, Jr, 'Geometric Figure Terms: their Universality and Growth', *Jnl of Anthropology* 1.2 (1979), 18–41.

Earl R. Anderson

Similar universal patterns in vocabulary development have been identified for basic colour words and for categorical names of plants and animals.[14]

Burris's study was based on contemporary non-European languages. However, Anglo-Saxonists will recognize that the language of Old English poetry belongs at stage two, while the prose texts show evidence of a transition to stage three. Two words in the core vocabulary, *beag* and *hring*, refer to a curve or circle. OE *circul* (< Lat. *circulus*) is used exclusively as an astronomical term meaning 'zodiac'.[15] In Ælfric's *Passio sancti Thomae apostoli* a well-carpentered window (*egðyrle*) is described as *ælteowe* 'well-finished' (< Gmc *tawjan*; cf. Go. *taujan*, OE *teon* 'to make', applied to a wide variety of crafts), rather than in terms of angularity.[16] OE *feowerscyte* 'square' appears as a calque in the Alfredian translation of Orosius's *Historiae adversum paganos* II.6 where the city of Babylon is described as 'swiþe ryhte feowerscyte', rendering 'moenibus paribus per quadrum disposita'.[17] Ælfric, in the *Catholic Homilies*, writes of a church built by Xerxes which was 'eahta-hyrnede' and 'eal of fiðerscitum marmstanum geworht'.[18] *Feowerscyte*, *fiðerscite* and *hyrnede*, terms suggestive of a square or of angularity, appear in prose but not in the extant poetry. Like other early Indo-European languages, Old English has no distinctive word for 'geometric shape'; OE *hiw* (Go. *hiwi*) has the more generic sense of 'appearance'.[19]

Because of the paucity of geometric terms in Old English, buildings in poetry may be described in terms of their height or magnitude, but rarely in terms of shape. Thus, Heorot was a 'medoærn micel' (*Beowulf* 69a); 'Sele hlifade / heah ond horngeap' (81b–82a).[20] In those few cases when the shape of

14 See B. Berlin and P. Kay, *Basic Color Terms: their Universality and Evolution* (Berkeley, CA, 1969); C. Brown, 'Folk Zoological Life-Forms: their Universality and Growth', *American Anthropologist* (1979), 791–817; C.H. Brown, *Language and Living Things: Uniformities in Folk Classification and Naming* (New Brunswick, NJ, 1984); S.R. Witkowski, C. Brown and P.K. Chase, 'Where Do Tree Terms Come From?' *Man* 16 (1981), 1–14.

15 *Ælfric's De Temporibus Anni*, ed. H. Henel, EETS os 213 (London, 1942), 16; 'ðam bradan circule þe is zodiacus gehaten' *ibid.* p. 20; *Byrhtferth's Manual*, ed. S.J. Crawford, EETS os 177 (London, 1929), 'se circul þe ys *zodiacus* gehaten' (p. 8).

16 *Ælfric's Lives of Saints*, ed. W.W. Skeat, 2 vols., EETS os 76, 82, 94 and 114 (London, 1881–1900) II, 402, line 69. With *ælteowe* compare Gothic *fulla-tojis* (calque of Latin *perfectus*) Matt. V.48; H.V. Velten, 'Studies in the Gothic Vocabulary with Especial Reference to Greek and Latin Models and Analogues', *JEGP* 29 (1930), 332–51 and 489–50, at 344.

17 Paulus Orosius, *Historiarum adversum paganos libri VII*, ed. C. Zangemeister, CSEL 5 (Vienna, 1882), 96; *The Old English Orosius*, ed. J. Bately, EETS ss 6 (London, 1980), 43, line 25.

18 'Eight-cornered' and 'all of quadrangular marble stones'; *Ælfric's Catholic Homilies: The Second Series, Text*, ed. M. Godden, EETS ss 5 (London, 1979), 287, lines 264 and 266.

19 C.D. Buck, *A Dictionary of Selected Synonyms in the Principal Indo-European Languages: a Contribution to the History of Ideas* (Chicago, 1949), p. 874.

20 'Great meadhouse... the dwelling towered up, high and wide-gabled'; *Beowulf and Judith*, ed. E.V.K. Dobbie, ASPR 4 (New York, 1953). Except where noted otherwise, quotations

68

a structure is referred to, it is described as rounded or curved, like the 'hringmere' in *The Ruin* 45a.[21] The adjective *geap*, usually translated as 'wide', was associated with angularity by Hotchner,[22] but in Latin glosses it translates either *curuus* or *pandus*, 'curved' or 'bent', or *callidus* 'clever', 'skilfully made', and *geaplice* glosses *callide, ingeniose*.[23] The wall (*wag*) in *The Ruin* 9b, described as *steap* and *geap* (11b), is thought of as curved by R.F. Leslie, who points out that *geap* refers to a 'wall' which is actually a mountain in *Solomon and Saturn* 255–7.[24] In *Beowulf*, Heorot is described as 'geap ond goldfah' (1800a), 'heah and horngeap' (82a); its roof is 'geapne' (836b); and the temple in *Andreas* is 'heah and horngeap' (668a). In these cases, *geap* could mean 'wide', 'curved' or 'arched', or 'skilfully made'. This is true, also, of the gem in Cotton Gnomes 22b–23a: 'Gim sceal on hringe / standan steap and geap'.[25]

Against this linguistic background we can observe three features about buildings in Old English poetry which together constitute the 'uncarpentered' perspective. First, the poets express an awed regard for Roman ruins, considered to be the products of a technologically superior culture. Second, buildings may be homologized to natural structures such as mounds or caves, and conversely, natural structures may be described in architectural terms. Third, when a building is described in detail, the emphasis is on its internal construction, described in terms of twisted rings or curved arches mounted on supports, rather than in terms of angular shapes that are prominent in the products of carpentry (and even masonry). These three features of the uncarpentered world at times overlap in the same poetic texts, but in the interest of clarity we will consider them separately here.

The theme of an awed regard for Roman ruins is expressed primarily in passages that describe buildings using the formulaic verse *(eald) enta geweorc*, a circumstance that supports the association of the uncarpentered perspective with oral tradition. P.J. Frankis has noted that in all five instances where *enta geweorc* refers to a building, Latin loan-words contribute to the impression that a technically superior architecture is being admired. In *Andreas* 1495a 'eald

---

from Old English poems are from G.P. Krapp and E.V.K. Dobbie, ASPR, 6 vols. (New York, 1931–53).

21 *Three Old English Elegies: The Wife's Lament, The Husband's Message, The Ruin*, ed. R.F. Leslie (Manchester, 1961).

22 C.A. Hotchner, *Wessex and Old English Poetry, with Special Consideration of The Ruin* (Lancaster, PA, 1939), pp. 35–6.

23 T. Wright, *Anglo-Saxon and Old English Vocabularies*, 2nd ed. rev. R.P. Wülcker, 2 vols. (London, 1884): *geap* for *cornas* (probably a miswriting), 369.6; for *curfa*, 377.37; for *pando*, 486.9; for *callidus*, 168.10, 274.4, 334.39; *geaplice* for *callide, ingeniose*, 197.26.

24 *Three Old English Elegies*, ed. Leslie, pp. 69–70.

25 ASPR 6, 55–7, *Maxims II* 22b–23a; see also *Gnomic Poetry in Anglo-Saxon*, ed. B.C. Williams (New York, 1914), pp. 127–9.

enta geweorc' refers to a prison, a *carcern* (1460a) where Andreas 'be wealle seah' (1492a); in *Beowulf* 2717b the 'enta geweorc' that Wiglaf 'bi wealle . . . seah' (2716a, 2717b) is the dragon's barrow; in *Cotton Maxims* the 'orðonc enta geweorc' are 'ceastra' (*Maxims II* 1b–2a), 'weallstana geweorc' (3a); in *The Ruin* details of the 'enta geweorc' (2b) include the 'wealstan' and 'torras' (1a and 3b); and in *The Wanderer* the 'eald enta geweorc' (87a) is also called a 'wealsteal' (88a). These ancient stone structures have endured the ravages of time, wind and weather, and are admired in part because of their antiquity.[26]

Anglo-Saxon admiration for Roman architecture is evident in Ælfric's *Passio S. Thomae*: Abbanes, the reeve of king Gundoforus of India, travels to Caesarea in Syria to recruit workers 'þa þe on stane cunnon and gecwemlice on treowe *þaet* hi on romanisce wisan æræere his cynebotl'.[27] Later the king asks, 'Miht þu me aræran on romanisce wisan cynelice gebytlu?' and Thomas responds with a catalogue of the various buildings that he can create: a hall, bath-house and kitchen, winter-house and summer-house, twelve houses together with good arches. Ælfric adds, 'ac swylc worc nis gewunelic to wyrcenne on englalande and for-þy we ne secgað swutellice heora naman'.[28] This narrative closely follows its Latin source, a *Passio S. Thomae* like the one printed by Mombritius,[29] but the phrase 'on romanisce wisan' (used twice) along with the contrast with English architecture, are Ælfric's contributions. Thomas's architectural skill symbolizes his mission to build 'cristes getimbrunge'[30] in India, and Ælfric's additional detail, 'on roman wisan', suggests the Roman Church and strengthens the theological theme of 'edification', a patristic commonplace based primarily on I Cor. XIV. Ælfric's contrast of Roman and English architecture suggests something more, however: that he understands and shares King Gundoforus's admiration for the *romanisce wise*.

While it is true that buildings are homologized to natural structures, conversely, the natural world can be described using architectural terms. This is possible because many basic architectural terms also refer to topographical or other features of the natural world. *Weall* can mean the wall of a building or

---

[26] P. J. Frankis, 'The Thematic Significance of *enta geweorc* and Related Imagery in *The Wanderer*', *ASE* 2 (1973), 253–69, at 256–7 and 267.

[27] *Lives of Saints*, ed. Skeat II, 400–2, lines 38–9: 'those who are cunning in stone, and approved of in wood, that they may erect his palace in the Roman fashion'.

[28] *Ibid.* p. 404, lines 91–2, 'Canst thou erect for me in the Roman fashion a royal dwelling?'; lines 100–1, 'but it is not customary to make such work in England, and therefore we shall not tell their names clearly'.

[29] *Sanctuarium, seu vitae sanctorum*, ed. B. Mombritius, 2 vols., 2nd ed. (Paris, 1910) II, 606–14. For an earlier Greek version, see *The Apocryphal New Testament*, ed. M. R. James (Oxford, 1924), pp. 364–77, and E. Hennecke, *New Testament Apocrypha*, ed. W. Schneemelcher, trans. R. McL. Wilson, 2 vols. (Philadelphia, 1965) II, 442–58.

[30] *Lives of Saints*, ed. Skeat II, 402, line 66.

city or fortress, but just as often a cliff (as in Old Saxon; cf. *Heliand* 2675a and 2684a).[31] *Hrof* can mean both 'roof' and 'sky', and more generally the 'summit' of a mountain. The formulaic expression *heofones hrof* or *wolcna hrof* 'roof of heaven' could be either a metaphor or a semantically reduplicative expression of the sort often used for intensification.[32] *Duru* could refer not only to a 'door', but also to a natural opening and particularly the mouth, as in *Lambeth Psalter* CXL.3, 'Duru [Lat. *ostium* 'opening'] ymbstandennesse welerum minum'.[33] *Muþ, muþa* could refer to the mouth but also to the door of a room or building: 'recedes muþan' (*Beowulf* 724a) refers to the door of Heorot, and 'merehuses muð' (*Genesis* 1364a) to the door of Noah's ark; *Cotton Gnomes* have 'Duru sceal on healle, rum recedes muþ' (*Maxims II* 37b–38a). The formulaic phrase *recedes muþ* probably should be thought of as a natural result of the semantic overlap of *duru* and *muþ*, rather than as a sensational image pointing to a supposed metaphor of 'building-as-body'. The metaphor of the human body as a building, however, appears in Cynewulf's *Elene* 1236b (*hus*), *Maldon* 297a (*feorhhus*) and *Dream of the Rood* 73a (*feorgbold*). The metaphor of the body as 'temple dryhtnes' in Advent Lyric VII (*Christ I* 186a) is based on St Paul's *corporale Dei templum* (II Cor. VI.16), a patristic commonplace.[34]

The homology of buildings and natural structures sometimes creates ambiguities that lead to difficulty in the interpretation of texts. In Exeter Riddle 29 (Moon and Sun), the Moon is pictured as attempting to build a *bur* 'bower' *on þære byrig* (line 5: 'in the stronghold [of the sky]'); but the Sun appears and drives her away: 'Ða cwom wundorlicu wiht ofer wealles hrof.' It is not clear whether the prepositional phrase means 'over the mountain top', 'over the horizon', or 'over the roof of the wall' referring exclusively to the figurative *byrig* of line 5.[35]

Beorg, beorh can refer to a mound or hill, a mountain or a barrow, with a

---

[31] *Heliand und Genesis*, ed. O. Behaghel, 9th ed. rev. B. Taeger (Tübingen, 1984).

[32] For collocation of near-synonyms as a device for intensification, see N. Peltola, 'Observations on Intensification in Old English Poetry', *NM* 72 (1971), 649–90, at 657 and 683–4.

[33] 'Keep the door of my lips'; *Der Lambeth-Psalter. Eine ae Interlinearversion des Psalters in der HS 427 der erzbischoflichen Lambeth Palace Library*, ed. U. Lindelöf, 2 vols. (Helsinki, 1909–14).

[34] See R.B. Burlin, *The Old English Advent: a Typological Commentary* (New Haven, 1968), pp. 123–4. For earlier background, see A.E. Hill, 'The Temple of Asclepius: an Alternative Source for Paul's Body Theology', *Jnl of Biblical Lit.* 99 (1980), 437–9.

[35] Exeter Riddle 29 in ASPR; no. 27 in *The Old English Riddles of the Exeter Book*, ed. C. Williamson (Chapel Hill, NC, 1977). R.K. Gordon, *Anglo-Saxon Poetry* (London, 1926), p. 299, translates 'over the mountain-top'. For 'over the horizon', see *Old English Language and Literature*, ed. A.H. Marckwardt and J.L. Rosier (New York, 1972), p. 198n., and J.J. Joyce, 'Natural Process in *Exeter Book* Riddle 29: "Sun and Moon"', *Annuale Medievale* 14 (1974), 5–8.

potential for ambiguity in *Beowulf* and particularly in *Guthlac A*.[36] The dragon's *beorh* in *Beowulf* clearly is an artificial structure, an *enta geweorc* supported by stone posts and arches: 'ða stanbogan stapulum fæst / ece eorðreced innan healde'.[37] When first used it was 'niwe be næsse, nearocræftum fæst'.[38] However, it is also called an *eorðsele* (2410a), *eorðscrafa* (3046a), *eorð[hu]se* (2232a) and *hlæw* (2296a, 2411a) and understandably was regarded by some early critics as a natural cave.[39] *Hlæw*, of course, would mean either 'barrow' or 'mound' and refers as well to Hnæf's funeral pyre in the Finn episode (1120a).

Guthlac's *beorg* in *Guthlac A* is probably the *tumulus* that had been excavated by greedy treasure-hunters ('hlaw mycel' in the prose *Guthlac*) and over which he built a *tugurium* or hut (Felix, *Vita S. Guthlaci*, ch. 28).[40] L. K. Shook and Karl P. Wentersdorf argue this position with emphasis on the possibilities that a barrow offers for religious symbolism, and A. H. Olsen emphasizes its role as part of a 'heroic' landscape.[41] In contrast, P. Reichardt argues that the *beorg* is a mountain, symbolic of eremetical values in the tradition of Cassian;[42] however, the *beorg* is hidden 'on bearwe', in a wood (148a) and obscured from view, 'bimiþen fore monnum' (147a) which is incompatible with the idea of a mountain. J. Roberts glosses *beorg* as 'mound' or 'hill' and rejects 'barrow', primarily because the text lacks supportive synonyms that point to a barrow, such as *eorðscræf* or *eorðsele* as are found in *Beowulf*, although she glosses *beorge* in *Guthlac B*, 1193b, as 'grave'.[43] The excavated *tumulus* with a hut built over it, in

---

36 L. Motz, 'Burg – Berg, burrow – barrow', *IF* 81 (1977), 204–20, has examined the linguistic evidence and proposed that IE *bhergh* and zero-form *bhrgh* have the basic sense of 'enclosure [providing protection]' rather than 'elevation' or 'mountain'. She notes that generally the *bhergh* derivatives apply to natural enclosures, and *bhrgh* derivatives to manmade habitations, but the two forms often alternate.

37 'The stone arches, secure on pillars, eternally held the earth-house within' (*Beowulf* 2718b–19).

38 'New by the headland, strengthened with cunning art' (*Beowulf* 2243).

39 The *beorh* was interpreted as a cave by L. Schücking, *Untersuchungen zur Bedeutungslehre der angelsächsischen Dichtersprache* (Heidelberg, 1915), but his arguments were answered by W. W. Lawrence, 'The Dragon and his Lair in *Beowulf*', *PMLA* 33 (1918), 569–80; see further his *Beowulf and Epic Tradition* (Cambridge, MA, 1928), pp. 208–12. Most subsequent commentators accept Lawrence's interpretation; see for example W. Sedgefield, 'The Scenery in *Beowulf*', *JEGP* 35 (1936), 161–9, at 164–7.

40 *Felix's Life of Saint Guthlac*, ed. B. Colgrave (Cambridge, 1956), pp. 92–4; *Das angelsächsische Prosa-Leben des hl. Guthlac*, ed. P. Gonser (Heidelberg, 1909), p. 117. See H. R. E. Davidson, 'The Hill of the Dragon', *Folklore* 61 (1950), 169–85, at 175, for buildings on the sites of barrows.

41 L. K. Shook, 'The Burial Mound in *Guthlac A*', *MP* 58 (1960), 1–10; K. P. Wentersdorf, '*Guthlac A*: the Battle for the *Beorg*', *Neophilologus* 62 (1978), 135–42; A. H. Olsen, *Guthlac of Croyland* (Washington, 1981), pp. 34–5.

42 P. F. Reichardt, '*Guthlac A* and the Landscape of Spiritual Perfection', *Neophilologus* 58 (1974), 331–8.

43 *The Guthlac Poems of the Exeter Book*, ed. J. Roberts (Oxford, 1979), pp. 21 and 132 [note to line 140].

Vita S. Guthlaci, corresponds well with the profile of a 'sunken hut', which archaeologists recognize as a common type of Anglo-Saxon house (discussed below). The advantage of the *tumulus* was that it presented Guthlac with a floor cavity already dug out. The description of Guthlac's home in a 'beorge on bearwe' (*Guthlac A* 148a), and as a 'bold on beorhge' (140a), a house built over a barrow, in a 'londes stow' (146b) that had been revealed or discovered, corresponds to Felix's text to such an extent that it cannot be dismissed as coincidence. This correspondence suggests that the *beorg* in *Guthlac A* is a barrow, although it must be conceded that 'hill' or 'mound' is equally consistent with other details in the poem.

Another example of a building homologized to a natural structure is the *eorðscræf* or *eorðsele* in *The Wife's Lament*:[44]

> Heht mec mon wunian   on wuda bearwe,
> under actreo   in þam eorðscræfe;
> eald is þes eorðsele,   eal ic eom oflongad.
> Sindon dena dimme,   duna uphea,
> bitre burgtunas   brerum beweaxne,
> wic wynna leas . . .
> þonne ic on uhtan   ana gonge
> under actreo   geond þas eorðscrafu . . .

An *eorðscræf* could be a cave, a barrow, a denehole (an underground storage pit of the sort described in Tacitus's *Germania,* ch. 16),[45] or a sunken workhouse of the sort described by Pliny (HN XIX.ii.9), who alludes to Germanic women manufacturing linen in underground structures, most likely during winter. Wentersdorf recently reviewed the evidence for these possibilities and settled in favour of a cave,[46] noting, among other things, that the simplex *scræf* means

---

[44] 'Someone ordered me to dwell in a grove of woods, under an oak tree in the earth-hut; old is this earth-dwelling, I am full of longing. The valleys are gloomy, the hills steep, the sharp hedges overgrown with briars, the settlement bereft of joys . . . Then at dawn I must pace alone under an oak tree, in the earth-hut' (*The Wife's Lament* 27–32a and 35–6, in *Three Old English Elegies,* ed. Leslie).

[45] Tacitus, *Opera minora,* ed. H. Furneaux and J.G.C. Anderson (Oxford, 1900).

[46] K.P. Wentersdorf, 'The Situation of the Narrator in the Old English *Wife's Lament*', *Speculum* 56 (1981), 492–516, at 498–503. Identification of the *eorðscræf* as a barrow, or by extension the grave, has its advocates among critics who believe that the narrator in the poem is a revenant or wandering spirit, or, alternatively, a mourner singing a death-song. See E. Lench, 'The *Wife's Lament*: a Poem of the Living Dead', *Comitatus* 1 (1970), 3–23; R.P. Tripp, Jr, 'The Narrator as Revenant: a Reconsideration of Three Old English Elegies', *Papers on Lang. and Lit.* 8 (1972), 339–61; 'Odin's Powers and the Old English Elegies', in *The Old English Elegies: New Essays in Criticism and Research,* ed. M. Green (Rutherford, NJ, 1983), pp. 57–68; and W.C. Johnson, Jr, '*The Wife's Lament* as Death-Song', in *The Old English Elegies,* ed. Green, pp. 69–81.

'cave'. However, *scræf* also means 'dwelling' more generally, although still with the connotation of a 'cavernous place' (Bosworth–Toller, s.v. *scræf* II): the word is used in metaphorical references to hell, e.g. 'sceaþena scræf' 'den of thieves', and glosses *domicilium* in Mark V.3 'Se hæfde on byrgenum scræf.'[47] Another possibility, proposed by J. Harris, is that the *eorðscræf* is a partially sunken hut,[48] essentially a carpentered structure used as a permanent dwelling. Tacitus alludes to such sunken huts as winter dwellings, and seems to regard them as structures of the same type as storage pits.[49] If there is confusion on his part it is understandable, since Tacitus, who had never been to Germany, based his description on reports by informants. However, archaeologists have confirmed the presence, throughout Germanic lands, of sunken dwellings of the sort that Tacitus refers to.[50] Such houses were widespread in early Anglo-Saxon England. They are in evidence in more than a hundred villages, variously with two posts, four posts or framed superstructures, and have been found wherever there are pagan Anglo-Saxon cemeteries[51] – in other words, throughout the early settlement area. Moreover although most were small hovels, some were substantial houses. One at Upton, Northamptonshire, for example, was thirty feet by eighteen feet with gabled end walls,[52] and evidence for other large structures has been found at Puddlehill, Dunstable.[53] The Wife's account of herself pacing the floor *geond eorþscrafu* suggests a larger structure, a requirement of the text that can be accommodated by archeological evidence. Since the *eorðsele* is called *eald* 'old', it may be one of the sunken houses that had been used in the early years of the Anglo-Saxon settlement. OE *eorþhus*, glossing *ypogaeum vel subterraneum* in a supplement to Ælfric's vocabulary,[54] must refer to the same type of house; Bald's *Leechbook* has:

[47] 'He [the madman of Gadara] had his dwelling among the tombs'. *The Gospel according to Saint Mark in Anglo-Saxon and Northumbrian Versions*, ed. W.W. Skeat (Cambridge, 1871).

[48] J. Harris, 'A Note on *eorðscræf*/*eorðsele* and Current Interpretations of *The Wife's Lament*', *ES* 58 (1977), 204–8.

[49] For this confusion on Tacitus's part, see *Germania*, ed. R. Much, 3rd ed. rev. H. Jankuhn and W. Lange (Heidelberg, 1967), p. 258.

[50] W.U. Guyan, 'Einige Karten zur Verbreitung der Grubenhäuser in Mitteleuropa im ersten nachchristlichen Jahrtausend', *Jahrbuch der schweizerischen Gesellschaft für Urgeschichte* 42 (1952), 174–97.

[51] J.G. Hurst, in *Deserted Medieval Villages: Studies*, ed. M. Beresford and J.G. Hurst (London, 1971), pp. 145–68.

[52] D.A. Jackson *et al.*, 'The Iron Age and Anglo-Saxon Site at Upton, Northants', *AntJ* 49 (1969), 202–21.

[53] C.L. Matthews, 'Saxon Remains on Puddlehill, Dunstable', *Bedfordshire Archaeol. Jnl* 1 (1962), 48–57. For a general survey of these and other such houses, see P.V. Addyman, 'The Anglo-Saxon House: a New Review', *ASE* 1 (1972), 273–307.

[54] *Anglo-Saxon and Old English Vocabularies*, ed. Wright and Wülcker, col. 187.32.

'Romane him worhton eorþhus for ðære lyfte wylme' ('the Romans built for themselves earth-houses because of the boiling heat of the air').[55]

The Wife's *eorðscræf* must be visualized in its larger context. Located *on wuda bearwe*, in a grove of trees, it is surrounded by *burgtunas*, fences or enclosures, and these are overgrown with briars, evidently because of neglect. Since Tacitus (*Germania*, ch. 16) mentions that Germanic settlements often were located in groves, it is easy to imagine the Wife's house shaded by a large oak tree. The setting is also called a *wic*. This word originally meant a 'dairy farm', that is, a small settlement removed from the village where cattle were tended and butter and cheese were made. By extension *wic* in place-names could be applied to a saltworks (cf. *Sealtwic*, the Anglo-Saxon name for Droitwich, Worcestershire) or other small settlement, such as a *berewic* 'barley-wick' or *huntan wic* 'hunting lodge', separated from the village and constructed for a specialized purpose. Often these settlements included dwellings, as evident from the place-name *wicham* (unless this refers to a *ham* near a Roman *vicus*),[56] and in Old English texts, *wic* often refers to a settlement or dwelling in a general sense. *Wic* as a small settlement distant from the village, however, is consistent with the Wife's solitary life. A comparable use of *wic* as an isolated settlement surrounded by woods and enclosures appears in the Old English translation of Bede's *Historia ecclesiastica* V.2, in a description of a *mansio secretior*, a retreat a mile and a half from the church at Hexham, used by monks as a place of meditation:

Sindon sumu deagol wiic mid walle 7 mid barwe ymbsealde, noht feorr from ðære ciricean Heagostealdes eac, ðæt is, huhuego in oðerre halfre mile fæcce; floweð Tiine seo ea betwihn. Habbað ða wiic gebædhus 7 ciricean S̄c̄e̅ Michaheles ðæs heahengles, in ðæm se Godes wer oft mid feaum broðrum his geferum stille wunude to biganne his leornunge 7 halig gebedu, and swiðust in ða tiid ðæs feowertiglican fæstenes ær Eastrum.[57]

---

[55] *Leechdoms, Wortcunning, and Starcraft of Early England*, ed. T.O. Cockayne, 3 vols., RS (London, 1864–6; repr. with new introduction by C. Singer, London, 1961) II, 146, line 16.

[56] G.B. Grundy, 'The Development of the Meanings of Certain Anglo-Saxon Terms', *ArchJ* 99 (1943), 86–8. For *wicham*, see M. Gelling, 'English Place-Names Derived from the Compound *wicham*', *MA* 11 (1967), 87–104.

[57] 'There are some retired habitations surrounded with a rampart and forest, not far from the church of Hexham, that is, about a mile and a half; the river Tyne flows between. These buildings comprise an oratory and a church of St Michael the archangel, at which the man of God often stayed with a few brethren as his companions in retirement, to pursue his studies and holy prayer, especially at the season of the forty days' fast before Easter.' *The Old English Version of Bede's Ecclesiastical History of the English People*, ed. T. Miller, 2 vols., EETS os 95 and 96 (London, 1890–1) II, 388; for Bede's text, *Bede's Ecclesiastical History*, ed. B. Colgrave and R.A.B. Mynors (Oxford, 1969), p. 456.

Earl R. Anderson

Again in the Old English *Durham*, after describing the Wear river well-stocked with various kinds of fish (3b–5), the encomiast describes wooded retreats stocked with various animals:

> And ðær gewæxen is wudafæstern micel;
> wuniað in ðem wycum wilda deor monige,
> in deope dalum deora ungerim.[58]

The triple-compound *wudafæstern* (emended to *wudafæsten[n]* in Bosworth–Toller) could mean 'a dwelling fast in the forest',[59] but probably refers more generally to the great forest that embraced Durham in medieval times.[60] An account of rivers, forests and rural retreats was part of the classical heritage of the *encomium urbis*.[61]

The setting in *The Wife's Lament*, then, is an isolated settlement (*wic*) in a grove (*on wuda bearwe*) surrounded by enclosures (*burgtunas*) that are overgrown with briars (*brerum beweaxne*) as a result of neglect. The Wife's dwelling in this *wic* is an old sunken house shaded by an oak tree, large enough for us to imagine her pacing the floor during times of distress. Her exiled spouse, the *geong mon* of lines 42–53, must endure greater suffering: he lives in a 'dreorsele . . . under stanhliþe'[62] and, lacking shelter, is reminded often of 'wynlicran wic'.[63] *Dreorsele* means 'dreary dwelling', not 'hall', and refers to the cliff that the *geong man* must use as shelter.[64] In the alternative, if the *eorðscræf* is a cave or barrow, we must understand *wic* in the general sense of 'place' or 'dwelling', and *burgtunas* as a metaphorical allusion to the nearby valleys and hills or other features of the landscape, and we must regard the scene as 'sketchy', 'surrealistic', or 'existential'[65] rather than as the precise, detailed description that it actually is.

---

[58] 'And there is established a great forest-fastness; many wild animals live in its retreats, countless animals in (its) deep dales' (*Durham* 6–8; ASPR VI, 27).

[59] Certainly it does not refer to Cuthbert's coffin, as proposed by C. B. Kendall, 'Let Us Now Praise a Famous City: Wordplay in the OE *Durham* and the Cult of St Cuthbert', *JEGP* 87 (1988), 507–21, at 520.

[60] Mentioned by Symeon of Durham, *The History of the Church of Durham*, trans. J. Stevenson (London, 1855), p. 673.

[61] For the encomiastic tradition in *Durham*, see M. Schlauch, 'An Old English *Encomium Urbis*', *JEGP* 40 (1941), 14–28, at 23 (for rivers and forests).

[62] 'A dreary dwelling under a cliff' (*The Wife's Lament* 50a and 48a).

[63] 'A more pleasant settlement' (52a).

[64] For *sele* as 'dwelling' rather than 'hall', see C. H. DeRoo, 'Old English *Sele*', *Neophilologus* 64 (1980), 113–20. The idea is that the *geong man* must live without shelter, not that he lives in a sort of 'anti-hall'. It should be noted that for the concept of 'anti-hall' in Old English poetry, in K. Hume, 'The Concept of the Hall in Old English Poetry', *ASE* 3 (1974), 63–74, at 68–70, most of the supporting examples are based on the view that *sele* means 'hall'.

[65] Examples of such metaphorical interpretations of details abound in the critical literature. P.

The description of the construction of buildings as a twisting of rings is found in at least one prose passage: King Alfred, in the account of his metaphorical 'house of learning' for which he had gathered timber and tools (in the Preface to his translation of Augustine's *Soliloquies*), advises his reader to gather materials 'þat he mage windan manigne smicerne wah and manig ænlic hus settan'.[66] The door of Heorot is 'fyrbendum fæst' (*Beowulf* 722a). The hall can withstand the violence of Beowulf's and Grendel's fight because it is secured with iron bands:

> he þæs fæste wæs
> innan ond utan   irenbendum
> searoþoncum besmiþod.[67]

Again when Heorot is repaired, only the roof having escaped damage, we recall that the hall remained standing because it was 'eal inneweard irenbendum fæst' (998). Similar details are found in the description of a helmet's crest (*hrof*) constructed with twisted wires:

> Ymb þæs helmes hrof   heafodbeorge
> wirum bewunden   walu utan heold.[68]

Gradon, in *Form and Style in Early English Literature* (London, 1971), p. 170, writes that the Wife 'uses language so generalised and conventional that we do not know what is actual and what is image'. Wentersdorf, 'The Situation', p. 514, who regards the *eorðscræf* as a cave, writes, 'One would expect the compound *burgtunas*, a hapax legomenon, to denote literally the defences (earthworks, ramparts, enclosures, walls) of a stronghold or settlement, and if so it may refer to the cliffs or beetling crags of the area . . . In the present context, a metaphorical interpretation of the hapax seems called for: "the confines of this joyless habitation are forbidding and overgrown with briars"'. M. Green, 'Time, Memory, and Elegy in *The Wife's Lament*', *The Old English Elegies: New Essays in Criticism and Research*, ed. Green, p. 125, regards the *eorðscræf* as a cave and refers to 'sketchy details of the surrounding landscape' including 'dim valleys and high hills that in the speaker's metaphoric association constitute a fortress (*burgtuna*, 31a)'. W.C. Johnson, in '*The Wife's Lament* as Death-Song' (*ibid.* p. 70), regards the *eorðscræf* as a barrow and the *burgtunas* as 'perhaps suggesting a group of burial mounds' and evoking 'an atmosphere of chthonic mystery'. D. Chase, '"The Wife's Lament": an Eighth-Century Existential Cry', *Univ. of South Florida Lang. Quarterly* 24 (1986), 18–20, comments that 'the existential character of the poem is also evident, symbolically, in the setting' (he interprets the *eorðscræf* as a cave).

[66] 'So that he may bind together many a fine wall and establish many a unique building.' *King Alfred's Version of St Augustine's Soliloquies*, ed. T. A. Carnicelli (Cambridge, MA, 1969), p. 47, lines 9–10. For a similar 'house of learning' metaphor, but without reference to geometric shapes, see *Byrhtferth's Manual*, p. 142.

[67] 'It was firmly, skilfully constructed within and without with iron bands' (*Beowulf* 773b–5a).

[68] 'Around the helmet's crest as a head-protection, the ridge held outside, wound with wires' (*Beowulf* 1030–1).

The construction of the Roman ruins at Bath are described thus in *The Ruin*:

Mod mo[nade]   myne swiftne gebrægd;
hwætred in hringas,   hygerof gebond
weallwalan wirum   wundrum togædre.
Beorht wæron burgræced,   burnsele monige,
heah horngestreon,   heresweg micel,
meodoheall monig   mondreama full,
oþþæt þæt onwende   wyrd seo swiþe.[69]

In a well-known article on imagery in the elegies, E.B. Irving argues that details in the construction of the ruin call attention to the nature of heroic society:

To the Germanic mind, what binds such a community together is the exchange of material wealth, the gold and silver and jewels mentioned later in the poem. It seems worth suggesting . . . that some connection may have been hinted at between the wires and rings that are part of the building's structure and wires in rings in the more usual sense (in poetic formulae, at least) of valuable artifacts and hence binders in the social structure.[70]

The description of the master builder as *hygerof* and *hwætred in hringas*, in particular, might seem to encourage this view. Such modifiers, however, indicating the enthusiasm of builders engaged in an ambitious project, are more properly referred to the encomiast tradition. In *Karolus Magnus et Leo Papa*, for example, a poem in praise of Charlemagne on the occasion of his meeting with Pope Leo I at Paderborn in 799, the poet, possibly Einhard, describes the building of Aachen, a second Rome, which was supervised personally by King Charles. In several places modifiers are used to indicate the enthusiasm of the builders:

Pars super in summis populi procul arcibus *ardens*
Saxa locat, solido coniungens marmora nexu;
Altera stat gradibus portantum sorte receptans
Pars onera atque *avidis manibus* praedura ministrat
Saxa . . .
Itque reditque operosa cohors, diffusa per urbem,
Materiam Romae *certatim* congregat altae.[71]

---

69 'A courageous one intended, a swift purpose set in motion; a resolute (builder) skilled in rings bound the foundation together wondrously with wires. The buildings of the city were bright, the bath-halls were many, the gilded horn-gables were high, the martial noise great, many a meadhall full of the revelry of men, until powerful Fate changed that' (*The Ruin* 18–24).

70 E.B. Irving, Jr, 'Image and Meaning in the Elegies', *Old English Poetry: Fifteen Essays*, ed. R.P. Creed (Providence, RI, 1967), p. 155.

71 'Some of the people *ardently* set stones far up at the top of the towers, joining the marble in solid slabs; others stand on the steps receiving in turn the loads that the porters bring, and

These passages illustrate the point that *hygerof* and *hwætred in hringas*, applied to the builders in *The Ruin*, are not sensational descriptors that require a symbolic explanation, but are, rather, conventional ways of indicating the skill and dedication of the builders.

The description of a structure in terms of curves or bends is seen again in the dragon's barrow in *Beowulf*, an *enta geweorc* that was held in place within by stone arches, *stanbogan* (2718a). The ruin in *The Wanderer* is described as a 'weal wundrum heah, wyrmlicum fah'.[72] *Wyrmlicum* could refer to decorative patterns in stone,[73] or to the herring-bone masonry in Roman walls, in zigzag patterns created by thin bricks or tiles laid along opposite diagonals on each horizontal course.[74] In either case the visual impression is one of curved or twisted shapes, consistent with descriptions of buildings elsewhere in the poetry. A common denominator among these buildings is their ability to withstand the ravages of time, warfare and weather. Heorot withstood the violence of Beowulf's fight with Grendel because the hall was secured with iron bands. The dragon's barrow was supported *ece* 'eternally' by pillars and arches. The walls of the ancient ruin in *The Wanderer*, the *eald* works of giants, still stand, although ravaged by wind and weather,

> winde biwaune,   weallas stondaþ
> hrime behrorene,   hryðge þa ederas.[75]

In *The Ruin*, 'Stanhofu stodan' (38a) wondrously bound together with wires, even though the buildings and repairers have perished and the buildings are ravaged by weather and warfare.

As this review has shown, there is a close connection between the details associated with buildings in Old English poetry and the limitations and

---

with eager hands pass on the heavy stones . . . The busy throng comes and goes, scattered about the city, *eagerly* gathering material to build lofty Rome'. *Karolus Magnus et Leo Papa, Ein Paderborner Epos vom Jahre 799*, ed. H. Beumann, F. Brunhölzl and W. Winkelmann (Paderborn, 1966), lines 114–18 and 123–4.

[72] 'A wall wondrously high, ornamented with serpent-like [shapes]' (*The Wanderer* 98).

[73] R. O. Bower, '*The Wanderer* 98', *Explicator* 13 (Feb. 1955), 26, suggests that the *weal* is a stone gravestone, and that *wyrmlicum fah* refers to 'maggot like pattern decoration of Neolithic burial monuments common throughout Britain'. C. Dean, '*Weal wundrum heah, wyrmlicum fah* and the Narrative Background of the *Wanderer*', *MP* 63 (1965–66), 141–3, suggests that the *weal* refers to a wall of stones around a grave, set up by the last survivor of a city (the *anhaga*), and that some of these stones had serpent-like ornamentation. P. J. Frankis, 'The Thematic Significance of "enta geweorc"', pp. 268–9, suggests a wall painted with images of dragons, symbolic of destruction. S. L. Clark and J. N. Wasserman, 'The Imagery of *The Wanderer*', *Neophilologus* 63 (1979), 291–6, at 295 propose that 'the serpents embossed upon the ruin represent the symbolic attempts which were made to bind up the now crumbling walls'.

[74] T. Millns, '*The Wanderer* 98: "*Weal Wundrum Heah Wyrmlicum Fah*"', *RES* 28 (1977), 431–8.

[75] 'Blown upon by wind, the walls stand covered with frost, snow-swept buildings' (*The Wanderer* 76–7).

possibilities afforded the poet by his language. So far as geometric forms are concerned, Old English provided 'core' vocabulary for circles or curves, and loan-translations for a 'square'; in terms of anthropological linguistics, the language was in a state of transition from stage 2 to stage 3. The language of Old English poetry, however, was at stage 2, with terms for circularity only. Moreover in both prose and poetry the language was limited in technical architectural terminology. However, alternative linguistic resources were available as sources of artistic power: buildings could be homologized to natural structures, and although their exterior shapes could not be described in terms of angularity, their interior construction could be described in terms of twists and curves, allowing for emphasis on their durability. The most significant conclusion to be drawn from this study is the evidence that it presents for cultural archaism in the poetry. It provides the perspective of an 'uncarpentered' world, with its vocabulary of geometric forms limited to curves and circularity, and with its awed regard for the products of a technologically superior culture. To a certain extent the 'uncarpentered' perspective is supported by the formulaic theme of the ancient *enta geweorc* that has withstood the ravages of time, warfare and weather. Another contributing factor is an element of conservatism in the language itself, which preserved the geometric vocabulary of an earlier age, together with its limitations.

The use of modal verbs in complex sentences: some developments in the Old English period

HIROSHI OGAWA

In his oft-quoted study of indirect discourse (dependent statements, dependent desires[1] and dependent questions) in Old English, J.H. Gorrell concludes the section on 'the use of the auxiliaries' by observing in his statistics an increasing frequency of their use in the period, which he relates to the loss of distinctive subjunctive inflexions:

The conclusions to be drawn from these statistics are very evident . . . Regarding *CP.*, *Or.*, *Boe.*, and *Bede* as representatives of Alfredian prose and *AH.*, *Boe.* [*sic*], *W.*, and *BH.* as types of the language of the later period, the above statistics show that the relative proportion of the subjunctive to the auxiliary forms in the former period is as 3 to 1, while at the time of Ælfric the proportion is as 2 to 1. This postulates, therefore, a growing tendency in the language to make use of the auxiliary constructions, and this tendency was fostered by the gradual breaking-down of the old subjunctive forms, until in course of time the periphrastic constructions almost entirely replaced the inflectional forms.[2]

This conclusion, though 'evident', calls for reconsideration. For, as I argue in detail in another publication,[3] Gorrell's statistics themselves, like those of most other scholars dealing with the problem, are subject to serious reservations in that they are not based on any clear statement of what he defines as 'auxiliaries' and 'subjunctives'. Any definition of 'modal auxiliaries', as far as it is based on the alleged equivalence of meaning to the inflexional form of a simple verb, leaves room for subjective interpretation and arbitrary decision in the individual examples, a point which is particularly true for Old English in which 'modal auxiliaries' can still often be used as full verbs. Hence the necessity of a new formulation of the problem, so that the resultant statistics can be objective and reliable. The one I adopt in the above-mentioned study – by comparing 'modal verbs' and other simple verb forms *in toto* rather than the pre-selected examples of 'modal auxiliaries' and the 'subjunctives' – gives a totally different picture from the one Gorrell gave of the changing frequency

---

[1] The term is defined below. See also B. Mitchell, *Old English Syntax*, 2 vols. (Oxford, 1985), §1937 (hereafter *OES*).

[2] J.H. Gorrell, 'Indirect Discourse in Anglo-Saxon', *PMLA* 10 (1895), 342–485, at 458.

[3] *Old English Modal Verbs: a Syntactical Study*, Anglistica 26 (Copenhagen, 1990), Introduction and §6.1.1.

of the words in question during the period. The selected early and late Old English prose texts contain, respectively, 1,989 modal verbs and 17,179 simple verb forms, and 2,116 modal verbs and 21,444 simple verb forms that occur in the whole variety of independent and subordinate clauses; the incidence of modal verbs is 10.4 per cent in early prose but only 9.0 per cent in late prose.[4]

One might object that this new result is largely an outcome of the different sets of clauses for which Gorrell's figures and mine are collected. However, that this is not so is strongly suggested by the usage in the narrower context of dependent desires, that is, those dependent clauses that are introduced by expressions of volition, which form a subset of Gorrell's indirect discourse and which usually 'govern' the subjunctive mood. The incidence of modal verbs here – 242 instances against 1,146 simple verb forms, or 17.4 per cent, in early prose and 386 against 1,584, or 19.6 per cent, in late prose[5] – might appear to support Gorrell's conclusions, but the rise in late prose is not as decisive as he leads us to believe. Further, this slight rise itself is counterbalanced by other evidence which does not allow us to see it as related immediately to the decay of the distinctive subjunctive inflexions from early to late Old English. For example, Table 1 below examines the alleged relationship between this morphological process and the employment of modal verbs, by analysing the frequency in the relevant clauses in early and late prose works of the preterite plural forms of modal verbs in relation to the total number of their instances and to the number of the preterite plural forms of simple verbs.

TABLE 1[6]

	MV (total)	MV (pret. pl.)	IF (pret. pl.)
Orosius	40	21	52
Ælfric's narrative prose	72	14	54

The relationship could be recognized, if anywhere, in this part of conjugation, where the morphological process in question is in evidence very clearly. But, contrary to what Gorrell's argument leads us to expect, it is in *Orosius* that the relative frequency of modal verbs is higher in either of the two ways

4 *Ibid.* §§2.2 and 3.2. My *modal verbs* in this book, as in the present study, include nine words: *agan, cunnan, *durran, magan, *motan, *sculan, þurfan, willan* and *wuton.*

5 *Ibid.* §§5.1.1 and 6.1.1. A list of Old English volitional expressions (as I define them) is given in the introduction to Part II of the same book.

6 In this table, as in other relevant ones in this study, MV and IF stand respectively for modal verbs and inflexional forms of simple verbs. For Ælfric's prose, I have examined all his non-liturgical narrative pieces as set out in P. Clemoes, 'The Chronology of Ælfric's Works', *The Anglo-Saxons: Studies in Some Aspects of Their History and Culture Presented to Bruce Dickins*, ed. P. Clemoes (London, 1959), pp. 212–47, esp. 218.

mentioned above, despite the original distinction between the subjunctive and the indicative (-*en*/-*on*) which is preserved much better in this 'Alfredian' text than in Ælfric's prose.[7] This, together with the evidence quoted at the end of the last paragraph, speaks against believing in simple chronological developments of Old English modal verbs as grammatical substitutes for ambiguous inflexional forms of simple verbs; the 'substitution theory', of which Gorrell's conclusion provides an example, is not valid at any rate for Old English, even in the 'subjunctive contexts' to which it should be expected to apply first and foremost.

If this is so, the question arises whether there is any other sense in which one can speak of developments in the Old English period. In what follows, I shall consider this problem with particular reference to usage in prose in dependent desires, to which some attention has already been paid.

THE USAGE OF MODAL VERBS IN DEPENDENT DESIRES

Dependent desires express desired relationship in the form of a finite clause, in place of the infinitive construction which would normally replace it in Modern English, and, as such, it is a particular stylistic trait of Old English. Use of a modal verb is often an important feature of such style, giving double expression to the sense of volition for which the introducing verb or phrase in the main clause alone would seem to us today to suffice – a tendency which may be assumed to reflect the original paratactic sentence construction of Old English. In Standop's words:

Es kommt hinzu, daß ae. noch eine deutliche Vorliebe für eine Ausdrucksweise besteht, die für unser Sprachgefühl pleonastisch wirkt und dazu neigt, syntaktische Funktionen überzudefinieren. In dem Satztyp 'Ich befehle, daß du gehen sollst' ist ja die Willensäußerung doppelt ausgedrückt: durch 'befehlen' and 'sollen'. Dafür setzt die moderne Sprache: 'Ich befehle dir zu gehen', und zwar im Deutschen wie im Englischen. Das Ae. aber geht noch einen Schritt weiter, indem es den gleichen Satztyp bei identischem Subjekt in Haupt- und Nebensatz verwendet: 'ich beabsichtige, daß ich ... will'; 'ich bitte, daß ich ... darf', usw. Der Infinitiv, obwohl ae. schon gebräuchlich, ist nicht so charakteristisch wie diese Nebensatzfügungen es sind. Sie sind ein weiterer Beweis für die bekannte Tatsache, daß das ae. Satzgefüge der Parataxe noch recht nahe steht.[8]

---

[7] For the dominance of the pret. pl. -*en* ending in dependent desires in *Orosius* (ed. Sweet; see n. 15), see my article 'Modal Verbs in Noun Clauses after Volitional Expressions in the Old English *Orosius*', *Stud. in Eng. Lit.* (Tokyo), English Number 1979, pp. 115–37, esp. 117. For later usage, I find, for example, some fifty forms ending in -*on*/-*an* but only one in -*en* in the corresponding contexts in *Ælfric's Lives of Saints*, ed. W. W. Skeat, EETS os 76, 82, 94 and 114 (London, 1881–1900). For ambiguous preterite plural forms in general, see A. Campbell, *Old English Grammar* (Oxford, 1959), §735(g).

[8] E. Standop, *Syntax und Semantik der modalen Hilfsverben im Altenglischen: Magan, Motan, Sculan, Willan*, Beiträge zur englischen Philologie 38 (Bochum-Langendreer, 1957), 45: 'What is

As Standop aptly points out, this 'pleonastic' use of modal verbs is best in evidence in those cases where the subject of the noun clause is identical with the subject of the main clause or at any rate with the logical subject of the volitional expression; I have presented full statistical evidence elsewhere[9] that modal verbs tend to occur much more frequently in the type just mentioned – the 'identical-subject type' – than in the other, 'non-identical-subject type' of clauses of the relevant groups (see below) in early as well as late Old English prose (and poetry). What I propose to do here is to examine whether or not this overall characteristic of Old English usage does in fact contain any sign of change to the contrary as one passes from the early to the late period.

We may begin with the frequency of modal verbs. The figures for dependent desires as a whole are given in the last section. These are analysed below according to the six groups into which dependent desires may be conveniently divided (Table 2). The groups (1) to (3), by their nature, almost always express the 'non-identical-subject type' of desired relationship and may consequently be left out of consideration in what follows. It is in the remaining three groups, expressing what one asks, wishes and guarantees to do as well as what one asks, wishes and guarantees somebody else to do, that we may hope to find evidence of immediate relevance for our present concern. The total for these three groups is given along the bottom of the table.

It can be seen, first, that while there is a continued preference for the usage in the 'identical-subject type' of requesting-, wishing- and swearing-groups of clauses into late Old English, the proportion of such examples in the total of modal verbs has decreased: from 102 out of 127 (= 80.3 per cent) in early Old English to 129 out of 200 (= 64.5 per cent) in late Old English. Secondly, both the 'identical-subject type' and the 'non-identical-subject type' record an internal rise of incidence of modal verbs, but the rate of the rise is not as high in the former (from 41.1 per cent to 56.3 per cent, with the rate of 137 per cent) as in the latter (from 5.7 per cent to 8.5 per cent, with the rate of 149 per cent). Taken together, these figures would point to some change that has taken place

more, there still remains in Old English a distinct preference for a mode of expression which, to our linguistic instinct, works pleonastically and tends to 'overdefine' syntactic functions. Indeed, in the sentence type 'Ich befehle, daß du gehen sollst [I command, that you shall go]', desired relationship is doubly expressed: through 'befehlen [to command]' and 'sollen [shall]'. Modern language replaces this by 'Ich befehle dir zu gehen [I command you to go]', and this is so in German as well as in English. However, Old English goes even a step further in that it uses this self-same sentence type for principal and subordinate clauses of which the subjects are identical: 'ich beabsichtige, daß ich . . . will [I intend that I will . . .]'; 'ich bitte, daß ich . . . darf [I pray that I may . . .]', and so on. The infinitive, though in use already in Old English, is not so characteristic as are subordinate constructions. These are another indication of the well-known fact that sentence construction in Old English still remains very close to parataxis.'   9 *OE Modal Verbs*, Tables 22, 29–31 and 38–40.

TABLE 2

Subjects of main and dependent clauses		Early prose		Late prose	
		IF/MV	(MV%)	IF/MV	(MV%)
(1) Commanding		219/58		319/104	
(2) Advising		299/21		261/29	
(3) Granting		67/36		138/53	
(4) Requesting	Identical	15/10 ·		24/50	
	Non-identical	253/13		515/38	
(5) Wishing	Identical	113/43		54/24	
	Non-identical	161/9		235/19	
(6) Swearing	Identical	18/49		22/55	
	Non-identical	1/3		16/14	
(4) + (5) + (6)	Identical	146/102	(41.1%)	100/129	(56.3%)
	Non-identical	415/25	(5.7%)	766/71	(8.5%)

during the period, so that usage in the 'identical-subject type' of clause has become less dominant in dependent desires in late Old English.

In trying to understand the nature of this change, it is perhaps significant to see modal verbs in the 'identical-subject type' of clause in relation to usage in the original stage of parataxis of which they are generally assumed to be the more obvious residues.[10] Decrease of such 'paratactic' uses would mean a development away from parataxis in the area of modal verbs as in sentence construction of the language in general. This is difficult to prove, since 'paratactic' uses in our sense can hardly be delineated with certainty. By limiting oneself to the most obvious of such uses, however, one can give some particulars, defining them, after Standop's suggestion,[11] as those examples of modal verbs in the 'identical-subject type' whose meanings are parallel (*gleichgerichtet*) to that of the expression of volition in the main clause, i.e. forms of **motan* and *þurfan* (the latter always with *ne*) in the requesting-group, and of *willan* in the wishing- and swearing-groups. As Table 3 demonstrates, these uses (called simply 'paratactic' there) are on the decline in the late period (53.0 per cent) compared with the early period (54.3 per cent).[12] The difference,

---

[10] See, e.g., the quotation from Standop on p. 83. [11] *Syntax und Semantik*, p. 169.

[12] We could have included **motan* and (*ne*) *þurfan* in what may be called the variant of the 'identical-subject type' in which one asks for permission on behalf of somebody else; the percentage of 'paratactic' uses is then 59.1 per cent in early prose (with six such examples) and 56.5 per cent in late prose (with seven examples).

TABLE 3

	Early prose		Late prose	
	'paratactic'	others	'paratactic'	others
Requesting	7	16	49	39
Wishing	13	39	4	39
Swearing	49	3	53	16
Total	69 (54.3%)	58 (45.7%)	106 (53.0%)	94 (47.0%)

albeit slight, also suggests that there may well be a change in the variety of modal verbs that occur in each of the two types of dependent desires in early and late Old English prose.

THE USAGE OF MODAL VERBS WITH IDENTICAL AND NON-IDENTICAL SUBJECTS

The main significance of the statistical evidence of the previous section lies in the fact that what appears as a change in terms of usage with identical/non-identical subjects may be seen further as related to a general development of the language away from parataxis. This development means, in usage of modal verbs in dependent desires, a less dominant part played by the 'pleonastic' uses – uses where a modal verb is simply parallel in meaning to the volitional expression in the main clause which it only reinforces – in favour of other uses which are perhaps more pregnant in the sense of being not immediately expected from the syntax of the sentences in which they are found. It will be important to examine what new uses there are which illustrate such a development of which statistics seem to give evidence.

The question concerns, on the most obvious level, the number of different modal verbs that occur in the two types of dependent desires. Comparison of those that do occur, marked with the symbol + in Table 4, reveals almost opposite tendencies in early and late Old English prose. While in the early period a greater number are used with identical subjects than with non-identical subjects in clauses of requesting- and wishing-groups, the tendency is completely reversed in the late period; in the swearing-group, where a greater number is found in the 'non-identical-subject type' even in the early period, the tendency has become more pronounced in the late period. In a word, the variety of modal verbs as a means of expressing shades of desired relationship proves to be more useful for the 'non-identical-subject type' in late prose – a preference which contrasts remarkably with the situation in, for example, the

86

TABLE 4. SUBJECTS OF MAIN AND DEPENDENT CLAUSES

			Early prose			
	cunnan	*magan*	**motan*	**sculan*	*þurfan*	*willan*
Requesting						
Identical		+	+	+	+	
Non-identical			+	+	+	
Wishing						
Identical	+	+	+	+	+	+
Non-identical		+		+		
Swearing						
Identical						+
Non-identical			+	+		

			Late prose		
	cunnan	*magan*	**motan*	**sculan*	*willan*
Requesting					
Identical		+	+		
Non-identical	+		+	+	+
Wishing					
Identical	+		+	+	+
Non-identical	+	+	+	+	+
Swearing					
Identical	+				+
Non-identical		+	+	+	+

'Alfredian' translation of Orosius. Here in the wishing-group of clause, for example, 'there are . . . two [examples] of **motan* and one of *magan* and **sculan* each' which occur after the verb *wilnian*, and 'in these four examples . . . as well as one [of *willan*] after *beon geornfull* . . . the four different modal verbs are all used when the Wisher is identical with the Doer'.[13]

Such a shift of emphasis to the usage with non-identical subjects is, above all, an outcome of two clusters of change – loss of some old uses in the 'identical-subject type' of clause and rise of new ones in the 'non-identical-subject type' itself in the late period. As Table 4 demonstrates, the former includes **sculan* in the requesting-group and *þurfan* in the requesting- and

---

13 Ogawa, 'Modal Verbs in *Orosius*', p. 133. Wisher and Doer in the quotation refer to the two key agents in desired relationship.

swearing-groups, both of which are always found with *ne*, meaning 'to be not obliged to, need not',[14] in the early period, as in:

Bede 242.26 [Ecgberht] of inneweardre heortan God̄ wæs biddende, þæt he ða gena sweltan ne sceolde . . .

GD 53.25 ic þe halsige þurh þone, þe þu to færst, þæt ic ne þurfe lybban .VII. dagas ofer þe in þisum middanearde.

CP 457.26 Gif ðu wille ðæt ðu ne ðyrfe ðe ondrædan ðinne Hlaford, do tela.[15]

On the other hand, the late Old English developments in favour of the usage with non-identical subjects include *willan* in the requesting-group[16] and *willan* in the swearing-group. It is this last that calls for particular attention. Here, *willan* would appear, if anything, logically impossible, just as it is to be expected in the identical-subject construction of the same group. But the unique example occurs in Ælfric's translation of the Old Testament narrative of the Israelites coming to terms with the Hivites without knowing who they really were:

Josh. IX.14–15 Hi undorfeng ða Iosue, 7 ne befran his Drihten. 7 hi ealle him sworon ðæt hi man slean nolde.

Latin IX.15 fecitque Iosue cum eis pacem et inito foedere pollicitus est quod non occiderentur.

The Vulgate version certifies that it is Joshua and the people he leads (the second *hi*) who promise the Hivites (*him*) peace in verse 15; the indefinite

---

14 Some more examples of this kind of negation of modal verb, as opposed to negation of main verb as in ModE *should not, must not*, occur in *Bo* 18.26, *ÆCHom* II (ed. Godden) 37.120, *WHom* 13.34; cf. *Mart* 20.17, *WHom* 4.25 (for these abbreviations, see below, n. 15). See also Standop, *Syntax und Semantik*, p. 104. Restriction of *þurfan* with *ne* to early Old English is also seen in the 'non-identical-subject type' of requesting. The total absence of *þurfan* in dependent desires strikingly characterizes the late usage.

15 Citations from the main texts in this study are made from the following editions: *The Old English Version of Bede's Ecclesiastical History of the English People*, ed. T. Miller, EETS os 95 and 96 (London, 1890–1); *Bischof Wærferths von Worcester Übersetzung der Dialoge Gregors des Grossen*, ed. H. Hecht, Bibliothek der angelsächsischen Prosa 5 (Leipzig, 1900 and Hamburg, 1907); *King Alfred's West-Saxon Version of Gregory's Pastoral Care*, ed. H. Sweet, EETS os 45 and 50 (London, 1871); *King Alfred's Orosius*, ed. H. Sweet, EETS os 79 (London, 1883); *The Old English Version of the Heptateuch*, ed. S. J. Crawford, EETS os 160 (London, 1922); and *Two of the Saxon Chronicles Parallel*, ed. C. Plummer (Oxford, 1892–9). For *Orosius*, the edition by Sweet has been cited because the detailed statistics were originally compiled from his edition, but the examples and figures are not significantly affected if the more recent edition by J. Bately (*The Old English Orosius*, EETS ss 6 (London, 1980)) is used instead. The texts are referred to by the short titles set out in B. Mitchell, C. Ball and A. Cameron, 'Short Titles of Old English Texts', *ASE* 4 (1975), 207–21. References are to chapter and verse of Ælfric's translation of Joshua but are otherwise to page and line (followed, in the case of the *Chronicle*, by annal in parentheses). 16 See below, p. 90, n. 20.

pronoun *man* in the noun clause in question forms a periphrasis for the Latin passive verb *occiderentur*[17] whose implied subject is rendered by the objective *hi* meaning the Hivites. In other words, *man* is not indefinite here in the usual sense of being unknown or unspecifiable but stands, evidently, for what *hi* in the main clause refers to, that is, the Israelites.[18] The sequence of the main and noun clauses thus expresses, logically speaking, the 'identical-subject type' of swearing; hence the use of *willan* to emphasize the sense of determination, despite the different grammatical subjects in the two clauses. It gives stylistic variation – variation with the characteristic use of a modal verb to maintain the original logical relationship – to what could well have been expressed simply in the form of the identical-subject construction; though this might have risked a potentially more confusing sequence of four third person plural pronouns (of, say, *hi ealle him sworon ðæt hi hi slean noldon*) which is dispensed with in the sentence as it stands. At any rate, it illustrates what is in fact the 'identical-subject type' in disguise or the 'quasi-identical-subject type', which, in this example, combines the proper 'identical-subject type' usage of *willan* with a different construction of which the passive verb in the Latin original appears to be the model.

It is important to note that the 'quasi-identical-subject' construction is not attested at all in early Old English prose, even in *Orosius* which is well-known for its prolific use of the indefinite pronoun *man*.[19] This work provides forty-four inflexional forms of simple verbs and two modal verbs that occur in those dependent desires the subject of which is *man*. These examples are discussed in the next section; suffice it to mention in this connection that among them is found nothing that comes closer to the 'quasi-identical-subject type' than examples like:

Or 290.9 On þæm færelte Firmus wearð gefangen, 7 forþgelæded to sleanne. Þa bæd he self þæt hiene mon ær gefulwade . . .

Or 246.28 hio [Cleopatra] þæt for þæm dyde þe hio nolde þæt hie mon drife beforan þæm triumphan wiþ Rome weard.

Here, as in the example from Joshua, the *man* construction renders periphrastically the passive *wære gefulwod* and *wære gedrifen* in which the noun clauses would have resulted if styled in the identical-subject construction, with the

---

17 For OE *man* as a substitute for the passive construction in general, see Mitchell, *OES*, §§369 and 747; J. Fröhlich, *Der Indefinite Agens im Altenglischen* (Bern, 1951), throughout.
18 It is thus an example of what Fröhlich calls *man5*, i.e. *man* is 'definierbar' (*Der Indefinite Agens*, p. 102, and throughout). By contrast, *man* in *Or* 264.8 and 226.15 (to be discussed later) are classified by him as *man3* (*man* is 'allgemein') and *man4a* (*man* is 'speziell' but 'unbekannt und nicht erschließbar'), respectively (*ibid.* pp. 51 and 78).
19 See L. G. Frary, *Studies in the Syntax of the Old English Passive with Special Reference to the Use of Wesan and Weorðan*, Language Dissertations 5 (Baltimore, MD, 1929), 22.

subject *he* and *hio* respectively. However, these and other relevant examples from *Orosius* are distinguished from *Josh*. IX.15 first by the fact that in them *man* is never co-referential with the subject of the main clause (which is in fact rendered as object in the noun clause); and, secondly, by the total absence of the modal verb in them. They might have been expected to use **sculan*, for example, just as this modal verb is occasionally used when the subject of the noun clause is not *man*, in the wishing-group in *Orosius* and in the requesting- and wishing-groups in some other early prose works.[20] In particular, the absence of any modal verb in the requesting-group here is all the more striking because of the contrast to usage in the 'identical-subject type' with a 'definite' subject in the same group, where its logical relationship of asking to be or to do something is regularly expressed by the use of the modal verb **motan* in *Orosius*. As it happens, the contrast is not quite complete, since those examples of **motan* include none with a passive infinitive, such as an hypothetical *he moste beon gefulwod* in place of *Or* 290.9, forming an exact counterpart to the *man* construction with a simple verb as illustrated above.[21] But examples with an active infinitive such as

Or 202.9 [Hannibal] hrædlice for to Cartaina, 7 biddende wæs þæt he moste wið Scipian sprecan . . .

Or 212.3 he wæs vi dagas on þa burg feohtende, oþ þa burgware bædon þæt hie mosten beon hiera underþeowas, þa hi hie bewerian ne mehton

represent a pattern which is distinct enough to demonstrate the close

---

[20] For details see Ogawa, *OE Modal Verbs*, §§5.5.3 and 5.6.3. *Willan* to ask for favour in dependent requests (*OED* s.v.v. 6b, 26b) is not attested in Old English except in two sentences in late prose; on this see my 'OE **Sculan/Willan* in Dependent Requests: a Note', *Philologia Anglica: Essays Presented to Professor Yoshio Terasawa on the Occasion of His Sixtieth Birthday*, ed. K. Oshitari *et al.* (Tokyo, 1988), pp. 53–9.

[21] However, this absence of **motan* with a passive infinitive does not seem to mean that the resultant voice of a verb determines the choice between the 'identical-subject type' of clause with a 'definite' subject and **motan* on one hand and the non-identical-subject construction with *man* and a simple verb on the other, with the latter to be used as an 'automatic substitute' for the former when this would result in the 'unidiomatic' passive infinitive with the modal verb. Basic paradigms of Old English verbs do allow such a form, though examples are more common in works of translation; see Mitchell, *OES*, §§751–2; M. Callaway, Jr, *The Infinitive in Anglo-Saxon* (Washington, DC, 1913), pp. 83–8. For examples, see (dependent desires) *El* 686 'Ic þæt geswerige þurh sunu meotodes, / . . . þæt ðu hungre scealt / for cneomagum cwylmed weorðan'; *Bede* 374.2 'he . . . wæs ða broðor biddende, þæt he ðær . . . bebyrged beon moste', and (other clauses) *Or* 128.5 'Þa Darius geseah ðæt he oferwunnen beon wolde'; and *ÆCHom* I, 282.19 'Fæder, and Sunu, and Halig Gast ne magon beon togædere genamode'; we also find a simple passive verb in the 'identical-subject type' in *Chron A* 8.19 (167) 'bæd þæt he wære Cristen gedon'. As we shall see, choice of the *man* construction is very much a matter of style.

association of a modal verb with the 'identical-subject type' of clause as opposed to the 'non-identical-subject type' of which the *man* construction is an example.

The examples in *Orosius* thus tend to emphasize the degree to which the 'quasi-identical-subject type' as represented by *Josh.* IX.15 is innovative both in the use of the word *man* to form that construction and of the use of *willan* which accompanies it. The developments it embodies point to the rise in late Old English of a syntactic possibility which goes beyond the simple, 'identical-subject type' of subordination.[22] As we shall see, there are other examples elsewhere in prose of the period which argue for such a development.

THE USAGE OF MODAL VERBS IN DEPENDENT DESIRES WHOSE SUBJECT IS *MAN*

The appearance in late Old English of *willan* with the 'quasi-identical subject' *man* and its implications may further be considered by comparing usage in a particular text of the period with that in an earlier one. For this purpose, an examination is made below of the 'Alfredian' *Orosius* and the late Old English part of what is known as the Copied Annals of the Peterborough Chronicle (the annals 892 to 1121),[23] with particular reference, as before, to those dependent desires whose subject is the indefinite pronoun *man*.

Table 5 below gives the number of modal verbs and simple verb forms that occur in the relevant clauses in the two texts. It can be observed that modal verbs, though very rare in *Orosius*, outnumber simple verb forms in the *Chronicle*, a change which is best in evidence in clauses after *bebeodan* and other

TABLE 5

		bebeodan, etc.	*biddan,* etc.	*geweorþan, rædan*	*wilnian,* etc.	Total
Or	MV/IF	1/30	0/10	1/1	0/3	2/44
ChronE	MV/IF	5/0	—	5/8	1/0	11/8

[22] An early Old English example of *man wolde* in subordinate clauses occurs in *GD* 219.11 'þa gesawon hi unfeor þanon ænne ofen inæledne, se wæs gegearwod to þon þæt man wolde bacan'. Here, however, *man* is, as Mitchell (*OES*, §2978) points out, identical with the 'logical subject of the preceding adjective clause' which is understood. See also *LS* 10 (Guthlac) 18.4.

[23] The last part of the material thus belongs in fact to the Middle English period. But for practical purposes it is treated collectively as late Old English. For the character of the language in the Copied Annals, see C. Clark, *The Peterborough Chronicle 1070–1154*, 2nd ed. (Oxford, 1970), pp. xli–xlv.

expressions of commanding. It is particularly noteworthy here that the single modal verb that occurs in *Orosius* does so with the infinitive of an intransitive verb: *Or* 264.8 'he bead þæt man on gelice to him onbugan sceolde swa to Gode', whereas the examples in the *Chronicle* all involve a transitive verb, viz. *ChronE* 143.19 (1013), 221.8 (1086), 222.24 (1086) and:

ChronE 138.4 (1008) Her bebead se cyng þ man sceolde ofer eall Angel cynn scipu feastlice wircean.

ChronE 142.19 (1012) [the bishop] forbead þ man nan þing wið him syllan ne moste.

The contrast could possibly be accidental, of course, in the light of the fact that **sculan* with a transitive verb does occur once elsewhere in *Orosius* (see below). But one might also wonder if it does not demonstrate how a modal verb can now be used, at least with a greater frequency than before, with *man* as a stylized equivalent to the passive construction as opposed to its use as the indefinite pronoun in the literal sense, of which *Or* 264.8 with the intransitive *onbugan to . . . swa to . . .* would seem to be an example. The distinction between the two uses just mentioned can be subtle. But it seems at any rate important to note that against the single transitive **sculan* mentioned above are forty-one inflexional forms of transitive simple verbs in *Orosius*, including twenty-nine after expressions of commanding and ten after expressions of requesting discussed in the previous section. As can be inferred from Table 5, the proportion is far more in favour of a modal verb construction in the *Chronicle*; the work has, in fact, only six transitive simple verb forms in dependent desires with *man* as a whole and none after expressions of commanding.

While the point just made has no direct bearing on the problem of usage with identical/non-identical subjects in early and late Old English, a second group of dependent desires – noun clauses dependent on *geweorþan* (in *Orosius*) and *(ge)rædan* (in the *Chronicle*) meaning 'to agree, decide' – deserves close attention on that score. Here the single modal verb in *Orosius* – the one mentioned above in connection with the intransitive/transitive distinction – occurs in a clause of the 'non-identical-subject type': *Or* 226.15 'þa gewearð þa senatos þæt mon eft sceolde getimbran Cartainam'.[24] But it should be noted at the same time that the verb *geweorþan* considered as a whole, like most other relevant ones in *Orosius*, tends to take a modal verb more frequently in the 'identical-subject type' than in the 'non-identical-subject type' of clause that follows it: there are four examples of *willan* in the former type (*Or* 178.7, 234.14, 280.20 and 280.21) but one of **sculan* in the latter (*Or* 208.28) which

---

[24] *Man* in this sentence is rightly classified by Fröhlich as *man4a* (see n. 17). It distinguishes itself from the use as 'quasi-identical subject' evidenced in *Josh*. IX.15 and the *Chronicle* (see below) in that it is not the senators who do the building. Gorrell ('Indirect Discourse', p. 406) appears to mistake the sentence for an example of *hit gewearð* 'it happened'.

follow the verb when *man* is not its subject. This situation contrasts with that in the *Chronicle*, where the relevant examples – four of **sculan* and one of **motan* with the subject *man* and one of *willan* with a 'definite' subject, after *(ge)rædan* – all occur in the 'non-identical-subject type' of clause, except the last.[25] What is more, these uses with the non-identical subject *man* are all found after some formulaic phrases, such as 'se cyng gerædde 7 his witan' and 'se cyng gerædde wiþ his witan',[26] which report agreements and decisions made at the witenagemot. Use in such a pattern may give the examples a certain significance which calls for examination.

In two of the examples, *man* stands for whoever is outside the council and is expected to carry out its decisions, representing the 'non-identical-subject type' in the strict sense:

ChronE 133.3 (999) Ða rædde se cyng wið his witan þ man sceolde mid scipfyrde. 7 eac mid landfyrde him ongean faran. ac ða þa scipu gearwe wæron. þa elkede man (C: þa ylcodan þa deman) fram dæge to dæge.

ChronE 177.8 (1052) gerædde se cyng 7 his witan þ mann sceolde forðian ut to Sandwic scipu.

Here in the latter example, for instance, we learn from what immediately follows that Earl Ralph and Earl Odda were commissioned to captain the ships. But in

ChronE 174.20 (1048) Ða gerædde se cyning 7 his witan þ man sceolde oðre syðan habban ealra gewitena gemot on Lundene to hærfestes emnihte,

man, described as having been decreed to hold another meeting, stands logically for nobody else than the king and his *witan* who are named as such in the main clause; the sentence represents what I have called above the 'quasi-identical-subject type'. In this, it parallels the development shown in *Josh.* IX.15 discussed earlier but shows another aspect of this late Old English construction by employing **sculan* rather than *willan* in it. **Sculan* so used is no simple means of 'express[ing] duty imposed by the adviser', as Gorrell says on

---

[25] There is another example of *willan* in a remotely related clause dependent on *unrædes* (*ChronE* 141.18 (1011)). But this is not included in the figures of Table 5.

[26] One is reminded here of expressions common in laws such as *LawAtr* I Prol 'Ðis is seo gerædnys, ðe Æþelred cyning 7 his witan geræddon.' But there seems to be little need to assume that the use in the *Chronicle* of *man* after such expressions of royal agreement could not have developed without the basis of a legal idiom; the laws contain only one example of the construction being discussed (*Forf 2*), as far as we can tell from F. Liebermann's Wörterbuch (*Die Gesetze der Angelsachsen*, 3 vols. (Halle, 1903–16) II, s.v. *gerædan*). For the use of the word *ræd* in laws and chronicles, see F. Liebermann, *The National Assembly in the Anglo-Saxon Period* (Halle, 1913), p. 12.

this example.[27] On the contrary, it serves to certify the sense of being authorized by a royal decree that is perhaps to be accorded to the sentence, so that it should not sound too much like a personal determination, which it would do if put in the 'identical-subject type' of clause as in the following hypothetical form, with the personal and co-referential *hi* and the volitional *willan* to express that emphasis on identical subjects in the desired relationship: 'Ða geræðde se cyning 7 his witan þ hi woldon oðre syðan habban ealra gewitena gemot . . .' The distinction, if subtle, is one that is obviously crucial in chronicle writing. It may well be important enough to have called, for its overt expression, for a new development in the choice of the type of clause and concomitantly of a modal verb that should accompany it.

It should be emphasized that the development which *ChronE* 174.20 is here assumed to embody is thus largely stylistic. One could perhaps prefer to argue that the example has nothing special about it any more than, say, *ChronE* 177.8, using as it does, like this latter, *man* with an active verb as a substitute for the passive voice. It is one thing to know that both may well be translated using a Modern English passive construction.[28] But what is essential here is that this 'substitute for the passive' is now used, with an appropriate choice of modal verb, in contexts which could well have used the 'identical-subject type' of active construction, with a 'definite' subject with which *man* is identical in reference. It is this co-referentiality that allows us now to call the example of *man* being discussed a stylistic variant of the 'identical-subject type'; it is something that is not evidenced at all in the early prose of *Orosius*, as we saw above. Moreover, even apart from that difference which seems clear enough to me, modal verbs have come to be used more frequently in the *Chronicle* than in *Orosius* in the *man* construction as a whole (see above, Table 5). Here, at any rate, the development from early to late prose is indisputable.

In fact, the development of the 'quasi-identical-subject type' of clause is sometimes recognized in Modern English translation itself. Whitelock's translation 'Then the king and his councillors determined to send to them and promise them tribute and provisions' for *ChronE* 129.10 'Þa geræðde se cyng 7 his witan þ him man to sende. 7 him gafol behete 7 metsunge' is one such example.[29] While Whitelock's translation does not claim any further possibi-

---

[27] 'Indirect Discourse', p. 367. Gorrell gives a wrong reference to his truncated version of the example ('se cyning geræðde þæt man *sceolde* habban gemot') as '*Chr.*, 250, C, 20'. What he means – *ChronC* 250.20 (ed. Thorpe) – is parallel to our *ChronE* 133.31 discussed below.

[28] See, e.g. D. Whitelock *et al.*, *The Anglo-Saxon Chronicle: a Revised Translation* (London, 1961), pp. 120 and 118 respectively.

[29] *Ibid.* p. 83. As this example shows, the 'quasi-identical-subject type' of dependent desires need not be supported by the use of a modal verb. See also *ChronE* 145.1 (1014).

lity, Garmonsway makes the case for the remaining two examples of modal verb in the *man* construction in the *Chronicle*, which he translates as follows:[30]

ChronE 133.31 (1002) se cyng gerædde 7 his witan. þ man sceolde gafol gyldon þam flotan. 7 frið wið hi geniman ('the king and his councillors decided to pay tribute to the˚ fleet and to make peace')

ChronE 137.21 (1006) Ða gerædde seo cyng 7 his witan eallum þeodscipe to þearfe. þeah hit him eallum lað wære. þ man nyde moste þam here gafol gyldan ('Then the king and his councillors agreed that they were compelled by circumstances to pay tribute to the host for the good of all the people, however distasteful it might be to them all').

The likelihood of this interpretation is high, if not as high as in *ChronE* 174.20 above, because both examples involve paying tribute – a proper thing, one might suppose, for a king to do; 'eallum þeodscipe to þearfe' in the second example seems to imply this royal function as against the need of his people. One might also include an example in a noun clause after *willan* 'to will' as a fourth case, because it has the same context:

ChronE 137.23 (1006) Ða sende se cyng to þam here. 7 him cyþan het þ he wolde þ... him man gafol and metsunge syllan sceolde.

The last three examples all represent paying tribute as impersonal necessity rather than as willing action of a king; the stylistic advantage of being able to avoid the 'identical-subject type' of clause with *willan* is obvious.

Clearly, then, it is significant that the quasi-identical subject *man* with *sceolde/moste* should occur where it does in the *Chronicle*. It is a development which may well have arisen out of the very characteristics of its own style and its special use of the word *man* in particular, on which Liebermann, discussing a very different problem, long ago observed: 'The indefinite *man*, a substitute for the passive mood wanting in Anglo-Saxon, very often hides the subject of a govermental action, and at least in one place it must mean the witena gemot',[31] that is, *ChronC* 160.13 (1037) 'Her man geceas Harald ofer eall to cinge, 7 forsoc Harðacnut.' Here we have something that constitutes an additional argument for the 'quasi-identical-subject type' by suggesting an aspect of the general context for its development. Taken together with *willan* in *Josh.* IX.15, *sculan and *motan in this type represent a certain variety of possibilities that are now added to the language by a new development in late Old English.

---

[30] *The Anglo-Saxon Chronicle*, trans. G.N. Garmonsway, 2nd ed. (London, 1954), pp. 133 and 137. He extends the interpretation to *ChronE* 133.3. But I should prefer not to take it as of the 'quasi-identical-subject type'; see above, p. 93.

[31] *The National Assembly*, p. 12. The reference is given as a footnote.

Hiroshi Ogawa

While the examples from the *Chronicle* so far discussed illustrate the tendency for a modal verb to be associated with what is at least *not* the strictly 'identical-subject type' of clause, there is no single clause after *(ge)rædan* in the *Chronicle* that is of that type in which *man* is the identical subject of the main and noun clauses and takes a modal verb – say, *willan* – in the latter clause;[32] the only relevant case is *ChronE* 127.2 (991) 'on þam geare man gerædde þ man geald ærest gafol Deniscan mannum', in which the indicative of a simple verb is used. In fact, *willan* with the identical subject is found only once in clauses after *(ge)rædan* in the *Chronicle* as a whole; its subject is then not indefinite: *ChronE* 210.13 (1075) 'Ðær wæs Roger eorl. 7 Walþeof eorl. 7 biscopas 7 abbotes. 7 ræddon þær swa þ hi woldon þone cyng gesettan ut of Englelandes cynedome.' Again, the other verb of the group under consideration, *geweorþan*, is restricted in the *Chronicle* to a single sentence in which *man* plays no part. There it is followed by a modal verb – not *willan* with the identical subject, but **sculan*: *ChronE* 145.16 (1014) 'gewearð him [Cnut] 7 þam folce on Lindesige anes. þ hi hine horsian sceoldan. 7 syððan ealle ætgædere faran 7 hergian';[33] the subject *hi*, being exclusive of Cnut (*hine*), is not strictly identical with the logical subject of the main clause, 'him 7 þam folce', though for the second half of the noun clause it is probably to be taken in the inclusive sense ('ealle ætgædere').

To summarize, it can be seen that the association of modal verbs with the 'non-identical-subject type' of clause (including the 'quasi-identical-subject type', where appropriate) as opposed to the strictly 'identical-subject type' remains much stronger in the *Chronicle* than in *Orosius* even in clauses after *geweorþan/(ge)rædan* considered as a whole, be it with the indefinite subject *man* or not: *Orosius* has four modal verbs (178.7, 234.14, 280.20 and 280.21) in the 'identical-subject type' and two (226.15; and 208.28) in the 'non-identical-subject type', but the *Chronicle* has one (210.13) and six (133.3, 177.8, 174.20, 133.31, 137.21; and 145.16) in the respective types. Here again the different tendency between early and late prose seems decisive.[34]

CONCLUSIONS

Usage in our selected area of dependent desires tends to confirm the statistical evidence that modal verbs in complex sentences with non-identical subjects

---

32 The third clause in *ChronE* 177.20 (1052) '7 gerædde man þa þ þa scipu gewendan eft ongean to Lundene. 7 sceolde man setton oðre eorlas 7 oðre hasæton to þam scipum' could be taken as one such case. But, on the grounds of its inverted word order (which is parallel to the initial '7 gerædde man') and the contrast to a simple verb in the preceding noun clause, I should prefer to take it as an independent clause.

33 The C version has *woldon* here.

34 Comparison in terms of the number of modal verbs as against that of simple verb forms

have become a more frequent pattern in late Old English than they were in early Old English – a change which is perhaps seen at its clearest in the rise of what I have called the 'quasi-identical-subject' construction as a logical substitute for the 'identical-subject type' in the strict sense; the originally non-identical subject *man* is now occasionally preferred, with a distinctive use of *willan* (*Josh*. IX.15) and **sculan/*motan* (e.g. *ChronE* 174.20 (1048)), to express what might equally well have taken the form of the identical subject in the main and dependent clauses. Appearance of such a construction is partly a matter of style and genre of individual texts, as the relevant cases of **sculan/ *motan* in the *Chronicle* clearly show. But style itself can vary chronologically, as in fact it does in the earlier and later parts of the text just mentioned.[35] That our 'quasi-identical-subject' construction does not occur in early Old English but rather in late Old English within the single genre of narrative texts (*Orosius* on one hand and Ælfric's translation of Joshua and the Copied Annals in the Peterborough Chronicle on the other) suggests strongly that here we may speak of a development during the Old English period rather than a purely stylistic variation among particular texts. Although one of the examples occurs in Ælfric's biblical translation to render a Latin passive verb, there is nothing that prevents us from assuming that it is essentially a native development; it is a development which consists in the widening of the syntactic possibilities of the word *man* as it is used, both indefinitely and impersonally, to denote agency.

If modal verbs in dependent desires point to a development during the period which implies shift of emphasis from the 'identical-subject type' of usage to the 'non-identical-subject type' of usage, we may perhaps relate it to a larger drift of the language from parataxis to hypotaxis of which it presumably

within each type does not prove as decisive (see the table below). But the decline of modal verbs in the 'identical-subject type' is at any rate clear enough.

	Subjects of main and dependent clauses	MV	IF
Orosius	Identical	4	0
	Non-identical	2	1
ChronE	Identical	1	2
	Non-identical	6	10

[35] See, e.g. G. Rübens, *Parataxe und Hypotaxe in dem ältesten Teil der Sachsenchronik*, Studien zur englischen Philologie 56 (Halle, 1915); C. Clark, 'The Narrative Mode of *The Anglo-Saxon Chronicle* before the Conquest', *England before the Conquest: Studies in Primary Sources Presented to Dorothy Whitelock*, ed. P. Clemoes and K. Hughes (Cambridge, 1971), pp. 215–35.

formed a part. In his *Ergebnisse*, Standop, after summarizing his own account of the 'pleonastic' use of modal verbs which I quoted earlier (see above, p. 83), immediately continues: 'Die Wechselwirkung in umgekehrter Richtung besteht darin, daß der jeweilige Hv.-Gebrauch den Sinn der übergeordneten Verben, insbesondere solcher der Mitteilung, der Wahrnehmung und der Willensäußerung, mit bestimmt'.[36] This change 'in the reverse direction' may be said to have already begun in Old English in that, as we have seen, a less dominant part has come to be played in late prose by those uses in the 'identical-subject type' of clause in which the meaning of a modal verb is simply parallel to that of the expression of volition in the main clause. It is also in this sense that developments of modal verbs in the Old English period seem to point forward to their later developments in the language, as reported, for example, by Wilde on usage in Middle English to Modern English: 'Die Objekt- und Subjektsätze mit Umschreibung . . . stellen einen eigenen, den sog. divergenten Typ dar. Je stärker der Vordersatz Neutralität und Möglichkeit ausdrückt, um so größer und notwendiger wird der Gebrauch der Umschreibung'.[37] The present study suggests a way in which future work on Old English modal verbs may be undertaken in reference to such larger developments of the language.

---

[36] *Syntax und Semantik*, p. 169: 'The interaction [between modal verbs in dependent clauses and introductory verbs in principal clauses] in the reverse direction consists in the fact that the respective use of modal verbs is a contributory determinant of the sense of the principal verbs, particularly those of informing, perceiving and desiring.'

[37] H.-O. Wilde, 'Aufforderung, Wunsch und Möglichkeit', *Anglia* 63 (1939), 209–391 and 64 (1940), 10–105 (the quotation occurs on p. 67 of the latter volume): 'The object clauses and subject clauses with modal periphrasis . . . represent a special, so-called divergent type. The more strongly the preceding clause expresses neutrality and eventuality, the greater and more necessary the use of periphrasis becomes.' An aspect of the decreasing use of the 'identical-subject type' of noun clause in favour of the infinitive construction in Middle English is discussed in my article 'The Periphrastic Subjunctive in ME *were/had lever* Constructions', *Stud. in Eng. Lit.* 49 (Tokyo, 1972), 55–66 [in Japanese].

Anonymous polyphony and *The Wanderer*'s textuality

CAROL BRAUN PASTERNACK

Old English manuscript poetry, including the text that we now call *The Wanderer*, remains close to its oral roots in its reliance on audible structures and traditional expressions, in its fluid relationship to other compositions and in its anonymity. It is not oral, however, and its existence in a manuscript is more than a physical fact. This change in medium has begun to affect the poetry's semiotics. Having lost the social context of oral performance, the poet attempts to provide a viewpoint in other ways. But this manuscript presentation does not share all the workings of a modern printed composition.[1]

The layout of the poetry in modern editions shows we have confused the manuscript with print media. The modern reader knows Old English poetry as a discrete number of poems, each of which has a title (we know the title is modern but print it anyway), a definite beginning (even if it has been lost), a middle and an end (which may again be lost but still exists as an idea for which we simply cannot find the physical manifestation). Even when printed with other poems from the same manuscript, the text's separateness appears in the visual signs of a preceding blank space, a centred title which becomes a running title at the top of each page, and the numbering of lines which begins at the start of each 'poem'. The format implies coherence, a fixed text reflective of a single poet's intentions (we see the struggle to achieve that ideal in the textual notes),[2] and a meaningful existence independent of context.[3] But both

---

[1] K. O'Brien O'Keeffe, in *Visible Song: Transitional Literacy in Old English Verse*, CSASE 4 (Cambridge, 1990), appropriately breaks down the opposition often hypothesized between the oral and the literate: 'The conditions "orality" and "literacy" are the end points on a continuum through which the technology of writing affects and modifies human perception. The immediate consequence of such a definition is that it admits the possibility that residual orality might be encoded in early manuscripts' (p. 13). She examines the differing 'graphic conventions' in Anglo-Saxon vernacular and Latin manuscripts to show that 'early readers of Old English verse read by applying oral techniques for the reception of a message to the decoding of a written text' (p. 21).

[2] See A. J. Frantzen, *Desire for Origins: New Language, Old English, and Teaching the Tradition* (New Brunswick, NJ, 1990), for discussion of the relationship between the concept of authorial intentionality and modern practices in textual editing.

[3] That these poems are never printed with prose found in the same manuscript reflects our modern classification of poetry as fine arts, distinct from the practical art of expository prose.

oral theory and intertextual theory show us a different vision of the Old English manuscript compositions in which the text is neither fixed nor self-contained nor an authorial production.

The poet, then, is *not* one who originates a text that may then be transmitted from one manuscript to another or copied down from a definitive performance and then transmitted by manuscript. Rather, it is possible to theorize three types of poets for Anglo-Saxon England: those who perform in front of an audience, shaping their versions in performance or beforehand;[4] those who perform their versions by inscribing them in manuscripts; and those who perform from manuscripts (these poets, too, would have shaped a new version, perhaps simply in their choosing of an occasion and modulations of voice, perhaps cutting, rearranging and expanding what they found, as the other types would have). The poetry that survives must by the nature of its existence be the work of the second type, poets who perform their versions by inscribing them in manuscripts. By implication, the spheres of poet and scribe merge, just as the spheres of poet and performer do.[5] These poets shape texts that are provisional and specific to their performance or manuscript contexts.

The key to the manuscript poetry's peculiar textuality is the structural prominence of sections of a composition, which I will call 'movements'. These building blocks stand out as formally distinct, semi-independent units, contrasting in style or content with the text that precedes and follows.[6] In oral poetry, they facilitate composition, assist the memory and connect the performance to community traditions. As a structural convention, they persist in manuscript poetry and continue to function in and maintain a matrix of concepts regarding composition and the poet's task. Because the movements

---

[4] See J. Opland's discussion of the controversy about memorized versus improvised performances, *Anglo-Saxon Oral Poetry* (New Haven, CT, and London, 1980), pp. 75–9.

[5] O'Keeffe also argues that scribes contribute to a text's creation. Examining poems that appear in multiple manuscripts, she asserts 'that in the cases where variants are metrically, semantically and syntactically appropriate, the scribe has "read formulaically" and has become a participant in and a determiner of the text' (*Visible Song*, p. 191), much as an oral performer would compose formulaically and create a new version of a poem. See also J. Dagenais, 'That Bothersome Residue: toward a Theory of the Physical Text', in *Vox intexta: Orality and Textuality in the Middle Ages*, ed. A.N. Doane and C.B. Pasternack (Madison, WI, and London, forthcoming), pp. 246–59. In discussing manuscripts he argues, 'One way of getting a grip on the physical text is, paradoxically, by viewing the manuscript text as a variety of oral performance. Curiously, that most ephemeral of literary events, an oral performance, comes closest to imitating that solidly physical text we seek: in its uniqueness, in the impossibility of its iteration, in its vulnerability to accidents of time and environment' (p. 255). Cf. T.W. Machan, 'Editing, Orality, and Late Middle English Texts', in the same volume.

[6] A.C. Bartlett recognizes a number of rhetorical patterns that create these divisions. See *The Larger Rhetorical Patterns in Anglo-Saxon Poetry*, Columbia Univ. Stud. in Eng. and Comparative Lit. 122 (Morningside Heights, NY, 1935). She characterizes the poetry as a 'tapestry' constructed in panels (p. 7).

are traditional in what they say and how they say it, they contribute to the anonymity of manuscript compositions. Because poets collocate and juxtapose these various expressions, the compositions are polyphonic as well. This anonymous polyphony characterizes Old English poetry.

The oral poet, according to Albert B. Lord, 'thinks of his song in terms of a flexible plan of themes, some of which are essential and some of which are not'.[7] These 'themes' or 'type-scenes' present a narrative scene or exposition of wisdom according to a conventional set of elements and structure. In either case, they have, as Lord has said, 'a semi-independent life of their own'.[8] Although poets adapt them to their present work, they draw them from a repertoire of scenes that exist in their memories and in tradition. Acoustics contribute to the distinctiveness of the movements. According to Lord, oral poets use assonance, alliteration, syntax and rhythm to create patterns which unify a movement either by developing a series of parallel and balanced lines or by developing a pattern different from that of the previous and following units.[9] They also employ patterns which mark the beginning and end of the unit. For example, a singer may end a descriptive unit with a 'last line, beginning with a shout and sung in a different and cadential rhythm'.[10] Their unitary structure allows the movements to function as units of knowledge in what Eric Havelock calls a 'tribal encyclopedia'.[11]

The aural distinctiveness of movements persists in manuscript texts. In a longer study, I describe and classify the stylistic and semantic patterns that create the movements.[12] Since the disjunctive effect of this structural conven-

---

[7] A. B. Lord, *The Singer of Tales*, Harvard Stud. in Comparative Lit. 24 (Cambridge, MA, 1960), 99. Although a great deal of valuable work has been done in the thirty years since Lord published *The Singer of Tales*, his discussion of theme and its relation to song is still widely accepted. Useful overviews of oral theory can be found in W. J. Ong, *Orality and Literacy: the Technologizing of the Word* (London, 1982) and J. M. Foley, *Oral-Formulaic Theory and Research: an Introduction and Annotated Bibliography* (New York, 1985).

[8] Lord, *Singer of Tales*, p. 94. Lord discusses movements that structure narrative scenes (an assembly, a battle, a marriage), which he calls 'themes'. D. K. Fry, 'Old English Oral-Formulaic Themes and Type-Scenes', *Neophilologus* 52 (1968), 48–54, contributes the useful term 'type-scene' to distinguish between the set structures of certain scenes and the broader concept to which we more commonly refer with the term 'theme'. I am using the musical term 'movement' because I wish to refer more broadly to any structural unit that has a distinct formal and semantic structure, whether its content is narrative or expository. For discussion of such units in oral or orally based poetry, see Fry, *ibid.*, Lord, *Singer of Tales* and A. Renoir, *A Key to Old Poems: the Oral-Formulaic Approach to the Interpretation of West-Germanic Verse* (University Park, PA, 1988).   [9] Lord, *Singer of Tales*, pp. 55–8.

[10] *Ibid.* p. 55.   [11] E. A. Havelock, *Preface to Plato* (Cambridge, MA, 1963), p. 185.

[12] See my dissertation, 'Disjunction: a Structural Convention in Old English Poetry' (unpubl. PhD dissertation, Univ. of California at Los Angeles, 1983). In 'Stylistic Disjunctions in *The Dream of the Rood*', *ASE* 13 (1984), 167–86, I attempted to show in detail the way a poet can define distinct syntactic modes to differentiate movements.

tion has always been clear enough for critics to agree about where the divisions are, here I will concentrate on the contribution the movements make to the poetry's textuality.

In *The Wanderer*, as in other Old English poetry, most critics agree on the poem's basic structure. We can easily perceive a frame (1–5 and 111–15), a first-person rendering of a lone-dweller's cares (6–29a), and a third-person description of the feelings of isolation (29b–57).[13] At line 58, the first person returns, marking the midpoint in the composition. Although some critics say that 58–65a conclude the first half, some that these verses begin the second, and some place the division in the middle between 62a and b, readers generally concur that the return marks a change, drawing a boundary here.[14] The next section (65b–87) proffers wisdom about the importance of moderation in a fleeting and difficult world. Then a speaker is again introduced, one who 'considers deeply this dark life' and declaims about the disappearance of all

[13] Some people conceive of this third-person description as a kind of straw-man figure that the *eardstapa* uses in his speech. See, for example, S.B. Greenfield, '*The Wanderer*: a Reconsideration of Theme and Structure', *JEGP* 50 (1951), 451–65, at 459. R.M. Lumiansky, 'The Dramatic Structure of the Old English *Wanderer*', *Neophilologus* 34 (1949), 104–12, at 108, similarly thinks that the *eardstapa* is 'widening the application' here of his own loss and grief. R.F. Leslie, *The Wanderer*, Old and Middle Eng. Texts (Manchester, 1966), thinks that although the lines are part of the monologue they constitute a 'change of tone' (p. 7); J. Mandel, *Alternative Readings in Old English Poetry*, Amer. Univ. Stud., Ser. 4, Eng. Lang. and Lit. 43 (New York, 1987), asserts that 'at l. 29b the poem shifts perceptibly but not significantly . . . the point of view from which we understand the events of the poem remains that of the wanderer' (p. 21). Dunning and Bliss note no structural division at this point (T.P. Dunning and A.J. Bliss, Introduction to *The Wanderer*, Methuen's OE Lib. (London, 1969), pp. 82–6).

[14] Most critics think that a major change takes place somewhere between 58a and 65b. E. Sieper (*Die Altenglische Elegie* (Strassburg, 1915), p. 197) and W.A. Craigie ('Interpolations and Omissions in Anglo-Saxon Poetic Texts', *Philologica* 2 (1923), 5–19, at 15) thought that the original poem ended with line 57, before the more universal reflections begin. B.F. Huppé analyses 58–62a as completing the *eardstapa*'s monologue and 62b–65a as an 'introductory generalization' for the next section ('*The Wanderer*: Theme and Structure', *JEGP* 42 (1943), 516–38, at 533); Lumiansky says 58–62a 'mark an important step' in the speaker's development into a wise man (p. 108); Greenfield believes 58–62a must be part of the *eardstapa*'s speech because of the reappearance of the first person but also declares that they 'begin, as it were, to ripple across the waters of all human experience' ('Reconsideration', p. 458); Dunning and Bliss believe the poem's second of two movements begins at 58 and that 58–63 expresses its 'distinctive character' and is a 'generalization . . . leading to the universalization of lines 62b–63' (*The Wanderer*, pp. 86–7); J.C. Pope proposes, in an analysis he later retracts, that the first person of line 58 introduces a second speaker and new character ('Dramatic Voices in *The Wanderer* and *The Seafarer*', *Franciplegius: Medieval and Linguistic Studies in Honor of Francis Peabody Magoun, Jr.*, ed. J.B. Bessinger, Jr and R.P. Creed (New York, 1965), 164–93, at 168; Mandel believes the *ic* at 58 is 'the same speaker who began the poem, speaking now from a different point of view . . . the poet now adopts a contrastive point of view, looks outward, and focuses on the anguish of all men' (p. 32).

that is joyful and dear on this earth (88–110). The closing frame reminds us of our true honour and security in heaven (111–15).

As with other poems, this structure has faced critics with a problem, how to account for stylistic shifts in what is supposed to be a single poem. The answers so far divide into two classes: either it is not really a single poem (or not a good one) or, alternatively, this structure uniquely fits this poem's thematic purpose. Early scholars analyse the stylistic shifts as a fault in manuscript transmission or poetic skill. In 1915, for example, Ernst Sieper argued that *The Wanderer* has within it an original ('echt') poem (lines 8–57) that has no organic connection ('organische Verbindung') with lines 58–115. He calls it a patchwork with highly visible seams ('Es ist Flickarbeit, deren Nähte deutlich sichtbar sind') which has been put together not by a poet but a mere compiler ('Kompilator').[15] By the 1950's, these same features become a sign of the poet's individual genius. Thomas C. Rumble, for example, characterizes this same disjointed text as a soliloquy in which the speaker 'projects himself' into diverse imaginary situations in what are 'dreamlike fragments'; hence, the poem's discontinuities 'seem the height of logic itself; for in the poem the reveries of the speaker are imperfectly realized, just as in life the projection of one's self into any wholly imaginary situation must inevitably be imperfectly realized', and we now realize 'that it is a considerably more skilfully wrought poem than has hitherto been supposed'.[16] Both of these critics rely on the concept of organic structure, evidently believing it to be a universal criterion of excellence, and both see *The Wanderer*'s shifting styles as *sui generis*. But organic structure is not universal – it is a quality cultivated for a time in printed literature – and *The Wanderer*'s polyphony, far from being unique, is conventional for its time.

Fortunately, this kind of text has come around once again in modernism, and modernist theory clarifies its operation.[17] Among others, Julia Kristeva favours these texts and analyzes their virtues. She singles out as writers of polyphonic texts Joyce, Proust and Kafka, and we might add Woolf, Faulkner and many others. She praises these texts because they promote a different kind

---

[15] Sieper, *Die Altenglische Elegie*, pp. 197–9.
[16] T. C. Rumble, 'From *Eardstapa* to *Snottor on Mode*: the Structural Principle of "The Wanderer"', *Mod. Lang. Quarterly* 19 (1958), 225–30, at 229–30.
[17] I distinguish between 'modern' and 'modernist'. 'Modern' contrasts with 'medieval' and more specifically 'Anglo-Saxon' and refers to the Enlightenment and later. 'Modernist' refers to that specific type of literature written between the wars and the criticism that came later but similarly challenged ideas of coherence and unity. T. Moi uses the term '"modernist theory" as distinct from a mere theory of modernism' in describing the group of structuralist and post-structuralist theorists who gravitated around *Tel Quel* in the late sixties, including Roland Barthes, Jacques Derrida, Michel Foucault and Julia Kristeva; see Moi's Introduction to *The Kristeva Reader*, ed. T. Moi (New York, 1986), pp. 1–22, at 4.

of thinking from the monological literature of Virgilian epic and nineteenth-
century novels, in which a single perspective dominates the whole.[18] Polyphonic texts employ 'the logic of *distance* and *relationship* between the different units
of a sentence or narrative structure'.[19] Theirs 'is a logic of *analogy* and *nonexclusive opposition*, opposed to monological levels of causality and identifying
determination'.[20] Their mosaic-like structure breaks the continuity that
represents chronology and causality and so demands that the readers invent
the connections themselves. As Roland Barthes would say, the readers must
write the text because they cannot read it.[21] To gain this participation, the
writer sacrifices control over the meanings his or her text conveys. Barthes
says that the 'plural' (that is, polyphonic) text 'practices the infinite deferral of
the signified', not in order to refer to 'some idea of the ineffable (of an
unnamable signified) but to the idea of *play*'. This play connects the text to
'enjoyment (*jouissance*), to pleasure without separation'.[22]

The Anglo-Saxon practice differs from the modernist in that they do not
seem to have indulged, consciously at any rate, in this kind of literary pleasure.
Their polyphonic poetry, while not attempting to fix meaning like a monological text, does orchestrate relationships among movements. A system of
verbal echoes stretches across disjunctions in a web that implies thematic
relationships[23] and promotes the possibility that the reader or listener might

---

[18] As soon as I give voice to Kristeva's generalization I can hear the objections. Of course,
Madame Bovary, among others, does not fit the term, but on the whole the distinction holds
true.

[19] J. Kristeva, 'Word, Dialogue and Novel', *The Kristeva Reader*, p. 42.   [20] *Ibid.*

[21] See R. Barthes, *S/Z*, trans. R. Miller (New York, 1974), pp. 3–13. Compare W. Iser's
discussion of 'gaps' in 'The Reading Process: a Phenomenological Approach', *New Lit. Hist.*
3 (1972), 279–99; repr. in his *The Implied Reader: Patterns of Communication in Prose Fiction from
Bunyan to Beckett* (Baltimore, MD, 1974), pp. 274–94. He implies that we follow the text's
directions: 'Whenever the flow is interrupted and we are led off in unexpected directions, the
opportunity is given to us to bring into play our own faculty for establishing connections –
for filling in the gaps left by the text itself.' 'Modern texts', as he says, 'frequently exploit' this
quality (p. 280). One part of the reading dynamic that they encourage is 'the process of
grouping together all the different aspects of a text to form the consistency that the reader will
always be in search of ... By grouping together the written parts of the text, we enable them
to interact, we observe the direction in which they are leading us, and we project onto them
the consistency which we, as readers, require' (pp. 283–4).

[22] R. Barthes, 'From Work to Text', *Textual Strategies: Perspectives in Post-Structuralist Criticism*,
ed. and trans. J. V. Harari (Ithaca, NY, 1979), pp. 73–81, at 75 and 80.

[23] This method of creating associations has been discussed generally by E. R. Kintgen in
'Echoic Repetition in Old English Poetry, especially *The Dream of the Rood*', *NM* 75 (1974),
202–23, and more specifically for *The Wanderer* by J. L. Rosier in 'The Literal-Figurative
Identity of *The Wanderer*', *PMLA* 79 (1964), 366–9; M. Cornell in 'Varieties of Repetition in
Old English Poetry, especially in *The Wanderer* and *The Seafarer*', *Neophilologus* 65 (1981),
292–307; R. E. Bjork in '*Sundor æt rune*: the Voluntary Exile of the Wanderer', *Neophilologus* 73
(1989), 119–29; and Kintgen in 'Word-Play in *The Wanderer*', *Neophilologus* 59 (1975), 119–27.

reach some understanding of the ineffable.[24] This technique is conventional throughout the canon and complements the disjunctions that the polyphony creates.

Normally, a composition's introductory section initiates a large portion of the thematic echoes.[25] In *The Wanderer*, it introduces themes of customary isolation ('oft . . . anhaga'), anticipation of God's grace ('are gebideð, / metudes miltse'), and the locations of suffering ('geond lagulade').[26] The subsequent sections bring back these concepts, replaying them in similar but new form any number of times as is useful. I will trace these three strands in detail as examples of the associational web and the variety of functions the echoes perform.

The text's first phrase, 'oft him anhaga', introduces one of the most dominant themes, the isolation that is always with a person. The figure is defined as *an*, alone, and he is repeatedly, *oft*, doing something in relation to that aloneness (addressed in the next phrase). That isolation becomes in the first-person narrative 'oft ic sceolde ana . . . / mine ceare cwiþan' (8–9a), linking the difficulty of speaking to isolation. This idea comes back again in this movement when the speaker explains the virtue that the 'domgeorne' practise 'oft' in binding fast ('bindað fæste') their breast-coffers (17–8) and again in his statement that he has 'oft' had to fetter his heart (19–21). At line 40, in the second movement, sleep often binds the lone-dweller ('earmne anhogan

---

See also C. B. Hieatt's work in this area in 'Dream Frame and Verbal Echo in *The Dream of the Rood*', *NM* 72 (1971), 251–63, and 'Modþryðo and Heremod: Intertwined Threads in the *Beowulf*-Poet's Web of Words', *JEGP* 83 (1984), 173–82. For a discussion of the method's cognitive aspects, see 'The Question of Unity' in Pasternack, 'Disjunction'. For a discussion of echoes in relation to oral formulae, see J.M. Foley, 'Genre(s) in the Making: Diction, Audience and Text in the Old English *Seafarer*', *Poetics Today* 4 (1983), 683–706, who designates this kind of system as 'modern' to the Anglo-Saxons, as opposed to the traditional, oral-generated system of echoes that resound among poems. (The traditional system that he looks at includes metrical as well as semantic parameters, though he distinguishes these traditional phrasings from the accepted definitions of formula.)

24 See how Cynewulf describes his experience composing *Elene*, 1236–56a, as an experience of mystery revealed.

25 There are others as well; see Kintgen, 'Word-Play'; Cornell, 'Varieties'; and Bjork, '*Sundor æt rune*', for more comprehensive discussions.

26 I interpret 'are gebideð' as 'awaits grace'. Dunning and Bliss point out that whether *gebideð* means 'experience' or 'wait for' is a matter of critical judgement that depends on how one understands the poem as whole. See Dunning and Bliss, pp. 41–2; B. Mitchell, 'Some Syntactical Problems in *The Wanderer*', *NM* 69 (1968), 172–98; and Greenfield, 'Reconsideration', pp. 464–5. In general, my analysis of the text is based on *The Wanderer* in *The Exeter Book*, ed. G.P. Krapp and E.V.K. Dobbie, ASPR 3 (New York and London, 1936), 134–7. I have also consulted Leslie's and Dunning and Bliss's editions, as well as the facsimile edition, *The Exeter Book of Old English Poetry*, ed. R.W. Chambers, M. Förster and R. Flower (London, 1933), 76v–78r. All translations of *The Wanderer* are my own.

oft gebindað'),[27] cutting him off from the world. When he awakens, even the seabirds 'swimmað oft onweg' (53b).[28] At line 90, when the poetry's focus shifts from the individual to the general condition, the repetition of *oft* associates the *anhaga*'s isolation with what a wise person thinks who *oft* thinks about the multitude of deaths that characterize this world ('feor oft gemon / wælsleahta worn'). *Oft*, pointing to what is customary, in each of these cases combines with isolation and loss, asserting that they characterize earthly life.

The text's second phrase, 'are gebideð', does not find its echo until the closing frame when the poet proclaims, 'Wel bið þam þe him are seceð' (114b). This simple framing echo works by 'nonexclusive opposition' rather than analogy. In the opening frame the *anhaga* simply waits for God's grace while he searches for an earthly treasure-giver, a search that can only lead to lament. At the end, the poetry turns the audience toward the only permanent remedy and stability – 'frofre to fæder on heofonum' (115).[29] The echo and reversal contribute to the composition's closure.

The third echoic set, like the first, highlights a central theme – the locations of suffering. 'Geond lagulade' (3a) is a synecdoche for this world that immediately names it as a place characterized by the cold seas of exile. The subsequent phrases – 'geond þas woruld' (58b), 'þes middangeard' (62b), 'in woruldrice' (65a), 'ealre þisse worulde wela' (74a), 'geond þisne middangeard' (75b), 'þisne eardgard' (85a), 'eorþanrice' (106b), 'weoruld under heofonum' (107b), 'eal þis eorþan gesteal' (110a) – repeatedly remind the audience that isolation and destruction are a part of this world and that they permeate all the regions of the world.

These linked phrases serve a second structural function: their sweeping scope gives them the power to conclude movements. One cluster (58–65a) comes at the end of the first two perspectives, joining forces with the first person's return. The second group (74a, 75b and 85a) forms an envelope that concludes the wisdom poetry. The beginning and end of this subsection declare the wealth and the towns throughout this world desolate and useless, weaving into the locating phrases the irony that walls stand on this earth only to be ravaged by wind and frost, and that the creator of men ('ælda scyppend', 85b) destroys until the old works of giants stand useless ('idlu stodon', 87).

---

[27] See Leslie, *The Wanderer*, p. 65, and Dunning and Bliss, *The Wanderer*, pp. 37–40, for discussions regarding the precise meaning and derivations of *anhaga* and *anhoga*. They both note possibilities for separate derivation but also explain their interchangeable semantics in this poem and others.

[28] With Leslie, I retain the manuscript's 'oft', in part because emendation is not necessary and in part because it continues the theme of repeated, customary experiences of isolation.

[29] For this analysis I draw on Kintgen, 'Wordplay'.

The following section of lamentation has a similarly ornamented closure in which once again the world is connected to its *idelnesse* (uselessness or vanity):

> Eall is earfoðlic eorþan rice,
> onwendeð wyrda gesceaft weoruld under heofonum.
> Her bið feoh læne, her bið freond læne,
> her bið mon læne, her bið mæg læne,
> eal þis eorþan gesteal idel weorþeð! (106–10)[30]

The repeated *her* adds force to the designations 'eorþan rice', 'weoruld under heofonum' and 'eal þis eorþan gesteal'. Up to this point, the echoes have stressed the similarity that binds together all the poetry has expressed, but the last echo will reverse all that by shifting locations from 'her' to 'þær' (115b), from 'under heofonum' (107b) to 'on heofonum þær us eal seo fæstnung stondeð' (115). This statement's impact comes from the weight of all the parallel statements that precede this last parallel opposite. The reversal puts the period on the poet's performance.

These and other echoic sets prompt a play of associations that work through similarity and difference and in this way allow the audience to spin out the threads which can interconnect the poem's polyphony. The audience's freedom to play out the threads may not reach the joyous anarchy Barthes describes, but it does allow them the latitude to weave any number of poems.[31]

The sense the audience makes from the composition depends in large part on the relationships individuals perceive with other texts already heard and read. Oral theory and modernist intertextuality both explain this mechanism. The oral-formulaic and thematic construction of Old English manuscript poetry dictates that both small and large segments of text have a life not just in the present text but in many other texts as well. John Miles Foley describes this relationship in 'oral and oral-derived poems' as a kind of referentiality or 'metonymy' which provides 'access to extratextual meaning' by tapping into the theme's or formula's own tradition.[32] Kristeva contends that this sort of intertextual relationship contributes to the significance of all texts. Working

---

[30] 'All is difficult in the kingdom of earth, the ordained course of fates turns the world under the heavens. Here wealth is transitory, here a friend is transitory, here man is transitory, here a kinsman is transitory, this entire foundation of earth becomes useless.'

[31] Compare Bjork in '*Sundor æt rune*', Huppé in '*Wanderer*: Theme and Structure' and Kintgen in 'Word-Play' for three diverse readings that make similar use of repetitions and structure.

[32] J.M. Foley, 'Orality, Textuality, and Interpretation', in *Vox intexta*, ed. Doane and Pasternack, pp. 34–45. See also Foley's discussion of theme and metonymy in 'Tradition and the Collective Talent: Oral Epic, Textual Meaning, and Receptionalist Theory', *Cultural Anthropology* 1 (1986), 203–22, and of formula in 'Genre(s) in the Making', and Renoir on type-scenes in *A Key to Old Poems*.

from Bakhtin but coining the term herself, she explains intertextuality this way: 'Any text is constructed as a mosaic of quotations; any text is the absorption and transformation of another.'³³ The meaning of a group of words comes from its intertextual position – in part from its position in the present text and in part from its position in what Kristeva calls 'exterior texts'.

But the intertextualities of printed and manuscript texts differ, and that difference flows from the manuscript poetry's oral derivation.³⁴ Considering the implications of Kristeva's definition reveals the discrepancy. The term 'quotation' implies that a phrase or group of phrases is taken from an earlier statement and that the audience is meant to recognize that previous existence. Oral and manuscript compositions are mosaics not of quotations but of traditional, shared expressions. One expression echoes similar ones in other texts, but which one came first is neither discoverable nor relevant because of the fluidity of related performances. In certain cases, where the text partici-pates in the literary tradition of the church, one text is 'the absorption and transformation of another' specific text, as Martin Irvine argues – for example, Cynewulf's *Elene*, *Juliana* and *Ascension* absorb and transform specific Latin texts,³⁵ and *Genesis*, *Exodus* and *Daniel* do the same with their biblical precedents. But often an Old English text does not absorb and transform another because it is in the nature of formulaic language for an indefinite number of intertexts to exist, written and oral.³⁶

The Wanderer's first movement following the frame illustrates well one kind of intertextuality which often operates. This first person speech takes its content and its expressions from the formulaic theme of exile. As Stanley B. Greenfield demonstrates, the *Wanderer*-poet uses in this speech three of the

---

³³ Kristeva, 'Word, Dialogue and Novel', p. 37.
³⁴ See A.N. Doane, 'Oral Texts, Intertexts, and Intratexts: Editing Old English', *Influence and Intertextuality*, ed. E. Rothstein and J. Clayton (Madison WI, and London, forthcoming) and also M. Irvine, 'Anglo-Saxon Literary Theory Exemplified in Old English Poems: Interpreting the Cross in *The Dream of the Rood* and *Elene*', *Style* 20 (1986), 157–81, for two other discussions of intertextuality and Old English poetry that differ considerably from each other and from mine.
³⁵ Irvine, 'Anglo-Saxon Literary Theory'. English translations of those Latin texts can be found in M. J. B. Allen and D. G. Calder, *Sources and Analogues of Old English Poetry: the Major Latin Texts in Translation* (Cambridge and Totowa, NJ, 1976).
³⁶ M. Riffaterre's definition is more linear than Kristeva's. As he conceives of it, an intertext is 'an implicit reference without which the text would not make sense: either the text is incomplete and can be deciphered only through the intertext or the text is linguistically deviant, and the scandal of this departure would be a gratuitous and random ungrammatica-lity without the authority and the focus given it by its grammatical correspondent in the intertext' ('Relevance of Theory/Theory of Relevance', *Yale Jnl of Criticism* 1 (1988), 163–76, at 169). In Old English compositions, however, one text is not the key to another, nor is the text ungrammatical without the intertext. The meaning is simply less full.

'four aspects or concomitants of the exile state': 'deprivation', 'state of mind' and 'movement in or into exile'.[37] 'Status', the first aspect that Greenfield lists, has been expressed in the poem's first line, 'anhaga'. In the speech itself, the expressions 'eðle bidæled' (20b), 'earmcearig' (20a), 'wintercearig' (24a) and 'hean' (23b) fit into the formulaic systems for indicating the exile's deprivation and state of mind.[38] 'Freomægum feor' (21a), 'hean þonan' (23b) and 'sohte seledreorig sinces bryttan' (25) fulfil three of the five categories for 'movement in or into exile'.[39] This theme does not go back to an original version or to any other single text. The strongest echo for one person might be *The Seafarer* and the idea of the *peregrinatio pro amore Dei*;[40] for another person *The Wife's Lament* might bring to mind imposed and unremedied isolation; another might relate to the text his own experience at sea.[41] It is also possible that a person's experience of *The Wanderer* colours his or her understanding of *The Wife's Lament*, making the wife's vision appear limited in her refusal to see that her plight is universal and that the only security is in heaven.

Such themes or movements have no one primary context that a later text calls upon because a different kind of relationship exists among both oral and manuscript texts from that in print culture. Oral theory and manuscript evidence imply that no fixed boundary exists between what statements belong to text A and what to text B. Nor is there a fixed definition as to what movements text A includes and how long or ornamented each movement is. For oral poets, the work is a fluid concept. An oral composition varies in length and content from one performance to another, depending on the

---

[37] S.B. Greenfield, 'The Formulaic Expression of the Theme of "Exile" in Anglo-Saxon Poetry', *Speculum* 30 (1955), 200–6, at 201.

[38] Greenfield's article came out before D.K. Fry published his piece, 'Old English Formulas and Systems', *ES* 48 (1967), 193–204, defining the term 'formulaic system', but Fry's definition fits Greenfield's way of describing families of phrases expressing certain ideas.

[39] Greenfield, 'Formulaic Expression', pp. 203–4.

[40] See D. Whitelock, 'The Interpretation of *The Seafarer*', *The Early Cultures of Northwest Europe: H.M. Chadwick Memorial Studies*, ed. C. Fox and B. Dickins (Cambridge, 1950), pp. 259–72; repr. in *Essential Articles for the Study of Old English Poetry*, ed. J.B. Bessinger, Jr and S.J. Kahrl (Hamden, CT, 1968), pp. 442–57.

[41] Such a theme does not differ much from a topos, which is to say that Old English intertextuality takes in the Latin as well as the Germanic traditions. For example, P. Clemoes, '*Mens absentia cogitans* in *Thè Seafarer* and *The Wanderer*', *Medieval Literature and Civilization: Studies in Memory of G.N. Garmonsway*, ed. D.A. Pearsall and R.A. Waldron (London, 1969), pp. 62–77, discusses in this light the poem's second movement, the third-person description of a lonely person's dream of being once again with his companions, who, on his waking, disappear as do the seabirds all about him. He demonstrates that the poet follows a topos expressed in Latin and in Old English 'that this consciousness of objects beyond immediate physical surroundings is of the essence of mental activity' (p. 62). He cites *The Seafarer* 58–64a, two of Ælfric's homilies, Alcuin's *De animae ratione*, a number of Augustine's works, and what he believes to be the source for *The Wanderer*'s image, Ambrose's *Hexaemeron*.

performance context and the audience's attention span. Yet if one asks those present at two differing performances, they will say the poet has sung the same song.[42] This 'illusion of repeatability', as Paul Zumthor says, 'constitutes the principal characteristic of oral poetry'.[43] Although elements are carried over from one performance to another, the compositions are 'provisional'. The idea of unity, according to Zumthor, is 'adventurous', since 'this type of unity in performance is less a matter of positing a necessary organicity in the text than of situating it among its possible variants'.[44]

A manuscript text only seems stable because most poems survive in only one version. In a very few instances, however, closely related compositions still exist: the Junius *Daniel* and Exeter *Azarias*, the Ruthwell Cross poem and the Vercelli *Dream of the Rood*, the Vercelli and the Exeter versions of *Soul and Body*.[45] Although traditionally scholars have treated the pairs as imperfect copies of one fixed poem, a view to oral performances instructs us to analyse them as related compositions which vary as to the length and shape of the whole but share extensive movements. Since, like jazz or folk musicians, the performers or writers may vary which movements they include and how much they expand and ornament movements, individual movements may be relatively stable, but what constitutes the whole is not. The dividing line between two compositions and two performances of one composition blurs. Like an oral performance, each manuscript composition is unique and is provisional.[46]

Unfortunately, we do not have other versions of *The Wanderer*, but we can get an idea of just how fluid the boundaries are that divide text from text by

---

[42] See Lord, *Singer of Tales*, pp. 99–123.

[43] P. Zumthor, 'The Impossible Closure of the Oral Text', *Yale French Stud.* 67 (1984), 25–42, at 26.   [44] *Ibid.* p. 27.

[45] The poetry called *Azarias* in the Exeter Book resembles very closely a movement in the Junius manuscript's *Daniel* (279–371). See A. Jones, '*Daniel* and *Azarias* as Evidence for the Oral-Formulaic Character of Anglo-Saxon Poetry', *MÆ* 35 (1966), 95–102, for the argument that they are related oral productions. A.N. Doane sees them as products of 'different performative situations' ('Oral Texts, Intertexts, and Intratexts', p. 86). The Ruthwell Cross has inscribed on it text that corresponds to lines 39–64 of the Vercelli *Dream of the Rood*. See É. Ó Carragáin, 'Crucifixion as Annunciation: the Relation of "The Dream of the Rood" to the Liturgy Reconsidered', *ES* 63 (1982), 487–505. The Exeter Book's *Soul and Body* corresponds to lines 1–126 of the Vercelli text.

[46] I agree with J. Dagenais that neither the manuscript nor the oral performance represents 'some underlying text' and they should be 'set . . . free of a system of representation and differences' ('That Bothersome Residue', p. 249). Foley has taken a similar stance: 'We cannot assume that a single text is "the poem", since it is only a version of the narrative, only one possible recension of a multiform which will forever evade the fossilization of print . . . To establish any one text or textual feature as standard is to mistake the ontology of oral traditional structure' ('Editing Oral Epic Texts', p. 81).

observing some intertexts for one movement. In the wisdom poetry movement (lines 65b–87), there is a list of what happens to bodies when battle has taken their lives. This list echoes its intertexts in syntax as well as diction; many comparable passages are extant in Latin and Old English. In this instance we are told that the wise man must perceive how ghastly it will be when the world's wealth stands waste, even as now walls stand whipped by the wind, the wine-hall decays, the ruler and the *duguþ* are dead alongside the wall. The scene gathers force by means of a list of fates such a *duguþ* meets:

> Sume wig fornom,
> ferede in forðwege,　　sumne fugel oþbær
> ofer heanne holm,　　sumne se hara wulf
> deaðe gedælde,　　sumne dreorighleor
> in eorðscræfe　　eorl gehydde.　　(80b–84)[47]

In their form and content, these lines resemble a number of other passages in extant Old English poems. One appears in Cynewulf's *Elene*. Constantine has engaged the Huns in a difficult and uncertain battle. But after a vision of the cross, he wins the battle, and the Huns' defeat is described using the same *sum* figure and many of the same images:[48]

> 　　　　　　Wurdon heardingas
> wide towrecene.　　Sume wig fornam.
> Sume unsofte　　aldor generedon
> on þam heresiðe.　　Sume healfcwice
> flugon on fæsten　　ond feore burgon
> æfter stanclifum,　　stede weardedon
> ymb Danubie.　　Sume drenc fornam
> on lagostreame　　lifes æt ende.　　(130b–37)[49]

The same figure appears in a gnomic instead of a narrative context in *The Fortunes of Men*. As the modern title suggests, the phrases take in a wide range of misfortunes, not just those that war can bring. The poem begins with a life's beginning, explaining that a man and a woman can bring a child into the world, nurture and raise that child, but God alone knows what winter will

---

[47] 'Battle has taken some, carried them on the way forth, one a bird has carried off across the high sea, one the grey wolf has shared with death, one a sad-faced earl has hidden in an earth-cave.'

[48] All quotations of Old English poetry other than *The Wanderer* are as they appear in ASPR, ed. G. P. Krapp and E. V. K. Dobbie, 6 vols. (New York and London, 1931–53).

[49] 'The soldiers were widely destroyed. Some battle took. Some not easily saved their lives in that battle. Some half-alive fled into the forest and protected their lives under the stone cliffs, guarded the place along the Danube. Some drowning took in the water-stream at the end of life.'

bring to that growing creature. Then it continues on this theme of uncertain endings:

> Sumum þæt gegongeð   on geoguðfeore
> þæt se endestæf   earfeðmæcgum
> wealic weorþeð.   Sceal hine wulf etan,
> har hæðstapa;   hinsiþ þonne
> modor bimurneð.   Ne bið swylc monnes geweald!
> Sumne sceal hungor ahiþan,   sumne sceal hreoh fordrifan,
> sumne sceal gar agetan,   sumne guð abreotan.   (10–16)[50]

The poem goes on listing deaths in this manner, using the *sum* pattern, for another fifty lines. These words are not identical to *The Wanderer*'s, the precise use of the passage differs, but the rhetorical figure is the same and the content is similar enough for one to remind us of the other (for example, the 'beasts of battle' theme is invoked with the image of the wolf eating the corpse).

In addition to this figure being used to express the theme of deaths and disasters, it is also used for a complementary theme usually called 'the gifts of men'. It appears that way later in *The Fortunes of Men*:

> Swa missenlice   meahtig dryhten
> geond eorþan sceat   eallum dæleð,
> scyreþ ond scrifeð   ond gesceapo healdeð,
> sumum eadwelan,   sumum earfeþa dæl,
> sumum geogoþe glæd,   sumum guþe blæd . . .
>   Sume boceras
> weorþað wisfæste.   Sumum wundorgiefe
> þurh goldsmiþe   gearwad weorþað.   (64–8 and 71b–73)[51]

In addition, the poem *The Gifts of Men* (which follows *The Wanderer* in the manuscript) is developed entirely in this mode. And Cynewulf's *Christ* poem has a beautiful passage about the gifts that God sows like seeds in the spirits of men:

> Sumum wordlaþe   wise sendeð
> on his modes gemynd   þurh his muþes gæst,
> æðele ondgiet.   Se mæg eal fela
> singan ond secgan   þam bið snyttru cræft

---

[50] 'To some it happens in youth that the end comes woeful to the wretched. The wolf shall eat him, the hoary heathstepper. Then the mother mourns his journey hence. Such a thing is not under a person's control! One hunger shall rob of life, one shall a storm drive to destruction, one shall a spear destroy, one battle break.'

[51] 'So variously the Mighty Lord across the earth dispenses to all, allots and decrees and governs fates, for some blessed riches, for some a portion of hardships, for some the gladness of youth, for some glory in battle . . . Some become learned scholars. For some wondrous gifts are prepared by the goldsmith.'

bifolen on ferðe.   Sum mæg fingrum wel
hlude fore hæleþum   hearpan stirgan,
gleobeam gretan.   Sum mæg godcunde
reccan ryhte æ.   Sum mæg ryne tungla
secgan, side gesceaft.   Sum mæg searolice
wordcwide writan.   Sumum wiges sped
giefeð æt guþe,   þonne gargetrum
ofer scildhreadan   sceotend sendað,
flacor flangeweorc.   (664–76a)[52]

The series continues, taking in those who sail the seas, make engraved swords and know the far-reaching plains. Clearly *The Wanderer's* poet did not invent his list nor did he invent his manner of listing. One might say that using *sum*, *sume* or *sumum* is the obvious way of constructing a list of possibilities, but the figure's use goes beyond that. In Old English poetry, these instances all have to do with human possibilities, the gifts given in life or the fates that can bring the body's life to an end.[53] Reading one instance easily brings to mind others that have been heard or read. One of these texts does not unlock another's meaning; they are, rather, meaningful con-texts.

The meaningful contexts include Latin ones as well – for those who were able to understand Latin. Cynewulf's version, as is well known, is an expansion of a list he had found in his main source, Gregory the Great's 'Ascension Homily':

Dedit vero dona hominibus, quia, misso desuper Spiritu, alii sermonem sapientiae, alii sermonem scientiae, alii gratiam virtutum, alii gratiam curationum, alii genera linguarum, alii interpretationem tribuit sermonum. Dedit ergo dona hominibus.[54]

[52] 'To some he sends wise eloquence into his heart's thought through his mouth's spirit, excellent understanding. He can sing and say a great many things to whom the skill of wisdom is committed in the spirit. One can strike the harp well with fingers, loudly before men, touch the joy-wood. One can expound divine law correctly. One can tell the course of the stars, the wide creation. One can skilfully write word-sentences. To one he gives success of war in battle, when a storm of spears above the shield shooters send, flying arrows.'

[53] It is possible that there are a number of themes or type-scenes that are related in complementary pairs. C. B. Hieatt, 'Cædmon in Context: Transforming the Formula', *JEGP* 84 (1985), 485–97, develops criteria for a creation and for a destruction type-scene that have formal similarities. E. Tuttle Hansen, *The Solomon Complex: Reading Wisdom in Old English Poetry* (Toronto, 1988), sees in such texts 'a conventional association of theme and structure', which she calls the '*swa missenlice* theme' (p. 97).

[54] 'But "He gave gifts to men", because, when the Holy Spirit was sent from above, it allotted the word of wisdom to one, to another the word of knowledge, to another the grace of virtues, to another the grace of healings, to another the various kinds of tongues, to another the interpretation of tongues (I Cor. XII.8). So He gave gifts to men.' Gregory the Great, *Homiliae .xl. in evangelia*, Hom.xxix: 'Habita ad populum in basilica beati Petri apostoli, in Ascensione Domini' (PL 76, cols. 1213–19, at 1218; trans. Allen and Calder, *Sources and Analogues*, pp. 79–81, at 80).

The two are quite close, except that Cynewulf has expanded individual items, varied his grammatical structure from one item to the next, and added to the list the warrior, the seaman and others. The same expression appears in I Corinthians (XII.7–11) and, no doubt, in other Latin texts as well. We can add to the list of such texts another sermon of Gregory's that Ælfric used as a source for one of his sermons.[55] There too Gregory lists the talents God has given using the term *alius* to introduce each, and there too Ælfric translates his list using *sum*.

The scholarly tradition looks at these Latin texts as sources for Cynewulf's text and perhaps the other Old English ones as well.[56] Irvine suggests a second option, to view the Old English poetry as 'a supplementary or complementary text which seeks to disclose some hidden discourse or subtext in [the] earlier text'.[57] The third option, the one I am arguing for, takes the perspective of a listener or reader who may or may not know Gregory's sermon. In this one, Cynewulf's version joins the matrix of similar statements, potentially including Gregory's but not necessarily.

To return to *The Wanderer*'s version of the list and its reception, the listener's or reader's mind can connect the list with a number of varied intertexts – with the unpredictability and waywardness of fate or with the variety of God's gifts or with the ravages of war or with the degeneration that will precede the Second Coming. It is one aspect of this sort of intertextuality that we cannot say about the Anglo-Saxon texts that one precedes another or that one is alluding to another.[58] The ability to date and order texts could be a casualty of history. But the free circulation of such movements implies that the

---

55 Gregory's is *Homiliae .xl. in evangelia*, Hom. ix: 'Habita ad populum in basilica sancti Silvestri, in die natalis ejus' (PL 76, cols. 1105–9); Ælfric's *In natale unius confessoris*, *Ælfric's Catholic Homilies: the Second Series*, ed. M. Godden, EETS ss 5 (London, 1979), 318–26.

56 See J. E. Cross, 'On *The Wanderer* lines 80–84: a Study of a Figure and a Theme', *Vetenskaps-Societeten i Lund Årsbok* (1958–59), 75–110; 'The Old English Poetic Theme of "The Gifts of Men"', *Neophilologus* 46 (1962), 66–70; and *Latin Themes in Old English Poetry* (Bristol, 1962). G. R. Russom, 'A Germanic Concept of Nobility in *The Gifts of Men* and *Beowulf*', *Speculum* 53 (1978), 1–15, musters a convincing argument against patristic writings influencing the Old English theme and cites Norse material that shows the theme's connection with 'endowments regarded as marks of aristocratic distinction' (p. 2).

57 Irvine, 'Anglo-Saxon Literary Theory', p. 158.

58 J. E. Cross takes a different position. Finding it logical to identify a single source and meaning, he differentiates the various themes using this figure of *repetitio* and decides that catalogues of *The Wanderer*'s type were used in homilies 'to reiterate the dogma of the resurrection of the body, whose ultimate scriptural source was Apocalypse XX.13 . . . The list, reflecting, as it does, an objection to the dogma of resurrection, would demand in the Christian listeners' minds the only answer', that security will come in the heavenly home (*Latin Themes*, p. 6). I am not sure that prose necessarily has interpretative priority, providing the answer that excludes other associations and interpretations.

concepts of originality and influence simply do not operate here. This theme of fortunes and fates belongs just as much to one performance as to another.

If originality does not make sense for Anglo-Saxon poetry, then neither does authorship as most people understand the concept. We tend to accept the anonymity of Anglo-Saxon poetry as an absence of information when actually it is a fact of the poetry's semiotics. Once again, Kristeva's discussion of intertextuality explains the issue. She asserts that 'the notion of *intertextuality* replaces that of intersubjectivity'.[59] What we see in a text is not communication between two subjectivities, author and reader, but a horizontal textual relationship between writing subject and addressee, as the text constructs these positions, as well as a vertical relationship between text and exterior texts. The writing subject structures discourse in relation to another, the addressee, and in doing so constructs a code in which in he or she is 'reduced ... to an *anonymity* mediated by ... the *he/she* character' who utters the words in the text. In reading, the addressee makes this code his or her subject and uses it to construct the 'author'.[60] This analysis may seem a roundabout way of saying that the narrator of a text is not the author but a persona, but it says something more, that the way we conceive a text's author is a separate issue from whether we can name the person who wrote it. Old English poetry is anonymous not because we do not have names of writers but because the texts do not present such a code and do not create such a character.

Ironically, Cynewulf's signed poems prove the point. Although he names himself in runic puzzles, these naming movements do not present us with a code out of which we can construct an author. Since *Juliana* precedes *The Wanderer* in the Exeter Book, it will serve as my example. The poem's account of Juliana's life ends with her burial and the assertion that in that same place the saint's praise has been raised throughout the years unto this day (692–5a). Then a first person proclaims great need for the saint's help: 'Is me þearf micel / þæt seo halge me helpe gefremme' (695b–96). Cynewulf works the runes indicating his name into the following statement of need. The necessity, however, is not peculiar to one person's life but to all human lives, for the first person tells about terror at the Last Judgement and nothing in the telling differentiates this life from that of any other sinner. This last movement serves two purposes, to ask each person who recites the poem to pray for Cynewulf by name (718–22) and to provide a position from which all reciters or listeners can comprehend the saint's life. In fact, as the poem closes, the request to pray for God to help 'me' slides into a description of the Trinity judging all people:

> ond meotud bidde
> þæt me heofona helm   helpe gefremme,

[59] Kristeva, 'Word, Dialogue and Novel', p. 37.   [60] *Ibid.* p. 45.

Carol Braun Pasternack

meahta waldend,   on þam miclan dæge,
fæder, frofre gæst,   in þa frecnan tid,
dæda demend,   ond se deora sunu,
þonne seo þrynis   þrymsittende
in annesse   ælda cynne
þurh þa sciran gesceaft   scrifeð bi gewyrhtum
meorde manna gehwam.   (721b–29a)[61]

The poem concludes with an explicit merging of the first person with all others in the direct prayer,

Forgif us, mægna god,
þæt we þine onsyne,   æþelinga wyn,
milde gemeten   on þa mæran tid.   Amen. (729b–31)[62]

Although we can find in these lines the name Cynewulf, we cannot find here a character out of which we can construct someone different from others.[63] The use of such a code comes only gradually with the change from oral to written texts. For the oral composition the poet is present, speaking the text, and so he or she does not need to embody a fictional speaker within the text. Rather than using such a speaker as a point of view from which to take in the text, the audience can use as their viewpoint the context of the performance

---

[61] 'And pray the creator that the protector of heavens may give me help, the mighty ruler, on that great day, the father, the spirit of comfort, in that terrible time, the judge of deeds, and the beloved son, when the Trinity, sitting in glory, in unity, for the race of men through bright creation will decree according to (their) deeds reward for each of men.'

[62] 'Grant us, God of hosts, that we may your face, joy of nobles, find mild in that great time.'

[63] To be fair, *Elene* has been the major resource for biographical insights. See, for example, B. ten Brink, *History of English Literature I; to Wiclif*, trans. H.M. Kennedy (London, 1895), pp. 51–9. Both E.R. Anderson, *Cynewulf: Structure, Style, and Theme in his Poetry* (Rutherford, NJ, 1983), p. 115 and D.G. Calder, *Cynewulf*, Twayne's Eng. Author Ser. 327 (Boston, MA, 1981), 136, characterize these sections as autobiographical, Anderson placing the epilogue into a classical 'tradition of autobiographical epilogues' (p. 116). There is, however, no more of an authorial code here than in *Juliana*. Although Cynewulf introduces a first person to speak about the poem's production, he does not assert that he has created it: he has gathered his thought (1236–39a), not devised it; his poetry is an undeserved gift from God (1242b–50a) and so not personal to him, and what he has expressed about the cross he found in books (1251b–56a). The movement's highly ornamented style undercuts any sense of naturalness that might derive from the grammatical first person, the *a* and *b* verses rhyming in thirteen out of twenty-one lines. In the next movement, the first person disappears, and Cynewulf combines his runic signature with details about a 'secg' (1256b) that conform to a type such as we also see in *The Seafarer*. Through this figure we are reminded of three facts about life: treasures of the mead-hall do not allay the sorrows of human life, the joy of youth departs and all joy of life is transitory. As in *Juliana*, the signature movement provides no autobiography in the modern sense but rather a figure for how all people should understand earthly life, and the third and last movement turns us toward the Last Judgement on all humanity.

116

and their own presence at it. When poets entrust texts to manuscripts, they must compensate for the loss of their own presence and the performance context. Ursula Schaeffer argues convincingly that a fictional first-person speaker is a way of staging the oral poet's presence.[64] Other techniques may substitute for performance context. Éamonn Ó Carragáin shows that the Ruthwell Cross poem functioned within a context of liturgy as it was performed and as it was depicted iconographically on the cross, so that context provided a meaningful setting for the Cross's account of the crucifixion, but when that poetry appeared in manuscript (in the version we call *The Dream of the Rood*) the meaning implicit in the liturgy had to be supplied by additional sections of poetry.[65] Although eventually poets learn such techniques and more, by adding contextual sections or inserting a fictional first-person speaker, the poet is at the same time recognizing the necessity of a sense of oral presentation.[66] The fundamental workings of the oral poetics persist, including the polyphony of composing poetry out of movements.

We can see the adaptations as well as the polyphony in *The Wanderer*. As the first movement, the poet gives us the 'eardstapa' (6) speaking in the first person so that we can use his position as an orientation for the topic. But whereas normally a modern first person presents what is supposed to be a peculiar viewpoint, the manuscript poem gives voice to a traditional position, the speech taking its content and its expressions from the formulaic theme of exile. The first person returns briefly after the second movement to tell the audience what to think about the presentation so far:

[64] U. Schaeffer, 'Hearing from Books: the Rise of Fictionality in Old English Poetry', *Vox intexta*, ed. Doane and Pasternack, pp. 117–136.

[65] É. Ó Carragáin, 'Liturgical Innovations Associated with Pope Sergius and the Iconography of the Ruthwell and Bewcastle Crosses', *Bede and Anglo-Saxon England: Papers in Honour of the 1300th Anniversary of the Birth of Bede, Given at Cornell University in 1973 and 1974*, ed. R.T. Farrell, BAR Brit.ser. 46 (Oxford, 1978), 131–47. He also argues that the manuscript that preserves *The Dream of the Rood*, the Vercelli Book, provides another meaningful context, the compiler's intention of assembling homiletic and poetic texts on a certain theme. See 'How Did the Vercelli Collector Interpret *The Dream of the Rood?*', *Studies in English Language and Early Literature in Honour of Paul Christophersen*, ed. P.M. Tilling, Occasional Papers in Ling. and Lang. Learning 8 (Coleraine, 1981), pp. 63–104. See also M.P. Richards on the *The Battle of Maldon* manuscript, BL, Cotton Otho A. xii: '*The Battle of Maldon* in its Manuscript Context', *Mediaevalia* 7 (1981), 79–89; J.R. Hall on the Junius manuscript: 'The Old English Epic of Redemption: the Theological Unity of MS Junius 11', *Traditio* 32 (1976), 185–208; and K. Lochrie on the Exeter Book: '*Wyrd* and the Limits of Human Understanding: a Thematic Sequence in the *Exeter Book*', *JEGP* 85 (1986), 323–51.

[66] See Schaeffer, 'Hearing from Books', esp. p. 124. W. Parks argues that the novel's heteroglossia 'has reified dialogue' since as a print genre it cannot participate in the 'person speaking to person' dialogue of oral performance ('The Textualization of Orality in Literary Criticism', in *Vox intexta*, ed. Doane and Pasternack, pp. 146–61, at p. 56.).

Forþon ic geþencan ne mæg   geond þas woruld
for hwan modsefa   min ne gesweorce,
þonne ic eorla lif   eal geondþence . .   (58–60)[67]

But this voice does not dominate the entire composition. Other styles come forward and polyphony dominates the text.

In addition to the first-person *eardstapa*, two other speaking positions direct our attention. These three presentations resemble the speeches of modern fiction in that they are introduced by forms of *cweðan*. But they are neither dramatic nor interactive; rather, they serve to present diverse perspectives on a theme,[68] and the introductions to the speeches tell us how to understand the words that follow. Each is more formalized than 'and then Jane said to Tom' and more substantial than the directives in a play indicating which speech belongs to whom.

In the *eardstapa*'s instance, a three-verse modifier helps to set up the movement that follows. It does not provide a series of details as one would expect in a novel or story but rather a series of variations on one term:

Swa cwæð eardstapa,   earfeþa gemyndig,
wraþra wælsleahta,   winemæga hryre.   (6–7)[69]

The varied terms, 'earfeþa', 'wælsleahta', 'hryre',[70] do not specify who the wanderer is: they specify the topic that the speech will address, and they give weight to the subject.

[67] 'Therefore I am not able to think throughout this world why my mind should not grow dark when I the life of men all consider . . .' Dunning and Bliss's note to this line discusses an ongoing debate about whether 'gesweorce' means 'does grow dark' and is subjunctive only because it is dependent on 'geþencan' or whether 'gesweorce' itself conveys a subjunctive meaning. In my analysis, the 'I' here is speaking about the appropriate way of evaluating the world, not simply how he as one man feels.

[68] See Pope, 'Dramatic Voices'; Greenfield's argument against the idea of dramatic voices, '*Min, Sylf*, and "Dramatic Voices" in *The Wanderer* and *The Seafarer*', *JEGP* 68 (1969), 212–20; and Pope's modification of his position, 'Second Thoughts on the Interpretation of *The Seafarer*', *ASE* 3 (1974), 75–86. See R. E. Bjork, *The Old English Verse Saints' Lives: a Study in Direct Discourse and the Iconography of Style*, McMaster OE Stud. and Texts (Toronto, 1985), for a discussion of how the style used in speeches is iconographically rather than dramatically or naturalistically shaped.

[69] 'So spoke the wanderer, mindful of hardships, of fierce slaughters, (mindful) about the fall of friend-kinsmen.'

[70] As Dunning and Bliss say in their note to line 7, '*winemæga hryre* has been much discussed' (p. 106). The problem is, in Leslie's words, 'In place of MS. *hryre* we should expect after *gemyndig* a genitive form *hryres*, in apposition to *earfeþa* (6) and *wælsleahta*' (7) (p. 67); instead we have a dative form. Dunning and Bliss follow Kershaw in taking it as a comitative dative dependent on 'wælsleahta', translating the phrase, 'remembering the fierce battles accompanying the deaths of his kinsmen' (p. 106). I prefer Leslie's analysis that 'hryre' is 'a dative after *gemyndig*, despite the genitive constructions which precede it', and is dative because that is its usual form in phrases with a dependent genitive (p. 67). According to this analysis, 'winemæga hryre' functions as the third item in a variational series.

The second instance is the most formalized and projects the greatest magnitude:

> Se þonne þisne wealsteal   wise geþohte
> ond þis deorce lif   deope geondþenceð,
> frod in ferðe,   feor oft gemon
> wælsleahta worn,   ond þas word acwið.   (88–91)[71]

It comes at the juncture of the wisdom poetry (65b–87) and the exclamatory lament (92–110). Again, the varied phrases convey the type of situation and the type of thoughts that form the response.[72] The *wealsteal* that this speaker gazes on is not a specific one but one of those that stand in various places on this earth (75–6); it is a synecdoche for 'this dark life' (88) and those two phrases transmute into the 'large number of slaughters' that he remembers. This elaborate figure tells us that the following thoughts come from pondering deeply the dark life that the poem has already spelled out.[73]

The third announcement of a speech is the briefest, 'Swa cwæð snottor on mode, gesæt him sundor æt rune' (111). This one stands out because of its shift from regular to hypermetric verse. As its principal function, it initiates an envelope-style conclusion by recalling 'Swa cwæð eardstapa', the first announcement of speech, which initiated the poem's first movement. Contrary to what would be expected in a dramatic situation, the speech's end does not bring any consequences; it is a prelude, instead, to the poem's conclusion. All told, these indicators of speech function as opportunities to call attention to a new division, to ornament that dividing line, and to use the expansiveness of variation or enumeration to stress certain ideas important to the poem's conceptual structure.

There is another important clue that these speeches are without dramatic dimensions; namely, that the poet has not bothered to make unambiguous their precise dimensions. Poems such as *Beowulf* show many ways of indicating

---

[71] 'He who this wall-foundation has wisely considered and this dark life deeply ponders, wise in heart, far back often remembers the large number of slaughters, and these words says.' Leslie takes this instance of 'feor' as an adverb of time analogous to *Beowulf* 1701a, 'Feor eal gemon' (p. 85).

[72] According to strict definition, 'þisne wealsteal', 'þis deorce lif' and 'wælsleahta worn' are not in variation with each other. The first two noun phrases are in compound phrases that define 'se' (he who), and the third is part of the main clause, the object of the verb 'gemon' (remembers). But all of these terms dwell on the same concept, defining it by shifting the terms that refer to it, which is what variation does.

[73] E.G. Stanley, 'Old English Poetic Diction and the Interpretation of *The Wanderer*, *The Seafarer* and *The Penitent's Prayer*', *Anglia* 73 (1955), 413–66, discusses the ways in Old English poetry in which the thought evokes the flower, not the flower the thought: 'the finest OE. figurative diction is that in which a state of mind or moral concept evokes in the poem the description of a natural phenomenon, associated by the Anglo-Saxons with that mood or moral concept' (pp. 427 and 434).

in audible words (i.e. without punctuation marks) where a speech ends; for example, a *þa* may indicate a new action, a second person's speech may begin with an indication of who that character is and a new verb indicating speech, or a phrase may refer to the words just spoken ('æfter ðam wordum', for example). But *The Wanderer*'s poet has not been so clear, and so scholars have debated whether 'swa cwæð eardstapa' refers back to the poem's first five lines as well as to the words that follow, similarly whether 'swa cwæð snottor on mode' refers to the preceding or following words or both, whether the one who wisely considers 'ond þas word acwið' is a different speaker from the *eardstapa* or is the *eardstapa*'s 'straw man', and exactly where that straw man's speech might end.[74] If, however, we remove the necessity for imagining a dramatic situation that naturalizes the differences in the poem's sections, an announcement of speech can simply mark the end or beginning of a perspective it also characterizes: 'This is the *eardstapa*'s way of perceiving when he is *earfeþa gemyndig*'; 'A person who wisely considers this crumbling wall and this dark life will have this perspective'; 'This was how someone wise in his spirit sees the situation when he has removed himself from society, *sundor æt rune*'.[75] It does not matter much whether the same person speaks these words because the text does not indicate people speaking to each other so much as it indicates speaking positions or perspectives framed and juxtaposed.

None of these introductions sets up a character or voice that controls the text. The composition persists as a disjunct set of movements, thematically associated but open in their thematic interrelationships. Because of its inherent anonymity and the traditional outlines of its polyphony, it participates with any number of other compositions in its intertextual play of meaning. This interplay cannot be limited even by the name of an author. With modernist polyphony, readers use the name of the author to compare several texts and build a sense of an author's distinctive handling of polyphony, managing to construct a sense of Woolf or Joyce though in a way different from monological texts. In Old English manuscript poetry, with the one exception of Cynewulf's texts, this author function cannot restrict the associations an audience makes in understanding a composition.[76]

---

[74] As Stanley says, such precision is beside the point: 'The poet is writing on the subjects of mutability and misery, and there are two ways open to him: direct moralizing or the use of imagery. He uses both in this poem.' The wanderer and the wise man serve him in his direct moralizing, but 'it is the poet's teaching, whoever may be speaking' (*ibid*. p. 463). For a syntactical analysis, see B. Mitchell, 'Some Syntactical Problems'.

[75] For this reading, see Leslie's note on this line (*The Wanderer*, p. 89).

[76] On the author function, see M. Foucault, 'What Is an Author?' *Textual Strategies*, ed. and trans. Harari, pp. 141–60, who says that the concept allows us to construct 'a relationship among the texts . . . a relationship of homogeneity, filiation, authentification of some texts by the use of others, reciprocal explication, or concomitant utilization', all of which contribute to the circle out of which we construct the author.

The manuscript layout itself shows the weakness of boundaries that divide compositions. There poetic texts are only lightly separated from those that precede and follow, and the distinction between a poem and a section of a poem barely exists.[77] In the Exeter Book the punctuation for sections of the longer poems about Christ, Guthlac, the Phoenix and Juliana looks the same as that distinguishing many of the shorter poems from each other (the beginning of *The Wanderer* has the same size capitalized word as the sections in *Juliana*). Of course, no poets' names and no titles mark the beginnings of any of these poetic divisions (Cynewulf integrates the runes pointing to his name into sentences some fifty verses before the poem's end and sixteen lines before the end of the folio and its all-capitalized 'AMEN'). Verbal framing rather than punctuation and page layout communicates a performance's beginning and end. *Juliana*, the composition before *The Wanderer*, draws to a close because of what the words say:

> forgif us mægna god þæt we þine onsyne æþelinga wyn
> milde gemeten onþa mæran tid:-AMEN:ᚷ[78]   (76r)

After these words, 'Oft him anhaga' at the top of 76v must start something new. The scribe's use of all capitals for *oft* confirms this impression.[79] Two-thirds of the way down 78r we pick up an echo of 'swa cwæð eardstapa' (6a), the phrase that marked the end of *The Wanderer*'s introduction, and the following verses reinforce the sense that the performance is closing:

> Swa cwæð snottor onmode gesæt him sundor æt
> rune til biþ seþe his treowe gehealdeþ nesceal næfre
> his torn torycene beorn ofhis breostum acyþan nem
> þe he ærþa bote cunne eorl mid elne gefremman wel
> biþ þam þe him are seceð frofre tofæder on heofonum
> þær us eal seo fæstnung stondeð:-:ᚷ[80]   (78r)

---

[77] See F. C. Robinson's discussion of this phenomenon in '"The Rewards of Piety": Two Old English Poems in Their Manuscript Context', *Hermeneutics and Medieval Culture*, ed. P. J. Gallacher and H. Damico (Albany, NY, 1989), pp. 193–200. He asks us to consider *An Exhortation to Christian Living* and *A Summons to Prayer* as 'one continuous text rather than a pair of separate poems' (p. 195) so that he can 'illustrate how important it can be to reconsider long-studied Old English texts in light of their manuscript settings' (p. 198).

[78] 'Grant us, God of hosts, that we may your face, joy of nobles, find mild in that great time. Amen.'

[79] The 'O' is two lines high and has moderate ornamentation, the 'F' one and a half lines, the 'T' one line. All three letters are bolder than those that follow. This description is based on observation of the manuscript's facsimile.

[80] 'So spoke the one wise in heart, sat apart at his counsel. Good is he who his truth keeps. A man must never his care too quickly from his breast make known unless he beforehand the remedy may know, the earl [know] how to perform it with courage. Well it is for him who seeks grace, comfort at the Father in the heavens where for us all that security stands.'

121

As was true for the preceding text, a simple turning towards hope for eternal joy concludes the performance. These endings, so much like each other and so much like the endings of many other poetic and homiletic texts, are not organically connected to the middle parts of the performances. What comes between beginnings and ends differs in length and in content, and the meanings we make of these collocations alsó differ.

The fluid interrelationships among compositions, their polyphonic structure and their anonymity function as connected elements in a cultural matrix. In some ways these qualities contribute to the distance between Anglo-Saxon poetic experiences and our experiences of their extant texts. We cannot recover a full sense of a composition's contexts, verbal and lived, and we cannot erase the other contexts of intervening centuries. That only texts filtered through the church survive increases our distance. In other ways, modernist aesthetics and critical theory may bring us closer to the earliest English texts than we have been since Anglo-Saxon studies began. We might now be ready to accept these surprisingly modernistic texts as they are, but doing so requires that we recognize historical and aesthetic discontinuities as well as similarities. For example, we must remember that our ideas of authorship are an historical as well as a semiotic phenomenon, a concept that did not jell before the eighteenth century and the institution of copyright laws.[81] We must accept the specificity of a manuscript text without insisting on qualities that are unique to poet and poem. As a corollary, we must stop looking for an original text that the manuscript badly represents,[82] and instead look for multiple ways of composing and performing a text. We should accept the poetry's anonymity and polyphony and add to our critical vocabulary 'harmony' and 'virtuosity'.[83]

[81] On the development of the concept and the law, see M. Rose, 'The Author as Proprietor: *Donaldson v. Becket* and the Genealogy of Modern Authorship', *Representations* 23 (Summer 1988), 51–85.

[82] See Dagenais, 'That Bothersome Residue' and Doane, 'Oral Texts, Intertexts, and Intratexts', for further arguments supporting this position.

[83] I must thank an anonymous reader for the term 'harmony' and H. Tartar of Stanford University Press for 'virtuosity'. I also wish to thank D.G. Calder, J. Carlson, A.N. Doane, F.C. Gardiner and J. Grossman for their comments on earlier versions of this essay.

The geographic list of *Solomon and Saturn II*

KATHERINE O'BRIEN O'KEEFFE

Solomon and Saturn II, the second verse dialogue between Solomon and Saturn in Cambridge, Corpus Christi College 422, has long enjoyed a rather dubious reputation as an exotic work. In part, the poem suffers a guilt by association with the two other Solomonic dialogues in the manuscript, both of which are fanciful treatments of the powers of the Pater Noster. Kemble's 1848 edition of *Solomon and Saturn II* formed part of an ambitious survey of the sources and analogues of the later, Latin Solomon and Marculf dialogues.[1] Although the subject matter of *Solomon and Saturn II* ranges widely from bizarre monsters to proverbial wisdom, Menner's 1941 edition influenced the modern reception of the work by presenting the poem in a predominantly 'oriental' context.[2] Menner's learned introduction to both the Solomon and Saturn verse dialogues focused on the mass of exotic legends associated with Solomon. In his opinion, both Solomon and Saturn poems were 'dependent on lost Solomonic Christian dialogues in Latin'.[3]

Without a doubt *Solomon and Saturn II* is a distinctly peculiar poem, and it is curious in another way as well. In its opening lines the poem presents itself as an oral contest between two formidable heroes, Solomon and Saturn:

> Hwæt, ic flitan gefrægn   on fyrndagum
> modgleawe men,   middangeardes ræswan,
> gewesan ymbe hira wisdom.[4]   (170–2a)

Its exchanges are recognizably agonistic in tone, and its often riddling wisdom is situational rather than abstract, and aggregative rather than analytic – to use Walter Ong's now familiar definition of the oral mindset.[5] Such features suggestive of orality notwithstanding, the poem contains an extraordinary geographic *list* of places which Saturn has visited.[6] The present study examines two implications of this list: that the nature of the list implies that it

---

[1] *The Dialogue of Solomon and Saturnus*, ed. J. M. Kemble (London, 1848).
[2] *The Poetical Dialogues of Solomon and Saturn*, ed. R. J. Menner (New York and London, 1941), pp. 21–35.
[3] *Ibid.* p. 26. Unless otherwise indicated, all references to the text of *Solomon and Saturn II* are to this edition.
[4] 'Lo, I have heard that wise men contended in the days of old, princes of the world contended about their wisdom.'
[5] W. J. Ong, *Orality and Literacy: the Technologizing of the Word* (London and New York, 1982), pp. 31–77.   [6] Cf. *ibid.* p. 42: 'An oral culture has no vehicle so neutral as a list.'

was compiled in writing, and that the geographic knowledge underlying the list suggests that the origins of *Solomon and Saturn II* are less exotic than has previously been thought.

The best way to highlight the character of this geographic list is to compare it with its more famous counterpart in *Widsith*. The differences are instructive. In *Widsith*, peoples and places are arranged in catalogues distinguishable by their controlling verbs.[7] These verbs shape the catalogues into narratives: the phrase 'ic wæs mid' structures the catalogue of tribes which Widsith claims to have visited; the phrase '[name] *weold* [tribe]' shapes a catalogue of kings; and 'sohte ic' governs a catalogue commemorating heroes. Classifying the catalogues in this way draws attention to the distinction between the mode of listing in *Widsith* and that in *Solomon and Saturn II*. In *Widsith*, geographic information is inseparable from its narrative framework and is presented as a story in series governed by a verb. Normally the verb in question governs two or three verse lines. For example:

Swa ic geondferde fela   fremdra londa
geond ginne grund.   Godes ond yfles
þær ic cunnade   cnosle bidæled,
freomægum feor   folgade wide.
Forþon ic mæg singan   ond secgan spell,
mænan fore mengo   in meoduhealle
hu me cynegode   cystum dohten.
Ic wæs mid Hunum   ond mid Hreðgotum,
mid Sweom ond mid Geatum   ond mid Suþdenum.
Mid Wenlum ic wæs ond mid Wærnum   ond mid wicingum.
Mid Gefþum ic wæs ond mid Winedum   ond mid Gefflegum.
Mid Englum ic wæs ond mid Swæfum   ond mid Ænenum.[8]   (50–61)

In this passage, the names of peoples are fixed within a travel-narrative in which both people and places are provided an appropriate ethical situation ('godes ond yfles / þær ic cunnade'). The heavy parallelism of this catalogue

---

7 For a study of the catalogue in *Widsith*, see N. Howe, *The Old English Catalogue Poems*, Anglistica 23 (Copenhagen, 1985), esp. 174–5.
8 *The Exeter Book*, ed. G.P. Krapp and E.V.K. Dobbie, ASPR 3 (New York and London, 1936), 151. Subsequent citations of *Widsith* are from this edition. 'So I travelled many foreign lands over the spacious earth. There, deprived of my kin, I experienced good and evil, far from my kinsmen I was in service in many places. Therefore, I may sing and recount a tale, declare before many in the meadhall how the noble benefited me with generosity. I was with the Huns and with the *Hreðgotan*, with the Swedes and with the Geats and with the South-Danes. With the Vendils I was and with the *Wærne* and with the Vikings. With the *Gefthan* I was and with the Wends and with the *Gefflegan*. With the Angles I was and with the Swabians and with the *Ænenas*.' On the names of these tribes, see *Widsith*, ed. K. Malone, Anglistica 13 (Copenhagen, 1962), 92.

(which continues thus for another twenty-seven lines, now and again relieved by a further bit of narrative) works mnemonically.

In the poem's account of (predominantly) Northern peoples, framed by the fictive wanderings of the scop, Widsith, there are two short sections especially pertinent to the material in the Saturn list. Thus we are told that the poet travelled in Asia:

> Mid Israhelum ic wæs ond mid Exsyringum,
> mid Ebreum ond mid Indeum ond mid Egyptum.
> Mid Moidum ic wæs ond mid Persum[9] (82–4a)

In his edition, Malone regards lines 82–3 as an interpolation and reads 'Moidum' as 'residents of the Danish Island of Møn' and 'Persum' as a scribal misunderstanding of 'Wersum'.[10] Similarly, he rejects lines 14–17 on Alexander, regarding both (on the basis of metrics) as being the work of the same person.[11] Malone's discomfiture with the lines he rejects stems from his conception of the poem's genesis and his belief that its unity of interest lay in the cataloguing of Germanic peoples.[12] Whatever one's opinion on theories of interpolation, both the eruption of Asian place-names into a text otherwise focused on northern Europe and the subsequent reference to Alexander argue a compelling interest in Asian material at some point in the textual history of *Widsith*. They also suggest that the content of the geographic list in *Solomon and Saturn II* may have a more mundane origin than lost Solomonic legend.[13] In *Widsith*, the presentation of geographic information within a narrative framework recalls several features characteristic of oral thought: the redundancy of its controlling verbs, its additive style of presenting information and its situational 'location' of information in a frame of experience, to name an obvious few. This is not to suggest, however, that such features necessarily indicate oral composition; they merely make it impossible to rule out. By

---

[9] 'I was with the Israelites and the Assyrians, with the Hebrews and with the Indians and with the Egyptians. I was with the Medes and with the Persians.'

[10] *Widsith*, ed. Malone, pp. 45–7.

[11]

> Þara wæs Hwala hwile selast,
> ond Alexandreas ealra ricost
> monna cynnes, ond he mæst geþah
> þara þe ic ofer foldan gefrægen hæbbe. (14–17)

See also *Widsith*, ed. Malone, pp. 37–8.

[12] *Widsith*, ed. Malone, p. 112: 'The author of *Widsith* was a cleric, at home in vernacular poetry sacred and profane . . . With the accuracy of a scholar and lover of the past he put three old thulas into the mouth of his scop of olden days and in the added parts (which he himself composed) he kept strictly to the limits of the heroic age . . .'

[13] In the Old English poem *Daniel*, for example, we find a particular interest in the rule of the Chaldeans and their subsequent overthrow by the Medes and Persians.

contrast, the simple listing of places in *Solomon and Saturn II* one after the other makes original oral composition unlikely.[14]

Although the opening of *Solomon and Saturn II* presents itself as a contest between wise men in which they debate about their wisdom, the text leaves little question but that Solomon will be the victor. On the conceptual level, the description of Solomon as 'bremra' ('the more famous', 173b) indicates his advantage in the debate, and on the visual level, the scribe of Cambridge, Corpus Christi College 422, acknowledges this perception about half-way through the dialogue by writing Solomon's name in ornamented capitals while leaving Saturn's name in plain small capitals.[15] Saturn, however, is given credentials to make the debate appear a challenge, for he is learned in books and is very widely travelled in the East. The lands he has visited make up the list in question:

Land eall geondhwearf:

Ind(ea) mer(e),	(Ea)st-Corsias,
Persea rice,	Palestinion,
Niniuen ceastre,	and Norð-Predan,
Meda maððumselas,	Marculfes eard;
Saulus rice,	swa he suð ligeð
ymbe Geallboe	and ymb Geador norð,
Filistina flet,	fæsten Creca,
wudu Egipta,	wæter Mathea[n],
cludas Coreffes,	Caldea rice,
Creca cræftas,	cynn Arabia,
lare Libia,	lond Syria
Bitðinia,	Buðanasan,
Pamphilia,	Pores gemære,
Macedonia,	Mesopotamie,
Cappadocia;	Cristes [eþel],
Hierycho, Galilea,	Hierusa[lem].[16]	(176b–92b)

The list breaks off with the first three syllables of 'Jerusalem' at the bottom of CCCC 422, p. 13. Because the text on the verso was thoroughly scraped off and

[14] On decontextualized lists as a characteristic feature of early writing, see J. Goody, *The Interface between the Written and the Oral* (Cambridge, 1987), p. 99. See also J. Goody, *The Domestication of the Savage Mind* (Cambridge, 1977), p. 75.

[15] See K. O'Brien O'Keeffe, *Visible Song: Transitional Literacy in Old English Verse*, CSASE 4 (Cambridge, 1990), 71–3.

[16] Following Menner's conventions, italics signal emendations for existing letters, parentheses mark emendations of illegible letters, and square brackets indicate conjectures for scribal omissions. 'He travelled throughout all lands: the Indian ocean, the East *Corsias*, the kingdom of the Persians, Palestine, the city Nineveh, and the North-Predans [Parthians?], the treasure-halls of the Medes, Marculf's native land, Saul's kingdom, as it lies south at Mt

replaced with a Latin formula for excommunication, there is no way of knowing if the list continued much further. However, one curious feature is immediately apparent upon reading the surviving list. Syntactically, the thirty-two items in the list are in apposition to *land* and should be variations on it. Yet not every item is a land; some are people, and some, oddly, are neither people nor places but abstractions such as 'Creca *cræftas*' and '*lare* Libya'. Towards the end of what remains of the list there are simply place-names without modifiers of any sort. Lying behind the statement of Saturn's qualifications as Solomon's opponent in the supposedly oral exchange of riddles and wisdom is apparently a written list. The source(s) of such a list could potentially reveal much about the method of compilation which produced the list and the learning which made it possible.

Menner did not speculate on the source of places which Saturn was supposed to have visited. He cites occasionally a biblical passage and now and again the Eusebius-Jerome *Onomasticon*.[17] In his notes to the poem, Friedrich Wild cites passages in the biblical books of Kings where many of the listed places are mentioned.[18] While the list is primarily composed of locations in Asia Minor, it nonetheless reflects some interesting learning, quite possibly deriving from several different texts.

Knowledge of geography was transmitted to the early Middle Ages by a variety of sources. The richest, most varied and most influential of these was Pliny's *Naturalis historia*, an encyclopaedic work of the first century treating geography, natural history and assorted marvels.[19] A much briefer (and slightly earlier) treatment of geography and marvels was available in Pomponius Mela's *Chorographia*.[20] Julius Solinus's widely popular *Collectanea rerum memorabilium* (s. iii?)[21] derived most of its information from Pliny, and to a lesser extent, from Mela. The anonymous treatise *De situ orbis* draws on Solinus and Martianus Capella.[22] A rather different, though equally derivative, treatise, whose intent was to present Roman measurements of the earth, was

---

Gilboa and north at Gadara, the dwelling of the Philistines, the stronghold of the Greeks, the forest of Egypt, the waters of Midian, the rocks of Horeb, the kingdom of the Chaldeans, the skills of the Greeks, the race of Arabia, the learning of Libya, the land of Syria, Bithinia, *Buthanasan*, Pamphilia, Porus's borders, Macedonia, Mesopotamia, Cappadocia, Christ's [?native land], Jericho, Galilea, Jerusalem . . .'

[17] See *The Poetical Dialogues*, ed. Menner, pp. 118–20, and *The Anglo-Saxon Minor Poems*, ed. E.V.K. Dobbie, ASPR 6 (New York and London, 1942), 164.

[18] F. Wild, *Solomon und Saturn*, Österreichische Akademie der Wissenschaften, phil.-hist. Klasse: Sitzungsberichte 243 (Vienna, 1964), 40–4.

[19] *Pliny. Natural History*, ed. H. Rackham *et al.*, 10 vols. (Cambridge, MA, 1938–62).

[20] *Pomponii Melae de Chorographia*, ed. C. Frick (Leipzig, 1880).

[21] *C. Iulii Solini Collectanea Rerum Memorabilium*, ed. T. Mommsen, 2nd ed. (Berlin, 1895).

[22] *Anonymi de Situ Orbis*, ed. M. Manitius (Stuttgart, 1884).

compiled in the early ninth century by the Irishman Dicuil.[23] In addition to these works, a number of geographic epitomes were enormously influential. Orosius opened his *Historiae aduersum paganos* (I.2) with a geography of the world which was independent of Pliny, perhaps derived through intermediate sources from Strabo.[24] Isidore, drawing on Orosius, Pliny and Solinus, among others, dedicated the fourteenth book of his *Etymologiae* to a geographic description of the earth and its three regions.[25] The sixth book of Martianus Capella's *De nuptiis Philologiae et Mercurii* condenses a standard outline of geography mainly from Solinus and Pliny.[26] Various anonymous texts abstracted from these works provide lists of places, peoples, towns, rivers, mountains.[27] And at least some Greek geography was available in translation through the verse of Avienus and Priscian.[28]

An additional text, one which I will argue is connected to the Saturn list, requires attention in this survey of the sources of early medieval geographic information. The *Cosmographia* of Aethicus Ister is an extraordinarily peculiar work of cosmography, ethnography and geography, purporting to be composed by one Aethicus the Istrian and translated from the Greek by St Jerome.[29] Although early editors accepted Aethicus as an author who pre-dated St Jerome, the work, which appears to draw heavily on the *Etymologiae*, must obviously post-date Isidore.[30] It is unclear when the text got to England.

---

23 *Dicuili Liber De Mensura Orbis Terrae*, ed. J. J. Tierney, Scriptores Latini Hiberniae 6 (Dublin, 1967), 27: 'As Parthey points out in his preface, Dicuil personally consulted, apart from the work of the commissioners of Theodosius and the *Cosmography* of Caesar, only Isidore, Pliny, Priscian, and Solinus.'

24 *Pauli Orosii Historiarum Aduersum Paganos Libri VII*, ed. C. Zangemeister (Leipzig, 1889).

25 *Isidori Hispalensis Episcopi Etymologiarum siue Originum, libri XX*, ed. W. M. Lindsay, 2 vols. (Oxford, 1911).

26 *Martianus Capella. De Nuptiis Philologiae et Mercurii*, ed. J. Willis (Leipzig, 1983). For a translation, see W. H. Stahl and R. Johnson, *Martianus Capella and the Seven Liberal Arts*, 2 vols. (New York, 1971–7), esp. vol. II.

27 See *Geographi Latini Minores*, ed. A. Riese (Heilbrun, 1878).

28 Both poets were translating the Greek coastal survey of Dionysus Periegetes. See *La Périégèse de Priscien*, ed. P. Van de Woestijne (Bruges, 1953) and *La Descriptio Orbis Terrae d'Avienus*, ed. P. Van de Woestijne (Bruges, 1961). On the contraction of geographic information available to early Christian Europe, see M. L. W. Laistner, 'The Decay of Geographical Knowledge and the Decline of Exploration, A.D. 300–500', in *Travel and Travellers of the Middle Ages*, ed. A. P. Newton ([n.p.], 1926), pp. 19–38, at 23 and 26; see also C. R. Beazley, *The Dawn of Modern Geography*, 2 vols. (Oxford, 1897–1901) I, 244.

29 *Die Kosmographie des Istrier Aithikos im lateinischen Auszüge des Hieronymus*, ed. H. Wuttke (Leipzig, 1853).

30 For defence of Aethicus as a genuine author, see H. Wuttke, *Die Aechtheit des Auszugs aus der Kosmographie des Aithikos* (Leipzig, 1854). K. Hillkowitz, *Zur Kosmographie des Aethicus*, 2 vols. (Cologne, 1934 and Frankfurt am Main, 1973) I, 69, proposes a date for composition at the end of the eighth century. H. Löwe (*Virgil von Salzburg und die Kosmographie des Aethicus Ister*, Akademie der Wissenschaften und der Literatur in Mainz, Abhandlung der geistes- und

The earliest surviving manuscript known to have been copied in England is Leiden, Bibliotheek der Rijksuniversiteit, Scaliger 69, whose copying T. A. M. Bishop dates to the second half of the tenth century and locates at St Augustine's, Canterbury.[31] A second English manuscript is London, British Library, Cotton Vespasian B. x, fols. 31–124, and this he dates s. x/xi, suggesting that it was copied at Worcester, perhaps from the manuscript now in Leiden.[32] Neither manuscript divides the text into books, but both have glossed headings in the margin.

The contents of the *Cosmographia* (like its vocabulary and style) are fairly strange and rather disorganized. The work begins conventionally with the creation of the world, treating heaven, earth and hell, the sun, the moon and the stars. In Wüttke's edition, based on the earliest known manuscript, the work is divided into six books. The second begins an account of Aethicus's journeys as he travels about the world, beginning with Hibernia, Britain and western regions, and then moving to Germany. The third book claims (in a heading) to include peoples not in the Bible. Also included here is Alexander material. The fourth book treats various kinds of ships. The fifth includes more unknown peoples and places, mostly in Asia. Treated here in lengthy fashion are griffins and the best technique for catching and killing them. The sixth book deals at length with Greece, further Alexander material, and a final summary of places in Asia which Aethicus visited.

While the widely popular works treated above collected, re-arranged and transmitted a body of essentially post-classical geographic information, another sort of geographic writings, itineraries, provided descriptions of important places of pilgrimage in the Holy Land.[33] Such itineraries range in form from simple lists of staging places on the pilgrimage to narrative

---

sozialwissenschaftlichen Klasse 11 (1951), 903–88) identifies Virgil of Salzburg as the author of the *Cosmographia*, although this identification has been disputed in recent years. Michael Richter discusses 'Hiberno-Latin' elements in the *Cosmographia* in 'Sprachliche Untersuchung der Kosmographie des Aethicus Ister', *Virgil von Salzburg: Missionar und Gelehrter*, ed. H. Dopsch and R. Juffinger (Salzburg, 1985), pp. 147–53. For an evaluation of the current state of Aethicus scholarship, see M. Herren, 'Wozu diente die Fälschung der Kosmographie des Aethicus?', in *Lateinische Kultur im VIII. Jahrhundert*, ed. A. Lehner and W. Berschin (St Ottilien, 1989), pp. 145–59, at 146 and 159.

[31] *Aethici Istrici Cosmographia Vergilio Salisburgensi rectius adscripta. Codex Leidensis Scaligeranus 69*, ed. T. A. M. Bishop, Umbrae Codicum Occidentalium 10 (Amsterdam, 1966). M. Lapidge, 'The Present State of Anglo-Latin Studies', in *Insular Latin Studies: Papers on Latin Texts and Manuscripts of the British Isles, 550–1066*, ed. M. W. Herren, Papers in Med. Stud. 1 (Toronto, 1981), 45–82, at 57–8, regards it 'very probable' that Vatican City, Biblioteca Apostolica Vaticana, Reg. lat. 1260 was the exemplar for Scaliger 69.

[32] *Aethici Istrici Cosmographia*, ed. Bishop, p. xii.

[33] For a selection, see *Itineraria et Alia Geographica*, ed. P. Geyer *et al.*, 2 vols. CCSL 175–6 (Turnhout, 1965).

accounts of the journey and the significance of the places visited.[34] Yet another source of specifically contextualized geographic information on the Holy Land is found in primarily exegetical works. Pre-eminent among these is Jerome's *De situ et nominibus locorum Hebraicorum*, a geographic dictionary arranged by letter and subdivided by book of the Bible.[35] Bede redacted this work for his short exposition of biblical place names.[36] A second, important geographic dictionary by Bede, his *Nomina regionum atque locorum de actibus apostolorum*, drew on Orosius, Isidore and Pliny, among others.[37]

This brief survey of the more common sources of standard information on geography, by no means exhaustive, suggests at once the popularity of geographic information and the conservative nature of its preservation. From the end of the Roman empire up to the time of the Crusades, the same information on places, peoples and locations was rearranged, rephrased or recombined, but essentially repeated, from text to text. While the repetitive character of early medieval geographic writing complicates any analysis of the sources of the *Solomon and Saturn* list, two features of the list give helpful directions – the unusual combination of individual place-names and the choice of descriptive detail within half-lines. There is probably little significance in the overall arrangement of the list, since the requirements of alliteration have mostly determined the ordering of places. But two groupings of biblical names in the poem parallel similar groupings in a potential source and should be considered evidence of its use.

Three popular works suggest themselves immediately as potential sources for the greater part of the list of Saturn's travels. Orosius's *Historiae adversum paganos* recommends itself as a source generally by its popularity in the Middle Ages and particularly by King Alfred's selection of it for translation as one of the works most important for men to know.[38] As was traditional, Orosius divided the world into three regions (Europe, Asia and Africa) and then offered a brief geographical survey, rather atypically presenting Africa first. In Zangemeister's edition of the Latin text, there are thirteen places listed in

---

[34] See M. B. Campbell, *The Witness and the Other World: Exotic European Travel Writing, 400–1600* (Ithaca, NY and London, 1988), pp. 20–33, on some narrative features in Egeria's *Peregrinatio*.

[35] PL 23, 903–76.

[36] *Nomina locorum ex beati Hieronimi presbiteri et Flavi Iosephi collecta opusculis*, ed. D. Hurst, CCSL 119 (Turnhout, 1962), 273–87.

[37] *Nomina regionum atque locorum de Actibus Apostolorum*, ed. M. L. W. Laistner, CCSL 121 (Turnhout, 1983), 167–78. Bede's *De locis sanctis* is a description of pilgrim sites heavily derivative of Adomnán, Jerome, Hegesippus and pseudo-Eucherius; it is ed. J. Fraipont, CCSL 175 (Turnhout, 1965), 245–80, at 247.

[38] On the popularity of Orosius's *Historia*, see *The Old English Orosius*, ed. J. Bately, EETS ss 6 (London, 1980), lv–lvi.

Orosius's geographic survey (I.2) which match the identifiable places in *Solomon and Saturn II*.[39] The Old English version offers eleven matching places mentioned close together in the first chapter and several others scattered in other parts of the Old English translation.[40] The possibility that *Solomon and Saturn II* had a connection with the Old English Orosius is intriguing, but both orthographic and lexical evidence are ambiguous and put such a connection in doubt. One orthographic peculiarity of the OE Orosius as preserved in London, British Library, Add. 47967 (s. x[1]) is the frequent substitution of 'ð' for 'd'.[41] While the form of 'Meðas' in the OE Orosius shows replacement of intervocalic 'd' by 'ð', *Solomon and Saturn II* maintains the Latin 'd' in 'Meda' (180a). Yet 'Mathea[n]' (for Vulgate *Madian*, the land of the Midianites, 184b) in *Solomon and Saturn II* shows precisely the opposite shift from voiced dental stop to voiced dental fricative. While the writing of 'Bithinia' as 'Pitðinia' in *Solomon and Saturn II* also shows the devoicing of 'b' (which Bately cites as characteristic of the Lauderdale text), the single instance of 'Biþþinia' in the Old English Orosius preserves the 'b'.[42] A suggestive piece of lexical evidence is offered by the half-line 'Creca cræftas' (186a). The only other combination of 'Creca' and 'cræft[]' in the surviving records of Old English occurs in the Old English Orosius. Yet, the appearance of 'Creca cræftum' in the Orosius occurs in a very different context and at considerable distance from the geographic survey of I.2.[43] 'Indea mere' (177a) may

---

[39] In Asia: India, Persia, Media, Mesopotamia, Chaldea, Arabia, Cappadocia, Aegyptus, Syria and Palestina; in Europe: Macedonia; in Africa: Libya Cyrenaica. 'Attica' occurs in the first list, but 'Graecia' is not named until later (I.11). Other relevant names mentioned later in the *Historiae* include Pamphylia (III.23), Bithinia (IV.20) and Hierusalem (VII.2). Porus, king of India, is treated with Alexander (III.19). Crete, Corsica and Parthia all occur in the list – an interesting fact in view of potential emendations for lines 177b, 179b and 183b.

[40] See *Old English Orosius*, ed. Bately, pp. 9–12 and 18–20. In order of occurrence: [in Asia] India (p. 9.29), *Persiða* (p. 10.3), *Meðia* (p. 10.3), *Caldea* (p. 10.11), Mesopotamia (p. 10.11), Arabia (p. 10.15), *Egypte* (p. 10.18), *Palestina* (p. 10.20), Syria (p. 10.21), *Capodocia* (p. 10.22); [in Europe] *Creca lond* (p. 12.21) (and separated by the report of Ohthere and Wulfstan); *Macedonie* (p. 18.10); [in Africa] *Libya Cirimacia* (p. 19.33). Later in the Old English text are found: *Pamphilia* (p. 77.28), *Biþþinia* (p. 118.7), *Hierusalem* (p. 125.24) and *Poros* (p. 72.13–23). The names suggested by emendation – Parthia, Crete and Corsica – all occur in the early list (pp. 10.3, 20.29 and 21.12).

[41] *Old English Orosius*, ed. Bately, p. cx and J. Bately, 'The Old English Orosius: the Question of Dictation', *Anglia* 84 (1966), 255–304, at 294, where she suggests that the dictator of the OE Orosius 'may well have been' a Welshman.

[42] *Old English Orosius*, ed. Bately, p. 118.7. In *Solomon and Saturn II*, the writing of 'Cofor' for 'Chebar' and 'Choreff[es]' for the genitive of 'Choreb' shows a normal use of 'f' to represent intervocalic Latin 'b'. See T. Pyles, 'The Pronunciation of Latin Learned Loan Words and Foreign Words in Old English', *PMLA* 58 (1943), 891–910, at 901.

[43] 'Creca cræftum' appears, in the Old English Orosius, in an account of Hercules's campaign against the Amazons: '. . . hie gecuron Ercol þone ent þæt he sceolde mid eallum Creca cræftum beswican . . .' (ed. Bately, p. 30.14–16).

conceivably reflect 'India gemæro' in the OE Orosius, but it is equally true that the Indian ocean also appears in a wide variety of other geographic lists.[44] In any case, there are other texts which offer richer lists.

A slightly stronger possibility for the source of the places mentioned in Saturn's list is Isidore's *Etymologiae* XIV.ii–v. In his treatment of the geography of Asia (and subsequently of Europe), Isidore offers among others eighteen places named in Saturn's list of travels. In order of appearance these places are: India, Mesopotamia, Media, Persia, Chaldea, Arabia, Syria, Egypt, Cappadocia, Palaestine, *Philistim*,[45] Jerusalem, Galilea, Bithynia, Pamphilia; Libya (here referring to the whole of Africa); Greece and Macedonia. The last two places are found in the text quite far away from the places grouped under the heading 'Asia' and are treated with Europe.[46]

A survey of the popular geographic compilations shows that most of the places listed above occur routinely in outlines of Asian topography. It also makes clear that missing from this sub-group are the places which Saturn visited in the Holy Land. A useful supplement to whatever text supplied the core of the list in *Solomon and Saturn II* may well be the *Nomina locorum ex beati Hieronimi presbiteri et Flaui Iosephi collecta opusculis*, a work which Hurst has attributed to Bede on the basis of its appearance as part of the two earliest manuscripts of Bede's commentary on the book of Samuel.[47] This brief collection of extracts, principally drawn from Jerome's *De situ*, is an alphabetical list and explanation of names in Kings. Two circumstances suggest that this short collection, rather than Jerome's longer work, may lie behind part of our geographic list. Bede's collection concentrates on the book of Kings, which is of particular relevance to this narrative about Solomon, and it groups the relevant place-names closely together. Particularly suggestive is the close juxtaposition of 'Gelboe' and 'Gadar' in the *Nomina locorum*. 'Gabaath', defined as 'domus Saul', immediately precedes 'Gelboe' in Bede's alphabetical list, and 'Gadar' is only some six entries away.[48] Further, of the entire list of

---

[44] *Old English Orosius*, ed. Bately, p. 9.29. The expression is fairly common; for example, Mela, 'ex illo oceano quem Indicum diximus' (I.9); Avienus: 'indicum ab eois mare feruere . . .' (line 153); and Orosius, *Historiae*, 'Indico oceano' (I.2.15–16).

[45] Cf. *Etym*. IX.ii.20 and 58. Here 'Philistim' is a city, whereas 'Philistiim' refers to the people. Hence 'Filistina flet'?

[46] Parthia is mentioned in connection with Media. Crete and Corsica are mentioned under the heading 'De insulis' in *Etym*. XIV.vi.15–16 and 41.

[47] CCSL 119, v.

[48] In Bede, the relevant entry on Saul simply reads: 'Gabaath in tribu Beniamin ubi erat domus Saul' (CCSL 119, 280). This definition significantly reduces the information contained in Jerome's *De situ* (PL 23, 948).

place-names beginning with 'g', these two are linked by orientation from Scythopolis.[49] The result is the neat juxtaposition of lines 181–2 in *Solomon and Saturn II* where Saul's kingdom extends south from Mt Gilboa and north from Gadara. Similarly, the same *Nomina locorum* also juxtapose the waters of 'Madian' and the rocks of Horeb found in 184b–5a.[50]

To this point the list of Saturn's travels has been considered simply as a collection of names, but a number of half-lines in *Solomon and Saturn II* attribute particular details to the places cited, and these details broaden our awareness of the reading behind the list. 'Cynn Arabia' (186b) illustrates the complexity of the problem before us. That the combination of *cynn* with *Arabia* is more than metrical filler seems indicated by the unusual form of the half-line. In every other instance where *cyn(n)* is combined with the genitive plural of a people's name, *cyn(n)* occupies second position in the half-line.[51] Most of these half lines are Sievers's Type E. 'Cynn Arabia' is the only instance of a half-line which places *cyn(n)* in first position.[52] One might conclude from these facts that 'cynn Arabia' is no simple formulaic combination, but rather owes its form to a desire to accommodate specific detail. The common geographic surveys listed earlier, however, do not provide much information on the peoples of Arabia as such. The Old English Orosius appears to confuse its translation, and lists 'þæt land Arabia 7 Sabei 7 Eudomane'.[53] Both Pliny and

---

49 CCSL 119, 280.269–70: 'Gelboe montes alienigenarum in sexto lapide a Scythopoli in quibus et uicus est grandis qui appellatur Gelbus'; p. 280.295–6: 'Gadar urbs trans Iordanen contra Scythopolim et Tiberiadem ad orientalem plagam sita in monte . . .'
50 CCSL, 119, 277. Bede is using Jerome's compilation (PL 23, 935). If Menner's emendation of MS '*claudas* Coreffes' to 'cludas Coreffes' is correct, then the 'rocks of Horeb' echoes Jerome's explanation of the word as it occurs in Judges: 'Sur Choreb, quod interpretatur, petra Choreb' (PL 23, 969). 'Petra Choreb' may well have been available to the Old English poet in a marginal gloss in one of his source manuscripts.
51 These are: 'Caldea cyn': *Dan* 42a; 'Egypta cyn': *Exo* 145a; 'Isra(h)ela cyn(n)': *Aʒ* 147b, *Dan* 23a and 69a, *Ex* 198b and 265b, *PPs* 77.59 3a and 80.13 1b; 'Faraones cyn': *Exo* 14b; 'swa he Fresena cyn': *Beo* 1093b; 'Isra(h)eles cyn(n)': *PPs* 104.9 4b, 113.1 1b and 134.4 2b; 'Iudea cyn(n)': *And* 560a, *El* 209a. Given these instances, the unique order of 'cynn Arabia' in *Solomon and Saturn II* 186b is striking.
52 Menner scans the line as 'a D-type with resolution of *Arab-*. *Arabia* had the chief stress on the first syllable, for the Latin stress is not followed in the anglicization of such names' (*The Poetical Dialogues*, p. 120).
53 See *Old English Orosius*, ed. Bately, p. 10.15 and note. Zangemeister's text of Orosius lists Arabia as part of a group including Mesopotamia, Babylonia, Chaldaea and '. . . nouissime Arabia Eudaemon, quae inter sinum Persicum et sinum Arabicum angusto terrae tractu orientem uersus extenditur. In his sunt gentes xxviii' (I.2): '. . . last of all, Arabia Eudaemon, which stretches towards the east in a narrow tract of land between the Persian Gulf and the Arabian Gulf'. Isidore (*Etym.* XIV.iii.13) simply lists 'novissime Arabia εὐδαίμων'.

Solinus offer slightly fuller information, including names of some tribes.[54]

There is, however, an even closer match to 'cynn Arabia' in Bede's *Nomina regionum*: 'Arabia: regio inter sinum maris rubri qui Persicus et eum qui Arabicus uocatur habet gentes multas, Moabitas, Ammanitas, Idumaeos, Sarracenos aliasque quam plurimas . . .'[55] This work provides separate entries for several other identifiable names in Saturn's list of travels: *Cappadocia, Syria, Pamphylia, Aegyptus, Arabia, Libya, Macedonia, Chaldaeorum regio, Bithynia, Graecia, Hierusalem, Medi, Madian, Sina* (= Choreb). In addition, *Palaestina, Galilaea* and *Persis* are mentioned as parts of other entries. The entry for 'Chaldaeorum regio' also offers the appropriate level of specificity for 'Caldea rice' (185b), but is not in itself evidence for the use of *Nomina regionum*, since this formulation with 'rice' and its appearance in two other half-lines in the list (178a, 181a) may suggest that the word was a filler.[56]

The phrase 'wudu Egipta' (184a) is another which repays attention. 'Wudu' may gloss a variety of Latin words, including both 'lignum' and 'arbor'.[57] If 'wudu' should be taken as 'lignum', its referent is not hard to find. Although Pliny lists a number of individual trees for which Egypt is noted, the *ficus* seems to have caught the imagination of succeeding writers. Apparently contrary to nature, the marvellous property of its wood is to become buoyant only after it has been saturated with water.[58] Even more marvellous, however,

---

[54] Solinus: 'verum haec Arabia procedit ad usque illam odoriferam et divitem terram, quam Catabani et Scaenitae tenent Arabes' (xxxiii.2: 'indeed Arabia extends all the way to that fragrant and rich land, which the Catabanes and the Scenitae tribes of Arabs hold'). Pliny: 'haec Cattabanum et Esbonitarum et Scenitarum Arabum vocatur . . .' (V.xii.65: 'This bears the name of the Cattabanes, Esbonitae and Scenitae tribes of Arabs . . .' p. 269) and elsewhere, 'multis gentibus eorum [i.e. Arabum] deductis illo a Tigrane Magno' (VI.xxxii.142: 'many of the Arabian races having been brought to that country by Tigranes the Great' p. 445).

[55] *Nomina regionum*, ed. Laistner, p. 167. 'Arabia: the region between the gulf of the Red Sea called "Persian" and that called "Arabian" has many peoples: Moabites, Ammonites, Idumaeans, Sararcens and many others . . .'

[56] In contrast to the combination 'cynn Arabia', the pattern gen. + *rice(s)* is very common. Half-lines with *rice* include: 'heofna rice': *GenB* 512b; 'engla rice': *El* 1230b, *Creed* 11b; 'rodera rice': *GuthA* 682a and 792a, *Phoen* 664a; 'eorþan rice': *Wan* 106b; 'gumena rice': *Wid* 133b, *Met* 9.41b; 'hæleþa rice': *Beo* 912b; 'maga rice': *Beo* 1853a; 'Gotena rice': *Met* 1.5A [gen. pl. by emendation from 'Gotene']. Half-lines with *rices* include: 'he(o,a)f(e,o)na rices': *GenA* 33b, *Dan* 441b, *And* 1683b, *MSol* 37b and 52a, *Exhort* 21a, *KtHy* 29b; 'eorðan rices': *Dan* 762b, *ChristB* 879b, *Sea* 81b, *LPr III* 11b, *Instr* 157b and 205b; 'rod(e,o)ra rices': *Sat* 346a and 687a; 'Gotena rices': *Deor* 23a; 'Creca rices': *Met* 26.11a; 'Indea rices': *MSol* 4b. No instances of *rice* + gen. are recorded in J.B. Bessinger and P.H. Smith, *A Concordance to the Anglo-Saxon Poetic Records* (Ithaca, NY and London, 1978).

[57] J. Bosworth and T.N. Toller, *An Anglo-Saxon Dictionary* (Oxford, 1898), p. 1277, senses I.1 and I.2.

[58] See Pliny, *Naturalis historia* XIII.xiv.57 ('materies'); Solinus, *Collectanea* xxxii.35 ('materia'); Augustine, *De civitate Dei* XXI.5 ('lignum cuiusdam ficus Aegyptiae'); Isidore, *Etymologiae* XVII.vii.17 ('cuius lignum in aquam missum ilico mergitur . . .').

is the tree which Aethicus Ister ascribes to Egypt: 'Ubi sunt arbores magnae quae picini dicuntur, unde in anno bis vellera carpunt et optimas vestes ex ipsis faciunt.'[59] While common usage might argue that the tree in question is an ordinary *ficus* (rather than an extraordinary clothes-tree), there is, however, another phrase in the Saturn list which may be firmly tied to Aethicus's peculiar work.

'Fæsten Creca' (183b) is a problematic half-line for a number of reasons. 'Creca' appears twice in Saturn's list, and one appearance is clearly redundant. Menner speculated in his note to this line that one of the two instances of 'Creca' should be 'Creta', and he cites Grein in the apparatus to the effect that 183b could be so emended. Certainly, 'Creca cræftas' ('skills of the Greeks') seems a more explicable combination than 'fæsten Creca' ('fortress of the Greeks'), and the combination is supported by its appearance elsewhere in the OE Orosius. If the emendation 'fæsten Creta' be allowed, the problem of understanding the half-line is simply transferred from Greece to Crete. Most of the geographic sources discuss Crete as an island with a hundred cities, 'unde et Hecatompolis dicta est'.[60] The *Cosmographia* focuses on another, quite possibly unique, detail. In this travel narrative, Crete is a prosperous, pleasant island where no dangerous animals grow, and which is secured by ninety-three well-defended cities situated at the four compass points. Odder still, it has 'in medio autem Anthiopolim urbem munitissimam atque metropolim celeberrimam et famosissimam, ubi sagittarum usus ac iacula plurima et utilia, fabros et artefices gnaros esse adfirmat.'[61] This fiction about Crete, I suggest, lies behind the 'fæsten Cre*t*a' of our poem.

While Isidore's popular *Etymologiae* or Orosius's *Historiae* are obvious choices for the text from which the *Solomon and Saturn II* poet began to build his list, there is the nagging problem of context. It is, of course, possible to imagine an author deciding on a topic and proceeding immediately to a handy geographic extract. But most literature is not generated from a dictionary. As I will argue below, both hard and soft evidence suggest possible connections between the *Cosmographia* and *Solomon and Saturn II*. The hard evidence consists in the list of places which Aethicus is said to have visited in bk VI. The relevant names occur in two groups. The first (in order) includes: *Bithinia*

---

59 *Kosmographie*, ed. Wuttke, p. 82: 'In that place there are huge trees which are called *picini*, from which twice a year they cull the fleeces and make from them excellent clothes.' K. Hillkowitz, *Zur Kosmographie* I, 41, traces some of the vocabulary of the passage to Isidore, *Etymologiae* XIV.iii.27–30, but Aethicus's odd, pitched trees appear to be his own fantasy.

60 Isidore, *Etymologiae* XIV.vi.16. See also Pomponius Mela, *Chorographia* II.112; Solinus, *Collectanea* xi.4; Pliny, *Naturalis historia* IV.xii.58; Bede, *Nomina regionum*, CCSL 121, 169.77.

61 *Kosmographie*, ed. Wuttke, VI. xci. '. . . in the middle is Anthiopolis, a highly fortified city and a most famous and celebrated centre, where the value of its arrows and the many useful javelins [each] attest that its smiths and craftsmen are expert.'

(lxxi), *Pamphilia* (lxxxi), *Graecia* (lxxii) *Macedonia* (lxxvii), *India* (lxxxiv), *Aegyptus* (lxxxiv), *Chaldea* (lxxxiv), *Syria* (lxxxiv), *Persi* (lxxxiv), *Medi* (lxxxiv), *Mesopotamii* (lxxxiv). These are separated from the following cluster by some Alexander material (and other information), and finally an intriguing account of a land which Aethicus was prevented from seeing. The second cluster includes: *India* (cvii), *Mesopotamia* (cvii), *Media* (cvii), *Persida* (cvii), *Nineveh* (cvii), *Arabia* (cviii), *Chaldea* (cviii), *Syria* (cviii), *Aegyptus* (cviii), *Cappadocia* (cviii), *Palastina* (cviii), *Hierusalem* (cviii), *Galilaea* (cviii), *Libia* (cix), with some overlap from the earlier section.[62]

The difference between the list extracted from the *Cosmographia* and that from the *Etymologiae* lies in two items. Aethicus lists Nineveh but not the Filistiim, Isidore lists Filistim (the city) but not Nineveh. Since both are readily available in the *Nomina locorum* the difference is not helpful in resolving the question at hand. There are, however, unusual names in several difficult half-lines of *Solomon and Saturn II*: 'East-Corsias', 'Norð-Predan', 'Marculfes eard' and 'Pores gemære'. The first two are unhelpful in establishing any connection between the *Cosmographia* and the Old English poem. 'East-Corsias' (177b), is almost certainly the product of corruption. Menner, following Holthausen, suggests that 'Corsias' is an error for 'Cossaei', according to Strabo a people neighbouring the Medes. These peoples do not figure in the narratives of the common geographic surveys, but are mentioned in the lists contained in the so-called *Liber generationis* and Fredegar's *Chronicon*.[63] I note in passing that Corsica (glossed in the margins of the English manuscripts of the *Cosmographia*) is one of a set of islands mentioned between the two clusters contributing to our list. Similarly, 'Norð-Predan' (179b) is a corruption, possibly a misreading for 'Parthian'. But 'Marculfes eard' is, I believe, identifiable from the *Cosmographia*.

In his commentary, Menner suggested that 'Marculfes eard' was Chaldea, since he understood Saturn to be a substitute for Marculf and Saturn is identified as 'Caldea eorl' in the disputed ending of *Solomon and Saturn I*.[64] As long ago as 1848, Kemble used the *Cosmographia* to establish a connection between 'Morcholon' and Saturn. Aethicus's strange ethnography of peoples omitted from the Bible describes the customs of the Turks, who 'fecerunt

---

[62] Parthia, Crete and Corsica are also mentioned.

[63] 'Liber generationis', in *Geographi Latini Minores*, ed. Riese, pp. 160–9, at 166; *Fredegarii et aliorum chronica*, ed. B. Krusch, MGH, SS rer. Merov. 2 (Hanover, 1888), 1–193, at 23.

[64] In the Solomonic dialogues other than those composed in England, Solomon's opponent is Marculf: '. . . there can hardly be any doubt that both Marculf and Marcolfus are equivalents and substitutes for *Marc(h)olus* (Morcholus), the deity identified with Saturn by Aethicus', *Poetical Dialogues*, ed. Menner, p. 119. See O'Keeffe, *Visible Song*, pp. 68–9, on Menner's editorial decision to move lines 170–9 of *Solomon and Saturn I* to the end of *Solomon and Saturn II*.

acervum magnum lapide ac bitumine conglutinatum, aedificantes pilas prae-grandes mirae magnitudinis et cloacas subtus marmore constructas, phyrram fontem glutinantes et appellaverunt Morcholom lingua sua, id est stellam deorum, quo derivato nomine Saturnum appellant'.[65] Both Menner and Kemble seized on this problematic passage as a way to explain how the English Solomonic dialogues featured a contest between Solomon and *Saturn* when the later, continental dialogues made Marculf Solomon's opponent. By claiming an equivalence between Saturn and Marculf on the basis of the *Cosmographia*, they tried to support a case for *Solomon and Saturn II* as a translation of a lost Latin Solomonic dialogue, despite the fact that the Old English poem is nothing like any of the surviving continental dialogues. While it is relatively easy to understand how Saturn could be understood as a Chaldean,[66] it is more difficult to see how the poet would equate Marculf with Saturn the Chaldean. The passage makes it quite clear that the land in question is Turkey. (The Turks were a people very new to geographic writing, and their appearance in the Tiberius world map may be owing to the *Cosmographia*.[67]) And the list of travels in *Solomon and Saturn II* makes 'Marculfes eard' a

---

[65] *Kosmographie*, ed. Wuttke, p. 19. 'They made a great pile in stone, cemented with bitumen, building colossal pillars of great size and drains assembled from below in marble, joining a stone fountain, and named it 'Morcholon', that is, 'star of the gods' by which derived name they invoke Saturn.' Wuttke emends his text to read 'fonte[m] glutinant*es*' and, further on, 'quo', but gives no apparatus to indicate the manuscript readings. Kemble, *Dialogue*, p. 119, cites the late manuscript London, BL, Cotton Caligula A. iii as reading 'pyrrham fortem et glutinatam' and 'quod derivato nomine Saturnum appellant'. Both Leiden Scaliger 69 and Cotton Vespasian B. x read *quod* as well. Wuttke's reading might be translated 'by which derived name they invoke Saturn'. With *quod* the translation would awkwardly be 'which, by a derived name, they call Saturn'. A full collation of the manuscripts would indicate the degree of instability of transmission at this point.

[66] Isidore's widely available *Etymologiae* identifies Saturn with an idol of the Babylonians: 'Bel idolum Babylonium est, quod interpretatur vetus. Fuit enim hic Belus pater Nini, primus rex Assyriorum, quem quidam Saturnum appellant; quod nomen et apud Assyrios et apud Afros postea cultum est, unde et lingua Punica Bal deus dicitur. Apud Assyrios autem Bel vocatur quadam sacrorum suorum ratione et Saturnus et Sol' (VIII.xi.23: 'Bel, which translates as 'old', is an idol of the Babylonians. This Belus was indeed the father of Ninus, first king of the Assyrians, whom some call Saturnus; in this respect the name is reverenced among both the Assyrians and later the Africans, whence in the Punic language Bal is said to be a god'). He later indicates the connection of Babylon with Chaldea: 'Babyloniae regionis caput Babylon urbs est, a qua et nuncupata, tam nobilis ut Chaldaea et Assyria et Mesopotamia in eius nomen aliquando transierint' (XIV.iii.14: 'The capital of the region of Babylon is the city Babylon, from which it is named; it is so celebrated that Chaldaea, Assyria and Mesopotamia in their time left it untouched in its name').

[67] See *An Eleventh-Century Anglo-Saxon Illustrated Miscellany (British Library Cotton Tiberius B. V part I)*, ed. P. McGurk, D.N. Dumville, M.R. Godden and A. Knock, EEMF 21 (Copenhagen, 1983), 83. McGurk tentatively assigns the miscellany to Christ Church, Canterbury (p. 109).

place which Saturn has visited. If 'Marculf' and 'Marcolfus' are, as Menner claims, 'equivalents and substitutes for Morcholus' – the *Morcholon* of our text – then he has connected *Solomon and Saturn II* not with a lost Latin dialogue source, but with the *Cosmographia*. Marculf's land would then be Turkey, the savage land of the Saturn-worshipping people whom Aethicus visited in bk III.

The remaining problematic half-line is 'Pores gemære' (189b). The word 'pores', showing the normal translation of a second declension masculine Latin noun to the a-declension in Old English, must refer to Porus, king of India.[68] Porus figures prominently in the various Latin histories and accounts of Alexander's conquests in the East and figures as well in the *Letter of Alexander to Aristotle*.[69] But though India is ubiquitous in the primary geographic texts, of these only Orosius adds an account of Porus's combat with Alexander, fairly late in the *Historiae*.[70] Aethicus does, in bk VI, visit the king of India, whose name here presents a particular difficulty. Aethicus reports:

Indiae regionibus valde felicibus repperimus, quod *in i*llis partibus Eden nemus dei coeli et hortus inaccessibilis carnale creaturae situs esset. Vale fecimus deis deabusque Indiae et aulae regis Ferzetis, qui bona fecit nobis, palatia et coenacula suа nobis ostendit ex auro et gemmis.[71]

As Hillkowitz has demonstrated, the *Cosmographia* is indebted to the *Epistola Alexandri ad Aristotelem* for this account, but the name of the king is otherwise unique.[72] Thus, if the poet of *Solomon and Saturn II* was using the *Cosmographia* at this point, he would have to have known that Porus was king of India and made the appropriate correction. Grammatically, such a correction might be suggested by an inflectional echo. A marginal gloss in Leiden Scaliger 69 presents the perplexing lemma 'Ferezis' in the ablative: 'Fereze rege indorum' (83v). The dative form of Porus 'Porose', bears just enough similarity with its 'r', voiced, intervocalic 's' and final 'e' to assist the jump to 'Porus'.[73] But this is mere speculation.

Two types of 'soft' influence suggest a connection between the Old English

[68] A. Campbell, *Old English Grammar* (Oxford, 1959), § 519.

[69] *Three Old English Prose Texts in MS. Cotton Vitellius A. xv*, ed. S. Rypins, EETS os 161 (London, 1924), 5–6.

[70] *Orosius*, ed. Zangemeister, III.xix.3–4; *Old English Orosius*, ed. Bately, p. 72.13–23.

[71] *Kosmographie*, ed. Wuttke, VI.cvi (p. 79): 'We learned about the extraordinarily fortunate regions of India, that in those parts Eden was located, the sacred grove of the god of heaven and garden inaccessible to any fleshly creature. We bid farewell to the gods and goddesses of India and to the royal court of king ?Ferzes, who treated us well, who showed us his palace and its upper chambers of gold and gems.'

[72] Hillkowitz, *Zur Kosmographie des Aethicus* I, 65 and II, 35–6.

[73] *Old English Orosius*, ed. Bately, p. 72.13: 'Porose þæm strengstan Indea cyninge.'

poem and the *Cosmographia*. *Solomon and Saturn II* is a contest between wise men in which Saturn claims his qualifications from his wide travels. The first (surviving) 102 lines of the poem are devoted to 'oriental' material (the lands travelled, the riddle on the land where no-one can travel, the *vasa mortis*) and remaining 223 lines treat general riddling questions. The *Cosmographia* claims to be a text recounting the travels and experiences of the very learned Aethicus. In one particularly apposite experience in bk VI, the *Cosmographia* waxes lyrical about Greece, so attractive a place that Aethicus stayed there five years disputing with one Fabius,

qui eo tempore in cuncta Graecia praeclarus inter caeteros nitebat. Propter quod praedictus philosophus Aethicus illuc, audita eius fama, advenisse se et per annos quinque inibi stationem fecisse adserens et in multis enigmatibus saepius ac subinde simul temptando disputaverunt, sed in cunctis coniecturis et problematibus Aethicus superior. Et in multis redarguebat universos decertando scrupolissimis ironiis; quam plurimas difficillimas quaestiones et nonnulla interpretare nequiverunt aut nescientes aut nolentes. Sed ille reprehendit ignorantes . . .[74]

In his contests of wisdom Aethicus took on all comers and 'rebuked the ignorant'. These learned disputations, with their debates 'in enigmatibus', present a travelling wise man in a context similar to that of Saturn in *Solomon and Saturn II*.

The first riddle which Solomon poses to Saturn is to tell him about the land where no man can step with his foot. Saturn's reply is a notoriously difficult passage in which one Wulf slays twenty-five dragons from which various kinds of 'atercynn' arise (211a–15b). These poisonous creatures make the land inaccessible to man and beast. Immediately preceding the geographic summary in the *Cosmographia*, Aethicus descends from the summits of the Caucasus and complains bitterly that he had not found what he was seeking. He had wished to visit a land of indescribable wealth, but entry was impossible because implacable guardians had made the region inaccessible. These guardians are dragons, ostriches (!), griffins, serpents, ants, lizards and venomous animals.[75] 'Atercynn' indeed. But for all this mystery, Solomon's

---

[74] *Kosmographie*, ed. Wuttke, VI. lxxix (pp. 59–60): 'who at that time in the whole of Greece stood out most eminent among the rest [of the philosophers]. For this reason, the aforementioned philosopher Aethicus, having heard of his fame, went there and took up residence for five years, and they debated in many *enigmata* very often and also by testing each other repeatedly, but in all disputed points and propositions Aethicus was victorious. And he refuted everyone by fighting it out in many most precise figures; they could not interpret so many most difficult questions, either being unable or unwilling. But he rebuked the ignorant.'

[75] *Kosmographie*, ed. Wuttke, VI.cv (p. 79): 'Submotus ab his eminentissimis montibus, aureis iugis noctem cum facibus adfui propter metum draconum et strucionum. Grifas et serpentes inibi iugiter invigilant. Formicas more canum rapacissimas centauriasque lacertas venenatas

reply is a joke on Saturn. Solomon corrects Saturn's attempted answer to the riddle about the land where no man can tread by observing that no man can set foot in deep water because he cannot reach bottom with his feet.[76]

In counterbalance to the extreme orientalism of Menner's study, I have suggested two very different texts which seem to have contributed to the information in *Solomon and Saturn II*. The little collection of names in the *Nomina locorum* not only provides place-names which are juxtaposed precisely as they are in the poem, but the work also seems to have travelled (at least early on) with Bede's commentary on Samuel.[77] In this commentary, Bede devotes considerable attention to Dagon, the fish-god of the Philistines, perhaps of relevance to the genesis of the whale-bodied Vasa Mortis. The *Cosmographia* is attractive as a source not because it is likely, but precisely because it is not. While it is not to be numbered among usual geographic sources, it was certainly in England by the middle of the tenth century, and its two tenth-century English manuscripts and probable connection with the Tiberius world map attest to its popularity. Its attraction as a source lies in its combination of materials (lists, beasts, the Alexander legend, riddling contests, abstruse knowledge) and a deliberately exotic mystique.

Menner posited as a source for *Solomon and Saturn II* a lost Latin Solomonic dialogue with Irish forebears, but such a source is simply an assumption. As Menner himself candidly notes, no Latin dialogue remotely resembling the poem has ever been discovered.[78] The opposite assumption, that *Solomon and Saturn II* is a largely original Old English composition, yields rather more interesting results. The structure of the list in itself is significant insofar as the arrangement of items includes places, peoples and abstractions in no discernible order. They have been objectified, removed from the ethical oral narrative which characterizes the catalogues of *Widsith*. Furthermore, the ordering of the names in the list accommodates the requirements of metre and alliteration. This rearrangement implies that the place-names were not merely lifted from their source texts, but abstracted, listed, alphabetized and manipulated to integrate them from at least two texts into one. The facts of the list point, I believe, overwhelmingly, to composition in writing. If there is merit as well in

valde reliqui cum sociis meis viris Achademicis et inquiens retuli: O inaccessibiles thesauros maximos, tam avaros et crudeles habentes custodes!' ('Having left these loftiest of mountains, I arrived at the golden mountains during the night with torches for fear of dragons and ostriches. Griffins and serpents are on guard there continually. I, along with my philosopher companions, left behind ants ravenous in the manner of dogs, centaurs and exceedingly venomous lizards, and I made a report, saying, "O most abundant and inaccessible treasure-troves, having such cruel and avaricious guardians"'.)

76 *Solomon and Saturn II*, 218b–19a.
77 *In Primam Partem Samuhelis libri IV*, ed. D. Hurst, CCSL 119 (Turnhout, 1962), v.
78 *Poetical Dialogues*, ed. Menner, p. 26.

my argument that the *Cosmographia* and perhaps the *Nomina locorum* supplied the names in the Saturn list, such a connection strongly suggests that composition of the verse list took place at a desk where the poet had access at least to an English recension of the *Cosmographia*, Bede's *Nomina locorum* and probably Isidore's *Etymologiae*.

Certainly the learning behind the poem is considerable and suggests access to a number of books, but my suggestion of a possible connection between the *Cosmographia* and *Solomon and Saturn II* remains necessarily preliminary. The *Cosmographia* requires a critical text with a full collation to assist further study. For the time being, the *Cosmographia* offers a chance to re-evaluate our impression of the local interests and cultural context out of which *Solomon and Saturn II* emerged. If we indeed find in it a source for part of *Solomon and Saturn II*, we have also acquired a tool to evaluate the nature and quality of the literacy which lies behind the writing of the poem.[79]

[79] The Interdisciplinary Group for Historical Literary Study (Texas A&M University) provided me with research time during which I was able to complete this article. I am very grateful to Professor Michael Lapidge both for his helpful criticism of the argument and his many useful suggestions for its improvement.

Latin learning at Winchester in the early eleventh century: the evidence of the Lambeth Psalter

PATRICK P. O'NEILL

Aside from its Old English gloss,[1] the Lambeth Psalter has largely been ignored. Yet this manuscript furnishes valuable evidence about Latin learning in late Anglo-Saxon England, specifically at Winchester. And it can lay claim to be the most important surviving witness to psalter scholarship from this period.

THE MANUSCRIPT

Physical Description

London, Lambeth Palace Library, 427 is a composite manuscript, now consisting of an eleventh-century psalter, a fifteenth-century gathering and two leaves from another eleventh-century manuscript.[2] The main part, the psalter proper, has dimensions 212 × 158 mm (written space 166 × 111 mm), with sixteen lines per page, a format which allows for generous spacing between the lines. Its script is a round Anglo-Caroline minuscule, dated by Ker to the first half of the eleventh century, apparently all written by a single scribe.

Collation

The manuscript consists of 212 medieval parchment leaves, foliated 1–211 by an eighteenth-century hand;[3] the final leaf, a pastedown, is not foliated. There

---

[1] U. Lindelöf, *Der Lambeth-Psalter: eine altenglische Interlinearversion des Psalters in der Hs 427 der erzbischöflichen Lambeth Palace Library: I, Text und Glossar, II, Beschreibung und Geschichte der Handschrift; Verhältnis der Glosse zu anderen Psalterversionen; Bemerkungen über die Sprache des Denkmals*, 2 vols., Acta Societatis Scientiarum Fennicae 35.i and 43.iii (Helsinki, 1909–14). Hereafter cited as 'Lindelöf' with volume and page number.

[2] For descriptions of the manuscript, see Lindelöf II, 1–2, and 14–15; M.R. James and C. Jenkins, *A Descriptive Catalogue of the Manuscripts in the Library of Lambeth Palace* (Cambridge, 1932), pp. 588–90; and N.R. Ker, *Catalogue of Manuscripts Containing Anglo-Saxon* (Oxford, 1957), pp. 432–3 (no. 280).

[3] Wanley gives no foliation references in his description of the manuscript (*Librorum veterum septentrionalium catalogus*, in G. Hickes, *Linguarum vett. septentrionalium thesaurus*, 2 vols. (Oxford, 1705) II, 268–9), presumably because the present foliation had not yet been entered.

are some irregularities in foliation: fols. 32 and 174 are doubled, while fol. 188 is incorrectly written on 187v. Besides four leaves at the beginning and four more at the end, the manuscript has 26 gatherings (most of eight leaves), the last of which is a fifteenth-century addition. The full collation is as follows: four half sheets (fols. 1–4); 1^8 + one leaf after 7 (fols. 5–13); 2^8 (fols. 14–21); 3^8 (fols. 22–9); 4^4 (fols. 30–2; fol. 32 is doubled); 5^8 (fols. 33–40); 6^8 (fols. 41–8); 7^8 + one leaf after 2 (fols. 49–57); 8^6 + one leaf after 5 (fols. 58–64); 9^8 (fols. 65–72); 10^8 (fols. 73–80);[4] 11–21^8 (fols. 81–168); 22^8 (fols. 169–75; fol. 174 is doubled); 23^8 (fols. 176–83); 24^8 (fols. 184–92;[5] fol. 188 is written on the verso of fol. 187); 25^8 + one leaf after 6 and one leaf after 7 (fols. 193–202); 26^8 lacks one leaf after 5 and one leaf after 7 (fols. 203–8); one conjugate (fol. 209 and the final leaf) enclosing two singletons (fols. 210–11).

Present Contents

The contents of Lambeth 427 are as follows:

1. Three prefaces to the psalter (fols. 1–2):

(i) (acephalous) Jerome's Letter to Paula and Eustochium on his edition of the Latin psalter subsequently known as the *Gallicanum*;

(ii) pseudo-Augustine psalter preface, entitled 'Dicta Sancti Agustini que sint virtutes psalmorum';

(iii) another psalter preface, inc. 'Suscipere dignare Domine Deus omnipotens hos psalmos consecratos quos ego indignus . . . ad uitam aeternam et remissionem'.

The remaining space of 2v is filled by a collect in a fifteenth-century hand, 'Tibi Domine commendamus animas . . .'

2. Lunar prognostications and tables (fols. 3–4).

The space remaining at the bottom of 4v was filled by the psalter preface, 'Suscipere dignare' (in the same hand as the collect of no. 1. iii above), which continues onto the upper part of 5r.

3. The Latin psalms (I–CLI), a Latin prayer entitled 'Confessio pro peccatis ad Deum',[6] and fifteen canticles, all (except for ps. CLI) with a near-contempor-

---

A century later the present foliation appears in H. J. Todd's *A Catalogue of the Archiepiscopal Manuscripts in the Library at Lambeth Palace* (London, 1812), p. 54, who mentions (p. x) that 'many Codices also have now received the advantage of foliation'.

[4] This gathering has a fifteenth- or sixteenth-century supply leaf (fol. 78), incorrectly identified by Ker, *Catalogue*, p. 343, as '12^6' instead of '10^6'.

[5] Incorrectly given as '25' by James, *A Descriptive Catalogue*, p. 588.

[6] Not in Lindelöf, but ed. M. Förster, 'Die altenglischen Beigaben des Lambeth-Psalters', *ASNSL* 132 (1914), 328–35, at 329–31.

ary interlinear Old English gloss (fols. 5–202). Within this section are found various additions:

(i) The lower third of 65r and all of 65v (before ps. LI) contain two collects, and two versions of the proper for the *Missa pro sancta cruce*, added in thirteenth- and fourteenth-century hands.

(ii) The lower third of 141v and all of 142r (before ps. CIX) contain a Latin prayer 'O summe Deus miserorum consolator omnium . . .' with a contemporary, partial Old English gloss,[7] added in the first half of the eleventh century.

(iii) Most of 183v (between the Latin prayer 'Confessio' and the first canticle) contains part of an Old English prayer in alliterative verse, 'Eala drihten leof, eala dema god . . .',[8] added in the second half of the eleventh century.

4. A Latin litany[9] (on 202v, written over an earlier litany)[10] and fifteen prayers in two hands of the late fourteenth/fifteenth centuries (202v–205v).

5. Fols. 206–9 are blank (though partially ruled) except for 209v which has in fifteenth-century hands four antiphons for the minor Hours and some scribblings, including the words 'R. Lanthonie'.

6. Two fragments (on non-adjacent leaves) in Old English of a history of Kentish royal saints, in a hand of the second half of the eleventh century, from another manuscript[11] (fols. 210–11).

---

[7] Ed. Förster, *ibid*. pp. 328–9.

[8] The Lambeth fragment is ed. H. Logeman, 'Anglica Minora', *Anglia* 11 (1889), 103; R. Wülker, *Bibliothek der angelsächsischen Poesie II* (Leipzig, 1894), 211–12; and E. van K. Dobbie, *Anglo-Saxon Minor Poems*, ASPR 6 (New York, 1942), 94–6, who supplies only its variant readings as part of an edition of the full text from London, British Library, Cotton Julius A. ii. Dobbie (p. lxxxvi) thinks that the Lambeth Psalter once contained a complete text (seventy-nine lines) of the prayer, but that 'a folio or more, containing the missing matter, has been lost after fol. 183'. He notes that the text immediately following, the first canticle, has no rubric and speculates that it may have been a casualty of the same loss. However, since fol. 183 marks the end, and fol. 184 the beginning, of integral gatherings of eight leaves, Dobbie's theory is doubtful.

[9] Discussed by M. Korhammer, *Die monastichen Cantica im Mittelalter und ihre altenglischen Interlinearversionen: Studien und Textausgabe*, Texte und Untersuchungen zur Englischen Philologie 6 (Munich, 1976), 239–40, who suggests that it originated in a monastery of southern England. The litany is ed. M. Lapidge, *Anglo-Saxon Litanies of the Saints*, HBS 106 (London, 1991), no. XXVII.

[10] Compare the Salisbury Psalter, where at the bottom of 151v the original litany after the canticles was erased and replaced by a twelfth-century litany; see C. and K. Sisam, *The Salisbury Psalter*, EETS os 242 (London, 1959), 2; this litany is ed. Lapidge, *Anglo-Saxon Litanies of the Saints*, no. XLIII.

[11] Ker, *Catalogue*, no. 281 (p. 343). These leaves were added to the Lambeth Psalter probably at the same time as (or after) no. 5, as indicated by the presence of their opening words among the fifteenth-century scribblings on 209v.

7. The final folio has some scribbles.

Original Contents

In attempting to establish the original contents of this composite manuscript, items 4–7 certainly can be eliminated from consideration. Likewise, item 2 should almost certainly be eliminated. Although matter similar to it is occasionally found in other eleventh-century psalters, item 2 breaks the logical sequence of psalter prefaces to psalter text. The impression that it is a later addition is strengthened by the evidence that its two leaves do not have holes found on fols. 1 and 2, while at the same time they show the loss from the bottom right corner of a strip which is intact on fols. 1, 2 and 5. Moreover, none of its several hands can be identified with the main hand and are considerably later (late eleventh- and early twelfth-century).[12] This means that items 1 and 3 constituted the original manuscript.

Two aspects of the latter require explanation. First, the spaces left by the original scribe before ps. LI, ps. CIX, and the first canticle,[13] which were subsequently filled by the additions listed under item 3. i–iii. Since these spaces coincide with well-known divisions of the psalms, often marked in other psalters by illumination or drawings, it could be argued that they were intended for similar treatment. Such elaborate decoration, however, would be out of keeping with the austere character of the manuscript, which contains only a single illuminated letter. More likely the spaces were intended for Latin prayers which the scribe did not have immediately at hand. Significantly, he did enter one prayer, the 'Confessio', at another major division of the psalter (after ps. CLI), treating it as an integral part of the Psalter.[14]

Second, did the litany immediately after the canticles (202v), which was erased to make way for the present one, form part of the original psalter? It was entered on the lower part of 202v immediately after the canticles, without a break, quite out of keeping with the generous spacing normally allowed by the main scribe between important divisions in this psalter. Moreover, its inclusion meant beginning another quire, thereby ruining the original scribe's plan to avoid this difficulty by adding two extra leaves to the final quire (no.

---

[12] Dr T. Webber (pers. comm.) would date the hand of 3r to the first quarter of the twelfth century and that of 4r to the late-eleventh/early-twelfth century. Note also the foliation 'I.10' (seventeenth-century hand?) at the bottom of 3r, which does not harmonize with either the 'A. 2' numbering of the gathering immediately preceding or the 'B' numbering of that following.

[13] Marking, respectively, the first part of a tripartite division of the 150 psalms; the beginning of a series of psalms used for daily Vespers in the Roman and Benedictine Office; and the end of the psalms proper.

[14] As indicated by the individual rubric and by the generous spacing which he allotted to it.

25) in order to fit in the last of the canticles. Arguably, the erased litany was a later addition.

Thus, the manuscript originally consisted of the psalms and canticles and was probably meant to include three Latin prayers, two of which were never entered. It also had prefatory psalter material (probably including at least one more item now lost),[15] written by the main scribe, though added after the completion of the psalms and canticles.[16] Whether it was also meant to contain an interlinear Old English gloss is uncertain, since the latter is slightly later and in a different hand. But the generous spacing between the lines in the texts of psalter and canticles,[17] especially in relation to the narrower spacing of the prefatory material,[18] suggests that an interlinear gloss was planned.

THE PSALMS

Text

Lindelöf correctly identified the Lambeth Psalter text as Gallicanum (Gall.), but in the absence of a critical edition of the latter his analysis of its readings is virtually worthless.[19] A collation against the recent Benedictine critical edition

---

[15] The acephalous Letter, which now begins fol. 1, would require eleven more lines (twelve if a title were included) to be complete. This suggests that at least one folio, with space for text of seven to eight lines on its verso and eighteen lines on its recto, is now missing.

[16] As suggested by the tidy arrangement whereby the psalms begin on the recto of the first folio of the first full quire, with a large decorated initial 'B' (of BEATUS, ps. I.1). Such an appropriate position would be hard to arrive at if the scribe had been encumbered by the preceding texts. Furthermore, Jerome's Letter has none of the readings which might be expected from its association in the Lambeth Psalter with a Carolingian recension of the *Gallicanum* (see below, pp. 147–8); e.g. in its readings 'uirgulam uiderit' (Carolingian texts of the Letter invert the order and supply an illustration of *uirgulam*: ÷); 'prespexerit' (Carolingian, 'perspexerit'), 'et uobis' (Carolingian, 'uobis'), 'de turbulente' (Carolingian, 'e turbulente'). These differences suggest that the Lambeth scribe supplied the Letter from a source other than the exemplar for the psalms, after he had written the latter. For a similar practice with gospels, compare York, Minster Library, Add. 1 (s. x/xi), where the first gathering, containing prefatory (gospel) matter, was added later; and see P. Mc Gurk, *Latin Gospel Books from A.D. 400 to A.D. 800*, Publications de Scriptorium 5 (Paris, Brussels, Antwerp and Amsterdam, 1961), 8.

[17] The Lambeth Psalter shares roughly the same ratio of length of written space to number of lines with three psalters containing an interlinear Old English gloss. Thus, Lambeth Psalter, 166 (mm.):16 (10.38); Oxford, Bodleian Library, Junius 27, 185:20 (9.25); London, British Library, Royal 2. B. V, 202:19 (10.63); and Stowe 2, 227:20 (11.35).

[18] Which has eighteen lines, rather than sixteen, per page in the same written space, arguably because here there was no need to allow for an Old English gloss.

[19] Lindelöf II, 16–18. For example, relying on Migne's edition of the Gallicanum, where *sed tu* is the reading for ps. VI.4, Lindelöf labelled the Lambeth Psalter's corresponding reading *et tu* as a Romanum contamination; the latter, in fact, is also the Gallicanum reading. Likewise, he labelled Lambeth's original reading *uirtutem tuam* (ps. LXVII.29) as Romanum and the correction *uirtuti tuae* as Gallicanum, whereas the opposite is true.

shows that Lambeth generally agrees in its variant readings with the Carolingian psalters produced in the Frankish kingdoms from the late eighth through the ninth century. For example, with them it omits *mihi* before *omnes* (ps. XV.3), has *autem* for *uero* (ps. XIX.9), *glorificate* for *magnificate* (ps. XXI.24), *despicies* for *spernet* (ps. L.19), *aquae quae super caelos sunt* for *aqua quae super caelum est* (ps. CXLVIII.4). This broad identification of Lambeth Psalter's text (a more precise determination is hardly possible) agrees well with the hypothesis that Gallicanum psalters from France and the Low Countries circulated in England in the tenth century, especially after the Benedictine Reform.[20] Further evidence of the influence of Carolingian psalters can be found in another constituent of the Lambeth text of the psalms, the critical signs.

The Critical Signs

In preparing the Gallicanum, Jerome used the obelus ($\div$) and the asterisk (*) to identify, respectively, words which occur in the Septuagint text but not in the Hebrew, and words which occur in the Hebrew but not in the Septuagint.[21] Despite Jerome's exhortation not to neglect these critical signs, they do not appear regularly in psalter texts until Carolingian times.[22] But then scarcity gave way to excess, with scribes adding spurious signs which cannot have been in Jerome's original, as is evident from a comparison with the Septuagint and Hebrew. The Lambeth Psalter also has the spurious signs characteristic of Carolingian, especially Alcuinian, psalters.[23] For example ps. XXIX.11 $\div$ *factus:*, ps. XXXIV.20 * *terrae:*, ps. LXXIII.8 $\div$ *quiescere:*, ps. XCVIII.8 $\div$ *in:*, ps. CXIII.5 $\div$ *tibi:*, ps. CXVII.28 $\div$ *es:* (1⁰). In fact the Lambeth Psalter has many more spurious obeli. Nor are they arbitrary; they occur in precisely those places where the text has words which are not found in another Latin version of the Psalter, the Hebraicum (Heb.), Jerome's direct translation from the Hebrew. For example, ps. XVI.15 $\div$ *autem:* (om. Heb.), ps. XX.7 *in saeculum*

---

[20] See C. and K. Sisam, *The Salisbury Psalter*, pp. 48–9.

[21] '... ubicumque virgulam [= obelus] viderit praecedentem, ab ea usque ad duo puncta quae inpressimus sciat in Septuaginta translatoribus plus haberi; ubi autem stellae similitudinem perspexerit, de hebraeis voluminibus additum noverit, aeque usque ad duo puncta...' (*Biblia Sacra iuxta Latinam Vulgatam Versionem ad Codicum Fidem: Liber Psalmorum* (Rome, 1953) X, 3–4: '... wherever he sees the preceding virgule (*scil.* obelus), let him understand that from there up to the two dots which we have marked represents what the Septuagint has in excess; but where he notices the symbol of the asterisk, let him recognize an addition from the Hebrew books, which likewise extends to the two dots'.

[22] See B. Fischer *et al.*, *Der Stuttgarter Bilder-Psalter* (Stuttgart, 1968), p. 265.

[23] Identified by collating the Lambeth Psalter against the Benedictine critical edition of the Gallicanum (*Biblia Sacra*, as cited above, n. 21). This edition has been criticized for its excessive rigour in omitting doubtful signs; see Fischer, *Der Stuttgarter Bilder-Psalter*, pp. 265 and 286, n. 31.

÷ *saeculi:* (cf. Heb. *sempiternum*), ps. LXXXV.10 *magnus* ÷ *es tu:* (Heb. *magnus tu*), ps. CVI.26 ÷ *usque:* (om. Heb.), CXIII.26 ÷ *qui uiuimus:* (om. Heb.).

Although this method of collating the Gallicanum against the Hebraicum is well attested from Irish and continental (especially double and triple) psalters, it is unlikely that any of these served as the direct source for the Lambeth Psalter, which has apparently unique obeli, e.g. ps. CV.21 ÷ *qui saluauit eos:* (Heb. *salvatoris sui*) and ps. CVII.7 *saluum* ÷ *fac:* (Heb. *salua*). Entered by the original scribe,[24] these obeli may well be the product of his own collation of the Gallicanum against the Hebraicum. By so doing he was, in effect, securing a rough working copy of the 'Hebrew Verity', the most faithful and accurate of Jerome's translations of the psalms. Seen in this light, his choice as prefatory matter of Jerome's Letter (item 1.i), which explained the function of the critical signs, was very appropriate. And his use of the critical signs is in harmony with other evidence in the Lambeth Psalter of a special interest in the different versions of the Latin psalter. Thus the glosses, Old English and Latin, frequently introduce readings from the Romanum and the Vetus Latina, the pre-Hieronymian Latin psalter.[25]

Other Entries

The Lambeth Psalter also has accompaniments to its text of the psalms: before each psalm a biblical *titulus*; between major divisions of certain psalms the abbreviation 'DP' for *Diapsalma*,[26] an obscure word marking stanzaic divisions; and within the acrostic ps. CXVIII the names (with Latin explanations) for the twenty-two letters of the Hebrew alphabet. Although an integral part of Jerome's Gallicanum, these items were often omitted in early medieval, especially liturgical, psalters. Their presence in the Lambeth Psalter offers further evidence of scholarly interest in Jerome's original text.

THE CANTICLES

Besides the original ten biblical canticles which belonged to the Roman Office used in England,[27] the Lambeth Psalter contains a group of five non-biblical

---

[24] Many other obeli in the Lambeth Psalter, distinguished from those of the original scribe by their thin hand and frequently by their location above the line and on the margin, are of uncertain date, but probably from the Anglo-Saxon period, since Gallicanum psalters of the twelfth century and later, in keeping with a new, more scientific approach to scriptural studies, tend to demonstrate a conservative attitude towards the use of the critical signs.

[25] See below, p. 153.

[26] Probably added by the rubricator at the same time as he added the biblical *tituli*. The latter was done after the completion of the main text, as evident from numerous instances where the *tituli* had to be continued onto the margin, e.g. pss. V, VIII, XV, because the main scribe did not allow enough space for them.

[27] See H. Schneider, *Die Altlateinischen Biblischen Cantica*, Texte und Arbeiten 29–30 (Beuron, 1938), esp. 46–50 and 75–88.

canticles. First attested in Carolingian psalters, these canticles gradually became a canonical series.[28] In England the new series begin to appear in psalters from the mid-tenth century on,[29] though at first incompletely. Prior to the Lambeth Psalter the only two complete Anglo-Saxon witnesses are Salisbury, Cathedral Library, 150 (? Sherborne, s. x²) and London, British Library, Harley 2904 (? Winchester, s. x^ex). But the Lambeth Psalter registers a text more in tune with contemporary continental psalters than either. Thus it has the 'new' readings *filiis* for *filius* (Cant. II.19), *parasti* for *preparasti* (Cant. X.30), *suscepturus* for *suscepisti* (Cant. XI.23, *Te Deum*). A glimpse at when and how these textual changes were being effected in England can be caught from Abbo of Fleury's *Quaestiones Grammaticales*. Among the grammatical issues which Abbo discusses is the Latin future perfect, which he illustrates with the reading *suscepturus* in the *Te Deum*. This reading, he argues, is grammatically superior to the alternative *suscepisti*;[30] and to drive home his point he provides a personal illustration modelled on the relevant verse of the *Te Deum*, 'uisitaturus fratres Anglicos, maxime Os⟨waldum⟩, archiepiscopum, non horrui maris periculum'.[31] His argument and illustration were probably based on his experience at the monastery of Ramsey (985–7) where he would have encountered the reading *suscepisti* and initiated a campaign to remove it. The new reading *suscepturus* is first attested in the Bosworth Psalter, London, British Library, Add. 37517 (Canterbury, s. x²), but this psalter contains only two of the 'new' canticles.[32]

Thus among English psalters the Lambeth Psalter is innovative in having both the full series of 'new' canticles and the most recent continental readings, a combination likely to have come from a centre in close contact with the Continent. A clue as to the identity of this centre may be provided by the order of the canticles, which is very unusual in locating the 'new' canticle *Te Deum* between the canticle for Saturday Lauds (*Audite caeli*) and that of Sunday Lauds (*Benedicite*), instead of somewhere after the latter. This awkward

[28] See J. Mearns, *The Canticles of the Western Church* (Cambridge, 1916), pp. 62–7. Throughout the present paper the numbering of Canticles in the Lambeth Psalter follows that of Mearns.
[29] No doubt under the influence of the Benedictine Reform, as evident from textual agreements between the English canticles and those found in later Carolingian psalters. For example, in the *Quicumque*, they share the readings *tertia die resurrexit* (v. 38) instead of *surrexit* of the *textus receptus*; *sedet* (v. 39) instead of *sedit*; *Dei patris omnipotentis* (v. 39) instead of *patris*; see C. H. Turner, 'A Critical Text of the *Quicumque Vult*', *JTS* 11 (1900), 401–11, at 404. In the *Te Deum*, they agree on *uerum et* (v. 12) instead of *uerum*, *suscepturus* (v. 16) instead of *suscepisti*; see J. Julian, *A Dictionary of Hymnology*, 2nd ed. (London 1907), pp. 1120–1.
[30] On the relative merits of the two readings, see Julian, *Hymnology*, p. 1123b.
[31] *Abbo Floriacensis: Quaestiones Grammaticales*, ed. A. Guerreau-Jalabert (Paris, 1982), p. 263 (§42) and n. 189.
[32] On this psalter, see P. M. Korhammer, 'The Origin of the "Bosworth Psalter"', *ASE* 2 (1973), 173–87.

position, which breaks the liturgical sequence, is attested in several Carolingian psalters,[33] but among Anglo-Saxon psalters only in London, British Library, Cotton Vitellius E. xviii and Harley 863, the one certainly written in Winchester, the other probably copied from a Winchester exemplar.[34]

ADDITIONS IN LATIN

Throughout the psalms and canticles occur numerous additions,[35] explanations and corrections, entered soon after the writing of the main texts. They not only reveal much about the sources which went into the making of the Lambeth Psalter, but also shed light on the uses to which it was put. Functionally, they divide into three main categories.

Latin glosses

Lindelöf noted the presence of some 130 Latin glosses, most of them supplied by the same scribes who glossed in Old English. Unfortunately, he did not print them,[36] although in some instances the Old English gloss is clearly dependent on them, rather than the lemma in the Latin psalter text, e.g. IN BREVI (ps. II.13): '.i. repente *hrædlice*'; SION (ps. LXXII.28): '.i. ecclesiae.[37] *þæt is gesamnunge*'; AETHAM (ps. LXXIII.15): 'i. diaboli. *sceapan*'.[38] They serve the following functions.

(i) *Grammatical*. These 'clarify the grammatical property of a word'.[39] Most common in Lambeth is the interjection *o*, inserted interlinearly as near as possible to the Latin lemma to which it refers,[40] e.g. FILIA (ps. XLIIII.11): 'o *dohtor*', where *o* indicates that FILIA is a vocative. These and similar *o*-glosses in other Latin works of Anglo-Saxon origin bear witness to the problem for Anglo-Saxon readers of recognizing a Latin vocative.[41]

---

[33] Oxford, Bodleian Library, Douce 59 and Rheims, Bibliothèque Municipale, 4, both ninth-century from France.

[34] See C. and K. Sisam, *The Salisbury Psalter*, p. 5, n. 3.

[35] Omitted from the present discussion are the numerous construe glosses (dots and signs) in the Lambeth Psalter, on which see F.C. Robinson, 'Syntactical Glosses in Latin Manuscripts of Anglo-Saxon Provenance', *Speculum* 48 (1973), 443–75, esp. 454–7; and M. Korhammer, 'Mittelalterliche Konstrukionshilfen und Altenglische Wortstellung', *Scriptorium* 34 (1980), 18–58, esp. 38–9.   [36] Except for twenty-three examples given in Lindelöf II, 2–3.

[37] *Pace* Lindelöf I, 115, n. 3, 'ecclesiae', written directly over SION, is in the same hand as the Old English gloss.

[38] Note that Latin and Old English gloss even correspond in number (singular) and case (genitive).

[39] G.R. Wieland, *The Latin Glosses on Arator and Prudentius in Cambridge University Library MS Gg. 5. 35* (Toronto, 1983), p. 48.

[40] Sometimes the Old English equivalent, *eala*, is also supplied.

[41] Old English did not have a separate inflection for the vocative; see Wieland, *The Latin Glosses*, pp. 51–3.

(ii) *Syntactical.* These clarify elliptical constructions, smooth the syntactical flow, and generally facilitate reading and understanding of the Latin text. Most common is the addition of copulative *est* (often accompanied by a corresponding Old English gloss) as in

EGO AUTEM (ps. V.8): 'scilicet, sum';
PARATUM COR (ps. CVII.2): 'scilicet, est: *is*'.

Others supply a subject (often in the vocative), object, adverbial phrase, or verb:

DOMINE USQUEQUO (ps. VI.4): 'scilicet, differs';
NE VIDEAT (ps. IX.32): 'scilicet, sanctos suos';
CARBONES IGNIS (ps. XVII.13): 'scilicet, succens[i] ab e[o]' (from v. 9)
NON ERO (ps. XXXVIII.14): 'scilicet, in hoc mundo';[42]
QUAM DULCIA (ps. CXVIII:103): 'o domine'.

(iii) *Lexical.* These explain words of the Latin Psalter, usually offering several 'synonyms':

AMMIRABILE (ps. VIII.10): 'mirificum ł paradoxum admirabile';
CIRCUMDEDERUNT ME (ps. XVII.5): 'uallauerunt me';
IRACUNDUS (ps. XVII.48): 'abrepticius ł furiosus';
AMICI . . . PROXIMI (ps. XXXVII.12): '.i. propinqui ł contribulos ł parentes';
OPEM (ps. XL.4): 'ł auxilium ł amminiculum ł suffragium';
SONUS (ps. XLI.5): 'bombus ł uox'.

Most have close correspondences among the Latin glossaries which circulated in the early Middle Ages. Thus, with the gloss on SONUS, compare the Abstrusa Glossary s.v. *bombus* (BO 10), 'sonus aut vox';[43] with the gloss on OPEM, compare Abstrusa (OP 8), 'Opem: auxilium',[44] and the Vatican/ Affatim Glossaries, 'Suffragium. auxilium. adminiculum aut interuentum'.[45] Yet the Lambeth glossator, who must have had access to similar glossaries,[46] differs from all of them in one fundamental respect: instead of clarifying

---

[42] Cf. *Magni Aurelii Cassiodori Expositio Psalmorum I–CL*, ed. M. Adriaen, CCSL 97–8 (Turnhout, 1958), 362, lines 348–9, 'utique in hoc mundo'.
[43] *Glossaria Latina*, ed. W. M. Lindsay *et al.*, 5 vols. (Paris, 1926–31) III, 15.
[44] *Ibid.* III, 62.
[45] *Corpus Glossariorum Latinorum*, ed. G. Goetz, 7 vols. (Leipzig, 1888–1923) IV, 178, line 28, and 570, line 30.
[46] The possibility that he found all of his material already combined in a single source is fairly remote. Certainly, of the major Latin alphabetical glossaries which have survived from Anglo-Saxon England no one glossary by itself can account for all of the Lambeth glosses. On these glossaries, see M. Lapidge, 'The School of Theodore and Hadrian at Canterbury', *ASE* 15 (1986), 45–72, and J. D. Pheifer, 'Early Anglo-Saxon Glossaries and the School of Canterbury', *ASE* 16 (1987), 17–44.

difficult and obscure words he tends to explain well-known with less common words, as in the glosses on SONUS and PROXIMI. His methodology[47] not only implies considerable knowledge of glossarial lore (since instead of tracking down glosses from alphabetically arranged lemmata he had to do the opposite), it also suggests a fairly advanced exercise in Latin lexicography, using the text of the psalms as starting-point.

(iv) *Textual.* These provide alternatives to the readings of the main psalter text, either variants found in other Gallicanum psalters or readings from other versions of the Latin psalter. The most frequently cited of such versions is the Romanum, the psalter in general use throughout most of the Anglo-Saxon period, which was probably still being used at Christ Church, Canterbury, and perhaps among the secular clergy at the time when the Lambeth Psalter was written.[48] Examples are DOLOSA (ps. XI.2) glossed 'mala: *yfel*'; (IN CIVITATE) MUNITA (ps. XXX.22): 'circumstantiae'; A DIRIPIENTI-BUS (ps. XXXIV.10): 'i. a rapientib[us]'. Other glosses agree with the Vetus Latina, but since all of them occur in the psalter commentaries of Augustine and Cassiodorus, they probably derive from these sources rather than a Vetus Latina psalter. Examples are IN INTERITU (ps. IX.16): 'in corruptione'; CUM PERUERSO PERUERTERIS (ps. XVII.27): 'scilicet, eris'; PRO ADSUMPTIONE (*titulus*, ps. XXI): '꜔ susceptione'.[49]

(v) *Interpretative.* They explicate individual words (often proper names) rather than offer broad lines of interpretation; and are drawn mainly from the psalter commentaries of Cassiodorus (Cass.), Augustine (Aug.) and the pseudo-Jerome *Breviarium in Psalmos* (Brev.).[50] Examples are:

SION (ps. II.7): '꜔ sanctam ecclesiam' (cf. Cass. 43, 160–1, '*Sion* hic Ecclesiam debemus accipere');
LEO (ps. IX.30): 'i. antixps' (cf. Brev. 893C, 'oculi Antichristi');
CONPUNGAR (ps. XXIX.13): '(. . .)witnod ꜔ plangat' (cf. Aug. 173, §13,2, 'Vt iam non plangat').

Not so orthodox, however, are certain other glosses which show dependence on the Antiochene exegesis of Theodore of Mopsuestia. Unlike the Western

---

[47] A similar type of gloss in London, British Library, Harley 110 is noted by R.I. Page, 'The Study of Latin Texts in late Anglo-Saxon England [2]: The Evidence of English Glosses', *Latin and the Vernacular Languages in Early Medieval Britain*, ed. N. Brooks (Leicester, 1982), pp. 141–65, at 151.

[48] It was certainly being copied at this time, as evidenced by London, British Library, Harley 603 and Arundel 155, and Paris, Bibliothèque Nationale, lat. 8824. See further C. and K. Sisam, *The Salisbury Psalter*, p. 49, n. 1.

[49] Cf. respectively, *Sancti Aurelii Augustini Enarrationes in Psalmos I–CL*, ed. E. Dekkers and J. Fraipont, CCSL 38–40 (Turnhout, 1956), 66, lines 7–8, and 98, line 2; and Cassiodorus, *Expositio Psalmorum*, ed. Adriaen, p. 188, line 1.   [50]Ed. PL 26, cols. 863–1382.

exegetes cited above, Theodore (d. 428) applied the psalms primarily to various persons and events of the Old Testament, rather than to Christ or the Church.[51] His original Greek commentary reached the West through a Latin translation by Julian of Eclanum (*c.* 410), and an epitome of the latter.[52] With these two Latin versions the Lambeth glosses show the following agreements:[53]

IN SPIRITU (ps. XXXI.2): '*on gaste.* .i. in anima' (cf. Julian 140,23 '*in spiritu eius*, id est in anima eius'; Epitome 140,12, '*nec est in ore eius* usque *dolus.* Id est: in anima');

TOTA DIE (ps. XXXI.3): '*singallice.* i. continue ł *ealne dæg*' (cf. Julian 141,36, 'iugiter . . . continue'; Epitome 140,18, '*dum clamarem tota die.* Pro: continue');

DIXI (ps. XXXI.5): 'i. statui. *ic cwæð*' (cf. Epitome 141,28, '*dixi* . . . statui et proposui');

COGITANTES MIHI MALA (ps. XXXIV.4): '*þa þencendan me yflu.* non errore, sed studio' (cf. Epitome 156,24, '*Cogitantes mihi mala.* Non errore nocentes, sed studio').

Only two other instances of dependence on Theodoran exegesis have been verified for Anglo-Saxon England, in a psalter commentary written in Northumbria in the first half of the eighth century;[54] and in the Old English prose translation of the first fifty psalms,[55] now widely accepted as the work of King Alfred. Neither seems likely as a direct source for the Lambeth glosses.[56] A recent suggestion[57] that Theodoran exegesis was taught by Theodore of

---

51 On Theodore's exegesis, see R. Devreesse, *Essai sur Theodore de Mopsueste*, Studi e Testi 141 (Vatican City, 1948), 55–78.

52 Both ed. L. De Coninck, *Theodori Mopsuesteni Expositionis in Psalmos, Iuliano Aeclanensi Interprete in Latinum Versae quae supersunt*, CCSL 88A (Turnhout, 1977). From this edition are taken the citations of Julian's work and its epitome, which follow.

53 It is not possible to determine from these few examples whether the Lambeth Psalter glossator had access to Julian's work or its epitome, or a combination of both, such as is attested in certain Hiberno-Latin manuscripts.

54 See *Glossa in Psalmos: The Hiberno-Latin Gloss on the Psalms of Codex Palatinus Latinus 68 (Psalms 39:11–151:7)*, ed. M. McNamara, Studi e Testi 310 (Vatican City, 1986), 48–51.

55 First established by R. L. Ramsay, 'Theodore of Mopsuestia in England and Ireland,' *Zeitschrift für celtische Philologie* 8 (1912), 452–97, at 480–5. See further P. P. O'Neill, 'The Old English Introductions to the Prose Psalms of the Paris Psalter: Sources, Structure and Composition,' *SP* 78 (1981), 20–38, esp. 22–3.

56 The former may have passed to the Continent at an early date (see *Glossa in Psalmos*, ed. McNamara, p. 18) and in any case tends to borrow interpretations rather than individual phrases such as those found in the Lambeth Psalter. The latter has Theodoran interpretations in an Old English paraphrase.

57 G. T. Dempsey, 'Aldhelm of Malmesbury and the Paris Psalter: a Note on the Survival of Antiochene Exegesis', *JTS* 38 (1987), 368–86.

Tarsus at Canterbury, and thence brought back to Malmesbury by Aldhelm, to reappear in the Old English prose translation, might seem to provide a possible explanation for these Lambeth glosses, but unfortunately the theory has no concrete evidence to support it. Although known to have been interested in material aspects of the Old Testament, Theodore of Tarsus did not (as far as we know) use Theodore of Mopsuestia's exegesis. Nor was he likely to have done so: as Rome's representative in England, he presided over the Council of Hatfield (680) which reiterated the condemnation of Theodore of Mopsuestia's works originally issued by the Fifth Council of Constantinople (553); and he would have known that the latter Council had singled out for condemnation passages from Theodore of Mopsuestia's Greek commentary on the Psalms.

The Christian tituli

In addition to the biblical *titulus* written in red capitals before each psalm, the Lambeth Psalter has for most psalms a corresponding 'Christian *titulus*'[58] entered in the margin. Although they postdate the biblical *tituli*, as evident from their location adjacent to and around the latter, it cannot be by any great interval of time since they were almost certainly in place before the near-contemporary marginal Old English glosses were added.[59] Instead of providing an Old Testament background (as did the biblical *tituli*), they present the psalms as sung by Christ or the Church, e.g. 'Vox Christi ad patrem', 'Vox ecclesiae de Iudaeis'. Visually they are distinguished in the Lambeth Psalter from both biblical *tituli* and marginal Latin glosses by the use of different colours, green, violet, blue;[60] or script, Anglo-Caroline or capital. On these criteria, at least four sets can be identified, all incomplete.[61]

---

[58] This is the name used for *tituli* not originating in the biblical text in *Les "Tituli Psalmorum" des manuscrits latins*, ed. P. Salmon, Collectanea Biblica Latina 12 (Vatican City, 1959).

[59] To judge by ps. LXXIII.1, the Latin text of which begins on the upper margin of 91r with the Old English gloss above, and the Christian *titulus* in turn entered above the latter. An Old English addition (*uel utaneddest þu*) to the main gloss˙(*utadræfdest þu*) of the first line, is squeezed in before the Christian *titulus* on the far left margin, far away from its referent. Normally, such additions to a first-line gloss are entered in the upper margin immediately above the word being elaborated (e.g. *para* on 92v, ps. LXXIII.22) but not in this instance because the space was already occupied by the *titulus*.

[60] The use of different colours recalls a similar practice for marking the initials of liturgical rubrics and psalms; see Ker, *Catalogue*, pp. xxxvii–xl.

[61] They were edited by J. Lawlor, 'The Cathach of St. Columba', *Proc. of the R. Irish Acad.* 33C (1916), 241–437, appendix iv (pp. 413–36), but neither accurately nor fully. For example, Lawlor incorrectly distinguished the green and violet *tituli* as different series while lumping together two different sets as a single series ('the black').

Set I, with seventy-one *tituli*, is written in either green or violet ink by one scribe.[62] It derives from a single source, not one of the six series of Christian *tituli* which were current in the early Middle Ages, but a set of psalter introductions, the pseudo-Bede *Argumenta*.[63] This work provides for each psalm a brief historical, allegorical and moral interpretation. Set I of the Lambeth Psalter draws on all three, though favouring the allegorical interpretation.[64] A somewhat similar use of the *Argumenta* in the rubrics of Paris, Bibliothèque Nationale, lat. 8824 (? southwest England, s. xi[med])[65] raises the possibility of a connection, but the two psalters often differ in wording,[66] or choose a different part of the *argumentum* for a particular psalm.[67] Moreover, the Paris Psalter quite frequently combines the historical and allegorical parts of the same *argumentum* under one rubric,[68] whereas Set I shows a marked predilection for the allegorical interpretation.[69]

Set II has forty-seven *tituli*, written by a different hand, in blue ink. Besides the pseudo-Bede *Argumenta*,[70] it draws on other sources, notably the Columban Series (Series I) of Christian *tituli*. This series (so called because it is first attested in an Irish psalter attributed to St Columba of Iona) enjoyed wide

---

[62] Edited by Ramsay, 'Theodore of Mopsuestia in England and Ireland', pp. 493–5. Ramsay did not mention the indecipherable *tituli* in green at pss. XCV and CXLIII, or the insertion of the word 'propheta' in blue before the green *titulus* to ps. LXXIII. In his identification of the source for the *titulus* to ps. LVII, read 'Arg. (b)' not 'Arg. (a)'.

[63] Of uncertain date and origins, perhaps seventh-century Ireland. See B. Fischer, 'Bedae de Titulis Psalmorum Liber', *Festschrift Bernhard Bischoff zu seinem 65. Geburtstag*, ed. J. Autenrieth and F. Brünholzl (Stuttgart, 1971), pp. 90–110, esp. 93–6 and 107. The *Argumenta* are edited in PL 93, 483–1102, and again by J. W. Bright and R. L. Ramsay, *The West-Saxon Psalms, Being the Prose Portion, or the 'First Fifty,' of the So-Called Paris Psalter* (Boston, 1907).

[64] Thus sixty-two are borrowed from the allegorical, seven from the historical, and two from the moral interpretations of the *Argumenta*.

[65] *The West-Saxon Psalms*, ed. Bright and Ramsay.

[66] For example, for ps. IV, the Paris Psalter has 'Vox x̄p̄i in cruce quando positus fuit'; the Lambeth Psalter 'Aliter, Deus [iusti]cie exaudiuit [in cru]ce positum [filium] suum'. (Words in square brackets are no longer legible, but conjecturable.)

[67] For example, for pss. XXVI, XXXVII and LVIII, Paris uses the historical interpretation, Lambeth the allegorical; conversely, at pss. XLV and XLIX.

[68] For example, ps. XV, 'Vox x̄p̄i ad patrem; Ezechias orauit Dominum in egritudine', which combines the allegorical and historical.

[69] Even when using the historical interpretation of the *Argumenta*, Set I often qualifies it. For example, in ps. XLIII, 'Profeta sanctorum pressuras s[uppli]cationes[que comme]morat', the vague 'sanctorum', which could apply to any Christian, replaces 'Machabaeorum' of the source, presumably because the historical application to anyone other than David was deemed objectionable. Likewise, in ps. XLV, '[Ex per]sona canitur sanctorum [pro liber]atione sua gratias [agen]tium', 'sanctorum' replaces the specific historical reference to the Two Tribes ('duarum tribuum') in the original. See further Ramsay, 'Theodore of Mopsuestia', p. 496.   [70] Including its historical interpretations for pss. VII and CL.

distribution. Clearly distinguishable among its numerous manuscript witnesses is a 'Carolingian' recension with distinctive readings.[71] These same
readings are found in Set II of the Lambeth *tituli*, for example at ps. XLI 'Vox
paenitentis', where the main tradition has 'Ante baptismum vox Christi est'.[72]

Set III, with twenty-three *tituli*, written in black-brown ink and capitals,[73] is
virtually confined to the final fifty psalms. In addition to the Columban series
(again with Carolingian readings)[74] it uses the pseudo-Jerome *Breviarium in
Psalmos* (Brev.),[75] a commentary also used in the Lambeth Latin glosses.[76] Set
IV, a medley of some twenty-six *tituli* confined mainly to the first fifty psalms,
is written in dark brown ink and Caroline minuscule by at least two different
hands.[77] Its primary source is the *Breviarium*, especially the latter's opening
comment on an individual psalm.[78] It also uses the Columban Series.

None of these four sets is complete, quite often they overlap,[79] and
collectively they do not cover the full 150 psalms,[80] all of which might suggest
that the process of entering them was haphazard. And yet their relationship is
somewhat more complex. For example, at ps. CXXVI, the scribe of Set I
expanded the *titulus* of Set II, '[Vox] Christi', with the addition in green, '[ad
f]uturam [aecclesi]am', making it agree with the *Argumentum* (and the
Columban Series); at ps. CXXXIV, he expanded 'Vox aecclesiae' with the
addition, 'quae increpat operantibus idol[a]', bringing it into line with the
Argumentum.[81] Conversely, at ps. L, the scribe of Set II added in blue to the Set
I *titulus*, 'Vox Pauli apostoli p[enitentis]' (= the corresponding *Argumentum*),
the words 'prophetae uel', above 'Vox', thereby enlarging it with a reference
to the corresponding Columban Series, 'Legendus ad lectionem Esaiae
prophetae . . .'. At ps. LXXII, in addition to entering his 'own' *titulus*, he

---

[71] See *Les "Tituli psalmorum"*, ed. Salmon, pp. 49 and 51.

[72] Likewise ps. LXXIII, 'Aliter uox aecclesiae de Iudeis', where the main tradition has 'Vox
Christi ad patrem'.

[73] In two different scripts, though possibly by the same hand. The first is distinguished by
heavily written, consistently sized capitals, the second by slenderly shaped, mixed capitals.

[74] For example, ps. CIV, 'Vox apostolorum de Iudeis', where the main series has 'Vox Christi
ad apostolos de Iudeis'; ps. CXXX, 'Vox sanctae Marie', where the main series has 'Vox
ecclesiae rogantis'.

[75] Compare for ps. CXLV, Lambeth's 'Hic anima ipsam ortatur et ipsas sibi respondit' with
Brev., 'Ipsa se hortatur, et ipsa respondet' (PL 26, 1323D).   [76] See above, p. 153.

[77] Most in a thick hand, the remaining four in a small neat hand similar to that of the marginal
Latin glosses.

[78] For example, ps. XXI, 'Hic humanitas loquitur Christi' (= Brev. 931C).

[79] In more than twenty instances, e.g. pss. VII, LIV and CXXIII.

[80] Twelve psalms lack a Christian *titulus*, e.g. pss. LXVIII–LXIX and CX.

[81] Likewise, ps. CXLIX, 'Vox Christi ad fideles', was made into the full text of the *Argumentum*
(allegorical) and Columban Series by the addition in green, 'de futuro et resurr[ectione]'.

emended that of Set I, 'sanctorum et pericula narrantur et preces connectuntur', by adding 'propheta' initially, presumably as an indirect subject.[82] Moreover, both scribes emended other sets of *tituli*. At ps. CXXV, the scribe of Set I made the original Set III *titulus*, 'Vox apostolorum', conform to the *Argumentum* (ànd main tradition of the Columban Series) by adding 'de impiis Iudeis'. At ps. CXLV, the scribe of Set II completed the rubric 'Vox Christi' (mistakenly entered as a biblical *titulus*, in reality the corresponding Christian *titulus* of the 'Carolingian' Columban Series) with the words 'ad populum', making it agree with the main tradition of the Columban Series. Thus, the intervention of these two scribes was not haphazard. The Set I scribe modified other Sets (especially Set II) to bring them into conformity with his favoured source, the mystical interpretation of the pseudo-Bede *Argumentum*; the Set II scribe did the same to Set I, in accordance with the Columban Series.[83]

All of this textual activity with the Christian *tituli* provides important clues about the place of origin of the Lambeth Psalter. Among the twenty-five or so surviving Anglo-Saxon psalters,[84] the use of the Columban Series (and the closely related allegorical *Argumenta*) is relatively rare; besides the Lambeth Psalter, it is found in only six other witnesses. Four of the six have Carolingian readings: London, British Library, Cotton Vitellius E. xviii, has throughout a very full text of the Carolingian recension; two others, London, British Library, Cotton Tiberius C. vi and Stowe 2, although with few *tituli* (respectively, nine and four), are also good textual witnesses; a fourth witness, the Paris Psalter, has some thirteen *tituli* with Carolingian readings, but confined to the second part of the psalter, with a sporadic pattern of distribution which suggests incidental borrowing from a secondary source; the fifth witness, London, British Library, Arundel 155, has a few readings. Thus the pre-eminent witness and thereafter the two next best witnesses are the Vitellius, Tiberius and Stowe Psalters, all written *c.* 1050–75 at Winchester.[85] Moreover, these same psalters stand apart in how they use these *tituli*.

---

[82] He also emended Set I at pss. LXXXIV and CL.

[83] Obviously, they did not perceive their work in these terms. They may not even have been aware that the allegorical *Argumenta* and Series I were separate works, since the two have so much in common (the latter is the source of the former; see *Les "Tituli psalmorum"*, ed. Salmon, pp. 47–8).

[84] Listed by H. Gneuss, 'Liturgical books in Anglo-Saxon England and their Old English Terminology', in *Learning and Literature in Anglo-Saxon England: Studies presented to Peter Clemoes on the Occasion of his Sixty-Fifth Birthday*, ed. M. Lapidge and H. Gneuss (Cambridge, 1985), pp. 91–141, at 114–16.

[85] On the Winchester origins of these three psalters, see, most recently, W. Hofstetter, *Winchester und der spätaltenglische Sprachgebrauch*, Texte und Untersuchungen zur Englischen Philologie 14 (Munich, 1987), 69–73; and 'Winchester and the Standardization of Old

While other Anglo-Saxon psalters have before each psalm a biblical *titulus* or a Christian *titulus* or nothing, the three Winchester psalters combine as a single rubric the biblical and Christian *titulus*. This kind of rubric originated in Carolingian psalters;[86] presumably the latter provided the model for the Winchester rubrics as well as the source of their Carolingian readings. The Lambeth Psalter rubrics, although originally consisting of only biblical *tituli*, subsequently were enlarged with Christian *tituli*, entered adjacently and in coloured ink and capitals, clearly an effort to imitate this Carolingian model. Thus the Lambeth Psalter's Christian *tituli* and their Carolingian readings point to dependence on a Winchester exemplar.

Textual emendations

In addition to the textual glosses already discussed under 'Latin Glosses', the Lambeth Psalter text of the psalms was directly altered by fairly numerous corrections and additions. They are written (mainly in the margin) in a large, bold hand in Anglo-Caroline script, probably to mark them as true emendations to the sacred text, rather than textual glosses. Their script is very similar to that of the main text,[87] which suggests that they were probably entered soon afterwards. The following are the most significant:

ps.	XXVI.2	CLAMAUI: addition of AD TE
	XXX.21	TABERNACULO: addition of TUO
	LIII.6	ME: addition of ET
	LIV.13	INIMICUS: addition of MEUS
	LXX.9	DEFICIET: emended to DEFECERIT
	LXXIV.9	BIBENT: addition of EX EO
	LXXV.12	AFFERENT: emended to AFFERTIS
	LXXV.13	SPIRITUS: emended to SPIRITUM
	LXXV.13	APUD: addition of OMNES
	LXXIX.2	TAMQUAM OUES: emended to UELUT OUEM
	XCI.14	ATRIIS: addition of DOMUS
	CV.32	AD AQUAS: emended to AD AQUAM.

Since many of these emendations are also found in the Romanum, it would seem logical to suppose[88] that they are the product of a collation of the Lambeth Psalter's Gallicanum text against a Romanum. But this theory fails to

---

English Vocabulary', *ASE* 17 (1988), 139–61, at 157–8. The close textual relationship between the Christian *tituli* of these three Psalters was recognized by R.L. Ramsay, 'Theodore of Mopsuestia', pp. 496–7, though he was unaware of the separate existence of a Series I or of its Carolingian recension.

[86] See B. Fischer, *Der Stuttgarter Bilder-Psalter*, pp. 261–2.

[87] Especially in the use of the rather high 'e', as in the readings AD TE and EX EO listed below. I am grateful to Dr T. Webber for advice on the script.   [88] As did Lindelöf II, 17–18.

explain why the collator should have chosen some Romanum readings and ignored many others, for example at ps. XLIII.14, where the Romanum has the addition IN before OBPROBRIUM, and SUNT after NOSTRO, neither of which appears among Lambeth's emendations; likewise with Romanum AB EIS (ps. LXXVII.38). In fact, the Lambeth emendations are precisely the 'new' readings (no more, no less) which appear in twelfth-century continental Gallicanum psalters[89] and psalter commentaries, setting them apart from the earlier, Carolingian psalters. One emendation stands out because it is not recorded in any Romanum or Vetus Latina psalter and therefore cannot be explained as a borrowing from them, the addition OMNES after APUD (ps. LXXV.13). Its earliest appearance (as far as I can tell) is in a psalter commentary attributed to Master Anselm of Laon (*c*. 1050–1117). The reading must have been of recent vintage, since Anselm introduces it into a comment which he borrowed from his teacher, Master Manegold (d. *c*. 1110), where the latter does not have it. Thus, on APUD REGES (ps. LXXV.13), Manegold comments, 'apud illos qui bene regunt suam terram',[90] but Anselm, 'apud OMNES illos qui bene regunt suam terrenitatem'.[91] Not only OMNES but all of the Lambeth emendations are present in the Gallicanum text of Anselm's commentary.

Whether the Lambeth emendator had access to Anselm's commentary is a moot question.[92] The real significance of his emendations is that they reflect the influence of a new type of exegesis of which Anselm is representative. Characterized by the 'blending of the two principles of patristic authority and logical realism',[93] it finds concrete expression in emendation of the sacred text

---

[89] Compare the readings of the psalters with sigla V, D and Ω in the Benedictine critical edition.

[90] PL 93, cols. 485–1098, at 888C. The true authorship of this commentary was plausibly established by G. Morin, 'Le pseudo-Bède sur les Psaumes et l'opus super Psalterium de Maître Manegold de Lautenbach', *RB* 28 (1911), 331–40; see also Fischer, 'Bedae de Titulis', p. 90. For Anselm's dependence on Manegold, see B. Smalley, *The Study of the Bible in the Middle Ages* (Notre Dame, IN, 1964), p. 49.

[91] PL 116, 193–696, at 452C, where the commentary is erroneously attributed to Haimo of Halberstadt. For its true authorship, see A. Wilmart, 'Un Commentaire des Psaumes restitué à Anselme de Laon', *Recherches de théologie ancienne et médiévale* 8 (1936), 325–44; Smalley, *The Study of the Bible*, p. 67, n. 2; and V.I.J. Flint, 'The "School of Laon": A Reconsideration', *Recherches de théologie ancienne et médiévale* 43 (1976), 89–110, at 92, n. 11. The reading OMNES still had some standing in England in the thirteenth century, as witnessed by the testimony of the English biblical scholar William de la Mare (d. 1290) who felt the need to explain why he rejected it: 'neque ante id quod dicitur REGES premittunt hebr. et grec. quod dicitur OMNES' (cited in the apparatus to ps. LXXV.13 of the Benedictine *Gallicanum*).

[92] Probably not, since Anselm's *floruit* (*c*. 1100) is somewhat later. In any case the psalter text used by Anselm was probably already in circulation when he wrote his commentary.

[93] See H.H. Glunz, *History of the Vulgate in England from Alcuin to Roger Bacon* (Cambridge, 1933), pp. 86–7.

based on grammatical considerations, such as Abbo's championing of *suscepturus* over *suscepisti*;[94] and, more strikingly, in the incorporation of words from patristic commentary into the sacred text because they were believed to enshrine the true meaning of the latter. Herein lies the significance of the addition OMNES before REGES (ps. LXXV.13) found in Anselm's commentary and the Lambeth Psalter. Its ultimate source and justification is Augustine's proposal to combine vv. 12 and 13 as a single unit of meaning, so that OMNES of v. 12 is extended into v. 13, 'offeremus munera terribili super *omnes* reges terrae, id est, super *omnes* regentes carnem suam'.[95]

But how did the Lambeth corrector gain access to these readings? The answer must be sought in four Gallicanum psalters produced at Winchester in the period 1050–1075, the Vitellius, Tiberius and Stowe Psalters already noted,[96] as well as London, British Library, Arundel 60. All contain in their main text virtually all of the emendations present in the Lambeth Psalter including the reading OMNES.[97] The presence in these four psalters of Old English glosses which accurately translate the 'new' readings makes a pre-Conquest date for the latter likely. So, too, does the evidence marshalled by Glunz[98] from a study of Anglo-Saxon gospel manuscripts, that Winchester was the centre of a distinct school of scriptural studies during the first half of the eleventh century. Significantly, the same textual stratification which Glunz[99] identified as distinctive of Winchester gospelbooks can also be recognized in these Winchester psalters: a basic Alcuinian text; Vetus Latina (the equivalent for the psalms being Romanum) readings received into this text as a result of the textual criticism practised in the French schools in the ninth and tenth centuries; and new readings (such as OMNES of ps. LXXV.13) generated by the scholastic exegetes of the eleventh century. And just as Glunz identified a distinctive 'Winchester Gospels', so it is possible to speak of a 'Winchester Psalter', whose distinctive readings were used to emend the Lambeth Psalter.[100]

---

[94] See above, p. 150. Another example in the Lambeth Psalter is the marginal gloss, 'o inique', which proposes an alternative grammatical reading of the lemma INIQUE (ps. XLIX.52) as a vocative noun rather than an adverb. Cf. Anselm, 'EXISTIMASTI INIQUE, vel *vocativus* vel adverbium' (PL 116, col. 367D).

[95] *Enarrationes in Psalmos*, p. 1052, lines 40–1.　　[96] See above, p. 158 and n. 85.

[97] The Stowe Psalter, perhaps reflecting its origins in a different Winchester house (see A.C. Kimmens, *The Stowe Psalter*, Toronto Old English Ser. 3 (Toronto, 1979), xix), does not have OMNES. The Tiberius Psalter (in its corrected state) is closest to the Lambeth Psalter, sharing with it all but one of the thirteen listed emendations. The one reading which they do not have in common, the addition EX EO (ps. LXXIV.9), is also absent from the other three Winchester psalters.　　[98] *History of the Vulgate*, pp. 133–48.　　[99] *Ibid.* p. 141.

[100] It is hardly suprising that the psalter should come in for such close textual scrutiny at Winchester, since after the gospels it was the most widely used book of the Bible, especially in a monastic setting as part of the Divine Office.

CONCLUSIONS

From the preceding study certain deductions can be made about the uses for which the Lambeth Psalter was intended. The lack both of the paraphernalia required for the liturgical observance of the psalms (hymns, calendar), and of decoration,[101] especially at important liturgical divisions of the psalter, almost certainly rules out liturgical use. This conclusion is positively supported by the presence of *Diapsalma* and the critical signs which normally do not appear in liturgical psalters. The unusually large number of such signs in a pattern which records differences from the Hebraicum, suggests a psalter intended for textual study. Likewise, the economy of the original contents, psalter prefaces, psalms and canticles with a learned interlinear Old English gloss, points to a book for study, reminiscent of the Regius Psalter (? Winchester, s. x^med) which has similar contents.[102]

Yet to posit one use for a psalter does not necessarily rule out others. The Lambeth Psalter may have served a private, devotional function, as evidenced by the contemporary prayer before the canticles, with its first person singular pronouns, and perhaps also by the allotting of a space (for a prayer?) before ps. CIX which marked the first psalm of the week's cursus for Vespers.[103] Likewise the Christian *tituli*, with their emphasis on the psalms as prayers uttered by Christ or the church, suggest a devotional interest in the psalms. A dual function would fit well with the contents of the Lambeth Psalter preface, where Jerome's Letter anticipates scholarly interest in the psalter text, while pseudo-Augustine's encomium on the virtues of the psalms, and the prayer following, reflect a devotional emphasis. Also compatible with private use are the tidy dimensions of the Lambeth Psalter, 212 × 158 mm. (written space 166 × 111 mm.), which make it the smallest of the surviving Old English glossed psalters. While too large to be described as a pocket-book, it would be extremely portable and consequently well suited to personal use for prayer and study.

Yet another use has been proposed for the Lambeth Psalter: as a classroom

---

[101] The one exception, the decorated initial 'B' of BEATUS (ps. I), which combines animal heads, plaited interlace, and acanthus, is a type normally found in non-liturgical manuscripts; see F. Wormald, 'Some Decorations from Manuscripts of the Winchester School', *Archaeologia* 91 (1945), 107–35, at 122.

[102] See *Der altenglische Regius-Psalter*, ed. F. Roeder, Studien zur englischen Philologie 18 (Halle, 1904), xi–xii.

[103] In both the Roman and Benedictine Office. The first page of ps. CIX, a protected inner leaf, shows the kind of wear compatible with daily use. Unfortunately, it is not possible to determine whether the wear occurred during the Anglo-Saxon period or later. See also the marginal note accompanying ps. CXVIII, discussed below, p. 165.

book. Such a claim can no longer be made lightly; in reaction to an earlier view that any manuscript containing glosses must have been used in the classroom (either by students or teacher), strict guidelines have been proposed for identifying classroom books.[104] How does the Lambeth Psalter measure up to these guidelines? Certainly, its interlinear Old English gloss could be described as a traditional 'repository of learning'. Its marginal Latin glosses touch on the main topics a teacher of the psalms might be expected to treat, notably grammar, syntax, lexicography (note especially the interest in supplying more difficult 'synonyms', perhaps to expand the student's vocabulary)[105] and orthodox allegorical interpretation. The fact that these glosses tend to be gathered in the early psalms need not tell against their use for the classroom, since a master could teach from selected passages.[106] Perhaps most telling for some scholars, the Lambeth Psalter has construe marks, a relatively simple system which would be eminently suitable for teaching Latin (and even Old English) syntax.[107] And since the scribe who inserted the construe marks presumably did not need the system for himself,[108] it must have been intended as an aid for others.[109]

Yet the Lambeth Psalter lacks two pedagogical aids normally found in Anglo-Saxon classroom manuscripts. The first is the accent marks which assisted the teacher in reading the text aloud to his students for dictation; but perhaps for a text so familiar as the psalms this dictation would not be needed. The second is the *q:* or *quare hoc* gloss, which prompted the teacher to ask questions about passages where it occurs. Despite these omissions the balance of evidence suggests that the Lambeth Psalter at some time served a pedagogical purpose, though not necessarily in a formal classroom setting.

Finally, the question of the Lambeth Psalter's place of origin. Unfortunately, the only direct evidence, the mention in a note (209v) of the Augustinian priory of Lanthony (*secunda*) near Gloucester, sheds no obvious light on the manuscript's history or provenance during the Old English period, since

---

[104] See G.R. Wieland, 'The Glossed Manuscript: Classbook or Library Book?', *ASE* 14 (1985), 153–73. [105] See above, p. 153. [106] See Wieland, *The Latin Glosses*, pp. 191–2.
[107] See Robinson, 'Syntactical Glosses', p. 465; and Korhammer, 'Konstrukionshilfen', pp. 39, 48 and 50.
[108] Since he must have known Latin syntax very well in order to do his work.
[109] If so, probably for students at a fairly advanced stage of study. The possibility that the Lambeth Psalter might have been used as reading material for monks – a suggestion made for certain glossed Anglo-Saxon manuscripts of well-known Christian poetic texts, by M. Lapidge, 'The Study of Latin Texts in late Anglo-Saxon England: the Evidence of Latin Glosses', *Latin and the Vernacular Languages in early Medieval Britain*, ed. Brooks, pp. 99–140 – is very unlikely, since it does not have the clean appearance of these 'library books' and in any case the psalter was a text which every monk would be expected to know by heart.

Lanthony was founded in 1136. One promising line of enquiry is the Lambeth Psalter's Old English interlinear gloss, which agrees very closely in word-choices and vocabulary with the interlinear Old English gloss to the *Expositio Hymnorum* and the Monastic Canticles, both found in British Library, Cotton Vespasian D. xii (? Canterbury, s. xi^med). All three interlinear glosses reflect the usage of Æthelwold's 'Winchester school'.[110] Unfortunately, 'Winchester' usage does not necessarily prove Winchester origin, since it was carried to monasteries founded or re-established by Æthelwold's pupils. It is in such a foundation, rather than Winchester, that both Gneuss and Korhammer would locate the Lambeth Psalter. For Gneuss the lack of any special relationship with the three Winchester psalters (Vitellius, Tiberius and Arundel) tells against a Winchester origin for the Lambeth Psalter. But this objection has been answered by Hofstetter's study of Winchester vocabulary, demonstrating a close relationship between the Lambeth Psalter and these three Winchester psalters.[111] For Korhammer the presence in the Lambeth Psalter of certain non-West-Saxon linguistic features (phonological and morphological)[112] and its close agreement in word-choices with the Monastic Canticles in Cotton Vespasian D. xii, the exemplar of which he would locate in East Anglia (probably Ely or Peterborough), points to the same place of origin for the Lambeth Psalter. But the departures from standard late West Saxon are relatively few overall; and they admit of other explanations, notably dependence on non-West Saxon sources.[113]

---

110 See H. Gneuss, *Hymnar und Hymnen im englischen Mittelalter* (Tübingen, 1968), pp. 186–7, and 'The Origin of Standard Old English and Æthelwold's School at Winchester', *ASE* 1 (1972), 63–83 at 77; and Korhammer, *Die Monastichen Cantica*, pp. 235–45.

111 See Hofstetter, *Winchester Sprachgebrauch*, p. 86: 'weist PsI [Lambeth Psalter] ganz auffallende Übereinstimmungen mit den in Winchester entstandenen Psalterversionen PsF, PsG und PsJ auf'.

112 In particular Korhammer, *Die Monastichen Cantica*, pp. 236–7, notes relatively frequent occurrences (as percentages) in the Lambeth Psalter of *weoruld* and *syndon* instead of West Saxon *woruld* and *synt*. However, patterns of distribution may tell more than absolute percentages. Thus *woruld* is the normal form in the first part of the Lambeth Psalter (pss. I–XLV); while *syndon* does not occur in pss. LIII–LXXVIII.3 or in the Canticles (both constituting scribally discrete sections), and infrequently (5 × out of 37 ×) in the marginal Old English glosses. This evidence suggests that the occurrence of non-West Saxon forms depends either on the scribe of an individual section or on his source and does not necessarily reflect the usage of the scriptorium where the Lambeth Psalter was written. For a similar conclusion based on textual and lexical evidence, see next note.

113 See C. and K. Sisam, *The Salisbury Psalter*, p. 72, who describe the Lambeth Psalter gloss as the product of 'a process of collection and accretion'. Likewise, Hofstetter, *Winchester Sprachgebrauch*, p. 87, would attribute the non-West Saxon features of vocabulary to dependence on non-West Saxon sources.

Given the uncertainty surrounding the origins of the Old English gloss, what can the Latin contents reveal about the origins of the Lambeth Psalter? First, that it belonged to a Benedictine monastery. The evidence is a marginal note at the beginning of ps. CXVIII, 'Hic inchoat cursus cotidianalis',[114] which reflects the Benedictine practice of beginning the first Hour of the week, Prime on Sunday, with ps. CXVIII (vv. 1–4).[115] Second, its Latin contents indicate that the compilers of the Lambeth Psalter must have had access to a first-class library since they were able to draw on an impressive range of texts relating to psalter study: the three main versions of the Latin Psalter, Romanum, Hebraicum, and Gallicanum; the principal Latin Psalter commentaries of the early Middle Ages, Augustine, Cassiodorus, and pseudo-Jerome's *Breviarium*, as well as the rare work of Julian of Eclanum with its Antiochene exegesis; the Columban Christian *tituli* and the pseudo-Bede *Argumenta*; and one or more Latin glossaries. Even more significant, two of these sources, the textual emendations based on a 'Winchester psalter', and the Carolingian readings of the Christian *tituli*, are otherwise attested only in Winchester psalters. Add to this evidence two peculiarities found only in the Lambeth Psalter and in Winchester psalters, the unusual position of the *Te Deum* in the sequence of canticles, and the curious division of ps. LXXVII at verse 40 (instead of 36).[116]

Could all this evidence of Winchester influence be explained by supposing that the Lambeth Psalter was copied in a monastery not located at Winchester but having access to an exemplar from Winchester? It might, if only a single text were involved, but the fact is that at least three scribes[117] of the Lambeth Psalter at different times used different 'Winchester' sources that were probably not contained in one exemplar.[118] Such activity almost certainly required immediate and continuous access to these sources. That requirement,

---

[114] At the bottom of 149r in a hand similar to that which entered some of the Set IV *tituli*.

[115] 'Prima hora dominica, dicenda quattuor capitula psalmi centesimi octaui decimi' ('At Prime on Sunday the first four verses of ps. CXVIII are to be recited': *Regula S. Benedicti*, ch. 18). The Roman Office begins the same Hour with ps. LIII.

[116] See C. and K. Sisam, *The Salisbury Psalter*, §6. In the Lambeth Psalter no division, either at v. 36 or 40, was marked by the main scribe, presumably because the psalter was not meant for liturgical use. But someone subsequently added a cross before v. 40 and a marginal note (indecipherable to me), both in dry-point.

[117] Namely, the scribes of (i) the *tituli* with Carolingian readings; (ii) the 'Winchester Psalter' readings; and (iii) the Old English gloss.

[118] Thus, the exemplar of the Old English gloss was probably not that which supplied the 'Winchester' readings, since the former does not reflect the innovations of the latter; and the Set I and II Christian *tituli*, with their different readings for the same psalms, almost certainly came from different sources.

and the accumulated evidence of Winchester influence, is best explained by accepting that the Lambeth Psalter was produced at Winchester.[119]

[119] One potential objection remains: if the Lambeth Psalter was at Winchester, it seems odd that later Old English glossators (of the Vitellius, Tiberius and Arundel Psalters) who are believed to have worked there, did not use such an excellent aid. The most obvious answer is the evidence that these glossators did, in fact, use the best of the Lambeth Psalter, but in the form of its underlying Winchester source; see C. and K. Sisam, *The Salisbury Psalter*, pp. 67–71, F.–G. Berghaus, *Die Verwandtschaftsverhältnisse der altenglischen Interlinearversionen des Psalters und der Cantica* (Göttingen, 1979), pp. 76–90, and Hofstetter, *Winchester Sprachgebrauch*, pp. 69–74. Another possible explanation is that the Lambeth Psalter had already left its original (Winchester) home by the mid-eleventh century; see K. Wildhagen, 'Das Psalterium Gallicanum in England und seine altenglischen Glossierungen', *Englische Studien* 54 (1920), 35–45, at 40–2, though his evidence is dubious and inaccurate. For example, he claims that the manuscript was at Lanthony as early as the eleventh century, and that the inclusion of St Mildred in item 6 (which he did not recognize as a fifteenth-century addition to the Lambeth Psalter) indicated that the manuscript was previously owned by a woman.

I am grateful to the American Council of Learned Societies for a grant-in-aid (Summer, 1983); to the Librarian of Lambeth Palace Library for permission to publish from the contents of the Lambeth Psalter; and to Dr M. Lapidge for corrections and editorial suggestions.

Poetic language and the Paris Psalter: the decay of the Old English tradition

M.S. GRIFFITH

The metrical version of psalms LI–CL, known as the Paris Psalter, is a pedestrian and unimaginative piece of poetic translation. It is rarely read by students of Old English, and most Anglo-Saxonists make only passing reference to it. There is scarcely any literary criticism written on the text, although some work has been done on its vocabulary and metre. I hope to show in this article, however, that its stylistic peculiarities mark an important stage in the disintegration of the Old English poetic mode, and that analysis of these may go some way towards answering the difficult questions which surround the manner and the cause of the style's disappearance at the end of the Anglo-Saxon period. In particular, I shall examine this poet's selective use of the poetic diction normally associated with the form, and the impact of this selectivity on the systems of rank and formula.

In order to achieve a wider assessment of the poetic language of the Paris Psalter, a comprehensive list of the traditional vocabulary of the poetry is required. Poetic words are sometimes asterisked by editors and lexicographers: Klaeber's glossary to his edition of *Beowulf* and Sweet's *The Student's Dictionary of Anglo-Saxon* are probably the best known works which do this.[1] Though Klaeber and Sweet are useful in this respect, such labelling was extremely difficult in the absence of concordances to the extant texts, and both wrongly label some words and exclude others as a result. The appearance of the microfiche concordance to Old English has radically simplified this task, and I have used it to draw up a full list.[2] Neither Klaeber nor Sweet give any guide to the point at which occurrence only in verse can be taken to indicate words which were not used by prose writers, because they were aware that such words properly belonged to the different register of poetry, and the establishment of such a limit is the greatest problem that the analysis faces. The aim here has been to establish a minimum limit of occurrence in verse (coupled with maximum absence from prose) above which the significance of the

---

[1] *Beowulf and The Fight at Finnsburg*, ed. F. Klaeber, 3rd ed. (Boston, 1936); *The Student's Dictionary of Anglo-Saxon*, ed. H. Sweet (Oxford, 1896).

[2] See Appendix I, below pp. 183–5. I hope to publish elsewhere a full analysis of this list, and of the definition of 'poetic' used to draw it up. For the concordance, see R. L. Venezky and A. diPaolo Healey, *A Microfiche Concordance to Old English* (Toronto, 1980).

distribution is unclouded by the possibility of alternative explanation. The words listed in Appendix I are those whose occurrence is confined to poetry, with a minimum of four occurrences in at least two poems, or which appear mainly in poetry, with a ratio of occurrence of at least four citations in verse to one in non-poetic texts. The following qualifications should be noted:

(a) All compounds have been treated as the sum of their component lexemes, and only these components are listed. Thus, a compound whose elements are non-poetic has also been regarded as non-poetic, even though its occurrence may be confined to verse. The matter is arguable, but such compounds may be regarded as products of a technique of compounding, rather than forms which were remembered by the poets as part of the word-hoard.

(b) Personal names and place-names are excluded; words like *gar* and *guþ* which are otherwise poetic often appear in the specialized context of personal names, but are extremely rare outside this context in non-poetic texts.

(c) Some latitude has been allowed where non-poetic occurrences are in the glosses and glossaries: these texts cannot simply be defined as prosaic in register as they sometimes gloss Latin poetic words with Old English ones.

(d) Multiple citations in prose at parallel points in different manuscripts of the same text have been counted singly.

These criteria produce a corpus of some 350 words which may reasonably be regarded as constituents of the word-hoard. The word-hoard may have been larger than this: some words may have disappeared, others may have been incorporated into prose style, but this cannot be ascertained by empirical analysis.

Beowulf uses 268 of these words, *Andreas* 221 and *Genesis A* 177: these long narrative poems thus employ more than 50 per cent of this vocabulary, and frequently use many of these words. By contrast, the Paris Psalter uses 106 of these words – remarkably fewer than *Beowulf* and considerably fewer than *Genesis A* – but this still represents 30 per cent of the available poetic vocabulary. The poet of the metrical psalms was at least acquainted with the conventional terminology, therefore, and it is possible that he had a full working knowledge of it, but was deliberately selective in its use. Krapp, commenting on the use of poetic diction in this text, notes that 'the poetical word *metod*, so common in older poetry as one of the designations of the Deity, occurs so rarely, perhaps only once, in the metrical parts of the Paris Psalter',[3] and it is true that many poetic words which are very common elsewhere appear extremely rarely, or not at all, in the Paris Psalter. In the former category are

---

[3] *The Paris Psalter and the Meters of Boethius*, ed. G. P. Krapp, ASPR 5 (New York, 1932), xvii.

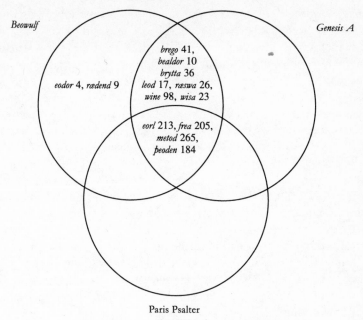

Fig. 2   Words for 'lord' in the Paris Psalter, *Beowulf* and *Genesis A*

eorl (68.20.3, 71.15.2), *fæge* (135.15.1), *firas* (134.3.2), *gar* (54.20.3, 90.6.2), *guma* (74.6.1, 93.10.1), *heapo-* (145.6.6), *metod* (127.5.2), *nergend* (113.9.1), *rand* (105.8.2), *secg* ('man', 110.7.1), *sinc* (67.27.4) and *þeoden* (118.52.2); and *beado*, *brego*, *brytta*, *eafora*, *frod*, *guþ*, *heoru-*, *hild*, *ides*, *maþelian*, *rinc*, *rof*, *sin*, *wiga* and *wine* are entirely absent. Even given the relative scarceness of poetic diction, instances of the latter group, and many occurrences of all of these words, should certainly have been expected in an Old English poem that is more than five thousand lines long. This is especially so, as many of these are convenient synonyms for common ideas in the poetry, like 'warrior', 'ruler' and 'God', which the alliterative poet found highly apt for his requirements. The peculiarity of this distribution – the rareness or absence of many of the best known poetic words – obviously suggests that the poet knew the vocabulary, but was reluctant to use it.

The surprising absence of common poetic words for set ideas is readily illustrated by the use of the available poetic words for 'lord' or 'noble man', in *Beowulf*, *Genesis A* and the Paris Psalter, as shown in fig. 2. The numbers in this figure represent the total occurrence of these items in the whole corpus, and demonstrate that only the commonest items are shared by all three texts, whilst the rarest appear only in *Beowulf*. The numbers include occurrences in compounds. The richness of the poetic vocabulary of *Beowulf* is shown by the

169

fact that it alone of these three poems uses poetic words for the set idea which do not occur in the other two (*eodor, rædend*), and only it uses all the poetic words which appear in the other two. Indeed, *hearra* is the only poetic word for this idea which cannot be found in *Beowulf*, and, as this word is mainly confined to *Genesis B*, and occurs frequently in the *Heliand*, it is possible that it was borrowed from the closely related Old Saxon poetic tradition.[4] The conventional character of the poetic vocabulary is exemplified by the large lexical overlap between *Beowulf* and *Genesis A*, and the relative distance of the metrical psalms from this tradition is shown by the slightness of the overlap with the other two texts. There is not a single poetic word for 'lord' in this text which does not occur in the other two, nor does it share vocabulary with either *Beowulf* or *Genesis A* in the way that they share with each other. Of the four words found in all three, *metod* and *þeoden* appear only once each in the psalms, and *eorl* only twice.

Many of the most productive of the poetic words – those which generate great numbers of compounds – are also largely absent from this text. The most productive poetic lexemes are *guþ* (53 different compounds), *hild(e)* (52), *hyge* (37), *bealo* (36), *ferhþ* (35), *sele* (31), *mere* (29), *beado* (25), *heaþo-* (24) and *gar* (22). *Guþ, hild, beado* and *gar* do not occur in compounds in this text, and only *gar* appears as a simplex. The remaining six generate only *hygeclæne, hygecræft, hygeþanc, haþyge, oferhyge; unbealo, bealoinwit; ferhþcleofa, ferhþcofa, ferhþlic; seledream, selegescot; merestream* and *heapogrim*, which all occur only once, with the exception of *hygecræft* (three times) and *selegescot* (eight times). By contrast, *The Fates of the Apostles*, a poem of a mere 122 lines, employs *guþhwæt, hildcorþor, hildheard, hygeblind, collenferhþ, beadocræftig* and *beadorof*. Certainly, the longest Old English poetic text should have provided large numbers of such compounds. Their absence from the metrical psalms is marked, and is connected with the paucity of heavy metrical types. It should be noted too that it is precisely this kind of vocabulary that lends the poetry the resonance of the heroic, even where the theme is not explicitly so.

The absence of heroic terminology from a text which uses almost a third of the available poetic vocabulary may, at first sight, seem contradictory, but the situation is clarified by a grammatical analysis of the poetic words. Fig. 3 shows how *Beowulf, Genesis A* and the Paris Psalter use the available poetic weak nouns. The number of nouns in this class that are poetic is small enough to suit this kind of presentation, but the distribution is typical of the poetic nouns. The numerical distribution is similar to that in fig. 2, with the commonest items in the centre, and the least common mainly confined to

---

4 B. J. Timmer, in *The Later Genesis, edited from MS Junius 11* (Oxford, 1954), notes that the meaning of *hearra* in *Genesis B* has been strongly influenced by Old Saxon (p. 38).

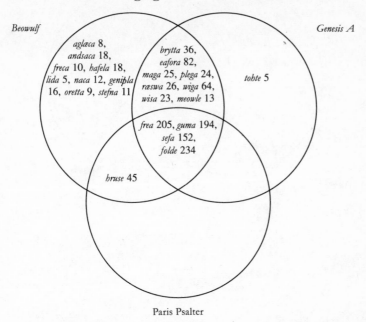

Fig. 3 Use of weak nouns in the Paris Psalter, *Beowulf* and *Genesis A*

Beowulf; the metrical psalms make use of only the most frequently occurring poetic nouns. *Beowulf* is remarkable for its extensive use of the poetic weak nouns. *Hearra*, the only poetic word for 'lord' not used by the *Beowulf*-poet, is also one of only three such nouns that he does not use (with *tohte* and *woma*). Remarkable, too, is the degree of overlap between *Beowulf* and *Genesis A*. With the sole exception of *hruse*, no poetic weak noun occurs in the metrical psalms that does not occur in either of the other two. This text cannot match either the range of poetic nouns to be found in *Beowulf*, or the closeness of the lexical relationship between *Beowulf* and *Genesis A*. Indeed, the Paris Psalter uses as many poetic adjectives and adverbs, and almost as many poetic verbs, as *Genesis A*, but uses only 57 of the poetic nouns, beside 117 in *Genesis A*, and 158 in *Beowulf*. Given that there are 183 available poetic nouns, it is clear that *Beowulf*, and to a slightly lesser extent *Genesis A*, emphasize the nominal poetic element, where the poet of the metrical psalms avoids it.

Fig. 4(a) and (b) shows the distribution in the same poems of poetic weak verbs of Classes I and II which are not prefixed. Although only three verbs are shared in common – a number similar to the shared element seen in figs. 2 and 3 – it is clear that, in its use of the verbal element of the poetic lexicon, the Paris Psalter engages much more closely with the poetic tradition as represented by *Beowulf* and *Genesis A*, for, unlike the situation presented in the two previous

171

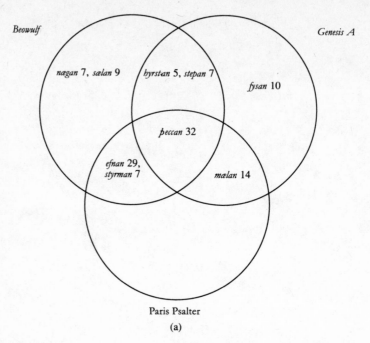

Fig. 4*a*   Distribution of Class I weak verbs in the Paris Psalter, *Beowulf* and *Genesis A*

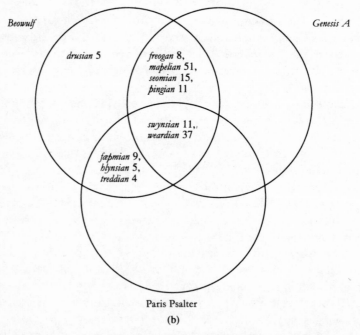

Fig. 4*b*   Distribution of Class II weak verbs in the Paris Psalter, *Beowulf* and *Genesis A*

172

figures, and despite the fact that poetic verbs occur less frequently than poetic nouns, figs. 4(a) and 4(b) show a text that shares poetic verbs both with *Beowulf* and with *Genesis A*. Fig. 3 suggests a tradition dominated by *Beowulf*, but here we see what we would expect from a tradition: the great majority of the lexical items are shared by the texts. Thus, the metrical psalms stand apart from the tradition in their scant use of poetic nouns, but are a normal part of that tradition in their use of the poetic verbs. The Paris Psalter is part of the poetic tradition, but, paradoxically, is not part of the heroic tradition, and this suggests a deliberate policy of selection by the poet, rather than ignorance of the poetic vocabulary.

This peculiar situation would appear to be at least partly a consequence of the poet's method of translation. It is well-known that Old English poets had at their disposal large groups of poetic and non-poetic words for commonly occurring ideas. When translating *homo* and *vir* in the psalms, we would expect a normal poet to have made extensive use of the considerable vocabulary for 'man' or 'warrior'. In fact, in sixty-two of the sixty-seven uses of *homo* in psalms LI–CL the poet translates *mann*, and in eleven of the twelve occurrences of *vir* he translates *wer*.[5] In the majority of the forty or so instances where the poet uses *beorn, eorl, firas, guma, hæleþ, hysse, nippas, secg* and *ylde* he is expanding, or making a complete addition to, the Latin. Almost all of these additions are in the first alliterating stave of the b-verse. The psalms offer fewer opportunities for the employment of poetic words for weapons, but the position is very similar: *scutum* is translated *scyld* (75.3.2, 90.5.1), whilst *rand* (105.8.2) is an addition to the Latin in the first stave of the b-verse, and *bord* and *lind* are never used; *gladius* is translated *sweord* on nine occasions, but never appears as *heoru, bill* or *secg*;[6] *iaculum* occurs once as *gar* (54.20.3). The poetic vocabulary is rich in words for 'crowd', 'troop' or 'band' – *corþor, gedræg, dryht, gedryht, hwearf, sweot, teohh* and *worn* – but the poet translates *grex* by *folc* (77.52.1, 77.70.1), *multitudo* generally by *menigeo* and *congregatio, synagoga* and *multi* variously, but never poetically. *Corþor* (54.15.2) is an addition, but looks very much like a mistake, and *teohh* (70.17.3) is also an addition. The Old English psalters most frequently gloss *homo*: *mann, vir*: *wer, scutum*: *scyld, gladius*: *sweord* and *multitudo*: *menigeo*. Where the poet resorts to poetic vocabulary, he still uses it for the traditional purpose of establishing alliteration, but he rarely uses such vocabulary when translating directly from the Latin. In direct translation he prefers to follow the conventional and prosaic translations of

---

[5] The exceptions are 65.4 *ylda*, 93.10 *guman*, 108.16 *þearfendra*, 127.5 *beorna*, 146.9 *haeleþa* and 75.4 *hi*.

[6] Nor is it translated as *mece*, a word often regarded as poetic which appears frequently in the glosses and glossaries.

Table 1

The number and percentage of poetic words in each metrical position

Text	First position	Second position	Third position	Fourth position	Light verses a-verse	Light verses b-verse	Positions of Secondary stress
Beowulf	453 (23.6%)	376 (19.6%)	394 (20.6%)	168 (8.8%)	178 (9.3%)	62 (3.2%)	283 (14.8%)
Andreas	184 (19.6%)	193 (20.6%)	213 (22.7%)	121 (12.9%)	67 (7.1%)	48 (5.1%)	112 (12%)
Genesis A	240 (24.3%)	181 (18.3%)	274 (27.7%)	109 (11%)	63 (6.4%)	29 (2.9%)	85 (8.6%)
Paris Psalter	57 (10%)	56 (9.8%)	286 (50%)	65 (11.4%)	62 (10.8%)	18 (3.1%)	22 (3.8%)

The number and percentage of prosaic words in each metrical position in the Paris Psalter

First position	Second position	Third position	Fourth position	Light verses	Positions of secondary stress	Unstressed positions	Defective
22 (19%)	6 (5%)	8 (7%)	34 (29%)	37 (31%)	3 (3%)	1 (1%)	7 (6%)

the psalter gloss tradition. A full list of the common nouns that this poet avoids using might provide a reliable guide to the vocabulary that a late Anglo-Saxon felt to be heroic, but, more importantly, this reluctance to deploy a large part of the word-hoard whilst using poetic metre, which is one of the most striking features of this text, suggests that, though the conventional metre still conveyed a powerful resonance for this poet, much of the traditional vocabulary evoked unacceptable heroic connotations. The Paris Psalter exemplifies a poetics in which rhythm and meaning have come to stand in an oblique, divergent relationship, where, for the *Beowulf* poet, these were harmonious and mutually enriching. This could be construed as a symptom of a poetic mode in its death throes.

It is inherently probable that any major change in the use of the conventional poetic language would have commensurate impact on the use of the system of rank, for this system is the set of principles that governs the meeting point of that language and the alliterative system. As such, it has two main aspects: a general and a specific. The general system is that by which poetic words (that have since largely disappeared from the language) are mainly used in alliterating positions, whilst 'synonymous' colloquial words (which the language has mainly retained) are allowed to appear freely in the non-alliterating position.[7] The development of this system must have been connected with the growth of the formulaic system, and with the need to find synonyms to fill the three alliterating positions. In its specific aspect, although certain poetic words are free to appear in all the alliterating positions, others are tied to specific positions in the alliterative line, and this situation probably came about because Old English poets felt that a particular word properly belonged to a particular position in the line because it commonly appeared in formulae which placed it in such a set position. Table 1 lists the number and percentage of poetic words in each metrical position of the line in *Beowulf*, *Andreas*, *Genesis A* and the Paris Psalter, and the number and percentage of prosaic words (as defined by E. G. Stanley)[8] across the line in the Paris Psalter. The general system of rank is illustrated by the contrast between the proportion of poetic and prosaic words that appear in the fourth, non-alliterating position in these texts. In normal verses in the Paris Psalter, prose words most frequently appear in this position, although this poet is perfectly normal in the low priority he gives to poetic words in the same position. The

---

[7] On poetic rank, see A. Brink, *Stab und Wort im Gawain* (Halle, 1920), M. Borroff, *Sir Gawain and the Green Knight: a Stylistic and Metrical Study* (New Haven, CT, 1962), pp. 52–90 and T.A. Shippey, *Old English Verse* (London, 1972), pp. 102–3.
[8] See 'Studies in the Prosaic Vocabulary of Old English Verse', *NM* 72 (1971), 385–418. Professor Stanley tells me that he would now revise his definition of 'prosaic'. I am grateful to Professor Stanley for a number of helpful criticisms of this article.

Table 2

The commonest poetic words in the Paris Psalter, and their distribution

Poetic word	First position	Second position	Third position	Fourth position	Light verses	Total occurrence
neod	3	1	54	0	3	61
awa	2	0	41	0	0	43
fæle	9	1	19	0	1	30
sneome	4	2	10	11	0	27
byge	3	8	14	0	1	26
folde	2	2	8	3	9	24
ealdor ('life')	5	2	0	1	11	19
langre	2	2	13	0	0	17
hæleþ	0	1	14	0	0	15
Totals	30	19	173	15	25	262

fact that, in all four texts, no more than 13 per cent of the poetic words are found in the final position graphically illustrates that poetic words do not occur randomly across the line, but are marked for use in alliterating positions, and that the poet of the metrical psalms also understood the closeness of this relationship. This is confirmed by the fact that forty-eight of the fifty-six poetic words which occur in the second stave of the a-verse of this text alliterate, even though the metrical psalms show markedly less double alliteration in this verse than is normal.[9] In the other positions, however, the distribution in the psalms is startlingly discrepant. Poetic words appear here much less frequently in positions of secondary stress, and this is causally connected with the lack of poetic compounds in this text. More important, however, is the fact that poetic words in the psalms are not spread evenly across the three alliterating positions: 18–28 per cent of these words in the other three poems are to be found in each of the first three positions of the normative line, and these figures are higher than for any other position, but half of the total number in the psalms are clustered in the first stave of the b-verse whilst their use is as rare in the two staves of the a-verse as it is in the second stave of the b-verse. So few poetic words appear in the a-verse of the psalms, and so low a proportion of its poetic vocabulary appears in this verse, that the system of rank can hardly be said to have had any impact upon its construction. Although the poet was aware of the general relationship that existed between the word-hoard and the alliterative structure, he limited its range principally to the construction of the b-verse.[10] As his use of the poetic words for 'man' shows, the word-hoard allowed him to pad out the line, and to make close translation seem something like poetry. The implications of this for the specific system of rank, are brought out by table 2, which gives the distribution across the line of the most commonly occurring poetic words in the metrical psalms. In *Genesis A*, *eafora*, *frea*, *metod*, *ides*, *hæleþ*, *eorl*, *rinc* and *þeoden* are all amongst the commonest poetic words and all are nouns suggestive of heroic theme, but only four of this poet's favourite words are nouns. The dominance of adverbs (*awa*, *sneome*, *lungre*) and of the adverbial (*neode*) in the poetic language of the psalms is noteworthy, for it contrasts with the rest of the poetry, and shows also the extent to which the poetic vocabulary is no longer integral to the language, but has been subordinated to the role of bleached padding. *Neode*, *awa*, *lungre* and *hæleþ* rarely appear here outside the third position in the line, and of the remainder only *ealdor* fails to show a large proportion of its occurrence in this position.

[9] See M.S. Griffith, 'The Method of Composition of Old English Verse Translation, with Particular Reference to the Metres of Boethius, The Paris Psalter and Judgment Day II' (unpubl. DPhil dissertation, Univ. of Oxford, 1985), pp. 46–57.

[10] On the difficulty the poet had with the first stave of the b-verse, see F.H. Whitman, 'A Major Compositional Technique in Old English Verse', *ELN* 11 (1973), 81–6.

This contrasts in a number of cases with the distribution in the rest of the corpus. *Awa* generally occurs elsewhere in the first stave of the a-verse in the formula *awa to ealdre; lungre* is also commonly found in this stave; all eight uses elsewhere of *fæle* fall in the first stave, all of them in verses with double alliteration, and five of them in the formula *faele freopo-* X. *Hyge, folde* and *hælep* are commonly found elsewhere in all three alliterating positions. *Ealdor* commonly occurs here in light verses, but is generally found elsewhere in the second stave of the a-verse in formulae such as *awa to ealdre, ece to ealdre* and *æfre to ealdre* which do not appear in this text. Thus it is not merely that the specifics of the system of rank are different in the metrical psalms, but also that the increasing detachment of this system from the a-verse and from the formula shows the extent to which the poetic system is becoming unravelled here. This text is not a reliable guide to the Old English system of rank, and should be handled with care in any analysis of it.[11]

The restriction in the use of poetic vocabulary, and the constriction placed on the system of rank, have a major effect on the use of the formula in this text. R. E. Diamond believed that the metrical psalms were not dissimilar from the rest of the poetry in their use of formulaic techniques, but, for a variety of reasons, his arguments cannot be accepted.[12] This is not the place for a complete analysis of the formulae to be found in the psalms, but, by the selective illustration of the occurrence of poetic words in certain types of formula, I hope to demonstrate that the Paris Psalter is not formulaic in any ordinary, or perhaps in any meaningful, sense. I shall concentrate on two groups of formulae: first, on the poet's use of epithets for God, because the poetry provides a great variety and wealth of formulae which contain this common, essential idea, and these ought to have been very useful to a translator of the psalms; and secondly, on the poet's use of some kinds of varied formulae, for these could not be produced by rote, and their presence, or absence, ought to test a poet's facility with formulaic technique.

The absence, noted above, of the usual formulae associated with *awa, ealdor* and *fæle* might suggest that the poet was happy to use poetic words as fillers, but was unwilling to use the formulae associated with those same words.

---

[11] There are also occasional violations of general rank. Only four of the forty-four occurrences of *hreper* outside the psalms fail to alliterate, but it fails in four of the six occurrences here. *Efnan* alliterates without exception elsewhere, but occurs here four times finally in the line, and three times in lines that lack alliteration.

[12] See *The Diction of the Anglo-Saxon Metrical Psalms*, Janua Linguarum, Series Practica 10 (The Hague, 1963). More than a third of the formulae quoted by Diamond are supported only by reference to verses elsewhere in the metrical psalms, and many of these represent repetitions in the source. More than a quarter are light verses which show repetition of the word in the position of main stress only.

Furthermore, the appearance of the repeated phrases *awa to feore*, *awa to worulde*, *fæle fultum*, *fæle sceap* and *fæle dryhten*, which are common in this text but are not to be found anywhere else in verse, might suggest that this poet still had a liking for repetition, despite his distaste for the traditional formulae. That this is the simplest explanation of the available evidence is most clearly demonstrated by the poet's use of epithets for God. As most of the poetry is concerned with the subject of Christianity, it is to be expected that in this area it will be varied and dense in its formulaic system, and nowhere more so than in a poetic version of the psalms in which the psalmist continually calls upon his god, and that god is the jealous and vengeful champion of the Israelites, the mighty and warlike god of the Old Testament, whose nature is well-suited to the traditional Old English heroic epithets for the divinity. Here, then, the poetic heritage could have provided the translator with great help in his composing, but, in the most obvious fashion, the poet avoids the conventional poetic language. By not using *brego* or *brytta*, he deprives himself of the common formulas *brego engla*, *brego moncynnes*, *lifes brytta* and *swegles brytta*. Not one of the formulae of the type *X engla* – such as *frea engla*, *metod engla*, *engla drihten*, *scyppend engla*, etc. – occurs in this text, even though some of them do not contain poetic words. The situation is as unusual in the single uses of the poetic *nergend* and *þeoden*, where the well-known formulae *sawla nergend*, *niþþa nergend*, *nergend god*, *nergend usser*, *engla þeoden*, *rice þeoden*, *mæra þeoden*, *þrymfæst þeoden*, *þeoden leofesta*, are not used, and the words appear in the otherwise unattested *nergend drihten* (113.9.1) and *þeoden drihten* (118.52.2). Likewise, *scyppend* does not occur in the formulae *scyppend engla*, *heofena scyppend*, *weroda scyppend*, *gasta scyppend*, but only once, and in the unique phrase *scyppend mære* (103.23.4). Epithets with explicit military or heroic flavour, like *sigora wealdend*, *sigora weard*, *sigora frea*, *sigora sopcyning*, *weroda wealdend*, *weroda drihten*, *weroda wuldorcyning*, are used either not at all, or very sparingly (only *sigora wealdend* once at 70.21.2, and *weroda drihten* three times). There are nonetheless hundreds of epithets for God in the metrical psalms, but almost all of them are produced using *god* or *drihten*, and a number of them are frequent here but occur nowhere else in Old English poetry (e.g. *bealde drihten*, *bliþe drihten*, *fæger drihten*, *se goda god*, *Isræla god*, etc.). Their lack of semantic and metrical variety (most with *drihten* are type 2A1 in the b-verse),[13] contributes much to the insipid quality of the verse; and yet, many of the missing formulae, especially those like *engla drihten*, which are common and lack poetic words, ought to have been produced by accident in such a large text with such frequent invocation, and their absence, and replacement by anodyne phrases often

---

[13] Type 2A1 is the commonest sub-division of type A in the metrical framework given by A. J. Bliss in *The Metre of Beowulf* (Oxford, 1967).

179

confined in verse to this text, is the strongest evidence of the psalter poet's deliberate avoidance of the formulaic heritage. The poet's religious ideology persuaded him to translate the word of God closely and faithfully, and to avoid the heroic image, but this is constantly threatened by the poetic mode in which it is expressed, for the many repetitions that are confined to this poetic translation indicate a poet with a sense of the formulaic contradictorily coupled with a desire to avoid well-known formulae. The Paris Psalter, therefore, occupies an incongruous position in its relationship with the tradition, and the effect on an Anglo-Saxon accustomed to the poetic mode must have come close to the grotesque.

Incongruity manifests itself in many aspects of this text's style. It is apparent, for example, in non-standard, internal repetitions like *fæle sceap* which bizarrely combine poetic words and prosaic ones, but it is nowhere better seen than in the poet's handling of formulaic systems. Appendix II (below, pp. 185–6) contrasts the appearance of formulaic systems in the Paris Psalter with the same in *Genesis A* (chosen because it too is a translation of part of the Bible), and concerns itself with verses in which there is repetition of only one word, which is the poetic word, and which is fully stressed, but in which other types of constraint demonstrate that these are members of formulaic systems. These can be sub-divided into three groups. Varied formulae are those which repeat a stressed poetic word and part of a compound, but vary the compound's other element (e.g. *tirfæst metod*: *wærfæst metod*). Where a formula's existence is supported only by repetition elsewhere within a larger metrical structure, or where a complete formula is found fixed in a heavier metrical unit, these are termed 'embedded' formulae.[14] The division between varied and embedded formulae is clear: typically, in the first category, the repetition does not constitute an entire metrical unit, and the variation does not affect the metrical type; conversely, in the second, the repeated element is a complete metrical structure, and the embedding always changes the metrical type. The embedded formulae have been grouped according to their general metrical shape: that is, into normal, heavy and hypermetric verses. Constrained formulae show repetition of a single element only, but the context always provides evidence of morphological, syntactic or metrical repetition. For example, a verse such as *Abraham maþelode* uses the poetic verb *maþelian*, which always appears in Old English poetry in the third person, singular, preterite, indicative *maþelode*, and, with only two exceptions, is always preceded by a stressed subject which is a proper noun. The verb never occurs in light verses, or in b-verses, but always occupies the second stave of the a-verse.

14 On this type of formula, see L. E. Nicholson, 'Oral Techniques in the Composition of Expanded Anglo-Saxon Verses', *PMLA* 78 (1963), 287–92.

180

It is essential to the production of these formulae that the poet should have a working knowledge of various conventional kinds of variation in the use of the poetic language, and it is precisely here that the psalms are most deficient, providing only one varied formula, one embedded formula and not a single constrained formula. Many of the changes in the poetic style contribute to this deficiency – the lack of a -verse formulae, the grouping of poetic words in the first stave of the b-verse, the absence of poetic compounds, and the rareness of heavy and hypermetric types – and it is likely that the poet was incapable of reconciling the exigencies of close translation with the demands imposed by this complex poetic mode. Oral-formulaists used to regard oral and literary modes of production as incompatible, and it is likely that, in this more specialized sense, they were correct: amplification lies at the heart of the Old English poetic style, but close translation forbids it. The subject matter of the psalms would have provided many difficulties for an Anglo-Saxon poetic paraphraser, but so does the content of Genesis, which is often not readily compatible with heroic style. The poet of *Genesis A* allows himself to amplify his source, and it is this that makes his composing approximate to the normal style. This text provides ten varied formulae, ten embedded formulae, and nineteen constrained formulae. The varied formulae show large systems emerging. For example, the formula *X-fæst metod* provides the following system:

. . . *tir metod*	*Gen A*	2377b
. . . *soþ metod*	*Gen A*	1414b, 2793b, 2807b
. . . *soþfæst metod*	*Gen A*	2654a
. . . *wærfæst metod*	*Gen A*	1320a, 1549a, 2901a
. . . *tirfæst metod*	*Gen A*	1044a
. . . *tirfæst hæleþ*	*DEdg*	13a, *Ex* 63b
. . . *wærfæst hæleþ*	*Gen A*	1740a, 2026a
. . . *wærfæst rinc*	*Gen A*	1011b[15]

This system could, doubtless, be extended, but there is sufficient evidence to show that the poets could readily vary standard formulae, often without substantially altering the meaning. The psalms do not use any of the above formulae, and no similar systems can be found in it; where the poet uses *soþfæst*, for example, it is in the repeated phrases *soþfæst weorc* and *soþfæst word*, which are unattested elsewhere.

The formulae in *Genesis A* that show the operation of morphological constraint all contain strong verbs that are restricted to one morphological

---

[15] The abbreviations of the titles of the poems are those given by B. Mitchell, C. Ball and A. Cameron, *ASE* 4 (1975), 207–21, revised *ASE* 8 (1979), 331–3.

form. *Bedreosan* and *beleosan* (with one exception) always occur in the poetry in the past participle; *ahycgan* (with one exception) is limited to the infinitive; and *ahlyhhan* (again with one exception) is confined to the third person, singular, preterite, indicative. Of the poetic verbs that show this kind of conditioning, only *ahlyhhan*, *hropan*, *mælan*, *neotan* and *towrecan* occur in the psalms. *Towrecan* appears, as elsewhere, in the past participle (58.15.2, 91.8.3), but it is remarkable that in the other four instances, the text provides examples, which are otherwise extremely rare, of breaches of constraint. Here is the only example of *ahlyhhan* not in the third person, singular, preterite, but in the present tense (85.11.1 *Heorte min ahlyhheð*); here is the sole instance of *hropan* not in the third person, plural, preterite, but in the present participle (146.10.2 *þonne heo hropende*); and 84.7.2 *mælan wille* is one of only two exceptions to the tendency of this verb, illustrated in fifteen occurrences, to appear in the third person, singular, preterite, often in the formula *wordum mælde*, with which the other exception, *El* 537 *wordum mældon*, is still associated. Only four out of eighteen occurrences of *neotan* are not in the infinitive, and one of these is 88.42.1, *þæt feores neote*. Just as this poet knows much of the poetic vocabulary but refuses to use most of the formulae linked with these words, so he knows many of the poetic verbs but refuses to accept the constraints governing their use. This underlines the extent of his detachment from the tradition, and the effect must have been to heighten the reader's (or listener's) sense of incongruity.

A number of conclusions are evident. The psalter poet can be demonstrated to have known much of the usual poetic diction, but was often reluctant to use it. His decision to translate closely and to follow in many instances the conventional and prosaic translations of the psalter gloss tradition, coupled with his apparent distaste for the heroic, inevitably led to restricted use of this vocabulary. The especially limited occurrence of the nominal element of this lexicon best illustrates this distaste, and removed from his language those words most productive in the formation of compounds. His mechanical deployment of the diction in order to carry the alliteration into the b-verse had, as its necessary consequences, the erosion of the system of rank, and the substantial destruction of the formulaic system. Hence formulae with poetic words are much rarer than might have been expected, even given his limited use of this diction. The many repetitions confined to the metrical psalms are partly the product of repetitions in the source, but also suggest a poet who, with such a marked liking for repetition, still had a sense of the formulaic. On the other hand, the absence of varied, embedded and constrained formulae, the breaches of morphological constraints, and, in particular, the lack of the usual epithets for God, indicate that the poet tried to distance his composition from the tradition, and to produce a translation which had only the faintest echoes of the heroic.

Elizabeth Salter commented on *Piers Plowman* that 'even if [Langland] had been familiar with and practised in the most extreme forms of alliterative rhetoric, it is hardly likely that he would have used them in a poem designed to reach not a small courtly audience, but the widest kind of public'.[16] Where Langland does use the normal Middle English alliterative poetic diction, he does not employ it in the mechanical fashion seen in the Old English metrical psalms, but the connection between absence of alliterative poetic diction and the interests of the audience is of possible relevance to an understanding of the psalms. The evidence here points to an audience which felt that such poetic language, and the heroic effect that it created, was out of place in a rendition of a sacred text, but one which also felt that the usual metre and a repetitive style were the only proper media for poetic translation in the vernacular. This new contradictory attitude to the ancient tradition must have been an important factor in its disappearance, and in the development of rhythmical prose, where a sense of rhythm is combined with the language of prose.

APPENDIX I

POETIC WORDS IN OLD ENGLISH

The following are the relevant poetic words. They are listed in alphabetical order, except that words beginning with *ge-* are listed under the first letter of the stem. Meanings and parts of speech are given only where a form gives rise to ambiguity, or where only one meaning or part is poetic. Poetic words in the Paris Psalter are marked with the symbol +.

geaclian, acol, ædre, æled, æsc ('spear'), *ætheran, afysan, agetan, aglac, aglæca, ahlyhhan +, ahycgan, andlean, andsaca, ar* ('messenger'), *aswebban, atol +, awa +*

bæl, beado, bealdor, bealo +, bearhtm ('noise'), *bedreosan, befæpman, beleosan, belipan, bemurnan, benc, beneotan, benn, beorn +, bereofan, besteman, beteldan, betlic, bepringan, bewitian, bewrecan, bill* ('sword'), *gebland, geblandan, blican, bord* ('shield'), *brant, brego, brim +, bryten, brytta, byre*

clamm, corpor +, gecost +, cringan, cumbol, cwanian, cymlic(e) +

darop, deall, demend, deor ('brave'), *gedræg, dreor, dreorig* ('bloody'), *gedreosan +, drusian, dryht, gedryht*

---

[16] *Piers Plowman, an Introduction* (Oxford, 1969), p. 23.

183

ead, eafora, eafoþ, ealdor + ('life'), *ealh* + , *ear* + , *earh, earp, efnan* + , *geefnan* + , *ellor, eodor* ('prince'), *eorl* + ('warrior')

fæge + , *fæle* + , *gefælsian, fær* ('ship'), *fæted, fæþm* + ('embrace', 'bosom'), *fæþmian* + , *fah* + , *faroþ, ferhþ* + , *gefeterian* + , *fifel, firas* + , *flah, folde* + , *forlacan, forþgesceaft, forþweg, gefræge, frea* + , *freca, freod, freorig, freoþo* + , *frigan* ('love'), *frige, frod, fus, fyrn* + , *fysan, gefysan*

gad, gamol + , *gar* + , *geador, geap* ('spacious'), *geatolic, geahþ, gegnum, gegnunga, gehþo, geoc, geocian, geocor, geofen, geomor* + , *geondhweorfan, geondwlitan, gifeþe, gifl, ginn, glæm, gnorn* + , *gnyrn, grap, greotan, grorn, guma* + , *guþ, gyllan, gyrn*

hador + , *hædre, hæleþ* + , *hæst, hafela, hasu, hearra, heaþo-* + , *gehegan, helm* ('protector'), *heolfor, heoru, hettend, hild, hleoþor* + , *hleow* + , *hlymman, hlynsian* + , *hnag, holm* + ('sea'), *horsc, hremig, hreþ(-ig), hreþer* + , *gehroden, hropan* + , *hror* + , *hroþor, hruse* + , *hwearf, hwearft* + , *hwopan, gehygd* + , *hyge* + , *hyrst, hyrstan, hysse* +

ides, iren ('sword')

gelac + , *lacan, gelad* ('way'), *lagu* + ('sea'), *leod* ('prince'), *(ge)leodan* + , *lid, lida, lind* ('shield'), *linnan, liss, lungre* +

mæcg + , *mæg* ('kinswoman'), *mægeþ* ('woman'), *mæl* + ('time'; 'sword'), *(ge)mælan* + , *mæþel, maga, mago, maþelian, mearh, meowle, mere* + ('sea'), *metan* ('traverse'), *metod* + , *meþe, mirce, missere, mund* ('hand')

naca, nægan, genægan, nearo (noun), *neotan* + , *nergend* + , *niod* + ('desire'), *niþan, niþ, geniþla, niþþas* +

ofermægen, onhæle, onspannan, onþeon, onwadan, or, oretta, orgeate, orlege, oþberan, oþferian, oþlædan + , *oþþringan*

pæþþan, plega ('battle-play')

rædend, ræswa, rand + ('shield'), *reced, reodan, reonig, reord* + ('speech'), *reotan, rinc, rof, gerum*

saed + , *sæl* ('hall'), *sælan, scealc* + ('warrior', 'servant'), *sceotend, scriþan* + , *scyne* + , *sealo, secg* + ('man')', *sefa* + , *sele* + , *seomian, sid* + (adj.), *sin, sinc* + , *sinnan, sliþe* + , *sliþen, sneome* + , *sneowan, snude, stefna, steþan, streamas* + ('sea'), *styrman* + ('cry aloud'), *sund* ('sea'), *swæs* ('dear'), *swat* ('blood'), *swatig* ('bloody'), *swearte* (adv.), *swefan* + ('sleep', 'die'), *swegl, sweot, geswing, geswiþan* + , *swylt* + , *swynsian* +

teohh + , *tiber* + , *toginan* + , *tir* + , *(ge)tohte, torht* + , *torn* + , *toscufan, towrecan* + , *træf, trag* + , *treddian* + , *getwæfan*

þeccan + , *þeoden* + , *geþingan, þingian* ('speak'), *þracu, geþræc* ('press', 'heap'), *þrag* + , *þroht, þryþ* + , *þurhwadan*

unbræce, unforcuþ + , *unhwilen, unscende, unwaclic(e), unweaxen, upheofon* + , *uprodor, upweg, urig-*

vadan, gewadan, wæcnan, wæd, wæfre, wæg+, wæge, wæpan, wap, wapum, weardian+
'guard', 'occupy'), wergþo+, wicg, wiga, wiggend, wine, wir, wisa, wiþerhycgende, wiþhyc-
ȝan+, wlitan+, woma, worn, woþ, wræst+, wrætt, wrætlic(e), wrasen, wudu ('ship')
ȝlde+ ('men'), ymbsittend+, yrman

APPENDIX II

FORMULAIC SYSTEMS USING POETIC WORDS IN *GENESIS A* AND THE PARIS PSALTER

The Paris Psalter
Varied formulae

105.28.2b *misdædum fah*
    cf. *Sat* 185b *iudædum fah*

Embedded formulae

54.22.2b, 142.4.4b *innan hreðres*
    cf. *Christ* B 539b, *Guth* B 979b, *Beo* 2113b *hreðer innan weoll, Guth* B 938b *Hreþer innan born, Guth* B 1052b *Hreþer innan swearc*

Genesis A
Varied formulae

1502a *torhtmod hæle*
    cf. *Finn* 23a *deormod hæleþ*
1044a *tirfæst metod*
    cf. 1320a, 1549a, 2901a *wærfæst metod,* 2654a *soþfæst metod; L Pr I* 8b, *And* 386b, *soþfæst metod*
1898a *heardum hearmplega*
    cf. *Ex* 327a, *Brun* 25a *heard handplega*
1011b *wærfæstne rinc*
    cf. *Men* 44a *rincas regolfæste, OrW* 13a *rincas rædfæste*
1740a, 2026a *wærfæst hæleþ*
    cf. *DEdg* 13a, *Ex* 63b *tirfæst hæleþ*

Embedded formulae

2383b *ac heo gearum frod*
    cf. *Phoen* 154a *gomol, gearum frod*
2904a *bearne sinum*
    cf. *Aȝ* 116a *sinum bearnum to brice*

157b *frea engla heht,* 1711a *frea engla bam*
    cf. *El* 1307b *Moton engla frean*

2156a *ham hyrsted gold*
    cf. *Beo* 2255b *hyrsted golde*
1194a *wine wintres frod*
    cf. *Mnl* 66b *ac sceal wintrum frod*
121b *Metod engla heht*
    cf. *Guth B* 1132b *þe him meotud engla*

1015a *awyrged to widan aldre*
    cf. *And* 938b, 1721b *to widan aldre, Jud* 347a *wuldor to widan aldre*
1523a *oðrum aldor oðþringeð*
    cf. *Jul* 500b *þam ic ealdor oðþrong.*
2174a *dædrof drihtne sinum*
    cf. *Beo* 2789a *dryhten sinne, GenB* 295a *dollice mid drihten sinne*

Constrained formulae

Morphological Constraint

2382a *þa þæt wif ahloh*
    cf. *And* 454b, *Jul* 189a, *Beo* 730b, *MSol* 178b
2031b, 2182a *ræd ahicgan*
    cf. *Dan* 130b, 147a, *Christ C* 902b, *Gifts* 44b
1998b *leofum bedrorene,* 2082a *dome bedrorene,* 2099a *eorlum bedroren*
    cf. *GenB* 582b, 823b, *Guth A* 626a, *Guth B* 901a, *Wan* 79a, *Sea* 16a
86a *leohte belorene*
    cf. *And* 1079a, *Guth B* 1170a, 1327a, *Beo* 1073a
Syntactic constraint

1133b, 1578a, 1629a, 1646a, 1682a, 2054a, 2834b *eafora X*
    cf. *Beo* 19a, 897a, 1068a, etc., *Met* 26.35a, *Brun* 7a, *Capt* 13a, *Men* 136a
2164a, 2836a *Ebrea leod*
    cf. *Beo* 341a, 348b, 625a, etc., *El* 20a, *Fins* 24b
2817a *Wine Ebrea*
    cf. *Beo* 30b, 148a, 170b, etc., *Wld* 2.14b
Mixed constraint

1820a, 2893a *Abraham maþelode*
    cf. the use of *maþelian* elsewhere in the poetry

A new Latin source for the Old English 'Three Utterances' exemplum

MARY F. WACK AND CHARLES D. WRIGHT

The so-called 'Three Utterances' exemplum, which tells of the exclamations of a good and a bad soul to the angels or demons who lead them to heaven or hell at the moment of death, was adapted independently by three Anglo-Saxon homilists. Versions of this legend survive in an Old English Rogationtide homily in Oxford, Bodleian Library, Hatton 114, 102v–105v,[1] in a homily *Be heofonwarum and be helwarum* in London, British Library, Cotton Faustina A. ix, 21v–23v, and Cambridge, Corpus Christi College 302, pp. 71–3,[2] and in a Lenten homily in Oxford, Bodleian Library, Junius 85/86, fos. 25–40.[3] In 1935 Rudolf Willard published a study of the exemplum, with a detailed comparison between the three Old English versions, an Irish version, and a single Latin version in Paris, Bibliothèque Nationale, lat. 2628 (s. xi).[4] Two years later Willard published a second Latin version from Oxford, University College 61 (s. xiv).[5] Other texts of the Latin sermon have subsequently come to light. In 1966 Réginald Grégoire edited a version from the Homiliary of Toledo (London, BL, Add. 30853, s. xi), and identified five additional

[1] See N. R. Ker, *Catalogue of Manuscripts containing Anglo-Saxon* (Oxford, 1957), no. 331, item 53. The manuscript is assigned the siglum 'O (Hatton)' by D. G. Scragg, 'The Corpus of Vernacular Homilies and Prose Saints' Lives before Ælfric', *ASE* 8 (1979), 223–77, at 253–5. The homily was first ed. R. Willard, *Two Apocrypha in Old English Homilies*, Beiträge zur englischen Philologie 30 (Leipzig, 1935), 38–54 (Willard's Text H), and has been re-edited by J. Bazire and J. E. Cross, *Eleven Old English Rogationtide Homilies* (Toronto, 1982), pp. 115–24.

[2] Ker, *Catalogue*, nos. 153, item 4 and 56, item 10. The manuscripts are Scragg's J and K ('Corpus', pp. 245–7). This homily has not been fully edited, but the 'Three Utterances' portion was ptd from the Cotton Faustina manuscript by Willard, *Two Apocrypha*, pp. 38–56 (Willard's Text C). Willard also printed the introductory section of the homily (p. 68), as well as another part (pp. 24–5) in connection with the Seven Heavens apocryphon.

[3] Ker, *Catalogue*, no. 336, item 6 (Scragg's C, 'Corpus', pp. 235–6). The homily was partially ed. Willard, *Two Apocrypha*, pp. 39–57 (Willard's Text J); the complete text is ed. A. M. Luiselli Fadda, *Nuove omelie anglosassoni della rinascenza benedettina*, Filologia germanica, Testi e studi 1 (Florence, 1977), 8–21.

[4] *Two Apocrypha*, pp. 31–149. The Paris text was first published by L. Dudley, *The Egyptian Elements in the Legend of the Body and Soul* (Baltimore, MD, 1911), pp. 164–5.

[5] 'The Latin Texts of *The Three Utterances of the Soul*', *Speculum* 12 (1937), 147–66. In their edition of the Rogationtide homily, Bazire and Cross designate the Paris text as D, the Oxford text as K.

manuscripts.[6] In 1979, R. E. McNally, who was unaware of Willard's study, published another text from two early Vatican manuscripts, as part of a group of sermons which McNally regarded as Hiberno-Latin.[7] We have been able to identify more than twenty additional Latin manuscripts of the 'Three Utterances', including a third manuscript of the McNally collection in East Berlin, Deutsche Staatsbibliothek, Phillipps 1716.[8]

Of the three Old English versions of the exemplum, the Rogationtide homily and the homily *Be heofonwarum and be helwarum* are closest to the previously edited versions of the Latin sermon, although both have significant divergences and are clearly not translated directly from any known Latin text.[9] The homily in Junius 85/86, however, has a drastically abbreviated variant version of the exemplum, omitting the initial struggle between the devils and angels that occurs in all other versions except the Irish, as well as the escort and chant of the devils who lead the damned soul away to hell, and incorporating unique variants within the series of utterances for both the damned and just souls.

A ninth-century manuscript, Munich, Bayerische Staatsbibliothek, Clm. 28135 (s. ix[in]), preserves a text of the abbreviated recension of the 'Three Utterances' consulted by the author of the Junius homily. This composite manuscript, from Freising, contains a series of promulgations of Bavarian synods from about A.D. 800, followed by theological extracts and sermons.[10] On 44r-47r occurs a text of the 'Three Utterances' sermon, essentially similar

---

6 *Les Homéliaires du moyen âge*, Rerum ecclesiasticarum documenta, Series maior: Fontes 6 (Rome, 1966), 224–5; for the additional manuscripts identified by Grégoire, see p. 177. See also Grégoire's *Homéliaires liturgiques médiévaux* (Spoleto, 1980), pp. 310–11. P. Courcelle printed variants from another text in Orléans, Bibliothèque municipale, 149 (126), pp. 155–8: 'Fragments non identifiés de Fleury-sur-Loire (III)', *Revue des études Augustiniennes* 2 (1956), 541–2.

7 R. E. McNally, '"In Nomine Dei Summi": Seven Hiberno-Latin Sermons', *Traditio* 35 (1979), 121–43, at 134–6 (McNally's Document I). McNally's two manuscripts are Vatican, Bibliotheca Apostolica, Pal. lat. 212 (s. viii[ex]), on which see E. A. Lowe, *Codices Latini Antiquiores*, 11 vols. and suppl. (Oxford, 1934–71; 2nd ed. of vol. II, 1972) (hereafter abbreviated *CLA*) I, no. 85; and Pal. lat. 220 (s. ix[in]).

8 See C. D. Wright, 'Apocryphal Lore and Insular Tradition in St Gall, Stiftsbibliothek MS 908', in *Irland und die Christenheit: Bibelstudien und Mission*, ed. P. Ní Chatháin and M. Richter (Stuttgart, 1987), pp. 124–45, at 134–7. V. Rose, *Verzeichnis der lateinischen Handschriften der Königlichen Bibliothek zu Berlin* I (Berlin, 1893), p. 72, dates the manuscript s. viii/ix, but it is not included in *CLA*.

9 See, in addition to Willard, Bazire and Cross's comparisons of the homily in O (Hatton) with the published Latin versions (*Rogationtide Homilies*, pp. 116–19).

10 On the manuscript, see B. Bischoff, *Die südostdeutschen Schreibschulen und Bibliotheken in der Karolingerzeit I: Die Bayrischen Diözesen* (Wiesbaden, 1960), p. 93. The contents are described by A. Werminghoff, 'Zu den bayrischen Synoden am Ausgang des achten Jahrhunderts', *Festschrift Heinrich Brunner* (Weimar, 1910), pp. 39–55; for addenda to Werminghoff's description, see G. Morin, 'Un nouveau feuillet de l'*Itala* de Freising', *RB* 28 (1911), 221–3.

A *new source for the 'Three Utterances' exemplum*

to the versions published by Willard, Grégoire and McNally. Earlier, however, on fol. 13, in a section of the manuscript identified by Werminghoff only as 'Auszüge aus Augustin', is an abbreviated version of the 'Three Utterances' which corresponds closely to the Old English version of the exemplum in the Junius manuscript. We print this text below, in parallel with the relevant portion of the Old English homily.[11]

Junius 85/86

Clm. 28135

anima homines peccatores cum exierat de corpore . . . Hit gelimpeð þanne þæs synfullan mannes saul gæð of his lichaman, ðonne bið heo seofon siðum sweatre ðonne se hræfen. And hit is cweden on ðissum godspelle þæt deofla lædan ða saule ond þanne heo spreceð wependre stæfne to ðam deoflum ond hyo cweþ: 'Micle siendon þa ðyostre þe ge me tolædað'. Ond þanne andsweriað hire ða deoflo and hie cweðað: 'Maran þe siendan toweard in helle'. Þanne cweð seo saul eft: 'Micel is ðeos unrotnes þe ge me tolædað'. Ond þanne andsweriað hiere þa deofle ond hie cweðað: 'Maran gewin ond mare unblis þe is gegearwod on helle'. Ond þanne æfter þysum wordum hie lædað þa saule on helle witu.

[13r] Anima hominis peccatoris cum exigerit de corpore septies nigrior erit quam coruus. Et demones[1] qui ducunt eam [†]infernus qui dicitur[2].[†] Et anima[3] dicit cum lacrimis et gemitu, 'Magne[4] sunt tenebre.' Et respondent demones[1] et dicunt, 'Maioresque erunt et tibi apud demones[1].' Et iterum dicit anima, 'Magna est tristitia.' Et respondent demones[1], 'Maiorque[5] erit[6] tibi apud demones[1].' Haec sunt trea uerba peccatorum quando ducuntur ad infernum.

Ond þanne bið ðæs halgan mannes saul wutodlice, þanne heo of ðam lichaman gangeð. Seofon siðum heo bið beorhtre þanne sunne, and þa halgan Godes

Anima autem hominis sequitur; cum exierit de corpore septiens splendior [*sic*] erit quam[7]

---

[11] In the Latin text we have supplied punctuation and expanded abbreviations silently. The Old English text is from Fadda's edition (*Nuove omelie*, pp. 19.169–21.198), but we do not follow her emendation in line 195, as explained below, n. 30. In the Old English homily the speech of the angels to the blessed soul continues with praise of God and the Trinity (*Nuove omelie*, ed. Fadda, pp. 21.198–23.209).

ænglas hie lædað to Paradysum and
þanne cwyð seo saul to ðam ænglum þe
hie lædað: 'Eala, micel is ðeos blis þe ic
on gelædad eam'. Ond þanne andswergeað hire þa ænglas and cweðað:
'Mara blis þe is on heofonum
gegearwad'. Ond þanne seo saul eft
cweð: 'Micel is þes þrym þe we on
syndan'. Ond þanne andswergeað hiere
þa ænglas and cweðað: 'Þu cymest ful
ær to maran þrymme'. Ond þanne cwyð
seo saul þriddan siðe: 'Mycel is þis leoht
þe ic on eam'. Ond þanne andswergeað
hiere þa ænglas and hie cweðað: 'Þu
gemetst mare leoht mid Gode'. Ond
þanne syngað þa halgan ænglas swiðe
gastligne [*sic*] sang ond berað ða clænan
sawle to Gode on heora fæðmum ond
hie cwæðað to ðære sawle: '*Beatus quem
elegisti; replebimur*'. Hie cweðað: 'Eadig
eart ðu sawl, ðu name Gode eardunge in
ðinum huse. Ond we nu gefyllað mid
gode ðin hus, ðin templ his halig ond
wundorlicre ðrymnesse'. Ond hie
cweðað eft be ðare sawle: 'Eadig eart
ðu, sawl, ðu geheolde ðines Drihtnes
bebodu, ond ðu dydest geornlice æfter
ðines Godes willan'.

[13v]

sol. Et sancti angeli qui
ducunt[8] eam ad
†paradysus quo[9]
dicitur[2].†Et dicit anima,
'Magna est laetitia'. Et
respondent angeli,
'Maiorquę erit tibi apud
deum'. Et iterum dicit
anima, 'Magna est
magestas in qua sumus.'
Et dicunt[10] angeli,
'Maiorque erit[11] tibi
apud deum.' Et tertia
dicit anima, 'Magna est
lumen'. Et respondent
angeli, '[. . .] apud
deum'. Et sancti angeli
cantabunt canticum
spiritalem, portantes
eam in sinu suo et
dicentes ad animam,
'Beatus quem elegisti
domine et adsumpsisti,
inhabitauit in
tabernaculis tuis.
Replebimur in bonis
domus tuae; sanctum est
templum tuum, mirabile
in aequitate. Et beatus es
qui mandata seruasti dei
tui et fecisti ea diligenter
secundum uoluntatem
dei tui.'

[1]demonis [2]*see below* [3]m *added
above line* [4]magna [5]maiorisque
[6]erant [7]quem [8]dicunt [9]d *erased*
[10]dicent [11]erat *with* i *added above
line*

This new source allows us to answer many of the questions raised by Willard, who entitled a chapter of his study 'The Problem of J' (i.e., the Junius text).[12] From the Latin *incipit* preserved in the Old English rendering Willard assumed, correctly, that the homilist was 'working from a Latin original', and that the details peculiar to this version were derived from his Latin source.[13] The version in Clm. 28135 shows that the omissions peculiar to J – of the struggle of the demons and angels over the souls, of the shout of triumph of the victorious side in each case, and of the description of the bringing forth of each soul from its body[14] – are due to the Latin source. The new text also shows just how closely the Anglo-Saxon homilist was following his source for the details of his description and for the content and sequence of the utterances.

The description of the colour of the damned soul as 'seven times blacker than a raven' and of the just soul as 'seven times brighter than the sun' derives from the Latin, which therein differs from the other published Latin versions of the sermon, in which the demons (not the souls) are said to be as black (but not seven times as black) as a raven (or an Ethiopian), the angels as white (but not seven times as white) as snow.[15] The Irish version, however, also compares the good and bad souls to the sun and to a raven, but does not say they are seven times as black or bright.[16]

---

[12] *Two Apocrypha*, pp. 118–21. Willard's sigla for the manuscripts do not correspond to Scragg's (Willard's C = Scragg's J and K; his J = Scragg's C). To avoid confusion we here follow Willard's designation of the homily in Junius 85/86 as J.   [13] *Ibid.* p. 78.

[14] For these three episodes, see *Two Apocrypha*, pp. 82–94, 95–7 and 98–105. The Irish version, however, lacks some of the same episodes, while the homily *Be heofonwarum and be helwarum* lacks the entire portion of the exemplum dealing with the just soul.

[15] On the colour of the souls, see *Two Apocrypha*, pp. 77–81. That the sinful soul is blacker than a raven and the just soul whiter than snow is a commonplace of medieval question-and-answer dialogues. See L. W. Daly and W. Suchier, *Altercatio Hadriani Augusti et Epicteti Philosophi*, Illinois Stud. in Lang. and Lit. 24 (Urbana, IL, 1939), 124. For an example in Irish, see Whitley Stokes, 'Irish Riddles', *The Celtic Review* 1 (1904), 132. In two Old English texts, Blickling Homily XIII and the Martyrology, souls are described as seven times brighter than snow. For the passage in the Blickling homily (referring to the soul of the Virgin), see Willard, *Two Apocrypha*, p. 80; for the Martyrology, see *An Old English Martyrology*, ed. G. Herzfeld, EETS os 116 (London, 1900), 96, lines 9–11. (We are grateful to Thomas Hall of the University of Illinois for drawing our attention to the latter reference, and for the reference to the article by J. E. Cross cited in the following note.)

[16] The Irish version is ed. and trans. C. Marstrander, 'The Two Deaths', *Eriu* 5 (1911), 120–5. The Rogationtide homily also states that the just soul will be as bright as the sun. The idea that the just soul is seven times brighter than the sun may have been suggested by a theme, based on Is. XXX.26 and common in Irish and Anglo-Saxon writers, that the sun was seven times brighter before the Fall and will regain its original brightness after the Judgment. For a discussion of this theme in the Irish tract *De ordine creaturarum* and in two Old English texts, see J. E. Cross, '*De Ordine Creaturarum Liber* in Old English Prose', *Anglia* 90 (1972), 132–40, at 135–6 and 139–40. In the *De ordine*, as also in a late Old English homily (Belfour XI), the

The sequence of utterances for each soul likewise reflects the Latin source, even down to the accidental omission of the third utterance of the damned soul. It is clear that the Latin text is deficient here, not only because of the lack of symmetry, but because the sequence of utterances of the damned soul concludes with the statement, 'Haec sunt trea uerba peccatorum . . .', even though only the first and second utterances have been given. The Anglo-Saxon homilist must have been aware of the lacuna, since he replaced the specific reference to a sequence of three utterances with the noncommital phrase 'æfter þysum wordum', but he did not attempt to make it good by his own invention. The remaining utterances correspond exactly to the Latin:

Latin	*Old English*	
The Damned Soul:		
Utterance	Utterance	Response
1. tenebre	1. ðyostre	1.
2. tristitia	2. unrotnes	2. gewin/unblis
3. —	3. —	3. —
The Just Soul:		
Utterance	Utterance	Response
1. laetitia	1. blis	1. blis
2. magestas	2. þrym	2. þrym
3. lumen	3. leoht	3. leoht

The first utterance of the damned soul (*tenebre/ðyostre*), answering to the third utterance of the just soul (*lumen/leoht*), is unproblematic, since all versions agree in including this pair of utterances.[17] As for the second utterance of the damned soul, the Latin source shows that Willard was correct when he speculated that 'The *unrotnes* of J probably translates some word like *tristitia*, which would be appropriate enough in antithesis to the *laetitia* of the righteous soul'.[18] His further speculation, whereby *unrotnes* is supposed to represent an original *angustia*, may possibly have been true for the archetype of the sermon, but clearly was not so for J's immediate source, which must have had *tristitia*. The second utterance of the damned soul (*tristitia/unrotnes*) therefore corresponds to the first utterance of the just soul (*laetitia/blis*). The Old English,

theme is linked with the transfiguration of the just with reference to Mt. XIII.43, although neither text states explicitly that the just will shine seven times as brightly as the sun. In the Apocalypse of Peter, Christ says that he will come to Judgment 'shining seven times as bright as the sun'; see E. Hennecke and W. Schneemelcher, *New Testament Apocrypha*, trans. R. McL. Wilson, 2 vols. (Philadelphia, 1965) II, 668.
17 See Willard, *Two Apocrypha*, p. 113.   18 *Ibid.*

however, in making explicit the terms of the utterances in the response of the devils, substitutes the roughly synonymous terms *gewin* and *unblis* for *unrotnes*. Willard suggested that the term *gewin* in the devils' response might be a vestige of a missing *iter*-utterance, a feature of all other versions except for the homily *Be heofonwarum and be helwarum*, perhaps a rendering of the adjective of an *asperum iter* utterance.[19] It is true that *gewin* is a rather loose equivalent for *unrotness* or *tristitia*, and is the only such doublet used by J, but since the Latin text in the Munich manuscript has no trace of an *iter*-utterance, it seems unlikely that the manuscript consulted by the homilist would have preserved such an utterance and that his term *gewin* is a displaced vestige of it.

The third utterance of the damned soul, which must correspond to the second utterance of the just soul, is more problematic. Since the Latin source, like the Old English, is also defective for this utterance, it does not help us to determine what the second utterance of the just soul, *prym*, corresponds to. It does, however, reveal what the term *prym* itself designates. According to Willard, if *prym* means 'glory' or 'magnificence', it should be a synonym for *laetitia*. But since J already has a *laetitia*-utterance (*blis*), Willard suggested that *prym* here might mean 'throng' or 'host', corresponding to an elaboration of the *laetitia*-response in his Latin text, which refers to the 'multitude' of angels coming to meet the soul. J would therefore have made two utterances and responses from a single *laetitia*-utterance and response of the original.[20] However, since all other versions have an *iter*-utterance, Willard preferred to interpret the word *prym* as a rendering of an adjective modifying *iter*, such as *dulce* (as in the Rogationtide homily) or *suave* (as in the Latin version known to Willard).[21] The Latin text in Clm. 28135, however, shows that the homilist's *prym* corresponds precisely to a distinct *magestas*-utterance in the Latin, and has not been manufactured from a *laetitia*-utterance; nor does it translate the adjective of an *iter*-utterance. Since this *magestas*-utterance is unique among the surviving Latin versions of the exemplum, there is no comparable evidence to establish what the corresponding term in the third utterance of the damned soul would have been, but an *iter*-utterance would not afford a satisfactory correspondence. The lack of an *iter*-utterance in J is therefore not an accident of transcription in the Old English, but reflects instead a substitution in the Latin original.

As for the sequence of the utterances, Willard argued that J 'reveals a most obvious displacement, in that it gives *lumen* as the third utterance of the just

---

[19] *Ibid.* pp. 118–20. In the Rogationtide homily the third utterance of the damned soul is 'asperum est iter'. In the homily *Be heofonwarum and be helwarum* the narrow or arduous 'way' (*iter* or *via*) has been replaced by a reference to a *gimlic hus*, by attraction to the *habitatio* or *tabernacula* to which the road leads (*ibid.* pp. 114–17).

[20] *Ibid.* pp. 119–20.   [21] *Ibid.* p. 120.

soul, which the other texts agree should be the first'.[22] Willard is probably correct in his reconstruction of the original sequence, since moving *leoht* from the third to the first position would not only make J conform to the normal order, but would also correct the asymmetry within J itself, so that the matching utterances of the damned and just souls would appear in the same order. Here again, however, the Latin text shows that the disruption cannot be attributed to the homilist, but had already occurred in his source.

In the previously published Latin versions, after the utterances, the angels and devils divide into two groups, the angels escorting the just soul and chanting the words of Ps. LXIV.5, *Beatus quem elegisti*, and the devils escorting the damned soul to the gloomier accompaniment of Ps. LI.3, *Quid gloriaris in malitia*.[23] Of the vernacular versions, the Rogationtide homily retains the escort and chant for both souls; the homily *Be heofonwarum and be helwarum* retains neither (although Willard argues that a fragment of the devils' chant is preserved in the third response); the Irish version retains the escort and chant for the damned soul, but not for the just soul;[24] and J, on the contrary, retains the escort and chant for the just soul, but not for the damned soul. Willard argued that 'the text of J is probably defective', but conceded the possibility that the escort and chant of the damned soul 'may never have existed in J, though in that case the loss must have occurred in the sources of J, for, since J preserves the *Beatus quem elegisti*, it is reasonable to assume that it possessed at one time the *Quid gloriaris* in the parallel episode of the wicked soul'.[25] As the new Latin text shows, the loss had indeed occurred in J's source, but Willard is undoubtedly correct in assuming that the original version had both escorts and chants. The allusion to the chant of the angels and to the *Beatus quem elegisti*, Willard further argued, demonstrates 'that J is derived from a version of the Three Utterances which at one time must have contained the details of the actual bringing forth of the soul, certainly with the *Dividite* and the *Beatus quem elegisti*, and probably with the *Noster hic homo* and *Suscitate*'.[26] Again, the original form of this recension may have included all these elements, but the text of Clm. 28135 confirms that only the *Beatus quem elegisti* was part of the homilist's immediate Latin source.

As Willard pointed out, J, like the Rogationtide homily, paraphrases the *Beatus quem elegisti*, so that it 'is no longer a hymn to God, but a song praising and encouraging the soul, who had chosen to serve God and to lay up for itself goodness in its heavenly mansion'.[27] Willard suggests that 'J seems to be translating something more like *Beatus, quoniam assumpsisti*', but the Latin text

---

[22] *Ibid.* p. 124.   [23] On the escort and chant, see Willard, *Two Apocrypha*, pp. 106–12.
[24] The Irish text states merely that the just soul 'was borne to heaven with a choir of angels' (see *Two Apocrypha*, p. 107).   [25] *Ibid.* p. 106.   [26] *Ibid.* pp. 99–100.   [27] *Ibid.* p. 110.

in Clm. 28135 does not show such a variant, and in any case the Latin psalm verse is quoted correctly in J itself, so it is more likely that the homilist has taken the liberty to remodel the verse to accord better with the context. Following Förster, Willard suggests that the author of J, or a subsequent copyist, has altered an original 'Eadig þone ðu ðe gecure' to 'Eadig eart ðu', on the model of the concluding commendation of the soul which begins with these words.[28] The new Latin text shows that this commendation, unique to J, is not original but is based upon an addition to the psalm verses in the Latin, beginning 'Et beatus es qui mandata seruasti', which occurs in no other version.[29] Unlike the Rogationtide homily, J continues after the *Beatus quem elegisti* with *Replebimur* (abbreviated in Latin but translated in full in Old English), which, as Willard noted, required no alteration to conform to the context.[30]

These comparisons show that the Latin text in Clm. 28135 preserves the recension of the 'Three Utterances' translated in J, but that the Anglo-Saxon homilist's manuscript had slight variant readings, as is clear even from the morphological differences in the Latin *incipit* incorporated by the homilist. Whether the minor verbal differences in the Old English reflect variant readings in the homilist's manuscript, or instead are the homilist's own alterations, is difficult to decide. The addition of the terms of each utterance in all the responses save the first is a natural expansion of the Latin, in which the terms must be understood. So too is the addition of the phrase *to Gode* in the description of the angels bearing the just soul in their bosom. In the utterances of the souls, J adds the phrase *þe ge me tolædað* in the two surviving utterances of the damned soul, and the similar phrases *þe ic on gelædad eam – þe we on syndan – þe ic on eam* in the three utterances of the just soul, where the Latin has the corresponding phrase only in the second utterance ('Magna est magestas in qua sumus'). In the responses of the devils and angels, the Old English has *in/ on helle* instead of the expected *mid deoflum* (corresponding to the Latin *apud demones*), and *on heofonum* for the first response of the angels instead of *mid Gode* (corresponding to *apud deum*). These renderings may reflect variant readings *in inferno* and *in caelo*, but it is more likely that the homilist has made this alteration

---

[28] *Ibid.* p. 111.
[29] According to Willard (*ibid.* pp. 66–7), the commendation in J is based ultimately on the *Visio S. Pauli*, in which the angels greet the righteous soul in similar terms.
[30] *Ibid.* p. 110. The Old English translation of this verse is obscure, however, and may be read, with Willard, 'thy temple is holy' (taking *his* as *is*), or, with Fadda, 'we fill . . . thy temple with his saints' (emending *halig* to *halig<re>*). Willard's rendering seems preferable, as conforming more closely to the sense of the psalm verse. Fadda's objection to the dative *wundorlicre ðrymnesse* may be met by emending to *wundorlic in ðrymnesse*, corresponding to the Latin *mirabile in aequitate* (ps. LXIV.6).

himself, since in the third utterance of the angels he reverts to *mid Gode*, corresponding to *apud deum*. In the description of the just soul, the adjective *halgan* in the phrase *ðæs halgan mannes saul* probably does reflect a variant reading, since the adjective is necessary to signal the transition from the bad to the good soul, and since a reading such as *anima . . . hominis [sancti]* is required to balance the phrase *anima hominis peccatoris* in the Latin. Finally, a lacuna in the third response of the angels in the Latin is made good by the homilist, whose manuscript probably preserved the response in full.[31]

A more difficult problem in the Latin text, not reflected in the Old English version, is posed by the similarly faulty construction of the clauses referring to the demons and angels who lead the souls. In the description of the damned soul, the Old English version seems to reflect a reading, 'Et demones ducunt eam (ad infernum)', paralleled by the description of the just soul, which presupposes a reading 'Et sancti angeli ducunt eam ad paradysum'. Instead, the Latin text has abortive relative constructions with *qui* after *demones* and *angeli*, continuing with the verbal phrase *ducunt eam* or *ducunt eam ad*[32] followed not by the expected accusatives, but by the nominatives *infernus* and *paradysus*, and concluding not with the main clauses required to complete the sense of the relative clauses but with the curious phrases *qui dicitur* and *quo dicitur*.

We can make no sense of these clauses as they stand, but believe we can demonstrate how the corruption originated in an imperfect adaptation of another text. A florilegium in Vatican, Bibliotheca Apostolica, Pal. lat 556 (s. ix[in]), written in Anglo-Saxon script and containing a series of homilies and moral extracts mostly ascribed to St Augustine,[33] includes one short piece consisting of a series of three triads. The second and third triads list the three worst and best things:[34]

---

[31] The praise of God and the Trinity which concludes the angels' speech to the just soul in the Old English (Fadda, *Nuove omelie*, pp. 21.198–23.209) may well be the homilist's elaboration.

[32] Presumably *ducunt eam ad* is the intended construction in both cases, but the preposition *ad* is omitted in the description of the damned soul.

[33] Ed. G. Di S. Teresa, 'Ramenta patristica 1: Il florilegio pseudoagostiniano palatino', *Ephemerides Carmeliticae* 14 (1963), 195–241; for the date, see p. 199. The editor, following Wilmart, considers the manuscript's place of origin to be Fulda (see pp. 196–7, n. 7), but notes that Paul Lehmann assigned it to Lorsch (p. 200, n. 23a). B. Bischoff gives the *Schriftheimat* as 'deutsch-angelsächsisches Gebiet'; see his 'Lorsch im Spiegel seiner Handschriften', in *Die Reichsabtei Lorsch*, 2 vols. (Darmstadt, 1977) II, 7–128, at p. 112. Professor J. E. Cross points out to us that another piece in Pal. lat. 556 has a close parallel for an image in the introduction of the Rogationtide 'Three Utterances' homily (for details, see the preface to the forthcoming reprint of Bazire and Cross, *Eleven Old English Rogationtide Homilies*).

[34] Di S. Teresa, 'Ramenta patristica', pp. 219–20. We have incorporated in brackets the emendations suggested in the editor's apparatus. Immediately following the triads is a variation of the 'thought, word and deed' triad so favoured by Irish and Anglo-Saxon authors; see P. Sims-Williams, 'Thought, Word and Deed: an Irish Triad', *Eriu* 29 (1978), 78–111.

Et tres sunt in hoc mundo deteriora omni malo: anima peccatoris, quae nigrior est coruo in septimo; et maligni demones qui eam adducunt; et infernus, cui dicitur [ducitur]:[35] non est enim deterius his trib*us*. Eadem anima conspicit putridinem [putredinem] sua*m*; carit [<et> canit]: *Conputrierunt [computruerunt] et corrupti [corruptae] sunt cicatrices meae a facie insipientiae meae* [ps. XXXVII.6].

Tres sunt in hoc mundo meliora omni bono: anima s*an*c*ti* in septimo sole specior [speci<osi>or]; et s*an*c*ti* angeli qui eam in sinu suo suspiciunt [suscipiunt]; et paradisus cui dicit*ur* [ducitur] et expectatio regni caelestis: his tribus n*on* est melius in hoc mundo. Et s*an*c*ti* angeli dilectantur [delectant?] anima*m* spiritali cantico et dicunt: *Beatus quem elegisti et adsumpsisti*, domi*n*e: *inhabitauit [inhabitabit] in tabernaculis tuis. Replebimur in bonis domus tuae* [ps. LXIV.5]. ...

This pair of triads clearly circulated in florilegia of moral extracts, for we encounter them again in closely similar form in Paulinus of Aquileia's *Liber exhortationis*.[36] A related but briefer version of the triads occurs in question-and-answer form in a Hiberno-Latin dialogue entitled *Prebiarum de multorium exemplaribus*:[37]

Quod sunt quae pessima sunt in hoc mundo? Id, III. Anima peccatoris post mortem, et demones uenientes in obuiam ei, et bene non deficiens ab eis in perpetuum.

Quod sunt qui meliora sunt in hoc mundo? Id, tres. Anima iusti post exitum de corpore, et angeli uenientes in obuiam ei, et regnum perpetuum possidere sine fine.

It appears that the author of the expanded version of the pair of triads preserved in Pal. lat. 556 was familiar with a version of the 'Three Utterances', and has slightly revised an existing pair of triads as in the *Prebiarum* to conform more closely in detail to the apocryphon: thus he specifies the colour of the damned and just souls as seven times blacker than a raven[38] and seven times brighter than the sun, just as in the version of the 'Three Utterances' in Clm. 28135,[39] and he emphasizes the escort of the souls by the angels and demons, by using the phrases *qui eam adducunt* and *qui eam . . . suspiciunt [suscipiunt]* instead of *uenientes in obuiam ei*[40] and by including the chant of the angels to the just soul of the *Beatus quem elegisti* and *Replebimur*.[41] The angels' chant of the verses from Ps. LXIV is proof of the compiler's familiarity with the 'Three Utterances'.

---

[35] The editor's apparatus here reads '*leg.* dicitur', obviously a misprint for '*leg.* ducitur', as is confirmed by the apparatus for the corresponding phrase in the following triad, which reads, '*leg.* ducitur (*cf. l. 11*)'.

[36] PL 99, 253–4. This text confirms most of the emendations proposed for Pal. lat. 556; significant variants will be noted below.

[37] Ed. R. E. McNally, *Scriptores Hiberniae Minores Pars I*, CCSL 108B (Turnhout, 1973), 164. On the Irish character of this text, see McNally's preface, *ibid.* pp. 129–32.

[38] This formula recurs later in the homilies (Di S. Teresa, 'Ramenta patristica', p. 222, lines 39–40).   [39] The version in Paulinus of Aquileia, however, lacks the phrase *in septimo*.

[40] Paulinus has *qui eam rapiunt* and *qui eam suscipiunt*.

[41] Paulinus adds the concluding part of the verse, 'sanctum est templum tuum, mirabile in aequitate', as in Clm. 28135.

Comparison of the expanded triads with the phrasing in Clm. 28135 shows how closely related these texts are:

Pal. lat. 556	Clm. 28135
. . . anima peccatoris quae nigrior est coruo in septimo;	Anima hominis peccatoris . . . septies nigrior erit quam coruus.
et maligni demones qui eam adducunt; et infernus cui dicitur [ducitur]. . . .	Et demones qui ducunt eam infernus qui dicitur.
. . . anima sancti in septimo sole [speci < osi > or];	Anima autem hominis . . . septiens splendior [*sic*] erit quam sol.
et sancti angeli qui eam . . . [suscipiunt]; et paradisus cui dicitur [ducitur]. . . .	Et sancti angeli qui ducunt eam ad paradysus quo dicitur.

Since the version of the 'Three Utterances' consulted by the compiler of the triads in Pal. lat. 556 agrees with the version in Clm. 28135 in the description of the colour of the souls, it would seem logical to conclude that the corrupt phrases *qui/quo dicitur* in the Munich manuscript are the source of the twice-repeated error *cui dicitur* in the triads. But this does not seem to be the case. In the triads the phrase *cui dicitur* is certainly an error for *cui ducitur*, as the editor suggests in his apparatus. So emended, it makes perfect sense in context: the third thing is *infernus/paradisus cui ducitur*, 'to which [the soul] is lead'. The nominatives *infernus* and *paradisus* are appropriate in this context in a way they clearly are not in Clm. 28135. So too are the relative clauses *qui eam adducunt/suspiciunt* [*suscipiunt*] in the second item of each list, which make no sense at all in Clm. 28135: the second thing is the *demones/angeli* 'who lead/receive it'. That this must have been the original reading of the triads is confirmed by the version in Paulinus of Aquileia, where the crucial phrases read 'et infernus in quem [*var.* in quo] ducitur' and 'et paradisus, in quem [*var.* in quo] ducitur'.

Our conclusion must therefore be that the redactor of the 'Three Utterances' in Clm. 28135 has attempted to use a pair of triads very similar to those in Pal. lat. 556 as the introductions to his abbreviated descriptions of the going-out of the damned and just souls, but has imperfectly revised the syntax of his source. He begins well enough, omitting the numerical tags of the triads, and supplying the first item in each list with the temporal clause *cum exi(g)erit de corpore* and with the finite verb *erit* necessary to make independent clauses out of the relative clauses in the lists. But he neglects to delete the relative constructions in the second item of each list, which do not make sense in their new context. As a way to link the second and third items of the lists, at least in the description of the just soul, he substitutes the preposition *ad* for the connective *et*, thereby creating a verbal phrase *ducunt eam ad* for which 'paradise' (and 'hell', assuming that the preposition *ad* has accidently been left off in the description of the damned soul) can be the object, merely forgetting to change the nominatives *infernus* and *paradisus* (which are correct in the lists) to the accusatives required by the new construction. Finally, he fails to omit the already corrupt phrase *cui* (or perhaps *in quo*) *dicitur* which concluded the third item of each list. Our redactor may be forgiven for being confused by this phrase, but he was obviously careless, since he could have perfected his revision simply by omitting in each case the relative *qui* and the phrase *qui/quo dicitur*, and by changing the nominatives *infernus* and *paradysus* to accusatives. He would then have arrived at the very simple construction he seems to have had dimly in mind: 'Et demones/angeli ducunt eam ad infernum/paradysum.'

The reconstruction suggested above is complex, but seems inescapable. The compiler of the triads in Pal. lat. 556 must have known a version of the 'Three Utterances', probably a full text of the same variant type which the author of the text in Clm. 28135 abbreviated, since both texts agree against all other versions in two respects: the description of the colour of the souls, and the description of the angels conducting the just soul *in sinu suo* (*on heora fæðmum* in the Old English).[42] But since the parallel syntax of the two texts is perfectly correct for a list, as in the triads, but nonsensical in Clm. 28135, we are forced to assume that the redactor of Clm. 28135 has borrowed the phrasing from the triads. The fact that the triads incorporate a chant of the damned soul (Ps. XXXVII.6) not found in Clm. 28135 proves that the compiler of the triads drew independently on a longer text of the 'Three Utterances'. In sum, the redactor who created the abbreviated version of the 'Three Utterances' in Clm. 28135 has conflated the triads with material drawn independently from a text of the 'Three Utterances' similar to the version known to the compiler of the triads, but has imperfectly adapted the syntax of the triads to the demands of the new context.

The Old English translator has finished the job, or perhaps it had already been done for him by his immediate Latin source. His 'and deofla lædan þa

---

[42] Paulinus's text does not have this phrase.

saula' simplifies the badly mixed construction of the Munich manuscript, and the corresponding phrase for the just soul, 'and þa halgan Godes ænglas hie lædað to Paradysum' makes the necessary change in case in the Latin word *paradysus*, even though the verb is of course Old English. Our translator evidently set higher standards.

According to Willard, the 'Three Utterances' sermon 'reflects, in its early history at least, the Celtic culture of the British Isles',[43] and his view has been confirmed independently by McNally, who considered the sermon Hiberno-Latin.[44] Among the additional manuscripts which we have identified, many of the earliest show Insular palaeographical symptoms, or are transmitted in manuscripts which contain other Hiberno-Latin texts. These manuscripts suggest that the Irish and Anglo-Saxon missions played an important role in the early transmission of the sermon on the Continent.[45] They include St Gallen, Stiftsbibliothek 908 (s. viii/ix), which contains a Hiberno-Latin Genesis commentary and other apocryphal material common in Irish tradition;[46] Karlsruhe, Badische Landesbibliothek, Aug. perg. 254 (s. ix), which contains the *Apocrypha Priscillianistica* for which M. R. James and many other scholars have suggested Irish origins;[47] and Munich, Clm. 6433 (s. viii[ex]), written by the Anglo-Saxon scribe Peregrinus, which contains a florilegium compiled from Hiberno-Latin sources, the *Florilegium Frisingense*.[48]

---

43 Willard, 'The Latin Texts', p. 160; cf. *Two Apocrypha*, p. 145. Willard believed, on linguistic grounds we do not consider conclusive, that the sermon was translated from a Greek apocryphon (see 'The Latin Texts', pp. 158–61). It seems clear, however, that the ultimate origins of the legend are to be sought in Eastern apocrypha, whether Coptic, Syriac or Greek.

44 See McNally, 'Seven Hiberno-Latin Sermons', pp. 121–32, for discussion of the Irish background of the sermons. M. Lapidge and R. Sharpe, *A Bibliography of Celtic-Latin Literature 400–1200* (Dublin, 1986), accept McNally's identification of the sermons, which they include under the section 'Celtic *Peregrini* on the Continent' (no. 803). See further Wright, 'Apocryphal Lore', pp. 134–5.

45 One of McNally's manuscripts, Vatican, Pal. lat. 220, from the Rhineland, was written in Anglo-Saxon script, and in McNally's view may be descended from an Irish exemplar. This manuscript contains other apocryphal material which circulated in Ireland and Anglo-Saxon England, including the interpolated version of the Apocalypse of Thomas and a Celtic-Latin text *De die dominico*, in addition to a unique Redaction of the *Visio S. Pauli* recently ptd M. E. Dwyer, 'An Unstudied Redaction of the *Visio Pauli*', *Manuscripta* 32 (1988), 121–38. See now C. D. Wright, 'Some Evidence for an Irish Origin of Redaction XI of the *Visio Pauli*', *Manuscripta* 34 (1990), 34–44.   46 For details, see Wright, 'Apocryphal Lore'.

47 On the Irish connections of the *Apocrypha Priscillianistica*, see Wright, 'Apocryphal Lore', pp. 135–6, and the references cited there. The collection includes the Seven Heavens apocryphon, versions of which occur in Old Irish and Old English. See Willard, *Two Apocrypha*, pp. 1–30, and D. Dumville, 'Towards an Interpretation of *Fís Adamnán*', *Studia Celtica* 12/13 (1977–78), 62–77.

48 See Wright, 'Apocryphal Lore', p. 135, n. 58. The *Florilegium Frisingense* has now been ed. A. Lehner, *Florilegia*, CCSL 108D (Turnhout, 1987); for the Irish character of the florilegium, see pp. xiii–xxxviii. On the manuscript, see *CLA* IX, no. 1283. On the Anglo-Saxon scribe Peregrinus, see also Bischoff, *Schreibschulen*, pp. 61–3 and 73–5.

Munich, Clm. 28135 also contains material connected with Irish traditions. These include not only the abbreviated version of the 'Three Utterances', but also a fuller text corresponding to the version published by McNally.[49] In addition, among the other anonymous homilies transmitted in the manuscript is a much-expanded version of another of the group of seven sermons which McNally considered to be Hiberno-Latin.[50] The manuscript also has extracts corresponding to the Hiberno-Latin *Liber de numeris*, including a lengthy series *de via iustorum et via peccatorum* (11v–13r, immediately preceding the abbreviated version of the 'Three Utterances'),[51] and some half-dozen enumerations,[52] along with the well-known Irish sequence of the twelve abuses (15r).[53]

Clm. 28135 also includes a version of a popular Doomsday sermon[54] which at an early period often circulated together with the 'Three Utterances' sermon. It appears, for example, as the first item in all three manuscripts of the larger collection of sermons from which McNally edited the seven sermons he considered Hiberno-Latin, and in several early manuscripts the two sermons are paired.[55] No scholar has specifically identified the Doomsday sermon as Hiberno-Latin, but its frequent manuscript association with the 'Three Utterances' suggests at least that it was a popular item in Insular circles. Moreover, as J. E. Cross has shown,[56] the Lenten homily in Junius 85/86 containing the 'Three Utterances' exemplum also incorporates a translation of this Doomsday sermon, thereby confirming their close association and Insular circulation.

A further possible connection with Irish traditions in the Lenten homily is a brief passage on the theme of the food of the soul. In her edition of the homily, Fadda drew attention to analogues of the theme in the *Apocrypha Priscillianis-*

---

[49] See above, pp. 188–9.

[50] On 51v–54r, corresponding to McNally's Document IV, p. 140. According to Bischoff (*Schreibschulen*, p. 93), this part of the manuscript (fos. 51–80) is a nearly contemporary addition to the original codex.

[51] See R. E. McNally, *Der irische Liber de numeris: Eine Quellenanalyse des pseudo-Isidorischen Liber de numeris* (Munich, 1957), pp. 41–2. McNally considered the passage in Clm. 28135 to be an extract from the *Liber de numeris*.

[52] For these parallels, see McNally's index, *ibid.* p. 206.

[53] This list is based on the Hiberno-Latin treatise *De duodecim abusivis saeculi*, ed. S. Hellmann, Texte und Untersuchungen 34 (Leipzig, 1909), 32–60. For bibliography, see Lapidge and Sharpe, *Bibliography of Celtic-Latin Literature*, no. 339.

[54] On 63v–65r, corresponding to pseudo-Augustine, *Sermo App.* ccli (Pl 39, 2210), inc.: 'O fratres karissimi, quam timendus est . . .'.

[55] On the Doomsday sermon, see Wright, 'Apocryphal Lore', pp. 136–7, who lists several early manuscripts in which the two sermons occur in sequence.

[56] J. E. Cross, 'A Doomsday Passage in an Old English Sermon for Lent', *Anglia* 100 (1982), 103–8. The Old English passage is Fadda, *Nuove omelie*, pp. 27.262–29.303.

tica, and part of this material occurs in other florilegia, including, again, McNally's seven Hiberno-Latin sermons.[57]

These further indications, together with the presence of the 'Three Utterances' exemplum itself, argue strongly for an Irish background for the Lenten homily. Nor is the Lenten homily in Junius 85/86 the only homily in the manuscript that draws on Irish sources: the body-and-soul homily in the same manuscript incorporates a sequence contrasting the teachings of God and of the devil which corresponds to yet another of McNally's Hiberno-Latin sermons.[58] These various parallels demonstrate that a florilegium containing a core of items from Irish tradition, including several pieces corresponding to sermons in the McNally collection, must have been available to Old English homilists. Among these Hiberno-Latin sermons was a distinctive abbreviated version of the 'Three Utterances', closely similar to that in Clm. 28135, which was translated by the author of the Lenten homily in the Junius manuscript.

---

[57] Fadda, *Nuove omelie*, pp. 2–3 (the Lenten sermon is there mistakenly identified as from Hatton 114). The Old English passage (*ibid.* p. 17.127–33, 143–51) corresponds in several significant phrases to two passages in the *Apocrypha Priscillianistica*, but must derive through an intermediary, with some expansion and alteration of wording. One of the two passages in the *Apocrypha Priscillianistica* occurs in McNally's Document VI, p. 142. See C. D. Wright, '*Docet Deus, Docet Diabolus*: A Hiberno-Latin Theme in an Old English Body-and-Soul Homily', *N&Q* 232 (1987), 451–3, at 453, n. 14.

[58] The sermon is ed. Fadda, *Nuove omelie*, pp. 163–73. The passage on the teachings of God and of the devil (*ibid.* pp. 169.72–171.83) corresponds to McNally's Document V, p. 141, lines 5–22. This passage was in turn borrowed by the composite homily Assman XIV (see Wright, '*Docet Deus*', p. 452, n. 10).

Wulfstan's *De Anticristo* in a twelfth-century Worcester manuscript

J. E. CROSS

Cambridge, St John's College 42 (B. 20) is a Latin manuscript, dated as twelfth century and tentatively placed at Worcester.[1] It contains 136 folios, closely written in double columns of forty-five lines each, in which a range of abbreviations has been used. By these means a quantity of material has been presented, including two collections of homilies/sermons, a calendar, extracts from the works of named authors and miscellaneous smaller items. The most notable of the sermons for Anglo-Saxonists is a new text of Archbishop Wulfstan's Latin composition, *De Anticristo*,[2] but it keeps company with other anonymous sermons, some of which are variant texts of sermons copied or composed in English manuscripts of the Anglo-Saxon historical period. The manuscript needs a closer study than those done by M. R. James,[3] who catalogued the anonymous items without identification, or by H. Schenkl,[4] whose catalogue is incomplete although it includes some identifications. Identification of the anonymous items, with notice of parallel texts in other manuscripts where possible, helps to confirm the date of the manuscript, suggests that its place of origin was Worcester, and allows speculation on the canon of Wulfstan's Latin writing.

CONTENT

Named items

Named items in the manuscript can be recorded but play no part in the assignment of date or identification of place of origin. These include a section from Isidore, *De differentiis rerum* (6r-12v) under the rubric: 'Incipit liber Ysidori iunioris de differentiis' (6r), chapters of Defensor, *Liber Scintillarum*, with omissions within the sections (121r-130v) and a title: 'Hic incipiunt capitula libri Scintillarum' (121r), and part of pseudo-Seneca, *De institutione*

---

[1] M.R. James, *A Descriptive Catalogue of the Manuscripts in the Library of St John's College, Cambridge* (Cambridge, 1913), pp. 57–64.
[2] D. Bethurum, *The Homilies of Wulfstan* (Oxford, 1957), pp. 113–15 (no. Ia).
[3] James, *A Descriptive Catalogue*, pp. 57–64.
[4] H. Schenkl, *Bibliotheca patrum Latinorum Britannica*, 3 vols. (Vienna, 1891–1901) II. 2 (Fortsetzung, 1898), pp. 49–51.

morum (136r-v) so entitled (136r). The manuscript also contains a text of the *Gesta Saluatoris* (62v-70v) and some psalms and prayers at the end of the manuscript (130v-135v).

The calendar

M. R. James[5] printed merely a selection of names from the calendar (3r-4r), from which he chose two to suggest a connection with Worcester: Oswald (28 February), bishop of Worcester from 961 and archbishop of York from 971 to 992,[6] and Ecgwine (30 December), bishop of Worcester at uncertain dates within the seventh and eighth centuries.[7] He also noted the addition of *Uulstan* (19 January), that is Wulfstan II of Worcester who died 19 or 20 January 1095.[8] Other names in the complete calendar appear to have no distinctive connection with Worcester, but the above names were sufficient for James to 'suggest a connexion with Worcester'[9] for the manuscript.

The first sequence of homilies/sermons

The first set of sermons, or reading-pieces for preachers (13r-62v), is a copy of a sermonary, composed after the 820s and regarded as Carolingian by Henri Barré,[10] who numbered the items as from its fullest early representative, Cambridge, Pembroke College 25 (Bury St Edmunds, s. xi).[11] Recently I have been able to consider the sermonary in detail[12] and to demonstrate its value for the composition of Old English vernacular sermons, but make brief points in relation to St John's 42 here.

In comparison with Pembroke 25, in Barré's numbering (accepted by me), St John's 42 omits Pembroke 25, nos. 1, 2, 6, 28, 49, 56–63 (now one sermon),[13] 64 and 77. Folios may also have been missing from the exemplar of St John's 42, since the equivalent item to Pembroke no. 46 ends incompletely at St John's 42, 48rb, but the following item (as Pembroke no. 47) continues immediately without a break in the script, but with loss of material at its

---

5 James, *A Descriptive Catalogue*, pp. 58–9.
6 *Handbook of British Chronology*, ed. E. B. Fryde, D. E. Greenway, S. Porter and I. Roy, 3rd ed. (London, 1986), p. 224. 7 *ibid.* p. 223.
8 James, *A Descriptive Catalogue*, p. 64, noting the later addition of the name; *Handbook*, ed. Fryde *et al.*, p. 224, noting Wulfstan's dates. 9 James, *A Descriptive Catalogue*, p. 64.
10 H. Barré, *Les homéliaires carolingiens de l'école d'Auxerre*; Studi e Testi 225 (Vatican City, 1962), 17–25, discusses and catalogues the collection.
11 M. R. James, *A Descriptive Catalogue of the Manuscripts in the Library of Pembroke College, Cambridge* (Cambridge, 1905), pp. 25–9; *On the Abbey of S. Edmund at Bury*, trans. of the Cambridge Ant. Soc. 33 (1895), no. 168.
12 J. E. Cross, *Cambridge, Pembroke College MS. 25: a Carolingian Sermonary used by Anglo-Saxon Preachers*, King's College, London, Medieval Studies 1 (London, 1987).
13 A sermon on All Saints now published by J. E. Cross, '"Legimus in Ecclesiasticis Historiis": a Sermon for All Saints and its Use in Old English Prose', *Traditio* 33 (1977), 101–35.

beginning.[14] St John's 42 has no direct filiation with the Bury manuscript, and could have been linked with an exemplar in another scriptorium, since the sermonary is extant already in four other manuscripts of English origin, two of these earlier than St John's 42.[15] Other manuscripts of this sermonary will undoubtedly be discovered, since it was also well-used by vernacular preachers.[16]

St John's 42, however, includes one item in this first set of sermons which is missing from other representatives of the sermonary, and is clearly a twelfth-century intruder within an original collection which was certainly available in England before the second half of the tenth century.[17] This is a sermon for the Nativity on 14r: 'Apparuit benignitas et humanitas saluatoris', which is a variant text of one printed under the name of Hildebert, archbishop of Tours.[18] The Hildebert collection, however, is now regarded as a mélange of sermons from different authors, and the item 'Apparuit benignitas' has now been firmly assigned by Jean-Paul Bonnes to Geoffrey du Loroux, alias Babion, a preacher of the twelfth century.[19] Its intrusion into this first set of sermons is explicable from the demonstration below that the second set of sermons (70v-121r) contains many sermons attributed to this same Geoffrey.

The intruder merely confirms the twelfth-century date of the manuscript, but the calendar together with the second set of sermons indicate association with Worcester and, indeed, with Archbishop Wulfstan.

The second sequence of homilies/sermons[20]

The second sequence, mainly of sermons (70v-121r), is a mixture of old and new. A full analysis, within present knowledge, is made as a prelude to a discussion of items which are significant for the placing of the manuscript.

---

[14] See Cross, *Cambridge, Pembroke College 25*, p. 50, for the comparison with St John's 42.

[15] Canterbury Cathedral, Add. 127/12, fragment (s. xi[in]); London, British Library, Royal 5. E. XIX (Salisbury, probably 1089–1125), 21r-36v (twelve sermons from a full collection); Lincoln, Cathedral Chapter Library, 199 (C. 3.3) (s. xii[med]), 213r-345r; Oxford, Balliol College 240 (s. xiv), 56r-136r.

[16] The sermonary was used for eight Old English vernacular sermons; see Cross, *Cambridge, Pembroke College 25*, pp. 91–3.

[17] Since it was used for four items in the so-named *Vercelli Codex* (Vercelli, Biblioteca Capitolare, CXVII), dated s. x[2] by N. R. Ker, *Catalogue of Manuscripts Containing Anglo-Saxon* (Oxford, 1957), p. 460 (no. 394).   [18] PL 171, 390–4.

[19] J.-P. Bonnes, 'Un des plus grands prédicateurs du XIIe siécle: Geoffrey du Loroux dit Babion', *RB* 56 (1945–6), 174–215.

[20] Abbreviations used in the catalogue below are as follows:
Bonnes: as quoted above, n. 19
Caesarius: *Sancti Caesarii Arelatensis Sermones*, ed. G. Morin, 2 vols., CCSL 103–4 (Turnhout, 1953), cited by sermon number, volume and page
Sauer: H. Sauer, 'Zur Uberlieferung und Anlage von Erzbischof Wulfstans "Handbuch"', *DAEM* 36 (1980), 341–84.

(1)   70v   Predicatio communis omnibus populis: Hic incipit: Iuxta qualitatem audientum . . . / . . . quod nobis paratum est ab initio mundi. Hęc nobis prestare . . . qui cum patre etc. Amen.

As Cambridge, Pembroke College 25, 166r-168r and Oxford, Balliol College 240, 129v-130v (this latter begins incompletely).[21]

(2)   71v   Sermo puplicus: Non est potestas . . . resistit (cf. Rom. XIII.1–2). Audite, fratres karissimi, quid apostolus . . . / . . . et una ecclesia, unum corpus efficiatur in secula seculorum.

Geoffrey du Loroux, alias Babion, no. 41 (Bonnes, p. 202).[22]

(3)   73r   Sermo magni Augustini de ebrietate: Licet propitio Cristo, fratres karissimi, credam uos ebrietatis malum . . . / . . . in pauperum refectionem proficiat, prestante domino . . . qui cum patre.

Pseudo-Augustine, *Sermo* ccxciv,[23] now Caesarius, *Sermo* xlvi (ed. Morin I, 205). The sermon was used in Old English as Assmann XII.[24]

(4)   74r   Sermo communis de criminalibus peccatis: Peccata criminalia hec sunt sacrilegium, homicidium . . . / . . . non plangimus quam possumus ad statum pristinum reuocare.

Caesarius, *Sermo* clxxix (ed. Morin II, 725–8), extracts from cc. 2, 3, 5, 6 and 7, with variant readings from the printed text.

Manuscripts

Barlow 37: Oxford, Bodleian Library, Barlow 37, fols. 1–47 (?Worcester, s. xii/xiii), now most fully analysed by Sauer

Châlons 31 (33): Châlons-sur-Marne, Bibliothèque Municipale, 31 (33) (Saint-Pierre-aux-Monts, s. xi²), partially analysed by G. Philippart, 'Manuscrits hagiographiques de Châlons-sur-Marne', *AB* 89 (1971), 71–3

Copenhagen 1595: Copenhagen, Royal Library, Gamle Konglige Samlungen 1595 (Worcester, s. xiⁱⁿ), described by E. Jørgensen, *Catalogus Codicum Latinorum Medii Aevi Bibliothecae Regiae Hafniensis* (Copenhagen, 1926), pp. 43–6. The date and place of origin is deduced from N. R. Ker, 'The Handwriting of Archbishop Wulfstan', *England before the Conquest: Studies in Primary Sources presented to Dorothy Whitelock*, ed. P. Clemoes and K. Hughes (Cambridge, 1971), pp. 315–31, at 319–21

Vespasian D. ii: London, British Library, Cotton Vespasian D. ii, inadequately described in J. Planta, *Catalogue of the Manuscripts in the Cottonian Library deposited in the British Museum* (London, 1802); dated by Bethurum, *Wulfstan*, p. 7, as s. xi/xii, but redated by Michelle Brown of the British Library, in written communication, as s. xii²/⁴

[21] The sermon listed Cross, *Cambridge, Pembroke College 25*, pp. 41–2 (no. 89).
[22] Ptd PL 147, 221–4 and 171, 792–6.   [23] PL 39, 2303–6.
[24] B. Assmann, *Angelsächsische Homilien und Heiligenleben*, Bibliothek der angelsächsischen Prosa 3 (Kassel, 1889; repr. Darmstadt, 1964), 144–50. The source was noted by K. Jost, 'Einige Wulfstantexte und ihre Quellen', *Anglia* 56 (1932), 307–12.

(5) 74v Castigatio quedam: Quotiens iuxta sepulchra diuitum transimus, considerate . . . / . . . si ad penitentiam conuertatur consequi ueniam posse creditur nullus de bonitate desperet.

A composite sermon.[25]

(6) 74v Augustinus: Non de loco ad locum querendus est Deus . . . Short excerpts from named authors – 74vb: Augustinus; 75ra: Ysidorus, Augustinus de laude innocentie, Rabanus, Gregorius; 75rb: Arnouius, Effrem, Beda, Effrem, Beda, Beda; 75va: Ysidorus, Ysidorus, Augustinus, Seruius, Maximus, Gregorius, Celestinus papa, Ysidorus.

(7) 75v Omelia Beati Augustini episcopi: Dilectissimi fratres de errore huius seculi . . . / . . . ut filium suum unigenitum misit in mundum, qui credit in eum non pereat sed habeat uitam ęternam.

A composite sermon.[26]

(8) 77r Sermo de penitentia contra quosdam in diuina pagina titubantes et plane contra claues ęcclesię predicantes: Si quis predicat et predicando temere . . . / . . . lapide percuciatur, percussus comminuatur, comminutus redigatur.

Theobaldus Stampensis (Étampes), *Epistola* I *ad episcopum Lincolniensem.*[27]

(9) 78r De filiis sacerdotum et aliis ex lapsu carnis generatis; Quoniam sacerdotum filios . . . / . . . ad dexteram suam collocat et collocando coronat in cęlis.

Theobaldus Stampensis (Étampes), *Epistola* V *ad Roscelinum.*[28]

---

25 (i) 74va 3–17, phrases from Caesarius, *Sermo* xxxi.2 (ed. Morin I, 135), cf. *Sermo lxvi ad fratres in eremo* (PL 40, 1352) and *De rectitudine catholicae conversationis* (PL 40, 1183). Caesarius considers the topos 'Look at the tomb'; on this topos in Old English, see J. E. Cross, 'The Dry Bones Speak – a Theme in some Old English Homilies', *JEGP* 56 (1957), 434–9.

(ii) 74va 27 – 74vb 24 phrases from Caesarius, *Sermo* clviii. 3–6 (ed. Morin II, 646–8), as noted for me by Abbé Raymond Étaix.

(iii) 74vb 24–36 statements from pseudo-Augustine, *Sermo* ccliv. 2–3 (PL 39, 2215–16), as in Alcuin, *De virtutibus et vitiis liber* cc. xii (*De confessione*) and xiii (*De penitentia*) (PL 101, 622). Alcuin probably abstracted from the sermon; on this see L. Wallach, 'Alcuin on Virtues and Vices', *Harvard Theol. Rev.* 48 (1955), 175–95, at 183–4.

26 Some sources are:

(i) 76ra 37–40, ultimately from Isidore, *Synonyma* II.91 (PL 83, 865), but adapted.

(ii) 76rb 'Augustinus ait: nec superbia . . . sine superbia', a phrase from Julianus Pomerius, *De vita contemplativa* III.4 (PL 59, 479), as noted for me by Abbé Raymond Étaix.

27 PL 163, 759–63.   28 PL 163, 767–70, omitting words of address.

(10)   79r   De ecclesia et monasterio quid sit: In primis si uales bene ualeo . . . /
. . . ueniat ad Augustinum, et uiuat de communi quod Deus est.
Theobaldus Stampensis (Étampes), epistle to Thurstan, archbishop of York.[29]

(11)   79v   De penitentia: Quid sit penitentia unus accipit nomen . . . / . . . qui
similiter sunt asperi sicut caprarum et pelles alii sicut sanctus
Martinus.
Unidentified.

(12)   80v   Versus de auaritia: Tortor auaricie uestigia tempnere . . . / . . .
uiuens non uiuit uite sibi gaudia demit.
Unidentified.

(13)   80v   Hic incipiunt [81r] prouerbia patrum: Dei omnipotentis filius inter
cetera sacramenta . . .
Short excerpts from named authors – 81ra: Ysidorus, Beda, Sixtus de contemtu
mundi, Gregorius, Augustinus, Sixtus, Ysidorus, Sixtus, Gregorius, Seneca,[30]
Gregorius; 81rb: Ieronimus; 81va: Gregorius, Sixtus, Gregorius de ordina-
tione, Augustinus; 81vb: Ieronimus, Gregorius, Sixtus, Augustinus, Beda,
Gregorius, Beda, Gregorius; 82ra: Gregorius, Laurentius, Gregorius; 82 rb:
Ieronimus, but the passage quoted: 'Caue honores . . . fulminatur', is almost as
Isidore, *Synonyma* II.88–9 (PL 83, 865); 82va: Sixtus, Sixtus. See below, no. 14,
on Seneca.

(14)   82v   Exceptum [sic] ex epistola beati Gregorii ad Secundinum, seruum
Dei inclusum, de callidi hostis insidiis: Antiquus hostis . . .
Short excerpts from named authors – more than once – Augustinus,
Gregorius, Ieronimus, Ysidorus, Iohannes, Seneca, Beda, Albinus, Sixtus,
Prosper, Ylarius, Salomon, Apostolus; once only: Maximus, Cesarius,
Saluius, Dionisius Ariopagita, Celestinus papa, Ciprianus, Ambrosius, exem-
pla Clementis ad Iacobum.

(15)   91r   De ieiunio quatuor temporum: Quattuor esse tempora totius anni
manifestum est . . . / . . . si bene fecerint percipietis ęternam

---

[29] Published by R. Foreville and J. Leclercq, 'Un débat sur le sacerdoce des moines au XIIe
siècle', *Studia Anselmiana* 41 (1957), 8–118, at 52–3, omitting words of address.

[30] On Seneca (cited in nos. 13 and 14), see B. Munk Olsen, 'Les classiques latins dans les
florilèges médiévaux antérieurs au XIIIe siècle', *Revue d'histoire des textes* 10 (1980), 115–64, at
140, who identifies five (out of six) of the quotations named as Seneca, as from Publilius
Syrus, *Sententiae*.

beatitudinem, prestante . . . Deus per omnia secula seculorum. Amen.

The first part of this sermon (on the historical reasons for the four fasts), is a text in manuscripts of Archbishop Wulfstan's 'Commonplace Book', ptd B. Fehr,[31] from Cambridge, Corpus Christi College 190, pp. 225–7, and also presented in facsimile, from London, British Library, Cotton Nero A. i, 173r-174v, by H. R. Loyn.[32] But the whole sermon as in St John's 42 is extant also in Copenhagen 1595, 23v-25r, Châlons 31 (33), 6v-8v, Vespasian D. ii, 19v-20v and Barlow 37, 39r-40r (with insertions). Barlow 37 is rightly regarded as a witness of the 'Commonplace Book' by Sauer, but on this item (his no. 33, p. 354), he did not realise that Barlow 37 presented the whole sermon.

(16)   91v   Sermo de decimis: Propitio Cristo, fratres karissimi, iam prope sunt dies . . . / . . . pro uestra bona uoluntate et obedientia deuota, prestante . . . qui in trinitate.

The sermon is in two parts. The first part is a variant text of pseudo-Augustine, *Sermo* cclxxvii. 1–3 inclusive,[33] now Caesarius, *Sermo* xxxiii (ed. Morin I, 143–6), §§1–3. But Caesarius §4 does not continue on tithing and our sermon adds a different ending on tithes. The whole sermon, as in St John's 42, is extant also in Copenhagen 1595, 43r-45v.

(17)   92v   De predicatione et fide: Oportet uos scire et intelligere, fratres karissimi, quia spiritus . . . / . . . ad ęternam gloriam uenire nobiscum ualeatis, ipso adiuuante . . . I.C., qui in trinitate.

Unidentified; also in Châlons 31 (33), 8v-11r and Cotton Vespasian D. ii, 20v-21v.

(18)   93r   De episcoporum et presbiterorum ordine predicationis: Dei omni-potentis sermo ad Ezechielem . . . / . . . retributionem bonam accipere mereamur, illo largiente . . . Deus per omnia.

Unidentified; also in Cotton Vespasian D. ii, 21v-23r.

(19)   94r   De Anticristo et eius signis: Omnis qui secundum Cristiane professionis rectitudinem . . . / . . . resistere per fidem ualeant, adiuuante . . . in secula seculorum.

Archbishop Wulfstan, *Sermo* Ia,[34] also in Copenhagen 1595, 51r-52r, Cotton

---

[31] *Die Hirtenbriefe Ælfrics*, ed. B. Fehr, Bibliothek der angelsächsischen Prosa 9 (Hamburg, 1914; rev. ed. Darmstadt, 1966), 240–1.

[32] *A Wulfstan Manuscript*, EEMF 17 (Copenhagen, 1971).

[33] PL 39, 2266–8.   [34] Bethurum, *Wulfstan*, pp. 113–15.

Vespasian D. ii, 28v-29r, Cambridge, Corpus Christi College 201, pp. 66–7 and Oxford, Bodleian Library, Hatton 113, 31v-33r. Abbé Étaix has informed me that the sermon is also copied in Madrid, Real Biblioteca del Escorial T.I.12 (s. xiv), 176r-v,[35] within a section containing other items found in Cotton Vespasian D. ii. St John's 42, 94r, in the right-hand margin, contains a well-executed line-drawing of Antichrist, in man's dress of flowing gown, in upright stature, but with a wolf's head, paws and feet. Its caption in later English, 'Of Antichriste and his signes', indicates a much later reading of Wulfstan's sermon.

(20)   94v Sermo sancti Gregorii de ligandi soluendique potestate: Sciendum est, fratres, quod sancti apostoli . . . / . . . ex ipsa tumide reprehensionis superbia culpa quę non erat fiat.

Gregory, *Homilia .xl. in Evangelia*,[36] extracts from no. xxvi.4–6, with variant readings from the printed text.

(21)   95r Sermo contra iniquos iudices et falsos testes: Auscultate, iudices terrę, sermones meos . . . / . . . sed cum iustis gaudia eterna per eum qui in trinitate . . . in secula seculorum. Amen.

Unidentified; also in Copenhagen 1595, 45v-47v, Châlons 31 (33), 11r-13v and Cotton Vespasian D. ii, 23r-v.

(22)   95v: Exortatio ad plebem: Audiuimus cum euangelium legeretur . . . / . . . ad eterna gaudia feliciter peruenire, ubi est gloria in secula seculorum.

Pseudo-Augustine, *Sermo* lxxviii,[37] now Caesarius, *Sermo* clviii (ed. Morin II, 645–8), with variant readings from the printed text.

(23)   96r De uitandis peccatis et de iuditio futuro: Fratres karissimi, tempus est transeundi de malo . . . / . . . pro bonis operibus supradictis et his similibus ibunt in uitam ęternam.

Compare pseudo-Bede, *Homiliae Subdititiae*, ciii.[38] Pseudo-Bede, ciii appears to be a greatly abbreviated version of St John's 42, no. 23, which, in long form, is extant also in Copenhagen 1595, 62r-65r, in Vespasian D. ii, 27v-28v and, judging by length, probably also in Madrid Escorial T. I. 12, 174v-176r.

---

[35] On this manuscript, see G. Antolín, *Catálogo de los Códices Latinos de la Real Biblioteca del Escorial* IV (Madrid, 1916), 106. Antolín does not place the manuscript but it contains some originally English material, notably a *translatio* of Thomas Becket (fol. 306) and a homily and prayers for the saint. I have not seen this manuscript.

[36] PL 76, 1199–201.   [37] PL 39, 1897–9.   [38] PL 94, 504–5.

(24)   97r   Sermo Augustini de die iudicii: Fratres karissimi, quam timenda est dies illa . . . /. . . de quo loco nos Deus omnipotens eripere dignetur qui in trinitate . . . secula seculorum. Amen.

Pseudo-Augustine, *Sermo* ccli,[39] extant also in Copenhagen 1595, 57r-58r and in Madrid Escorial T. I. 12, 178v-179r. The sermon, however, was extremely popular.[40]

(25)   97v   De resurrectione mortuorum: Uerba domini nostri I.C., fratres karissimi, que in lectione . . . / . . . iusti autem in uitam ęternam et regnabunt cum Deo in secula seculorum. Amen.

Unidentified; also in Copenhagen 1595, 56r-57r.

(26)   97v   Sermo: Popule meus quid feci tibi . . . / . . . ubi feliciter gaudeatis, iuuante . . . regnat in secula.

Geoffrey du Loroux, alias Babion, no. 24 (Bonnes, p. 201).[41]

(27)   99v   Sermo in dedicatione: Fundamenta eius in montibus sanctis . . . / . . . qui loquuntur pacem cum proximo suo, mala autem in cordibus eorum (Ps. XXVII.3).

Geoffrey du Loroux, alias Babion, no. 48 (Bonnes, p. 203).[42]

(28)   100v   De hoc quod omnes homines dicuntur fures: Propterea, fratres karissimi, aliud est de diuitibus . . . / . . . ite ergo maledicti et cetera (cf. Matt. XXV.31).

Unidentified.

(29)   100v   Sermo de ecclesia in dedicatione: Facta sunt encenia in Ierosolimis . . . / . . . abiit dominus sabbato persata.

See below, no. 34.[43]

(30)   101r   De tenacitate: Discipuli autem eius esurientes . . . / . . . non pro rapina sed pro tenacitate.

See below, no. 34.[44]

---

[39] PL 39, 2210.

[40] On other Latin manuscripts containing the text, see J. E. Cross, 'Towards the Identification of Old English Literary Ideas: Old Workings and New Seams', *Sources of Anglo-Saxon Culture*, ed. P. E. Szarmach (Kalamazoo, MI, 1986), p. 84; on its use in Old English, see J. E. Cross, 'A Doomsday Passage in an Old English Sermon for Lent', *Anglia* 100 (1982), 103–8.

[41] Ptd PL 171, 828–33, as Hildebert, *Sermo* cvi.

[42] Ptd PL 171, 733–6, as Hildebert, *Sermo* lxxxiii.

[43] This section is ptd PL 171, 731–2.   [44] This section is ptd PL 171, 732–3.

(31) 101r De rapina: Est et aliud contrarium genus . . . / . . . sed non propter elemosinas peccata committere.

See below, no. 34.[45]

(32) 101r De sacrificio: Nec solum raptores insaniunt . . . / . . . et domum reconciliationis destruis.

See below, no. 34.

(33) 101v De ultione rapine: Ecce habetis auctoritatem ab apostolo . . . / . . . pauperis non tamen erit in finem.

See below, no. 34.

(34) 101v De ultione sacrilegii male tractatis uasa domini: Sed quia mentionem fecimus . . . / . . . ad regales nuptias, iuuante domino nostro, et cetera.

Items 29–34 are Geoffrey du Loroux, alias Babion, no. 47 (Bonnes, p. 203).[46]

(35) 102r Incipit sermo ad sacerdotes: Ve pastoribus qui dispergunt . . . / . . . nomen sacerdotis retinere studeatis, iuuante Deo nostro qui tecum.

Geoffrey du Loroux, alias Babion, no. 55 (Bonnes, p. 203).[47]

(36) 103r Sermo ad sacerdotes: Designauit . . . pauci (Luke X.1–2). Elegit, fratres karissimi, dominus in primitiua ęcclesia duodecim . . . / . . . cum seruis suis quibus talenta tradidit ponet, qui uiuit et regnat Deus per.

Geoffrey du Loroux, alias Babion, no. 46 (Bonnes, p. 203)[48]

(37) 103v Alius ad sacerdotes: Factum est . . . oues meę (Ezek. XXXIV.1–5,

---

[45] Items 31–4 are unpublished.

[46] Bonnes (p. 203, n. 16) comments that item 29, printed in PL 171, is frequently followed by a section headed: *De tenacitate*, and then other sections entitled: *De rapina, De sacrilegis, De ultione rapinae, De ultione male tractantium uasa domini*, as in two of the manuscripts considered by him. Note that the benediction is entered only after item 34.

[47] Ptd PL 147, 224–6 ('Incerti auctoris sermones sex ad populum', *Sermo* ii).

[48] Two sermons by Babion have the same incipit, nos. 46 and 54. No. 54 has been printed in PL 171, 926–9 and is presented in St John's 42, 114r–115v, as our item 47 below. This sermon, item 36 (Bonnes, no. 46), is the other sermon with the same incipit, but is unpublished. See, on the two sermons, B. Hauréau, *Notices et extraits de quelques manuscrits latins de la Bibliothèque Nationale* 1 (Paris, 1890), 247, commenting on Paris, BN, lat. 3833, a manuscript containing Babion's sermons.

with omission). Sed ego super pastores ... / ... mundum et purum, offeratis ei in die iudicii, qui.

Geoffrey du Loroux, alias Babion, no. 56 (Bonnes, p. 203).[49]

(38) 105r Sermo de sinodo ad sacerdotes; Quantas commissis uobis ouibus debeatis excubias ... / ... et agnoscere familiam suam, cum uenerit iudicare uiuos ac m < ortuos > .

Hildebert, *Sermo* lxxxviii.[50]

(39) 107r Ad sacerdotes: Homo . . . domini sui (Matt. XXV.14–18). Hęc parabola, fratres karissimi, dicta a domino ... / ... fideles in cęlo cum aliis remuneret dominus . . . qui uiuit.

Geoffrey du Loroux, alias Babion, no. 42 (Bonnes, p. 202).[51]

(40) 108r Incipit sermo sancti Augustini de periculo sacerdotis, et de illo diuite qui purpura induebatur, et de illo diuite cuius uberes fructus attulerat. Diligenter attendite, fratres karissimi, omnes sacerdotes domini ... / ... ad eterna premia feliciter peruenire, prestante ... Cristo et cetera.

Pseudo-Augustine, *Sermo* cclxxxvii,[52] now Caesarius, *Sermo* clxxxiii (ed. Morin II, 744–8).

(41) 109r Alius ad sacerdotes: Locutus ... sunt domino (citations from Lev. XXI.16–21, XXII.4). Fratres karissimi, hec omnia que in ueteri lege de sacerdotio ... / ... cauete ne pro omnibus dignitati officii inueniamini indigni (110ra23)

Geoffrey du Loroux, alias Babion, no. 44 (Bonnes, p. 203).[53]

(42) No title, text continues without break.
110ra23 Dicit apostolus Paulus: Non est potestas ... / ... et discordias seminando unionem pacis extinguere.

Part of Geoffrey du Loroux, alias Babion, no. 41 (Bonnes, p. 202), copied whole as item 2 above (71v).

(43) 110v Gregorius Iohanni Constantinopolitano episcopo de superbia: Diabolus despectis angelorum legionibus secum ... / ... ubi non dico multa tractare sed mihi uix respirare liceat.

49 Ptd PL 171, 915–18, as Hildebert, *Sermo* cxxviii.   50 PL 171, 751–8.
51 Ptd PL 171, 779–83, as Hildebert, *Sermo* xcv.   52 PL 39, 2287–8.
53 Ptd PL 147, 226–9 ('Incerti auctoris sermones sex ad populum', *Sermo* iii).

J. E. Cross

Geoffrey du Loroux, alias Babion, no. 68 (Bonnes, p. 204), being an extract from Gregory I, *Epist.* V.44.[54]

(44) 111v Sermo ad sacerdotes in sinodo: Deus . . . diiudicat (ps. LXXXI.1). Fratres karissimi, cum Dominus noster . . . / . . . et cum eis correctis in cęlo uiuatis, iuuante . . . qui uiuit et regnat.
Geoffrey du Loroux, alias Babion, no. 57 (Bonnes, p. 203).[55]

(45) 113r Sermo de synodo: Labia . . . exercituum est (Mal. II.7). Audite, fratres karissimi, quantum thesaurum . . . / . . . magna multitudine redeatis, ubi regnat dominus . . . cum angelis et sanctis per omnia.
Geoffrey du Loroux, alias Babion, no. 73 (Bonnes, p. 204).[56]

(46) 114r Incipit sermo synodalis qui in singulis synodis presbiteris enunciandus est: Fratres presbiteri et sacerdotes Dei, cooperatores . . . / . . . infirmitas bonis studeatis operibus adimplere, prestante . . . Cristo.
Admonitio synodalis.[57]

(47) 114v Sermo ad sacerdotes: Designauit . . . pauci (Luke X.1–2). Elegit, fratres karissimi, dominus in primitiua ecclesia . . . / . . . sale doctrine. Uobis dicit dominus: Negotiamini dum ego uenio. (cf. Luke XIX.13).
Geoffrey du Loroux, alias Babion, no. 54 (Bonnes, p. 203).[58]

(48) 115v Sermo ad penitentes: Rogo, fratres karissimi, et cum grandi humilitate admoneo . . . / . . . hoc enim solum aduersarii timent, illud solum expauescunt.
Eligius of Noyon (pseudo?), *De rectitudine catholicae conversationis*,[59] sentences from §§ 1–4, 7 and 8, with variant readings from the printed text.

[54] MGH, Epist. I, ed. P. Ewald and L.M. Hartmann (Berlin, 1891), 340, line 12 to the end.
[55] Ed. Bonnes, pp. 205–9.
[56] Ptd PL 147, 229–31 ('Incerti auctoris sermones sex ad populum', *Sermo* iv).
[57] An address ptd PL 115, 675–84, as *Homilia*, attributed to *Leo papa*, but now ed. from many manuscripts by R. Amiet, 'Une "Admonitio synodalis" de l'époque carolingienne', *MS* 26 (1964), 12–82. The text in St John's 42 is as Amiet, text H, which is nearest to the archetype. Our text has none of the later insertions, and differs from H only in benediction (apart from scribal errors and translocation of some phrases). On the popularity of the address, see T.L. Amos, 'The Origin and Nature of the Carolingian Sermon' (unpubl. PhD dissertation, Michigan State Univ., 1983), p. 218.
[58] Ptd PL 171, 926–9, as Hildebert, *Sermo* cxxxii. See above, n. 48.   [59] PL 40, 1169–74.

(49) 116r Ad reddendas decimas: Iam, fratres karissimi, prope sunt dies in quibus debetis messes colligere . . . / . . . libenter audite et, Cristo auxiliante, implere stude.

Caesarius, *Sermo* xxxiii (ed. Morin I, 143–7) an abbreviation with adaptation but many verbal echoes.[60]

(50) 116v Sermo sancti Augustini: R<ec>ogitemus, fratres karissimi, cuncta mala que fecimus . . . / . . . adiuuet et ad cẹlestia regna mereamur peruenire cui est . . . seculorum.

Pseudo-Augustine, *Sermo* ccl.[61]

(51) 117r Sermo: Audiuimus, fratres karissimi, in ewangelio dominum dicentem: In primis . . . sicut teipsum (cf. Matt. XXII.37 etc.). Fratres karissimi quomodo possumus . . . / . . . in ignem ẹternum, de quo nos liberet omnipotens Deus qui uiuit et regnat.

A composite sermon.[62]

(52) 117v Sermo: Rex Sirie cum excercitu magno obsedit . . . / . . . sed alii gaudium cẹlorum, adiuuante eo qui uiuit . . . seculorum.

Unidentified.

(53) 118v Sermo: /119r/De patrefamilias qui exiit summo mane . . . / . . . possidete regnum cum patre qui uiuit . . . seculorum. Amen.

Unidentified.

(54) 119r Item sermo: Ve uobis qui depredaberis quia depredabimini . . . / . . . qui tota die fugat et in uespere facto papilionem capit.

Unidentified.

(55) 120r Ad contemplatiuos: Cum egrederetur Loth . . . te fac (cf. Gen. XIX.17–20). Nouistis, fratres karissimi, quia Loth nepos . . . / . . . in celeste regnum feliciter permanere, qui uiuit et regnat (121r).

Geoffrey du Loroux, alias Babion, no. 36 (Bonnes, p. 202).[63]

---

[60] It is not, however, the shortened form of Caesarius, *Sermo* xxxiii, ptd PL 67, 1078–9 as pseudo-Caesarius, *Homilia* xvi.   [61] PL 39, 2209–10.

[62] The sermon has echoes of Gregory, *Homilia .xl. in Evangelia*, no. xvi, PL 76, 1134–8, and pseudo-Caesarius, *Sermo* xvii, PL 67, 1079–80, with other material.

[63] Ptd PL 171, 880–3, as Hildebert *Sermo* xcviii, with an addition at the end.

J. E. Cross

Date

The inclusion of many sermons by Geoffrey of Loroux, alias Babion (d. 1158),[64] and one sermon by Hildebert of Lavardin, archbishop of Tours (d. 1133),[65] obviously confirms the twelfth-century date of the manuscript, but the copying of some letters of Theobald of Étampes helps to indicate the earliest date of composition. Item 9 to Roscelin, teacher of Abelard, and a man known to Anselm, is interesting, but the mere naming of the recipient does not allow closer dating. Apparently, the bishop of Lincoln addressed in item 8 is more likely to be Robert Bloet (d. 9 January 1123) than his successor Alexander and, if so, the letter was written before 1123.[66] Item 10, however, is to Thurstan, who was archbishop of York from 1119,[67] but it is argued[68] that the contents of the letter, and the opposition which it aroused, date it as not before the Lateran Council of 1123 at which Thurstan was present. If such suggestions by commentators on Theobald are well-founded, it appears that the manuscript was copied after 1123.

Wulfstanian items in the collection

De Anticristo (no. 19)

A number of items (nos. 15–19, 21 and 23–5) cohere as a group, at the centre of which is the new copy of Wulfstan's Latin De Anticristo (item 19, 94r-v). Dorothy Bethurum[69] edited this sermon from four manuscripts known to her: CCCC 201 (s. xi^{med} for this section); Bodley, Hatton 113 (s. xi$^{3/4}$); Vespasian D. ii (s. xii$^{2/4}$); and Copenhagen 1595 (s. xi^{in}, before 1023). Of these manuscripts Hatton 113 was written at Worcester,[70] Corpus 201 'has some connexion with Worcester or York',[71] and the earliest manuscript, Copenhagen 1595, contains a short passage in Old English on 66v in Wulfstan's own hand, and exhibits corrections and interpolations to other Latin texts in the same hand elsewhere in the manuscript.[72] De Anticristo, a Wulfstan composition, immediately

---

[64] Bonnes, p. 198.   [65] New Catholic Encyclopedia VI (Washington, 1967), 1116.
[66] Foreville and Leclercq, 'Un débat', p. 14.
[67] Handbook of British Chronology, ed. Fryde et al., p. 295.
[68] Foreville and Leclerq, 'Un débat', p. 14.   [69] Bethurum, Wulfstan, pp. 113–15.
[70] Ker, Catalogue, p. 399.   [71] Bethurum, Wulfstan, p. 2.
[72] Ker, 'Handwriting', pp. 319–21. C.E. Hohler rejects Ker's identification in 'Some Service-books of the later Saxon Church', Tenth-Century Studies, ed. D. Parsons (London and Chichester, 1975), pp. 60–83 and 217–27, at 225, n. 59. P. Wormald, 'Æthelred the Lawmaker', in Ethelred the Unready: Papers from the Millenary Conference, ed. D. Hill (Oxford, 1978), pp. 47–80, at 52, also offers a caveat. But the rejection and caveat are based on debatable evidence. See J.E. Cross and A. Brown, 'Wulfstan and Abbo of Saint-Germain-des-Prés', forthcoming in Medievalia, and the introduction to the facsimile edition of Copenhagen 1595 by J.E. Cross and J. Morrish, EEMF, forthcoming.

216

indicates association with, or ultimate influence from, the Worcester scriptorium for any manuscript which contains the sermon. The palaeographical comments on Hatton 113 and Corpus 201 confirm this.

De ieiunio quatuor temporum (no. 15)

Another sermon in St John's 42, which appears in the Wulfstan manuscript Copenhagen 1595, is also associated with other Wulfstan material. Item 15, *De ieiunio quatuor temporum*, is extant also in Barlow 37, a manuscript which contains many items found in other manuscripts of Wulfstan's so-named 'Commonplace Book.'[73] The beginning only, on the historical reasons for the four fasts, is also extant in two other manuscripts of the 'Commonplace Book', CCCC 190, which Bethurum thought was nearest to the archetype of the collection,[74] and in London, British Library, Cotton Nero A. i, which contains corrections in Wulfstan's hand.[75] A comparison of the five manuscript-texts is suggestive. Within the normal range of scribal variation,[76] all five run parallel to the words *decretum est* (St John's 42, 91va; Fehr, p. 241, line 2), at which point CCCC 190 and Cotton Nero A. i contain a sentence citing Gregory which is omitted from the other three manuscripts. All five then continue parallel to *que opinio discutatur* (St John's 42, 91va8; Fehr, p. 241, line 10). Here Barlow 37 alone inserts a short and irrelevant sequence of three items from the *Excerptiones Pseudo-Ecgberti*,[77] a text found whole in manuscripts of the 'Commonplace Book'. All then continue with a short passage, 'Haec ergo ieiunia. . .constitute sunt' (St John's 42, 91va8–13; Fehr p. 241, lines 10–14, reading *colendi* for *constitute*). At this point Copenhagen 1595 has an erasure of two half-lines, and St John's 42 reads 'omne tempus constitutum est', a phrase which is missing from Barlow 37. St John's 42, Copenhagen 1595 and Barlow 37 then continue in sermonizing manner, quite differently from CCCC 190 and Cotton Nero A. i. This section of item 15 exhorts the faithful to obey their priests and not to contemn commands on fasting, by recalling a scriptural exemplum (the story of Jonathan who broke Saul's command by tasting a little honey and thus being prevented from concluding a victorious battle (I Kings XIV) and a scriptural statement, a near-quotation of Luke X.16 ('Qui uos

[73] D. Bethurum, 'Archbishop Wulfstan's Commonplace Book', *PLMA* 57 (1942), 916–29. For a close analysis of Barlow 37, see now Sauer, 'Wulfstans "Handbuch"'.
[74] Bethurum, 'Commonplace Book', p. 928.
[75] Ker, 'Handwriting', pp. 321–4.   [76] Fehr's edition has some inaccuracy.
[77] The items are now ptd R. A. Aronstam, 'The Latin Canonical Tradition in late Anglo-Saxon England' (unpubl. PhD dissertation, Columbia Univ., 1974), no. 80 (p. 83) on the age for ordination of priests; no. iii (p. 119) on admittance of virgins and ordination of deacons; no. 82 (p. 84) on the time and place for ordination of bishops. Aronstam nos. 80 and 82 are ptd B. Thorpe, *Ancient Laws and Institutes of England*, 2 vols. (London, 1840) II, 111 (nos. 97 and 98).

audit me audit . . .')). Here Barlow 37 alone inserts another statement on fasting in Lent from the 'canons', the closest analogue for which is a similar reference to the 'canons' in Abbo (of Saint-Germain-des Prés), *Sermo* xii,[78] a sermon copied in two Wulfstan manuscripts, Copenhagen 1596 and CCCC 190. The sermon in St John's 42 and its collateral texts now concludes with a final command for the congregation or readers to obey priests and precepts of God in order to receive eternal blessedness at judgement. It is worth recalling also that the exemplum of Jonathan was used in an Old English sermon on fasting in Rogationtide, published as Napier, no. 36,[79] which Dorothy Whitelock described as being 'in Wulfstan's style'.[80]

Sermo de decimis (no. 16)

In manner of composition item 16, *Sermo de decimis*, is the same as item 15. Ellen Jørgensen[81] identified this item as pseudo-Augustine, *Sermo* cclxxvii,[82] now known to be Caesarius of Arles, *Sermo* xxxiii (ed. Morin I, 143–7), an authoritative statement on tithes,[83] but it is not exactly so. Caesarius preached his sermon before John the Baptist's day, 24 June (*Solstitia*), a notable day for the celebration of pagan practices. Caesarius spoke about tithing for the first three paragraphs of his sermon (as in Morin's edition),[84] but in the final paragraph he condemned the 'impious bathing' in fountains, marshes and rivers at night or early morning. Such a castigation of a 'wretched' pagan custom was irrelevant for a sermon on tithes, so item 16 runs parallel with Caesarius §§ 1–3 and then adds a new ending on tithes, referring to the precepts of God to Moses and Melchisedech, and even to the practical matter of dividing tithes, in this case, in four ways, for the repair of the church, for the priests and clerics, for other various uses of the church, for the poor and strangers.

Authorship of items 15 and 16

Although all the evidence presented below is circumstantial, I find it difficult to believe that Wulfstan himself was not responsible, either by personal direction or even draft, for the original composition of items 15 and 16. Their

---

[78] Abbo's sermon is now ptd U. Önnerfors, *Abbo von Saint-Germain des-Prés: 22 Predigten*, Lateinische Sprache und Literatur des Mittelalters 16 (Frankfurt am Main, etc., 1985), *Sermo* xii, at p. 120 for the passage, on the severity of breaking a day of fast in Lent, where Abbo cites 'sancti canones'. Abbo's sermon is in Copenhagen 1595, 39r-40v and CCCC 190, p. 249.   [79] See *Wulfstan*, ed. A. Napier (Berlin, 1883), p. 174 for the story.

[80] *Sermo Lupi ad Anglos*, ed. D. Whitelock, 3rd ed. (London, 1963), p. 21.

[81] See above, n. 20.   [82] PL 39, 2266–8.

[83] See R. Willard, 'The Blickling-Junius Tithing Homily and Caesarius of Arles', *Philologica: the Malone Anniversary Studies*, ed. T. A. Kirby and H. B. Woolf (Baltimore, 1949), pp. 65–78.

[84] See above, n. 20.

inclusion in the manuscript which is now bound as Copenhagen 1595 is crucial to this opinion. Jennifer Morrish[85] has now analysed the Copenhagen manuscript and indicates that it was created as a loose-quire volume, the individual sections of which originally had a separate existence and were later bound together. In Copenhagen 1595, *De ieiunio quattuor temporumn* (23v-25v) is in section II, and *De decimis dandis* (43r-45v) is in section IV, but both were copied by one scribe whose hand is found in other manuscripts already associated with Wulfstan, namely in BL, Cotton Tiberius A. xiii, pt 1, in which the Wulfstan hand occurs persistently,[86] and BL, Cotton Vespasian A. xiv, principally a collection of Alcuin's letters, with corrections in the Wulfstan hand.[87] Since the Wulfstan hand also interpolates in Copenhagen 1595, section IV,[88] the copyist is closely associated with the distinctive corrector in three manuscripts. The material copied in the two sections also points, directly or indirectly, towards Wulfstan. Preceding *De ieiunio* in section II are three items, with rules for priests, on the ecclesiastical grades and for bishops,[89] which are found also in that part of Boulogne-sur-Mer, Bibliothèque Municipale, 63 which was a copy of one composed by Ælfric,[90] Wulfstan's correspondent and aide. Following *De decimis* in section IV are four brief sermons, entitled *Contra iniquos iudices et falsos testes, Sermo ad coniugatos et filios, De dominis et seruis* and *Sermo ad uiduas.* All of these are similar in structure, drawing together appropriate scriptural quotations and presenting firm rules of conduct, and none of them have identifiable whole sources, at least at present. But the *Sermo ad coniugatos* uses either Pirmin, *De singulos libros scarapsus*,[91] or its extract in the *Excerptiones pseudo-Ecgberti*,[92] both of which works were among Wulfstan's sources elsewhere.[93] And, for the very passage from Pirmin or pseudo-Ecgbert, the Wulfstan hand has inserted a phrase in the margin which the scribe omitted.[94] It could be helpful for a skilled Latinist to consider features of style in these brief sermons (and some others of similar structure in Copenhagen 1595)[95] against those of known Latin works by Wulfstan, since their topics were certainly of concern to the archbishop.

---

[85] Detailed analysis will be presented in a forthcoming volume on Copenhagen 1595 (see above, n. 72).   [86] Ker, 'Handwriting', pp. 324-6.

[87] *Ibid.* pp. 326-7. Ker comments that the collection 'was almost certainly made for Wulfstan'.

[88] *Ibid.* p. 320, noting the marginal insertion on 48r.

[89] The material will be analysed in detail by J.E. Cross and J. Morrish (see above, n. 72).

[90] See P. Clemoes, 'Supplement to the Introduction', *Hirtenbriefe*, ed. Fehr, p. cxxvii.

[91] PL 89, 1037–80.

[92] *Ancient Laws*, ed. Thorpe II, 115 (no. 121); Aronstam, 'The Latin Canonical Tradition', pp. 93–4 (no. 105).

[93] On Pirmin, see K. Jost, *Wulfstanstudien*, Swiss Stud. in English 23 (Bern, 1950), 45–62.

[94] See above, n. 88.

[95] Other short sermons of this kind in Copenhagen 1595 are *De conuersione et penitentia et communione* (54r-56r), *De resurrectione mortuorum* (56r-57r), *De adiutorio Dei et libero arbitrio* (59r-

J. E. Cross

Since the sections of the Copenhagen manuscript were also in one place for their binding, it should be added that the whole manuscript has many connections with Wulfstan, notably and firmly, copies of his accepted Latin works *De Antecristo et eius signis* (51r-52r), *De baptismo* (78r-79r), his Latin excerpts from scripture entitled *De visione* (65v-66v), Latin letters related to Wulfstan (41r-42r), the writing in Old English on 66v in the Wulfstan hand,[96] and two Latin letters from Ælfric to Wulfstan (67r-77v), one of which was 'modified in Wulfstan's possession'.[97] It could be argued that other items are connected with Wulfstan and/or Worcester.[98] Doubts may remain about the actual authorship of items 15 and 16 in St John's 42, but no doubt should remain about their close association with Wulfstan.

The other items in the group, *De predicatione et fide* (no. 17), *De episcoporum et presbitorum ordine predicationis* (no. 18), *Sermo contra iniquos iudices et falsos testes* (no. 21), *De uitandis peccatis et de iuditio futuro* (no. 23), (the 'long version' of pseudo-Bede, *Hom.* ciii), *Sermo Augustini de die iudicii* (no. 24) (pseudo-Augustine, *Sermo* ccli) and *De resurrectione mortuorum* (no. 25), are extant in one or more of a group of manuscripts, Copenhagen 1595, Cotton Vespasian D. ii and Châlons 31 (33),[99] the first two of which contain other items associated with Wulfstan.

Centring on *De Anticristo*, as indicated above, and supported especially by items 15 and 16, the copying of these sermons in St John's 42 points towards Worcester as place of origin, substantiating hints raised by the St John's 42 calendar. All this information, when added together, strongly suggests that St John's 42 is another example of the continuity of Anglo-Saxon traditions at Worcester over the historical divide of the Norman Conquest.

60v). The last of these was copied by the scribe who transcribed sections II and IV; the first two were copied by a scribe who was associated with him and whose hand is also found in Cotton Vespasian A. xiv.   [96] Ker, 'Handwriting', p. 320.

[97] Clemoes, 'Supplement', *Hirtenbriefe*, ed. Fehr, p. cxxxvii.

[98] See J. E. Cross and A. Brown, 'Literary Impetus for Wulfstan's *Sermo Lupi*', *Leeds Stud. in English* ns 20 (1989), 271–91. Other suggestions will be made in the volume on Copenhagen 1595 (see above, n. 72).

[99] Châlons-sur-Marne 31 (33) may appear to be an oddity in this group, but since the scriptorium did not begin until the eleventh century, the dissemination could have been from Worcester to Châlons-sur-Marne.

A pair of inscribed Anglo-Saxon hooked tags from the Rome (Forum) 1883 hoard

JAMES GRAHAM-CAMPBELL and ELISABETH OKASHA, with an introductory note by MICHAEL METCALF

The importance of the hoard found in the excavations in the Forum at Rome in 1883, just outside the the the House of the Vestal Virgins, has long been recognized by Anglo-Saxon numismatists, for it is the largest recorded source for the coinage of Æthelstan and Edmund. Archaeologists, art-historians and epigraphers have, however, failed to appreciate the significance for Anglo-Saxon studies of the pair of silver tags found with the coins (pl. VIII), bearing between them the name of Pope Marinus, despite their having been illustrated (in uncleaned condition) by Christopher Blunt in his 1974 account of the hoard.[1] The tags themselves are described and discussed here by Dr James Graham-Campbell and their inscriptions by Dr Elisabeth Okasha, both working from photographs kindly made available to us by Dottoressa Silvana Balbi de Caro, of the Museo Nazionale in Rome, through the agency of Dr Michael Metcalf.[2]

A NOTE ON THE HOARD by MICHAEL METCALF

The Rome (Forum) hoard of 1883 consisted of some 833 silver coins and one Byzantine gold solidus, found together in a pot with the pair of tags discussed here. All but six of the coins are English, and there need be no doubt that they represent an offering to the papacy, sent to Rome during or very shortly after the pontificate of Marinus II (942–6). The strays may have been picked up en route or they may, more probably, have been added to the sum after their

---

[1] C. E. Blunt, 'The Coinage of Athelstan, 924–939: a Survey', *BNJ* 42 (1974), 35–158, at 141–55 (Appendix I: 'The Forum Hoard, Found in Excavations near the House of the Vestal Virgins 1883'); the tags are illustrated (enlarged) on p. 141, where they are identified wrongly as bronze 'fibulae'. The original account of the hoard was by G. B. De Rossi, *D'un tesoro di monete anglo-sassone trovato nell' Atrio delle Vestali* (Rome, 1884), and in English as 'A Hoard of Anglo-Saxon Coins Found in Rome', *NChron* 3rd ser. 4 (1884), 225–55. See also C. E. Blunt, 'Anglo-Saxon Coins Found in Italy', *Anglo-Saxon Monetary History: Essays in Memory of Michael Dolley*, ed. M. A. S. Blackburn (Leicester, 1986), pp. 159–69, at 161 (Hoard No. 4).

[2] Dr M. Metcalf has completed a full publication of the hoard, with illustrations of all the coins, for the *Bollettino di Numismatica*, to which the photographs of the tags belong and with whose permission they are published here (pl. VIII).

arrival in Rome. The English coins are of Alfred (6), Edward the Elder (213), Æthelstan (396), Edmund (200), Archbishop Plegmund (4), Anlaf Guthfrithsson (1), Anlaf Sihtricsson (4), and Sihtric Sihtricsson (1). They are from all regions of England, in proportions which suggest that the whole is unlikely to have been withdrawn from the currency of any one region (since such hoards as we have show that the currency was regionally weighted in its composition). The hoard may, therefore, be from a treasury which drew upon taxation nationally. The obvious hypotheses are that it is from either the royal treasury or that of the archbishop of Canterbury.

THE HOOKED TAGS by JAMES GRAHAM-CAMPBELL

Description

The two silver hooked tags from the Forum hoard form a pair, having the same incised ornament and a shared inscription inlaid with niello; recent cleaning has revealed them to be in excellent condition (see pl. VIIIa and b). Each tag consists of an oval plate, with a pair of perforated lugs extending from one end and a plain hook from the other. Both are incised with two concentric, approximately circular lines, framing a single row of text, with the outer of these margins extended around the lugs; the central field is filled with a trilobate foliate motif. The text, which is executed in Anglo-Saxon capitals, is split between the two tags, reading on the first (i): + DOMNOMA (pl. VIIIa); and on the second (ii): RINOPAPA + (pl. VIIIb). In both cases the letters read clockwise around the tags, with the cross placed at the top, immediately below the hook. The reverse of both tags is unornamented, except that the first tag (i) has a crudely executed V-shaped arrangement of seventeen small punchmarks, alongside and partly over a V of incised lines (pl. VIIIa). The first tag is slightly larger than the second. Approximate lengths: (i) 44 mm; (ii) 42 mm.

Discussion

These tags represent a well-known type of middle to late Anglo-Saxon hooked fastener, with perforations that are always unriveted, suggesting that in use they were attached to cloth by sewing. In many cases the hooks themselves appear to be of little strength, suggesting that their main purpose was simply for closure rather than for holding something fast under strain. The finest examples of Anglo-Saxon hooked tags are those of niello-inlaid silver in the ninth-century Trewhiddle style; a close parallel in form and size for the Forum hoard examples is provided by one such from Canterbury, Kent.[3] However,

---

[3] J. Graham-Campbell, 'Some New and Neglected Finds of 9th-Century Anglo-Saxon Ornamental Metalwork', *MA* 26 (1982), 144–51, at 144–5, fig. 2.2 and pl. ivb.

simpler tags continued to be made during the tenth and eleventh centuries.[4] The central design on the Forum hoard tags consists of a bud between two leaves, a foliate motif popular in ninth-century ornament, as in the standard fan-shaped field at the butt-end of numerous Trewhiddle-style strap-ends (such as those from Whitby Abbey, North Yorkshire).[5] The same motif is used to fill roundels on the smaller of the two silver disc brooches from the hoard found in Beeston Tor Cave, Staffordshire, where it had been deposited *c*. 875.[6] In consequence, the combination of this foliate design with the fashion for niello-inlaid silver would have suggested, in the first instance, a ninth-century date for the Forum hoard tags. However, the use of niello-inlaid silver remained a standard technique in the tenth century, and the motif is too simple for precise dating, even allowing for its marked difference from the ragged acanthus-leaf designs that were to become established in Anglo-Saxon art of the tenth century (as on the niello-inlaid silver plates around the base of the Canterbury censer-cover).[7]

As argued below by Dr Okasha, the text on the Forum hoard tags is primary and reads ' + DOMNO MARINO PAPA + ', probably to be translated as 'to Lord Pope Marinus'. The form and style of these tags, as well as their script, would have accorded with their being contemporary with Marinus I (882–4), but these features are also perfectly consistent with their dating to the pontificate of Marinus II (942–6), as suggested by the evidence of the associated coins. On this basis, they are the only known pieces of tenth-century Anglo-Saxon metalwork to be dated by an inscription naming a known historical person, and their manufacture may be placed securely in the 940s.

The Forum hoard tags cannot therefore be far removed in date from the only other pair of hooked tags to have been found together with Anglo-Saxon coins, those deposited *c*. 963 in a chalk container, at Tetney, Lincolnshire.[8] However, the Tetney hooked tags are simpler, being of plain silver, and are triangular in form, without lugs (as would appear to be the case with the majority of the later examples). It is of particular interest that a pair of tags constitutes the *only* non-numismatic element of silver in both these mid-tenth-century hoards, strongly suggesting that they had functioned in both instances as bag or purse fasteners. Indeed, traces of fabric survived at Tetney and on at least one coin in the Forum hoard.

---

[4] For a general discussion of hooked tags, see D. A. Hinton, 'Hooked Tags', in M. Biddle, *Artefacts from Medieval Winchester, pt 2: Object and Economy in Medieval Winchester*, 2 vols., Winchester Stud. 7.ii (Oxford, 1990) II, 548–52, with particular reference to examples found at Winchester.

[5] D. M. Wilson, *Anglo-Saxon Ornamental Metalwork, 700–1100, in the British Museum* (London, 1964), pl. xl, nos. 116–22.   [6] *Ibid*. pl. xi, no. 2.

[7] *Ibid*. pl. xii, no. 9.   [8] *Ibid*. p. 178, pl. xxxii, nos. 86 and 87.

Two silver tags with gilt edges, both triangular in form and without lugs (although not a matched pair), form part of the unpublished hack-silver in the mixed hoard from List on the island of Sylt (Nordfriesland), which also includes fragments of Anglo-Saxon disc brooches. The hoard was deposited in the early eleventh century, on the basis of a group of freshly struck English and German coins, but the hack-silver and ingots are to be associated with an earlier group of fragmented English, Arabic, German and Scandinavian coins, all belonging to the tenth century.[9] A mixed silver hoard, buried at Gerete, Fardhem, on Gotland (with a suggested end-date for its coins of 1099 x 1112), contains a single disc-shaped hooked tag, unornamented and without lugs.[10] It seems reasonable to suggest that the Gerete example had originally been associated with the Anglo-Saxon coins in that hoard which have the earlier end-date of *c*. 1050 x 1053; indeed, only two other silver hooked tags of late Anglo-Saxon origin have been found in Scandinavian Viking-age contexts. These are both disc-shaped, but one is a classic Trewhiddle-style, lugged example from a Birka cremation grave (Grave 348), Sweden,[11] while the other, from a midden at Vesle Hjerkinn in the Dovre mountains, Norway, represents a later type, with linear, rocker-engraved ornament and no lugs.[12]

The best known pair of Anglo-Saxon hooked tags are the fine examples in niello-inlaid silver, of triangular form with triple lugs, found at the knees of a skeleton (Grave 67) in the Old Minster cemetery at Winchester, Hants.[13] In this case, there is no doubt that they will have been in use as fasteners for gartering, as also the pair found at the knees of the skeleton in Birka Grave 905, Sweden, which represents a unique Scandinavian tenth-century variant in the form of animal masks.[14] In contrast, however, a single hooked tag was found 'beside the right hand' of Skeleton No. 4, in the late Anglo-Saxon execution cemetery at Meon Hill, Hants,[15] and was thus interpreted as a 'wrist

---

9 I am most grateful to Ralf Weichmann (Institut für Ur- und Frühgeschicte der Christian-Albrechts-Universität, Kiel) for information on the List hoard in advance of the completion of his Ph.D. thesis, entitled 'Edelmetalldepots der Wikingerzeit in Schleswig-Holstein'.
10 M. Stenberger, *Die Schatzfunde Gotlands der Wikingerzeit*, 2 vols. (Stockholm, 1947) II, 58–60, fig. 249.5.
11 H. Arbman, *Birka I: Die Gräber* (Stockholm/Uppsala, 1940–3), p. 99, fig. 52.1 and pl. 99.4; J. Graham-Campbell, *Viking Artefacts: a Select Catalogue* (London, 1980), pp. 90 and 266, no. 311.
12 B. Weber, 'Vesle Hjerkinn – A Viking Age Mountain Lodge? A Preliminary Report', *Proc. of the Tenth Viking Congress: Larkollen, Norway, 1985*, ed. J. E. Knirk (Oslo, 1987), pp. 103–11, at 105–6, fig. 4.
13 D. M. Wilson, 'Late Saxon Metalwork from the Old Minster, 1964', *Ant J* 45 (1965), 262–4, at 263–4, pl. lxxix*c*; Hinton, 'Hooked Tags', no. 1407, fig. 148, and pl. xlv*a*.
14 Arbman, *Birka*, p. 353, fig. 304, pl. 91.6.
15 D. M. Liddell, 'Excavations at Meon Hill', *Papers and Proc. of the Hampshire Field Club and Archaeol. Soc.* 12 (1933), 127–62, at 135 and 153–4, fig. 15.M4.

fastener', but the hands were bound together so that the tag in fact lay in the pelvic area, and another such 'wrist fastener' was found 'close to the right wrist' of Skeleton No. 24, with its arms to its side, in the nearby execution cemetery on Stockbridge Down, Hants.[16] The use of a single hooked tag on one wrist only, as at first suggested by these two discoveries, represents an unlikely dress fashion and it seems more reasonable to look for an alternative explanation for the presence of single tag when found at the waist region of a late Anglo-Saxon burial, such as also that from the pelvic area of Grave 36 of the pre-Chapter House cemetery of St Albans Abbey, Herts.[17] Their use in these instances as purse fasteners would seem to be a reasonable explanation, given the Forum hoard and Tetney associations of hooked tags with coins.

It seems clear, therefore, that there was no specialized function for these somewhat delicate fasteners which would have been used variously, either singly or in pairs, as required for different purposes. However, there is one argument to indicate that the Forum hoard tags were designed for use together on a single object, rather than on two separate objects (like the Winchester garters). This is the fact that their text is split between them, a feature of no other Anglo-Saxon inscription, whilst, as Dr Okasha comments below, 'a text divided between faces or sides of a single object is, however, fairly common'. In this light, the Forum hoard tags would most likely have been sewn, side by side, onto a single cloth object – most plausibly a purse or money-bag, as suggested above.

THE TEXTS by ELISABETH OKASHA

Description

The two hooked tags (pl. VIII*a* and *b*) each contain a text, and both texts are placed in a similar position on the tag. In both cases the text is contained in the border formed between two approximately circular margins. The letters touch neither margin, although the cross of text (i) does touch the inner margin. The crosses are placed in those parts of the border nearest to the hooks. The letters read clockwise around the borders with the bottoms of the letters facing inwards. The letters have been incised and filled with niello. All the letters, including those damaged, are clearly legible.

The margins of the tags are set carefully around the central foliate motif and around the lugs. These margins appear to be primary, that is, to be an integral

---

[16] N. Gray Hill, 'Excavations on Stockbridge Down, 1935–36', *Papers and Proc. of the Hampshire Field Club and Archaeol. Soc.* 13 (1937), 247–59, at 250 and 255, pl. i.

[17] M. Biddle and B. Kjølbye-Biddle, 'England's Premier Abbey: the Medieval Chapter House of St Albans Abbey and its Excavation in 1978', *Hertfordshire's Past* 11 (1981), 3–27, at 23, fig. 18.

part of the design of the tags. Like the letters, the margins and central motif have been incised and then filled with niello. It does not seem likely that a border would be deliberately formed by margins in order to be left plain. It follows that, if the margins are primary, the texts are also likely to be primary.

The letters of both texts are unevenly spaced around the borders, but the spaces between letters do not indicate word divisions. In text (i) the letters of the first half of the text, + DOM, are set close together taking up about one third of the available border. The remaining four letters, NOMA, are widely spaced around the remainder of the border. Text (ii) is similar: the letters + RINO are set close together followed by the more widely spaced letters PAPA. This suggests that the metalworker was unsure of how much space was available for each letter. In my view, he probably started in each case by incising the cross next to the hook and then proceeded cautiously clockwise until he had inscribed about half of the text. He could then estimate what remained and space the rest of the letters around the remaining border.

It is likely that the metalworker was copying a written exemplar, and some assumptions concerning this exemplar can be made. If the exemplar had contained the texts already arranged around a circle then the unevenness in spacing could have been rectified at that stage. The exemplar is therefore likely to have contained the texts written in a straight line. The exemplar must have had the texts divided into two parts. Had this not been done, then the clustering of letters in the first half of each text, as described above, would have occurred on one text, not on both. We may assume that the written exemplar contained the text written in two straight lines, perhaps in a similar way to the transliteration given below. The placing of the cross beside the hook in each case was presumably to preserve uniformity of design; the decision to do this could have been taken by either the metalworker or the scribe who wrote the exemplar.

Script

The script used on the tags is known as Anglo-Saxon capitals. There are two or more occurrences of each of the letters, A, M, N, O and P. With the exception of the instances of M and N, the occurrences of these letters are consistent in form with each other. The M of MARINO (see text (i) below) has a small vertical medial line which the M of DOMNO lacks, but both these forms of M are common in Anglo-Saxon capitals.[18] In MARINO the N has the cross-bar meeting both verticals, while in the N of DOMNO the cross-bar

[18] E. Okasha, 'The Non-Runic Scripts of Anglo-Saxon Inscriptions', *Trans. of the Cambridge Bibliographical Soc.* 4 (1964–8), 321–38.

meets the left vertical but the lower right serif. Although such differences in the shape of the letter N can be an indication of date, two examples are quite insufficient for this purpose. The script offers no firm dating evidence. All that can be said is that it lacks typically early features such as Insular letters and angular letter-forms.[19] The script is consistent with the tenth-century date for the tags indicated by the identification of the name MARINO with Pope Marinus II (see below).

Texts[20]

(i) + DOMNOMA|

(ii) RINOPAPA + |

Discussion

The texts read together, '+ DOMNO MARINO PAPA +', probably to be translated, '+ to Lord Pope Marinus +'. *Domnus* is a well-attested medieval spelling for *dominus*, and the phrase *domnus apostolicus* is recorded in reference to the Pope.[21] On the tags it is presumably used as a title of respect. The phrase *domno marino* could be dative or ablative. While *papa* looks like an ablative rather than a dative form, confusion of endings is common in medieval Latin inscriptions; alternatively, *papa* as a title might be left undeclined. The whole phrase *domno marino papa* is probably best taken as dative, as in the translation suggested above. There were two popes called Marinus: Marinus I (= Martin II), 882–4, and Marinus II (= Martin III), 942–6. It is on the evidence of the date of the coins that the *Marinus* of the inscription is to be identified with Pope Marinus II.

No other Anglo-Saxon inscription contains one text divided between two separate objects. A text divided between faces or sides of a single object is, however, fairly common. The Brussels Cross, for example, has the long text set around the thickness of the cross on faces at varying angles to each other; bands of interlace decoration also split up the text, sometimes occurring in the middle of a word.[22] The nearest parallel for the treatment of the inscription on the pair of hooked tags is the pair of silver spoons from the Sutton Hoo ship-

---

[19] *Ibid.*

[20] The texts are transliterated using the following system: A indicates a legible letter A; *A* indicates a letter A, damaged but legible; | indicates the end of a text.

[21] R. E. Latham and D. R. Howlett, *Dictionary of Medieval Latin from British Sources: Fascicule III, D-E* (London, 1986), pp. 718–19, no. 8.

[22] E. Okasha, *Hand-List of Anglo-Saxon Non-Runic Inscriptions* (Cambridge, 1971), no. 17, pp. 57–8 and figs.

burial, Suffolk. They contain two separate but connected texts, the names *saulos* and *paulos* inscribed in Greek letters.[23]

CONCLUSIONS

Hooked tags are, by their nature, functional objects, and this pair is no exception. It is remarkable to find the name of the pope inscribed on such small and everyday objects. Blunt concluded that the Forum hoard coins represented 'a payment of Peter's pence to the Holy See'[24] and his suggestion is entirely consistent with the translation of the text given above, ' + to Lord Pope Marinus + '. The evidence thus combines to suggest that this pair of hooked tags was commissioned in England during the pontificate of Marinus II (942–6), as fasteners for a special purse to contain some form of national papal payment. They would thus have been made either at royal command or to the order of the archbishop of Canterbury, as suggested above by Dr Metcalf.

The use of hooked tags was widespread in southern England at this period (as already noted, for example, at both Canterbury and Winchester), although there has so far been little evidence for their manufacture other than in the form of a remarkable ninth-century design on a bone 'motif-piece' found in London (pl. IX). This was recovered in 1974 from a riverfront revetment dump, dating from the late twelfth to the early thirteenth century, on the site of Seal House, 106–8 Upper Thames Street.[25] It comprises part of a cow longbone into which has been incised the outline of a small hooked tag, consisting of an oval plate with a pair of lugs. The plate has a plain border and its central field is filled with a spreadeagled animal – an unusual collared quadruped, whose head (with oval eyes) forms the base of the hook – executed in a version of the Trewhiddle style. Although a few other ninth- to early tenth-century Trewhiddle-style 'motif-pieces' are known, from York as well as London, none carries such an artefact design.[26]

In conclusion, London, Canterbury and Winchester present themselves as chief amongst England's principal centres of learning and fine metalwork where this remarkable pair of silver tags, with their unique papal inscription,

---

[23] R.E. Kaske, 'The Silver Spoons of Sutton Hoo', *Speculum* 42 (1967), 670–2 and figs.; R. Bruce-Mitford and S.M. Youngs, 'Late Roman and Byzantine Silver', in R. Bruce-Mitford, *The Sutton Hoo Ship Burial* III, pt 1, ed. A. Care Evans (London, 1983), 1–201, at 125–46 and figs. [24] Blunt, 'Coinage of Athelstan', p. 141.

[25] I am grateful to Frances Pritchard, of the Museum of London (with whose permission pl. IX is published here), for information concerning this motif-piece, in advance of her own publication in *Aspects of Saxo-Norman London, II: Finds and Environmental Evidence*, ed. A.G. Vince, London and Middlesex Archaeol. Soc. Special Paper 12 (London, 1991).

[26] U. O'Meadhra, *Early Christian, Viking and Romanesque Art. Motif-Pieces from Ireland, II: A Discussion on Aspects of Find-Context and Function* (Stockholm, 1987), pp. 78–83, figs. 57–9.

might have been commissioned during the 940s on the authority of king or archbishop, specifically to fasten an official purse destined for Pope Marinus II (942–6).

In the words of Professor Loyn,[27] this date 'has a special interest because it was King Edmund (940–46) who laid down in his laws that *Romfeoh* should be among the compulsory dues paid by the church', although Loyn was not prepared himself to accept the Forum hoard as an actual payment of Peter's Pence, as Blunt had described it,[28] suggesting that it might be no more than 'a portion of a routine royal or ecclesiastical treasure hoard'. It is our belief that the arguments presented here have been sufficient to demonstrate that the Forum hoard represents no 'routine' treasure, consisting instead of royal or ecclesiastical alms (as had been paid under Alfred)[29] or, more probably, dues of the kind for which Edmund legislated – even if not strictly speaking of Peter's Pence, the tax paid to Rome in the form of a single penny from each free household, for this, as Loyn concluded, only 'grew into institutional shape in the tenth and early eleventh centuries'.[30]

---

[27] H. R. Loyn, 'Peter's Pence', *Friends of Lambeth Palace Library Ann. Report 1984*, pp. 10–20, at p. 19.
[28] Blunt, 'Coinage of Athelstan', p. 141.
[29] Loyn, 'Peter's Pence', p. 18; see also S. Keynes and M. Lapidge, *Alfred the Great: Asser's 'Life of King Alfred' and Other Contemporary Sources* (Harmondsworth, 1983), p. 237, n. 37, and p. 268, n. 206.   [30] Loyn, 'Peter's Pence', p. 13.

Bibliography for 1990

CARL T. BERKHOUT, MARTIN BIDDLE,
MARK BLACKBURN, SARAH FOOT,
SIMON KEYNES and ALEXANDER RUMBLE

This bibliography is meant to include all books, articles and significant reviews published in any branch of Anglo-Saxon studies during 1990. It excludes reprints unless they contain new material. It will be continued annually. The year of publication of a book or article is 1990 unless otherwise stated. The arrangement and the pages on which the sections begin are as follows:

1. GENERAL AND MISCELLANEOUS   *page* 233
2. OLD ENGLISH LANGUAGE   236
3. OLD ENGLISH LITERATURE   242
   General, 242; *Poetry*, 242 (*General*, 242; '*Beowulf*', 244; *Other poems*, 245); *Prose*, 247
4. ANGLO-LATIN, LITURGY AND OTHER LATIN ECCLESIASTICAL
   TEXTS   249
5. FONTES ANGLO-SAXONICI   250
6. PALAEOGRAPHY, DIPLOMATIC AND ILLUMINATION   251
7. HISTORY   253
8. NUMISMATICS   257
9. ONOMASTICS   260
10. ARCHAEOLOGY   262
   General, 262; *Towns and other major settlements*, 264; *Rural settlements, agriculture and the countryside*, 265; *Pagan cemeteries and Sutton Hoo*, 267; *Churches, monastic sites and Christian cemeteries*, 267; *Ships and seafaring*, 270; *Sculpture on bone, stone and wood*, 270; *Metal-work and other minor objects*, 271; *Inscriptions*, 272; *Pottery and glass*, 273
11. REVIEWS   273

Carl Berkhout has been mainly responsible for sections 2, 3 and 4, Alexander Rumble for sections 6 and 9, Sarah Foot for section 7, Mark Blackburn for section 8 and Martin Biddle for section 10. Section 5 has been compiled on the basis of information supplied by Don Scragg; Section 10 has been compiled with help from Birthe Kjølbye-Biddle. References to publications in Japan have been supplied by Professor Yoshio Terasawa. Simon Keynes has been responsible for co-ordination.

The following abbreviations occur where relevant (not only in the bibliography but also throughout the volume):

AAe   *Archaeologia Aeliana*
AB   *Analecta Bollandiana*
AC   *Archæologia Cantiana*

AHR	American Historical Review
AIUON	Annali, Istituto Universitario Orientale di Napoli: sezione germanica
AntJ	Antiquaries Journal
ArchJ	Archaeological Journal
ASE	Anglo-Saxon England
ASNSL	Archiv für das Studium der neueren Sprachen und Literaturen
ASSAH	Anglo-Saxon Studies in Archaeology and History
BAR	British Archaeological Reports
BBCS	Bulletin of the Board of Celtic Studies
BGDSL	Beiträge zur Geschichte der deutschen Sprache und Literatur
BIAL	Bulletin of the Institute of Archaeology (London)
BN	Beiträge zur Namenforschung
BNJ	British Numismatic Journal
CA	Current Archaeology
CBA	Council for British Archaeology
CCM	Cahiers de civilisation médiévale
CMCS	Cambridge Medieval Celtic Studies
CSASE	Cambridge Studies in Anglo-Saxon England
DAEM	Deutsches Archiv für Erforschung des Mittelalters
EA	Études anglaises
EconHR	Economic History Review
EEMF	Early English Manuscripts in Facsimile
EETS	Early English Text Society
EHR	English Historical Review
ELN	English Language Notes
EPNS	English Place-Name Society
ES	English Studies
FS	Frühmittelalterliche Studien
HS	Historische Sprachforschung
HZ	Historische Zeitschrift
IF	Indogermanische Forschungen
JBAA	Journal of the British Archaeological Association
JEGP	Journal of English and Germanic Philology
JEH	Journal of Ecclesiastical History
JEPNS	Journal of the English Place-Name Society
JMH	Journal of Medieval History
JTS	Journal of Theological Studies
LH	The Local Historian
MA	Medieval Archaeology
MÆ	Medium Ævum
MLR	Modern Language Review
MP	Modern Philology
MS	Mediaeval Studies
MScand	Mediaeval Scandinavia
N&Q	Notes and Queries

Bibliography for 1990

NChron   Numismatic Chronicle
NCirc   Numismatic Circular
NH   Northern History
NM   Neuphilologische Mitteilungen
OEN   Old English Newsletter
PA   Popular Archaeology
PBA   Proceedings of the British Academy
PMLA   Publications of the Modern Language Association of America
PQ   Philological Quarterly
RB   Revue bénédictine
RES   Review of English Studies
SBVS   Saga-Book of the Viking Society for Northern Research
SCBI   Sylloge of Coins of the British Isles
SCMB   Seaby's Coin and Medal Bulletin
SettSpol   Settimane di studio del Centro italiano di studi sull'alto medioevo (Spoleto)
SM   Studio Medievali
SN   Studia Neophilologica
SP   Studies in Philology
TLS   Times Literary Supplement
TPS   Transactions of the Philological Society
TRHS   Transactions of the Royal Historical Society
YES   Yearbook of English Studies
ZAA   Zeitschrift für Anglistik und Amerikanistik
ZDA   Zeitschrift für deutsches Altertum und deutsche Literatur
ZVS   Zeitschrift für vergleichende Sprachforschung

1. GENERAL AND MISCELLANEOUS

Alexander, Jonathan J.G., 'Thomas Julian Brown 1923–1987', PBA 75 (1989), 341–59

[Anon.], 'John Nowell Linton Myres, 1902–1989', Bodleian Lib. Record 13, 267–8

Antonsen, Elmer H., ed., The Grimm Brothers and the Germanic Past, Stud. in the Hist. of the Lang. Sciences 54 (Amsterdam and Philadelphia)

Bammesberger, Alfred, and Alfred Wollmann, ed., Britain 400–600: Language and History, Anglistische Forschungen 205 (Heidelberg)

Bammesberger, Alfred, 'SKANOMODU: Linguistic Issues', Britain 400–600, ed. Bammesberger and Wollmann, pp. 457–66

Bately, Janet Margaret, 'Medieval English Studies at King's College London', Med. Eng. Stud. Newsletter (Tokyo) 22, 10–11

Bennett, Helen T., Clare A. Lees and Gillian R. Overing, 'Anglo-Saxon Studies. Gender and Power: Feminism and Old English Studies', Med. Feminist Newsletter 10, 15–25

Berkhout, Carl T., 'Old English Bibliography 1989', OEN 23.2, A1–A24

Berkhout, Carl T., Martin Biddle, Mark Blackburn, Sarah Foot, Simon Keynes and Alexander Rumble, 'Bibliography for 1989', ASE 19, 247–88

233

Bibliography for 1990

Biggam, C.P., *Anglo-Saxon Studies: a Select Bibliography*, Bocgetæl Engliscra Gesiþa (Worthing, West Sussex, 1989)

Biggs, Frederick M., Thomas D. Hill and Paul E. Szarmach, ed., *Sources of Anglo-Saxon Literary Culture: a Trial Version*, Med. & Renaissance Texts & Stud. 74 (Binghamton)

Binski, Paul, 'Reflections on *La estoire de Seint Aedward le rei*: Hagiography and Kingship in Thirteenth-Century England', *JMH* 16, 333–50

Bradley, James, 'Sorcerer or Symbol? – Weland the Smith in Anglo-Saxon Sculpture and Verse', *Pacific Coast Philol.* 25, 39–48

Bradley, S.A.J., 'Grundtvig, Anglo-Saxon Literature, and "Ordets Kamp til Seier"', *Grundtvig-Studier* 1989–90, pp. 216–45

Brehe, S.K., 'Reassembling the *First Worcester Fragment*', *Speculum* 65, 521–36

Bremmer, Rolf H., Jr, 'Late Medieval and Early Modern Opinions on the Affinity between English and Frisian: the Growth of a Commonplace', *Folia Linguistica Historica* 11, 167–91

Brett, Caroline, 'John Leland, Wales and Early British History', *Welsh Hist. Rev.* 15, 169–82

Breuker, Ph. H., 'On the Course of Franciscus Junius' Germanic Studies, with Special Reference to Frisian', *Amsterdamer Beiträge zur älteren Germanistik* 31–2, 42–68

Brewer, Derek, 'Geoffrey Thomas Shepherd, 1918–1982', *Med. Eng. Stud. Newsletter* (Tokyo) 22, 30–3

Britton, Derek Alan, 'Medieval English Studies in Edinburgh', *Med. Eng. Stud. Newsletter* (Tokyo) 22, 5–10

Burns, Marjorie, 'J.R.R. Tolkien: the British and the Norse in Tension', *Pacific Coast Philol.* 25, 49–59

Cameron, Kenneth, 'Obituary: Professor J. McN. Dodgson', *JEPNS* 22, 54–5

Cavendish, Richard, 'Articles of Association: the English Companions', *Hist. Today* (February), pp. 62–3

Clayton, Mary, *The Cult of the Virgin Mary in Anglo-Saxon England*, CSASE 2 (Cambridge)

Conner, Patrick W., 'Notes from ANSAXNET, Again', *OEN* 24.1, 32–5 [see also 36–9]

Conner, Patrick W., Marilyn Deegan and Clare A. Lees, 'Computer-Assisted Approaches to Teaching Old English', *OEN* 23.2, 30–5

D'Aronco, M.A., A.M. Luiselli Fadda and M.V. Molinari, ed., *Studi sulla cultura germanica dei secoli IV–XII in onore di Giulia Mazzuoli Porru* [= *Romanobarbarica* 10] (Rome)

Del Pezzo, Raffaella, Maria Grimaldi and Valeria Micillo, 'Studi italiani di filologia germanica [1978–87]', *AIUON: Filologia germanica* 30–1, 259–390

Donoghue, Daniel, 'Laȝamon's Ambivalence', *Speculum* 65, 537–63

Fazzini Giovannucci, Elisabetta, 'La denominazione del mese di dicembre in tedesco antico e medio', *Studi sulla cultura germanica*, ed. D'Aronco *et al.*, pp. 133–59

Finkenstaedt, Thomas, 'Medieval English Studies in Germany', *Med. Eng. Stud. Newsletter* (Tokyo) 22, 11–16

Frantzen, Allen J., *Desire for Origins: New Language, Old English, and Teaching the*

Tradition (New Brunswick and London)

Gendre, Renato, 'Bibliografia degli scritti di G. Mazzuoli Porru', *Studi sulla cultura germanica*, ed. D'Aronco *et al.*, pp. ix–xi

Glosecki, Stephen O., comp., 'Middle Saxon England', *OEN* 23.2, 26–9 [summary of conference proceedings]

Gneuss, Helmut, *Die Wissenschaft von der englischen Sprache: Ihre Entwicklung bis zum Ausgang des 19. Jahrhunderts*, Bayerische Akademie der Wissenschaften, Philosophisch-historische Klasse, Sitzungsberichte 1990.1 (Munich)

'The Study of Language in Anglo-Saxon England', *Bull. of the John Rylands Univ. Lib. of Manchester* 72, 3–32

Godden, M. R., 'Money, Power and Morality in Late Anglo-Saxon England', *ASE* 19, 41–65

Gransden, Antonia, 'Prologues in the Historiography of Twelfth-Century England', *England in the Twelfth Century*, ed. Daniel Williams (Woodbridge), pp. 55–81

Hall, J. R., 'William G. Medlicott (1816–1883): an American Book Collector and His Collection', *Harvard Lib. Bull.* ns 1, 13–46

[Hill, Joyce, *et al.*], 'Fifth Progress Report: *Fontes Anglo-Saxonici*', *OEN* 23.2, 20–1

Hines, John, 'Philology, Archaeology and the *adventus Saxonum vel Anglorum*', *Britain 400–600*, ed. Bammesberger and Wollmann, pp. 17–36

Howe, Nicholas, 'Introduction [to special OE issue]', *ANQ* ns 3, 43–5

Jin, Koichi, *et al.* (ed.), *Studies in English Philology in Honour of Shigeru Ono* (Tokyo) [in English & Japanese]

Lawton, David, 'Harold Leslie Rogers 1925–1990', *Med. Eng. Stud. Newsletter* (Tokyo) 23, 1–2

Lendinara, Patrizia, and Michael Lapidge, 'Record of the Fourth Conference of the International Society of Anglo-Saxonists, at Durham, 7–11 August 1989', *ASE* 19, 1–3

Luiselli Fadda, Anna Maria, '*Cithara barbarica, cythara teutonica, cythara anglica*', *Studi sulla cultura germanica*, ed. D'Aronco *et al.*, pp. 217–39

Magennis, Hugh, and Ivan Herbison, *Discovering Old English: Guided Readings* (Belfast)

Mitchell, J. Lawrence, ed., *Specimen of an Etymological Dictionary Attributed to John Mitchell Kemble* (Saint Paul, MN)

Oizumi, Akio, and Toshiyuki Takamiya, ed., *Medieval English Studies – Past & Present* (Tokyo)

Owen-Crocker, Gale R., 'Designing for the Seventh Century', *Costume* 24, 3–14

Pollington, Stephen, *The Warrior's Way: England in the Viking Age* (London, 1989)

Pulsiano, Phillip, 'Research in Progress', *OEN* 23.2, B1–B4

Richards, Mary P., 'International Society of Anglo-Saxonists', *Med. Eng. Stud. Newsletter* (Tokyo) 23, 16–18

Robinson, Fred C., 'Herbert Dean Meritt, 1904–1984', *Med. Eng. Stud. Newsletter* (Tokyo) 22, 24–6

'In Memoriam: Norman E. Eliason (1908–91)', *OEN* 24.1, 12

'Robert Earl Kaske, 1921–1989', *Med. Eng. Stud. Newsletter* (Tokyo) 22, 33–5

Rowland, Beryl, 'Rossell Hope Robbins, 1912–1990', *Med. Eng. Stud. Newsletter* (Tokyo) 22, 28–9

Schendl, Herbert, 'Hans Ernst Pinsker, 1908–1987', *Med. Eng. Stud. Newsletter* (Tokyo) 22, 26–7

'Medieval English Studies in Vienna', *Med. Eng. Stud. Newsletter* (Tokyo) 22, 16–20

Schichler, Robert L., ed., 'Abstracts of Papers in Anglo-Saxon Studies', *OEN* 23.2, C1–C33

Schipper, William, 'The Early Dictionaries of Old English and the Worcester Tremulous Scribe', *International Christian Univ. Lang. Research Bull.* 4, 81–98

See, Klaus von, 'Andreas Heusler in seinen Briefen', *ZDA* 119, 379–96

Shook, Laurence K., 'Ashley Crandell Amos (1951–1989)', *MS* 52, ix–xi

Simmons, Clare A., *Reversing the Conquest: History and Myth in Nineteenth-Century British Literature* (New Brunswick, NJ, and London)

Simpson, Hassell A., 'Steinbeck's Anglo-Saxon "Wonder-Words" and the American Paradox', *Amer. Lit.* 62, 310–17

Smaczay, Jan, '*Alfred*: Dvořák's First Operatic Endeavour Surveyed', *Jnl of the R. Musical Assoc.* 115, 80–106

Stanley, E.G., comp., *British Academy Papers on Anglo-Saxon England* (Oxford and New York)

Stanley, E.G., 'J. Bosworth's Interest in "Friesic" for his Dictionary of the Anglo-Saxon Language (1838): "The Friesic is Far the Most Important Language for my Purpose"', *Aspects of Old Frision Philology*, ed. Rolf H. Bremmer Jr, Geart van der Meer and Oebele Vries, Estrikken 69: Amsterdamer Beiträge zur älteren Germanistik 31–2 (Amsterdam and Atlanta, GA), 428–52

'Old English Studies for Japan', *Med. Eng. Stud. Newsletter* (Tokyo) 22, 1–5

Szarmach, Paul E., ed., *Old English Newsletter* 23.1–2 (Binghamton)

Tashjian, Georgian R., David R. Tashjian and Brian J. Enright, *Richard Rawlinson: a Tercentenary Memorial*, with foreword by E.G. Stanley (Kalamazoo, MI)

Torti, Anna, 'Medieval English Studies in Italy', *Med. Eng. Stud. Newsletter* (Tokyo) 22, 20–4

Whatley, E. Gordon, 'Hagiography in Anglo-Saxon England: a Preliminary View from *SASLC*', *OEN* 23.2, 36–46

2. OLD ENGLISH LANGUAGE

Adamson, Sylvia, Vivien Law, Nigel Vincent and Susan Wright, ed., *Papers from the 5th International Conference on English Historical Linguistics, Cambridge, 6–9 April 1987*, Current Issues in Ling. Theory 65 (Amsterdam and Philadelphia)

Alekseeva, G.G., 'O strukturnykh modeliakh slozhnykh predlozheniĭ s posledova-tel'nym podchineniem i sopodchineniem v drevneangliĭskom iazyke', *Vestnik Leningradskogo Universiteta* 1988, seriia 2.1.2, 114–16

Amos, Ashley Crandell, 'Old English Words for *old*', *Aging and the Aged in Medieval Europe*, ed. Michael M. Sheehan, Papers in Med. Stud. 11 (Toronto), 95–106

Anderson, Earl R., 'The Etymology of OE *serc*, *syrce*, *syric*, ON *serkr*', *Neophilologus* 74, 635–6

Baxter, Andrew R.W., 'Phonetic Similarity and Paradigmatic Levelling in Old

Bibliography for 1990

English', *Amsterdamer Beiträge zur älteren Germanistik* 29 (1989), 19–27

Blockley, Mary, 'Old English Language', *ANQ* ns 3, 45–8

'Uncontracted Negation as a Cue to Sentence Structure in Old English Verse', *JEGP* 89, 475–90

Bremmer, Rolf H., Jr, 'Is de Nederlandse meervoud-*s* van Engelse komaf?', *Amsterdamer Beiträge zur älteren Germanistik* 28 (1989), 77–91

'Two Early Vernacular Names for the *aves beati Cuthberti*: Middle English *lomes* and Middle Low German/Old Frisian *eires*', *ES* 71, 486–95

Brinton, Laurel J., 'The Development of Discourse Markers in English', *Historical Linguistics and Philology*, ed. Jacek Fisiak, Trends in Ling., Stud. and Monographs 46 (Berlin and New York), 45–71

Cable, Thomas, 'Philology: Analysis of Written Records', *Research Guide on Language Change*, ed. Edgar C. Polomé, Trends in Ling., Stud. and Monographs 48 (Berlin and New York), 97–106

Coleman, Robert, 'The Assessment of Lexical Mortality and Replacement between Old and Modern English', *Papers*, ed. Adamson *et al.*, pp. 69–86

Cronan, Dennis, 'Old English Water-lands', *ELN* 27.3, 6–9 [*ealand, igland*]

Crystal, David, *The English Language* (London and New York, 1988) ['Old English', pp. 145–60; 'Casting the Runes', pp. 161–5]

D'Aronco, Maria Amalia, 'Divergenze e convergenze lessicali in inglese antico: il caso di *elehtre*', *Studi sulla cultura germanica*, ed. D'Aronco *et al.*, pp. 65–102

Dekeyser, Xavier, 'Adjacent and Distant Antecedents and the Compound Relative *sepe* in Old English Prose', *Leuvense Bijdragen* 78 (1989), 385–99

'Preposition Stranding and Relative Complementizer Deletion: Implicational Tendencies in English and the Other Germanic Languages', *Papers*, ed. Adamson *et al.*, pp. 87–109

Dekeyser, Xavier, and Luc Pauwels, 'The Demise of the Old English Heritage and Lexical Innovation in Middle English: Two Intertwined Developments', *Leuvense Bijdragen* 79, 1–23

Del Pezzo, Raffaella, 'Ags. *winburg* "città del convivio"', *Studi sulla cultura germanica*, ed. D'Aronco *et al.*, pp. 103–14

Denison, David, 'Auxiliary + Impersonal in Old English', *Folia Linguistica Historica* 11, 139–66

'The Old English Impersonals Revived', *Papers*, ed. Adamson *et al.*, pp. 111–40

Derolez, René, 'Runic Literacy among the Anglo-Saxons', *Britain 400–600*, ed. Bammesberger and Wollmann, pp. 397–436

Dietz, Klaus, 'Die südaltenglische Sonorisierung anlautender Spiranten', *Anglia* 108, 292–313

Dresher, B. Elan, 'On the Unity of the Mercian Second Fronting', *Papers*, ed. Adamson *et al.*, pp. 141–64

Eichner, Heiner, 'Die Ausprägung der linguistischen Physiognomie des Englischen anno 400 bis anno 600 n. Chr.', *Britain 400–600*, ed. Bammesberger and Wollmann, pp. 307–33

Estival, Dominique, 'A Diachronic Study of the English Passive', *Diachronica* 6 (1989), 23–54

Fernández, Francisco, *Historia de la lengua inglesa* (Madrid, 1986)

Fischer, Andreas, 'Aspects of Historical Lexicology', *Meaning and Beyond: Ernst Leisi zum 70. Geburtstag*, ed. Udo Fries and Martin Heusser (Tübingen, 1989), pp. 71–91

Fisiak, Jacek, '*Domesday Book* and Late Old English Dialects', *Historical Linguistics 1987*, ed. Henning Andersen and Konrad Koerner, Current Issues in Ling. Theory 66 (Amsterdam and Philadelphia), 107–28

Francovich Onesti, Nicoletta, *L'inglese dalle origini ad oggi: le vicende di una lingua* (Rome, 1988)

Fujiwara, Hiroshi, 'Element Order in the *Peterborough Chronicle* 1070–1121', *Ann. Collection of Essays and Stud.* (Faculty of Letters, Gakushuin Univ.) 36, 99–118

'Parallelism in Old English Epic Poems', *Bull. of the Lang. Inst. of Gakushuin Univ.* 12 (1989), 46–58 [in Japanese]

Fujiwara, Yasuaki, *A Study of Old English Meter* (Tokyo) [in Japanese]

Fulk, R.D., *see* sect. 3*bi*

Garavelli, Rossana, 'Il lessico del mare nella poesia anglosassone', *AIUON: Filologia germanica* 30–1, 159–214

Goossens, Louis, 'Framing the Linguistic Communication Scene: *ask* vs. *acsian* and *biddan*', *Historical Linguistics 1987*, ed. Henning Andersen and Konrad Koerner, Current Issues in Ling. Theory 66 (Amsterdam and Philadelphia), 191–209

Griffiths, Bill, *A User-Friendly Dictionary of Old English* (Benbowbridge, Cowley, Middx, 1989)

Groussier, Marie-Line, 'La Polysémie de *of* en vieil anglais et la métaphore spatialisante', *Historical Linguistics 1987*, ed. Henning Andersen and Konrad Koerner, Current Issues in Ling. Theory 66 (Amsterdam and Philadelphia), 211–30

Grønvik, Ottar, 'Zwei archaische Züge im altwestnordisch Numerussystem', *Sprachwissenschaft* 15, 184–96

Gussenhoven, Carlos, and Jeroen van de Weijer, 'On V-Place Spreading vs. Feature Spreading in English Historical Phonology', *Ling. Rev.* 7, 311–32

Gwara, Scott, 'Old English *helm, hamel, healm*: Three Lexical Problems in Glosses to Aldhelm's Prose *De Virginitate*', *N&Q* 37, 144–52

Hall, Margaret Austin, 'Syntactic and Semantic Patterning with the Verb *be* in the Older Germanic Languages', *Jahrbuch für Internationale Germanistik* B11, 18–25

Harbus, Antonina, *see* sect. 3*c* [*olehtung*]

Hattori, Yoshiki, 'Anticipation of *þaet* Clauses in Wulfstan's *Homilies*', *Ono Festschrift*, ed. Jin, pp. 195–208

Healey, Antonette diPaolo, 'Dictionary of Old English: Support', *OEN* 23.2, 17–18

Holland, Joan, 'Dictionary of Old English: 1990 Progress Report', *OEN* 24.1, 20–1

Ide, Mitsu, '"*And + Hæfde + the Past Participle*" in ChronA', *Ono Festschrift*, ed. Jin, 141–52

Jack, George, 'The Reflexes of Second Fronting in the AB Language', *ES* 71, 289–306

Jin, Koichi, '*Hwa* and *Hwæt* – A Syntactic Case', *Ono Festschrift*, ed. Jin, pp. 65–78

Kastovsky, Dieter, 'The Typological Status of Old English Word-Formation', *Papers*, ed. Adamson *et al.*, pp. 205–23

'Typological Changes in the History of English Morphology', *Meaning and Beyond:*

Bibliography for 1990

Ernst Leisi zum 70. Geburtstag, ed. Udo Fries and Martin Heusser (Tübingen, 1989), pp. 159–78

'Whatever Happened to the Ablaut Nouns in English – and Why Did It Not Happen in German?', *Historical Linguistics 1987*, ed. Henning Andersen and Konrad Koerner, Current Issues in Ling. Theory 66 (Amsterdam and Philadelphia), 253–64

Kitson, Peter, 'On Old English Nouns of More than One Gender', *ES* 71, 185–221

Klar, Kathryn A., 'A Note on a Possible Anglo-Saxon Pun in *Branwen*', *Celtic Language, Celtic Culture: a Festschrift for Eric P. Hamp*, ed. A. T. E. Matonis and Daniel F. Melia (Van Nuys, CA), pp. 305–7 [*hlæfdige*]

Kniezsa, Veronika, 'The Orthographic Aspect of the Runes', *Historical Linguistics and Philology*, ed. Jacek Fisiak, Trends in Ling., Stud. and Monographs 46 (Berlin and New York), 245–59

Koopman, Willem F., 'The Double Object Construction in Old English', *Papers*, ed. Adamson *et al.*, pp. 225–43

'Old English Constructions with Three Verbs', *Folia Linguistica Historica* 11, 271–300

Kortlandt, Frederik, 'The Germanic Third Class of Weak Verbs', *North-Western European Lang. Evolution* 15, 3–10

Kytö, Merja, and Matti Rissanen, 'The Helsinki Corpus of English Texts: Diachronic and Dialectal', *Med. Eng. Stud. Newsletter* (Tokyo) 23, 11–14

Laur, Wolfgang, 'Zur Frage nach frühen Unterschieden zwischen Nordgermanisch und Westgermanisch', *Sprachwissenschaft* 15, 197–225

Lendinara, Patrizia, see sect. 6 (two entries)

Lucas, Peter J., 'On the Role of Some Adverbs in Old English Verse Grammar', *Papers*, ed. Adamson *et al.*, pp. 293–312

McCarren, Vincent P., and Robert N. Mory, 'The *Abecedarium* from British Museum Cotton MS. Titus D 18', *MP* 87, 266–71

McCully, C. B., and R. M. Hogg, see sect. 3*bi*

Makino, Teruyoshi, 'On Prepositions of the *Parker Chronicle*', *Jnl of the Faculty of Foreign Lang.* (Komazawa Univ.) 31, 13–25 [in Japanese]

Matzel, Klaus, 'Ae. *weorod*, as. *werod*, ahd. **werot*', *HS* 103, 106–7

Meid, Wolfgang, 'Englisch und sein britischer Hintergrund', *Britain 400–600*, ed. Bammesberger and Wollmann, pp. 97–119

Mirarchi, Giovanni, see sect. 3*bi* (second entry) [*swa . . . swa*]

Mitchell, Bruce, *A Critical Bibliography of Old English Syntax to the End of 1984 including Addenda and Corrigenda to 'Old English Syntax'* (Oxford and Cambridge, MA)

'*Old English Syntax*: a Review of the Reviews', *NM* 91, 273–93

Moessner, Lilo, *Early Middle English Syntax*, Linguistische Arbeiten 207 (Tübingen, 1989)

Momma, Haruko, 'Old English *cirm* and *cirman*: Can a Sound Change Affect a Semantic Change?', *Eng. Lit. in Hokkaido* 35, 87–96

'Old English *ungemete(s)*: an Immeasurably Long Word?', *Med. Eng. Stud. Newsletter* (Tokyo) 23, 10–11

Moriya, Yasuyo, 'The Demonstrative Adverb *ða* in Old English as Seen in Ælfric's

Bibliography for 1990

Prose', *International Christian Univ. Lang. Research Bull.* 5.1, 37–47

Morris, Richard L., 'The Germanic Futures and Prototype Theory', *North-Western European Lang. Evolution* 16, 73–90

Mucciante, Luisa, 'Struttura e funzione dei glossari bilingui nel periodo anglosassone', *Studi in memoria di Ernesto Giammarco* (Pisa), pp. 219–41

Mukhin, Anatolij M., and Alla N. Shamanayeva, 'Groups of Transitive Verbs with Dative in Old English', *Folia Linguistica Historica* 11, 193–212

Murray, Robert W., 'The Shortening of Stressed Long Vowels in Old English', *Diachronica* 5 (1988), 73–107

Nevalainen, Terttu, 'Modelling Functional Differentiation and Function Loss: the Case of *but*', *Papers*, ed. Adamson *et al.*, pp. 337–55

Nielsen, Hans Frede, 'W.L. van Helten's *Altostfriesische Grammatik* Viewed from a Comparative Angle', *Amsterdamer Beiträge zur älteren Germanistik* 31–2, 349–56

Nishinarita, Michio, '*Nerian* and *Neriend*', *Ono Festschrift*, ed. Jin, pp. 119–28

Ogawa, Hiroshi, *Old English Modal Verbs: a Syntactical Study*, Anglistica 26 (Copenhagen, 1989)

'Ælfric's Use of **sculan* in Dependent Desires', *NM* 91, 181–93

'Notes on the Syntax in Late Anonymous Homilies: a Study in the Development of Old English Prose', *Ono Festschrift*, ed. Jin, pp. 79–92

Ogura, Michiko, 'Another Quest for OE *cweðan* – a Morphological Approach', *Ono Festschrift*, ed. Jin, pp. 107–18

'*Me cwæð* in MS Cotton Claudius B.iv', *N&Q* 37, 152–4

'OE *wyrm*, *nædre*, and *draca*', *Jnl of Eng. Ling.* 21 (1988), 99–124

'What Has Happened to "Impersonal" Constructions?', *NM* 91, 31–55

Ogura, Mieko, *Historical English Phonology: a Lexical Perspective* (Tokyo, 1987)

Ohta, Masako, 'On the Possesive Dative in Old English', *Ono Festschrift*, ed. Jin, pp. 129–40

Okasha, E., 'Vernacular or Latin? The Languages of Insular Inscriptions, AD 500–1100', *Epigraphik 1988*, Österreichische Akademie der Wissenschaften Philosophisch-Historische Klasse Denkschriften 213.2 (Vienna), 139–47

Ono, Shoko, 'The Repetition in *The Life of St. Guthlac* – Utilising "Oxford Concordance Program"', *Ono Festschrift*, ed. Jin, pp. 177–94

Paddock, Harold, 'On Explaining Macrovariation in the Sibilant and Nasal Suffixes of English', *Folia Linguistica Historica* 11, 235–69

Page, R.I., 'Dating Old English Inscriptions: the Limits of Inference', *Papers*, ed. Adamson *et al.*, pp. 357–77

Pintzuk, Susan, and Anthony S. Kroch, see sect. 3*bii*

Plank, Frans, 'Paradigm Arrangement and Inflectional Homonymy: Old English Case', *Papers*, ed. Adamson *et al.*, pp. 379–406

Poussa, Patricia, 'A Contact-Universals Origin for Periphrastic *do* with Special Consideration of OE-Celtic Contact', *Papers*, ed. Adamson *et al.*, pp. 407–34

Pulsiano, Phillip, 'OE Names of Winds', *ANQ* 3, 103–4

Rasmussen, Jens Elmegård, 'Germanic Verschärfung: Tying Up Loose Ends', *Historical Linguistics 1987*, ed. Henning Andersen and Konrad Koerner, Current Issues in Ling. Theory 66 (Amsterdam and Philadelphia), 425–41

Reddick, R. J., 'Clause-Bound Grammar and Old English Syntax', *SP* 87, 379–96

Rissanen, Matti, 'On the Happy Reunion of English Philology and Historical Linguistics', *Historical Linguistics and Philology*, ed. Jacek Fisiak, Trends in Ling., Stud. and Monographs 46 (Berlin and New York), 353–69

Sato, Akiko, '*Soðlice* and *witodlice*: Case of Functional Shift of Old English Adverbs', *Eng. Ling.* (Tokyo) 7, 39–55

Schabram, Hans, '*Electre* und *a(u)mber* zu den Bezeichnungen für Hellgold und Bernstein im Mittel – und Frühneuenglischen', *Anglia* 108, 1–18 [*eolhsand*, *smylting*, etc.]

Seebold, Elmar, 'Was ist jutisch? Was ist kentisch?', *Britain 400–600*, ed. Bammesberger and Wollmann, pp. 335–52

Sgarbi, Romano, 'Note sulla fonetica dei testi runici in inglese antico', *Rendiconti del'Istituto Lombardo*, Classe di lettere e scienze morali e storiche 122 (1989), 129–43

Stanley, E. G., 'Old English *belehycge*: a Ghostword', *N&Q* 37, 3–5

Stockwell, Robert P., and Donka Minkova, 'Verb Phrase Conjunction in Old English', *Historical Linguistics 1987*, ed. Henning Andersen and Konrad Koerner, Current Issues in Ling. Theory 66 (Amsterdam and Philadelphia), 499–515

Suzuki, Seiichi, 'On the Origin and Development of the Action Noun Forming Suffix *-nis* in Old English', *IF* 95, 184–207

Takeuchi, Shi'ichi, 'Some Notes on "*Geaf and Sealde*" in the Old English *Bede*', *Ono Festschrift*, ed. Jin, pp. 153–64

Taylor, Paul Beekman, *see* sect. 3*bi* [terms for beauty]

Teshima, Takeshi, 'Middle Voice in the Old Germanic Languages and its Development', *Stud. in Humanities* (Shinshu Univ.) 24, 91–104

Thorne, James P., 'Some Modern Standard English Filters', *Papers*, ed. Adamson *et al.*, pp. 471–80

Tieken-Boon van Ostade, Ingrid, 'The Origin and Development of Periphrastic Auxiliary *do*: a Case of Destigmatisation', *North-Western European Lang. Evolution* 16, 3–52

Trobevšek-Drobnak, Frančiška, 'Expanded Tenses in the Old English Orosius: a Syntactic Strengthening' *Linguistica* (Ljubljana) 30, 13–46

Unebe, Noriko, 'OE *Gan, Faran, Feran* in the Transition Period', *Ono Festschrift*, ed. Jin, pp. 285–98

van der Wurff, Wim, 'The *easy-to-please* Construction in Old and Middle English', *Papers*, ed. Adamson *et al.*, pp. 519–36

Warner, Anthony R., 'Reworking the History of English Auxiliaries', *Papers*, ed. Adamson *et al.*, pp. 537–58

Wårvik, Brita, 'On Grounding in English Narratives: a Diachronic Perspective', *Papers*, ed. Adamson *et al.*, pp. 559–75

'On the History of Grounding Markers in English Narrative: Style or Typology?', *Historical Linguistics 1987*, ed. Henning Andersen and Konrad Koerner, Current Issues in Ling. Theory 66 (Amsterdam and Philadelphia), 531–42

Wedel, Alfred R., 'The "Complexive Aspect" in Old West Germanic', *The Fifteenth*

Bibliography for 1990

LACUS Forum 1988, ed. Ruth M. Brend and David G. Lockwood (Lake Bluff, IL, 1989), pp. 424–33

Windross, Michael, '*Haver/rave*, . . . a Re-examination of the Old English Origins of h/r Alternation', *Linguistica Antverpiensia* 23 (1989), 215–30

Wollmann, Alfred, 'Lateinisch-Altenglische Lehnbeziehungen im 5. und 6. Jahrhundert', *Britain 400–600*, ed. Bammesberger and Wollmann, pp. 373–96

Yamanouchi, Kazuyoshi, 'Some Notes on *Fyrenful* as Old English Equivalent for Latin *Peccator*', *Ono Festschrift*, ed. Jin, pp. 93–106 [in Japanese]

Yoshino, Yoshihiro, 'Multiple Negation in Complex Sentences in OE Prose', *Ono Festschrift*, ed. Jin, pp. 47–64

3. OLD ENGLISH LITERATURE

a. General

Bremmer, Rolf, 'Hermes–Mercury and Woden–Odin as Inventors of Alphabets: a Neglected Parallel', *Amsterdamer Beiträge zur älteren Germanistik* 29 (1989), 39–48

Damico, Helen, and Alexandra Hennessey Olsen, ed., *New Readings on Women in Old English Literature* (Bloomington, IN, and Indianapolis)

Green, Eugene A., 'Enoch, Lent, and the Ascension of Christ', *De Ore Domini: Preacher and Word in the Middle Ages*, ed. Thomas L. Amos *et al.*, Stud. in Med. Culture 27 (Kalamazoo, MI, 1989), 13–25

Hasenfratz, Robert J., 'The Theme of the "Penitent Damned" and its Relation to *Beowulf* and *Christ and Satan*', *Leeds Stud. in Eng.* ns 21, 45–69

Hill, Joyce, 'Old English Literature [1987]', *Year's Work in Eng. Stud.* 68, 121–37

Meier, Hans Heinrich, 'Die Schlacht im "Hildebrandslied"', *ZDA* 119, 127–38

Pàroli, Teresa, 'Santi e demoni nelle letterature germaniche dell'alto medioevo', *Santi e demoni nell'alto medioevo occidentale (secoli V–XI)* = *SettSpol* 36 (1989), 411–98

Shepherd, Geoffrey, *Poets and Prophets: Essays in Medieval Studies by G. T. Shepherd*, ed. T. A. Shippey and John Pickles (Woodbridge and Rochester, NY) [collected papers]

Tristram, Hildegard L. C., 'The Early Insular Elegies: *item alia*', *Celtic Linguistics*, ed. Martin J. Ball *et al.*, Current Issues in Ling. Theory 68 (Amsterdam and Philadelphia), 343–61

b. Poetry
i. General

Blockley, Mary, *see* sect. 2 (second entry)

Bosse, Roberta Bux, and Norman D. Hinton, 'Cynewulf and the Apocalyptic Vision', *Neophilologus* 74, 279–93

Caie, Graham D., 'The Exile Figure in Old English Poetry', *Europa og de Fremmede i Middelalderen*, ed. Kurt Villad Jensen (Copenhagen, 1989), pp. 71–81

Donoghue, Daniel, 'Old English Meter', *ANQ* ns 3, 69–74

Foley, John Miles, ed., *Oral-Formulaic Theory: a Folklore Casebook*, Garland Folklore

Casebooks 5 (New York and London)

Frank, Roberta, 'Anglo-Scandinavian Poetic Relations', *ANQ* ns 3, 74–9

Fulk, R. D., 'Contraction as a Criterion for Dating Old English Verse', *JEGP* 89, 1–16

Garavelli, Rossana, *see* sect. 2 [marine and nautical terms]

González, José Manuel, 'Facticidad, mitología y heroicidad en la poesía del inglés antiguo', *Estudios de filología inglesa: homenaje al Doctor Pedro Jesús Marcos Pérez* (Alicante), pp. 247–57

Hill, Joyce, '"Þæt wæs geomuru ides!" A Female Stereotype Examined', *New Readings on Women*, ed. Damico and Olsen, pp. 235–47

Hill, Thomas D., '"The Green Path to Paradise" in Nineteenth-Century Ballad Tradition', *NM* 91, 483–6

'The "Variegated Obit" as an Historiographic Motif in Old English Poetry and Anglo-Latin Historical Literature', *Traditio* 44 (1988), 101–24

Jacobs, Nicolas, 'Celtic Saga and the Contexts of Old English Elegiac Poetry', *Etudes Celtiques* 26, 95–142

Jager, Eric, 'Speech and the Chest in Old English Poetry: Orality or Pectorality?', *Speculum* 65, 845–59

Kim, Suksan, 'Stress Assignment Rules for Old English (Poetry)', *Lang. Research* (Seoul National Univ.) 25 (1989), 729–74

Lucas, Peter J., *see* sect. 2

McCully, C. B., and R. M. Hogg, 'An Account of Old English Stress', *Jnl of Ling.* 26, 315–39

Mirarchi, Giovanni, 'Rapporto tra poesia ed eresia ariana nell'Inghilterra anglosassone', *Studi di letteratura e di linguistica* (Salerno) 4, 19–32

'Significato del costrutto "(swa) . . . swa . . . swa" nella poesia anglosassone', *Studi di letteratura e di linguistica* (Salerno) 4, 5–17

Muir, Bernard J., *see* sect. 6 [Exeter Book]

Nelson, Marie, *Structures of Opposition in Old English Poems*, Costerus ns 74 (Amsterdam and Atlanta, GA, 1989)

O'Keeffe, Katherine O'Brien, *Visible Song: Transitional Literacy in Old English Verse*, CSASE 4 (Cambridge)

Osborn, Marijane, '*The Fates of Women* from Four Anglo-Saxon Poems', *New Readings on Women*, ed. Damico and Olsen, pp. xi–xiii

Parks, Ward, *Verbal Dueling in Heroic Narrative: the Homeric and Old English Traditions* (Princeton)

Reichl, Karl, 'Formulaic Diction in Old English Epic Poetry', *Traditions of Heroic and Epic Poetry, II: Characteristics and Techniques*, ed. J. B. Hainsworth *et al.*, Publ. of the Mod. Humanities Research Assoc. 13 (London, 1989), 12–70

Robinson, Fred C., 'Old English Poetry: the Question of Authorship', *ANQ* ns 3, 59–64

Russom, Geoffrey, 'A New Kind of Metrical Evidence in Old English Poetry', *Papers*, ed. Adamson *et al.*, pp. 435–57

Taylor, Paul Beekman, 'The Old English Poetic Vocabulary of Beauty', *New Readings on Women*, ed. Damico and Olsen, pp. 211–21

ii. 'Beowulf'

Bammesberger, Alfred, 'Die Lesart in *Beowulf* 1382a', *Anglia* 108, 314–26

'The Conclusion of Wealhtheow's Speech (*Beowulf* 1231)', *NM* 91, 207–8

Bloom, Harold, ed., *'Beowulf': Modern Critical Interpretations* (New York, New Haven and Philadelphia, 1987)

Cherniss, Michael D., '"Beowulf Was Not There": Compositional Implications of *Beowulf*, Lines 1299b–1301', *Oral Tradition* 4 (1989), 316–29

Clark, George, *Beowulf*, Twayne's Eng. Authors Ser. 477 (Boston)

Creed, Robert Payson, *Reconstructing the Rhythm of 'Beowulf'* (Columbia, MO, and London)

Damon, John, 'The Raven in *Beowulf* 1801: Bird of a Different Color', *Work in Progress* (Dept of Eng., Univ. of Arizona) 1, 60–70

Duggan, Hoyt N., 'Scribal Self-Correction and Editorial Theory', *NM* 91, 215–27

Duncan, Ian, 'Epitaphs for Æglæcan: Narrative Strife in *Beowulf*', *'Beowulf'*, ed. Bloom, pp. 111–30

Fajardo-Acosta, Fidel, *The Condemnation of Heroism in the Tragedy of Beowulf: a Study in the Characterization of the Epic*, Stud. in Epic and Romance Lit. 2 (Lewiston, NY, Lampeter and Queenston, Ontario, 1989)

Foley, John Miles, *Traditional Oral Epic: the 'Odyssey', 'Beowulf', and the Serbo-Croatian Return Song* (Berkeley, Los Angeles and Oxford)

Galloway, Andrew, *'Beowulf* and the Varieties of Choice', *PMLA* 105, 197–208

Gerritsen, Johan, *see* sect. 6

Gómez Lara, Manuel José, 'The Death of Anglo-Saxon Secular Heroes: a Linguistic Discussion on *Beowulf* and *The Battle of Maldon*', *Revista canaria de estudios ingleses* 17 (1988), 269–80

Harris, A. Leslie, 'The Vatic Mode in *Beowulf*', *Neophilologus* 74, 591–600

Hasegawa, Hiroshi, *Beowulf – The Fight with Grendel* (Pt I) (Tokyo) [a dual edition]

Hasenfratz, Robert J., *see* sect. 3a

Hill, Thomas D., 'Beowulf as Seldguma: *Beowulf*, lines 247–51', *Neophilologus* 74, 637–9

'"Wealhtheow" as a Foreign Slave: Some Continental Analogues', *PQ* 69, 106–12

Howard, Patricia J., 'Irony of Fate in Cecelia Holland's *Two Ravens*: Echoes of *Beowulf* and Icelandic Saga', *The Comparatist* 14, 15–25

Hudson, Marc, *'Beowulf': a Translation and Commentary* (Lewisburg, PA, London and Toronto)

Irving, Edward B., Jr, *'Beowulf'*, *ANQ* ns 3, 65–9

Karibe, Tsunenori, *'Beowulf* with its Japanese Translation Facing the Original (I)', *Bull. of the Faculty of the Liberal Arts* (Niigata Univ.) 20, 239–84

Karkov, Catherine, and Robert Farrell, 'The Gnomic Passages of *Beowulf*', *NM* 91, 295–310

Kolb, Eduard, 'Schiff und Seefahrt im *Beowulf* und im *Andreas*', *Meaning and Beyond: Ernst Leisi zum 70. Geburtstag*, ed. Udo Fries and Martin Heusser (Tübingen, 1989), pp. 237–52

Lucas, Peter J., *'Beowulf* 224: *eolet æt ende*', *N&Q* 37, 263–4

Lundberg, Patricia Lorimer, 'The Elusive *Beowulf* Poet Self-Represented in the *I*-Narrator and the Scops', *Ball State Univ. Forum* 30 (1989), 5–15

Mitchell, Bruce, '*Beowulf*, line 1020b: *brand* or *bearn*?', *Studi sulla cultura germanica*, ed. D'Aronco *et al.*, pp. 283–92

North, Richard, *see* sect. 3*biii*

Oshitari, Kinshiro, *Beowulf* (Tokyo) [Japanese translation]
'Reading Between the Lines of *Beowulf*', *Ono Festschrift*, ed. Jin, pp. 415–34 [in Japanese]

Overing, Gillian R., *Language, Sign, and Gender in 'Beowulf'* (Carbondale and Edwardsville, IL)

Pigg, Daniel, F., 'Cultural Markers in *Beowulf*: a Re-evaluationof the Relationship between Beowulf and Christ', *Neophilologus* 74, 601–7

Pintzuk, Susan, and Anthony S. Kroch, 'The Rightward Movement of Complements and Adjuncts in the Old English of *Beowulf*', *Lang. Variation and Change* 1 (1989), 115–43

Pulsiano, Phillip, and Joseph McGowan, '*Fyrd, here*, and the Dating of *Beowulf*', *Studia Anglica Posnaniensia* 23, 3–13

Rowland, Jenny, 'OE *ealuscerwen/meoduscerwen* and the Concept of "Paying for Mead"', *Leeds Stud. in Eng.* ns 21, 1–12

Smith, Roger, 'Ships and the Dating of *Beowulf*', *ANQ* ns 3, 99–103

Stanley, E. G., '"Hengestes heap", *Beowulf* 1091', *Britain 400–600*, ed. Bammesberger and Wollmann, pp. 51–63

Swearer, Randolph, Raymond Oliver and Marijane Osborn, *Beowulf: a Likeness*, with introduction by Fred C. Robinson (New Haven and London)

Taylor, Paul Beekman, 'The Epithetical Style in *Beowulf*', *NM* 91, 195–206

Tristram, Hildegard L. C., *see* sect. 3*c*

Vickman, Jeffrey, *A Metrical Concordance to 'Beowulf'*, with preface by R. D. Fulk, OEN Subsidia 16 (Binghamton)

iii. Other poems

Belanoff, Patricia A., 'Women's Songs, Women's Language: *Wulf and Eadwacer* and *The Wife's Lament*', *New Readings on Women*, ed. Damico and Olsen, pp. 193–203

Benson, Garard, trans., 'Old English Riddle', Poems on the Underground (London) [Riddle 47]

Biggs, Frederick M., 'Unities in the Old English *Guthlac B*', *JEGP* 89, 155–65

Blake, N. F., ed., *The Phoenix*, revised ed. (Exeter)

Blockley, Mary, '*Seafarer* 82a: the Past as Perfect', *N&Q* 37, 2–3

Bradley, Daniel J., 'The Old English Rune Poem: Elements of Mnemonics and Psychoneurological Beliefs', *Perceptual and Motor Skills* 69 (1989), 3–8

Bundi, Ada, 'Una crux in *Deor* 1', *Atti dell' Accademia Peloritana dei Pericolanti*, Classe di lettere, filosofia e belle arti 62 (1988 for 1986), 257–84

Coppola, Maria Augusta, '. . . *gebleod wundrum, eadgum ond earmum ungelice*. La parusia nel *Cristo III*', *Studi sulla cultura germanica*, ed. D'Aronco *et al.*, pp. 31–63

Cucina, Carla, *Sulla struttura del 'Seafarer': la tipologia del contrasto come strategia compositiva*, Studi e ricerche di linguistica e filologia 3 (Pavia)

Bibliography for 1990

Garde, Judith N., '*Christ I* (164–195a): the Mary–Joseph Dialogue in Medieval Christian Perspective', *Neophilologus* 74, 122–30

Gendre, Renato, '*La Battaglia di Brunanburh* v. 54a: *dreorig daraða lāf*', *Studi sulla cultura germanica*, ed. D'Aronco *et al.*, pp. 161–77

Gómez Lara, Manuel José, *see* sect. 3*bii* [*Battle of Maldon*]

Hall, J.R., '*Exodus* 166b, *cwyldrof*: 162–167, the Beasts of Battle', *Neophilologus* 74, 112–21

Hasenfratz, Robert J., *see* sect. 3*a* [*Christ and Satan*]

Hieatt, Constance B., 'Transition in the Exeter Book *Descent into Hell*: the Poetic Use of a "stille" yet "geondflow[ende]" River', *NM* 91, 431–8

Izydorczyk, Zbigniew, 'The Inversion of Paschal Events in the Old English *Descent into Hell*', *NM* 91, 439–47

Jager, Eric, 'Invoking/Revoking God's Word: the *vox Dei* in *Genesis B*', *ES* 71, 307–21

'A *Miles Diaboli* in the Old English *Genesis B*', *ELN* 27, 1–5

Jensen, Emily, '"The Wife's Lament's" *eorðscræf*', *NM* 91, 449–57

Jones, John Mark, 'The Metaphor That Will Not Perish: "The Dream of the Rood" and the New Hermeneutic', *Christianity & Lit.* 38.2 (1989), 63–72

Keefer, Sarah Larratt, 'A Monastic Echo in an Old English Charm', *Leeds Stud. in Eng.* ns 21, 71–80 [Charm 6]

Keefer, Sarah Larratt, and David R. Burrows, *see* sect. 6 [*Kentish Psalm 50*]

Kiernan, Kevin S., 'Reading Cædmon's "Hymn" with Someone Else's Glosses', *Representations* 32, 157–74

Kolb, Eduard, *see* sect. 3*bii* [*Andreas*]

Liuzza, Roy M., 'The Old English *Christ* and *Guthlac* Texts, Manuscripts, and Critics', *RES* 41, 1–11

Lucas, Peter J., '*Landmenn* and the Destruction of the Egyptian Idols: Two Notes on the Old English *Exodus*', *N&Q* 37, 139–41

see also sect. 6 [*Judith*]

McEntire, Sandra, 'The Monastic Context of Old English "Precepts"', *NM* 91, 243–9

McPherson, Clair W., 'Spiritual Combat: the *Dream of the Road*', *Anglican Theol. Rev.* 71 (1989), 166–75

Mason, Lawrence, trans., *An Anglo-Saxon Genesis* (Lampeter) [reprint of 1915 translation and 1832 drawings]

Mirarchi, Giovanni, '*La Fenice*, v. 217a: *heore dreorges hus*', *AIUON: Filologia germanica* 30–1 (1987–8), 43–56

'*La Fenice*, v. 591b: *fuglas scyne*', *Studi sulla cultura germanica*, ed. D'Aronco *et al.*, pp. 267–82

Miyazaki, Tadakatsu, '*Sǣmanna sið* (l. 479) and *flodweard* (l. 494) in the Old English *Exodus*', *Ono Festschrift*, ed. Jin, pp. 435–50

Moffat, Douglas, ed. and trans., *The Old English 'Soul and Body'* (Wolfeboro, NH, and Woodbridge)

Molinari, Maria Vittoria, 'Sull'*Æcerbot* anglosassone. Rituale per la benedizione dei campi (ms. Londra, B.L., Cotton Caligula A.VII)', *Studi sulla cultura germanica*, ed. D'Aronco *et al.*, pp. 293–308

Morey, James H., 'Adam and Judas in the Old English *Christ and Satan*', *SP* 87, 397–409

Nedoma, Robert, 'The Legend of Wayland in *Deor*', *ZAA* 38, 129–45

Nelson, Marie, '*Judith*: a Story of a Secular Saint', *Germanic Notes* 21, 12–13

'King Solomon's Magic: the Power of a Written Text', *Oral Tradition* 5, 20–36 [*Solomon and Saturn I*]

North, Richard, 'Tribal Loyalties in the *Finnsburh Fragment* and Episode', *Leeds Stud. in Eng.* ns 21, 13–43

Orton, P.R., '*The Wife's Lament* and *Skírnismál*: Same Parallels', *Úr Dölum til Dala: Guðbrandur Vigfússon Centenary Essays*, ed. R. McTurk and A. Wawn, Leeds Texts and Monographs ns 11 (Leeds, 1989), 205–37

Overing, Gillian R., 'Of Apples, Eve, and *Genesis B*: Contemporary Theory and Old English Practice', *ANQ* ns 3, 87–90

Reifegerste, E. Matthias, 'Die altnordischen Rätsel', *Skandinavistik* 20, 20–3 [OE Riddles]

Renoir, Alain, 'Eve's I.Q. Rating: Two Sexist Views of *Genesis B*', *New Readings on Women*, ed. Damico and Olsen, pp. 262–72

Roberts, Jane, '*Guthlac A* 624: *lege biscencte*', *N&Q* 37, 264–5

Rodrigues, Louis J., ed. and trans., *Anglo-Saxon Riddles* (Lampeter)

Ross, Margaret Clunies, 'The Anglo-Saxon and Norse *Rune Poems*: a Comparative Study', *ASE* 19, 23–39

Rowland, Jenny, see sect. 3*bii* [*Andreas*]

Samuels, Peggy, 'The Audience Written into the Script of *The Dream of the Rood*', *Mod. Lang. Quarterly* 49, 311–20

Solari, Roberto, '*Ēoh . . . hyrde fȳres . . . wynan on ēþle*', *Studi sulla cultura germanica*, ed. D'Aronco *et al.*, pp. 429–39 [*Rune Poem*]

Sorrell, Paul, 'Oaks, Ships, Riddles and the Old English *Rune Poem*', *ASE* 19, 103–16

Stanley, E.G., '*The Rune Poem* 34: *beornum*', *N&Q* 37, 143–4

Welsh, Andrew, 'Swallows Name Themselves: Exeter Book Riddle 55', *ANQ* ns 3, 90–3

Wright, Charles D., 'The Lion Standard in *Exodus*: Jewish Legend, Germanic Tradition, and Christian Typology' *ASNSL* 227, 138–45

see also sect. 3*c* [*Elene*]

Yun Lee Too, 'The Appeal to the Senses in the Old English *Phoenix*', *NM* 91, 229–42

c. Prose

Bately, Janet, 'Those Books That Are Most Necessary for All Men to Know: the Classics and Late Ninth-Century England, a Reappraisal', *The Classics in the Middle Ages*, ed. Aldo S. Bernardo and Saul Levin (Binghamton), pp. 45–78

Berlin, Gail Ivy, 'Bede's Miracle Stories: Notions of Evidence and Authority in Old English History', *Neophilologus* 74, 434–43

Cameron, M.L., 'Bald's *Leechbook* and Cultural Interactions in Anglo-Saxon England', *ASE* 19, 5–12

Cross, J.E., 'A *Sermo de Misericordia* in Old English Prose', *Anglia* 108, 429–40

Del Lungo Camiciotti, Gabriella, 'Un brano confessionale in inglese antico: Laud Misc. 482, ff. 46r–47r, righi 22–21', *Aevum* 64, 175–82

Frederick, Jill, '"His ansyn wæs swylce rosan blostma": a Reading of the Old English *Life of St Christopher*', *Proc. of the PMR Conference* 12–13 (1989), 137–48

Green, Eugene A., 'Ælfric the Catechist', *De Ore Domini: Preaching and Word in the Middle Ages*, ed. Thomas L. Amos *et al.*, Stud. in Med. Culture 27 (Kalamazoo, M1, 1989), 61–74

Grundy, Lynne, 'Ælfric's *Sermo de Sacrificio in Die Pascae*: *Figura* and *Veritas*', *N&Q* 37, 265–9

Harbus, Antonina, 'The Use of the Noun *olehtung* in Vercelli Homily VII', *N&Q* 37, 389–91

Irvine, Susan E., 'Bones of Contention: the Context of Ælfric's Homily on St Vincent', *ASE* 19, 117–32

Jeffrey, J. Elizabeth, *Blickling Spirituality and the Old English Vernacular Homily: a Textual Analysis*, Stud. in Med. Lit. 1 (Lewiston, NY, Lampeter and Queenston, Ontario, 1989)

McGowan, Joseph, 'Apolloniana', *ASNSL* 227, 130–8

'The Old English *Apollonius of Tyre* and the Latin Recensions', *Proc. of the PMR Conference* 12–13 (1989), 179–95

Meyer, Marc A., *see* sect. 4 [penitentials]

Morini, Carla, 'Le fonti della *Passio S. Agathæ* di Ælfric', *AIUON: Filologia germanica* 30–1, 83–94

Moriya, Yasuyo, *see* sect. 2 [Ælfric]

Ogawa, Hiroshi, *see* sect. 2 (second and third entries)

Pilch, Herbert, 'The Last Vercelli Homily: a Sentence-Analytical Edition', *Historical Linguistics and Philology*, ed. Jacek Fisiak, Trends in Ling., Stud. and Monographs 46 (Berlin and New York), 297–336

Quinn, Karen J., and Kenneth P. Quinn, *A Manual of Old English Prose*, Garland Reference Lib. of the Humanities 453 (New York and London)

Richards, Mary P., and B. Jane Stanfield, 'Concepts of Anglo-Saxon Women in the Laws', *New Readings on Women*, ed. Damico and Olsen, pp. 89–99

Riedinger, Anita R., 'The Englishing of Arcestrate: Woman in *Apollonius of Tyre*', *New Readings on Women*, ed. Damico and Olsen, pp. 292–306

Robertson, Elizabeth, *Early English Devotional Prose and the Female Audience* (Knoxville, TN) ['The AB Texts and the Anglo-Saxon Tradition', pp. 144–80 and 208–10]

Szarmach, Paul E., 'Ælfric's Women Saints: Eugenia', *New Readings on Women*, ed. Damico and Olsen, pp. 146–57

'Old English Prose', *ANQ* ns 3, 56–9

see also sect. 6 [Vercelli Homily XX]

Tejada, Paloma, 'Traducción y caracterización lingüística: la prosa anglosajona', *Revista canaria de estudios ingleses* 18 (1989), 243–9

Tristram, Hildegard L. C., 'Der insulare Alexander', *Kontinuität und Transformation der Antike im Mittelalter*, ed. Willi Erzgräber (Sigmaringen, 1989), pp. 129–55

'More Talk of Alexander', *Celtica* 21, 658–63

Trobevšek-Drobnak, Frančiška, *see* sect. 2 [OE Orosius]

Wallace, D.P., 'King Alfred's Version of St Augustine's *Soliloquies*, III, 23–26, *The Vision of the Damned*', *N&Q* 37, 141–3

Wright, Charles D., 'The Three "Victories" of the Wind: a Hibernicism in the *Hisperica Famina, Collectanea Bedae*, and the Old English Prose *Solomon and Saturn* Pater Noster Dialogue', *Ériu* 41, 13–25

'The Pledge of the Soul: a Judgment Theme in Old English Homiletic Literature and Cynewulf's *Elene*', *NM* 91, 23–30

Yamagata, Hiromitsu, 'Some Emendations Proposed in the Prose *Life of St Guthlac*', *Ono Festschrift*, ed. Jin, pp. 165–76

4. ANGLO-LATIN, LITURGY AND OTHER LATIN ECCLESIASTICAL TEXTS

Amos, Thomas L., 'Preaching and the Sermon in the Carolingian World', *De Ore Domini: Preaching and Word in the Middle Ages*, ed. Thomas L. Amos *et al.*, Stud. in Med. Culture 27 (Kalamazoo, 1989), 41–60

Bejczy, István, 'Ein Zeugnis Alkuins: Die *Vita Willibrordi*', *Nederlands Archief voor Kerkgeschiedenis* 70, 121–39

Breen, Aidan, 'The Text of the Constantinopolitan Creed in the Stowe Missal', *Proc. of the R. Irish Acad.* 90.C4, 107–21

Chazelle, Celia M., 'To Whom Did Christ Pay the Price? The Soteriology of Alcuin's *Epistola* 307', *Proc. of the PMR Conference* 14 (1989), 43–62

Classen, Albrecht, 'Frauenbriefe an Bonifatius. Frühmittelalterliche Literaturdenkmäler aus literarhistorischer Sicht', *Archiv für Kulturgeschichte* 72, 251–73

Clausi, Benedetto, 'Elementi di ermeneutica monastica nel *De schematibus et tropis* di Beda', *Orpheus* ns 11, 277–307

Fell, Christine E., 'Some Implications of the Boniface Correspondence', *New Readings on Women*, ed. Damico and Olsen, pp. 29–43

Forman, Mary, 'Three Songs about St Scholastica by Aldhelm and Paul The Deacon', *Vox Benedictina* 7, 229–52

Gewalt, Dietfried, 'Der entstummte Bettler. Zu Beda Venerabilis, Historia Ecclesiastica Gentis Anglorum, V, 2', *Linguistica Biblica* 54 (1983), 53–60

Goffart, Walter, 'The *Historia Ecclesiastica*: Bede's Agenda and Ours', *Haskins Soc. Jnl* 2, 29–45

Grimes, Donald J., 'Petrine Primacy: Perspectives of Two Insular Commentators (A.D. 600–800)', *Proc. of the PMR Conference* 12–13 (1989), 149–58 [Bede, pseudo-Jerome]

Gwara, Scott, *see* sect. 2 [Aldhelm]

Herren, Michael W., 'Gildas and Early British Monasticism', *Britain 400–600*, ed. Bammesberger and Wollmann, pp. 65–78

Hill, Thomas D., *see* sect. 3*bi* (second entry)

Lambert, Pierre-Yves, 'Gloses en vieux-breton, 1–5', *Etudes Celtiques* 26, 81–93 [Bede]

Langosch, Karl, *Mittellatein und Europa: Führung in die Hauptliteratur des Mittelalters* (Darmstadt)

Lapidge, Michael, 'Anglo-Latin Studies: a Decennial Retrospective', *ANQ* ns 3, 79–85

'A New Hiberno-Latin Hymn on St Martin', *Celtica* 21, 240–51

'The Study of Greek at the School of Canterbury in the Seventh Century', *The Sacred Nectar of the Greeks: the Study of Greek in the West in the Early Middle Ages*, ed. Michael W. Herren, King's College London Med. Stud. 2 (London, 1988), 169–94

McNamara, Martin, *see* sect. 7

Martin, Lawrence T., trans., *The Venerable Bede. Commentary on the Acts of the Apostles*, Cistercian Stud. 117 (Kalamazoo, M1, 1989)

'The Two Worlds in Bede's Homilies: the Biblical Event and the Listeners' Experience', *De Ore Domini: Preacher and Word in the Middle Ages*, ed. Thomas L. Amos *et al.*, Stud. in Med. Culture 27 (Kalamazoo, MI, 1989), 27–40

Mason, Emma, *see* sect. 7 [Wulfstan of Worcester]

Meyer, Marc A., 'Early Anglo-Saxon Penitentials and the Position of Women', *Haskins Soc. Jnl* 2, 47–61

Sherley-Price, Leo, and D.H. Farmer, trans., *Bede. Ecclesiastical History of the English People, with Bede's Letter to Egbert and Cuthbert's Letter on the Death of Bede*, revised edition (Harmondsworth)

Stork, Nancy Porter, *Through a Gloss Darkly: Aldhelm's Riddles in the British Library MS Royal 12.C.xxiii*, Stud. and Texts 98 (Toronto)

Szarmach, Paul E., *see* sect. 6 [Alcuin]

Ward, Benedicta, *The Venerable Bede* (London)

Wright, Charles D., *see* sect. 3*c* (first entry)

5. FONTES ANGLO-SAXONICI

A Database Register of Written Sources used by Authors in Anglo-Saxon England, ed. D.G. Scragg and M. Lapidge (Univ. of Manchester)

Clayton, M., 'The Sources of Ælfric's Homily for the Nativity of the Blessed Virgin Mary (Assmann III)', 57 entries: nos. C.B.1.5.8.001–057

'The Sources of Blickling Homily i', 24 entries: nos. C.B.3.4.18.001–024

Doane, A.N., 'The Sources of the Anonymous Genesis A', 117 entries: nos. C.A.1.1A.001–117

Godden, M.R., 'The Sources of Ælfric's Catholic Homilies I.xxiii', 23 entries: nos. C.B.1.1.25.001–023

'The Sources of Ælfric's Catholic Homilies I.xxxv', 42 entries: nos. C.B.1.1.37.001–042

'The Sources of Ælfric's Catholic Homilies I.xxxviii', 46 entries: nos. C.B.1.1.40.001–046

Jackson, P., 'The Sources of the Anonymous *Vitas Patrum*', 12 entries: nos. C.B.3.3.35.001–012

Swan, M., 'The Sources of Ælfric's Life of St Thomas', 14 entries: nos. C.B.1.3.34.001–014

Wilcox, J., 'The Sources of the Anonymous *De temporibus anticristi*, Napier Homily xlvi', 26 entries: nos. C.B.3.4.34.001–026

6. PALAEOGRAPHY, DIPLOMATIC AND ILLUMINATION

Berry, Nigel, *see* sect. 7

Bischoff, Bernhard, trans. Dáibhí Ó Cróinín and David Ganz, *Latin Palaeography: Antiquity and the Middle Ages* (Cambridge)

Brown, Michelle P., *A Guide to Western Historical Scripts from Antiquity to 1600* (London)

Cahn, Walter, 'Ascending to and Descending from Heaven: Ladder Themes in Early Medieval Art', *SettSpol* 36 (1989), 697–724 [BL, Cotton Claudius B.IV, fol. 29]

Cross, J. E., 'Missing Folios in Cotton MS. Nero A.I', *Brit. Lib. Jnl* 16, 99–100

Dodwell, C. R., 'The Final Copy of the Utrecht Psalter and its Relationship with the Utrecht and Eadwine Psalters (Paris, B.N. Lat. 8846, ca. 1170–1190)', *Scriptorium* 44, 21–53

Gameson, Richard, 'The Anglo-Saxon Artists of the Harley 603 Psalter', *JBAA* 143, 29–48

Gatch, Milton McC., '*Fragmenta Manuscripta* and *Varia* at Missouri and Cambridge', *Trans. of the Cambridge Bibliographical Soc.* 9, 434–75

Gerritsen, Johan, 'Have with You to Lexington! The *Beowulf* Manuscript and *Beowulf*', *In Other Words: Transcultural Studies in Philology, Translation and Lexicography Presented to Hans Heinrich Meier*, ed. J. Lachlan Mackenzie and Richard Todd (Dordrecht, 1989), pp. 15–34

Gilbert, J. E. P., 'The Lindisfarne Gospels – How Many Artists?', *Durham Univ. Jnl* 82, 153–60

Gryson, Roger, and Paul-Augustin Deproost, 'La Tradition manuscrite du commentaire de Jérôme su Isaïe (livres I et II)', *Scriptorium* 43 (1989), 175–222

Henderson, George, '*Sortes Biblicae* in Twelfth-Century England: the list of Episcopal Prognostics in Cambridge, Trinity College MS R.7.5', *England in the Twelfth Century*, ed. Daniel Williams (Woodbridge), pp. 113–35 [also concerns Trinity B.10.4]

Heslop, T. A., 'The Production of *de luxe* Manuscripts and the Patronage of King Cnut and Queen Emma', *ASE* 19, 151–95

Hooke, Della, *Worcestershire Anglo-Saxon Charter-Bounds*, Stud. in AS Hist. 2 (Woodbridge)

Keefer, Sarah Larratt, 'The *Ex Libris* of the *Regius Psalter*', *ANQ* 3, 155–9

Keefer, Sarah Larratt, and David R. Burrows, 'Hebrew and the *Hebraicum* in Late Anglo-Saxon England', *ASE* 19, 67–80

Kiernan, Kevin S., 'Old English Manuscripts: the Scribal Deconstruction of "Early" Northumbrian', *ANQ* ns 3, 48–55

Lapidge, Michael, 'An Isidorian Epitome from Early Anglo-Saxon England', *Studi sulla cultura germanica*, ed. D'Aronco *et al.*, pp. 443–83

Lendinara, Patrizia, 'The Abbo Glossary in London, British Library, Cotton Domitian I', *ASE* 19, 133–49

'Il glossario del ms. Oxford, Bodleian Library, Bodley 163', *Studi sulla cultura germanica*, ed. D'Aronco *et al.*, pp. 485–516

Lockwood, Herbert Hope, 'One Thing Leads to Another: the Discovery of Additional Charters of Barking Abbey', *Essex Jnl* 25, 11–13

Lucas, Peter J., 'The Place of *Judith* in the *Beowulf*-Manuscript', *RES* 41, 463–78

Mažuga, V.I., 'Observations sur les techniques utilisées par les scribes latins du haut moyen âge', *Scriptorium* 44, 126–30

Muir, Bernard J., 'A Preliminary Report on a New Edition of the Exeter Book', *Scriptorium* 43 (1989), 273–88

Neuman de Vegvar, Carol L., 'The Origin of the Genoels-Elderen Ivories', *Gesta* 29, 8–24

Nice Boyer, Marjorie, 'The Humble Profile of the Royal Chariot in Medieval Miniatures', *Gesta* 29, 25–30 [BL, Cotton Claudius B.IV, Tiberius B.V, etc.]

O'Dwyer, B.W., 'Celtic-Irish Monasticism and Early Insular Illuminated Manuscripts', *Jnl of Religious Hist.* 15 (1989), 425–35

O'Keeffe, Katherine O'Brien, *see* sect. 3*bi*

Pelteret, David A.E., *Catalogue of English Post-Conquest Vernacular Documents* (Woodbridge)

Pulsiano, Phillip, 'The Scribes and Old English Gloss of *Eadwine's Canterbury Psalter*', *Proc. of the PMR Conference* 14 (1989), 223–60

Raw, Barbara C., *Anglo-Saxon Crucifixion Iconography and the Art of the Monastic Revival*, CSASE 1 (Cambridge)

Rutter, Jan, 'The Search for a Small Anglo-Saxon Bound at Shaftesbury', *Proc. of the Dorset Nat. Hist. and Archaeol. Soc.* 111, 125–7

Santosuosso, Alma Colk, 'Music in Bede's *De temporum ratione:* an 11th-Century Addition to MS London, British Library, Cotton Vespasian B.VI', *Scriptorium* 43 (1989), 253–7

Schneiders, Marc, 'Zur Datierung und Herkunft des Karlsruher Beda (Aug. CLXVII)', *Scriptorium* 43 (1989), 247–52

Szarmach, Paul E., 'The Latin Tradition of Alcuin's *Liber de Virtutibus et Vitiis*, cap. xxvii–xxxv, with Special Reference to Vercelli Homily XX', *Mediaevalia* 12 (1989), 13–41

Thomson, R.M., *Catalogue of the Manuscripts of Lincoln Cathedral Chapter Library* (Cambridge)

Voigts, Linda Ehrsam, 'Catalogue of Incipits of Scientific and Medical Writings in Old and Middle English', *Manuscripta* 34, 212–13 [project description]

Werner, Martin, 'The Cross-Carpet Page in the Book of Durrow: the Cult of the True Cross, Adomnan, and Iona', *Art Bull.* 72, 174–223

'On the Origin of the Form of the Irish High Cross', *Gesta* 29, 98–110

Wright, Charles D., 'Some Evidence for an Irish Origin of Redaction XI of the *Visio Pauli*', *Manuscripta* 34, 34–44

Bibliography for 1990

7. HISTORY

Arnold, Benjamin, 'England and Germany, 1050–1350', *England and Her Neighbours, 1066–1453*, ed. Jones and Vale, pp. 43–5

Bachrach, Bernard S., 'The Questions of King Arthur's Existence and of Romano-British Naval Operations', *Haskins Soc. Jnl* 2, 13–28

Bachrach, Bernard S., and Rutherford Aris, 'Military Technology and Garrison Organization: Some Observations on Anglo-Saxon Military Thinking in Light of the Burghal Hidage', *Technology and Culture* 31, 1–17

Bailey, Keith, 'Osyth, Frithuwold and Aylesbury', *Records of Buckinghamshire* 31 (1989), 37–48

Bassett, Steven, 'Churches in Worcester before and after the Conversion of the Anglo-Saxons', *AntJ* 69 (1989), 225–56

Bates, David, 'Two Ramsey Abbey Writs and the Domesday Survey', *Hist. Research* 63, 337–9

Beech, George, 'Aquitanians and Flemings in the Refoundation of Bardney Abbey (Lincolnshire) in the Later Eleventh Century', *Haskins Soc. Jnl* 1 (1989), 73–90
   'England and Aquitaine in the Century Before the Norman Conquest', *ASE* 19, 81–101

Berry, Nigel, 'St Aldhelm, William of Malmesbury, and the Liberty of Malmesbury Abbey', *Reading Med. Stud.* 16, 15–38

Biddick, Kathleen, *The Other Economy: Pastoral Husbandry on a Medieval Estate* (Berkeley, 1989) [Peterborough Abbey]

Blair, W. J., 'An Introduction to the Oxfordshire Domesday', *Oxfordshire Domesday*, ed. William, and Erskine, pp. 1–19

Bond, Richard, Kenneth Penn, and Andrew Rogerson, *The North Folk: Angles, Saxons, and Danes* (North Walsham)

Bremmer, Rolf H., Jr, 'The Nature of the Evidence for a Frisian Participation in the *Adventus Saxonum*', *Britain 400–600*, ed. Bammesberger and Wollmann, pp. 353–71

Bridbury, A. R., 'Domesday Book: a Re-interpretation', *EHR* 105, 284–309

Brown, Shirley Ann, 'The Bayeux Tapestry: Why Eustace, Odo and William?', *Anglo-Norman Studies XII*, ed. Chibnall, pp. 7–28

Cain, T. D., 'An Introduction to the Leicestershire Domesday', *Leicestershire Domesday*, ed. Williams and Erskine, pp. 1–21

Campbell, James, 'The Sale of Land and the Economics of Power in Early England: Problems and Possibilities', *Haskins Soc. Jnl* 1 (1989), 23–37
   'Was it Infancy in England? Some Questions of Comparison', *England and Her Neighbours, 1066–1453*, ed. Jones and Vale, pp. 1–17

Casey, P. J., and Michael G. Jones, 'The Date of the Letter of the Britons to Aetius', *BBCS* 37, 281–90

Chibnall, M., ed., *Anglo-Norman Studies XII: Proceedings of the Battle Conference 1989* (Woodbridge)

Cooke, Kathleen, 'Donors and Daughters: Shaftesbury Abbey's Benefactors, Endowments and Nuns, *c.* 1086–1130', *Anglo-Norman Studies XII*, ed. Chibnall, pp. 29–45

Darvell, T. C., and L. V. Grinsell, 'Gloucestershire Barrows: Supplement 1961–1988', *Trans. of the Bristol and Gloucestershire Archaeol. Soc.* 107 (1989), 39–105 [Anglo-Saxon land charters discussed]

Down, T. 'Tatworth Middle Field', *Proc. of the Somerset Archaeol. and Nat. Hist. Soc.* 133 (1989), 103–24

Dumville, David N., *Histories and Pseudo-Histories of the Insular Middle Ages* (Aldershot) [collected papers]

'Two Troublesome Abbots', *Celtica* 21, 146–52 [Aldfrith, king of Northumbria]

Dyson, Tony, 'King Alfred and the Restoration of London', *London Jnl* 15, 99–110

Eales, Richard, 'The Central Middle Ages, *c.* 900–1200, ii: British Isles', *Hist. Assoc., Ann. Bull. of Hist. Lit.* 74, 29–30 [publications of 1988]

Edgington, Susan, 'Siward–Sigurd–Sigrid: the Career of an English Missionary in Scandinavia', *Northern Stud.* 26 (1989), 56–9

Evans, A. K. B., 'Cirencester's Early Church', *Trans. of the Bristol and Gloucestershire Archaeol. Soc.* 107 (1989), 107–22

Foot, Sarah, 'What Was an Early Anglo-Saxon Monastery?', *Monastic Studies: the Continuity of Tradition*, ed. Judith Loades (Bangor), pp. 48–57

Forster, G. C. F., 'Review of Periodical Literature and Occasional Publications: Medieval', *NH* 26, 218–19

Gardiner, Mark, 'Some Lost Anglo-Saxon Charters and the Endowment of Hastings College', *Sussex Archaeol. Coll.* 127 (1989), 39–48

Gem, Richard, 'Documentary References to Anglo-Saxon Painted Architecture', *Early Medieval Wall Painting and Painted Sculpture*, ed. Cather *et al.*, pp. 1–16

Gibson, Margaret T. and Janet L. Nelson, ed., *Charles the Bald: Court and Kingdom*, 2nd ed. (Aldershot)

Gillingham, John, 'Chronicles and Coins as Evidence for Levels of Tribute and Taxation in Late Tenth- and Early Eleventh-Century England', *EHR* 105, 939–50

Glasscock, R. E., 'An Introduction to the Cambridgeshire Domesday', *Cambridgeshire Domesday*, ed. Williams and Erskine, pp. 1–17

Godman, Peter and Roger Collins, *Charlemagne's Heir: New Perspectives on the Reign of Louis the Pious (814–840)* (Oxford)

Goffart, Walter, *see* sect. 4 [Bede]

Gordon, Eric, *Eynsham Abbey 1005–1228: a Small Window into a Large Room* (Chichester)

Gosling, John, 'The Identity of the Lady Ælfgyva in the Bayeux Tapestry and Some Speculation Regarding the Hagiographer Goscelin', *AB* 108, 71–9

Green, Judith, 'Anglo-Scottish Relations, 1066–1174', *England and Her Neighbours, 1066–1453*, ed. Jones and Vale, pp. 53–72

Greengrass, Mark, and Joseph Smith, ed., *Hist. Assoc., Annual Bull. of Hist. Lit.* 73 [publications of 1987]

Greenslade, M. W., with D. A. Johnson, 'The City of Lichfield: the Anglo-Saxon

Ecclesiastical Centre', *The Victoria History of the County of Staffordshire* XIV, ed. M.W. Greenslade (Oxford), 5–8

Härke, Heinrich, '"Warrior Graves"? The Background of the Anglo-Saxon Weapon Burial Rite', *Past and Present* 126, 22–43

Hayashi, Hiroshi, 'The Lost Laws of Anglo-Saxon Kings. Part II. Some Observations on the Nature of Anglo-Saxon Laws (1)', *Gakushuin Rev. of Law and Politics* 25, 147–215

Hills, Catherine, 'Roman Britain to Anglo-Saxon England', *Hist. Today* (October), pp. 46–52

Hinton, David A., *see* sect. 10*a*

Hodges, Richard, 'Charlemagne's Elephant and the Beginnings of Commoditisation in Europe', *Acta Archaeologica* 59 (1988), 155–68

Holdsworth, Christopher, 'Hermits and the Powers of the Frontier', *Reading Med. Stud.* 16, 55–76

Hunter Blair, Peter, *The World of Bede* (Cambridge) [reissue of 1970 edition, with foreword and bibliographical addenda by Michael Lapidge]

Hyndman, C. Knox, 'The Celtic Church and Missionary Vision', *Reformed Theol. Jnl* 6, 55–61

James, Edward, 'Late Antiquity and the Early Middle Ages', *Hist. Assoc., Ann. Bull. of Hist. Lit.* 74, 17–23 [publications of 1988]

James, S.A.L., and D. Seal, 'An Introduction to the Sussex Domesday', *Sussex Domesday*, ed. Williams and Erskine, pp. 1–27

Jones, Michael E., 'St Germanus and the *Adventus Saxonum*', *Haskins Soc. Jnl* 2, 1–11

Jones, Michael, and Malcolm Vale, ed., *England and Her Neighbours, 1066–1453: Essays in Honour of Pierre Chaplais* (London and Ronceverte, 1989)

Keats-Rohan, K.S.B., 'The Devolution of the Honour of Wallingford, 1066–1148', *Oxoniensia* 54 (1989), 311–18

'The Making of Henry of Oxford: Englishmen in a Norman World', *Oxoniensia* 54 (1989), 287–309

Kelley, David H., 'The House of Æthelred', *Studies in Genealogy and Family History in Tribute to Charles Evans*, ed. Lindsay L. Brooks, Assoc. for the Promotion of Scholarship in Genealogy, Occasional Publication 2 (1989), 63–93 [a descendant of King Æthelred I]

Kelly, Susan, 'Anglo-Saxon Lay Society and the Written Word', *The Uses of Literacy in Early Mediaeval Europe*, ed. McKitterick, pp. 36–62

Keynes, Simon, 'Changing Faces: Offa, King of Mercia', *Hist.Today* (November), pp. 14–19

'Royal Government and the Written Word in Late Anglo-Saxon England', *The Uses of Literacy in Early Mediaeval Europe*, ed. McKitterick, pp. 226–57

Kleinschmidt, Harald, 'Formen des Heiligen im frühmittelalterlichen England', *Heiligenverehrung in Geschichte und Gegenwart*, ed. Peter Dinzelbacher and Dieter R. Bauer (Ostfildern), pp. 81–5

Lawson, M.K., 'Danegeld and Heregeld Once More', *EHR* 105, 951–61

Lewis, C.P., 'An Introduction to the Shropshire Domesday', *Shropshire Domesday*, ed.

Williams and Erskine, pp. 1–27

Lewis, C. P., 'The Earldom of Surrey and the Date of Domesday Book', *Hist. Research* 63, 329–36

Lifshitz, Felice, 'The *Encomium Emmae Reginae*: a 'Political Pamphlet' of the Eleventh Century?' *Haskins Soc. Jnl* 1 (1989), 39–50

Loyn, Henry, '1066: Should We Have Celebrated?', *Hist. Research* 63, 119–27

McDonnell, John, 'Upland Pennine Hamlets', *NH* 26, 20–39

McKitterick, Rosamond, ed., *The Uses of Literacy in Early Mediaeval Europe* (Cambridge)

McNamara, Martin, 'Monastic Schools in Ireland and Northumbria before A.D. 750', *Milltown Stud.* 25, 19–36

Mason, Emma, *St Wulfstan of Worcester c. 1008–1095* (Oxford)

Meckler, Michael, 'Colum Cille's Ordination of Aedán mac Gabráin', *Innes Rev.* 41, 139–50

Moore, John S., 'The Gloucestershire Section of Domesday Book: Geographical Problems of the Text: Part 3', *Trans. of the Bristol and Gloucestershire Archaeol. Soc.* 107 (1989), 123–48

Morillo, Stephen, 'Hastings: an Unusual Battle', *Haskins Soc. Jnl* 2, 95–103

Nelson, Janet L., 'Perceptions du pouvoir chez les historiennes du haut moyen âge', *La Femme au moyen-âge*, ed. Michel Rouche and Jean Heuclin (Paris), pp. 75–85

'Women and the Word in the Earlier Middle Ages', *Women in the Church*, ed. W. J. Sheils and Diana Wood, Stud. in Church Hist. 27 (Oxford), 53–78

O'Dwyer, B. W., *see* sect. 6

Ortenberg, Veronica, 'Archbishop Sigeric's Journey to Rome in 990', *ASE* 19, 197–246

Roffe, D. R., 'Domesday Book and Northern Society: a Reassessment', *EHR* 105, 310–36

'From Thegnage to Barony: Sake and Soke, Title and Tenants in Chief', *Anglo-Norman Studies XII*, ed. Chibnall, pp. 157–76

'An Introduction to the Derbyshire Domesday', *Derbyshire Domesday*, ed. Williams and Erskine, pp. 1–27

'An Introduction to the Nottinghamshire Domesday', *Nottinghamshire Domesday*, ed. Williams and Erskine, pp. 1–31

Sharpe, Richard, 'Goscelin's St Augustine and St Mildreth: Hagiography and Liturgy in Context', *JTS* 41, 502–16

Sims–Williams, Patrick, *Religion and Literature in Western England, 600–800*, CSASE 3 (Cambridge)

'Dating the Transition to Neo-Brittonic: Phonology and History, 400–600', *Britain 400–600*, ed. Bammesberger and Wollmann, pp. 217–61

Stafford, Pauline, 'Women in Domesday', *Medieval Women in Southern England* = *Reading Med. Stud.* 15 (1989), 75–94

Thompson, E. A., 'Ammianus Marcellinus and Britain', *Nottingham Med. Stud.* 34, 1–15

Thorn, F. R., 'Hundreds and Wapentakes', *Cambridgeshire Domesday*, ed. Williams and Erskine, pp. 18–26

'Hundreds and Wapentakes', *Derbyshire Domesday*, ed. Williams and Erskine, pp. 28–38

'Hundreds and Wapentakes', *Leicestershire Domesday*, ed. Williams and Erskine, pp. 22–30

'Hundreds and Wapentakes', *Nottinghamshire Domesday*, ed. Williams and Erskine, pp. 32–42

'Hundreds and Wapentakes', *Oxfordshire Domesday*, ed. Williams and Erskine, pp. 20–9

'Hundreds and Wapentakes', *Shropshire Domesday*, ed. Williams and Erskine, pp. 28–40

Hundreds and Wapentakes', *Sussex Domesday*, ed. Williams and Erskine, pp. 26–42

Whybra, Julian, *A Lost English County: Winchcombeshire in the Tenth and Eleventh Centuries*, Stud. in AS Hist. 1 (Woodbridge and Wolfeboro, NH)

Wickham, Chris, 'European Forests in the Early Middle Ages: Landscape and Land Clearance', *SettSpol* 37, 479–545

Williams, A., and R. W. H. Erskine, ed., *The Cambridgeshire Domesday* (London)

ed., *The Derbyshire Domesday* (London)

ed., *The Leicestershire Domesday* (London)

ed., *The Nottinghamshire Domesday* (London)

ed., *The Oxfordshire Domesday* (London)

ed., *The Shropshire Domesday* (London)

ed., *The Sussex Domesday* (London)

Witney, K. P., 'The Woodland Economy of Kent, 1066–1348', *Agricultural Hist. Rev.* 38, 20–39

Wood, Ian, 'The Channel from the 4th to the 7th Centuries AD', *Maritime Celts, Frisians, and Saxons*, ed. McGrail, pp. 93–7

'Ripon, Francia and the Franks Casket in the Early Middle Ages', *NH* 26, 1–19

Yorke, Barbara, *Kings and Kingdoms of Early Anglo-Saxon England* (London)

'"Sisters Under the Skin"? Anglo-Saxon Nuns and Nunneries in Southern England', *Medieval Women in Southern England* = *Reading Med. Stud.* 15 (1989), 95–117

8. NUMISMATICS

Archibald, Marion M., 'Pecking and Bending: the Evidence of British Finds', *Sigtuna Papers*, ed. Jonsson and Malmer, pp. 11–24

Bateson, J. D., 'Roman and Medieval Coins Found in Scotland, to 1987', *Proc. of the Soc. of Antiquaries of Scotland* 119 (1989), 165–88

Bendixen, Kirsten, 'The Coins from the Second Excavation in Oldest Ribe 1986', *Sigtuna Papers*, ed. Jonsson and Malmer, pp. 43–7 [incl. 34 'sceattas']

Berga, Tatjana, 'Grobe Nachahmungen westeuropäischer Münzen des 11. Jahrhunderts in Lettland', *Sigtuna Papers*, ed. Jonsson and Malmer, pp. 49–53 [incl. imitations of Anglo-Saxon coins]

Blackburn, Mark, 'The Anglo-Saxon Coins in Gotha Museum', *NCirc* 1990, 83–4

'The Blunt Collection of Medieval Coins acquired for the Fitzwilliam Museum', *NCirc* 1990, 119–21

'Do Cnut the Great's First Coins as King of Denmark Date from Before 1018?', *Sigtuna Papers*, ed. Jonsson and Malmer, pp. 55–68 [incl. an appendix: 'Die-cutting Styles and Weight Standards used at Lincoln in the *Last Small Cross* Type']

'The Earliest Anglo-Viking Coinage of the Southern Danelaw (late 9th Century)', *Proceedings of the 10th International Congress of Numismatics*, ed. Carradice, pp. 341–8

'Hiberno-Norse Coins of the Helmet Type', *Studies in Late Anglo-Saxon Coinage*, ed. Jonsson, pp. 9–24

'What Factors Govern the Number of Coins Found on an Archaeological Site?', *Coins and Archaeology. Medieval Archaeology Research Group, Proceedings of the First Meeting at Isegran, Norway 1988*, ed. H. Clarke and E. Schia, BAR International ser. 556 (Oxford, 1989), 15–24

'Znaleziska pojedyncze jako miara aktywności monetarnej we wczesnym średniow-ieczu (Single-finds as a Measure of Monetary Activity in the Early Middle Ages)', *Prace i Materiały Muzeum Archeologicznego i Etnograficznego w Łodzi, Seria Numizmatyczna i Konserwatorska* 9 (1989), 67–85 [with English summary]

Blackburn, Mark, and Michael Bonser, 'A Carolingian Gold Coin Struck From a Die of Chartres and Found at Congham, Norfolk', *NCirc* 1990, 304–6

Blackburn, M. A. S., and M. J. Bonser, *see* sect. 10*h*

Blunt, C. E., and C. S. S. Lyon, 'Some Notes on the Mints of Wilton and Salisbury', *Studies in Late Anglo-Saxon Coinage*, ed. Jonsson, pp. 25–34

Carradice, I. A., ed., *Proceedings of the 10th International Congress of Numismatics, London, September 1986*, International Assoc. of Professional Numismatists Publication No. 11 (London)

Chick, D. S., and D. J. Symons, 'A New Penny of Offa', *NCirc* 1990, 202

Colman, Fran, *see* sect. 9

Dolley, Michael, and Melinda Mays, 'Nummular Brooches', *Object and Economy in Medieval Winchester*, ed. Biddle, pp. 632–5

Fort, E. Tomlinson, 'Two more Ninth Century Imitations of Mercian Coins', *NCirc* 1990, 231

Gillingham, John *see* sect. 7

Graham-Campbell, James, 'The Coinless Hoard', *Coins and Archaeology. Medieval Archaeology Research Group, Proceedings of the First Meeting at Isegran, Norway 1988*, ed. H. Clarke and E. Schia, BAR International ser. 556 (Oxford, 1989), 53–61

Heslip, Robert, and Peter Northover, 'The Alloy of the Hiberno-Norse Coinage', *Sigtuna Papers*, ed. Jonsson and Malmer, pp. 103–11

Holman, David, 'The Late Saxon Mints of Kent: Part II', *Kent Archaeol. Rev.* 99, 193–8

Iversen, Mette, and Ulf Näsman, ed., *Nordic Archaeol. Abstracts 1988* [Viking Age, pp. 150–74, incl. ref. to Anglo-Saxon coinage]

Jonsson, Kenneth, 'Bror Emil Hildebrand and the Borup Hoard', *Studies in Late Anglo-Saxon Coinage*, ed. Jonsson, pp. 35–45

'The Import of German Coins to Denmark and Sweden *c.* 920–990', *Sigtuna Papers*, ed. Jonsson and Malmer, pp. 139–43

Jonsson, Kenneth, ed., *Studies in Late Anglo-Saxon Coinage*, Numismatiska Meddelanden 35 (Stockholm)

Jonsson, Kenneth, and Brita Malmer, ed., *Sigtuna Papers. Proceedings of the Sigtuna Symposium on Viking-Age Coinage 1–4 June 1989*, Commentationes de Nummis Saeculorum IX–XI in Suecia Repertis, ns 6 (Stockholm)

Jonsson, Kenneth, and Gay van der Meer, 'Mints and Moneyers *c*. 973–1066', *Studies in Late Anglo-Saxon Coinage*, ed. Jonsson, pp. 47–136

Jonsson, Kenneth, and Majvor Östergren, 'The Gotland Hoard Project and the Stumle Hoard – an Insight into the Affairs of a Gotlandic "Farman"', *Sigtuna Papers*, ed. Jonsson and Malmer, pp. 145–58

Kluge, Bernd, 'Das älteste Examplar von Agnus Dei-Typ', *Studies in Late Anglo-Saxon Coinage*, ed. Jonsson, pp. 137–56

Leimus, Ivar, 'A Fourteenth Agnus Dei Penny of Æthelred II', *Studies in Late Anglo-Saxon Coinage*, ed. Jonsson, pp. 157–63

Lindberger, Elsa, 'Nyförvärv av Anglosaxiska mynt till Kungl Myntkabinettet i Stockholm', *Nordisk Numismatisk Unions Medlemsblad* 1990, 94–100

'Skatten från Cuerdale: En saga i silver', *Svensk Numismatisk Tidskrift* 1990, 96–7

Malmer, Brita, 'Coinage and Monetary Circulation in Late Viking Age Scandinavia According to Recent Die-Studies', *Proceedings of the 10th International Congress of Numismatics*, ed. Carradice, pp. 357–60 [imitations of Æthelred II's and Cnut's coins]

'On Scandinavian Quatrefoil Imitations', *NCirc* 1990, 308–9

Metcalf, D. M., 'Can We Believe the Very Large Figure of £72,000 for the Geld Levied by Cnut in 1018?', *Studies in Late Anglo-Saxon Coinage*, ed. Jonsson, pp. 165–76

'The Fall and Rise of the Danelaw Connection, the Export of Obsolete English Coin to the Northern Lands, and the Tributes of 991 and 994', *Sigtuna Papers*, ed. Jonsson and Malmer, pp. 213–23

'How Sceattas are Attributed to their Mints: the Case of Series H, Type 48', *Proceedings of the 10th International Congress of Numismatics*, ed. Carradice, pp. 333–7

'A "Porcupine" Sceat from Market Lavington, with a List of Other Sceattas from Wiltshire', *Wiltshire Archaeol. and Nat. Hist. Mag.* 83, 205–8

Mikołajczyk, Andrzej, 'Anglosaskie monety w Polsce wczesnośredniowiecznej (Anglo-Saxon Coins in Early Medieval Poland)', *Prace i Materiały Muzeum Archeologicznego i Etnograficznego w Łodzi, Seria Numizmatyczna i Konserwatorska* 9 (1989), 87–102 [with English summary]

Molvogin, Arkadi, 'Normannische Fundmünzen in Estland und anderen Ostseeländern', *Sigtuna Papers*, ed. Jonsson and Malmer, pp. 241–9

Pagan, H. E., 'The Coinage of Harold II', *Studies in Late Anglo-Saxon Coinage*, ed. Jonsson, pp. 177–205

Petersson, H. Bertil A., 'Coins and Weights. Late Anglo-Saxon Pennies and Mints, *c*. 973–1066', *Studies in Late Anglo-Saxon Coinage*, ed. Jonsson, pp. 207–433

Philpott, Fiona A., *A Silver Saga: Viking Treasure from the North West*, ed. James Graham-Campbell (Liverpool) [catalogue of an exhibition commemorating the discovery of the Cuerdale hoard]

Pilet-Lemière, J., and J. Le Maho, 'Deux deniers du VIIIe s. dits "sceattas" découverts à Rouen', *Bulletin de la Société française de numismatique* 45, 737–9

Robinson, Paul, 'Two Medieval Coin Brooches from Wiltshire', *Wiltshire Archaeol. and Nat. Hist. Mag.* 83, 208–10 [one is Edward the Confessor, *Pyramids* Type, moneyer Sæbode, Salisbury mint]

Rudling, David, 'The Medieval Farm on Bullock Down', *Sussex Archaeol. Coll.* 126 (1988), 241–3 [penny of Edgar, *BMC* iii, moneyer Leofwold, Wilton mint]

'Three Pennies of Edward the Martyr', *Sussex Archaeol. Coll.* 129 (1989), 245–6

Sawyer, Peter, 'Coins and Commerce', *Sigtuna Papers*, ed. Jonsson and Malmer, pp. 283–8

Smart, Veronica, 'Osulf Thein and Others: Double Moneyers' Names on the Late Anglo-Saxon Coinage', *Studies in Late Anglo-Saxon Coinage*, ed. Jonsson, pp. 435–53

Stein, Anthony Asher, 'A Case for Reappraising Stewart Type 59', *NCirc* 1990, 273–4

Stewart, Ian, 'Coinage and Recoinage after Edgar's Reform', *Studies in Late Anglo-Saxon Coinage*, ed. Jonsson, pp. 455–85

'Ministers and Moneyers (Summary)', *Proceedings of the 10th International Congress of Numismatics*, ed. Carradice, pp. 339–40

Talvio, Tuukka, 'Agnus Dei: Mynt och Myntsmycken', *Nordisk Numismatisk Unions Medlemsblad* 1990, 83–5

'The Designs of Edward the Confessor's Coins', *Studies in Late Anglo-Saxon Coinage*, ed. Jonsson, pp. 487–99

'Stylistic Analyses in Anglo-Saxon Numismatics: Some Observations on the Long Cross Type of Æthelræd II', *Sigtuna Papers*, ed. Jonsson and Malmer, pp. 327–30

Zant, John, 'A Saxon "Sceat" from The Square, Winchester', *Winchester Museums Service Newsletter* 8 (October), 2–3 [Series J. Type 85]

9. ONOMASTICS

Bailey, Keith, 'The Madley Brook: Some Reflections on an Oxfordshire Stream-Name', *Oxoniensia* 54 (1989), 403–5

Chevenix Trench, John, 'Some Buckinghamshire Place-Names Reconsidered', *JEPNS* 22 (1989–90), 47–53

Clark, Cecily, 'Historical Linguistics – Linguistic Archaeology', *Papers*, ed. Adamson *et al.*, pp. 55–68

Cole, Ann, 'The Origin, Distribution, and Use of the Place-Name Element *ōra* and its Relationship to the Element *ofer*', *JEPNS* 22 (1989–90), 26–41

Colman, Fran, 'Numismatics, Names and Neutralisations', *TPS* 88, 59–96

Coplestone-Crow, Bruce, *Herefordshire Place-Names*, BAR Brit. ser. 215 (Oxford, 1989)

Cox, Barrie, 'Byflete', *JEPNS* 22 (1989–90), 42–6

'Rutland in the Danelaw: a Field-Names Perspective', *JEPNS* 22 (1989–90), 7–22

Del Pezzo, Raffaella, *see* sect. 2

Dietz, Klaus, 'Französisch-englische Namenkontakte im Bereich der Anthroponymie', *Dictionnaire historique des noms de famille romans. Actes du Ier Colloque (Trèves, 10–13 décembre 1987)*, ed. Dieter Kremer (Tübingen), pp. 217–46

Dodgson, John McNeal, 'Notes on Some Bynames in *Domesday Book*', *Proper Names at the Crossroads of the Humanities and Social Sciences: Proceedings of the XVIth International Congress of Onomastic Sciences, Québec, Université Laval, 16–22 August 1987*, ed. Jean-Claude Boulanger (Québec), pp. 221–8

English Place-Name Society, 'Bibliography 1987–90', *JEPNS* 22 (1989–90), 56–9

Fellows-Jensen, Gillian, '*Amounderness* and *Holderness*', *Namn och Bygd* 78, 23–30

'Place-Names as a Reflection of Cultural Interaction', *ASE* 19, 13–21

'Scandinavian Personal Names in Foreign Fields', *Recueil d'études en hommage à Lucien Musset*, Cahiers des Annales de Normandie 23, 149–59

Garrad, L. A., '"Borrane" as a Name for Ancient Sites in Man', *Proc. of the Isle of Man Nat. Hist. and Archaeol. Soc.* 9 (1987–9), 607 [Old English word]

Gelling, Margaret, 'The Historical Importance of English Place-Names', *Proper Names at the Crossroads of the Humanities and Social Sciences: Proceedings of the XVIth International Congress of Onomastic Sciences, Québec, Université Laval, 16–22 August 1987*, ed. Jean-Claude Boulanger (Québec), pp. 85–103

'Old English Topographical Terms', *Proceedings of the XVIIth International Congress of Onomastic Sciences*, ed. Närhi, I, 362–8

Gelling, Margaret, with H. D. G. Foxall, *The Place-Names of Shropshire* I: *the Major Names of Shropshire*, EPNS 62–3 (Nottingham)

Hooke, Della, 'The Interpretation of Minos Names in Charters and the Recognition of Regional Pays', *Proceedings of the XVIIth International Congress of Onomastic Sciences*, ed. Närhi, I, 423–30

see also sect. 6

Johnson, D. A., 'Lichfield: the Place-Name', *The Victoria History of the County of Staffordshire* XIV, ed. M. W. Greenslade (Oxford), 37–9

Lazzari, Loredana, 'A proposito di Manshead e *Mannesheved*', *Studi sulla cultura germanica*, ed. D'Aronco *et al.*, pp. 187–98

Lebecq, Stéphane, 'On the Use of the Word "Frisian" in the 6th–10th Centuries Written Sources: Some Interpretations', *Maritime Celts, Frisians and Saxons*, ed. McGrail, pp. 85–90

Lias, A. S., *Place-Names in England: a Critical Survey* (privately published)

McKinley, R. A., *A History of British Surnames* (London and New York)

Meid, Wolfgang, *see* sect. 2

Närhi, Eeva Maria, ed., *Proceedings of the XVIIth International Congress of Onomastic Sciences, Helsinki, 13–18 August 1990*, 2 vols. (Helsinki)

Sandred, Karl Inge, 'Language Contact in East Anglia: Some Observations on the Scandinavian Place-Names in -*thwaite* in Norfolk', *Proceedings of the XVIIth International Congress of Onomastic Sciences*, ed. Närhi, II, 310–17

Scherr, Jennifer, 'Names of Some English Holy Wells', *Proceedings of the XVIIth International Congress of Onomastic Sciences*, ed. Närhi, II, 318–23

Spittal, Jeffrey, and John Field, *A Reader's Guide to the Place-Names of the United Kingdom: a Bibliography of Publications (1920–89) on the Place-Names of Great Britain and Northern Ireland, the Isle of Man, and the Channel Islands* (Stamford)

Bibliography for 1990

10. ARCHAEOLOGY

a. General

Allen, T.G., 'Archaeological Discoveries on the Banbury East–West Link Road', *Oxoniensia* 54 (1989), 25–44

[Anon.] 'Excavation and Fieldwork in Wiltshire', *Wiltshire Archaeol. and Nat. Hist. Mag.* 83, 218–33 [includes Anglo-Saxon sites]

[Anon.] 'Research in 1989: i. Fieldwork, ii. Excavations', *Med. Settlement Research Group Ann. Report* 4 (1989), 28–46 [includes Anglo-Saxon sites]

Arnold, Christopher, 'The Anglo-Saxon Cemeteries of the Isle of Wight: an Appraisal of Nineteenth-Century Excavation Data, *Anglo-Saxon Cemeteries*, ed. Southworth, pp. 163–75

Boddington, Andy, 'Models of Burial, Settlement and Worship: the Final Phase Reviewed', *Anglo-Saxon Cemeteries*, ed. Southworth, pp. 177–99

Cadman, Graham, with Michel Audouy, 'Recent Excavations on Saxon and Medieval Quarries in Raunds, Northamptonshire', *Stone: Quarrying and Building in England*, ed. Parsons, pp. 186–206

Cather, Sharon, David Park and Paul Williamson, 'Introduction', *Early Medieval Wall Painting and Painted Sculpture*, ed. Cather *et al.*, pp. iii–xxi

    ed., *Early Medieval Wall Painting and Painted Sculpture in England*, Proceedings of a Symposium at the Courtauld Institute of Art, February 1985, BAR Brit. ser. 216 (Oxford)

Council for British Archaeology, *Archaeology in Britain 1989* (London)

    British Archaeological Abstracts 22.1, 2 (April, October, 1989)

    British Archaeological Abstracts 23.1, 2 (April, October)

    Report No. 40 for the Year Ended 30 June 1990 (London) [with reports on the activities of CBA committees and Regional Groups dealing with all periods]

CBA Regional Group 6, *Bulletin* (1989) [reviews work on all periods in Norfolk and Suffolk, 1988]

CBA Regional Group 8, *West Midlands Archaeology* 31 (1988) [reviews work on all periods in Hereford and Worcester, Shropshire, Staffordshire, Warwickshire and West Midlands, 1988]

CBA Regional Group 8, *West Midlands Archaeology* 32 (1989) [reviews work on all periods in Hereford and Worcester, Shropshire, Staffordshire, Warwickshire and West Midlands, 1989]

Devoy, Robert J.N., 'Controls on Coastal and Sea-level Changes and the Application of Archaeological-historical Records to Understanding Recent Patterns of Sea-level Movement', *Maritime Celts, Frisians and Saxons*, ed. McGrail, pp. 17–26

Evans, Jeremy, 'From the End of Roman Britain to the "Celtic West"', *Oxford Jnl of Archaeol.* 9, 91–103

Gaimster, David R.H., *et al.*, 'Medieval Britain and Ireland in 1989', *MA* 34, 162–252

Gardiner, Mark, 'The Archaeology of the Weald – a Survey and A Review', *Sussex Archaeol. Coll.* 128, 33–53

Gelman, P. J., ed., 'Excavations in Essex 1989', *Essex Archaeol. and Hist.* 21, 126–39

Hawkes, S. C., 'Bryan Faussett and the Faussett Collection: an Assessment', *Anglo-Saxon Cemeteries*, ed. Southworth, pp. 1–24

Hayes, P., and T. Lane, 'The Fenland Survey, Lincolnshire: the Northern Fens (Wrangle)', *Archaeol. in Lincolnshire* 4 (1988), 4–8

Healey, Hilary, 'Road Works and By-passes', *Archaeol. in Lincolnshire* 4 (1988), 17

Hills, Catherine, *see* sect. 7

Hinton, David A., *Archaeology, Economy and Society: England from the Fifth to the Fifteenth Century* (London)

Hodges, Richard, 'The Danish Contribution to the Origin of the English Castle', *Acta Archaeologica* 59 (1988), 169–72

Huggett, Jeremy, and Julian Richards, 'Anglo-Saxon Burial: the Computer at Work', *Anglo-Saxon Cemeteries*, ed. Southworth, pp. 65–85

Keevil, A. J., 'The Fosseway at Bath', *Proc. of the Somerset Archaeol. and Nat. Hist. Soc.* 133 (1989), 75–101

McGrail, Seán, ed., *Maritime Celts, Frisians and Saxons*, CBA Research Report 71 (London)

Manchester, Keith, 'Resurrecting the Dead: the Potential of Paleopathology', *Anglo-Saxon Cemeteries*, ed. Southworth, pp. 87–96

Martin, E., *et al.*, ed., 'Archaeology in Suffolk 1988', *Proc. of the Suffolk Inst. of Archaeol. and Hist.* 37 (1989), 59–77

'Archaeology in Suffolk 1989', *Proc. of the Suffolk Inst. of Archaeol. and Hist.* 37, 147–64

Mitchell, John, 'Early Medieval Wall Paintings Excavated in Germany, Italy and England: a Preliminary Survey', *Early Medieval Wall Painting and Painted Sculpture*, ed. Cather *et al.*, pp. 123–33

Parsons, David, 'Review and Prospect: the Stone Industry in Roman, Anglo-Saxon and Medieval England', *Stone: Quarrying and Building in England*, ed. Parsons, pp. 1–15

ed., *Stone: Quarrying and Building in England, AD 43–1525* (Chichester)

Philpott, Fiona A., *see* sect. 8 [Cuerdale hoard]

Raw, Barbara C., *see* sect. 6

Reece, Richard, 'Models of Continuity', *Oxford Jnl of Archaeol.* 8 (1989), 231–6

Rhodes, Michael, 'Faussett Rediscovered: Charles Roach Smith, Joseph Mayer, and the Publication of *Inventorium Sepulchrale*', *Anglo-Saxon Cemeteries*, ed. Southworth, pp. 25–64

Southworth, Edmund, ed., *Anglo-Saxon Cemeteries: a Reappraisal Proceedings of a Conference held at Liverpool Museum 1986* (Stroud)

Stocker, David, and Paul Everson, 'Rubbish Recycled: a Study of the Re-Use of Stone in Lincolnshire', *Stone: Quarrying and Building in England*, ed. Parsons, pp. 83–101

Thomas, Charles, 'Gallici Nautae de Galliarum Provinciis – A Sixth/Seventh Century Trade with Gaul, Reconsidered', *MA* 34, 1–26

Tooley, M. J., 'Sea-Level and Coastline Changes During the Last 5000 Years', *Maritime Celts, Frisians and Saxons*, ed. McGrail, pp. 1–16

Watson, Jacqui, and Glynis Edwards, 'Conservation of Material from Anglo-Saxon Cemeteries', *Anglo-Saxon Cemeteries*, ed. Southworth, pp. 97–106

Bibliography for 1990

White, Roger, 'Scrap or Substitute: Roman Material in Anglo-Saxon Graves', *Anglo-Saxon Cemeteries*, ed. Southworth, pp. 125–52

b. Towns and other major settlements

Allen, Tim, 'Abingdon', *CA* 121, 24–7

Allison, Enid, and Harry Kenward, 'Fleas from Archaeological Deposits', *Archaeol. in York* 15.1, 27–33

[Anon.] 'The Bell Tolls', *Yesterday's World* 2 (November/December 1989) 8 [Late Saxon buildings including a bell-pit at Timberhill, Norwich]

[Anon.] 'Saxon London', *Yesterday's World* 6 (June/July), 8

[Anon.] 'The Vikings in London', *Brit. Archaeol. News* 4.2 (March 1989), 18

Atkin, Malcolm, and A. P. Garrod, 'Archaeology in Gloucester 1988', *Trans. of the Bristol and Gloucestershire Archaeol. Soc.* 107 (1989), 233–42

Barker, Philip, ed., *From Roman Viroconium to Medieval Wroxeter. Recent Work on the Site of the Roman City of Wroxeter* (Worcester)

Bateman, Nick, 'The Discovery of Londinium's Amphitheatre: Excavations at the Old Art Gallery Site 1987–88 and 1990', *London Archaeologist* 6.9, 232–41 [discusses medieval topography and the theatre]

Biddle, Martin, *Object and Economy in Medieval Winchester*, 2 vols., Winchester Studies 7.ii (i)-(ii) (Oxford)

[Brisbane, Mark] 'A Southampton Update', *Winchester Museums Service Newsletter* 4 (June 1989), 15

Canterbury Archaeological Trust, *Canterbury's Archaeology 1987–1988* (Canterbury, 1989)

Canterbury's Archaeology 1988–1989 (Canterbury)

Chitwood, P., 'St Mark's Yard East', *Archaeol. in Lincolnshire* 4 (1988), 24–6 [includes timber buildings and finds of 10th to 12th cent.]

Davies, S. M., and A. H. Graham, 'Trowbridge Castle Excavations 1988: an Interim Report', *Wiltshire Archaeol. and Nat. Hist. Mag.* 83, 50–6

Durham, Brian, 'The City of Oxford', *CA* 121, 28–33

Dyson, Tony, *see* sect. 7

Gardiner, Mark, 'Excavations at Testers, White Horse Square, Steyning, 1985', *Sussex Archaeol. Coll.* 126 (1988), 53–76 [some evidence for pre-conquest development]

[Green, Frank] 'Saxon Romsey', *Winchester Museums Service Newsletter* 4 (June 1989), 14–15

Hair, Nick, 'Penrith Market Hall Excavations 1990', CBA Regional Group 3, *Newsbulletin* 3.14 (October), 33

Hassall, T. G., C. E. Halpin, and M. Mellor, 'Excavations in St. Ebb's Oxford, 1967–1976, Part I: Late Saxon and Medieval Domestic Occupation and Tenements, and the Medieval Greyfriars', *Oxoniensia* 59 (1989), 70–277

Heathcote, Jenni, 'Excavation Round-up 1989, Part 1: City of London', *London Archaeologist* 6.6, 160–7

Hunter-Mann, Kurt, 'Excavations at 5–13 Clifford Street', *Archaeol. in York* 15.1, 11–16

Keene, Derek, 'Medieval London and its Region', *London Jnl* 14 (1989), 99–111

Bibliography for 1990

Kipling, R.W., 'Southgate Hotel 1990', *Winchester Museums Service Newsletter* 8 (October), 3–4

Kipling, Roger, and Graham Scobie, 'Staple Gardens 1989', *Winchester Museums Service Newsletter* 6 (February), 8–9

Martin, Gerry, 'Water Lane, 1988–1989', *Winchester Museums Service Newsletter* 4 (June 1989), 10–11

Matthews, C.L., updated by Joan Schneider, *Ancient Dunstable* (Barton-le-Clay)

Milne, Gustav, 'King Alfred's Plan for London?', *London Archaeologist* 6, 206–7

Milne, Gustav, and Damian Goodburn, 'The Early Medieval Port of London AD 700–1200', *Antiquity* 64, 629–36

O'Connor, T.P., *Bones from Anglo-Scandinavian Levels at 16–22 Coppergate*, Archaeol. of York 15/3 (London, 1989)

Pearson, N.F., 'Swinegate Excavations', *Interim: Archaeol. in York* 14.4, 2–9
'Swinegate Excavations', *Archaeol. in York* 15.1, 2–10

Ponsford, Michael, *et al.*, 'Archaeology in Bristol 1986–89', *Trans. of the Bristol and Gloucestershire Archaeol. Soc.* 107 (1989), 243–51

Sandred, Karl Inge, 'Det anglosaxiska London i ny belysning', *Ortnamnssällskapets i Uppsala Årsskrift* 1990, pp. 63–9

Teague, S.C., 'Archaeological Excavations at The Square, 1988', *Winchester Museums Service Newsletter* 3 (February 1989), 3–5
'Excavations at Market Street 1987–88', *Winchester Museums Service Newsletter* 2 (September 1988), 6–8
'28–29 Staple Gardens', *Winchester Museums Service Newsletter* 6 (February), 6–8

Tranter, Margery, 'Of Cows and Churches: Reflections on the Origins of Derby', *Med. Settlement Research Group Annual Report* 4 (1989), 21–4

Tweddle, Dominic, 'Craft and Industry in Anglo-Scandinavian York', *Work in Towns 850–1850*, ed. Penelope J. Corfield and Derek Keene (Leicester), pp. 17–41

Ulriksen, Jens, 'Teorier og virkelighed i forbindelse med lokalisering af anløbspladser fra germanertid og vikingetid i Danmark', *Aarbøger for Nordisk Oldkyndighed og Historie* 20, 69–101 [discusses early trading towns in N. W. Europe including England; with German summary]

Vince, Alan, *Saxon London: an Archaeological Investigation* (London)

Ward, Alan, 'Archaeological Investigations at Tower Street, 1988', *Winchester Museums Service Newsletter* 3 (February 1989), 6–7

Zant, John, 'Excavations: High Street, Winchester, 1989', *Winchester Museums Service Newsletter* 6 (February), 2–6

c. Rural settlements, agriculture and the countryside

[Anon.] 'Raunds Area Project', *CA* 122, 61

Bassett, Steven, *The Wootton Wawen Project: Interim Report No. 7* (Birmingham)
'The Roman and Medieval Landscape of Wroxeter', *From Roman Viroconium to Medieval Wroxeter*, ed. Barker, pp. 10–12

Baxter, Alan, 'Village of Discovery', *Yesterday's World* 1 (September/October 1989), 28–30 [about reconstructing West Stow]

Beavitt, Paul, Deirdre O'Sullivan and Robert Young, 'Fieldwork on Lindisfarne,

Bibliography for 1990

Northumberland, 1980–1988', *Northern Archaeol.* 8.1–2 (1987), 1–23

Blair, John, *Ecclesiastical Topography*, Bampton Research Paper 3 (Oxford)

Bonnassie, Pierre, 'Consommation d'aliments immondes et cannibalisme de Survie dans l'Occident médiéval', *Annales. Économies, Sociétés, Civilisations* 44 (1989), 1035–56

Bowman, Paul, 'The Langton Area Survey – First Interim Report', *Trans. of the Leicestershire Archaeol. and Hist. Soc.* 64, 103 [Early Saxon settlement site]

Brown, A. E., and C. C. Taylor, 'The Origins of Dispersed Settlement: Some Results from Fieldwork in Bedfordshire', *Landscape Hist.* 11 (1989), 61–81

Crabtree, Pamela, *West Stow, Suffolk: Early Anglo-Saxon Animal Husbandry*, East Anglian Archaeol. 48 (Gressenhall, 1989)

Creighton, J., and P. Halkon, 'Excavation at Hawling Road, Market Weighton By-Pass, North Humberside, 1989', *Univ. of Durham and Univ. of Newcastle upon Tyne Archaeol. Reports* 13 (1989), 48–50 [possible Anglo-Saxon settlement]

Davison, Alan, *The Evolution of Settlement in Three Parishes in South-East Norfolk*, East Anglian Archaeol. 49 (Gressenhall)

Didsbury, Peter, 'Fieldwork in Cottam and Cowlam Parish', *Yorkshire Archaeol. Jnl* 62, 63–7 [Anglo-Saxon site]

Dyer, C., 'Dispersed Settlements in Medieval England: a Case Study of Pendock, Worcestershire', *MA* 34, 97–121

'Medieval Forests and Woodland: Settlement and Society', *Med. Settlement Research Group Annual Report* 4 (1989)

Fairbrother, J. R., *Faccombe Netherton. Excavations of a Saxon and Medieval Manorial Complex*, 2 vols., British Museum Occasional Paper 74 (i)–(ii) (London)

Farley, Michael, 'Windmill Field, Hitcham: the Early Saxon Grave and a Possible Settlement', *Records of Buckinghamshire* 31 (1989), 75–7

Ford, S., and A. Hazell, 'Prehistoric, Roman and Anglo-Saxon Settlement Patterns at North Stoke, Oxfordshire', *Oxoniensia* 54 (1989), 7–23

Haldenby, David, 'An Anglian Site on the Yorkshire Wolds', *Yorkshire Archaeol. Jnl* 62, 51–63

Hamerow, H. F., 'Anglo-Saxon Settlement Pottery and Spatial Development at Mucking, Essex, *Berichten van der Rijksdienst voor het Oudheidkundig Bodemonderzoek* 37 (1987), 245–73

Marshall, Alistair, 'Possible Roman/Medieval Road at Fulford near Withington, Gloucestershire', *Trans. of the Bristol and Gloucestershire Archaeol. Soc.* 107 (1989), 210–17

Martin, Edward, 'Deserted and Sparsely Populated Settlements in Suffolk', *Med. Settlement Research Group Annual Report* 4 (1989), 13–14

Matthews, Keith, and Gilbert Burleigh, 'A Saxon and Early Medieval Settlement at Green Lane, Letchworth', *Hertfordshire's Past* 26 (Spring 1989), 27–31

Rutledge, Paul, 'Colkirk: a North Norfolk Settlement Pattern', *Norfolk Archaeol.* 41.1, 15–34 [Late Anglo-Saxon settlement]

Sargent, Andrew, 'The Greater London Excavation Index', *London Archaeologist* 6.8, 216–21

Simmons, B. B., 'Extra-Mural Activities', *Archaeol. in Lincolnshire* 4 (1988), 18 [Late

Saxon site at Donington]

Stamper, Paul, ed., *Wharram Research Project. Interim Report on the 41st [and Final] Season* (London)

Winchester, Angus, *Discovering Parish Boundaries* (Princes Risborough)

d. Pagan cemeteries and Sutton Hoo

[Anon.] 'Survival of the Dead', *Yesterday's World* 2 (November/December), 8–9 [the Snape cemetery]

[Anon.] 'Sutton Hoo', *CA* 118, 353–8

Arrhenius, Birget, *et al.*, 'Vegetational Development and Land Use in Vendel and Sutton Hoo', *Norwegian Archaeol. Rev.* 23.1–2, 60–4

Atkinson, Helen, 'The Boat Grave Studies of Sutton Hoo and Vendel. A Palaeoenvironmental Study', *Norwegian Archaeol. Rev.* 23.1–2, 65–78

Carver, M.O.H., ed., *Bull. of the Sutton Hoo Research Committee* 7

Crossland, E.A., 'Saxon Finds at Ermyn Way, Leatherhead', *Proc. of the Leatherhead and District Local Hist. Soc.* 5.3, 83–5 [Anglo-Saxon cemetery of 7th cent., and a possible execution cemetery of the ?10th cent.]

Down, Alec, and Martin Welch, *Apple Down and the Mardens*, Chichester Excavations 7 (Chichester)

Filmer-Sankey, William, 'A New Boat Burial from the Snape Anglo-Saxon Cemetery, Suffolk', *Maritime Celts, Frisians and Saxons*, ed. McGrail, pp. 126–34
'Snape', *CA* 118, 348–52

Härke, Heinrich, '"Warrior Graves"? The Background of the Anglo-Saxon Burial Rite', *Past & Present* 126, 22–43

Kinsley, A.G., *The Anglo-Saxon Cemetery at Milgate, Newark-on-Trent, Nottinghamshire* (Nottingham, 1989)

Owen-Crocker, G.R., 'Early Anglo-Saxon Dress: the Gravegoods and the Guesswork', *Textile Hist.* 18.2 (1987), 147–58

Parfitt, Keith, 'Excavations at Mill Hill, Deal 1982–1989: an Interim Report', *Kent Archaeol. Rev.* 101, 9–18 [includes Pagan Saxon cemetery with a shield-mount in gilded bronze]

Smith, Paul S., 'Early Anglo-Saxon Burials from Stafford Road, Brighton, East Sussex', *Sussex Archaeol. Coll.* 126 (1988), 31–51

Stead, I.M., and Valerie Rigby, *Verulamium: the King Henry Lane Site*, English Heritage Archaeol. Report 12 (London, 1989) [contains a full account of a 7th- to 8th-century Anglo-Saxon cemetery overlying the Roman and Iron Age cemeteries]

Wilson, John, 'Rescue Excavations on the Anglo-Saxon Cemetery at Eastry 1989', *Kent Archaeol. Rev.* 100, 229–31

e. Churches, monastic sites and Christian cemeteries

Adams, Kenneth A., 'Monastery and Village at Crayke, North Yorkshire', *Yorkshire Archaeol. Jnl* 62, 29–50

Aldsworth, F.G., 'Recent Observations on the Tower of Holy Trinity Church, Bosham', *Sussex Archaeol. Coll.* 128, 55–72

Aldsworth, F. G., and R. Harris, 'The Tower and "Rhenish Helm" Spire of St. Mary's Church, Sompting', *Sussex Archaeol. Coll.* 126 (1988), 105–44 [present spire built in first quarter of the 14th cent. on a late 11th-cent. tower, and not in the Anglo-Saxon period]

Andrews, David, and Martyn Smoothy, 'Asheldham Church Revisited', *Essex Archaeol. and Hist.* 21, 146–51 [no Anglo-Saxon timber church as claimed by Rodwell and Drury, *AntJ* 58 (1978), 133–51]

[Anon.] 'Glass Key', *Yesterday's World* 2 (November/December, 1989), 8 [Anglo-Saxon minster at South Elmham]

Ballantyne, Ann, 'Conservation of the Anglo-Saxon Wall Painting at Nether Wallop', *Early Medieval Wall Painting and Painted Sculpture*, ed. Cather *et al.*, pp. 105–9

Biddle, Martin, and Birthe Kjølbye-Biddle, 'The Dating of the New Minster Wall Painting', *Early Medieval Wall Painting and Painted Sculpture*, ed. Cather *et al.*, pp. 45–63

'Early Painted Wall Plaster from St. Albans Abbey', *Early Medieval Wall Painting and Painted Sculpture*, ed. Cather *et al.*, pp. 73–8

'Painted Wall Plaster from the Old and New Minsters in Winchester', *Early Medieval Wall Painting and Painted Sculpture*, ed. Cather *et al.*, pp. 41–4

Blair, John, 'The Early Church at Cumnor', *Oxoniensia* 54 (1989), 57–70

'Saint Beornwald of Bampton: Further References', *Oxoniensia* 54 (1989), 400–3 *see also* sect. 10*c*

Cox, D. C., 'The Building, Destruction, and Excavation of Evesham Abbey: a Documentary History', *Trans. of the Worcestershire Archaeol. Soc.* 3rd ser., 12, 123–46

Cramp, R. J., and J. Cronyn, 'Anglo-Saxon Polychrome Plaster and Other Materials from the Excavations of Monkwearmouth and Jarrow: an Interim Report', *Early Medieval Wall Painting and Painted Sculpture*, ed. Cather *et al.*, pp. 17–30

Crawford, Sally, 'The Anglo-Saxon Cemetery at Chimney, Oxfordshire', *Oxoniensia* 54 (1989), 45–56

Davey, Norman, 'Medieval Timber Buildings in Potterne', *Wiltshire Archaeol. and Nat. Hist. Mag.* 83, 57–69 [with further comment on the pre-conquest church published *ibid.* 59 (1964), 116–23]

Drury, P. J., 'Anglo-Saxon Painted Plaster Excavated at Colchester Castle, Essex', *Early Medieval Wall Painting and Painted Sculpture*, ed. Cather *et al.*, pp. 111–22

Fernie, Eric, 'Archaeology and Iconography: Recent Developments in the Study of English Medieval Architecture', *Architectural Hist.* 32 (1989), 18–29 [Anglo-Saxon church at Repton]

Freke, D. J., and A. T. Thacker, 'The Inhumation Cemetery at Southworth Hall Farm, Winwick', *Jnl of the Chester Archaeol. Soc.* 70 (1987–8), 31–8

Hall, R. A., 'Recent Work at the Wilfridian Crypt, Ripon Cathedral', *Bull. of the CBA Churches Committee* 27, 12–13

Hartgroves, S., and R. Walker, 'Excavations in the Lower Ward, Tintagel Castle, 1986', *Cornish Stud.* 16, 9–30

Heighway, C. M., 'Painted Plaster and Sculpture from the Tenth-Century New Minster of St. Oswald at Gloucester', *Early Medieval Wall Painting and Painted*

Bibliography for 1990

Sculpture, ed. Cather *et al.*, pp. 79–88

Higgit, John, 'Anglo-Saxon Painted Lettering at St. Patrick's Chapel, Heysham', *Early Medieval Wall Painting and Painted Sculpture*, ed. Cather *et al.*, pp. 31–40

Holmes, John, 'A Saxon Church at Findon', *Sussex Archaeol. Coll.* 127 (1989), 252–4

'A Saxon Church at West Blatchington', *Sussex Archaeol. Coll.* 126 (1988), 77–91

Jones, R.H., 'Excavations at St. James' Priory, Bristol, 1988–9', *Bristol and Avon Archaeol.* 8 (1989), 2–7 [possible late Anglo-Saxon cemetery]

Meeson, R.A., and D. Sand, 'Two Capitals in Holy Trinity Church, Baswick, Stafford', *Trans. of the South Staffordshire Archaeol. and Hist. Soc.* 30 (1988–9), 21–2

Milner-Gulland, R.R., 'Clayton Church and the Anglo-Saxon Heritage', *Early Medieval Wall Painting and Painted Sculpture*, ed. Cather *et al.*, pp. 205–19

'Greatham Church: Fabric, Date, Dimensions, Implications', *Sussex Archaeol. Coll.* 126 (1988), 93–103 [discusses Old English length measurement]

Moffett, Cameron, 'The Anglo-Saxon Church of St. Andrew at Wroxeter', *From Roman Viroconium to Medieval Wroxeter*, ed. Barker, pp. 8–9

Morris, Christopher D., *Church and Monastery in the Far North: an Archaeological Evaluation*, Jarrow Lecture (1989)

'Tintagel Island', *Univ. of Durham and Univ. of Newcastle Archaeol. Reports* 14, 42–4

Morris, R.K., 'A Note on St. Gregory's Minster, Kirkdale, North Yorkshire', *Bull. of the CBA Churches Committee* 27, 4–6

Nowakowski, J., and C. Thomas, 'Tintagel Churchyard Excavations 1990', *Cornish Archaeol.* 29, 97–8

Oddy, W.A., 'The Conservation of the Winchester Anglo-Saxon Fragment', *Early Medieval Wall Painting and Painted Sculpture*, ed. Cather *et al.*, pp. 65–71

Park, David, 'Anglo-Saxon or Anglo-Norman? Wall Paintings at Wareham and Other Sites in Southern England', *Early Medieval Wall Painting and Painted Sculpture*, ed. Cather *et al.*, pp. 225–47

Poulton, Rob, *Archaeological Investigations on the Site of Chertsey Abbey*, Surrey Archaeol. Soc. Research Volume 11 (Guildford, 1988) [Anglo-Saxon monastery *not* under the Norman and later complex]

Rahtz, Philip, 'The Bones of St. Edward the Martyr', *Brit. Archaeol. News* 4.2 (March, 1989), 17–18

Rodwell, Warwick, *Church Archaeology* (London)

Scull, C., 'Excavation at Watchfield, Oxfordshire, 1989', *Univ. of Durham and Univ. of Newcastle Archaeol. Reports* 13 (1989), 51–2 [Anglo-Saxon cemetery]

Scull, C.J., and A.F. Harding, 'Two Early Medieval Cemeteries at Milfield, Northumberland', *Durham Archaeol. Jnl* 6, 1–29

Senior, J.R., 'Hildenley Limestone: a Fine Quality Dimensional and Artifact Stone from Yorkshire', *Stone: Quarrying and Building in England*, ed. Parsons, pp. 146–68

Sherlock, D., and H. Woods, *St. Augustine's Abbey: Report on Excavations, 1960–78*, Kent Archaeol. Soc. Monograph Series 4 (Maidstone, 1988)

Stanley, M.F., 'Carved in Bright Stone: Sources of Building Stone in Derbyshire', *Stone: Quarrying and Building in England*, ed. Parsons, pp. 169–85 [includes Repton]

Sutherland, Diana S., 'Burnt Stone in a Saxon Church and its Implications', *Stone:*

Bibliography for 1990

Quarrying and Building in England, ed. Parsons, pp. 102–13 [Brixworth]

Taylor, H. M., 'The Fabric of Some Sussex Churches with Early Wall Paintings', *Early Medieval Wall Painting and Painted Sculpture*, ed. Cather *et al.*, pp. 221–3

Thomas, Charles, 'The 1988 C. A. U. Excavations at Tintagel Island: Discoveries and their Implications', *Cornish Stud.* 16, 49–60

'The Archaeology of Tintagel Parish Churchyard', *Cornish Stud.* 16, 79–91

'Christians, Chapels, Churches and Charters – or, "Proto-Parochial Provisions for the Pious in a Peninsula" (Land's End)', *Landscape Hist.* 11 (1989), 19–26

Thomas, Charles, 'Minor Sites at Tintagel Island', *Cornish Stud.* 16, 31–48

Tudor-Craig, Pamela, 'Nether Wallop Reconsidered', *Early Medieval Wall Painting and Painted Sculpture*, ed. Cather *et al.*, pp. 89–104

Wakely, Jennifer, Keith Manchester, and Charlotte Roberts, 'Scanning Electron Microscope Study of Normal Vertebrae and Ribs from Early Medieval Human Skeletons', *Jnl of Archaeol. Science* 16 (1989), 627–42 [bones from Raunds, Northants. and Eccles, Kent]

f. Ships and seafaring

Carver, M. O. H., 'Pre-Viking Traffic in the North Sea', *Maritime Celts, Frisians and Saxons*, ed. McGrail, pp. 117–25

Crumlin-Pedersen, Ole, 'The Boats and Ships of the Angles and Jutes', *Maritime Celts, Frisians and Saxons*, ed. McGrail, pp. 98–116

Ellmers, Detlev, 'The Frisian Monopoly of Coastal Transport in the 6th–8th Centuries', *Maritime Celts, Frisians and Saxons*, ed. McGrail, pp. 91–2

Filmer-Sankey, William, *see* sect. 10d

g. Sculpture on bone, stone and wood

Batey, C. E., C. D. Morris and B. E. Vyner, 'A Tenth-Century Carved Boned Strip from Ferryhill, County Durham', *Durham Archaeol. Jnl* 6, 31–3

Butler, Lawrence, 'All Saints Church, Crofton', *Yorkshire Archaeol. Jnl* 62, 125–32 [Anglo-Saxon stone crosses]

Dinsmore, J. K., and W. A. Oddy, 'Report on the Reculver Cross Fragments', *Early Medieval Wall Painting and Painted Sculpture*, ed. Cather *et al.*, pp. 154–8

Eska, Joseph F., 'Towards an Integrated Interpretation of the Right Panel of the Franks Casket', *ANQ* ns 3, 85–7

Gibson, M. T., and E. C. Southworth, 'Radiocarbon Dating of Ivory and Bone Carvings', *JBAA* 143, 131–3

Heighway, C. M., *see* sect. 10e

Hines, John, 'Re-reading the Sculpture of Anglo-Saxon Cumbria', *SBVS* 22.7 (1989), 444–56

Lang, James, 'The Painting of Pre-Conquest Sculpture in Northumbria', *Early Medieval Wall Painting and Painted Sculpture*, ed. Cather *et al.*, pp. 135–46

Neuman de Vegvar, Carol L., 'The Origin of the Genoels-Elderen Ivories', *Gesta* 29, 8–24

Rodwell, Warwick, 'Anglo-Saxon Painted Sculpture at Wells, Breamore and Bartonupon-Humber', *Early Medieval Wall Painting and Painted Sculpture*, ed. Cather *et al.*, pp. 161–75

Salisbury, C.R., 'A Watching Brief at Hemington Fields, Castle Donington, SK 461 307', *Trans. of the Leicestershire Archaeol. and Hist. Soc.* 64, 97–9 [Roman and Anglo-Saxon sculpture fragments from a Norman mill]

Stalley, Roger, 'European Art and the Irish High Crosses', *Proc. of the R. Irish Acad.* 90.C6, 137–58

Tudor-Craig, Pamela, 'Controversial Sculptures: The Southwell Tympanum, The Glastonbury Respond, The Leigh Christ', *Anglo-Norman Studies XII*, ed. Chibnall, pp. 211–31

Tweddle, Dominic, 'Paint on Pre-Conquest Sculpture in South-East England', *Early Medieval Wall Painting and Painted Sculpture*, ed. Cather *et al.*, pp. 147–59

Williamson, Paul, and Leslie Webster, 'The Coloured Decoration of Anglo-Saxon Ivory Carvings', *Early Medieval Wall Painting and Painted Sculpture*, ed. Cather *et al.*, pp. 177–94

Wood, I.N., 'Ripon, Francia and the Franks Casket in the Early Middle Ages', *NH* 26, 1–19

Worssam, B.C., and T.W.T. Tatton-Brown, 'The Stone of the Reculver Columns and the Reculver Cross', *Stone: Quarrying and Building in England*, ed. Parsons, pp. 51–69

Yapp, W.B., 'The Font at Melbury Bubb: an Interpretation', *Proc. of the Dorset Nat. Hist. and Archaeol. Soc.* 111 (1989), 128–9 [regarded as late Anglo-Saxon]

h. Metal-work and other minor objects

Ager, Barry, 'The Alternative Quoit Brooch: an Update', *Anglo-Saxon Cemeteries*, ed. Southworth, pp. 153–61

[Anon.] 'Anglo-Saxon Treasure', *Yesterday's World* 3 (January/February), 4 [the Wasperton Collection bought by Warwickshire Museum]

[Anon.] 'Milton Keynes', *CA* 122, 69–72 [cemetery with Anglo-Saxon gold pendant]

[Anon.] 'Wiltshire Archaeological Registers for 1987 and 1988', *Wiltshire Archaeol. and Nat. Hist. Mag.* 83, 224–39

Ashley, Steven J., Kenneth Penn and Andrew Rogerson, 'Four Continental Objects of Early Saxon Date', *Norfolk Archaeol.* 41, 92–3

Austin, D., G.A.M. Gerrard, and T.A.P. Greaves, 'Tin and Agriculture in the Middle Ages and Beyond: Landscape Archaeology in St. Neot Parish, Cornwall', *Cornish Archaeol.* 28, 5–251

Blackburn, M.A.S., and M.J. Bonser, 'A Viking-Age Ingot from near Easingwold, Yorks.', *MA* 34, 149–50

Bradbury, J., and R.A. Croft, 'Somerset Archaeology 1989', *Proc. of the Somerset Archaeol. and Nat. Hist. Soc.* 133 (1989), 157–85 [cast copper-alloy censer from near Glastonbury Abbey]

Earl, Bryan, 'Reply [to Dr. Tom Greeves]', *Hist. Metallurgy* 24.1, 47–8 [tin smelting as early as 7th cent. claimed at Week Ford, Devon]

Graham-Campbell, James, 'Two Medieval Gold Finger-Rings from Great Wratting',

Proc. of the Suffolk Inst. of Archaeol. and Hist. 37.1 (1989), 55–7 [one ring perhaps 10th- or 11th-cent.]

'Two 9th-Century Anglo-Saxon Strap-Ends from East Sussex', *Sussex Archaeol. Coll.* 126 (1988), 239–41

'Two New 9th-Century Anglo-Saxon Strap-Ends from East Sussex', *Sussex Archaeol. Coll.* 127 (1989), 244–5

Greeves, Tom, '8th-Century Tin Smelting on Dartmoor: Do We Really Have the Evidence?', *Hist. Metallurgy* 24.1, 45–6

Griffiths, D. W., 'A Group of Late Anglo-Saxon Hooked Tags from Cheshire', *Jnl of the Chester Archaeol. Soc.* 70 (1987–8), 39–49

Hess, Wolfgang, 'A German Weight Bearing the Name of an Emperor Otto', *NCirc* 1990, 306–8 [found in London]

Hudson, H., and F. Neale, 'A Saxon Ring from Wedmore', *Proc. of the Somerset Archaeol. and Nat. Hist. Soc.* 133 (1989), 188–91

Leigh, David, 'Aspects of Early Brooch Design and Production', *Anglo-Saxon Cemeteries*, ed. Southworth, pp. 107–24

O'Sullivan, Deirdre, 'Two Early Medieval Mounts from the Crosthwaite Museum, Keswick', *MA* 34, 145–7

Richardson, Colin, 'A Catalogue of Recent Acquisitions to Carlisle Museum and Reported Finds from the Cumbrian Area', *Trans. of the Cumberland and Westmorland Ant. and Archaeol. Soc.* 90, 1–98 [includes 9th-cent. Anglo-Saxon strap-end, stone cross shaft, and other Anglo-Saxon material]

Tyler, Susan, 'A Supporting-Arm Brooch from the Field next to Cuton Hall, Springfield', *Essex Archaeol. and Hist.* 21, 144–6

White, Sally, 'An Anglo-Saxon Button Brooch from Lancing, West Sussex', *MA* 34, 144–5

Winchester Research Unit, 'Measuring Stick from Lower Brook Street', *Winchester Museums Service Newsletter* 4 (June, 1989), 7

Yapp, W. Brunsdon, 'Animals in Medieval Art: the Bayeux Tapestry as an Example', *JMH* 13.1, 15–75 [includes much Anglo-Saxon discussion]

'The Animals of the Ormside Cup', *Trans. of the Cumberland and Westmorland Ant. and Archaeol. Soc.* 90, 147–61

i. Inscriptions

Binns, J.W., E.C. Norton, and D.M. Palliser, 'The Latin Inscription on the Coppergate Helmet', *Antiquity* 64, 134–9

Derolez, René, *see* sect. 2

Eichner, Heiner, *see* sect. 2

Elliott, Ralph W.V., *Runes: an Introduction*, 2nd ed. (Manchester, 1989)

Higgitt, J., 'The Stone-Cutter and the Scriptorium. Early Medieval Inscriptions in Britain and Ireland', *Epigraphik 1988*, Österreichische Akademie der Wissenschaften Philosophisch-Historische Klasse Denkschriften 213.2 (Vienna), 149–61

Hines, John, 'The Runic Inscriptions of Early Anglo-Saxon England', *Britain 400–*

600, ed. Bammesberger and Wollmann, pp. 437–55
Okasha, E., *see* sect. 2

j. Pottery and glass

Blinkhorn, Paul, 'Middle Saxon Pottery from the Buttermarket Kiln, Ipswich, Suffolk', *Med. Ceramics* 13 (1989), 12–16

Campbell, Ewan, 'A Blue Glass Squat Jar from Dinas Powys, South Wales', *Bull. of the Board of Celtic Studies* 36 (1989), 239–45 [Anglo-Saxon glass vessel with discussion of type and distribution]

Henderson, Julian, 'The Nature of the Early Christian Glass Industry in Ireland: Some Evidence from Dunmish Fort, Co. Tyrone', *Ulster Jnl of Archaeol.* 51 (1988), 115–26

Mainman, Ailsa, 'Mayen't It Be . . .', *Interim: Archaeology in York* 14.4, 40–3 [8th-cent. Rhenish import]

Miles, Paul, Jane Young, and John Wacher, *A Late Saxon Kiln Site at Silver Street, Lincoln*, Archaeol. of Lincoln 17.3 (London, 1989)

k. Musical instruments

11. REVIEWS

Abels, Richard P., *Lordship and Military Obligation in Anglo-Saxon England* (Berkeley, 1988): N. Hooper, *History* 75, 293

Alcock, Leslie, *Economy, Society and Warfare among the Britons and Saxons* (Cardiff, 1987): J. L. Davies, *Hist. and Archaeol. Rev.* 5, 9–10; D. N. Dumville, *EHR* 105, 419–20

Amos, Ashley Crandell, Antonette diPaolo Healey *et al.*, ed., *Dictionary of Old English: C* (Toronto, 1988): J. Bately, *N&Q* 37, 213–14; A. S. G. Edwards, *MLR* 85, 679–81; M. Griffith, *MÆ* 59, 148–52; D. Hooke, *MA* 34, 295–6

Andrews, P., ed., *The Coins and Pottery from Hamwic* (Southampton, 1988): A. Mainman, *Med. Ceramics* 13, 53; A. Vince, *MA* 34, 253–5

Arnold, C. J., *The Anglo-Saxon Cemeteries of the Isle of Wight* (London, 1982): M.G. Welch, *Bull. of the Inst. of Archaeol. London* 25, 96

An Archaeology of the Early Anglo-Saxon Kingdoms (London, 1988): D. Clark, *Bull. of the Inst. of Archaeol. London* 26, 233–5; E. James, *History* 74, 498–9

Bammesberger, Alfred, ed., *Problems of Old English Lexicography* (Regensburg, 1985): R. H. Bremmer, Jr, *Amsterdamer Beiträge zur älteren Germanistik* 28, 121–4; K. Dietz, *ASNSL* 226, 421–5

Banting, H. M. J., ed., *Two Anglo-Saxon Pontificals* (London, 1989): P. Meyvaert, *Albion* 22, 461–4

Bassett, Steven, ed., *The Origins of Anglo-Saxon Kingdoms* (Leicester, 1989): E. Christiansen, *EHR* 105, 392–4; M. L. Faull, *Yorkshire Archaeol. Jnl* 62, 204–6; C. Heighway, *Hist. and Archaeol. Rev.* 5, 13–14; I Deug-Su, *SM* 3rd ser. 30, 962–3; H. R. Loyn, *AntJ* 69, 365–6; P. Wormald, *Oxoniensia* 54, 420–2

Beresford, Guy, *Goltho: the Development of an Early Medieval Manor c. 850–1150* (London,

1987): H. Hinz, *Germania* 67, 631–4

Bernstein, David J., *The Mystery of the Bayeux Tapestry* (London, 1986): B. S. Bachrach, *Speculum* 65, 123–4

Bieler, L., *Ireland and the Culture of Early Medieval Europe*, ed. R. Sharpe (London, 1987): D. N. Dumville, *JEH* 41, 82–3

Bischoff, Bernhard, *et al.*, ed., *The Epinal, Erfurt, Werden and Corpus Glossaries* (Copenhagen, 1988): M.-C. Garand, *Scriptorium* 43, 336–8; V. P. McCarren, *Speculum* 65, 941–4; I. C. McDougall, *RES* 41, 543–5

Blair, J., ed., *Minsters and Parish Churches* (Oxford, 1988): A. Boddington, *MA* 34, 263–4; S. Foot, *JEH* 41, 90–2; D. A. Stocker, *JBAA* 143, 140–3

Blunt, C. E., B. H. I. H. Stewart and C. S. S. Lyon, *Coinage in Tenth-Century England* (Oxford, 1989): K. Jonsson, *Nordisk Numismatisk Unions Medlemsblad* 1990, 101–3; R. McKitterick, *TLS* 1990, 538; D. M. Metcalf, *NChron* 150, 296–8

Bodden, Mary-Catherine, ed. and trans., *The Old English Finding of the True Cross* (Cambridge, 1987): D. Donoghue, *Speculum* 65, 368–9; J. Hill, *Anglia* 108, 205–9; R. M. Scowcroft, *Religious Stud. Rev.* 16, 267

Bonner, Garald, David Rollason and Clare Stancliffe, ed., *St Cuthbert, His Cult and His Community to AD 1200* (Woodbridge, 1989): D. H. Farmer, *JTS* 41, 274–6; R. M. Haines, *Canadian Jnl of Hist.* 25, 247–8; I. Henderson, *AAe* 5th ser., 18, 238–42; H. R. Loyn, *MA* 34, 261–3; P. Meyvaert, *Albion* 22, 461–4; H. Moisl, *Durham Archaeol. Jnl* 6, 81–2; A. E. Redgate, *N&Q* 37, 448–50

Bowden, Betsy, *Listener's Guide to Medieval English* (New York and London, 1988): M. Jennings, *Speculum* 65, 947–9

Brooks, Nicholas, *The Early History of the Church at Canterbury* (Leicester, 1984): E. John, *N&Q* 37, 214–15

Brown, George Hardin, *Bede the Venerable* (Boston, 1987): J. Campbell, *EHR* 105, 711; W. W. Dickerson, *Fides et Historia* 22.1, 92–4; R. W. Hanning, *Speculum* 65, 375–7

Brown, Shirley Ann, and Michael W. Herren, *The Bayeux Tapestry: History and Bibliography* (Woodbridge, 1988): M. Parisse, *CCM* 33, 285–7

Busse, Wilhelm, *Altenglische Literatur und ihre Geschichte* (Düsseldorf, 1987): L. W. Collier, *MÆ* 59, 152

Calder, Daniel G., and T. Craig Christy, ed., *Germania: Comparative Studies in the Old Germanic Languages and Literatures* (Wolfeboro, NH, and Woodbridge): D. H. Green, *RES* 41, 107–8

Cameron, Angus, *et al.*, ed., *Dictionary of Old English: D* (Toronto, 1986): M. Griffith, *MÆ* 59, 148–52

Davies, Wendy, and Paul Fouracre, ed., *The Settlement of Disputes in Early Medieval Europe* (Cambridge, 1986): R. C. Van Caenegem, *Le Moyen Âge* 96, 151–4

Donoghue, Daniel, *Style in Old English Poetry* (New Haven and London, 1987): R. P. Creed, *ELN* 27.4, 73–4; A. S. G. Edwards, *MLR* 85, 400–1; J. Roberts, *N&Q* 37, 453–5; E. G. Stanley, *RES* 41, 233–4

Drewett, Peter, and Mark Gardiner, *The South East to AD 1000* (London, 1988): [Anon.,] *CA* 118, 362; [Anon.,] *Yesterday's World* 1 (September/October, 1989), 39; D. G. Bird, *Britannia* 21, 410–11

Bibliography for 1990

Driscoll, Stephen T., and Margaret R. Nieke, ed., *Power and Politics in Early Medieval Europe* (Edinburgh, 1988): C.E. Batey, *Bull. of the Inst. of Archaeol. London* 26, 254–5; I. Henderson, *MA* 34, 283–4

Elliott, Ralph W.V., *Runes: an Introduction*, 2nd ed. (Manchester, 1989): E. Seebold, *Anglia* 108, 478–83

Evans, Angela Care, *The Sutton Hoo Ship Burial* (London, 1986): M.G. Welch, *Bull. of the Inst. of Archaeol. London* 25, 115

Fisiak, Jacek, *A Bibliography of Writings for the History of the English Language*, 2nd ed. (Berlin, New York and Amsterdam, 1987): F.C. Robinson, *IF* 95, 338–40; H. Sauer, *Kratylos* 35, 211–13

Francovich Onesti, Nicoletta, *L'inglese dalle origini ad oggi* (Rome, 1988): L. Lazzari, *AIUON* 30–1, 395–6

Füchs, R., *Das Domesday Book und sein Umfeld* (Stuttgart, 1987): H.R. Loyn, *EHR* 105, 713–15; J. Sarnowsky, *Historisches Jahrbuch* 110, 167–9

Gardiner-Stallaert, Nicole, *From the Sword to the Pen: an Analysis of the Concept of Loyalty in Old English Secular Heroic Poetry* (New York, Bern and Frankfurt am Main, 1988): M. Griffith, *MÆ* 59, 153; J. Hill, *Anglia* 108, 484–6

Gilmour, B.J.J., and D.A. Stocker, *St. Mark's Church and Cemetery* (London, 1986): C. Platt, *EHR* 105, 431

Gilmour, L.A., *Early Medieval Pottery from Flaxengate, Lincoln* (London, 1988): D.A. Hinton, *MA* 34, 287–8

Goffart, Walter, *The Narrators of Barbarian History (A. D. 550–800)* (Princeton, 1988): P. Fouracre, *History* 74, 497–8; M. Sot, *Annales. Économies, Sociétés, Civilisations* 44, 888–90

Grant, R.J.S., *The B Text of the Old English Bede: a Linguistic Commentary*, Costerus ns 73 (Amsterdam and Atlanta): D.G. Scragg, *RES* 41, 380–1

Greenhill, B., and S. Manning, *The Evolution of the Wooden Ship* (London, 1988): S. McGrail, *JBAA* 143, 144–5

Grierson, Philip, and Mark Blackburn, *Medieval European Coinage, I. The Early Middle Ages (5th–10th Centuries)* (Cambridge, 1986): S. Coupland, *History* 73, 286–7; J. Lafaurie, *Revue numismatique* 6th series 31, 279–84

Hall, Richard, *Viking Age Archaeology in Britain and Ireland* (Princes Risborough): R. Daniels, CBA Regional Group 3, *Newsbulletin* 3.4 (October), 37

Hansen, Elaine Tuttle, *The Solomon Complex: Reading Wisdom in Old English Poetry* (Toronto, Buffalo and London, 1988): J.M. Ziolkowski, *JEGP* 89, 210–11

Hawkes, Sonia Chadwick, *et al.*, ed., *Anglo-Saxon Studies in Archaeology and History* (Oxford, 1985): B. Gilmour, *JBAA* 143, 139; C. Hills, *Germania* 66, 268–9

Hawkes, Sonia Chadwick, ed., *Weapons and Warfare in Anglo-Saxon England* (Oxford, 1989): B. Gilmour, *JBAA* 143, 139

Hayfield, C., *An Archaeological Survey of the Parish of Wharram Percy, East Yorkshire 1. The Evolution of the Roman Landscape* (Oxford, 1988): J. Price, *NH* 20, 235–6

Heffernan, Carol Falvo, *The Phoenix at the Fountain* (Newark, DE, London and Toronto, 1988): H. Damico, *Speculum* 65, 994–7

Henderson, George, *From Durrow to Kells. The Insular Gospel Books 650–800* (London, 1987): P. McGurk, *History* 74, 114–15

Heyworth, P.L., ed., *Letters of Humfrey Wanley* (Oxford, 1989): J.P. Carley, *Univ. of Toronto Quarterly* 60, 118–20; M. Griffith, *MÆ* 59, 164–5; E.G. Stanley, *N&Q* 37, 70–2

Hinton, P., ed., *Excavations in Southwark 1973–76, Lambeth 1973–79* (London, 1989): A. Vince, *Med. Ceramics* 13, 55–6

Hodges, R., *The Anglo-Saxon Achievement* (London, 1989): C. Scull, *MA* 34, 288–9 *Primitive and Peasant Markets* (Oxford, 1988): S. Roskams, *MA* 34, 290

Hodges, R., and B. Hobley, ed., *The Rebirth of Towns in the West A. D. 700–1050* (London, 1988): D.A. Hinton, *MA* 34, 255–6

Holt, J.C., ed., *Domesday Studies* (Woodbridge, 1987): R. Fuchs, *HZ* 251, 125–7; D.J. A. Matthew, *EHR* 105, 997–9

Hooke, Della, *Anglo-Saxon Settlements* (Oxford, 1988): J. Hamshere, *Landscape Hist.* 13, 95–6; E. James, *History* 74, 498–9; K.E. Jermy, *Yesterday's World* 4 (March/April), 36; D.M. Palliser, *NH* 26, 236–7

Horsman, Valerie, *et al.*, *Aspects of Saxo-Norman London* I, *Building and Street Development near Billingsgate and Cheapside* (London, 1988): M. Gardiner, *London Archaeologist* 6.9, 249–50; D. Keene, *MA* 34, 258–9

Howe, Nicholas, *Migration and Mythmaking in Anglo-Saxon England* (New Haven and London, 1989): W.A. Chaney, *Albion* 22, 655–6; N. Jacobs, *N&Q* 37, 452–3; K.M. Schoening, *Comitatus* 21 (1990), 128–32

Hurst, H.R., *Gloucester, the Roman and Later Defences: Excavations on the East Defences and a Reassessment of the Defensive Sequence* (Gloucester, 1986): R.M. Isserlin, *Bull. of the Inst. of Archaeol. London* 26, 279

Irving, Edward B., Jr, *Rereading 'Beowulf'* (Philadelphia, 1989): A.H. Olsen, *Envoi* 2.1, 101–8; P. Stafford, *Lit. and Hist.* 2nd ser. 1.2, 85–6

Jeffrey, J. Elizabeth, *Blickling Spirituality and the Old English Vernacular Homily* (Lewiston, NY, Lampeter and Queenston, Ontario, 1989): P.J. Clements, *Christianity and Lit.* 39, 328–30

Jones, Charles, *Grammatical Gender in English: 950 to 1250* (London, New York and Sydney, 1988): F. Chevillet, *EA* 43, 204–6

Jones, Martin, *England Before Domesday* (London, 1986): M. Bell, *Hist. and Archaeol. Rev.* 4, 56–7

Jonsson, Kenneth, *The New Era, The Reformation of the Late Anglo-Saxon Coinage* (Stockholm, 1987): H.E. Pagan, *NChron* 150, 299–300

Ker, N.R., and Andrew G. Watson, *Medieval Libraries of Great Britain: a List of Surviving Books. Supplement to the Second Edition* (London, 1987): S. Krämer, *DAEM* 46, 191

Kerlouégan, François, *Le 'De Excidio Britanniae' de Gildas* (Paris, 1987): G. Silagi, *DAEM* 46, 203–4

Kiernan, Kevin S., *The Thorkelin Transcripts of 'Beowulf'* (Copenhagen, 1986): E.G. Stanley, *N&Q* 37, 323–4

Kinsley, A.G., *The Anglo-Saxon Cemetery at Millgate, Newark-on-Trent, Nottinghamshire* (Nottingham, 1989): C. Hills, *Germania* 68, 680–2; J. Richards, *MA* 34, 260–1

Lapidge, Michael, and Helmut Gneuss, ed., *Learning and Literature in Anglo-Saxon England* (Cambridge, 1985): Hans Sauer, *BGDSL* 112, 461–4

Law, Vivien, *The Insular Latin Grammarians* (Woodbridge and Totowa, NJ, 1982): J. van der Straeten, *AB* 108, 217

Lobel, Mary D., ed., *The British Atlas of Historical Towns*, 3, *The City of London from Prehistoric Times to c. 1520* (Oxford, 1989): G. Rosser, *London Jnl* 15, 179–81

Mandel, Jerome, *Alternative Readings in Old English Poetry* (New York, Bern and Frankfurt am Main, 1987): E. G. Stanley, *RES* 41, 379–80

Mikołajczyk, Andrzej, *Polish Museums, Anglo-Saxon and Later Medieval British Coins*, SCBI 37 (Oxford, 1987): K. Jonsson, *Svensk Numismatisk Tidskrift* 1990, 244–5; H. E. Pagan, *NChron* 150, 298–9

Milnes, P., *et al.*, *A Late Saxon Kiln Site at Silver Street, Lincoln* (London, 1989): D. A. Hinton, *MA* 34, 287–8

Mitchell, Bruce, *On Old English: Selected Papers* (Oxford, 1988): K. S. Kiernan, *Envoi* 2.1, 121–4; M. Ogura, *Stud. in Eng. Lit.* (English Number 1990) (Tokyo), 164–9; D. G. Scragg, *RES* 41, 378–9

Morris, Richard, *Churches in the Landscape* (London, 1989): J. H. Bettey, *AntJ* 69 (1989), 371–2

Myres, J. N. L., *The English Settlements* (Oxford, 1989): N. J. Higham, *Hist. and Archaeol. Rev.* 5, 78–9

Nelson, Janet L., *Politics and Ritual in Early Medieval Europe* (London and Ronceverte, 1987): J. Campbell, *JEH* 41, 403–5

O'Connor, T. P., *Bones from the General Accident Site, Tanner Row* (London, 1988): P. Halstead, *Yorkshire Archaeol. Jnl* 62, 216–7

Bones from Anglo-Scandinavian Levels at 16–22 Coppergate (London, 1989): J. Clutton-Brook, *Yorkshire Archaeol. Jnl* 62, 217

O'Donovan, M. A., ed., *Charters of Sherborne* (Oxford, 1988): S. Kelly, *JEH* 41, 85–9

Olsen, L., *Early Monasteries in Cornwall*, Studies in Celtic History 11 (Woodbridge, 1989): C. Brett, *CMCS* 19, 122–4

Orme, Nicholas, *Early British Swimming, 55 BC to AD 1719* (Exeter, 1983): P. Williams, *EHR* 105, 732

Owen-Crocker, Gale R., *Dress in Anglo-Saxon England* (Manchester, 1986): D. N. Adams, *Bull. of the Inst. of Archaeol. London* 25, 151–2; G. Clauss, *Germania* 66, 595–7

Padel, O. J., *A Popular Dictionary of Cornish Place-Names* (Penzance, 1988): M. J. Swanton, *Devon and Cornwall Notes & Queries* 36, 185–6

Parker, Mary A., '*Beowulf' and Christianity* (New York, 1987): H. Chickering, *Speculum* 65, 214; M. Griffith, *MÆ* 59, 153–4

Pelteret, David A. E., *Catalogue of English Post-Conquest Vernacular Documents* (Woodbridge): J. Green, *TLS* 1990, 1386

Peterson, Lena *et al.*, *Studia Onomastica: Festskrift till Thorsten Andersson den 23 Februari 1989* (Lund, 1989): H. Beck, *BN* 24, 420–1

Poulton, R., *Archaeological Investigations on the Site of Chertsey Abbey* (Guildford, 1988): M. Curtis, *Yesterday's World* 3 (January/February), 40; C. Norton, *MA* 34, 303–4

Renoir, Alain, *A Key to Old Poems* (University Park, PA, and London, 1988): A. S. G. Edwards, *MLR* 85, 679–81; P. F. Ganz, *RES* 41, 613; M. Griffith, *N&Q* 37, 72–3; E. R. Haymes, *Speculum* 65, 745–6; R. Kellogg, *JEGP* 89, 346–8

Bibliography for 1990

Richards, Mary P., *Texts and Their Traditions in the Medieval Library of Rochester Cathedral Priory* (Philadelphia, 1988): P-M. Bogaert, *Revue d'Histoire Ecclésiastique* 85, 395–7

Ridyard, Susan J., *The Royal Saints of Anglo-Saxon England* (Cambridge, 1988): D. Bradley, *Revue d'Histoire Ecclésiastique* 85, 559; J. Howe, *Catholic Hist. Rev.* 76, 338–9; E. J. Kealey, *The Historian* 53, 117–18; N. W. Nolte, *Albion* 22, 290–1; D. Rollason, *History* 75, 292; P. Sheingorn, *Envoi* 2.1, 1–29

Rodwell, W., *English Heritage Book of Church Archaeology* (London, 1989): [Anon.,] *JBAA* 143, 147

Rollason, David, *Saints and Relics in Anglo-Saxon England* (Oxford, 1989): [Anon.,] *CA* 120, 409; R. McKitterick, *TLS* 27 April, 448

Ronay, Gabriel, *The Lost King of England* (Woodbridge, 1989): E. Christiansen, *The Spectator*, 24 February, 29–30

Royal Commission on the Historical Monuments of England, *An Inventory of Historical Monuments in the County of Northampton* 3, *Archaeological Sites in North-West Northamptonshire* (London, 1981); 4, *Archaeological Sites in South-West Northamptonshire* (London, 1982); and 5, *Archaeological Sites and Churches in Northampton* (London, 1985): A. King, *Bull. of the Inst. of Archaeol. London* 25, 160–1

Russom, Geoffrey, *Old English Meter and Linguistic Theory* (Cambridge, 1987): P. S. Baker, *Speculum* 65, 490–1; B. R. Hutcheson, *Envoi* 2.1, 203–5; P. J. Lucas, *SN* 62, 113–15; S. D. Spangehl, *Language* 66, 427–8

Schneider, Karl, *Sophia Lectures on 'Beowulf'* (Tokyo, 1986): R. Frank, *Colloquia Germanica* 22, 302–3

Schofield, J., and R. Leech, ed., *Urban Archaeology in Britain* (London, 1987): B. Levitan, *Bull. of the Inst. of Archaeol. London* 25, 166–7; F. Verhaeghe, *Helinium* 30, 136–9

Sherlock, D., and H. Woods, *St. Augustine's Abbey: Report on Excavations 1960–78* (Maidstone, 1988): L. Butler, *AntJ* 69, 367–9

Silvester, R. J., *Norfolk Survey, Marshland and Nar Valley* (Gressenhall, 1988): C. C. Taylor, *MA* 34, 299–300

Spatt, D. A., and B. J. D. Harrison, *The North York Moors: Landscape Heritage* (London, 1989): P. Rahtz, *Yorkshire Archaeol. Jnl* 62, 220–1

Squires, Ann, ed., *The Old English 'Physiologus'* (Durham, 1988): H. Wirtjes, *MÆ* 59, 297–8

Stafford, Pauline, *The East Midlands in the Early Middle Ages* (Leicester, 1985): J. Campbell, *Midland Hist.* 15, 151

Unification and Conquest (London): F. Barlow, *The Times Higher Education Supplement*, 26 January, 20

Stenton, F. M., *Anglo-Saxon England*, paperback ed. (Oxford, 1989): P. Stafford, *Hist. and Archaeol. Rev.* 5, 98–9

Todd, Malcolm, *The South-West to AD 1000* (London, 1987): C. F. Slade, *History* 73, 473

Tylecote, Ronald Frank, *The Early History of Metallurgy in Europe* (London, 1987): H. Forshell, *Fornvännen* 84 (1989), 264–7

Vince, Alan, *Saxon London* (London): K. Wade, *AntJ* 69, 366–7

Bibliography for 1990

Wallace-Hadrill, J.M., *Bede's 'Ecclesiastical History of the English People': a Historical Commentary* (Oxford, 1988): M. Clayton, *RES* 41, 157; W. Goffart, *JEH* 41, 83–5; S.E. Kelly, *N&Q* 37, 450–2; R.W. Pfaff, *Church Hist.* 59, 228–9

Walton, Penelope, *Textiles, Cordage and Raw Fibre from 16–22 Coppergate* (London, 1989): F. Pritchard, *Yorkshire Archaeol. Jnl* 62, 222–3; J.P. Wild, *AntJ* 69, 367; J.P. Wild, *AAe* 18, 237–8

White, W.J., *The Cemetery of St. Nicholas Shambles* (London, 1988): M. Cox, *London Jnl* 15, 96

Whitelock, D., *et al.*, ed., *Councils & Synods with Other Documents Relating to the English Church, I: A. D. 871–1204* (Oxford and New York, 1981): H. Vollrath, *Annuarium Historiae Conciliorum* 21, 212–14

Whittock, Martyn J., *The Origins of England 410–600* (London, 1986): D.P. Kirby, *History* 73, 284–5

Wilson, David M., *The Vikings and their Origins*, rev. ed. (London, 1989): N.J. Higham, *Hist. and Archaeol. Rev.* 5, 108–9

Wolfram, Herwig, and Anton Scharer, ed., *Intitulatio III* (Vienna, 1988): P. Neumeister, *Deutsche Literaturzeitung* 111, 184–8

Yorke, Barbara, ed., *Bishop Æthelwold: his Career and Influence* (Woodbridge, 1988): R. McKitterick, *JEH* 41, 477–8; D. Rollason, *History* 74, 499–500

Index to volumes 16–20

Volume numbers in italic precede page numbers

Abbo of Fleury: author of *Quaestiones grammaticales*, *20*, 150, 161

Abbo of Saint-Germain-des-Prés: author of *Bella Parisiacae urbis*, *19*, 133, 139–141, 143–4; *Sermo* xii, *20*.218; Greek learning of, *17*.224; Latin glossary of, *see* glossaries

Abbotsbury Abbey, in Dorset: *18*.207–12; account of, in Thomas Gerard's 'Survey of Dorsetshire', *18*.221–3; cartulary of, *18*.215, 219, 221, 223–5, 233, 235–42; account of, in Dugdale's *Monasticon Anglicanum*, *18*.235–8; charters of, used by Sir Henry Spelman, *18*.233–4; dissolution of, *18*.212, 223; endowments of, *18*.209, 236, 239; foundation of, *18*.208, 221–3, 236–8; guild statutes of, *18*.208, 220, 237; new ownership under the Strangways of Melbury, *18*.212, 217, 219, 238; writs of, *18*.219, 233, 238

Abecedarium Normannicum, *19*.21

Abingdon: abbey of, *19*.129–32, 156, 162, 180, 182–3; liturgy of, *18*.67; cult of St Vincent at, *19*.125–9, 180, 182–3; *Chronicon monasterii de Abingdon*, *19*.126–7; *De abbatibus Abbendoniae*, *19*.128; monks from Corbie at, *18*.83; dispute with Oxfordshire, *17*.254; relationship to Winchester, *17*.159

Adam of Damerham, *16*.211

Adamnan, author of *De locis sanctis*, *18*.113

Adauctus, St, *see* Felix

Ademar of Chabannes, chronicler of Aquitainian history, *19*.84–6, 88, 93

adultery, in AS society, *20*.19–25; legal definition of *20*.19; influence of Christianity on attitudes to, *20*.20–2; on the Continent, *20*.23–5

Ælfgyth, queen, *19*.156

Ælfheah, bishop of Winchester, *17*.160; relics of, *19*.186

Ælfric, abbot of Eynsham, *18*.100, 104, 107, *19*.55–6, 122, 129, 226

author of Catholic Homilies; *18*.104, *19*.51–2, 54–5, 57, 59, 117–19, 176, 197n; vocabulary of, *17*.139–40, 145n, 152, 157–8, *20*.68, 70; lexis of, *17*.112, 116, 140, 143; etymologies in, *17*.35–44; rhetoric in, *17*.39, 40, 44; use of sources, *17*.36–44, *19*.42, 55–7, 59–61, 63–4; commemoration of All Saints in, *19*.60; of Annunciation in, *19*.60; Common of a Confessor in, *19*.123

Grammar of: fragment of, *16*.188–9, 195; etymologies in, *17*.44; prose style of, *17*.94, 138;

dating of, *17*.106–7; modal verbs in, *20*.82–3; translation of Old Testament: *20*.88–90, 93, 95, 97; of Genesis *17*.184n; of Hexateuch, *19*.99; author of *Hexameron*, *18*.107; author of *Judith*, *18*.117, 126; author of *Colloquy*, *19*.56, 58; author of *De falsis deis*, *19*.37; author of *Letter to Sigeweard*, *18*.117–18

author of OE *Lives of Saints*: of St Edmund, *18*.120; of St Oswald, king, *18*.131; of SS Peter and Paul, *19*.56–7; of St Swithhun, *19*.131; of St Vincent, *19*.117–19, 121, 123, 129–32

Ælfric Bata, author of *Colloquy*, *19*.177–8

Ælfsige, abbot of Peterborough, *19*.155n, 161, 177

Ælfweard, abbot of Evesham and bishop of London, *19*.82

Ælfwine, royal scribe, *19*.178n

Ælfwine, son of King Harold, *19*.100

Æthelberht, king of Kent, laws of: *20*.21; treatment of adultery in, *20*.20–5; Christianity's influence on, *20*.21–5; marriage of, described by Bede, *20*.29–30

Æthelflæd, 'Lady of the Mercians', conquests of, *18*.150, 157, 161, 167

Æthelgar, abbot of New Minster, *17*.160; bishop of Selsey, charter of, *18*.228; archbishop of Canterbury, *19*.197, 244

Æthelmær, ealdorman, *19*.64

Æthelnoth, archbishop of Canterbury, *19*.184–5

Æthelnoth, abbot of Glastonbury, *16*.198

Æthelred, king of Mercia, *18*.9, lawsuits during reign of, *17*.251, 276; *see also* charters

Æthelred II, 'the Unready', king of England, *18*.151, *19*.82, 125, 155, 186; lawsuits during reign of, *17*.280; lawcode of, at Wantage, *18*.150; charters of, concerning Abbotsbury, *18*.227–9, 238; concerning land in Hampshire, *18*.228; concerning Selsey, *18*.228; coinage of, *18*.186, *19*.96; *see also* coinage

Æthelswith, sister of King Alfred, *19*.236

'Ætheltrud', daughter of King Æthelwald, *19*.235

Æthelwald, king, *19*.235

Æthelweard, abbot of Glastonbury, *16*.198

Æthelweard, earldorman, *19*.64–5; author of *Chronicle*, *18*.143, 143n, 155–7: mention of Lincoln, *18*.9–10; mention of Lindsey, *18*.9–10; mention of Stamford, *18*.196–7; use of *Anglo-Saxon Chronicle*, *18*.9

Æthelwig, abbot of Evesham, *19*.82

Index

Æthelwine, abbot of Abingdon, *19*.183
Æthelwold, bishop of Winchester, *19*.123, 130, 139;
Benedictional of, *see* benedictionals; life of: Latin
prose, by Ælfric, *19*.130–1; Latin prose, by precentor Wulfstan, *19*.226; liturgical feasts of,
19.170; monasteries established by, *18*.48; script
inspired by, *see* script

 OE translation of Benedictine Rule, *17*.32,
141–2, *18*.88, *19*.50, 53; vocabulary of, *17*.152,
157; characteristics of, *17*.140–51; account of
King Edgar's establishment of monasteries,
vocabulary of, *17*.152, 157

Æthelwulf, ealdorman of Berkshire, *18*.155–7
Æthelwulf, king of Wessex, *18*.120, *19*.203
Aethicus Ister, author of *Cosmographia*, *20*.128–9; as
source for geographical list of *Solomon and Saturn
II*, *20*.128–9, 134–6, 138–41
Agatha, St, relics of, *19*.186
Agnes, St, cult of, *19*.226
Aidan, bishop of Lindisfarne, *19*.47–8
Alberic, of Rome, *19*.207, 217
Albuin (or Ælfwine), founder of priory in Aquitaine, *19*.94
Alcuin, of York, *19*.68, 68n; author of *Commentaria
in S. Ioannis euangelium*, *19*.122; lectionary of,
18.58; letter of, *19*.53; prayers of, *18*.79; York
poem of, *16*.192; author of *De orthographia*,
Greek terms in, *17*.229; author of *Disputatio de
rhetorica et uirtutibus*, view of rhetoric in, *16*.8–9;
collection of letters, *20*.219; use of classical rhetorical texts, *16*.133n; as source for Ælfric, *17*.40;
use of *Vetus Latina*, *17*.181; as reformer of biblical text, *17*.184
Aldfrith, king of Lindsey, *18*.1, 11
Aldhelm, abbot of Malmesbury, bishop of Sherborne, *19*.5, 104, 111, 226; glosses on works of,
16.28, *17*.221, 223, 233–46; hermeneutic vocabulary of, 16.29n; use of *Vetus Latina*, *17*.165–6,
180–1; use of Greek, *17*.228, 232

 author of *De uirginitate*, *16*.44, *19*.140; use of
Prudentius in, *16*.214, 217; author of *Enigmata*,
19.8; manuscript tradition of, *16*.202–3; letter on
Malmesbury property dispute, *17*.251
Aldred, bishop of Worcester, *see* Ealdred
Aldwych, settlement at London, *18*.16
Alexander III, pope, bull of 1163 to Lincoln, *18*.27
Alfred, ealdorman of Surrey, will of, *16*.157
Alfred, king of Wessex, *18*.88, *19*.6–7, 203, 205;
burhs of, *18*.152; coins of *18*.186, *19*.97n; laws of
(West Saxon laws), *20*.20, 22–3; preface to, *17*.96–
7; vocabulary of, *17*.110; will of, *17*.96; lawsuits
during reign of, *17*.250, 279–80

 educational reform of: *17*.93–4, 132, at court,
16.156–7; scribes of, *16*.159; script of, *16*.156–7;
circular letter of, *16*.156

 translations of: choice of, *20*.130; prose style
of, *17*.119, 138; of Boethius's *Consolation of Philos-*

ophy, *19*.45–6, 55, 58; prose style of, *17*.96, 118,
128–30, 133n; vocabulary of, *17*.155; view of
history in, *16*.131–2, 137; of Gregory the Great's
Pastoral Care, *16*.156, *17*.95, 98, 112, 120, 125–7,
133n, *19*.44, 174; preface of, *16*.157, *17*.93n, 104,
230; manuscripts of, *16*.162–3, 165; vocabulary
of, *17*.155–6, 175; of Orosius's *Historiae adversum
paganos*, idea of educational reform in *16*.128; idea
of moral action in, *16*.132; of Augustine's *Soliloquies*, vocabulary of, *20*.77; prose style of, *17*.96,
118, 130, 155; use of *Vetas Latina*, *17*.181
Alleluia, bilingual, *18*.76; repertory of, *18*.67
aloes, *19*.9–10
Amand, St, of Arras, cult of, *19*.244–6
Ambrose, St, commentaries of, *18*.122; author of *De
uiduis*, *18*.122; author of *De Elia et ieiunio liber unus*,
18.122–3; author of *Expositio in psalmum*, *19*.78n;
use of *Vetus Latina*, *17*.165, 173–4
Ambrosius Autpertus, author of *Liber de conflictu
uitiorum et uirtutum*, *16*.208
Anderson Pontifical, *see* pontificals
Andreas, OE poem, vocabulary of, *20*.69–70; poetic
language of, *20*.168, 174–5; military imagery in,
16.215
Andrew, St, *19*.169
Angers, graduals from *18*.68
Anglo-Saxon Chronicle, *18*.6–7, 9, 31–2, 113, 142–3,
150–1, 157, 167, 173, 176–7, 187, 189–90, 197,
199, 241, *19*.53, 158, 177, 187, 197; as early prose
work *17*.95, 97–8, 106, 108, 114–16, 118–20, 137–
8; vocabulary of, *17*.154; use of *anweald* ('authority') in, *16*.142–4; lawsuits in, *17*.249, 281
Anonymus ad Cuimnanum, early Insular commentary
on *Ars Donati*, *17*.226
Anselm of Laon, author of psalm commentary,
20.160
antiphonary, of Mont-Renaud, *18*.59, 67, 73–5, 81,
89, 91; Worcester Antiphoner, *18*.88
Apocalypse of Thomas (OE version of), prose style of,
17.99, 107
Apocrypha Priscillianistica, *20*.200–2
Apollinaris, St, relics of, *19*.125, 127
Apollinarius, St, of Rheims, cult of, *19*.246
Apollonius, riddle of, *19*.104; *Historia Apollonii*,
19.105
Appendix Vergiliana, in Glastonbury manuscript,
16.207–8
Aquitaine, trading contacts of, *19*.91, 96
Arabs, medicinal terms associated with, *19*.10–11;
trade with, *19*.9–11
Arator, author of *Historia Apostolica*, *19*.237n
Arculf, bishop, in Adamnan's *De locis sanctis*, *18*.113
Arenberg Gospels, *see* gospelbooks
Aristotle, logical categories of, *17*.133
Arundel Psalter, *see* psalters
Ars Phocae, as source for glossaries, *16*.19, 44
Ascension, homilies for, *18*.109, 112

Index

Ascension, OE poem, composition of, 20.108

Asser, author of *Life of King Alfred*; mention of Lindsey, 18.6–7, 31–2; account of Danish wars, 18.120; mention of Nottingham, 18.188, 190; use of *Anglo-Saxon Chronicle* in, 17.95; on Alfred's translations, 17.125n; descriptions of Alfred in, 17.138; use of *Vetus Latina* in, 17.181; on Werferth's translation of Gregory the Great's *Dialogues*, 17.120; possible influence on English script, 16.159–60

Athelstan, king, 19.120, 126; relations with Continent, 19.245; coinage of, 18.162, 167, 186, 192, 19.97n; diploma of, 16.173–4; relics of, 17.155

Augustine, St, of Hippo, 19.119; use of etymologies, 17.35; use of *Vetus Latina*, 17.165, 185; as source for Ælfric, 17.40; influence on psalter glosses, 20.153, 161, 165; florilegium of, 20.196–7; author of *De doctrina christiana*, 18.119; discussion of rhetoric in, 16.2, 6, 7–8, 13, 14–15; author of *Soliloquies, see* Alfred, translations of; in preface of Ælfric's *Catholic Homilies*, 17.35; relics of, 19.158; sermon on Judith, 18.126; sermon on St Vincent, 19.121; providential view of history, 16.131, 132

Augustine of Canterbury, mission to Kent, 18.173

Ausonius, manuscript of, at Glastonbury, 16.206–7, 209

Autbert, St, of Arras, cult of, 19.246

authority, concept of, in OE *Orosius*, 16.138–45; in OE *Boethius*, 16.138, 140–1; in OE *Pastoral Care*, 16.138

Avienus, geographical information in, 20.128

Azarias, OE poem, in relation to other poems, 20.110

Bale, John, antiquary, list of Frithegod's writings, 17.48

Bagford, John, antiquary, as collector of manuscripts, 16.188; collection of, 17.83; fragment formerly belonging to, script of, 16.181–3, 185–8; contents of, 16.182; description of, 16.182; date of, 16.186; provenance of, 16.188–92, 194–5

balsam, 19.8–9

Bamburgh, royal centre of Northumbria, 18.30

Bardney, abbey of, in Lincolnshire, 19.98, 100

Barnack, church of, in Northamptonshire, 19.99

Bartholomew, St, cult of, 19.227; relics of, 19.156, 169, 183–4

Basil, pseudo-, author of *Admonitio ad filium spiritualem*, 18.105n, 107

Battle of Maldon, OE poem, 18.118, 120, 19.52, 56; vocabulary in, 20.71

Bede: 19.8, 37, 67, 182; and classical literature, 16.1–15; knowledge of Cicero, 16.2, 7–8, 10–15; use of Vergil, 16.5; knowledge of Greek, 16.41, 17.228, 232; view of history, 16.130–1; and pagan rhetorical tradition, 16.1–2, 8–14; use of etymologies,

17.35–8; use of *Vetus Latina*, 17.165–6, 167n, 174–5, 181, 184n; as biblical critic, 17.184; as source for Ælfric, 17.36, 40–1, 43; acknowledged in preface of Ælfric's *Catholic Homilies*, 17.35; as source for Haymo, 17.36

writings of: *De die iudicii*, manuscripts of, 19.138; author of *De natura rerum*, 19.135; author of *De temporum ratione*, 19.211; author of *Historia ecclesiastica*, use of rhetoric in, 16.9; on Aidan, 19.155, 201, 203; on Colman, 19.47–8; on Egbert, 19.47–8; on Leeds, 18.31; on Lindsey, 18.1, 6, 8–9, 31–2; on Liudhard, 20.28–30; on Oswald, 18.131n; on Paulinus, mission of, 18.174; on lawcodes, 17.96; manuscripts of, 18.38, 86; OE translation of, *see* OE *Bede*; *Historia abbatum*, 18.112; *Homiliae*, 19.62; manuscript of, 20.55, 61; *Nomina locorum*, geographical list of, 20.132–4; as source for *Solomon and Saturn II*, 20.130, 132–4, 136, 140–1; martyrology of, 19.240, 245, 245n; grammatical treatises of, rhetoric in, 16.8; *De orthographia*, 17.223, 229; *De arte metrica*, use of Prudentius, 16.214; *Epistola ad Pleguinam*, as a polemic piece, 16.9–12

commentaries of, 18.131n; use of Tyconius, 18.119; *Expositio Actuum Apostolorum*, 18.112; use of rhetoric in, 16.12–13; *In primam partem Samuhelis*, as source for *Solomon and Saturn II*, 20.40; reference to classical learning, 16.2–6; *In Proverbia*, reference to classical learning, 16.6; *In Canticum canticorum*, criticism of Julian of Eclanum in, 16.7; *Explanatio Apocalypsis*, as source for Frithegod, 17.49

Benedict, of Aniane, author of *Memoriale*, gloss on, 17.159; vocabulary of, 16.153

Benedict, St, of Monte Cassino, 19.160n, 175

Benedict Biscop, 19.202–4; return from Rome, 19.227; as collector of books, 16.192

Benedictine reform, 16.149; 18.88–9; 19.76

Benedictine Rule, 18.86, 88; vocabulary of, 17.153; gloss on, 17.159; OE translation of, by Bishop Æthelwold, 18.88, 19.50, 53

benedictionals, 19.173; of Bishop Æthelwold, 18.90, 19.163n, 164–5, 170, 179, 190; its scribe Godeman, 19.169; Paris Benedictional, 19.153; of Ramsey, 19.170; of Archbishop Robert, 19.170–1

Beowulf, 18.99, 117, 129; 19.43; J.R.R. Tolkien on, 16.191; metre of compared to *Genesis B*, 16.68, 73–4; vocabulary of, 20.68–72, 77, 79; speeches in, 20.119–20; poetic language of, 20.168–75

Berhtfrith, in the *Life of Wilfrid*, 18.11

Berhtwald, *praefectus*, in the *Life of Wilfrid*, 18.11–12

Berhtwulf, king of Mercia, 18.156

Bern Riddles, *see* riddles

Bernicia, 18.30

Bertha, wife of King Æthelberht, 20.28, 30, 33, 40–1

Besançon Gospels, *see* gospelbooks

Index

bibles, from ASE, *18*.41–2; as used in ASE, *17*.165–6; *Codex Amiatinus*, *17*.184, *18*.41, *19*.67, *see also* manuscripts, Florence, **Amiatino 1**; Royal Bible, *18*.41–3;Tokyo, Takamiya Collection, fragment, *18*.33–43; Carolingian, *18*.42; of Moutier-Grand-val, *18*.42; of Rorigon, *18*.42; from Tours, *18*.43; Vivian Bible, *18*.42

Birinus, St, relics of, *19*.157, 186

Blæcca, *praefectus*, of Lincoln, *18*.11–12, 174

Blaise, St, relics of, *19*.203

Blicking Homilies, *18*.100, 124, 131n, *19*.42, 49–50, 53; no. 3, *18*.106; no. 4, *18*.101–6; copy of in a Junius manuscript, *18*.101–2; no. 5, *18*.99, 101, 105–8; no. 6, *18*.106; no. 10, *18*.101, 105, 108–12; no. 11, *18*.101, 112–14; on SS Peter and Paul, *19*.56; manuscript of, *18*.100–1; etymologies in, *17*.42–3; prose style of, *17*.100, 134; vocabulary in, *17*.154

Bobbio, *19*.104

Boethius, tomb of, in Pavia, *19*.237; commentaries of, *16*.132; *Consolation of Philosophy*, of, OE translation of, *see* Alfred

Boniface, martyr, church of, at Rome, and cult of at Rome, *19*.217–18

Boniface, St, mission of, *16*.191; requests for books, *16*.193

Book of Cerne, *see* prayerbooks

Book of Durrow, *see* gospelbooks

Book of Kells, *see* gospelbooks

booklists, *19*.138–9; of Canterbury, *see* Canterbury; of Glastonbury, *see* Glastonbury

Bosworth Psalter, *see* psalters

Bovi, grants of land to, *18*.230–2, 239; as witness to charters, *18*.230–2

breviaries, *19*.151; primitive, *17*.87–8; Nocturns in, *17*.87

Brigitte, St, relics of, *19*.186

Brihtmær, abbot, *19*.185

Brihtwine II, bishop of Sherborne, *18*.229

Brioude, abbey of Saint-Julian, *17*.64, *19*.96

Britwell, *19*.184

Brogne, influence of, on Benedictine Reform, *18*.89

Burghal Hidage, *18*.149

Burgred, king of Mercia, *18*.157; buried at Rome, *19*.212

burials, at Derby, *18*.160; at Leicester, *18*.163; at Nottingham, *18*.203; at Worcester, *18*.174; funerary urns, *18*.195

Burwell Priory, in Lincolnshire, *19*.98n

Bury Gospels, *see* gospelbooks

Bury St Edmunds, *19*.82, 90, 93, 180, 183; book attributed to, *18*.86; Leofstan, abbot of, pilgrimage to Rome, *19*.235; missal of, *18*.53

Byrhtferth of Ramsey, *19*.37; historical writings of, *18*.156; as used by Simeon of Durham, *18*.156; author of *Vita S. Ecgwini*, lawsuits in, *17*.256; Latin prose life of St Oswald, archbishop of

York, *18*.88; *Enchiridion (Manual)*, *19*.52; vocabulary of, *17*.155; sources of, *17*.224; story of St Wilfrid's relics by, *17*.45n

Britun, William, precentor of Glastonbury, *16*.200, 202n

Cædmon, *18*.99; manuscript of works attributed to, illuminations in, *19*.99; hymn of, compositional technique of, *20*.65

Cædwalla, king of Wessex, *19*.203; tomb of, in Rome, *19*.211

Caesarius of Arles, sermons of, *18*.102–5; *Rule* of, *20*.40n

Caistor, *18*.4

calendars, *18*.84–5, *19*.90, 92, 124, 184, 235; in Bosworth Psalter, *19*.123–4; from Christ Church, Canterbury, *19*.244; from Ely, *19*.89; from Evesham, *19*.89–90; from Glastonbury, *19*.89, 123–4; in New Haven, **Beinecke 578**, *17*.69–71; in the Portiforium of St Wulstan, *18*.77; from St Peter's Abbey, Glos., *17*.69; of Sarum, *17*.69; from Tewkesbury, *17*.70; from Wessex, *19*.241, 244; from Winchcombe Abbey, *17*.69; from Worcester, *17*.70, *19*.89–90

Cambridge Psalter, *see* psalters

Cambridge Songs, manuscript of, *16*.202–3

Canterbury, *19*.82, 91, 98–100, 139–40, 155, 162–3, 165–6, 169, 175–6, 178, 181–2, 203; charter relating to, *18*.4–5; economy, pre-Viking, *18*.176; manuscripts of, *18*.33, 38–9; booklist of, *17*.227; learning at, *20*.228–9

Canterbury, St Augustine's Abbey: *19*.85, 90, 93, 133–4, 143, 154n, 157, 174, 197; books from Winchester at, *18*.87; missal of, *18*.53; reconstruction of, by Abbot Wulfric, *19*.97

Canterbury, Christ Church (cathedral): *19*.90, 93, 124, 143, 154, 156–8, 162, 167, 169, 170n, 175, 181–4, 226n; archbishops of, *18*.40; visits to Rome by, *19*.205; books from Winchester at, *18*.87; books sent to Worcester from, *18*.87; crypt of, *19*.227; liturgical books of, *18*.59, 84–5; calendar of, *19*.244; relics of St Fursa at, *19*.243; texts attributed to, *18*.86; psalter written at, *20*.27; influence of Winchester on, *17*.159–60; booklist from, *17*.226; writ of, *see* writs; charters of, *see also* charters

Canterbury, St Martin's: hoard of, *20*.27

canticles, monastic, of Lambeth Psalter, *20*.147–51, 162; OE gloss of, *20*.164

Caprasius, St, of Aulla, in AS calendars, *19*.235; cult of, *19*.245

cassia, *19*.10

Cassiodorus, author of *Expositio psalmorum*, early AS manuscripts of, *20*.53; influence on psalter glosses, *20*.153, 165

Castra, *19*.15–16

Cecilia, St, cult of, *19*.227

284

Index

Cedd, St, monastery of, at Tilbury, *20*.10

cemeteries, *18*.2; at Lovedon Hill, *18*.2; at St Paul-in-the-Bail, Lincoln, *18*.173–4, 181; at Leicester, *18*.166; outside Lincoln, *18*.174; at Newark, *18*.2; outside Nottingham, *18*.187–8; *see also* burials, settlements

Ceolfrith, bible pandects of, *18*.41; death of, at Langres, *19*.245

Ceolwulf II, king of Mercia, *18*.142–3, 144n

Cerdic, arrival of, in Britain, *17*.94–5

Cerne Abbas, *19*.64; monks from, at Abbotsbury, *18*.239

Chad, St, Mercian prose work about, style of, *17*.99, 104–14, 118, 131–2; vocabulary of, *17*.154

Charles the Bald, bibles of, *18*.42; sacramentary of, *18*.76

charms, Irish, *19*.5

Charroux, abbey church of (Poitou), *19*.97–8, 100

charters, prose style in before 900, *17*.96, 134–7; Kentish, *17*.251, 253; vocabulary of, *17*.157; lawsuits in, *17*.248, 256–8, 271–5; of Rochester, by King Eardwulf of Kent, *17*.251; of Christ Church, *18*.39; of King Offa, *17*.251; of Worcester, *17*.251, 273, 276–7; of Malmesbury, *17*.251; of Sherborne, *17*.251, 277; of King Æthelred, *17*.277, 280; *see also* Abbotsbury

Cheshire, see of, *18*.22; *see also* Domesday Book

Chester, *19*.179; St John's minster church of, *18*.22

Childebert, king of the Franks, *19*.120

chrismons, in AS charters, *17*.39

Christ, OE poem, intertextuality of, *20*.112, 121

Christina, St, of Bolsena, cult of, *19*.229, 245

Christmas, feast of, *18*.58–66, 69, 74–6, 78–80; mass for, *18*.51–2; edition of, from **Royal 5. A. XII**, *18*.91–3; for First Sunday after, *18*.53–5, 58–9; edition of, from **Royal 5. A. XII**, *18*.96–7; for Octave of, *18*.53–4, 57–9, 68–71, 78; edition of, from **Royal 5. A. XII**, *18*.96

Christopher, St, homily on, Mercian prose work, style of, *17*.99, 112

Chrodegang, bishop of Metz, author of *Regula canonicorum*, manuscript of, *17*.84, 221; OE gloss on, *17*.141; OE translation of, *17*.158, *19*.50–1, 53; vocabulary of, *17*.153

Chrysogonus, St, cult of, *19*.227

Cicero, logical categories of, *16*.133; author of *Aratea*, in ASE, *17*.230

Circumcision, feast of, *18*.71

Ciriacus, St, relics of, *19*.157, 186

Claudius Pontificals, *see* pontificals

Cluny, gradual of, *18*.73n; influence on Saint-Denis, *18*.73

Cnut, king of England, *18*.208, *19*.81n, 82, 84, 86, 88–9, 91–3, 99, 126, 128, 155–9, 161, 170, 174, 177, 179–86, 203; charters of, *18*.219–20, 222, 226, 229–32, 237, 239; lawsuits of, *17*.280; treatment of adultery in laws of, *20*.25; coinage of, *see*

coinage, of Cnut; die-cutting in reign of, *18*.186; Scandinavian followers of, *16*.306, *18*.209, 230; pilgrim to Rome, *19*.86–7; promoting saints' cults, *19*.86–8; relations with Continent, *19*.245; in Stamford *18*.197

coinage, *18*.171, 176, *19*.41; Gaulish, *20*.28; Le Dorat hoard, *19*.96–8; at Mucking, *20*.14; Scandinavian, *16*.306, *18*.203; Visigothic, *20*.28–9

coinage of Æthelred II, *18*.186, *19*.96; of Alfred, *18*.186, *19*.97n; of Anlaf Guthfrithsson, *20*.222; of Anlaf Sihtricsson, *20*.222; of Athelstan, *18*.162, 167, 186, 192, *19*.97n, *20*.221–2; of Cnut, *16*.233–307; of Eadred, *19*.97n; of Edgar, *18*.162; of Edmund, *19*.97n, *20*.221–2; of Edward the Elder, *19*.97n, *20*.222; of Harold I, *16*.233–307; of Harthacnut, *16*.233–307; of Plegmund, *19*.97n, *20*.222; of Sihtric Sihtricsson, *18*.186, *20*.222

coinage minted at Canterbury, *20*.38; *see also* Liudhard, coin of; at Derby, *18*.162; at Leicester, *18*.163, 167; at Lincoln, *18*.24, 182, 185–7; at Nottingham, *18*.192–3; at Stamford, *18*.197, 201; at York, *18*.24, 176, 182

Coleman of Worcester, OE prose life of St Wulstan, *19*.159–60; *see also* Wulfstan II

Colman, *see* Bede, *Historia ecclesiastica*

Cologne, *19*.180, 182

Columbanus, St, at Besançon, *19*.240; in *Anglo-Saxon Chronicle*, *17*.116

comitatus, as source of imagery in OE poetry, *20*.65–6

computus, *19*.136; of Bede, *De temporum ratione*, *19*.211; of Byrhtferth of Ramsey, *Enchiridion* (*Manual*), *19*.52

Conques, abbey of, *19*.98n, 100; cartulary of, *19*.94

Copenhagen Gospels, *see* gospelbooks

Corbie, liturgical books of, *18*.59, 81, 83–4; *see also* graduals; monks of, at Abingdon, *18*.83, 90n

Cotton Gnomes, vocabulary of, *20*.71

Cotton Maxims, technical terms of, *20*.70

councils, of Arles, of 314, *18*.174; of Clovesho, settling disputes at, *17*.251; of 746/7, *17*.96n; of 803, *18*.173; Fifth Council of Constantinople, of 553, *20*.155; council of 567, *20*.40; of Hatfield, of 680, *20*.155; Great Council of Southern English, *17*.273, 275

Coventry, *19*.185

cross, symbolism of, *20*.41; types of, *20*.34–8, 41; hymns to, *see* Venantius Fortunatus, hymns; miracles of, *20*.32–3; reliquary of *20*.32–4, 37–41; Irish High Cross, *20*.41; Greek *Hetoimasia*, *20*.35–6; True Cross of St Radegund, *see* Radegund, cross of; Holy Cross, cult of, *19*.226; Brussels Cross, *20*.227

Crowland, *19*.90, 156; 185

Cuthbert, St, cult of, *16*.178

Cuthswith, abbess in Worcestershire, book of, *16*.193

285

Cyneheard, bishop of Winchester, *19*.7

Cynewulf, OE poet, *19*.107, *20*.115–16; use of military imagery by, *20*.65–6; *see also Ascension, Christ, Elene* and *Juliana*

Cynewulf, king of Wessex, diploma of, *16*.167

Cyprian, use of *Vetus Latina, 17*.165, 185

Danelaw, *18*.2, 137, 150, 152, 158, 161, 204; *19*.17

Daniel, OE poem, *20*.108; relation to other poems, *20*.110

Darley abbey, cartulary of, *18*.157–8

De mirabilibus urbis Romae, of Master Gregory, *19*.200

De situ orbis, source for *Solomon and Saturn II, 20*.127

De temporibus anticristi, vocabulary in, *17*.154

Defensor, author of *Liber scintillaris*, OE gloss on, *17*.156, *19*.52

Derby, burial remains at, *18*.160; coinage of, *18*.162; Iron Age history, *18*.201, Little Chester in, *18*.154–5, 160–1; origins of, *18*.153–5; Roman history of, *18*.153–4, 201; pre-Saxon history of, *18*.202; early and mid-Saxon history of, *18*.155–7, 190

Dernstall, St Martin's parish church in, *18*.24–5, 39

Dicuil, author of *Liber de mensura orbis terrae*, as source of *Solomon and Saturn II, 20*.127–8

Dionysius Exiguus, *20*.57–8

Pedanius Dioscorides, herbalist, author of *De materia medica, 17*.17, 19–21, 199, 204

Domesday Book, *18*.135, 137, 152, 157–8; lawsuits in, *17*.249, 252–5, 257, 271; concerning Abbotsbury, *18*.209–10, 226–7, 230, 233; concerning Cheshire, *18*.22; concerning Derby, *18*.161–2, 190; concerning Leicester, *18*.167–8; concerning Lincoln, *18*.177, 182; concerning Lincolnshire, *18*.20–3; concerning Nottingham, *18*.190, 192; concerning Scandinavian population, *18*.203; concerning Stamford, *18*.196–7; concerning York, *18*.23

Dominic of Evesham, author of *Vita S. Ecgwini*, as evidence of lawsuits, *17*.256

Donatus, author of *Ars maior*, as source of Greek in ASE, *17*.226

Dorchester, *18*.3n, 22–4

Dositheus, author of *Ars grammatica, 17*.225

Doué-la-Fontaine, pottery finds at, *19*.96

Downpatrick, Ireland, gradual from, *18*.59, *see also* graduals

The Dream of the Rood, OE poem, *19*.106; vocabulary of, *20*.71; military imagery in, *20*.65; relation to other OE poems, *20*.110

Dunstan, archbishop of Canterbury, *19*.76n, 139; as student at Glastonbury, *16*.197; abbacy at Glastonbury, *16*.198; as patron saint of Glastonbury, *16*.198n; and Glastonbury revival, *16*.197n; legal dispute of, *17*.255; liturgical feast of, *19*.170n; *see also* script

Durham, books from Winchester at, *18*.87; gradual

for cathedral priory, *18*.59; *see also* graduals

Durham, OE poem, vocabulary of, *20*.76

Eadburh, queen, refuge at Pavia, *19*.236

Eadgifu, queen, legal disputes of, *17*.252

Eadhæd, bishop of Ripon, *18*.9

Eadmer of Canterbury, *19*.183; discussion of Frithegod, *17*.47n, 48n, 57

Eadnoth I, bishop of Dorchester, *18*.23

Eadred, king, *19*.130, 183; campaigns of, *17*.45; coins of, *19*.97n

Eadric, king of Kent, laws of, *18*.16

Eadric Streona, law disputes of, *17*.251

Eadwald, scribe, *16*.166

Eadwig, king, charter of, concerning Abbotsbury, *18*.225–6, 238; lawsuits of, *17*.280; control of land south of the Thames, *18*.227

Eadwig Basan, scribe, *19*.155, 173–6, 178–9, 182; of Eadwig Gospels, *see* gospelbooks; of Eadwig Psalter, *see* psalters; of York Gospels, *see* gospelbooks

Eadwig Gospels, *see* gospelbooks

Eadwig Psalter, *see* psalters

Eadwine Psalter, *see* psalters

Eadwulf, bishop of Lindsey, *18*.3–5

Ealdred, bishop of Worcester and archbishop of York, relations with Continent, *19*.245; trip to Cologne, *19*.160

Ealhmund, in northern annals for 732–802, *18*.156; in Byrhtferth of Ramsey's historical writings, *18*.156; in *List of Saints' Resting Places, 18*.156; in Simeon of Durham's *Historia regum, 18*.156

Earnwig, abbot of Peterborough, *19*.177–8; psalter of (now lost), *19*.173; sacramentary of (now lost), *19*.173

East Anglia, *18*.137, 149, 150; episcopal succession of, *16*.149

East Midlands, *18*.150

Easter season, homilies for, *18*.106, 108–9

Ecgberht, *Poenitentiale Ecgberti, 17*.214; *see also* Bede

Ecgfrith, king of Northumbria, *18*.9; concerning Lindsey, *18*.173

Ecgwine, St, bishop of Worcester, cult of, *19*.84, 88, 101; in Worcester calendar, *20*.204; founder of Evesham, *19*.84; Latin prose life by Byrhtferth, *19*.84

Edda, see Snorri Sturluson

Edgar, king of England, *19*.125, 127, 131, 183, 206; accession to throne of Mercia and Northumbria, *18*.226; charters of, concerning Abbotsbury, *18*.220, 226–7, 238; coinage of, *18*.162, 167, 197; laws of, *18*.21; relations with Continent, *19*.245; monastic reform of, *17*.133; monetary reform of, *16*.233; lawsuits during reign of, *17*.278–81

Edith, queen, *19*.100; commemoration of, at La Chaise-Dieu, *19*.95; royal church of, at Stamford, *18*.196

Edith, St, of Wilton, Latin life of by Goscelin, in prose and verse, *19*.186; relics of, *19*.186; shrine of, *19*.157; taught by Radbod of Rheims, *19*.242

Edmund, St, King of East Anglia, at Bury St Edmunds, *19*.158; Latin prose life by Abbo, *19*.226; OE prose life by Ælfric, *18*.120

Edmund I, king, *18*.186, 207, *19*.156; laws of, *20*.229; coins of, *19*.97n; Viking conquests of, *18*.150, 176; at Derby, *18*.157; at Leicester, *18*.167

Edmund Ironside, great geld of, *16*.235

Edward the Elder, king, coins of, *19*.97n; foundation of *burhs*, at Nottingham, *18*.198, 204; at Stamford, *18*.204; reconquests of Viking lands, *18*.144, 153, 190–1

Edward the Confessor, king, *19*.95, 183–4; charters of, *18*.208; concerning Abbotsbury, *18*.220, 222, 228, 231–4, 238–9; concerning Shaftesbury, *18*.230; relics of, *19*.186; wife of, *18*.135; moneyers of, *16*.233; lawsuits during the reign of, *17*.280; *Vita Ædwardi*, legal dispute in, *17*.253

Edwin, king, politics of, *17*.253

Elder Edda, *19*.26

Eleanor of Aquitaine, *19*.81

Elene, OE poem, *18*.117, *19*.43; vocabulary of, *20*.71; composition of, *20*.108, 111

Eleusippus, Speusippus and Meleusippus, SS of Langres, entry in Bede's *Martyrology*, *19*.240, 245, 245n

Ely, *19*.90–1, 154, 157, 174, 185; calendar of, *19*.89; *Liber Eliensis*, *19*.174, 185; legal disputes in, *17*.257–8

Emerentiana and Eulalia, SS, cult of, *19*.227

Emma, queen, *19*.87–8, 92, 97, 156–9, 161, 169, 174, 177, 179–88

Encomium Emmae, *19*.180, 182

enigmata, of Aldhelm, *see* Aldhelm; of Symphosius, *see* Symphosius; *see also* riddles

Epiphany, feast of, *18*.53; chants for the Mass, *18*.69

Eucherius of Lyon, author of *Instructiones*, glosses on *16*.26n

Eulalia, St, *see* Emerentiana

Eusebius of Caesarea, history of, compared to Orosius, *16*.129

Evesham abbey, *19*.88–9, 93, 99–101, 185–6; calendars of, *19*.89–90; chronicle of, *17*.256, 258, *19*.82, 156; cults at, of St Ecgwine, *19*.84, 91; St Hilary, *19*.92, 94; St Odulf, *19*.82; St Radegund, *19*.91, 94; St Wigstan, *19*.82; pilgrims from Aquitaine at, *19*.89

Excerptiones Pseudo-Ecgberti, *20*.217, 219

Exeter, *19*.90, 92, 126; cult of St Vincent at, *19*.126; litany of, *19*.92; papal bull of Eugenius II, confirmation of lands of, *18*.242, 242n; relic list of, *19*.120

Exeter Book, *19*.104, .106–7, 109, 112, 116

Exodus, OE poem, compared to Latin source, *17*.169; *Vetus Latina* in, *17*.182–3; translation of, *20*.108

Expositio hymnorum, *see* glosses

Eynsham, *19*.64, 131

Fabian, St, entry in litany, *19*.161n

Faith, St (Sainte-Foi), of Conques, cult of, *19*.94; in English calendars, *19*.89

Faritius, abbot of Abingdon, *19*.128

The Fates of the Apostles, OE poem, poetic language in, *20*.170

Faversham, Kent, *19*.20

Felicity, St, relics of, *19*.186

Felix and Adauctus, SS, alleluia in the Mass for, *18*.67

Felix, author of *Vita S. Guthlaci*, *see* Guthlac, St, *vita* of

Ferriolus and Ferritiolus, SS, cult of, *19*.240–1

Five Boroughs, *18*.143, 201–5; English reconquest of, *18*.150; as part of Seven Boroughs, *18*.151; as Viking settlement, *18*.150, 152–3; *see also* Derby, Leicester, Lincoln, Nottingham and Stamford

Fleury-sur-Loire, *19*.76n, 81, 100, 138–9; influence on Benedictine Reform, *18*.89; at Worcester, *18*.88; AS books sent to, *18*.50

'Florence' of Worcester, chronicle of, *19*.187

Florentinus, St, relics of, *19*.155n, 161n

Florilegium Frisingense, *20*.200

Fordwich, settlement near Canterbury, *18*.16

Fortunatus, *see* Venantius Fortunatus

The Fortunes of Men, OE poem, *19*.106; intertextuality of, *20*.111–12

Fredegar, author of *Chronicon*, as source for *Solomon and Saturn II*, *20*.136

Frederick II, emperor, *19*.234

Frisian, Old, relationship to Old English, *17*.7–13

Frithegod, of Canterbury, *19*.95–6, 100; name of, *17*.46–7, 61–2, 65; writings of, *17*.48–9; use of Greek, *17*.50–1; later career of, *17*.61–5; origin of, *17*.61–5

    author of *Breuiloquium uitae Wilfridi*: description of, *17*.46; scholarship on, *17*.46; origin of, *17*.46–7; style and diction of, *17*.50–1; manuscripts of, *17*.51–6; origin of manuscripts, *17*.56–7; relationship of manuscripts, *17*.58–61; in Christ Church catalogue, *17*.57; in St Augustine's catalogue, *17*.57

Fulbert, bishop of Chartres, relations with Cnut, *19*.86, 180

Fulda, liturgy of, *18*.57

Fuldrad, abbot of Saint-Vaast, *19*.244

Fulgentius, as source of Ælfric, *17*.39; author of *Epistola II ad Gallam uiduam*, *18*.123

Fursa, St, founder of abbey of Péronne, 243; relics of, at Christ Church, *19*.243; *Vita S. Fursei*, *17*.116n

Geffrei Gaimar, author of *L'estoire des Engleis*, *19*.125

genealogies, AS royal, *18*.173

Genesis A, OE poem: sources of, *17*.177–9; as liturgy, *17*.183–4; Latin textual basis of, *17*.163–89; compared to Vulgate, *17*.163–4, 166–7, 170–89; compared to *Vetus Latina*, *17*.163, 166–89; compared to Greek bible, *17*.167–9, 186, 185n; compared to Hebrew bible, *17*.168–9; Hispano-Visigothic influence on, *17*.185; poetic language of, *20*.168–75, 180–1, 185

Genesis B, OE poem: metre of, scholarship on, *16*.67–8; compared to *Beowulf*, *16*.68, 73–4; compared to Old Saxon fragment, *16*.68–88; distribution of verbs, *16*.83; particles in, *16*.72–88; auxiliary verbs in, *16*.84–6; finite verbs in, *16*.80–4; adverbs in, *16*.76–80; adjectives in, *16*.75–6; infinitives in, *16*.86–8; verse types in, *16*.101–2; alliteration in, *16*.111–20, 121; poetic language of, *20*.170

Genesis, Old Saxon, description of, *16*.67–9, 102, 106

Geoffrey du Loroux, *alias* Babion, sermons of, *20*.205, 212–16

George, St, relics of, *19*.160–1n, 186

Germanus, monk of Fleury, influence at Worcester, *18*.88

Gervase of Canterbury, *19*.158, 181, 183–5

Gerward, librarian of Louis the Pious, booklist of, *16*.181; identity of, *16*.190–2, 195

Géry, St, of Arras, cult of, *19*.246

Ghent, influence on English monasticism, *18*.89, *19*.224

The Gifts of Men, OE poem, intertextuality of, *20*.112

Giles, St, of Provence, cult of, *19*.94; in English calendars, *19*.89

Giraldus Cambrensis, on Lincoln, in his *Vita S. Remigii*, *18*.20n

Giso of Wells, *see also* sacramentaries

Glastonbury Abbey, *19*.124–6, 129–30, 139, 156, 163, 165, 174, 186, 197, 244; pre-Conquest manuscripts of, *16*.197–212; books sent to Worcester, *18*.87; revival of learning at, *16*.197; calendar of, *19*.89, 123–4; cartulary of, *18*.207–8; plainchant at, *18*.90n; booklist of, *16*.198, 202; catalogue at, *16*.200–1, 203, 208; riddle collections at, *16*.202–3; chronicle by John of Glastonbury, *19*.125; crypt of, *19*.90; cult of St Vincent, *19*.125–9; massacre of monks at, in 1081, *19*.90n; 1184 fire at, *16*.198n; dissolution of, *16*.198–9

glossaries: list of, *16*.17n; Latin, *20*.152, 165; Anglo-Saxon, Irish influence on, *16*.29–30; Greek, *17*.219–21, 232; medical, *17*.32; of herbs, *17*.22

glossaries (individual): *AA Glossary*, *16*.32–4, 43; *Abavus Glossary*, *16*.32–3, 43; *Abba Glossary*, *16*.33–43; *Abolita Glossary*, *16*.19, 31–2, 38, 42; editions of, *16*.19n; *Abstrusa Glossary*, *16*.19, 31–2, 38, 42; editions of, *16*.19n; *Affatim Glossary*, *16*.30–3; *17*.152; *Arma Glossary*, *16*.38; *Cleopatra*

Glossary, medical glosses in, *17*.27; *Corpus Glossary*, relation to other Anglo-Saxon glossaries, *16*.17–18; editions of, *16*.17n, description of, *16*.19, 30–1, 44; medical glosses in, *17*.28; *Cyrillus Glossary*, *16*.42–3; *Epinal-Erfurt Glossary*, relation to other Anglo-Saxon glossaries, *16*.17–18; editions of, *16*.17n; date of *16*.18n; description of, *16*.19–44; medical glosses in, *17*.28; *Erfurt II and III*, *16*.18; editions of, *16*.18n; description of, *16*.19, 30–4, 44; *Grimm Glossary*, *16*.23–4; *Harley Glossary*, *17*.223; *Leiden Glossary*, as compiled in England, *16*.17; description of, *16*.19–44; *Liber Glossarum*, *16*.32–3; *Milan Glossary*, *16*.27, 44; *Paris Glossary*, *16*.24; *Philoxenus Glossary*, *16*.40, 42–3; *Scholica graecarum glossarum*, *17*.223–4, 232–46, *19*.133; *Werden Glossaries*, *16*.18; editions of *16*.17n; description of, *16*.19, 30–1, 34–44 of Abbo, *19*.133–4, 136–7, 139–44; of Placidus, *16*.31n, 32, 33

glosses: in OE, Kentish, *17*.75; Mercian, *17*.104, 110; Northumbrian, *17*.110; on the Continent, *16*.191; in Old High German, on the Continent, *16*.191

glosses: on the Bible, *16*.25; on Leviticus, *16*.26, 44; on the psalter, *17*.95, *20*.173–5, 182–3; in the Lambeth Psalter, in Latin, *20*.151–5, 163; in OE, *20*.143, 145, 147, 149, 151, 154–5, 161–4, 165n; on the Regius Psalter, *18*.86; on the Eadwine Psalter, *19*.71–2; on a Worcester psalter, *18*.84; on gospels, Lindisfarne, *17*.110, 144; Rushmore, *17*.110, 155; on the Durham Ritual, *17*.110; on the Durham Hymnal, *17*.153, 158–9; on Defensor's *Liber scintillaris*, *19*.52; on the *Expositio hymnorum*, *17*.140–1, 144, 153, 158–9, *20*.164; on Alcuin, *De virtutibus et vitiis*, *17*.156; on Isidore's *Synonyma*, *16*.193; on Nonius Marcellus's *Compendiosa doctrina*, *16*.31–2; on Orosius's *Historiae adversum paganos*, *16*.26, 28–9; on Greek in Boethius, *De consolatione Philosophiae*, *17*.222, 227; on Frithegod, *17*.52–6

Gloucester, books attributed to, *18*.86

Godwine, Earl, legal dispute of, *17*.257

Gnomes, OE, *19*.112

Godeman, scribe, *19*.169, 169n, 171, 190

Godgifu (Godiva), wife of Earl Leofric, *18*.23

Gorze, monastic reform at, *19*.242

Goscelin, monk of Saint-Bertin, *19*.186; author of *Vita S. Wulfsini*, legal disputes in, *17*.254–5; *see also* Edith, St

gospelbooks, *18*.45, 58, 90, *19*.151–2, 154, 157, 165, 168, 172–4, 176, 179, 227; OE, editions of, *17*.67n; West Saxon, *17*.67, *19*.42, 49–50, 53, 59, 63; Yale fragments of, *17*.72–82; description of, *17*.75–80; vocabulary of, *17*.155; Gothic, *Codex Argenteus Upsaliensis*, *20*.45, 53

gospelbooks (individual): Arenberg Gospels, *19*.153, 165, 169–70, 172, 182; Besançon Gospels,

19.153, 170–2, 179, 188–91, 195, 240; Bury Gospels, *19*.153, 175; Copenhagen Gospels, *19*.165–70, 172, 179, 181, 191–5; of the Earl of Chester, *19*.180–1; Book of Durrow, *20*.41; Eadwig Gospels, *19*.153; Grimbald Gospels, *19*.98, 166, 182; Hanover Gospels, *19*.175–6, 182; of Judith of Flanders, *19*.180–1; Kederminster Gospels, *19*.177n; Book of Kells, *20*.41; Lindisfarne Gospels, *18*.34, 42, *19*.63, *see also* glosses, gospelbooks; Rushmore Gospels, *19*.42, 63; *see also* glosses, gospelbooks; Trinity Gospels, *19*.166, 168, 172; York Gospels, *19*.166–7, 169, 170–2, 175, 179, 182

graduals, *18*.54; written at Christ Church, Canterbury, *18*.59, *see also* manuscripts, Durham, Univ. Lib., **Cosin v. v. 6**; of Cluny, *18*.73n, *see also* manuscripts, Paris, BN, **lat. 18010**; of Downpatrick, Ireland, *18*.59; *see also* manuscripts, Oxford, Bod. Lib., **Rawl. C. 892**; for Durham, *18*.59; *see also* manuscripts, Durham, Univ. Lib., **Cosin v. v. 6**; of Mont-Renaud, *18*.59, 67, 73–5, 81, 89, 91, *see also* manuscripts, Mont-Renaud, s.n.; of Nevers, *18*.61, 68; of Rheinau, *18*.68–9; of **Royal 5. A. XII**, *18*.58–77, 81–4, 89–90; of Saint-Denis, *18*.58–9, *see also* manuscripts, Paris, Bibl. Maz. **384**; of Saint-Vaast, *18*.58–9, 61, *see also* manuscripts, Paris, BN, **lat. 9436**; Cambrai, Bibl. Mun. **75**; of Worcester, *18*.59, *see also* manuscripts, Worcester, Cath. Lib., **F. 160**

Greek, knowledge of, in ASE, *17*.55, 61, 63, 217–46; learning of, *17*.230–2; monastic centres of, *17*.231–2; transliteration of, *17*.218–19; vocabulary of, *17*.219–24, 228, 231–2; syntax of, *17*.224–7, 232; etymologies based on, *17*.221–3; works wholly in, *17*.228–9; bilingual works in, *17*.229; bilingual Alleluia, *18*.60–6; glossaries of, *see* glossaries, Greek

Gregory the Great, pope, *19*.85, 160n; cult of, *19*.202–3; tomb of, at St Peter's, Rome, *19*.211; use of etymologies by, *17*.35; as source for Ælfric, *17*.37, 38n, 39–40, 42–3, *20*.114; as source for Cynewulf, *20*.113–14; letter to Bertha, in Kent, *20*.40; as acknowledged in Ælfric's preface to *Catholic Homilies*, *17*.35; as author of *Dialogi*, manuscript of, at Werden, *20*.55; OE translation of, *see* Werferth; as author of *Regula pastoralis*, *19*.174; OE translation of, *see* Alfred, *Pastoral Care*; author of *Homilia in Ezechielem*, manuscript of, *20*.56; author of *Moralia in Iob*, manuscript of, *20*.60; author of homily on Ascension, *18*.112; author of sermon for the feast of SS Nereus and Achilleus, *18*.111–12

Gregory of Tours, *19*.120, 212–13, 240; on Æthelberht and Bertha of Kent, *20*.30, 33; on the True Cross relics, *20*.39

Grimbald, St, of Saint-Bertin, *19*.171

Grimbald Gospels, *see* gospelbooks

Grímnismál, *19*.26

Guthlac B, OE poem, vocabulary of, *20*.72

Guthlac, St, office for his feast, *18*.85; sister of, *19*.212; *vita* of, by Felix, *18*.87; vocabulary in *20*.72–3; in Glastonbury catalogue, *16*.201; Mercian prose work about, style of, *17*.99, 112–13, 134

Guthrum, *18*.152

Hadrian, abbot of Canterbury, *19*.204

hagiography, lawsuits found in, *16*.249–50, 254, 256–8

Hanover Gospels, *see* gospelbooks

Harold Harefoot, king, *19*.94; legal dispute of *17*.276; *see also* writs, of Harold Harefoot

Harold I, king, *19*.95

Harold II, king, *19*.95

Harthacnut, king, *19*.177, 187; charters of, *18*.208, 231; legal dispute of, *17*.253, 257; coinage of, *see* coinage, of Harthacnut

Harwood, William, *16*.211–12

Hastings, battle of, *19*.81, 101

Hávamál, *19*.25, 26

Haymo of Auxerre, use of etymologies by, *17*.35–6, 38; as source for Ælfric, *17*.36–8, 40; acknowledged in the preface of Ælfric's *Catholic Homilies*, *17*.35; homiliary of, *see* homiliaries

Hebraicum, of Jerome, *see* psalters

Hegesippus, author of *De bello Iudaico*, *16*.191

Heiric of Auxerre, *19*.62

Helen, St, relics of, *19*.186, *20*.32, 40

Heliand, metrics of, *16*.106; vocabulary of, *20*.71; poetic language of, *20*.170

Henry of Anjou, king, *19*.81

Henry of Blois, abbot of Glastonbury, *16*.210–11; bishop of Winchester, *19*.157

Heptateuch, Werden fragments of, *20*.43–63; script of, *20*.52, 60

herb gardens, *17*.31

Herbarium, of pseudo-Apuleius, *17*.17–20, 28, 31, 100–2, 197–9, 204; OE translation of, *19*.5–6, 10; description of, *17*.16, 18–33, 210; *see also* medicine, works of

Herbert of Bosham, *19*.77

herbs, of Anglo-Saxon England, *see* medicine, herbs used in

Hermeneumata, definition of, *16*.19n; source of, *16*.26n, 43; in *Epinal-Erfurt Glossary*, *16*.23, 25–7

Hilary, St, of Poitiers, *19*.87; cult of, *19*.88, 92, 94, at Evesham, *19*.92, 94; at Poitiers, *19*.87; at Worcester, *19*.92, 94; entry of, in English calendars, *19*.89; life of, by Venantius Fortunatus, *19*.93

Hildebert, archbishop of Tours, *20*.205, 216

Hildigrim, bishop of Châlons-sur-Marne, *20*.55–7

Hincmar, archbishop of Rheims, building of churches, *19*.242

Hisperica famina, *19*.5

Index

Historia Apollonii, see Apollonius

Hlothhere, king of Kent, laws of, *18*.16

hoards, of Forum (House of the Vestal Virgins) in Rome, *20*.221–2; tags from, *see* tags; of Beeston Tor Cave, Staffs., *20*.223; of Gerete, Fardhem, Gotland, *20*.224

Holland, Lincs., *18*.2–3

Holme, parish church of St Benet's (Norfolk), *19*.158, 161

Holme Riddles, *see* riddles

Holy Cross, *see* Cross, Holy, cult of

Holy Innocents, Mass for the feast of, *18*.52, 54, 58, 59n, 67–8, 75–6, 78, 82–3; edition of, from **Royal 5. A. XII**, *18*.94–5

homiliaries, *18*.100: of Haymo of Auxerre, *19*.121; of Smaragdus, *19*.121–2; of Paul the Deacon, *17*.36–7, 39, 88, *19*.121–2

homilies, *18*.85–6, 88, 107; *see also* Ælfric, *Catholic Homilies*; Blickling Homilies; Vercelli Homilies

Honorius I, pope, *19*.200

Horncastle, *18*.4

Horsham-St Faith, parish church of (Norfolk), *19*.94, 98n

Hrabanus Maurus, *19*.68; use of *Vetus Latina*, *17*.181; author of *Expositio in Librum Iudith*, *18*.123, 125–6, 129

Hugh Candidus, author of chronicle of Peterborough, *19*.160n, 161

Hugsvinnsmál, *19*.25

Hwicce, *18*.9

hymnals, of Canterbury, *17*.158; Durham Hymnal, *see* glosses; *Expositio hymnorum*, *see* glosses; in New Haven, **Beinecke 578**, *17*.67; *Hymnarium Moissacense*, *17*.49

Ine, king of the West Saxons, books of, *16*.197; at Rome, *19*.203–4, 212

Ingulf, abbot of Abingdon, *19*.128, 183

Ipswich, trading centre, *18*.16

Irish missionaries, influence on biblical text, *17*.185–6

Isidore, bishop of Seville, *19*.26, 37; view on history, *16*.130, 132; theory of etymologizing, *17*.35; *Etymologiae*, manuscripts of, *16*.165–7, *20*.53; as source for *Solomon and Saturn II*, *20*.128, 132, 135–6, 141; as source of Greek terms, *17*.221, 223–4, 233–46; as source of Greek learning, *17*.231–2; as source of geographical information, *20*.132; author of *De differentiis uerborum*, *19*.135, 138; author of *De natura rerum*, *19*.134–6; author of *Synonyma*, *see* glosses; author of *De ortu et obitu patrum*, manuscript of, *20*.53; author of *Allegoriae*, manuscript of, *20*.53

itineraries, to Holy Land, *20*.129–30; *see also* Rome

James, St, *19*.169

Jerome, St, use of etymologies, *17*.35; Ciceronian dream of (*Ep.* xx), *16*.2, 4–5, 10, 14; and Cicero,

16.2; as translator of the Bible, *17*.164, 180; author of Gallicanum version of psalms, *see* psalters, versions of; author of *Hebraicum*, *see* psalters, versions of; use of *Vetus Latina*, *17*.165; acknowledged in preface of Ælfric's *Catholic Homilies*, *17*.35; author of *Epistola lxxxix ad Saluinam*, *18*.126; author of commentary on Ephesians, *17*.37; author of commentary on Ecclesiastes, *16*.193; author of commentary on Isaiah, manuscript of, at Werden, *20*.54, 61; author of *De situ et nominibus locorum hebraicorum*, as source for *Solomon and Saturn II*, *20*.130, 132; as source for Bede's *Nomina locorum*, *20*.132; author of *Liber interpretationis hebraicorum nominum*, *17*.37, 43; author of *Aduersus Heluidium*, Bede's knowledge of, *16*.10, 14; author of *Aduersus Iouinianum*, as source for William of Malmesbury, *17*.50

John the Evangelist, St, *19*.161n, 169, 176, 187; Mass for the feast of, *18*.59, 83; chants of, *18*.69; edition of, from **Royal 5. A. XII**, *18*.94

John the Baptist, St, liturgical feast of, *18*.102

John XII, pope, *19*.207

John XV, pope, *19*.207

John of Glastonbury, chronicle of, *19*.125

John Chrysostom, St, sermons of, *18*.47n

Judith, homily on, by Ælfric, *18*.117, 126; sermon on, by Augustine, *18*.126

Judith, biblical book, *18*.117, 124, 126, 129–31, 133

Judith, OE poem, *18*.117–18, 120–2, 19–43; allegory in *18*.118, 120–1; use of sources in, the battle, *18*.131–3; the beheading, *18*.126–8; the display of the head, *18*.129–31; the feast, *18*.122–6

Judith of Flanders, *19*.179

Judoc, St, *19*.171

Julian of Eclanum, as translator and transmitter of Theodore of Mopsuestia, *20*.254; influence on Lambeth Psalter, *20*.165

Julian, bishop of Toledo, author of *Prognosticon futuri saeculi*, in Glastonbury catalogue, *16*.201–3

Juliana, St, OE verse life by Cynewulf, *18*.118, 120, 127, *19*.43–4; composition of, *20*.108, 121

Jumièges, abbey church of, *19*.97, 181, AS books sent to, *18*.50

Junius Psalter, *see* psalters

Justinus, author of *Epitome*, tradition of, *16*.183; Weinheim fragment of, *16*.181–96; origin of, *16*.181, 183–4; provenance of, *16*.189–92, 194–5; script of, *16*.181, 183, 187–8

Juvenal, author of *Satirae*, in ASE, *17*.230

Karolus magnus et Leo papa, attributed to Einhard, vocabulary in, *20*.78

Kederminster Gospels, *see* gospelbooks

Kent, charters of, *18*.231; manuscripts associated with, *18*.43; script associated with, *18*.40

Kentish psalm 50, *19*.75–6, 79; *Hebraicum* psalter in, *19*.67–8; *Romanum* psalter in, *19*.70–1

Index

Kesteven, Lincs., *18*.2–3
Knutsford, place-name of, *19*.14–16
Kuhn's Law of Particles, *16*.67–8, 71–2, 78–9, 83–4, 88–103, 110

La Chaise-Dieu, abbey church of (Auvergne), *19*.94–6, 100
Lacnunga, *17*.16, 100, 102, 195, 205–6, *19*.5–6, 10, 12
Lambeth Psalter, *see* psalters
Lanfranc, archbishop of Canterbury, *19*.76
Lantfred, as author of poems, *16*.210; letter of, *16*.210; use of Frithegod's style, *17*.57n; author of *Translatio et miracula S. Swithuni*, *16*.204
Lathcen, author of *Moralia*, as represented by earliest Insular script, *20*.53
Lauderdale Orosius, *see* manuscripts, London, BL, **Add. 47967**
Laurence, St, cult of, *19*.120–3, 132, 226; in homiliaries, *19*.122; in litanies, *19*.121, 161n; in missals, *19*.122; relics of, *19*.121
lawcodes: prose style in, before 900, *17*.96, 119, 130, 137; Christianity's influence on, *20*.21; burial rights in, *20*.9; preface to the laws of Alfred, *see* Alfred, laws of
lawcodes, individual: of Æthelred II, *18*.150; of Alfred, *see* Alfred; of Eadric, king of Kent, *18*.16; of Edgar, *18*.21; of Hlothhere, *18*.16
lawsuits, AS, hand-list of, *17*.247–81
lectionaries, *18*.58, 85, *19*.152, 227; *Vetus Latina* and Greek readings of, *17*.183; *see Ordines Romani*
lectionaries, individual: of Alcuin, *18*.58; of Corbie, *18*.58; of Florence, *19*.173, 175, 182, 227; of Murbach, *18*.58; in **Royal 5. A. XII**, *18*.58, 75–6, 89; in Würzburg, *18*.58, 83
Leechbook, Bald's, *17*.16, 27, 32, 100, 101n, 102, 195, 197–9, 204–8, 214; *19*.5–8, 12; sources of, *17*.15
Leeds, place-name of, *18*.31
Legend of St Giles, OE vocabulary of, *17*.154
Legend of the Seven Sleepers, OE vocabulary of, *17*.154
legendaries, *Cotton-Corpus Legendary*, *19*.129–30
Leicester: coinage of, *18*.167; archaeology of, *18*.168; place-name of, *18*.163; see of, Middle Anglian diocese, *18*.166; defunct after 872, *18*.167
Leicester: history of, Iron Age, *18*.163, 201; Roman, *18*.163–5, 201; pre-Saxon, *18*.202; early and middle Saxon, *18*.165–7; Anglo-Scandinavian, *18*.135, 167–8
Leland, John, antiquary, compiler of Glastonbury booklist, *16*.198, 202
Leningrad Bede, script of, *16*.186–8; *see also* manuscripts, Leningrad, Public Lib., **Q. v. 1.18**
Lent, homilies for, *18*.101, 106
Leo IV, pope, and *Schola Saxonum* in Rome, *19*.205, 212
Leofric, bishop of Exeter, *19*.126; books of, *18*.50
Leofric, earl, *18*.23, *19*.185
Leofric Missal, *see* sacramentaries

Leofstan, abbot of Bury St Edmund's, pilgrimage to Rome, *19*.235
Leonard, St, of Saint-Léonard-de-Noblat, cult of, *19*.94; entry in English calendars, *19*.89
Letter of Alexander to Aristotle, Mercian prose work, style of, *17*.99, 112–13, 134; as source for *Solomon and Saturn II*, *20*.138
Liber Commonei, lesson for Genesis in, *17*.168; editions of, *17*.168; containing lessons in Greek and *Vetus Latina*, *17*.182; *see also* manuscripts, Oxford, Bodl. Lib., **Auct. F. 4. 32**
Liber Eliensis, *see* Ely
Liber Judith, *see* Judith
Liber de numeris, *20*.201
Liber pontificalis, *19*.200, 205, 212, 214, 216–17
Liber rotarum, *19*.135; *see also* Isidore, *De natura rerum*
Liber vitae, *see* Winchester, New Minster
Lichfield, bishopric of, *18*.22
Limoges, *19*.100; abbey church of Saint-Martial, *19*.85–6, 88, 98
Lincoln, as administrative centre for Lindsey, *18*.29–30; Anglo-Scandinavian history, *18*.29, 135, 152, 176–87, 203; coinage of, *18*.186; bishop of, at Council of Arles, *18*.174; castle of, *18*.28; under Ceolwulf, *18*.144n; charters and bulls of, *18*.27, 242n, in Domesday Book, *18*.20–3, 177, 182; under Edmund, *18*.177; place-name of, *18*.8, 10, 17, 31; mint of, *18*.205; trade and commerce, *18*.17, 205; history of, Iron Age, *18*.169, 201; Roman, *18*.7, 12, 15–17, 29–31, 169–76, 201; post-Roman, *18*.10–12, 14–15, 173–6; pre- and mid-Saxon, *18*.202; churches of, early church of, *18*.167, 174–5; St Mark's *18*.14; St Mary's *18*.20–9; St Mary Magdalene, *18*.27–9, 31; St Paul-in-the-Bail, *18*.11, 25, 173–4, 181; *see also* Wigford
Lindisfarne Gospels, *see* gospelbooks
Lindsey, *18*.3, 20–9, 173; bishops of, at St Mary's of Lincoln, *18*.26–9; episcopal succession of, *16*.149; economy of, *18*.176; kingdom of, *18*.1–3, 17, 30, 150, 172–3; place-names of, *18*.30–2; in Bede, *18*.1, 6, 8–9, 31–2; in Æthelweard's *Chronicon*, *18*.9–10; in Asser's *Life of King Alfred*, *18*.6–7, 31–2; at Lincoln, *18*.10, 20; at *Syddensis ciuitas*, *18*.4–6; at Wigford, *18*.30–1
List of Resting-Places of the Saints, *18*.156–7, *19*.129–30; *see also* relics
litanies, *19*.92, 121; entry of St Martial of Limoges in, *19*.93; entry of St Radegund in, *19*.92; of Exeter, *19*.92; of Ramsey, *19*.92; for Rogation Days, *18*.109; of Winchcombe, *19*.92, 241; of Winchester, *19*.92; in New Haven, **Beinecke 578**, *17*.67–9
literacy, definition of, *16*.50
Little Chester, *see* Derby
Liudger, bishop of Münster, *20*.50, 52, 54–8, 60; *Vita rhythmica S. Liudgeri*, *20*.55; *Vita S. Liudgeri*, by Atfrid, *20*.54, 55

Liudger, Frisian noble, identity of, *16*.193; books of, *16*.193–4

Liudhard, bishop, as described by Bede, *see* Bede, on Liudhard; coin (medalet) of, *20*.27–41; description of, *20*.28–9; cross on, *20*.34–41; at Canterbury, *20*.33

Lombards, laws on adultery of, *20*.19–20

London, *19*.82; economy of, pre-Viking, *18*.176; trade of, *18*.16; urban archaeology, *18*.150; scribal activity at, *16*.149

Lupus, abbot, letter of, *18*.120

Machutus, OE life of, *17*.116

Macrobius, works of, in ASE, *17*.230; author of *De differentiis et societatibus Graeci Latinique uerbi epitome*, comparing Greek and Latin verbs, *17*.225

Maellon, St, of Arras, cult of, *19*.246

magic, of the Anglo-Saxons, definition of, *17*.193–4; in medicinal recipes, *17*.193–215

Malchus, life of, Mercian prose work, style of, *17*.100

Malmesbury, *19*.82, 99, 183; charter of, *see* charters, Malmesbury

Manchester, place-name of, *19*.14–16

Manegold of Lautenbach, psalm commentary of, *20*.160

Mannig, abbot of Evesham, *19*.177

MANUSCRIPTS

Alençon, Bibliothèque Municipale
12: *17*.227n

Amiens, Bibliothèque Municipale
110: *19*.141, 143

Angers, Bibliothèque Municipale
91: *18*.68; 96: *18*.68

Antwerp, Plantin-Moretus Museum
M. 16. 8: *17*.22n, 222n

Arras, Bibliothèque Municipale
444: *18*.62–6, 82

Autun, Bibliothèque Municipale
2: *17*.86

Basel, Universitätsbibliothek
F. III. 15a: *17*.102n

Berlin
Deutsche Staatsbibliothek
Fragment 34: *20*.53n; Phillips 1716: *20*.188
Staatsbibliothek, der Stiftung Preussischer Kulturbesitz
Grimm 132, 2: *16*.23n, 24; Grimm 139, 2: *16*.23–5; theol. lat. fol. 322: *20*.58; theol. lat. fol. 346: *20*.53; theol. lat. fol. 354: *20*.60; theol. lat. fol. 355: *20*.54n; theol. lat. fol. 356: *20*.56; theol. lat. fol. 362: *20*.47n, 54n, 59; theol. lat. fol. 366: *20*.50; theol. lat. fol. 367: *20*.54n; theol. lat. qu. 139: *20*.56; theol. lat. qu. 505: *20*.47n

Bern, Burgerbibliothek
179: *17*.227n; 181: *17*.227n; 421: *17*.227n; 671: *16*.160n, 170

Besançon, Bibliothèque Municipale
14: *19*.153, 174, 182, 188–91

Bonn, Universitätsbibliothek
S. 366: *20*.55n, 57; S. 367: *20*.54n

Boulogne-sur-Mer, Bibliothèque Municipale
10: *16*.175; 63: *20*.219; 82: *16*.170, 175–7; 189: *17*.57, 62–4, 156

Brussels, Bibliothèque Royale
1650: *16*.28, *17*.154; 1828–30: *17*.22n, 219, 223; 8558–8563: *16*.175

Budapest, National Széchényi Library
Clmae 277: *20*.47n

Cambrai, Bibliothèque Municipale
61: *18*.61n; 75: *18*.61, 63–6, 82; 162–3: *18*.58

Cambridge
Corpus Christi College
9: *18*.88; 12: *16*.152n; 23: *16*.216, 218–30, *17*.154; 41: *17*.107n, 116n; 69: *16*.150n; 130: *17*.218; 140: *17*.77; 144: *16*.17n, 35n, *17*.154; 146: *18*.78n, 84; 153: *16*.150n, 151n, 160n; 162: *16*.153n; 173: *16*.163–4, 165n, 169–70, *17*.95n; 178: *18*.85; 183: *16*.148n, 150n, 174–5, 177–8; 190: *20*.209, 217–18; 191: *17*.84; 198: *18*.85; 201: *17*.108n, 153, 158, *20*.210, 216–17; 221: *17*.218n, 229, 231; 223: *16*.215–16, 218–21, 228–30; 260: *17*.219; 276: *17*.231; 286: *16*.150n, 171; 302: *20*.187; 307: *16*.166–7; 322: *17*.154; 326: *19*.140, 143–4; 330: *17*.229n, 230–1; 352: *16*.150n, *17*.229; 356: *16*.150n, *17*.219, 221n, 223, 230n, 232; 389: *16*.150n; 391: *18*.77, 84, *19*.245n; 422: *16*.150n, 153n, *17*.108n, *20*.123, 126; 448: *16*.149n, 150n, 175–6; 473: *18*.59–61, 63–9, 73–7, 82, 84

Gonville and Caius College
820 (h): *18*.41–2

Magdalene College
Pepys 2981: *18*.41–2

Pembroke College
25: *20*.204–5; 301: *19*.173, 181

Peterhouse
2. 4. 6: *16*.18n, 30n

St John's College
42: *20*.203–15

Sidney Sussex College
100: *16*.148n

Trinity College
B. 3. 5: *17*.231; B. 4. 27: *16*.151n; B. 10. 4: *19*.166, 181; B. 11. 2: *16*.176n; B. 14. 3: *19*.237n; B. 15. 33: *16*.165, 169–70, 174, *17*.220; B. 15. 34: *19*.176; B. 16. 3: *16*.175–6; O. 2. 30: *16*.151n, *17*.229; O. 2. 51: *16*.216, 218–21, 230, *17*.231; O. 3. 7: *17*.227n; O. 4. 10: *17*.219n; O. 4. 71: *17*.231; O. 7. 41: *17*.231; O. 10. 28: *17*.218; R. 5. 33: *16*.200n, *19*.126; R. 15. 32: *19*.124, 190

University Library
Additional 4543: *16*.160n; Ee. 2. 4: *16*.197n,

199n, *17*.85, 91, 229; **Ff. 1. 23**: *19*.226n; **Ff. 4.
42**: *16*.160n; **Gg. 5. 35**: *19*.140, 142, 144; **Gg. 3.
21**: *17*.70; **Gg. 3. 28**: *17*.38; **Gg. 5. 35**: *16*.202–3,
216–21, 225, 227–9, *17*.49; **Ii. 1. 33**: *19*.117–18;
Ii. 2. 11: *17*.76, 81; **Ii. 2. 19**: *17*.88n; **Ii. 3. 12**:
17.226; **Ii 4. 20**: *17*.87n; **Kk. 4. 13**: *17*.88; **Kk. 5.
16**: *16*.186; **Kk. 5. 32**: *16*.199n; **Kk. 5. 34**:
16.204–12; **Ll. 1. 10**: *17*.95n, *18*.33n, 38–9
Cambridge, Massachusetts, Harvard Law School
   2062: *18*.225
Canterbury
  Dean and Chapter Library
    Additional 12/12: *20*.205n
    Ant. C. 1282: *16*.171
Cava, Archivio della Badia
   1: *17*.86
Châlons-sur-Marne, Bibliothèque Municipale
   31: *20*.206n, 209–10, 220
Cheltenham, Phillipps Collection
   36183: *see* Tokyo, Takamiya Collection
Coburg, Landesbibliothek
   1: *16*.171
Cologne, Dombibliothek
   106: *20*.58
Columbia, Missouri, University of Missouri
Library
   Fragmenta Manuscripta 1: *17*.84–92; **Fragmenta Manuscripta 2**: *17*.83; **Plimpton 54**:
20.53n
Copenhagen, Royal Library
   G.K.S. 10.2: *19*.165–6, 191–5; **1595**: *20*.206n,
209–10, 216–20; **Ny Kgl. Saml. 1**: *19*.70, 73,
75
Darmstadt, Hessische Landes- und Hochschulbibliothek
   93: *20*.47n
Dresden, Sächsische Landesbibliothek
   Dc. 187 + 160 + 186 + 185: *17*.28n
Durham
  Cathedral Library
    A. iv. 19: *16*.168–9, *17*.108n; **B. iii. 32**: *17*.153,
159; **B. iv. 6**: *18*.41; **B. iv. 9**: *16*.216, 218–21,
230; **C. iv. 7**: *18*.41; **Hunter 100**: *17*.22n
  University Library
    Cosin v. v. 6: *18*.59, 67, 70, 91
Düsseldorf
  Landes- und Stadtbibliothek
    B. 212: *20*.53n; **B. 213**: *20*.55n; **B. 215**: *20*.53n;
C. 118: *20*.53n; **E. 32**: *20*.54n
  Hauptstaatsarchiv
    Fragment K 16: **Z4–2**: *20*.55n; **Fragment K
19**: **Z8–1**: *20*.55n
  Staatsarchiv
    Fragment 20: *20*.53n; **HS. Z. 4 nr. 1**: *20*.55n;
HS. Z. 4 nr. 2: *20*.53n; **HS. Z. 4 nr. 3, 1**: *20*.53n;
HS. Z. 4 nr. 8: *20*.55n; **s.n.**: *20*.53n
  Universitätsbibliothek

A. 19: *20*.43–52, 60–4; **B. 3**: *20*.58; **B. 81**:
20.47n; **B. 191**: *20*.47n; **B. 210**: *20*.53n; **E. 2**:
20.47n; **E. 3**: *20*.47n; **Fragm. K19**: **Z9/1**:
16.18n
Epinal, Bibliothèque Municipale
   72: *16*.17n; *17*.22n
Erfurt, Wissenschaftliche Allgemeinbibliothek
   Amplonianus 2° 42: *16*.17n, 18n, *17*.22n
Essen-Werden
   Pfarrhof: *16*.18n
Exeter, Dean and Chapter Library
   FMS/3: *16*.171
Florence, Biblioteca Laurenziana
   66. 21: *16*.194; **Amiatino 1**: *17*.184n; *18*.41;
Plut. xvii. 20: *19*.173, 227n
Geneva, Bodmer C. B.
   175: *17*.227n
Gerleve, Stiftsbibliothek
   s.n.: *20*.53n
Hanover, Kestner Museum
   Culem. 1 nr. 1: *20*.57; **WM XXIa 36**: *19*.175–6
Herrnstein über Siegburg, Gräflich Nesselrode'sche Bibliothek
   192: *17*.19
Ivrea, Biblioteca Capitolare
   60: *18*.66
Karlsrule, Badische Landesbibliothek
   Aug. perg. 254: *20*.200
Kassel, Landesbibliothek
   Anhang 19: *16*.162n, 163, 167, *17*.95n; **Theol.
fol. 21**: *16*.187, *20*.53n; **Theol. fol. 65**: *16*.191
Laon, Bibliothèque Municipale
   238: *19*.161; **444**: *17*.228n
Le Havre, Bibliothèque Municipale
   330: *18*.45–6, 60n
Leiden, Bibliotheek der Rijksuniversiteit
   Bibl. Publ. lat. 67E: *16*.38n; **Bibl. publ. lat.
67F**: *16*.30, 32; **Burmannus Q. 3**: *16*.218n;
Scaliger 69: *20*.129, 138; **Voss. lat. F. 24**:
17.229n; **Voss. lat. F. 111**: *16*.209
Leningrad, Public Library
   O. v. xiv.1: *16*.175, 177, *17*.53–5, 58–60; **Q. v.
i. 18**: *16*.186, *20*.53n
León, Archivo Catedralicio
   6: *17*.86
Lichfield, Cathedral Library
   Lich. 1: *16*.160n
Lincoln, Cathedral Chapter Library
   199: *20*.205n
London
  British Library
    Additional 10546: *18*.42; **23211**: *16*.156n,
158n, *17*.95n; **24193**: *17*.83, 85, 90, 92; **24199**:
16.216, 218–30, *17*.222, *19*.164; **30853**: *20*.187;
32246: *17*.22n; **34652**: *17*.221; **34890**: *19*.166;
37517: *20*.150; **37777**: *17*.184n, *18*.41; **40165 A.
2**: *16*.158n, *17*.95n; **40618**: *16*.161, 168; **43405**:

London (*cont.*)
17.87n; **45025**: *17*.184, *18*.41; **47967**: *16*.168,
170–1, *20*.131; **49598**: *19*.170, 190; **57337**:
19.169
Additional Charter 19801: *18*.77n
Arundel 60: *17*.153, *19*.124, *20*.161, 164; **155**:
17.156, *19*.124, 175–6, 182, *20*.153n, 158
Cotton
Augustus ii. 19: *17*.94n; **ii. 20**: *18*.40; **ii. 23**:
16.173; **ii. 65**: *16*.173; **ii. 94**: *18*.39–40
Caligula A. xiv: *19*.226n
Charter viii. 4: *16*.167; **viii. 16**: *16*.173–4; **viii.
22**: *16*.173
Claudius A. i: *16*.51–3, 58–61, 64; **A. iii**:
18.84; **B. iv**: *19*.99; **B. v**: *16*.175
Cleopatra A. iii: *16*.21n, 23n, *17*.22n, 27, 111n,
219n, 223; **A. vi**: *16*.157n; *17*.226; **C. viii**:
16.216, 218–29, *19*.164
Domitian A. i: *17*.224, *19*.133–4, 135, 138–9,
141–4; **A. vii**: *16*.158n; **A. viii**: *17*.154; **A. ix**:
16.149n, 150n. 158n, 167, *17*.98n
Faustina A. ix: *20*.187
Galba A. xviii: *16*.158n, 161n, 176; *17*.228
Julius A. ii: *20*.145n; **A. vi**: *17*.140, 153, 159
Nero A. i: *20*.177n, *20*.209, 217; **C. iii**: *17*.53n;
D. iv: *17*.108n, *18*.34; **E. i**: *18*.77, 84, 88
Otho B. ix: *16*.175; **B. x**: *18*.85; **B. xi**: *17*.100n,
102; **C. i**: *17*.77; **E. i**: *17*.221, 223, 230n
Tiberius A. ii: *16*.175; **A. iii**: *17*.153; **A. xiii**:
20.219; **A. xiv**: *16*.188, *20*.51n; **A. xv**: *16*.210; **B.
iv**: *18*.6n; **B. v**: *19*.197; **B. xi**: *16*.162n, 163, 167,
17.95n; **C. ii**: *16*.188, *18*.38; **C. vi**: *20*.158, 161,
174; **E. iv**: *17*.69n
Titus D. xxvi + xxvii: *19*.124, 190–1
Vespasian A. i: *17*.84, 95n, 154; **A. xiv**:
20.219; **B. x**: *20*.129; **D. ii**: *20*.206n, 209–10,
216, 220; **D. iii**: *20*.164; **D. vi**: *17*.75, 156, 219n,
19.75; **D. xii**: *17*.140, 153, 159, *20*.164; **D. xiv**:
16.150n, 172; **D. xx**: *17*.108n
Vitellius A. vi: *17*.59n; **A. xv**: *18*.117; **A. xviii**:
18.51; **A. xix**: *17*.219n; **C. iii**: *17*.18n, 19n; **E.
xviii**: *17*.152, *19*.124, *20*.151, 158, 161
Egerton 1046B: *18*.41–2; **2615**: *18*.61n; **2831**:
16.186
Harley 76: *19*.153, 182; **585**: *17*.19n; **603**:
19.175, 226n, *20*.153n; **652**: *17*.88n; **863**: *20*.151;
1960: *19*.103; **2892**: *19*.184, 203n; **2904**: *20*.150;
2965: *16*.159, 170–1, *17*.228; **3271**: *17*.219n;
3376: *17*.22n, 219, 219n, 222, 230n; **3826**:
17.218n, 220n, 221n, 230n; **3859**: *17*.231; **4664**:
17.87n; **5642**: *17*.225n, 228n; **5792**: *16*.42n;
5915: *16*.182, 188; **6258B**: *17*.19n; **7653**: *17*.228
Loan 81: *18*.41
Royal 1. A. XIV: *17*.76n, 78; **1. A. XVIII**:
16.175; **1. B. VII**: *16*.171; **2. A. X**: *17*.87n; **2. A.
XX**: *16*.149n, *17*.228; **2. B. V**: *17*.141, 155,
18.86–7, *20*.147n; **2. C. III**: *17*.88; **1. D. IX**:

19.177n, 181, 195; **1. E. VI**: *18*.41–2; **4. A. XIV**:
18.85–7; **5. A. XII**: *18*.47–84, 87–90; **5. E. XVI**:
17.218; **5. E. XIX**; *20*.205n; **5. F. III**: *16*.158n; **6.
C. I**: *17*.222; **7. C. XII**: *17*.140; **7. D. XXIV**:
16.174; **8. C. VII**: *17*.70; **12. C . XXIII**: *16*.201–
4; **12. D. XVII**: *17*.100n, 108n; **13. A. XI**:
17.231; **13. A. XV**: *16*.167n; **13. C. V**: *18*.86; **15.
A. XVI**: *17*.219, 220n, 221n, 222, 230n, 233–
46; **15. A. XXXIII**: *17*.219, 220n, 221, 221n,
229, 233–46
Sloane 4040: *16*.188n
Stowe 2: *17*.140, 152; **944**: *19*.191; *20*.147n, 158,
161, 161n
Stowe Charter 8: *17*.94n
Lambeth Palace Library
237: *16*.199n; **427**: *16*.140, 153, *20*.143–66;
1370: *16*.161n
Public Record Office
S.P. 46/125: *16*.170–1
Wellcome Historical Medical Library
573: *17*.19n
Louvain-la-Neuve, Université Catholique de Lou-
vain, Centre Général de Documentation
Fragmenta H. Omont 3: *16*.158n; *17*.22n
Lyon, Bibliothèque de la Ville
403: *17*.170–1, 185
Madrid, Real Biblioteca del Escorial
E. II.I: *17*.227n; **T. I. 12**: *20*.210–11
Milan, Biblioteca Ambrosiana
D. 36 sup.: *16*.218n; **M. 79 sup.**: *16*.23n, 27
Monte Cassino, Archivio della Badia
90: *16*.33, 40; **401**: *16*.33
Montpellier, Bibliothèque de l'Ecole de Médecine
H. 220: *16*.218n
Mont-Renaud
s.n.: *18*.59, 67, 73–5, 81, 89, 91
Munich, Bayerische Staatsbibliothek
Cgm. 187. III: *16*.18n, *20*.59n; **Clm. 601**:
17.225n; **Clm. 6433**: *20*.200; **Clm. 14324**:
17.227n; **Clm. 15825**: *17*.227n; **Clm. 18767**:
17.227n; **Clm. 19452**: *17*.227n; **Clm. 28135**:
20.188–202; **Clm. 29031b**: *16*.216, 220–2, 229n
Münster
Universitätsbibliothek
Paulinianus 271: *16*.18n
Staatsarchiv
Msc. 1. 243: *20*.58n
Naples, Biblioteca Nazionale
IV. G. 68: *16*.218n; **Latinus 1**: *17*.171
New Haven, Yale University, Beinecke Library
Beinecke 578: *17*.67–82
New York, Pierpont Morgan Library
M. 869: *19*.153
Williams S. Glazier Collection, G. 26: *16*.186
Orléans, Bibliothèque Municipale
127: *18*.50; **149**: *20*.188n; **159**: *16*.209; **271**:
17.227n

Index

Oslo, Universitetsbibliotek
Mi. 1: *18*.46–7
Oxford
Balliol College
240: *20*.205n
Corpus Christi College
197: *18*.86
Jesus College
10: *17*.69n
St John's College
17: *17*.213n
University College
61: *20*.187
Bodleian Library
Auct. D. 2. 16: *17*.155n; **D. 2. 19**: *16*.161n,
17.108n, 155n; **F. 1. 15**: *17*.218n, 226; **F. 3. 6**:
16.216, 218–21, 225–9; **F. 4. 32**: *16*.197n, 198n,
199n, 201n, *17*.91n, 168–9, 171–2, 181–2, 219,
228–30
Barlow 4: *18*.85; **35**: *17*.230n; **37**: *20*.206n, 209,
217–18
Bodley 163: *19*.182; **180**: *17*.227n; **343**: *19*.119;
441: *17*.77, 79; **579**: *16*.176, 199n, *18*.50n; **775**:
18.59–61, 63–7, 69, 73–5, 82, 89, 91
Digby 63: *16*.148n; **146**: *16*.28, *17*.154, 219,
220n, 223, 230, 233–46
Douce 59: *20*.151n; **125**: *17*.231; **176**: *20*.56n;
293: *17*.70n
Eng. bib. c. 2: *17*.79
E Mus. 79: *18*.225
Hatton 20: *16*.149n, 162–3, 167, 171, *17*.95n;
30: *16*.199n, *18*.87; **38**: *17*.76n, 78; **48**: *18*.88; **76**:
17.19n, 140–2, 154; **93**: *18*.43, 84; **113**: *18*.85,
20.210, 216; **114**: *18*.85, *20*.187; **115**: *18*.85
Junius 11: *17*.183, *19*.99; **27**: *16*.153n, 171,
17.111n, *20*.147n; **85 + 86**: *16*.154n, *18*.101–2,
20.187–96, 202
Lat. bib. c. 8: *18*.41–2
Laud grec. 35: *17*.228
Lat. hist. a. 2: *16*.204n
Lat. liturg. f. 5: *16*.149n
Laud misc. 263: *16*.185n; **567**: *17*.22n
Lat. theol. c. 3: *17*.91
Rawlinson C. 697: *16*.175, 199n, 203n, 215,
217–21, 225, 230; **C. 892**: *18*.59, 61, 63–5, 67,
70n, 81
Tanner 3: *17*.226n; **10**: *16*.168, *17*.98n, 116
Paris
Bibliothèque Mazarine
384: *18*.59, 67, 73–5, 81, 91; **404**: *18*.54n
Bibliothèque Nationale
lat. 1: *18*.42; **2**: *18*.42; **3**: *18*.42; **272**: *19*.173, 182;
528: *17*.228n; **887**: *18*.66, 67n; **909**: *18*.66; **987**:
19.153, 170, 173, 182, 191; **1084**: *18*.66; **1107**:
18.78, 78n; **1478**: *17*.227n; **2290**: *18*.56, 80;
2628: *20*.187; **2685**: *16*.24; **3833**: *20*.212n; **6401**:
17.227n, *19*.237n; **6401A**: *17*.222n, 227; **6503**:

17.228n; **6639**: *17*.227n; **7561**: *17*.228n; **7581**:
19.138; **7585**: *17*.230n; **7651**: *16*.40n; **8084**:
16.218n; **8087**: *16*.218n; **8431**: *17*.55–6, 58–60,
64; **8824**: *20*.153n, 156; **8846**: *19*.72; **9434**: *18*.56;
9436: *18*.58–9, 67–8, 76–7, 82–3, 90–1; **9439**:
18.54n; **9449**: *18*.68; **9527**: *16*.187; **10861**:
16.154n, *18*.39; **11937**: *19*.70, 73, 75; **12051**:
18.83n; **12052**: *18*.83n; **12961**: *17*.227n; **13252**:
18.66–7, 82; **13833**: *19*.139; **14088**: *17*.54–55;
14380: *17*.227n; **15090**: *17*.227n; **16093**:
17.227n; **17814**: *17*.227n; **18010**: *18*.59, 67, 73–
5; **nouv. acq. lat. 1298**: *16*.30n
Poitiers, Bibliothèque Municipale
250: *19*.98
Princeton, Scheide Library
71: *18*.99n
Rheims, Bibliothèque Municipale
4: *20*.151n
Rouen, Bibliothèque Municipale
Y. 6: *18*.50n, *19*.181, 195; **Y. 7**: *19*.191
Salisbury, Cathedral Library
117: *18*.41; **150**: *17*.156, *20*.150
Sankt Gallen, Stiftsbibliothek
17: *17*.228n; **136**: *16*.218n; **295**: *16*.26n; **902**:
17.225n, 228n; **908**: *20*.200; **912**: *16*.33, 39n, 40;
913: *16*.23n, 25–6; **1395**: *17*.228n
Speyer, Dombibliothek
s.n.: *20*.53n
Stockholm, Kungliga Biblioteket
A. 135: *17*.94n
Tokyo, Takamiya Collection, *see* bibles
Tours
Bibliothèque Municipale
184: *18*.55n
Petit Séminaire
s.n.: *18*.54n, 56
Uppsala, Universitetsbiblioteket
DG 1: *20*.53n
Urbana, University of Illinois Library
128: *16*.149n
Vatican City
Biblioteca Apostolica Vaticana
lat. 1468: *16*.39n; **lat. 1469**: *16*.39n; **lat. 3320**:
16.33; **lat. 3321**: *16*.19n, 38n; **lat. 3363**: *16*.176–
7, 199n, *17*.91n; **lat. 3865**: *17*.227n; **lat. 4770**:
18.70; **Pal. lat. 210**: *16*.191; **Pal. lat. 212**:
20.188n; **Pal. lat. 220**: *20*.188n; **Pal. lat. 259**:
16.186; **Pal. lat. 556**: *20*.196–9; **Pal. lat. 1877**:
16.190; **Reg. lat. 12**: *19*.175; **Reg. lat. 321**:
17.62–4; **Ross. lat. 204**: *18*.54n; **Ross. lat. 205**:
17.49n
Vercelli, Biblioteca Capitolare
CXVII: *20*.205n
Winchester, Winchester College Muniment
7. 2. 3: *16*.174
Wolfenbüttel, Herzog August-Bibliothek
Gud. lat. 125: *20*.47n

Index

Worcester, Cathedral Library
  F. 91: *18*.85; F. 160: *18*.59, 62–7, 81–2, 89; F.
  173: *18*.84, 87, 89, *19*.89. Q. 5: *18*.87; Q. 21:
  18.85; Q. 78b: *18*.85
Würzburg, Universitätsbibliothek
  M. p. th. f. 12: *16*.29n; M. p. th. f. 47: *20*.54n;
  M. p. th. f. 149a: *16*.184; M. p. th. q. 2: *16*.193
York, Cathedral Library
  Additional 1: *19*.166–7; *20*.147n
Zaragoza, Biblioteca del Cabildo
  17–94: *16*.208
Zürich, Zentralbibliothek
  Rh. hist. 27: *17*.89–90

Marcellus, *De medicamentis*, *17*.198–200
Margaret, St, of Antioch, cult of, *19*.229
Marinus II, pope, *20*.220, 223, 227–9
Martial, St, of Limoges, cult of, *19*.84–5, 93–4; entry
  in calendars, *19*.89; entry in litanies, *19*.151n,
  161n; life of, *19*.88; as patron of Gaul, *19*.84–5; for
  abbey church of, *see* Limoges
Martianus Capella, works of, in ASE, *17*.230;
  author of *De nuptiis Philologiae et Mercurii*, as
  source for *Solomon and Saturn II*, *20*.127
Martin, St, entry in the canon of the Mass, *19*.160n
Martin, St, of Tours, as patron saint of Tours, *20*.33;
  as culted at Canterbury, *20*.33
martyrologies, of Bede, *see* Bede, Martyrology of;
  Jeromian, *19*.90, 219; *see also* Old English
  Martyrology
Mary, Blessed Virgin, commemoration of, within
  Nativity season, *18*.52–4, 56, 70, 75, 80; Mass for,
  edition of, from Royal 5. A. XII, *18*.95; cult of,
  19.187
Mary Magdalene, cult of, *18*.28–9; in a lost work of
  Frithegod, *17*.49
Mary, St, of Egypt, relics of, *19*.186
Marycorn, Lincs., *18*.21–2, 27
Maurdramnus, abbot of Corbie, *18*.83
Maurice, St, and his companions, cult of, *19*.239,
  245–6
Maxims I, metre of, *16*.106
Maxims II, *19*.11–12
medicine: in Anglo-Saxon England, scholarship
  on, *17*.15n, 191–4; terminology of, *17*.16–33; in
  OE, *17*.21–3; Greek and Latin influence on,
  17.30, 33, 191, 193, 211; Germanic influence,
  17.23–5, 191, 211; knowledge of, *17*.15, 31; loan
  words of, *17*.25–9; formations of loan words,
  17.29–32; *see also* herbs used in, *17*.21, 23, 31;
  plants used in, *17*.20, 205–7, 209; plant-names,
  17.22–3, 26–33
medicine, works of: *Leechbook* (*Læceboc*), *see* Leechbook; *Lacnunga*, *see* Lacnunga; *Old English Herbarium*; *see* Herbarium; *Peri Didaxeon*, *17*.16; *De herba
  vettonica liber*, falsely attributed to Antonius
  Musa, *17*.18, 20; *De taxone liber*, *17*.18; *Liber*

medicinae ex animalibus, pecoribus et bestiis uel auibus,
  of Sextus Placitus Papiriensis, *17*.18–19, 100–2,
  198; *see* glosses, Placitus; *Liber medicinae ex herbis
  femininis*, falsely attributed to Dioscorides, *17*.19,
  20; *Hermeneumata medico-botanica*, *17*.32; Omont
  medical fragment, *17*.100, 102
Meleusippus, St, of Langres, *see* Eleusippus
Mercia, *18*.9, 136; bishoprics of, *18*.166, 173; conquest of Lincoln, *18*.17–18, 30; conquest of Lindsey, *18*.1–2, 17–18; conquest by West Saxons,
  18.40; conquest by Vikings, *18*.142, 152, 176;
  kings of, *18*.40; manuscripts associated with,
  18.43; script associated with, *18*.39; urban
  archaeology, *18*.149
Mercian prose texts, prose style of, *17*.99–134; *see
  also under individual works*
Mildred, St, feast of, *19*.170n, relics of, *19*.184
missals, *18*.47, 84–6, 89, *19*.151, 178; of Bayeux,
  18.54; of Bury St Edmunds, *18*.53, *19*.161, *see also*
  manuscripts, Laon, Bibl. Mun. 238; of Canterbury, St Augustine's, *18*.53; early fragments of,
  18.45, 46n, 46–7; of Italy, 18.70, *see also* manuscripts, Vatican City, BAV, lat. 4770; *for Missal of
  Robert of Jumièges*, *see* sacramentaries; *for Leofric
  Missal*, *see* sacramentaries; of Rennes, *18*.54; of
  Saint-Denis, *18*.78; of Saint-Eloi *18*.83n; of Saint-
  Martin of Tours, *18*.54; Sarum, *18*.53, 54n, 55n,
  19.122; of Winchester, New Minster, *18*.45, 50,
  19.122; *see also* Le Havre, Bibl. Mun., 330; of
  Tours, *18*.56–7; of Saint-Vaast, *18*.62; *see also*
  manuscripts, Arras, Bibl. Mun. 444
Moore Bede, script of, *16*.186–7; *see also* manuscripts,
  Cambridge, University Library, Kk. 5. 18
Morcar, *see* Sigeferth
Moutier-Grandval Bible, *see* bibles

narration, in OE poetry, *16*.45–63; definition of,
  16.46; in *Beowulf*, *16*.45n
Newington, *19*.184
Niall, *17*.114
Nicasius, St, of Rheims, cult of, *19*.245–6
Nicholas, St, liturgical feast of, office for, *18*.84
Nicholas II, pope, bull of 1061, *18*.22, 24
Northampton, history of, early Saxon, *18*.188;
  Scandinavian, *18*.145; size of, *18*.204; settlements
  at, *see* settlements
Northumbria, *18*.9, 30, 150; bibles of, *18*.41; con-
  quest of Lindsey by, *18*.1
Norwich, 18.204
notation, musical, *18*.65–6, 71–5, 81; AS, *18*.71–2;
  Breton, *18*.71–2; Lotharingian, *18*.71; Winches-
  ter, *18*.71; in Royal 5. A. XII, *18*.71–5, 77, 89
Nottingham: history, Iron Age, *18*.187, 201;
  Roman, *18*.187, 202; Saxon, *18*.187–90, 202;
  Anglo-Scandinavian, *18*.135, 190–3, 203–4; coin-
  age of, *18*.192–3; economy of, *18*.192–3; pottery
  of, *18*.192–3, 204

Index

Oda, archbishop of Canterbury, *19*.95, 139, 183; prefatory prose letter of, *17*.52, 55, 58, 62, 64; relics of Wilfrid, obtained by, *17*.45, 50; as dedicatee of Frithegod, *17*.46; journey to Continent of, *17*.62

Odo, abbot of Cluny, reformation of monasteries by, *19*.216–17

Odolric, abbot of Saint-Martial of Limoges, *19*.85

Odulf, St, cult and relics of, at Evesham, *19*.82

Offa, king of Mercia, *18*.150, 172; tomb of, at St Peter's, Rome, *19*.211; establishment of *pening*, *17*.101; charter of, *see* charters

Olaf, St, cult of, *18*.231, 232n

Olaf Guthfrithsson, campaign of, southern, *18*.205; conquests of, of Derby, *18*.157; of Leicester, *18*.167–8; of Nottingham, *18*.191

Old English Bede, *19*.46–8, 53–5; date of, *17*.98; manuscripts of, *16*.167–9; concept of *anweald* in, *16*.142–4; vocabulary of, *20*.75; prose style of, *17*.98, 103–4, 109, 111–15, 117–18, 123–7, 131–6, 138

Old English Hexateuch, vocabulary of, *17*.155; *see also* Ælfric

Old English Martyrology, *19*.44, 90, 93n, 123, 240; date of, *17*.103, 132n, 135, 137–8; vocabulary of, *17*.154; prose style of, *17*.95, 103–4, 105n, 109, 112, 114, 118–20, 132

Old English Orosius, *18*.120, *19*.44; dating of, *17*.97; description of, *16*.130, 144–5; compared to Latin original, *16*.127, 133–8, 141–3, 144–5; reason for translation, *16*.128, 137; vocabulary of, *17*.155–6, *20*.68; verbs in, *20*.82–3, 87–97; used by Alfred, *17*.97; prose style of, *17*.109, 115, 117, 119n, 128–9, 133n, 138

oral poetry, *see* poetry, oral

orality, definition of, *20*.99–100; tradition of, *20*.65–6; theory of, *20*.109–10; within textuality, *20*.100–102, 109–10

Orc, thegn of King Cnut, and Abbotsbury, *18*.208–9, 220–1, 223, 230–1, 232–3, 236–7, 239

Orderic Vitalis, *19*.158

Ordines Romani, *17*.86–7, *18*.69; Greek in, *17*.182

Orosius, author of *Historiae adversum paganos*, orthography in, *20*.131; view of history of, *16*.129–30, 132; intention of, *16*.129; used by Aldhelm, *16*.44; geographical list of, *20*.130–2, 135; as source for *Solomon and Saturn II*, *20*.128, 130–3, 138; glosses on, *see* glosses, Orosius

orthography, OE, as evidence for dating, *17*.102n, 105–7

Osgar, abbot of Abingdon, *19*.127

Oswald, king of Northumbria, prose life by Ælfric, *18*.131; in Bede, *see* Bede, *Historia ecclesiastica*

Oswald, archbishop of York, brought Germanus of Fleury to Worcester, *18*.88; Latin prose life by Byrhtferth, *18*.88; reforms of, at Worcester, *18*.88–9, 89n; at Winchcombe, *18*.89; commemor-

ation of, in calendar, *20*.204

Otto I, emperor, *19*.206–7

Ouen, St, entry in calendar, *19*.184; lost life of, by Frithegod, *17*.48, 65, *19*.183–4; liturgical feast of, *19*.170n; relics of, *19*.157–8, 183

Ovid, author of *Ars amatoria*, manuscript of in ASE, *16*.160

Oxford, churches of, *18*.28n

paganism, in ASE, attested in medical works, *17*.191–2; in OE poetry, *20*.65

pallium, *19*.206, 246; collection of, at Rome, by Dunstan, *19*.203; by Plegmund, *19*.203; by Sigeric, *19*.197, 203, 207, 222

Palm Sunday, homilies for, *18*.106

Pancras, St, cult of, *19*.227

Paris, Saint-Magloire, church of, troper from, *18*.66–7

Paschasius Radbertus, *19*.68

passionals, of Worcester cathedral priory, *18*.77, 84, 88

Paul, St, apostle, entry in litany, *19*.161n, 169; *see also* Peter and Paul, SS

Paul the Deacon, homiliary of, *see* homiliaries, Paul the Deacon

Paulinus, missionary work in Lincoln, *18*.11, 172, 174; foundation of church, *18*.174–5

Paulinus of Aquileia, author of *Liber exhortationis*, *20*.197–8

Pastor Hermae, Insular manuscript of, *20*.53

Peada, *princeps* of Middle Anglia, *18*.166

Pega, St, sister of Guthlac, *19*.212; tomb of, at St Peter's, Rome, *19*.212

penitentials, treatment of adultery in, *20*.25

Pentecost, *18*.108–9

pepper, *19*.8

pericopes, *17*.43

Perpetua, St, relics of, *19*.186

Persius, author of *Satirae*, manuscripts of, in ASE, *17*.230

Peter, St, apostle, cult of, *19*.202–3, 226; entry in litany, *19*.169

Peter and Paul, SS, apostles, Ælfric's OE life of, *19*.56–7; Blickling homily on, *19*.56

Peter's Pence (Romscot), *19*.205, 212; *20*.228–9

Peterborough, *19*.126, 139, 154–5, 159–61, 174–7, 181–2, 194; OE chronicle of, *20*.91–7

Philip and James, SS, cult of, *19*.227

pilgrimages, to Rome, *19*.225–6, 235–7, 246; *see also* itineraries, *pallium*

Pirmin, author of *De singulis libris scarapsus*, as source, *20*.219

place-names, *19*.17–20; as evidence of settlements, *20*.10, 15, 17; *see also* Knutsford, Leicester, Lincoln, Lindsey, Manchester, Rutland, York

plants, in ASE, *see* medicine, plants used in

Index

Plegmund, archbishop of Canterbury, *17*.103; coins of, *19*.97n

Pliny, as author of *Naturalis historia*, source for *Herbarium*, *16*.17, 198, 204, 208; as source for Alcuin's poem on York, *16*.192; as source for *Solomon and Saturn II*, *20*.127–8, 133–4; vocabulary in, *20*.73; medical recipe of, *16*.198

poetry, OE: origins of, *17*.93; as model for prose, *17*.132; world of, *20*.65–80; language of, *20*.67–80; vocabulary of, *17*.156–7, *20*.70–80; textuality, *20*.100–8; polyphony of, *20*.104–5; intertextuality of, *20*.107–8; metre of, *16*.68, 104–10, 67, 68n, 122–5, 76, 87; *see also Genesis B*, metre of; orality of, *16*.49; types of oral poets, *16*.47–63, *20*.100; style of, *20*.181; compositional technique of, *20*.101–2; viewpoint of, *20*.116–17

Poitiers, *19*.89, 100; cults of St Hilary and St Radegund, *19*.87; Hypogée des Dunes, chapel, crypt of, *19*.90; Saint-Hilaire, abbey church of, *19*.86, 92, 97; Sainte-Radegonde, church of, *19*.98–9; Sainte-Croix, convent, *19*.87; Saint-Savin, church of, near Poitiers, *19*.99

Pompeius, grammarian, in Alcuin's poem on York, *16*.192

Pomponius Mela, author of *Chorographia*, *20*.127

pontificals, *18*.84–6; Anderson, *19*.169–70; Claudius, *18*.84, 88; of Bishop Sampson, *18*.78n, 84

Porphyry, author of *Isagoge*, *16*.132

Portiforium of St Wulstan, *18*.77, 84, 88; *see also* manuscripts, Cambridge, **CCC 391**

pottery, from excavations, *20*.3, 5, 13–14

prayers, of *lorica* type, *17*.95

prayerbooks, Book of Cerne, *18*.33n, 38–40, 43, *20*.61

Prebiarum de multorium exemplaribus, Hiberno-Latin dialogue, *20*.197

Priscian, grammarian, geographical list of, *20*.128; author of *Institutio de nomine, pronomine et uerbo*, commentary on, by Remigius, *19*.137–8, 147–9, in BL, **Cotton Domitian i**, *19*.134, 137–8; 147–9; Greek terms of, *17*.224–6, 231

processions, liturgical, on Rogation Days, *18*.109

prose, OE: origins of, *17*.93; works of, *17*.94–118; lost works of, *17*.96n; West Saxon, *17*.95–118, 136–8, 141; Mercian, *17*.94, 97–118, 132–8; during Alfred's time, *17*.93–4; of the saga of Cynewulf and Cyneheard, *17*.93, 132n; characteristics for dating, linguistic, *17*.105–7; of vocabulary, *17*.108–112; varieties of, *17*.118–38; use of modal verbs in, *20*.81–98

Prouerbia Salomonis, glosses on, *see* glosses

Prudentius, life of, *16*.213; writings of, *16*.213–14; author of *Contra Symmachum*, *16*.213; scholarship on, *16*.213n, Vergilian language in, *16*.214; author of *Psychomachia*, description of, *16*.214 217; studies on, *16*.214n, influence on OE literature, *16*.214–15, 231; manuscripts of, in ASE,

16.215–17; description of, *16*.215–18; textual tradition of, *16*.218–21; illustrations of, *16*.221–5; in London, BL, **Add. 24199**, *19*.164; in **Cotton Cleopatra C. viii**, *19*.164, 167; glosses on, *see* glosses, Prudentius

psalters (general): *19*.19, 175, 179; Anglo-Saxon, *20*.151, 158–9; continental, *20*.147–51, 159–60

psalters (individual): Arundel Psalter, *19*.92n, 175, *see also* glosses; in **Beinecke 578**, *17*.67–8; Bosworth Psalter, *19*.123–4, 184, *20*.150; Cambridge Psalter, *19*.77n, Douce Psalter, *17*.70n; Eadwig Psalter, *19*.153; Eadwine Psalter, *19*.72, 75–6; glosses in *19*.78–9; Hebrew in *19*.77; psalter version in, *19*.68, 70–3, 76; glosses of, *19*.42, 51, 77n, 78, 80, 80n; of Earnwig (lost), *19*.173; Junius Psalter, *16*.168, 170, 176, *19*.77n, *see also* manuscripts, Oxford, Bodl. Lib., **Junius 27**; Lambeth Psalter, *19*.52, description of, *20*.143–66; vocabulary of, *20*.71; *tituli* of, *20*.155–9, 162; emendator of, *20*.159–61; psalms of, *20*.146–9; *see also* glosses; Paris Psalter, *20*.156, 158; language of, *20*.167–86; translation of, *20*.173–5; use of formulae, *20*.178–82; prose style of, *17*.97, 130–1, 155–6; *see also* glosses; Regius Psalter, *18*.86, *19*.80, 80n, *20*.162; *see also* glosses; of Robert, archbishop of Rouen (lost), *19*.158, 173; Salisbury Psalter, *19*.77n, *20*.145n; *see also* glosses; Stowe Psalter, *19*.77n, *see also* glosses; *see also* manuscripts, London, BL, **Stowe 2**; Vespasian Psalter, *19*.77n, *see also* glosses; Vitellius Psalter, *19*.77n, *see also* glosses; Winchcombe Psalter, *19*.226

psalters: versions of, Hebrew original, *19*.67; Greek, *19*.67, 72; Origen's Greek, *19*.67; *Vetus Latina*, *20*.153, 159–61, 165; Jerome's Latin *Romanum*, *19*.67, 71–2, 76; Jerome's Latin *Gallicanum*, *19*.67, 71–2, 76, *20*.147–9, 153, 159–60, 165; Jerome's Latin *Hebraicum*, *19*.67, 70–2, 74, 76–7, *20*.148–9, 162, 165; as available to Bede, *19*.67; in *Codex Amiatinus*, *19*.67; Theodulf's version, *19*.67–8, 70–7, 80n; as a school-text, *19*.79; commentary on, *18*.85

pseudo-Apuleius, *see Herbarium*

pseudo-Augustine, sermon of, *20*.209, 215

pseudo-Bede, *De psalmorum libro exegesis, argumenta* of, *20*.156, 158, 165

pseudo-Ingulf, author of *Historia Ingulfi*, *19*.185, 212n

pseudo-Jerome, author of *Breuiarium in psalmos*, influence on psalter glosses, *20*.153, 157, 165

Quaestiones hebraicae, anonymous, *19*.69

Quintilian, grammarian, *16*.8; categories of, *16*.133

Radbod, monk of Rheims, teacher of St Edith at Wilton, *19*.242

Radegund, St, *20*.31–3, 40–1; cult of, *19*.88, 92, 94;

Index

at Evesham, *19*.91, 94; at Poitiers, *19*.87, 98; at Worcester, *19*.91, 94; entry in English calendars, *19*.89–90; entry in English martyrologies, *19*.90; entry in litany, *19*.92; founder of Sainte-Croix, convent, *19*.87; Latin prose life of, by Venantius Fortunatus, *see* Venantius Fortunatus; church of, *see* Poitiers; cross of, *see* Cross, of Radegund

Ragyndrudis Codex, *16*.193

Rainham, Kent, *19*.20

Ramsbury, *19*.197

Ramsey, *19*.92, 100, 161; books received from Winchester, *18*.87; chronicle-cartulary of, *18*.224; lawsuits in, *17*.253, 258; foundation of, by Oswald, *18*.88–9; litany of, *19*.92

Ramsey Benedictional, *see* benedictionals

recipes, *19*.138

Regius Psalter, *see* psalters

regnal lists, *17*.95n

Regularis Concordia, veneration of the Holy Cross, *19*.226; OE translation of, *17*.153, 156, 158

relic-lists, of Abingdon, *19*.128; of Exeter, *19*.120; of Glastonbury, *19*.128; of Winchester, Hyde Abbey, *19*.125.

Rémi, St, Rheims, cult of, *19*.242, 245; liturgical feasts of, Natale, *19*.245; Translation, *19*.245

Remigius Fauius, *16*.207

Remigius of Auxerre, commentaries of, on Phocas, grammarian, *19*.137; on Priscian's *Institutio*, *19*.137–8, 147–9; on Martianus Capella, dating of, *16*.165n; Greek glosses in, *see* glosses, on Martianus Capella

Remigius, bishop of Lincoln, *18*.20–1, 27; acquisition of lands at Stow-in-Lindsey, *18*.23; construction of new cathedral, *18*.24, 26, 28, 31; consecration of, in 1092, *18*.31

Repton, Viking occupation of, *18*.155, 157, 203

resin, *19*.10

Rheinau, gradual of, *18*.68–9

rhetoric, study of in ASE, *16*.1, 8

Richard, duke of Gloucester, confirmation of Abbotsbury charter, *18*.211

Richard of Cirencester, *19*.186–7

riddles, of Apollonius, *19*.104; Bern Riddles, *19*.104; Holme Riddles, *19*.103; *see also* enigmata

Robert, Archbishop, Benedictional of, *see* benedictionals

Robert, archbishop of Rouen, *19*.158

Robert of Jumièges, archbishop of Canterbury, *18*.150; *19*.173

Robert Fitz Walter, *19*.94

Robert, St, of Turland, founder of La Chaise-Dieu, *19*.95

Rochester, influence of Winchester on, *17*.160; charter of, *see* charters, of Rochester

Rogation Days, homilies for, *18*.101. 109, 112; litany for, *18*.109

Rome: records of Roman churches, *De mirabilibus urbis Romae* of Master Gregorius, *19*.200; diary of Abbot Nikolás of Munkathverá in Iceland, *19*.200; Itinerary of Einsiedeln, *19*.200; Itinerary of Sigeric, *see* Sigeric; of John the Deacon, *19*.200; *Liber censuum* of Cencius Camerarius, *19*.200; *ordo* of Benedict the Canon, *19*.200; of Peter Mallius, *19*.200; *Itinerarium Salisburgense*, *19*.200–1; in William of Malmesbury, *Gesta regum*, *19*.200–1

Rorigon, Bible of, *see* bibles

Royal Bible, *see* bibles

The Ruin, OE poem, vocabulary of, *20*.69, 78–9

ruins, Roman, in OE poetry, *20*.69–70

Rune Poems, Icelandic, *19*.25–6, 30, 33, 35–8; OE, *19*.23–5, 27–8, 35–9, 105–6, 110–12, 114–16; Old Norse, *19*.23–5, 29, 31–5, 37–8

Ruthwell Cross, poem of, *20*.110

Rutland, principal site at Hambleton, *18*.137; place-name of, *18*.135–42, 146–8

sacramentaries, *18*.84, *19*.176; of Charles the Bald, *18*.76; of Earnwig (lost), *19*.173; Fulda Sacramentary, *18*.56–7; Gelasian sacramentaries, *18*.50–2, 54–7; 75–6, 78–80; of Giso of Wells, *18*.51, 53, 55; Gregorian sacramentaries, *18*.49–58, 68–71, 75–6, 78–80; Leofric Missal, *18*.50, 52–3, 76, 91, *19*.123–4, 163n, 244; Leonine Sacramentary, *18*.52, 56; Missal of Robert of Jumièges, *18*.50, 52–3, 76, *19*.90–1, 93n, 155, 160–2, 173; *Missale Gothicum*, *18*.50, 56; of Ratoldus, *18*.83n; *Rossianum*, *18*.53–4; in **Royal 5. A. XII**, *18*.49–58, 75–6, 78–81, 89; of Saint-Amand, *18*.57n; of Saint-Denis, *18*.58; of Saint-Vaast, *18*.58–9, *see also* manuscripts, Paris, BN, **lat. 9436**; of Senlis, *18*.76; of Tours, *18*.70; of Trente, *18*.76; of Winchester, *18*.50–3, 76, 80, 91, *19*.241

Saint-Amand, sacramentary of, *see* sacramentaries

Saint-Benoît-sur-Loire, *see* Fleury-sur-Loire

Saint-Bertin, books attributed to, *19*.152n

Saint-Denis, influence of, *18*.73, 80; liturgy of *18*.57n; liturgical books of, *18*.56, 58–9, 78, 80–2, 84; sacramentary of, *see* sacramentaries; *see also* graduals

Saint-Evroult, *19*.173

Saint-Magloire, *see* Paris

St Neots, pottery attributed to, found at Derby, *18*.160

Saint-Vaast, chants attributed to, *18*.82; liturgical books of, *18*.58–9, 61–2; *see also* graduals

saints' lives, collection of, *18*.39

Salisbury Psalter, *see* psalters

Saluius, St, of Arras, cult of, *19*.246

Sampson, bishop, *see* pontificals

Sandwich, *19*.184

Santiago, Spain, *19*.94

Saragossa, *19*.120

Saxon, Old, syntax of, *16*.110

299

Schola Saxonum (*Schola Anglorum*), of Rome, *19*.204–7, 212, 221, 225; church of S. Maria, *18*.205, 212
scripts
 uncial, books in, *16*.156; half-uncial, books in, *16*.156; Welsh reformed minuscule, *16*.160–1; Irish minuscule, *16*.161; Irish national hand, *16*.161
 AS minuscule, *16*.147, 156; *18*.34, 36–9, 43, 48–9, 77, *19*.134, 153, 162–6, 173–4, 176; AS minuscule compared to continental, *16*.184, *20*.52; Mercian, *18*.39; as seen in Tiberius group of manuscripts, *18*.33, 38–9, 42–3; under Wulfred of Canterbury, *18*.39; Anglo-Saxon reformed minuscule, styles of, *16*.157, 162–9; proto-square minuscule, *16*.163, 169–170, 172; Northumbrian, description of, *16*.186–8; Southumbrian, description of, *16*.158, 187–8, *18*.36, 39, 43; of Werden provenance, *20*.52–9
 English square minuscule, description of, *16*.153–5; development of, *16*.147–8, 155; origins of, *16*.149–50, 155–69; scholarship on, *16*.150–3; manuscripts of, *16*.150; flat-topped variety, *16*.150–1; Celtic influence on, *16*.151, 161; Phase I, development of, *16*.169–73; manuscripts of, *16*.170–1; Phrase II, development of, *16*.173.8; manuscripts of, *16*.173–6
 Caroline minuscule, introduction into England, *16*.147, *17*.90; popularity of, *16*.154–5; books of, *16*.157; at Glastonbury Abbey, *16*.197n, *17*.91; Dunstanesque, *19*.162–7; pre-Caroline, books with, *16*.157; Anglo-Caroline, *16*.148, 153; Æthelwoldan, *19*.162–5, 167, 174, 180; description of, *17*.84
 script of individual manuscripts: of Dunstan's *Classbook*, *17*.91; of *Parker Chronicle*, *16*.148; description of script, *16*.163, 165; dating of, *16*.164; scribal hands of, *16*.148n, 163–4, 170; of Lambeth Psalter, *20*.143, 146; of *tituli* in, *20*.155; of Cambridge, **CCC 422**, *20*.126; of **Cotton, Claudius A.i**, *17*.51–3, 58–60; of Leningrad, **O. v. xiv. 1**, *17*.53–4, 58–60; of Paris, BN, **lat. 8431**, *17*.55–6, 58–60; of Columbia, Missouri, **Fragmenta manuscripta 1**, *17*.84–5, 89; of New Haven, **Beinecke 578**, *17*.73–4; of London, BL, **Add. 24193**, *17*.83; of **Royal 15. A. XVI**, *17*.219n
The Seafarer, OE poem, *19*.35; intertextuality of, *20*.109
Seaxwulf, bishop of Lindsey, *18*.9
Sebastian, St, cult of, *19*.161n, 227
Second Lay of Guðrún, *19*.38
Sedulius Scottus, use of *Vetus Latina*, *17*.181
Senlis, liturgy of, *18*.84; sacramentary of, *18*.76
Septuagint, description of, *17*.164
sermons, OE anonymous, in Worcester manuscript, *20*.203–16; on the Nativity, *20*.205; on All Saints, *20*.204n
settlements, AS, patterns of, *20*.1–17; influence on

topography, *20*.12–15; model of 'Middle Saxon Shift', *20*.1, 11; 'wandering' type (*Wandersiedlungen*), *20*.5–7, 10; farming in, *20*.17; evidence of charters for, *20*.14–15; sunken huts of, *20*.1–2; of Puddlehill, Dunstable, *20*.74; of Upton, Northants., *20*.74; sunken houses in OE poetry, *20*.73–5; hill-top communities, of Church Down, *20*.15; of Chatherington, *20*.15; valley settlements, of Chalton, Hants., *20*.14–15; of Idsworth, *20*.15; of Blendworth, *20*.15; *see also* cemeteries
settlements (individual): of Barking, *20*.14; of Bishopstone, Sussex, *20*.9, 13; of Cassington, *20*.13; of Catholme, *20*.2, 7n; of Cowdery's Down, Hants., *20*.2, 7n; of Eynsham, *20*.13; of Meon Valley, *20*.15; of Maxey, Northants., *20*.5; of Mucking, Essex, *20*.1, 3–14; of New Wintles Farm, Oxon., *20*.5; of Pennyland, Bucks., *20*.5; of Purwell Farm, Oxon., *20*.5; of Sutton Courtenay, Berks., *20*.1; of Walton, Bucks., *20*.5, 16; of West Stowe, *20*.2, 5, 9; of Wicken Bonhunt, Essex, *20*.5, 14; of Walpole, *20*.16
settlements (continental): patterns of, in Denmark, *20*.7; in Germany and Netherlands, *20*.7; of Flögeln, Lower Saxony, *20*.7; of Gristede, Lower Saxony, *20*.7; of Norre Snede, Jutland, *20*.7; of Vorbasse, Jutland, *20*.7; of Odoorn, Drenthe, *20*.6–7; of Wijster, Drenthe, *20*.6–9
Seven Boroughs, *18*.151–2
Shaftesbury Abbey, lands of, *18*.230
Sherborne, *19*.90, 93; books received from Winchester, *18*.87; cartulary of, *18*.232; charter of, *18*.231; witness lists from, *17*.252; cult of St Olaf at, *18*.232n; liturgy of, *18*.67
Sigeferth and Morcar, thegns, *18*.151
Sigeric, archbishop of Canterbury, as dedicatee of Ælfric's *Catholic Homilies*, *17*.38; itinerary of, to Rome, churches visited, *19*.212–25; discussion of, *19*.197–202, 225–8; edition of, *19*.199–200; at the Lateran Palace, *19*.222; return journey, *19*.228–46; at Rome, *19*.207–8; route of, *19*.204; at the *Schola Saxonum*, *19*.206–7, 212, 221; at the Vatican, *19*.210
Sigeweard, *18*.117
Sigrdrifumál, *19*.26
Sigurðardrapa, *19*.33
Sigwulf, thegn, *18*.207
silk, *19*.8
Silvester, St, cult of, *19*.227; liturgical feast of, *18*.54; Mass for, *18*.53, 57, 59
Silvinus, St, cult of, *19*.245; entry in English calendars, *19*.244
Simeon of Durham, author of *Historia regum*, *18*.156
Skírnismál, *19*.36
Smaragdus, author of *Expositio in Regulam S. Benedicti*, manuscript of, *17*.91–2; use of etymologies, *17*.35; acknowledged in the preface of Ælfric's *Catholic Homilies*, *17*.35; homiliary of, *see*

homiliaries

Snorri Sturluson, author of prose *Edda*, *19*.26, 29–33, 37–8

Solarljoð, *19*.25, 27

Solinus, author of *Collectanea rerum memorabilium*, as source for *Solomon and Saturn II*, *20*.127–8, 133–4

Solomon and Saturn II, OE poem, *20*.123–41; sources of, *20*.127–41; composition of, *20*.140–1; geographical list of, *20*.123–41; description of, *20*.126; description of Saturn, *20*.126

Soul and Body, OE poem, *20*.110

Southampton, pre-Viking economy of, *18*.176; trading centre at, *18*.16–17

Southumbria, bibles associated with, *18*.41–2; manuscripts associated with, *18*.33, 43; script associated with, *see* script

Spearhavoc, abbot of Abingdon, *19*.177

Speusippus, St, of Langres, *see* Eleusippus

Stamford: history of, Iron Age, *18*.193–6, 201–2; Roman, *18*.193–6, 201–2; Saxon, *18*.202; reconquest by Edward the Elder, *18*.204; Anglo-Scandinavian, *18*.135, 196–201, 203–5; mint at, *18*.197, 201, 204–5; in Domesday Book, *18*.196–7; ware attributed to, found at Derby *18*.160

Stephen, St, liturgical feast of, *18*.89; Mass for, *18*.58, 59n, 66–7, 70, 74–5, 78, 83; chants of, *18*.69; edition of, in **Royal 5. A. XII**, *18*.93–4

Stephen of Ripon, author of *Vita S. Wilfridi*, as source for Frithegod, *17*.46, 58–61

Stigand, bishop of Winchester and Canterbury, *17*.160, *19*.157, 187

Stowe Psalter, *see* psalters

Stow-in-Lindsey, *18*.4; St Mary's, minster church of, *18*.23–4

Sutton Hoo, Suffolk, *18*.137; excavations at, *20*.13; spoons from, *20*.227–8; *see also* pottery; settlements

Sutton, Oliver, bishop of Lincoln, *18*.28

Swithun, St, bishop of Winchester, life of, in OE prose, by Ælfric, *19*.131; liturgical feast of translation of, *19*.170n

Symposius, author of *enigmata*, *19*.105, manuscript tradition of, *16*.202–3

Tacitus, author of *Germania*, role of women in, *20*.19; vocabulary of, *20*.73–5

tags: types of, *20*.223–5, 228; from Birka, *20*.224; from List, *20*.224; from Meon Hill, Hants., *20*.224–5; Old Minster cemetery, *20*.224; from Tetney, *20*.223; from Vesle Hjerkinn, *20*.224; from Forum Hoard, *20*.221–19; description of text on, *20*.225–8

Tamworth, *18*.197, 204

Tatwine, author of *enigmata*, manuscript tradition of, *16*.202–3

Tavistok, books received from Winchester, *18*.87

Thanet, *19*.184

Theobald of Etampes, letters of, *20*.216

Theodore of Mopsuestia, influence on psalter glossing, *20*.153–5

Theodore of Tarsus, archbishop of Canterbury, *16*.17, 44; *19*.204; *20*.154–5

Theodred, bishop of London, *19*.237

Theodulf of Orléans, *19*.67–8; *see also* psalters, versions of

Thetford, ware attributed to, found at Derby, *18*.160

Thiaterd, bishop of Dorestad, manuscript of Livy, *16*.191

Thomas Becket, *19*.77

Thorney, *19*.195; books received from Winchester, *18*.87

Three Utterances exemplum, origins of, *20*.222n; versions of, *20*.187–8, 201; OE versions of, *20*.187–96, 199–202; Latin sources for, *20*.188–202; Irish version of, *20*.188, 191, 191n, 194, 200–2

Thurstan, Norman abbot of Glastonbury, *16*.198

Tiburtius and Valerian, SS, cult of, *19*.227

Timothy, St, of Rheims, *19*.246

tithing, *18*.102–4

tituli, in psalters, definition of, *20*.155; Columban/Carolingian, *20*.156–8, 165; in Lambeth Psalter, *see* psalters, Lambeth

Tola of Rouen, wife of Orc, *18*.208–9, 223, 232–3, 236, 239

Torksey, *18*.9–10

Tours, liturgical books of, *18*.43, 56–7, 76; liturgy of, *18*.57n

Trente, sacramentary of, *see* sacramentaries

Tribal Hidage, *18*.3, 8, 32, 173

tropes and tropers, *18*.66; of Paris, Saint-Magloire, *18*.66–7; of Winchester, Old Minster, *18*.59; *see also* manuscripts, Cambridge, **CCC 473**; Oxford, Bodl. Lib., **Bodley 775**

Tyconius, *Rule* of, *18*.119–20

Ulf, son of King Harold, *19*.95

Vaast, St, *see* Vedast

Vafðruðnismál, *19*.26

Valentine, St, relics of, *19*.158, 187–8

Valerian, St, *see* Tiburtius

Vedast, St, cult of, *19*.244–6

Vegetius, author of *Epitome rei militaris*, in ASE, *17*.230

Venantius Fortunatus, author of life of St Radegund, *19*.92–3

Vivian Bible, *see* bibles

Vǫluspá, *19*.34, 36

Vulgate, *see* bibles

Wærferth, bishop of Worcester, as translator for Alfred, *17*.97, 109, 114, 120–3, 125, 127, 132;

Wærferth, bishop of Worcester (*cont.*)
translation of Gregory the Great's *Dialogi*, *19*.44, 53; prose style of, *17*.97–8, 103–4, 109, 111–12, 114, 118, 120–6, 128, 132–6; vocabulary of, *17*.154; anonymous revision of, at Winchester, *19*.52; vocabulary of, *17*.140–2, 154; invitation of, from Alfred, *17*.103; charters of, *17*.135

Wanderer, OE poem, vocabulary of, *20*.70, 79; orality of, *20*.99; structure of, *20*.102–5; polyphony of, *20*.103–5, 107, 117–18, 120, 122; themes of, *20*.105–7; intertextuality of, *20*.108–22; narrators of, *20*.117–22

Wearmouth/Jarrow, *18*.41; *19*.227; *19*.202n; study of grammar at, *16*.8

Wells, *19*.90

Werden, Benedictine Abbey, foundation of, *20*.50, 53; medieval library of, *20*.45; bindery of, *20*.46; bindings from, *20*.45–9; early manuscripts from, *20*.52–60

Werferth, bishop of Worcester, *see* Wærferth

wergeld, payment of, for adultery, *20*.20

Wessex, *burhs* of, *18*.149, 204; urban archaeology of, *18*.153

West Midlands, urban archaeology of, *18*.149

Westminster Abbey, *19*.95, 97, 156, 183, 186

Whitby, alleluia in the liturgy, *18*.67

Widsith, OE poem, geographical list of, *20*.124–6, 140

Wife's Lament, OE poem, vocabulary of, *20*.74–5; intertextuality of, *20*.109

Wigford, early administrative centre for Lindsey, *18*.16, 30; place-name of, *18*.16, 18, 18n; as see of Lindsey, *18*.3; parish churches of, *18*.18–19; St Benedict's, *18*.19; St Botolph's, *18*.19; St Mark's, *18*.19; St Mary-le-Wigford's, *18*.19, 27; St Peter-at-Gowts', *18*.19

Wigstan, St, of Mercia, cult of, at Evesham, *19*.82; relics of, at Evesham, *19*.82, 156

Wilfrid, St, Latin prose life by Stephen of Ripon, *18*.11–12; pilgrimage to Rome, *19*.202–4, 236; as collector of books, *16*.193; politics of, *17*.253; altar of, at Canterbury, *17*.45; theft of relics, *17*.45

William the Conqueror, and Abbotsbury, *18*.211, 22–3, 238; and Aquitaine, *19*.81, 101; and Derby, *18*.163; and Lincoln, see of, *18*.28

William the Great, duke of Aquitaine, *19*.81n. 86, 89, 91, 99, 158–9, 173; cults of saints, his patronage for, *19*.88; cult of St Hilary, *19*.87; relations with Cnut, *19*.84; saints lives, as a gift for (lost), *19*.173

William of Malmesbury, *19*.157; author of *De antiquitate Glastonie ecclesie*, *18*.207, *19*.125; author of *Gesta pontificum*, *18*.4, 12n, *19*.183, 185–6; author of *Gesta regum*, *17*.253, *19*.125, 179, 185–7, 200; Latin prose life of St Wulfstan, *see* Wulfstan, life of; on Glastonbury's book-list, *16*.198; descrip-

tion of Frithegod, *17*.50–1, 57; citing Plautus, *17*.50; on Alfred's translations, *17*.97–8

William II, and Abbotsbury, *18*.222–3

Willibald, St, *19*.8–9, 235; hand of, *16*.185

Willibrord, St, mission of, *16*.191

Wilton, *19*.157, 186; Radbod, monk of Rheims, teaching at, *19*.242

Winchcombe, churches of, *18*.28n; litany of, *19*.92; restoration by Oswald, *18*.89

Winchcombe Psalter, *see* psalters

Winchcombe Sacramentary, *see* sacramentaries

Winchester, *19*.76n, 82, 90, 92–3, 98–9, 124, 129, 157–8, 162, 170n, 171, 173, 175, 182; books sent, to Canterbury, *18*.87; to Durham *18*.87; influence of, *18*.84, 86, 89; litany of, *19*.92

Winchester, New Minster (later Hyde Abbey): *19*.124–5, 130–1, 155n, 157–8, 171, 187–8, 190–1; chronicle-cartulary of, *18*.224; cult of St Radegund, *19*.91–2; *Liber vitae* (Hyde Register), *19*.125, 129, 187–8; missal of, *18*.45, 50, *19*.122; notation of, *18*.71; charter of, *16*.174

Winchester, Old Minster: books written at, *18*.84; vocabulary of, *17*.156–61, *19*.53; under Æthelwold, *17*.144–54; lexical characteristics of, *17*.140–3; word groups of, *17*.143–51, text groups of, *17*.151–6; list of monks at, *17*.158; liturgy of, *18*.47; influence on other monasteries, *17*.159–60; Latin learning at, *20*.143, 164; psalters at, *see* psalters; gospels at, *see* gospels; Pontifical of Bishop Sampson written at, *18*.78n; tropers of, *18*.59; pottery of, *19*.96; urban archaeology, *18*.149, 204; decoration of, *16*.168

witan, at Nottingham, *18*.190

The Wonders of the East, OE text, *17*.99

Worcester, *19*.89, 93, 159–60; books attributed to, *18*.81–2, 86–8; books received from other centres, *18*.87; scribal activity of, *16*.149; as continuator of tradition, *20*.220; burials at, *18*.174; calendar of, *19*.89–90, *20*.203–5; charter written at, *18*.77n; *see* charters; Chronicle of 'Florence' of Worcester, *19*.187; cults of, St Ecgwine, bishop of Worcester, *19*.89, 91; St Hilary of Poitiers, *19*.92, 94; St Radegund of Poitiers, *19*.91, 94; liturgical books of, *19*.84–5; *see* graduals; passional, *18*.77, 84, 88; Pontifical of Bishop Sampson, *see* pontificals; Portiforium of St Wulstan, *see* Portiforium; liturgy of, *18*.88–9

writs, *19*.173; royal, *17*.248–9; concerning Abbotsbury, *18*.219n; of Edward the Confessor, *18*.208, 211, 232, 238; of Harold Harefoot, *17*.251–2; of William the Conqueror, *18*.210–11, 238

Wulfhere, king, of Mercia, *18*.9

Wulfred, archbishop of Canterbury, *18*.39

Wulfric, abbot of St Augustine's, Canterbury, *19*.97

Wulfstan I, archbishop of York, *18*.84, 89, 167–8, *19*.177; script of, *20*.219–20; canonical writings,

18.104; homilies, *18*.121; lawcode of (*Grið*), *19*.54; preaching and theology of, *18*.100; sermons of, *18*.120, *20*.203, 218–20; *Sermo Lupi ad Anglos*, *19*.53; *De anticristo*, *20*.203, 209–10, 216, 217; *Sermo de decimis*, *20*.218; *De ieiunio quatuor temporum*, *20*.217–19; *Commonplace Book* of, *20*.209, 217; prose style of, *17*.94, 138; vocabulary of, *17*.155, 157

Wulfstan II, bishop of Worcester, Latin prose life of, by William of Malmesbury, *19*.159–60, 162, 174, 177; in calendar of Worcester, *20*.204

Wulfstan, precentor of Winchester, author of *Narratio metrica de S. Swithuno*, *16*.204

Wulfwig, bishop of London, *18*.21

Wynnebald, St, *19*.235

Yeavering, Northumbria, *18*.195

York, *19*.17, 182; *Anglo-Saxon Chronicle*, D-version of, compiled at, *18*.32; archbishops of, lands of, *18*.23–4; churches of, *18*.167; cathedral church of St Peter's *18*.25; in Domesday Book, *18*.23; place-name of, *19*.17; Seven Boroughs, part of, *18*.151; trade centre at, *18*.16, 176, 184; urban archaeology of, *18*.150, 153; Vikings at, *18*.143n, 150, 152, 176

York Gospels, *see* gospelbooks